# EDWARD BELLAMY ABROAD:

*An American Prophet's Influence*

# EDWARD
# BELLAMY
# ABROAD

*An
American
Prophet's Influence*

**SYLVIA E. BOWMAN, et al.**

**Preface by
MAURICE LE BRETON**

**TWAYNE PUBLISHERS**

**NEW YORK**

To THE MEMORY OF

Professor Jean Simon of the Sorbonne who died
before he could complete the research
for his chapter of this book,

AND

Bellamy Earnshaw, the grandson of Edward Bellamy,
who followed the development of this volume
with interest until the day
he no longer could.

# Preface

All those interested in noting the diversity of individual reactions to a prophetic vision of man's future in this world will find Miss Sylvia E. Bowman's painstaking inquiry into the question of the reception granted the world over to Edward Bellamy's picture of the ideal state both challenging and thought-provoking.

Even when, as often happened, the reception of his ideas was unfavorable, it was nevertheless Edward Bellamy's fortune to elicit from his readers reactions far more passionate, and consequently far more stirring, than those the average writer can ever hope to draw forth from his audience. One cannot help feeling, in fact, when confronted with the huge amount of critical literature devoted to his books in widely different countries, that few writers, except among the very greatest, ever found so large and so responsive an audience as did modest, unassuming Edward Bellamy whose primary aim was certainly not literary fame.

The reason for this worldwide interest in his works is to be found, of course, not so much in the intrinsic literary value of Edward Bellamy's fiction as in the importance man has always attached to the problem which is at the core of Bellamy's creative activity, a problem which leaves no one indifferent, whether one agrees or disagrees with the author's treatment of it, and, also, in the indomitable spirit of earnest and ineradicable optimism which inspired his hopeful vision of a better future for mankind.

What Edward Bellamy attempted to do, in fact, was to offer a new version, as definite as he could make it, of that age-old human dream of a millenium, a nineteenth-century preview of that "brave new world" which had already been the fond dream of men for many generations before Shakespeare coined the phrase in an age which was more eager, even, than the nineteenth century to screen off the depressing picture of the present behind the more comforting image of a far-off Eldorado.

For although he has by now won a place among the prophets of the future, Edward Bellamy is, of course, the heir to many centuries, just as his own country, the United States of America, at present for many a symbol of the Future, owes its very existence as a nation to that old human dream of "God's kingdom on Earth." Edward Bellamy's dream would never have found a response in so many hearts and minds had it been nothing but a wanton display of his imagination. Both Americans and Europeans deeply felt the presence of the age-old longing for a millenium behind the simple words of the unpretentious fiction.

But this does not mean that everybody felt gratified by this presentation of a better world in a not too remote future. Mankind, as William James had come to realize toward the end of his life, can roughly be divided into two sharply opposite groups: the "tender-minded" and the "tough-minded" (*Pragmatism,* Lecture I). The former group would include the idealists, the optimists, the religious-minded people, while the "tough-minded" would rather favor the opposite tendencies. "They have a low opinion of each other," James adds; "the tough think of the tender as sentimentalists and soft heads. The tender feel the tough to be unrefined, callous or brutal." No wonder Edward Bellamy's sentimental vision of a purer state of civilization should have met with a very different reception according to the widely divergent types of readers who reacted to it.

That Bellamy's vision was largely a sentimental one is evident both from the writer's own statements on several occasions and from the fact that it originated in the feeling of indignation Bellamy experienced, as a tender-minded Jeffersonian idealist, at the prevailing conditions in contemporary America. As an idealist, he wanted to reawaken his countrymen to the true meaning of those much adulterated notions of "democracy," "liberty," and "equality" which, he thought, had suffered ill-treatment at the hands of the tough-minded since the days of the "Philosophes." No wonder Bellamy's humanitarian vision, suffused with eighteenth-century idealism, with its obvious reliance on good will and brotherliness, often clashed with the more "realistic" philosophy of the tougher-minded Europeans whose experience of mankind was, of course, less optimistic than his own. Theirs was, in most cases, a rougher experience of the forces which counteract man's emancipation; and they had, many of them, come to the conclusion that a new order, if it was to last, could only be established by doing away violently, first, with unreconcilable adversaries, and, next, seeing to it that they were silenced forever.

Needless to say, Edward Bellamy's tender mind, with its quasi-evangelistic vision of a peaceful evolution, was not calculated to give ample satisfaction to those who were for enforcing happiness on mankind by all means, however rough.

He had no patience, either, on the other side, with the callous indifference and disdainful smugness of many who simply dismissed the problem of an improvement in the future of mankind with the answer that man's nature would have to be changed first before any attempt of the kind could be thought of. One will easily recognize the two types of minds and their reactions to Bellamy's ideas as one reads the successive chapters of this book.

It was a good thing Edward Bellamy wrote as he did. People like him, whatever the reception granted to their ideas, are the salt of the earth. It does not much matter, after all, whether they are right (whatever that may mean) in every detail of their vision. It is the fact that they had a vision that counts, and also, that they were naïve and bold enough not to keep it to themselves, but to spread abroad the good news. Many a fine oak in our forests has grown from what one might well have thought to be a lost seed. Edward Bellamy's ideas may yet revive someday, somewhere, in an unexpected fashion. Miss Sylvia E. Bowman is to be thanked for her indefatigable labor in a field which may in the not too remote future prove more rewarding than a superficial estimate would allow.

MAURICE LE BRETON
*Director of the Institute of*
*English and American Studies*

*La Sorbonne, Paris*

# Acknowledgments

Aside from the authors who contributed chapters to *Bellamy Abroad*, I am indebted to the following persons who are not mentioned elsewhere but who aided me in one way or another in compiling material.

*Australia*—L. G. DeGaris, Professor Ian R. Maxwell, Professor Lloyd S. Churchward, J. R. Rowland, J. A. McMurtrie.

*Belgium*—Professor Irene Simon; Professor G. Schuerweghs; Professor Van der Heyden; Professor E. de Jonghe; Miss Paulette Michot; Professor Pee; Mr. Struyf; Mr. Camille Huysmans; Professor Hubaux; Mr. A. Joris, University of Liège; and members of the Bellamy Association of Ghent.

*Bulgaria*—Director in 1957 of the National Library of Sofia: "Vassil Kolarov."

*Canada*—P. A. Howard, Gilberte Cuté-Mercier, Douglas Carr, and Professor A. S. P. Woodhouse.

*Czechoslovakia*—Dr. Jan Petrmichl, Dr. René Křížkovská, Dr. Vilém Závada, and Dr. M. Grimmova of the National and University Library, Prague.

*Denmark*—Carlo Christensen, Mr. Borge Schmidt.

*England*—Robert Morris, Marcus Cunliffe, G. C. Allen, C. E. Ratcliffe, A. L. Morton.

*France*—Professor R. Asselineau, the Sorbonne; Jacques Duboin, editor of *La Grande Relève*.

*Germany*—Professor Erich Angermann, Professor Julius Schwietering, Professor Helmut Kuhn, Dr. Franz H. Link, Dr. Richard Brinkman, Dr. Heinz Walz, Professor Levin L. Shucking. I am also grateful to the staff of the American Institute of the University of Munich which provided a scholarship for Franz Riederer thereby enabling him to prepare the study which I have condensed from his doctoral dissertation resulting from his investigation of Bellamy's influence in Germany.

*Holland*—W. C. Postma, J. J. Dik, Professor Fred Polak, J. A. van Houten.

*Hungary*—J. Szentmihályi and A. Pálvölgyi, members of the Reference Department of the Egyetemi Könyvtár of Budapest, who supplied all the material about Bellamy in Hungary because, as they wrote, they felt it "their duty to make known some data to a work of scholarship" and added "we are glad to be able to do so."

*India*—Seetha Neelakantan, Adyar Library and Research Center; Sophia Wadia, editor of *P. E. N.*; Shri Pyarelal; K. D. Shahani; M. Pratap; Sibnarayan Ray; Professor A. G. Stock; Lucy Harlow.

*Israel*—Dr. G. Kressel, Professor Sholom J. Kahn, Ithamar Leef.

*Italy*—Professor Carlo Izzo, under whose direction the study in Italy was done; Bruno Orlando; Professor Mario Praz.

*Japan*—Iyoji Aono, University of Tokyo Library; Professor Masaki Yamamoto of Meiji University; Shirô Sugai, National Diet Library.

*Jugoslavia*—Branko Hanž, Matko Rojnic, University Library, Zagreb; Ljubica Nenadovic and Slobodan Jovanovic of the Narodna Biblioteka, Beograd.

*New Zealand*—E. Presland Tack; A. E. Hollay; W. J. Tasker; A. E. Turner; J. O. Wilson, Chief Librarian, General Assembly Library; Prime Minister Walter Nash; Stuart Perry, city librarian, Wellington; J. E. Colchin, Dominion Secretary, New Zealand Social Credit Political League.

*Norway*—Professor Sigmund Skard; Fredrik Wulfsberg.

*Poland*—Professor Stanislaw Helsztynski, Dr. Rosa Jablonska, W. Furmanczyk, J. Fisiak, and Mrs. Helena Dreszer and Mrs. Napinska, and Professor M. Schlauch. The preliminary work in Poland was done by Mr. Furmanczyk of the University of Warsaw, but it was completed by the author-editor of this volume after Furmanczyk received a grant to study the papers of Theodore Dreiser in the United States.

*Portugal*—A. de Castro e Abreu: Faculty of Letters, University of Lisbon.

*Rumania*—Professor G. Vlădescu-Răcoasa.

*Russia*—I. Anisimoff, Director of the Maxim Gorky Institute of World Literature, under whose direction the study of Bellamy in Russia was made; A. Kardashev; Evgeni A. Zaostrovtsev; Konstantin Chugunov; T. G. Mamedov; Vladimir Kuzmichev.

*Spain*—Justo Garcia Morales.

*Sweden*—Professor Erik Tengstrand.

*Switzerland*—Professor Werner Bleuler and Werner Reist contributed most of the material about their country. Reist published Bellamy's *Looking Backward* after World War II.

*United States*—Mr. and Mrs. Thomas Harris, who typed this manuscript; and Mr. Thomas Yates, who checked it for errors. Mr. Bruce Tone, who spent long hours helping me read proof, deserves more than expressions of gratitude. Miss Amanda Gerig, who performed many scholarly, clerical chores for me during the period of the composition of the book, must also be acknowledged and thanked.

# Contents

"Of this thing, however, be certain: wouldst thou plant for Eternity, then plant into the deep infinite faculties of man, his Fantasy and Heart; would thou plant for Year and Day, then plant into shallow superficial faculties, his Self-love and Arithmetical Understanding, what will grow there. A Hierarch, therefore, and Pontiff of the World will we call him, the Poet and Inspired Maker, who Prometheus-like, can shape new Symbols, and bring new Fire from Heaven to fix it there. Such too will not always be wanting; neither perhaps now are. Meanwhile, as the average of matters goes, we account him Legislator and wise who can so much as tell when a Symbol has grown old, and gently remove it."—Carlyle, *Sartor Resartus: The Life and Opinions of Herr Teufelsdröckh* (1835).

# Introduction

Although the literati may remember that Edward Bellamy's *Looking Backward* was a best-selling, widely translated novel in the nineteenth century and that in the 1930's Edward Weeks, Charles Beard, and John Dewey all listed it as being second only to Marx's *Das Kapital* as the most important book published after 1885, few have been concerned about or cognizant of its worldwide popularity and influence. *Bellamy Abroad* traces the story of the American Utopian's acclaim and, more important, it reveals his influence upon literary and political movements and the use of his Utopian novels by revolutionaries and reformers.

*Looking Backward* won greater fame than its sequel *Equality* (1897), which was Bellamy's answer to his critics, his cogent argument for the democracy of his egalitarian state, his outline for the transition to the ideal state he had delineated in his first Utopia, and his most devastating criticism of nineteenth-century capitalism. Because of the trenchant attack upon the profit system in the famous "Parable of the Water Tank," *Equality* also became famous. Because it was a very serious political-economic pseudo-novel, revolutionaries and reformers realized that it could not be so easily used as a whole as *Looking Backward*. The "Parable" was, however, easily comprehended by all people; and it was therefore translated, printed, and widely circulated by labor leaders, socialists, and Marxists—particularly by the Russian ones.

Because only brief mention is made of Bellamy's impact abroad in Elizabeth Sadler's "One Book's Influence: Edward Bellamy's 'Looking Backward'" (*New England Quarterly*, 1944), in Alyn Forbes' "The Literary Quest for Utopia" (*Social Forces*, 1927), in Arthur Morgan's *Edward Bellamy*, and in Frances T. Russell's *Touring Utopia*, the material comprising *Bellamy Abroad* is the result of the first attempt to trace thoroughly the role Bellamy's books played in countries other than his own. This documented and non-speculative study* of the impact of Bellamy's fiction upon literature and upon political, labor, and other reform movements should accomplish the following: (1) establish him as one of the United States' most

---

* Only the material which concerns one of the leaders of India is speculative, and it is labeled as such.

widely read and ideologically influential writers; (2) promote a reassessment of Bellamy in the literary histories of the United States; (3) encourage other studies of the history of political ideas; and (4) open the door for future comparative literature studies.

Other than accomplishing these objectives, *Bellamy Abroad* indicates that the world of chaos and conflict which exists today was in no small way generated by those who believed Bellamy's ideal state could become reality or by those who—realizing the effectiveness of *Looking Backward* in awakening dreams in the minds of men and hope in their hearts—used his books for their own nefarious or benevolent purposes. Bellamy was employed, for example, by such diverse groups as the Fabians of England; the Theosophists of the world; the labor leaders of Canada, Denmark, New Zealand, and Australia; and by the revolutionary Russians and Marxists.

But Bellamy's popularity was not limited to the nineteenth century, for there was a revival of interest in the 1930's in Canada, the United States, South Africa, Indonesia, and New Zealand. Furthermore, Bellamy societies still exist today in California and in Holland; and *Looking Backward*, which still sells six thousand copies or more a year in its native country, has since World War II been republished in Russia's East Berlin, in Japan, in France, in Italy, in Switzerland, and in Holland. As Dr. Hermann Duncker wrote in the introduction of the 1949 German edition, Bellamy is as little out of date today as he has ever been.

*Bellamy Abroad* does not pretend to be, therefore, the final study that will be made of Edward Bellamy's influence. First of all, more detailed studies, suggested in the final chapter of this volume, need to be made about sundry aspects of his influence. Second, investigations conducted in future decades may be more fertile; for, because of the present international political situation, many countries could not be fully investigated and many people in positions of power were hesitant to reveal the true influence of "a Utopian" upon their concepts. A notable exception is Prime Minister Walter Nash of New Zealand who stated in his letter of September, 1960, that he had not only read *Looking Backward* and *Equality* but that he considered Edward Bellamy "probably one of the greatest, if not the greatest, prophets of the development of world conditions." The Honorable Mr. Nash also added that he continued not only to read the books but that he often talked of Bellamy's "amazing qualities of prophecy."

Although Bellamy was considered by his famous contemporary Henry George to be a man who spun airy dreams about a cooperative world in which men worked for mere love of labor and to serve altruistically their fellow men, the existence of *Bellamy Abroad* signifies that Bellamy was not too mistaken. For the scholars and the librarians from the many countries of the world who have contributed their objective studies or their reports to this book have done so because of their devotion to knowledge—and have frequently risen above political barriers and conflicts to do so. Because of the geographical, political, and linguistic problems presented in making a study of Bellamy's round-the-globe influence, this book could not have been written without their help.

When I began in the early 1950's to compile an international bibliography of material written about Bellamy and of the translations of his novels, I soon realized that to make even a superficial investigation of his popularity and influence would be an imponderable, if not impossible, task. Before I had completed *The Year 2000: A Critical Biography of Edward Bellamy* (1958), I began, therefore, to write to different universities and libraries abroad to ask for the cooperation of some member of their staffs in making the study of Bellamy's influence. Because of the interest of the many, many people listed in the acknowledgments section preceding this introduction, or as authors of chapters, the information was assembled. As director, author, and editor of this volume, I have rewritten the material submitted; with the consent of the contributors, I have added to or subtracted from their reports; eliminated any evidence of influence which could not be documented; and published the chapters under the names of the major contributors.

We have, therefore, prepared in *Bellamy Abroad* chapters which indicate the Americanism and the anti-Marxism of Bellamy's ideas and which delineate his popularity—or reactions to it—in both major and minor geographical and ideological areas of influence. Chapters are devoted to the countries where his impact was greatest or where Bellamy societies existed; and two chapters—the next to the last—are concerned with his history in such countries as Japan, India, Jugoslavia, Hungary, Bulgaria, Poland, and Czechoslovakia. In the final chapter the patterns of Bellamy's influence are considered and related, where possible, to those in his own country; and, finally, suggestions for future studies are presented. At the end of the volume is an international bibliography which lists by countries not only translations of Bellamy's books but also articles and books written about him—or in reaction to his ideas. This bibliography, which could not be complete because of the devastation wrought by two world wars and because of the elementary state of bibliographies in some areas of the world, complements the extensive bibliography contained in *The Year 2000*.

A complicated study now in preparation—but one which cannot be completed for many more years—will consider exclusively Bellamy's tremendous impact in the United States upon literature—Utopian, muckraking, proletarian, and revolt; upon political movements—from the Bellamy club movement through the People's Party to and including the New Deal, the Technocrats, and the Townsendites; and upon various religious, labor, political, and reform groups. Although I intended, when *The Year 2000* was completed, to publish *Bellamy at Home and Abroad* as one volume, the widespread influence of Bellamy has made it necessary to release *Bellamy Abroad* as the second volume of what is now regarded as a three- or four-volume study of America's most famous Utopian novelist —and Christian, democratic socialist.

Since the study of Bellamy's life and influence was begun in an era which did not view with interest—or approval—research about a famous champion of socialism, I am particularly grateful for the scholarly objectivity and catholicity of the administration of Indiana University, which aided my efforts by giving me two research grants to help defray expenses and a sabbatical leave to gather much of the information this pioneer book presents. I should also like to acknowledge the encouragement given me at one time or another by the following professors: Ralph Broyles, Donald Carmony, Smith Higgins, James A. Work, Napier Wilt, Donald Bond, E. K. Brown, David Daiches, Joseph Schiffman, Everett W. MacNair, Harriet Stoddard, Carlo Izzo, and Maurice le Breton. Without stimulating teachers of character, encouraging friends and administrators, and the interest of others which leads to active participation or cooperation, most scholarly books would never be written— nor most lives very satisfactorily lived.

SYLVIA E. BOWMAN

*Indiana University*

# Chronology

1850 March 26th: Edward Bellamy was born in Chicopee Falls, Massachusetts. The son of the Reverend Rufus King Bellamy and of Maria Putnam Bellamy, he came of an old and distinguished American family.

1864 Edward, after a profound religious experience, became a member of his father's Baptist Church in Chicopee Falls.

1867 Edward, rejected for West Point, entered Union College, Schenectady, N. Y., as a special student who followed his own reading courses in literature, political science, history, and political geography. During this period he probably became interested in socialism and in the ideas of Auguste Comte.

1868- Edward with his cousin William Packer studied in Dres-
1869 den, Germany, and traveled in Europe. He later said that what he observed made him aware of the end results of the Industrial Revolution.

1869 Bellamy began the study of law in Springfield, Massachusetts.

1870 Bellamy recorded in his journal his loss of religion and his search for a religion. About 1873 he eventually wrote his "Religion of Solidarity," the personal philosophy which he reread and reaffirmed in 1887.

1871 Bellamy passed his bar examination with brilliance, refused a promising partnership, and opened his own office. After his first case, he retired from the legal profession; he stated that he could not be a "public blood hound."

1871 "Woman Suffrage," his first known article, was published in *Golden Age* (March 11).

1871 Bellamy went to New York City in November to write intermittently for the New York *Post*.

1872 March 30th issue of *Golden Age* contained his article "National Education."

1872 Bellamy returned to Chicopee Falls in June to assume the position on the *Springfield Union* as editorial writer and literary editor and reviewer. In this year he also gave a lyceum talk outlining his socialistic beliefs.

1875 Bellamy published his first known short story "The Cold Snap," in *Century Magazine* (September).

1876 Bellamy published "A Providence" in *Century Magazine* (July); "The Old Folks' Party" appeared in *Scribner's* (March).

1877 In this year many of his short stories appeared in *Appleton's, Lippincott's, Century,* and *Scribner's* magazines; they were "Extra-Hazardous," "A Midnight Drama," "A Superfluity of Naughtiness," "Hooking Watermelons," "Lost," "A Summer Evening's Dream."

1877 In December, Bellamy resigned from the *Union* because of ill health; his success in publishing short stories had, however, probably influenced him to chance a literary career.

1878 Edward traveled from January to April with his brother Frederick; they went to the Sandwich Islands and toured some areas of the West.

1878 In this year Bellamy's first novel *Six to One: A Nantucket Idyll* appeared; though considered a "summer idyll," this work showed the influence of his "Religion of Solidarity." In this year he also published "Deserted" which shows the influence of his trip to the West.

1878- *The Duke of Stockbridge* was serialized in the *Berkshire*
1879 *Courier;* this accurate interpretation of Shays' Rebellion was published posthumously in book form in 1900. During 1879, "Pott's Painless Cure," "Taking a Mean Advantage," "Two Days' Solitary Imprisonment," and "Jane Hicks" were published.

1880 *Dr. Heidenhoff's Process,* a remarkable psychological study of the effect of guilt upon the tender conscience, was published in book form after having been serialized in the Springfield *Union* (1878-79).

1880 Edward and Charles Bellamy founded in February the *Springfield Penny News,* a newspaper devoted to telling the people the truth. Edward also published "A Tale of the South Pacific" and "That Letter."

1881 In May, the *Penny News* became the *Daily News,* a newspaper still published in Springfield, Massachusetts.

1882 In May, Edward Bellamy married Emma A. Sanderson, who had been a ward of his father since 1874. This marriage marked a turning point in Bellamy's career.

1884   Bellamy retired from the *Daily News* to devote himself to literature. His son Paul was born on December 26th. In this year Edward published *Miss Ludington's Sister,* which had also been serialized in *The Literary World.*

1886   Bellamy began writing *Looking Backward;* his daughter Marion was born on March 4th. "The Blindman's World" appeared in November in the *Atlantic.*

1887   "At Pinney's Ranch" appeared in the *Atlantic.*

1888   *Looking Backward* was published by Benjamin Ticknor; and, in the summer of this year, plans were being made for the formation of the Bellamy Club of Boston which had its first meeting in the fall. "A Love Story Reversed" appeared in *The Century.*

1889   In May the first issue of *The Nationalist* appeared; it did not cease publication until April, 1891. During this year "An Echo of Antietam," "A Positive Romance," "To Whom This May Come," and "With the Eyes Shut" were published. After these stories, Bellamy gave up his literary career to devote himself to his reform movement.

1891   In January, Bellamy began publishing in Boston his own reform journal, *The New Nation,* which appeared until 1893.

1891   Bellamy followers from Boston attended the organization of the People's Party in May in Cincinnati, Ohio. Of this third party, William Dean Howells remarked that Bellamy "virtually founded" it.

1893   Bellamy began *Equality,* which was published in 1897; by December, 1897, it had sold 21,044 copies; by 1905, 41,000 copies.

1897   In August, Bellamy went to Denver, Colorado, for his health.

1898   In April, Bellamy returned to Chicopee Falls where he died May 22, 1898.

1898   *The Blindman's World and Other Stories* was posthumously published; these stories are those Bellamy himself selected as his best. W. D. Howells wrote the preface.

1900   *The Duke of Stockbridge* was published with a preface by the Reverend Francis Bellamy, a cousin of the author.

# EDWARD BELLAMY ABROAD:

## *An American Prophet's Influence*

# CHAPTER ONE

# Edward Bellamy, The American Prophet
## (1850-1898)

"IF YOU WILL KINDLY SELL 5,000 copies of Looking Backward for me, I will engage to give the voters of 1892 a platform worth voting for, and furnish the voters too" wrote Edward Bellamy on June 15, 1888,[1] to Benjamin Ticknor, his publisher, whom he had urged in August, 1887, to publish his novel as quickly as possible because "it was the accepted time" for a "publication touching on social and industrial questions to obtain a hearing."[2]

Although Bellamy in 1888 could hardly have foreseen that the Bellamy clubs then being formed because of the effect of Looking Backward would affect the formation of the People's Party or its platform, or that the novel would have been translated by 1892 into all major languages, he was astute in assessment of the reaction of the citizens of the chaotic world of the 1880's and 1890's who sought an inspiring solution to the problems of the conflict between capital and labor, of exploitation of the worker, of unequal distribution of wealth, of panics and depressions, and of winning in Europe and of maintaining in the United States a form of government which would guarantee for all "life, liberty, and the pursuit of happiness." Although reform movements were as popular as "corn on the cob" in the United States[3] and although Marxism had already raised the red flag in Europe and had found sympathizers in the United States, Looking Backward won not only millions of readers but ardent disciples who founded Bellamy clubs; socialists—Christian and Marxist—who adopted the book for propaganda and educational purposes; religious groups who saw in its ideal society the fulfillment of their principles; labor and farm leaders who wished to show their followers the equitable world which could be achieved; and humanitarian idealists who could not accept "traditional economics" and who aspired to end "man's inhumanity to man."

29

I  *The Appeal of* Looking Backward

*Looking Backward* had such a worldwide appeal not only because it was, said its author, "a bare anticipation in expression of what everybody was thinking and about to say"[4] but because of Bellamy's presentation of its contents: he chose the form of a Utopian romance. In simple, clear, concise prose Bellamy related the story of Julian West, a Bostonian plutocrat, who went to sleep in 1887 and awakened in the year 2000 to discover a society which had solved all the problems that had plagued his era. The anarchic, brutal, immoral exploitations of the competitive nineteenth century had been replaced by fraternal cooperation; and the inhumanity of man to man had been transposed into the consideration and kindliness which had once been reserved only for the family circle. The social and cultural divisions of 1887 had also been mitigated; for, since all the people were economically as well as politically equal, they had equal opportunity for self-development. Since all the people were employed in the nation's work forces and since all means of production and distribution were controlled by the state, unemployment, poverty, panics, depressions, and labor-capital conflicts had vanished.

Julian also discovered that the industrial democracy which had solved all these social, ethical, political, and economic problems had become a true government of, by, and for the people. With a peaceful, evolutionary, legal process, the citizens—motivated by Christian or humanitarian brotherly love—had replaced the plutocracy of 1887 by extending and reinforcing the rights guaranteed by the Constitution: they had given to all men and women the right of economic equality which they deemed necessary to safeguard their social equality, political freedom, and equality of opportunity. To make possible this economic equality—the cornerstone of the ideal society—they had organized to control industry as they had once before to conduct their own government. They had finally realized that "no business is so essentially the public business as the industry and commerce on which the people's livelihood depends, and that to entrust it to private persons to be managed for private profit is a folly similar in kind, though vastly greater in magnitude, to that of surrendering the functions of political government to kings and nobles to be conducted for their personal glorification."[5]

In the new industrial democracy, West discovered that wealth no longer had the power to corrupt the government; its officials were incorruptible because they had no need of money. The venal influence of monopolies upon the legislative, executive, and judicial branches of the government no longer existed; for there was now one Great Monopoly—the federal government. Since all the people were from birth joint stockholders in this monopoly, they were no longer lethargic, indifferent citizens. Their selfish interests prompted them to watch the government and to produce, as members of the industrial forces, to their capacity; for the welfare of all depended upon the government's efficient planning and operation and upon their own production.

As Julian West perceived the ethical, political, social, and economic improvements which religious motivation and the political-economic extension of the American Constitution had wrought, he realized the barbarism of nineteenth-century civilization and became a convert to the new way of life—to Christian, democratic, state socialism. Julian did not realize, however, that he had adopted socialistic theories; for Bellamy called his plan Nationalism. He had avoided the true cognomen for his society because he had desired, as he wrote to William D. Howells, to escape the prejudicial associations with the word "socialism": "the red flag," "sexual novelties," and an "abusive tone about God and religion."[6]

Bellamy's readers were as convinced as Julian West not only because the complex ideas and principles were presented in simple, effective exposition and dialogue but because Bellamy was logical, convincing, positive, and sincere. He was persuasive because of his legal and editorial training; his knowledge of history and political science; his freedom from "bias of sect and party"; and his penetrating understanding and delineation of the political, economic, and social problems of his day. These attributes made his plan, as W. F. Phillips wrote in 1898, "so thoroughly and admirably reasoned that rational dissent" was "impossible."

Both the logic and the practicality of his plan were enhanced by his "interpreting the purport and direction of the conditions and forces which were" tending in his own era toward the evolution of the new society.[7] Because the plan for the new society was so "cleverly woven out of the warp and woof of daily life," it fascinated the reader to such an extent that, when he had finished the book, he asked himself " 'Why not today?' "[8] Furthermore, as Charles Madison stated in 1942, *Looking Backward* was convincing because the ideal society was presented "as an accomplished fact"; the reader was "confronted not with an imaginary social scheme which is obviously impractical but with a perfected way of life based on the existing industrial system."[9]

*Looking Backward* was also vital and inspiring[10] because it was positive. As Laurence Gronlund[11] and Bellamy both asserted, it "suggests instead of denouncing . . . it proposes instead of merely opposing . . . it affirms rather than denies . . . and it is the most notable embodiment of the 'Everlasting Yea' against the 'Everlasting Nay.' "[12] Although the novel contained a forceful condemnation of private enterprise, it was more important, as John Dewey also observed, because of its concrete, contrasting picture of a better life; of a perfected humanity because of a changed environment; and of the social, political, and economic application of Christ's behest that men should love their brothers as themselves—and treat them accordingly!

Besides these constructive, positive aspects of *Looking Backward*, Bellamy's enthusiasm for his plan, his faith in it, and, as A. W. Levi and Joseph Dorfman observed, his "deep sincerity and . . . intense love of humanity . . . and a broad humanitarian social philosophy that transcended . . . specific proposals for reconstruction and reform"[13] contributed to the effectiveness of his Utopia. As Bellamy himself stated, the hope that filled him as he wrote must "in like manner move all who should come even in part to share it"—for "face answereth to face in water" and "the heart of man to man."[14]

That Bellamy was correct in his realization of the effect hope and faith would have upon his readers was established by the description of Thomas Wentworth Higginson who stated that *Looking Backward* inspired "a band of young proselytes who, instead of believing that what [Bellamy] . . . says is too good to be true, believe that it is too good not to be true; and are ready to proclaim its teachings as at least a temporary gospel of good news."[15] It was also confirmed by a journalist of the Chicago *Journal* who wrote: "Give every honest man a hearing. That is the lesson of the day. . . . Listen respectfully to him, if he speaks for better men and better deeds, even if you have difficulty in following the strange leaps of his imagination. The man who hopes for the development of the best traits of human nature may be crazy, but he is infinitely more lovable than the man who goes craftily ahead, gambling on the rule of the worst traits."[16]

Although *Looking Backward* appealed to its readers because of its graphic explanation of complex principles and because of its constructive, hopeful, and sincere message, its sale would probably have been greatly curtailed had it not been a Utopian

the sexes: "State socialism while undoubtedly favoring a great
reduction of social disparities, does not postulate the economical
equality of citizens or of sexes. It would abolish the unfair
advantage capital gives some individuals over others, but
would permit the natural inequalities in the endowments of
individuals and of the two sexes to have full effect in determining their larger or smaller possessions. Nationalism could
not permit this consistently with its fundamental principle,
which is the evolution of industry of the national or republican
idea. The nation, in whatever relation it assumes to its citizens,
can be no respecter of persons. As all law-abiding citizens,
without regard to disparities of powers, share equally in political power, and enjoy equally the benefit of all public services
and functions, so must it be when industrial production and
distribution shall also become national functions."[21] The Marxist motto was, stressed Bellamy, "from each laborer according
to his ability or to each according to his earnings"; the Nationalist motto was "from each man and woman equally to each
equally."

Bellamy also took issue with the Marxists because of their
solution to the industrial problems and because of their lack
of a concrete plan for the society to be achieved as a result of
a proletarian revolution. To Bellamy, as to Charles Bradlaugh,
" 'no scientific socialist pretends to have any scheme or detailed
plan of organization.' They only pretend to desire to destroy
existing society because of its evils; tomorrow may grow, if and
how it can, without the slightest precautions against the development of a worse state." Although the Marxists were "very
chary about defining the ultimate social ideal," they seemingly
thought it should be a "sort of confederation of industrial guilds,
each controlling for its own benefit some province of industry."[22] To have the unions own the industries collectively would
be dangerous, asserted Bellamy; for a selfish group would still
retain power over others.

To nationalize industries was, however, to place all production
and distribution under the control of the federal government
which was the agent of the people and which had as its chief
duty the safeguarding of the highest rights of *every* citizen—the
rights of life and of self-preservation. In order to give these
rights and to guarantee the liberties established by the American Constitution, the government had to be a universal employment bureau and a great insurance agency. Although Bellamy advocated state socialism, he never ceased to insist that
his form of industrial democracy had as its prerequisites and

novel and had Bellamy not called his form of government
Nationalism rather than socialism. Because Bellamy presented,
like Henry George, his ideas in "such a form as to seem once
removed from practical, immediate action,"[17] *Looking Backward*, though it was attacked, sold in the United States 400,000
copies from 1888 to 1897—the period in which the ideas of
socialists and philosophical anarchists were an anathema because of the "red scare" resulting from the Haymarket Riot.
In this period in which "a man who talked or wrote socialism
was in danger of being run into a corner and clubbed,"[18] people discussed and often sponsored Nationalism because they
did not know they were concerning themselves with socialistic
principles.

## II  *American, Anti-Marxian Socialism*

Bellamy felt, however, that ideologically and patriotically he
had pertinent reasons for distinguishing Nationalism from socialism. With the aid of Laurence Gronlund (the author of *The
Co-operative Commonwealth in Its Outlines: An Exposition of
Modern Socialism*) and of Mason Green (an editor of Bellamy's
reform journal, the *New Nation*), many articles were published
which highlighted the distinctive qualities of Nationalism. In
three articles which Bellamy wrote for the *New Nation* and in
one which he wrote for publication in Russia (published in
English for the first time in the appendix of this volume),
Bellamy showed how Nationalism differed from anarchism,
Christian Socialism, and, in particular, Marxism.

"Nationalism . . . or American socialism," he wrote, "differs
utterly from anarchistic socialism, both as to ends and to
means. Its social ideal is a perfectly organized industrial system which, by reason of the close interlocking of its wheels,
shall work at a minimum of friction with a maximum result of
wealth and leisure for all. This end it would not attain by
revolution but by an orderly evolution of the republican idea
of the equal interest of all in the State. This idea, already applied in the political organization of advanced states, nationalists
would carry into industry and economics."[19]

"As to Christian socialism, Nationalism differs from that only
in the greater definiteness and completeness of its program and
in the fact that the conclusions can be just as logically derived
from humanitarian as from theological premises."[20]

In his discussions of the way Nationalism varied from Marxism, Bellamy invariably stressed ten specific, major differences.
Only Nationalism promised absolute equality of income and of

its foundation the democratic government of the United States which had been conceived to guarantee the common welfare of all citizens.

In keeping with his objection of giving any one group control, Bellamy stressed that Marxism was a class movement appealing only to the proletariat; Nationalism, however, appealed equally to all and was equally for all.[23] Bellamy, therefore, rejected class conflict; and in this respect, he was, as Mason Green stated, "unique among the economic creeds which are generally classed as socialistic. He was not class conscious but race conscious—an economic universalist—and did not believe in the doctrine of election for any one class at the expense of another class. The proletarian socialists fight from the angle of the factory, the work bench, the mines, and the like. They advocate collective, not government ownership of the means of production, always nursing a hostility to employers as far as they represent capital. Down to Bellamy's day socialist writers assumed generally the proletarian attitude. This was true of leaders like Owen, Blanc, Marx, Engels, Bebel, Maurice, Morris, Hyndman, and others."[24]

Also in keeping with his attitude about conflict between groups was Bellamy's assertion that the revolutionary methods of the Marxists contrasted to those sponsored by the Nationalists, who desired to achieve their industrial democracy by a legal, evolutionary process which would develop along the "established lines of the national organism in its various grades of the municipal, state, and general administration" until eventually all facilities of production and distribution were under the control of the central government.[25]

Because the Nationalists did not condone bloody revolution and the creation of the violent hatred so necessary to incite one, they relied upon a religious revival which would fill the hearts of men with love of one another, give them solidarity, and motivate them to reform peacefully the economic system which had made the practice of love and other virtues impossible. Instead of considering religion as the "opium of the people," Bellamy—despite his independent, unorthodox religious convictions—stated that the world could only be "set right by love, and this demands confidence in goodness and trust in God. Positive forces are the saviors of humanity—clear, strong, mighty beliefs in the good time coming, and in the power of Christian truth and grace to bring it about. The doubters and the devilers cannot march in the van of this army."[26]

When men had applied the precepts of Christ to their eco-

nomic and political life and when they had experienced mutual
love and unselfishness in all their relationships,[27] they had then
and only then learned, wrote Bellamy in *Equality*, the true
significance of "God the Father" and of the words which expressed the religion of love. "'If We love one another God
dwelleth in us and his love is perfected in us.' 'He that loveth
his brother dwelleth in the light.' 'If any man say I love God,
and hateth his brother, he is a liar.' 'He that loveth not his
brother, abideth in death.' 'God is love and he that dwelleth
in love dwelleth in God.' 'Every one that loveth knoweth God.'
'He that loveth not knoweth not God.'"[28]

Although Bellamy sought to solve the material, economic
problems of the era with his industrial democracy, his major
objective was not to supply men with material comforts but
to free them from bondage to the world of the flesh and the
devil, and to lead them to the moral life of the true Kingdom
of God in which neither humanity nor Christ would any longer
be daily crucified. Because of the moral society in which men
would dwell, because of their lack of concern with material
problems, and because of their leisure and opportunities for development, Bellamy envisioned a spiritual, intellectual renaissance of humane individualism. Bellamy believed that history
and science proved man was perfectible and that his ideal
state would promote not only individuality but perfectibility.[29]

Because people had to be religiously and intellectually prepared and because the ideal society could best evolve if it were
established by a democracy and by people who loved their
country and their own countrymen, Bellamy stated that Nationalism was limited to the reform of the American society; it had,
therefore, no international pattern or intent—as did Marxism.
Bellamy asserted that love of men should first be shown at home
and that any advocated reform should reflect the national culture, mores, and needs. Love of country, wrote Bellamy in
"Looking Forward," "so often misdirected, is the grandest and
most potent form under which the enthusiasm for humanity has
yet shown itself capable of moving great masses, and in its
spirit is contained the promise and the potency of the world-
embracing love in which it shall some day merge."[30]

As this statement indicates, Bellamy did believe, however,
that the rest of the civilized world would eventually establish
the ideal state when its achievement in the United States had
demonstrated what it would guarantee materially, intellectually,
spiritually, and morally to its citizens. Eventually, dreamed
Bellamy, a federal system of autonomous states would provide

a world government—the ultimate form of society and the social ideal. The world federation would rule by law; and it would eliminate the wastes of economic and military wars.[31]b

With these differences, Bellamy adapted socialism to American democratic governmental principles and objectives; to the American respect for religion and dislike of bloody conflict; and to the American dream of plenty and equality for all. And to Bellamy, these were important changes; for he had written to William Dean Howells in 1888 that no reform group could or should succeed in the United States which was not "wholly and enthusiastically American and patriotic in spirit and suggestions."[32] In "Looking Forward" he had stated that "social reforms must follow National lines and will succeed as they are able to adapt themselves to National conditions and sentiments and adapt themselves with National traditions and aspirations."[33]

When we analyze Bellamy's views of the duty of the government, of the history of the United States, and of the role Nationalism was to play; when we review the intent of the early settlers, the social criticisms, and the social protest movements before and after the Civil War; and when we consider the intellectual ideas of nineteenth-century America and of Europe which Bellamy synthesized, we find that his ideal state was indeed in keeping with American traditions, aspirations, and rebellions.

### III  Bellamy's View of American Government

The duty of the government to Bellamy—as to Locke, Jefferson, and the fathers of the American Constitution—was to be concerned with the common good of its members; and the best government was not only that which made the most grass grow but that which furthered the citizens' morality, security, and personal liberty. Like Lord Acton, Bellamy regarded history as the record of man's struggles for freedom; and in each instance in which men had fought against king, priest, or master for political, religious, or personal liberty, Bellamy saw a step made toward the evolution of the true democracy of man. To him the logical result of the diffusion of learning, of Luther's triumph at the Diet of Worms, and of the English rebellion against priest, king, and nobility, had been the Declaration of Independence and the American Revolution which had instituted the first phase of modern democracy—political democracy.

Bellamy divided the history of American democracy into two

general phases: in the first or negative phase, democracy was merely a political substitute for monarchy and was really a pseudo-republic doomed to degenerate into a plutocracy; in the second or positive phase, the republican form of government evolved into democratic, state socialism. Bellamy also divided the history of the struggle for freedom in the United States into three specific periods: the American Revolution, which won political freedom from England and political equality for the people; the Civil War, which freed the chattel slave; and the Nationalist revolution, which emancipated all citizens from economic and industrial slavery by instituting economic equality to end the rule of the wealthy and to begin that of the rich in intellect and merit.

To Bellamy the negative phase of the development of democracy had been caused by the fact that the drafters of the American Constitution had not carried their idea of the "inalienable" equality of men to its logical conclusion: economic equality. They had failed to do so because they had not foreseen the Industrial Revolution, its impact upon the distribution of wealth, and the effect this economic inequality would have in distorting the freedoms and rights of men. The result of this lack of clairvoyance had been that the government of the United States had established freedom from England but not freedom of its citizens from one another; consequently, the rule of the king had merely been replaced by that of the plutocrats, whose power increased as the wealth of the nation became more concentrated in the hands of the few.

During the Industrial Revolution and the anarchical economic struggle which ensued, this spirit of mastership had become pronounced—so pronounced that the plutocracy had destroyed the republic by conducting its own revolution. As a result of the destructive force of what Bellamy termed the "business-wrecking, law-defying, man-crushing party of the trusts and syndicates," the rich minority had obtained rule over the majority. Because of this power of wealth and because of its unequal distribution—political equality, equality before the law, equality of opportunity and education, personal liberty, and the dignity of man had been destroyed. Because of the control by the capitalists of the churches, the newspapers, the schools, and the business of the nation—freedom of speech, of the press, and of enterprise had become nonexistent.

In order to restore the original purposes of the true constitution of the United States—the Declaration of Independence—

Bellamy proposed to inaugurate the positive period of democracy as a result of a counterrevolution. The objectives of this revolution would be: negatively, to end forever the political, social, industrial domination of people by the profit-seeking minority; and, positively, to establish freedom of speech and worship, freedom from fear and want, and equality of ownership and opportunity.

Because of these objectives, Bellamy maintained that Thomas Jefferson, had he been alive during the counterrevolution, would have regarded this "movement toward industrial self-government as the people's only escape from plutocracy" and that he would have realized that it was a "strictly logical and necessary development of the principles laid down in the Declaration of Independence" which in its preamble "logically contained the entire statement of the doctrine of universal economic equality guaranteed by the nation collectively to its members individually."

Bellamy argued, therefore, that this counterrevolution was a truly *conservative* American movement which would restore the original principles of the democratic government by rescuing it from the few for the few, and returning it to the people for all the people. Subsequently, the first "rounded, full-orbed, complete" republic—social, economic, and political—would be achieved. The responsible agents of the people of this government, the self-interested and enlightened public, and the economic equality of the citizens would preserve the society from future oppression of either economic or political nature. Bellamy regarded the economic democracy of his state as all important: it was the "corollary and the necessary supplement of political democracy, without which the latter must forever fail to secure to a people the equalities and liberties which it promises."

Bellamy's most succinct statement of the importance of this extension of the rights of men to include economic equality was made in *Equality:* "The cornerstone of our state is economic equality; and is not that the obvious, necessary, and only adequate pledge of these three birthrights—life, liberty, and happiness? What is life without its material basis, and what is an equal right to life but a right to an equal material basis for it? What is liberty? How can men be free who must ask the right to labor and to live from their fellow men and seek their bread from the hands of others? How else can any government guarantee liberty to men save by providing them a means of labor and of life coupled with independence; and how could that be done unless the government conducted the economic system upon which employment and maintenance depend? Finally, what is implied in the equal right of all to the pursuit of happiness? What form of happiness, so far as it depends at all on material facts, is not bound up with economic conditions; and how shall an equal opportunity for the pursuit of happiness be guaranteed to all save by a guarantee of economic equality?"

Although economic equality was the economic and political cornerstone of his ideal society, Bellamy's moral one was the brotherhood of man, and the motivating force was enthusiasm for humanity. Bellamy not only intended for the nation to become "an economical organism, but a *moral* organism as well"; and he wrote to Colonel T. W. Higginson in December, 1888, that "on this last point" he would lay extraordinary stress.

> This is of course necessarily an economical reform, but its most important aspect is that of a *moral* movement for uplifting, enlarging and ennobling the individual life by making every individual contribute his efforts first and directly to the common or national wealth, and himself dependent for his livelihood upon his equal share in it, so that he is rich as the nation is rich and poor as his fellow citizens are poor and never otherwise. Then all the issues of life will be first from the individual to the nation, then from the nation back to him. As the hand profits not directly by what it seizes nor the mouth by what it devours, but only by sending its booty to the common treasury to be nourished in return by the red blood from the heart, so the members of the coming nation will serve and live, in constant remembrance and realization of their common life and mutual dependence. The great heart will beat in the pulse of the smallest members.[34]

The final result of this solidarity of interest which resulted from economic equality, cooperation, interdependence, and enthusiasm for humanity was to be a social order which would be morally, socially, economically, and politically based—as we have noted—upon the precepts of Christ. In one of his unpublished manuscripts, Bellamy wrote that this was "no new scheme. The idea that men being brothers should live together as brothers is as old as the first aspirations of humanity. It is the heart of all religion and the express meaning of Christ. . . . All I have done in *Looking Backward*, all I aim . . . to do is to show certain ways whereby men can realize this ideal."[35]

Bellamy's moral, humane, and economic objectives led philosopher John Dewey to state in "The Great American Prophet" (1934) that Bellamy was

an American and a New Englander in more than a geographical sense. He was imbued with a religious faith in the democratic ideal. But for that very reason he saw through the sham and pretense that exists or can exist in the present economic system . . . . he exposes his profound conviction that our democratic government is a veiled plutocracy. He was far from being the originator of this idea. But what distinguishes Bellamy is that he grasped the *human* meaning of democracy as an idea of equality and liberty. No one has carried through the idea that equality is obtainable only by complete equality of income more fully than Bellamy. Again, what distinguishes him is that he derives his zeal and his insight from devotion to the American ideal of democracy.[36]

To American Marxist Laurence Gronlund, Bellamy wanted "Uncle Sam . . . to grow up on the very lines that were laid down by the Pilgrims when they landed on Plymouth Rock."[37] To Charles Madison, Bellamy "possessed a social conscience characteristic of a long line of New England Puritans—from Roger Williams to Wendell Phillips. . . . As a true believer in the teachings of both Jesus and Jefferson, he felt impelled to cry out against oppression and inequality, to expound the 'principle of human brotherhood—the enthusiasm of humanity.'"[38] To Professor A. W. Levi, Bellamy was "the very incarnation of the best of our American radical tradition" but he had also the American reactionary's love for his country and the appreciation for the historic value of its tradition.[39]

But to perceive fully the Americanism of Bellamy's plans and objectives, we must also review the history of American aspirations, social criticism, Utopian institutions, and the intellectual interests of his countrymen before and during his time; for all of these, as we shall see, contributed to his American, pragmatic, Transcendental vision of the ideal society.

## IV  *American Aspirations and Criticisms*

From the beginning of the settlement of America, the dreams of men were given a new horizon, and a land of promise beckoned the courageous to seek their fulfillment. The concepts of the new life to be achieved or enjoyed were as varied as the individuals and their environments; some dreamed of adventure, some of wealth, some of religious freedom and toleration, some of realizing the Kingdom of God upon the earth, and some

envisioned social equality and the horn of plenty for all men.
As Bellamy viewed the early history of his nation, he wrote:

> A new and grand theater had been opened up for the human
> achievement, where mankind, freed from the burdens of tradi-
> tion, prejudice, and old-world oppressions of every sort, might
> take a new departure in the search for the lost paradise of the
> race. In this new world men found that their aspirations for
> liberty, equality, and fraternity, and the reign of justice on
> earth, which countless centuries of wrong and tyranny had been
> unable to stifle, were to be fulfilled. The first three centuries
> after the discovery were full of bloodshed and wickedness;
> but about a hundred years ago, when the American republic
> was founded, it looked as if the dreams which Columbus' dis-
> covery had suggested were indeed to be realized by the suc-
> cessful working out here of the problem of free government
> and equal rights for all. We are today confronted by portentous
> indications in the conditions of American industry, society and
> politics that this great experiment, on which the last hopes of
> the race depends, is to prove, like all former experiments, a
> disastrous failure.[40]

To Bellamy the reasons for the impending ruin were the "political corruption . . . social rottenness . . . moral degeneracy . . .
industrial oppression . . . which . . . resulted from the overthrow of our republican equality by the money power."[41]

Bellamy's view of the early significance of his country and
of its impending downfall was that of a New Englander. In
their colonial literature, New Englanders had shown their
concern about the social and religious values of the colonies;
for they were struggling to create a new social order which
they believed would be blessed by God if its ends were good
and honorable. In the writings of John Cotton, William Bradford, Edward Johnson, and John Winthrop, the early settlers
evinced their belief that Christ intended to achieve greater
matters with this handful of settlers than the world knew—
and thus began the vision of America's destiny which may be
traced in its literature.

To realize the new social order, John Winthrop urged that
men live closely knit together in brotherly love; and such sermons as that delivered by Robert Cushman in 1621 begged the
people not to ask for their individual portions of land, for the
ideal would be for them—as Bellamy in almost identical words
wrote centuries later to Higginson—to live as one, "being of
one heart, and one soul; neither anything more resembles hellish
horror, than for every man to shift for himself; for if it be good

mind and practice, thus to affect particulars, *mine* and *thine*, then it should be best also for God to provide one heaven for thee, and another for thy neighbor." Although Cushman did not specifically advocate permanent communal ownership and stated only that it was "too soon to put men to their shifts," he, like his intellectual and spiritual descendant, Edward Bellamy, did preach that "particularizing" was first introduced into the world by Satan and that "nothing in the world doth more resemble heavenly happiness than for men to live as one, being of one heart, and one soul. . . ."[42]

Despite the biblical admonition of "Let no man seek his own: but every man another's wealth," the people of the colonies of Plymouth and Jamestown were not contented with the communal ownership that had been instituted by their charters for practical and not idealistic purposes. The lands were soon allotted to individuals and—recorded William Bradford in his *History of Plimouth Plantation* (1630-50)—a remarkable increase of diligence resulted. In the South where religious fervor had contributed little to its settlements, an economic feudal order developed. In the North—where a crusading religious spirit had instigated settlements by the English Separatists, virtuous middle-class people who believed in democratic institution; by the Puritans, Jacobean gentlemen who supported an autocratic church and state; and by the Quakers—the capitalistic spirit was to flourish. Although New England was to have its John Eliot, who wrote in the colonial period the earliest outline of an ideal commonwealth based on Christian principles in *The Christian Commonwealth* (1659), and its John Woolman, who would denounce and leave trade because of its wickedness and its furtherance of immorality, it was to produce its capitalistic John Sewall and eventually its great materialistic philosopher Benjamin Franklin.

The capitalistic spirit was protected and encouraged by the religion of its settlers which, according to Max Weber, R. H. Tawney, and Clive Day, harmonized the quests for profit and for God by providing an ethical basis for the acquisition of riches. Wealth was a danger only when enjoyed or when it encouraged laziness; but when it was used to beget more riches, the usage was virtuous. The emphasis upon the importance and virtue of work, the denunciation of idleness, the doctrine of "the call," the belief in the mastery of self, and the reliance upon individual conscience, all paved the way for capitalism— and for Edward Bellamy who used these Puritan ideas and ideals in waging war against capitalism and in creating his new society which, like that of the early Puritan, sought to restrict man's use of man for profit.

And the early colonists of New England, like the medieval church and the Calvinists of Geneva, sought to control economic endeavors for the good of the whole. The early theocracy of Massachusetts was "merciless alike to religious liberty and to economic license." As Clive Day has pointed out, the social significances of property were emphasized as "they never have been in our later life" and the "use of capital was closely restricted to serve social ends."[43] The awareness of the priority of the interests of the group over that of individuals which had been included in the Pilgrim Compact of 1620 and in John Winthrop's *Modell of Christian Charity* ( 1630) was reflected in economic legislation which fixed the wages that artisans could command, established prices, limited export or products needed by the colonies, and established the legal rate of interest. City markets were encouraged so that competition would give the consumer a fairer price; public granaries were maintained so that the grain could be distributed at a fair price; and grist mills were either built by the town or so regulated that they would be operated for the benefit of the public.

Like the Europeans before them, the New England colonists rebelled at the religious restrictions placed upon usury; and the rebels founded new colonies or migrated to Pennsylvania where the tolerant, utilitarian, and individualistic characteristics flourished and eventually undermined the theocracies. These rebel colonies, such as that of Roger Williams, and their leaders were, however, to be considered by historians not only as the true founders of American democracy but as the fathers of the capitalistic, utilitarian nation epitomized by what Tawney called "the golden common sense of Benjamin Franklin."

By the end of the American Revolution, which had been fought for economic as well as political reasons, even the clergy was being denounced for its materialism and its catering to wealth by Timothy Dwight in "The Triumph of Infidelity." By 1786 the first armed revolt against the unjust use of property was to occur in Shays' Rebellion—and Edward Bellamy was to write in the 1870's the *first* historically accurate interpretation of this affair in *The Duke of Stockbridge*. In this novel Bellamy pointed out that the people believed that they had merely exchanged the rule of the king for that of the plutocrat, and he also portrayed the corrupting effect wealth had upon legislatures. The spirit of mercantilism, which Jefferson had so much feared, had already set aside those liberties and the rights of the people which the Declaration of Independence had assured them.

By 1789, Thomas Paine in *Agrarian Justice* and Freneau had pointed out the undemocratic exploitation of the masses by "the few, the proud, the first"—the wealthy. Paine thought not only that the contrast of poverty and affluence was undemocratic but that the state, through taxation, should redistribute the wealth which was produced not individually but by the social organism—and these statements were repeated a hundred years later by Bellamy.

In the 1830's James Fenimore Cooper presented in his political novels *The Bravo* and *The Heidenmauer*, brilliant, analagous analyses and warnings of the role economic combinations could play in defeating the objectives of the American Revolution and the principles of the Constitution by producing a greedy financial aristrocracy. In *The Heidenmauer* Cooper very astutely presented the Reformation in Germany as an example of the corruption produced by economic power and greed for it; and this was the same subject which later was also to interest Bellamy, a student of history. In *The Bravo* Cooper presented the methods used by the Venetian republican plutocrats to maintain their power; and Bellamy in *The Duke of Stockbridge* depicted the way a dictator could be developed and then used by the plutocracy.

Not only Paine, Jefferson, and Cooper, but Whittier, Lowell, and other abolitionists were to indicate, as Walter Taylor states in *The Economic Novel in America*, that "political democracy is not enough to insure the welfare of the average man, and must therefore be reinforced by some measure of economic democracy."[44] As we shall see, these ideas—popular before and after the Civil War—found their fullest expression in the Utopian novels of Edward Bellamy.

## V  Pre-Civil War Socialism

Before the Civil War, the power of wealth, the growing inequities of its distribution, a religious revival, and the popularity of the ideas of St. Simon, Fourier, and Robert Owen nearly achieved, stated John Noyes, a socialistic revolution. Although this statement was gross exaggeration, the interest in socialism which produced the first American socialistic works might have attained more concrete results had it not been for the abolition movement which turned the attention of reformers to the economic institution of slavery. After the chattel slave had been freed, many of the men who had been associated with the socialistic and the abolition movements turned their attention to the freeing of the wage slave.

The "brief and abortive social experiments of the forties" were, however, effective, wrote Bellamy in *Equality;* for they paved the way for the period after the Civil War when the people, because of their economic insecurity, were ready to take notice of the new economic order for which people had been agitating in Europe during and since the American Revolution, and to give "serious attention to the idea of dispensing with the capitalist by a public organization of industry to be administered like other common affairs in the common interests."

As this and other statements and references which Bellamy made indicate, he—an avid reader and a student of political economy, history, and religion—was very well acquainted with the radical thinkers of Europe and of his own country. In his book reviews and in his editorials published in the *Springfield Union* in the 1870's, Bellamy mentioned such early radical leaders in America as Fanny Wright, Robert Owen and Robert Dale Owen, Albert Brisbane, John Noyes, Josiah Warren, Horace Greeley, Theodore Parker, Bronson Alcott, Emerson, Thoreau, and others who in the pre-Civil War period were associated with the Owenite, Fourieristic, Transcendentalist movements; two of them he many years later knew personally as his own followers: Thomas W. Higginson and John Orvis. In considering the Americanism of Bellamy's ideas, the socialist movements, Utopian colonies and literature, literature of social criticism, and intellectual interests of the nineteenth century become important.

Because of the influence of Fanny Wright, of Robert Owen, and of Fourier, and because of the growing material inequities, the period from 1820 to 1860 produced the first American socialistic writing. Thomas Skidmore in *The Right of Man to Property* (1829) sponsored in almost Marxian terms collective ownership of all property and machinery and created a short-lived socialist movement. Before him, however, L. Byllesby in *Sources and Effects of Unequal Wealth* (1826) had presented an excellent analysis of economic exploitation; and William Thompson in *Essay on the Distribution of Wealth* (1824) had portrayed the social evils which resulted from material inequities, and had advocated that mutual cooperation replace the capitalistic system. Adin Ballou in *Practical Christian Socialism* (1854) had advanced the theories of socialism which had been the basis of his colony at Hopedale, Massachusetts. In periodicals and in book form, George Henry Evans published his arguments against all forms of property accumulation through land, usury, or speculation; he maintained, like Jefferson, that men held land in usufruct only and that the right to live entailed the right to land.

Albert Brisbane—whose ideas (according to his brother Frederick) interested Edward Bellamy—published under the influence of Fourier his *Social Destiny of Man* (1840). After Brisbane had converted Horace Greeley, Brisbane published a column in the *Tribune;* and it became, stated Charles Sotheran in his biography of Greeley, "a collectivist newspaper." The other important publication which was "the immediate organ of the American Socialists" of the period was *The Harbinger,* which replaced the famous *Dial.* Among the contributors—although all of them did not espouse *the cause*—were such men as Nathaniel Hawthorne, Theodore Parker, Emerson, Greeley, Lowell, Whittier, William Wetmore Story, Thoreau, Brisbane, Parke Godwin, Alcott, Higginson, R. D. Owen, and Orestes Brownson.

The influence of German socialism was evidenced during this period by William Weitling who wished socialism to incorporate Christian principles; who published *Republik der Arbiter;* and who founded a communistic colony in Communia, Wisconsin. During the same period, the New York German Communist Club was founded (1857); and the Turnverein, which had as its avowed chief purpose "the promotion of socialism and the support of the socialistic democratic party," was organized on a national basis (1850).[45]

During this era many groups founded, like Weitling, religious or socialist Utopian colonies in the United States. In 1870, John Noyes estimated the number to be over a hundred; R. Brace Taylor computed the number from 1607 to 1894 to have exceeded two hundred—but most of these colonies were founded before the Civil War. The oldest and most successful communities were those of the Shakers, who, guided by the visions and doctrines of Ann Lee, established their first colony at Mt. Lebanon, New York, in 1792; by 1874, the Shaker colonies numbered fifty-eight and had a total membership of nearly twenty-five hundred people. Other successful communities were those founded by the Rappites (1805); the Zoarites or Baumelers (1817); by the Eben-Ezers or Amana Communists (1844), whose settlements still flourish in Iowa; by the Oneida Perfectionists (1848); and by the Aurora Commune (1852).

Influences from abroad furthered the founding of many of these colonies, and the most influential of these were François

Fourier (and his disciples Victor Considerant, Horace Greeley, Albert Brisbane); Robert Owen, the father of English socialism; and Etienne Cabet. As a result of Fourierism, which was really humanitarian and cooperative and not communistic, some forty small, poorly financed experiments in associationism were started in the 1840's. The most famous of these was Brook Farm but the longest lived were the Wisconsin Phalanx (1844-1850) and the North American (1843).

The dates of the Owenite communistic colonies cluster around the year 1826, but the influence of Owen was to last throughout the century because of the publications of his son Robert Dale Owen, whose biography of his father was reviewed by Bellamy; he interestingly enough remarked that Robert stated his father's theory of economic equality had not been successful. Like Owen, Etienne Cabet insisted upon strict economic equality; but, as Bellamy pointed out in a *New Nation* article, he did not permit the colonists enough personal freedom. Cabet's non-religious, communistic settlements of the 1840's were ill-starred; but the Iowa colony had achieved prosperity by 1874 when it was visited by Charles Nordhoff.

Three Utopian anarchistic colonies were also founded in this period from 1830 to 1860 by Josiah Warren, who had been a dissenting member of the Owen New Harmony Colony. Warren, who expounded ideas similar to those of Proudhon, became the founder of the Boston Anarchists and was, said John Stuart Mill, one of the writers who had influenced his thinking. As we have already noted, Bellamy was conversant with the ideas of Warren.

Bellamy was acquainted with all these settlements and with their guiding principles and innovations; for he reviewed Charles Nordhoff's *The Communistic Societies of the United States* for the *Springfield Union* in December, 1874; and, in his pre-publication notice of the book in April, he had stated that Nordhoff's book would probably be less biased than John Noyes' *History of American Socialism*, since the latter would no doubt have been prejudiced by his own ideas which had led to his founding the Oneida Colony.

In his review of Nordhoff's book, Bellamy wrote that prejudice against the words "socialism" and "communism" had prevented widespread knowledge of the nature and results of these experiments and that this book was, therefore, a valuable contribution to American literature. In view of what Bellamy attempted to achieve in his ideal society, it is interesting to note that he observed that the colonies had for the most part as "their bond some religious belief, but this is not necessarily Christianity, but may be as with the Icarians a principle of social philosophy. . . ." He also noted that the "chief healthful influence of communal life is its freedom from care and anxiety for the future or for personal prospects which are guaranteed by the commune. . . ."[46]

When Bellamy also reviewed a reissue of Hawthorne's *Blithedale Romance*, he remarked that it was concerned with "the ever-interesting passage in the history of New England opinion."[47] Bellamy, like Hawthorne, believed, however, that a colony was not the test of the workability of the doctrines it advanced; for, founded in the midst of a hostile environment, it would have difficulty experimenting with any new moral or economic system. Bellamy considered that only a complete, independent state could test the practicability of any plan and that, furthermore, a single step taken toward reform in society made a more permanent gain than the most successful colony, by contributing to the felicity of the many and by showing others what could be attained. Bellamy stated: "We do not believe in the colony idea as a help to the social solution any more than we believe in the monastic idea as an assistance to the moral solution. . . . We cannot help thinking they [men and women] would serve their generation better by staying at home and preaching the gospel to their neighbors."[48]

## VI  *Utopian, Critical, Humanitarian Literature*

Besides Hawthorne's *Blithedale Romance*, ten other Utopian novels were written in the United States from 1819 to 1860. Though they have very little literary value, some are of interest because of their criticisms, their variable doctrines, and their various suggested plans for the reformation of society. Of particular interest because of Bellamy's concepts are George Tucker's *A Voyage to the Moon* (1827) which depicts an ideal community in which land was equally divided, and Ezekiel Sanford's *Humours of Europea: A Tale of Colonial Times* (1828) which portrays—as had John Eliot in 1659—a state based on the law of God. Sanford shows, as Cooper later did in *The Crater* (1847), the disruptive influence of religious differences. Cooper, however, because of his own experiences with courts and newspapers, added—as did Bellamy—lawyers, irresponsible editors, and professional ministers to the divisive, destructive influences of any ideal commonwealth.

Mrs. Mary Griffith published *Camperdown: or News from Our Neighborhood* (1836) which contained the long story

"Three Hundred Years Hence" depicting an era in which women had equal rights, wars and monopolies were abolished, and the government owned the railroads. The most popular novel of the period was, however, Sylvester Judd's Transcendental novel, *Margaret* (1845), which transported the reader to Mons Christi, the ideal state based on the love of Christ. In 1846, Judge John Wells of New York published, with the aid of Horace Greeley, *Henry Russell: or the Year Two Thousand*. When the novel did not sell, Judge Wells destroyed the edition; but, after *Looking Backward* was published, some reviewers called attention to the resemblance between the two ideal societies. In 1856, David Moore described in *The Age of Progress* a New Eden which had been attained by the brotherhood of men, restrictions upon ownership of property, and birth control.

From 1860 to 1887, three non-fiction books and eleven Utopian novels were published. American Marxist Laurence Gronlund's *Co-operative Commonwealth* (1884) outlined a cooperative state which many reviewers thought quite similar to Bellamy's when *Looking Backward* was published. Other critics and reviewers were also to compare both *Looking Backward* and *Equality* to Lester Ward's *Dynamic Sociology* (1883) and to Henry George's *Progress and Poverty* (1877-79). There is no doubt that Bellamy was conversant with George's single-tax theory, a form of agrarian socialism; but there is no proof that Bellamy had read either Ward or Gronlund until after the publication of *Looking Backward* when he knew Gronlund personally and when he presumably corresponded with Ward.

Of the Utopian novels published in the 1860's, those of Alexander Lookup—*Excelsior* (1860) and *The Road Made Plain to Fortune for the Millions* (1860)—attacked in the first novel the banking system, foreclosures, and panics and in the second the party system which led to organized public plundering and to usurpation of the laws of both men and God. In *The Road,* the author also suggested that the people must stop not only this plunder but also the "rent and taxation" which created an irresponsible aristocracy. The anonymous *Equality, or a History of Lithconia* (1863) and Radical Freelance's *The Philosophers of Foufouville* (1868) presented egalitarian societies, but the latter also contained an indictment of reformers reminiscent of those of Hawthorne in *Blithedale Romance,* and of Edward Bellamy.

The Reverend Everett Hale, who was mentioned frequently by Bellamy in his articles and reviews of the 1870's, published two Utopias: *Sybaris* (1869), delineating the ideal society of an island off the coast of Italy which was ruled by the natural aristocracy, did not believe in commerce or war, and had the objective of educating people; and *Ten Times Ten Is One* (1870), which presented the brotherhood-of-man, lend-a-hand philosophy which had brought about the new social order.

Although Mark Twain anonymously published his critical, provocative *The Curious Republic of Gondour* in 1875, the most significant Utopian novel of this decade was T. Wharten Collens' *The Eden of Labor: or the Christian Utopia* (1876). After depicting the strife between capital and labor which made the world far from ideal, Collens advocated that labor and capital be united in the same body and that Christ's law of love be instituted. Like Collens, Bellamy was to believe that Christianity and Christian virtues were impossible in a capitalistic society and that charity and love were the principles upon which political economy should be based.

Of the five Utopian novels which appeared in the 1880's, one of these *supposedly* influenced Bellamy: John Macnie's imaginative *Diothas* (1883) which outlined a society that was not socialistic but one in which all the citizens worked at home and had ample time for social and intellectual pursuits. Although there is no actual proof that Bellamy read *The Diothas*, reviewers saw a resemblance because of the scientific improvements forecast; the labor force, which had already been suggested by Hale; and the use of mesmerism—a very popular topic at the time and one often employed, therefore, in literature.

A. D. Cridge in *Utopia* (1884) portrayed a planet state upon which war and want no longer existed, and the picture of men on earth criticized the slavery and injustice, the superstition, and the ignorance of the era. In the land of *A New Moral World* (1885) by James Casey, the people had abolished crime and poverty by banishing money from their world—a world in which the people owned all the land for their united use and in which the brotherhood of man was an actualtiy. In *The Key of the Industrial Cooperative Government* (1886) Henry Allen also delineated a social order in which no money and no competition existed. Production and distribution had been nationalized, labor was compulsory, and each person was given to according to his needs from the common fund.

Although Bellamy did not borrow from these Utopian novels, the basic criticisms and solutions of his predecessors were, like his, reflections of the age—of interests and plans with which Bellamy could have become acquainted in many, many ways. In fact, he doubtless was, but he mentioned only Hale's and

Hawthorne's novels among the many Utopias to which he frequently referred in his articles and editorials. Most of his references are to Plato's *Republic*, Lytton's *The Coming Race* and
*The Parisians*, and E. Maitland's *By and By*, which to Bellamy
contained "excellent social and moral speculation . . . food for
thought." Bellamy considered Bacon's *Atlantis* inferior to his
other works; but he had only praise for Hugo's *Ninety-three*,
which contains a picture of an ideal society comparable to
Bellamy's. He frequently referred to Rabelais, so it is more than
probable that he was acquainted with "The Castle of Thelemy";
and he not only mentioned but quoted Johnson's *Rasselas* in
his discussion of the Utopian plans of Ruskin. Other references
indicate that Bellamy had read Dr. Richardson's *City of Health*,
Swift's *Gulliver's Travels*, Kingsley's *Alton Locke* and *Yeast*,
and Fénelon's *Télémaque*—a writer very popular in the New
England of Bellamy's time and one to whom Bellamy attributed
great influence upon his ideas.

Bellamy was not only acquainted with the Utopists of all
time, but reviewed or read many of the novels of social criticism
of his period which dealt with the problems of woman's rights,
political corruption, cooperation as a means of solving the industrial problems, profit sharing, and exploitation of the laborer.
Bellamy's editorials in the *Springfield Union* and decades later
in the *New Nation* indicated his preoccupation with these problems and with their proposed solutions. Among the books which
he reviewed for the *Union* in the 1870's were Mark Twain's and
Charles D. Warner's *The Gilded Age*, Reverend J. G. Holland's
*The Story of Sevenoaks*, Bailey's *They All Do It*, and De Forest's *Honest John Vane*. Bellamy's comments in his reviews and
his articles show not only his awareness of the concern with the
problems of his era but his sources—as has been shown in *The
Year 2000: A Critical Biography of Edward Bellamy* (1958)—
for the developments he depicted as having already occurred
in *Looking Backward*.

These same articles and reviews also reveal his reading of
classical and humanitarian foreign literature. Of the foreign
writers, Bellamy was particularly fond of Charles Dickens
whom he mentioned in *Looking Backward* as the author who
first opened the eyes of humanity and stirred its heart by picturing situations as they actually existed. In his reviews of the
1870's, Bellamy noted that Hugo portrayed the depths of
human misery and had stressed enthusiasm for humanity; that
Turgenev in *Virgin Soil* had outlined the causes of revolution
and had consistently pled for the solidarity of humanity; and

that George Sand was a true republican who deserved high praise for the high principles she expressed in her fiction. Bellamy also praised Thackeray, enjoyed the novels of Hardy, and quoted such classical writers as Marcus Aurelius, Thomas Aquinas, Epictetus, Cicero, Virgil, Froude, Rochefoucauld, Goethe, Montesquieu, Plato, Plotinus, De Tocqueville, and others.

## VII  Socialism after the Civil War

Although many of the American socialistic, critical, or Utopian books before the Civil War had been the result of foreign influences and of native situations which had interested or concerned the intellectuals, socialism after the war became popular among the laborers. As John Orvis, who was associated with both periods, wrote in 1890 in The Nationalist, "the sleep of the ages" had been broken from 1830 to 1850 by St. Simon, Fourier, and Owen; but from 1850 to 1890 their

labors of the morning had been stimulated and augmented by the inspiration of Lassalle and Marx . . . and have been carried forward towards the noonday by the roused and marshalled working classes, engaged in efforts for the gradual application of the principles of socialism to existing commercial and industrial relations; some in promoting cooperative stores, as in England and the United States, others in cooperative industry, such as the Cooperative Carpenters' and Cooperative Saddlers' Associations, with Godin's Industrial Palace in France, and cooperative banking in Germany; others in promoting Christian socialism like Maurice, Kingsley, Hughes, Ruskin, and Morris in England; Ripley, Channing, Greeley, and James in the United States.

After the lapse of those early experiments in combined social order in England and the United States, such as that of New Lanark, and those of Brook Farm and the North American Phalanxes, socialism went down among the working classes, to whom it was a necessity; and has from that time been educating them into methods for its gradual application to the exigencies of their conditions. The outcome has been to establish a propagandism without a parallel among popular movements, especially in the United States.

The special agencies in this work have been such associations as the "Patrons of Husbandry," the "Sovereigns of Industry," "The Sociological Society," and the tremendous agitations among trades unions and other workingmen's organizations throughout the world. It is probable, however, that no other popular movement so clearly demonstrates the extent to which socialistic ideas pervade the minds of the working classes as that of the "Knights of Labor." Their declaration of principle is a masterly

programme of socialistic ideas and methods, adapted to the
present condition of the movement, and their gradual embodiment in improved social arrangements, according to the popular enlightenment and necessity. . . . It is these tremendous
forces, which have been silently working through society for
more than forty years, that have created the popular current
which is bearing on its bosom Messrs. George and Bellamy and
their works. . . .[49]

This postwar interest in socialism was, wrote James F. Hudson in 1887 in the *North American Review*, the result of monopolies, pools, and trusts which controlled the necessities of life.[50]
Basically, Bellamy agreed with Hudson, for he too saw that
from these combinations sprang mass production which produced impersonal relations between employee and employer,
the formation of unions, the bloody conflicts between capital
and labor, the startling inequities in the distribution of wealth,
the corruption of the state and national legislatures, and the
speculative frenzy and the glut of the market which created
panics, depressions, unemployment, insecurity, cynicism about
the efficacy of republican government, and multiple suggestions
for reform. As Bellamy viewed the national situation, he felt
that no single proposed reform measure would long rectify the
situation; and he also saw in industrial society "a stream of
tendencies through ever larger experiments in concentration
and combination toward the ultimate complete integration of
the nation for economic as well as for political purposes."
Since the economic reasons for consolidation were valid and
workable, Bellamy accepted this tendency as the basic principle
of association which through a peaceful, legal, evolutionary
process would lead to one Great Monopoly, the State.
As early as 1872 Bellamy had, however, outlined in a lyceum
speech what socialism might be able to accomplish in the creation of a more equitable, moral world. His book reviews and his
editorials of this same decade in the *Union* also indicate that
he was well acquainted with all the movements mentioned by
John Orvis and with some which were not: The Knights of St.
Crispin, the Molly Maguires, the International Working People's Association, other native and foreign cooperatives and
profit-sharing experiments, and state or municipal ownership
of public facilities.
As has been shown in *The Year 2000: A Critical Biography
of Edward Bellamy* and in Arthur Morgan's *Edward Bellamy*,
Bellamy was also aware of the Marxists. Although Marx's *Das
Kapital* had not been translated into English when Bellamy

wrote *Looking Backward*, his ideas had been popularized in pamphlets, newspapers, and brochures which, said Bellamy in 1874, made a "pile rivalling the pyramid of Cheops."[51] Bellamy's other comments in the *Union* also show that he was conversant with the work of Victoria Woodhull, who had published the first complete English version of *The Communist Manifesto* in *Woodhull and Claflin's Weekly*. Bellamy remarked, however, that when Woodhull and Stephen Pearl Andrews (a disciple of Josiah Warren, a Fourierist, a Swedenborgian, and a state socialist) had joined the International, they had done the organization inestimable damage by associating with it their doctrines about free love.

Among the many foreign radicals whose books were reviewed or mentioned by Bellamy were Charles Bradlaugh, Joseph Arch, Ruskin, J. S. Mill, Norman MacLeod, Charles Kingsley, Murray, William Morris, Thomas Cooper, Frederick Maurice, Sir Arthur Helps, and Thomas Hughes. He also reviewed such studies of radical leaders as R. J. Hinton's *English Radical Leaders*, Edward Young's *Labor in Europe and America*, and Giles G. Stebbins' *Bible of the Ages*. In his reviews and editorials Bellamy mentioned the ideas of St. Simon, Comte, Proudhon, Blanc, Hegel, Descartes, and others mentioned elsewhere in this chapter.

Bellamy's knowledge of the ideas of these American and European radicals and of the innovations sponsored by the various Utopian settlements and reform groups become extremely important to the student who seeks the sources for the ideas which he incorporated in his ideal society. For examples of the way he synthesized material, let us note the following concepts. Although Bellamy stated in *Equality* that the idea of the "integrated economic system coordinating the efforts of all for the common welfare" dated back in theory to Plato and had probably existed before him, Bellamy was also acquainted with the advocacy of collective ownership by the Icarian, Owenite, Shaker, and Oneida Perfectionist colonies and by the different labor and revolt groups of the United States. Of the radical thinkers with whom he was acquainted who sponsored collective ownership were—to mention a few—Owen, St. Simon, Lassalle, Hegel, J. S. Mill, Blanc, Proudhon, Comte, and, of course, Marx and Engels.

Although Bellamy stressed the importance of economic equality in the ideal state as one of his major differences with the Marxists, he—as Professor Richard Ely indicated in *Socialism and Social Reform*[52]—was not distinctively original. Although,

as we have already noted, American political writers and critics
had long urged comparative economic equality as a means of
assuring the other equalities and freedoms established by the
Constitution, it is probable that Bellamy borrowed the idea of
absolute economic equality from Cabet, who considered inequality the source of the world's ills and who founded his
society "*sur la base d'Égalité la plus parfaite*";[53] from Blanc,
who had instituted it in his association of tailors at Clichy in
1848; or from Proudhon, Owen, or Roscher. Bellamy also displayed, however, his debt to the American scene, for he but-
tressed his argument for economic equality by pointing out that
it was a logical extension not only of the Constitution but of
the wage system employed by the unions which realized that
an equal wage was the only system that would give unity
and contentment to men. For a broader application of the principle, Bellamy pointed to the policy of the federal government
of providing equal protection for all in time of war and of
disbursing the taxes to state-supported schools for the benefits
of the whole society.

Bellamy also supported his argument for economic equality
with the social fund theory—an idea which had been developed
by St. Simon. Bellamy insisted that, since the social organism—
"the machinery of associated labor and exchange"—which made
the production of wealth possible was the result of the work
and invention of many generations, it was "the indivisible inheritance of all in common" and hence should belong to society
collectively. This principle of the social fund made it impossible to give a man wages based wholly on the product of his
own labor since he utilized perforce the knowledge and the
inventions of the past. This impossibility of distinguishing each
man's contribution from the common inheritance of the social
organism made, therefore, equality of income a necessity; at
the same time, these factors also proved the mutual dependence
and support which existed in society and, moreover, the basic
wrongness of anyone's using any part of the social organism
for private profit. Like Marx, St. Simon, Proudhon, Rodbertus,
and Wendell Phillips, Bellamy regarded the profit system as
theft.

Because men had only a joint title to the social heritage,
Bellamy argued that private ownership was unjust. Like Lassalle, he asserted, however, that the equal income of wages
of the ideal state was private property and that it was more
firmly established and guaranteed by state capitalism than it
had been by private capitalism. The new system of ownership

and income was comparable to that of the corporations; but, argued Bellamy, it was not only psychologically beneficent since it freed all men and all women from worry and insecurity, but it was also morally so, since the divisive and anti-social influence of unequal wealth no longer existed. In order to maintain economic equality, it was necessary, however, that inheritance of any kind of property be discontinued—and here too Bellamy was using the ideas which had been proposed by labor groups and socialists as a means of distributing wealth more equitably.

In his creation of the industrial armies which were to supply the wealth guaranteeing equality of income, Bellamy could have been inspired by such men as Cabet, Blanc, Fourier, St. Simon, and Edward E. Hale who had all advocated productive organization of labor. In his early editorials of the 1870's, Bellamy had written about the great public works sponsored by Napoleon III, and decades later he had written about the law proposed to the Massachusetts legislature which would have made it possible for the state to establish industries for the employment of the unemployed. In his articles and later in his Utopias, Bellamy argued that the employment of laborers by the nation was merely the fulfillment of the government's duty to supply the source of life—work—to its citizens; and in presenting this argument Bellamy showed his acquaintance with Fichte, Blanc, Comte, and the labor-union spokesmen of his own era.

In his rules and regulations of the industrial armies Bellamy employed the merit system, which had been widely discussed in his epoch; the equality of women, which had been advocated by the radical suffragette leaders; the Puritan sense of the benefit of work for the individual and the duty of contributing to the community; and the idea of "the call" which meant in the ideal state that people would be given the work for which their innate abilities and interests prepared them.

These few examples of Bellamy's application of the trends and the ideas of his century and of the men he had studied not only indicate the method he used in creating his industrial democracy but they show—as Louis Hartz has stated in *The Liberal Tradition in America* (1955)—the very Americanism of Bellamy's synthesis. Bellamy, like other Americans before and after him, considered the trust as the source of all ills; and by turning the country into one Great Monopoly, he hoped to solve the problem and, at the same time, save the Locke-Jeffersonian republic,[54] insure "and vindicate the right of property on a scale never dreamed of," and create the industrial democracy which he had stated he hoped to create in 1873: one which would solve the problems of his time in a more "sagacious and sincere" fashion than that proposed by the Internationalists, whom he described as sponsoring "international demagoguism" and "communist violence."[55]

That Bellamy was sincere in his attitude toward the Marxists was evinced not only in his articles and journal entries of the 1870's, 1880's, and 1890's (which have already been reviewed) but by his reactions toward the socialists who had joined the Bellamy clubs: he tried to evict them. Letters from a member of the Washington, D. C., club[56] and from Cyrus Field Willard of the Boston one, attest to Bellamy's desire to expel the socialists because he feared that Laurence Gronlund and others would either capture the Nationalist movement or incorrectly interpret his ideas which, wrote socialist Willard, were recognized by him and by Gronlund as being "three-fourths Nationalism and one-fourth Communism."[57]

When Sylvester Baxter stated in *The Nationalist* in 1889 that Bellamy was "too utilitarian for the orthodox Marxist," Bellamy, who admired John Stuart Mill, must have agreed with him. Although Bellamy was a pragmatic evolutionist, he was also a New England moralist and mystic whose ideal state had intellectual, spiritual objectives which were the result of his *Religion of Solidarity* resulting in turn from the intermingled influence of Hegel, Comte, Swedenborg, Fénelon, Darwin, the Chartists, and Transcendentalism. Although these influences had often merged in one way or another in the ideas of individuals or in the intellectual movements before Bellamy, they received their fullest and most popular expression in the ideal state of the year 2000 which Bellamy presented in *Looking Backward*. Henry James, Sr., observed that Emerson proclaimed the good time coming but was incapable of stating the form it would take. Bellamy did so.

## VIII  *Philosophical Influences and Objectives*

Like Emerson, Thoreau, Alcott, Theodore Parker, and William E. Channing, whose books Bellamy read and reviewed in the *Union*, Bellamy in the "Religion of Solidarity" stressed the primacy of the human soul; but he also recognized the duality of man—the presence in him of the infinite or impersonal and of the finite or individual. Like Emerson, Alcott, Thoreau, and James, Bellamy rejected the selfish, divisive, amoral individualism of the market place; and, like James and Alcott, he dreamed of a society which would solve the economic problems of man and thereby free him to develop his spiritual and intellectual qualities. To Bellamy—as to Alcott, James, Fénelon, Comte, and the Hegelians—the salvation of mankind lay in the development of the impersonal—the unselfishness and the love for others which united man with man, and with God or the Absolute.

Like Henry James, Sr., Bellamy believed that man was part of the Universal Spirit to which he was joined by the spark of the universal or impersonal in him and which, with the right environment, could be developed. This universal force was the spirit of God existing in all men and which therefore united all men or made them brothers—and both Bellamy and James were not certain that there was either an impersonal or a personal God to be worshipped. Bellamy did believe, however, that men would discover—as has already been noted—the true significance of "God the Father" only when they had developed the impersonal to such an extent that they could create the society of love which would approach the Kingdom of God on earth. When they had achieved this ideal state, there would be no need for an organized Church or for a government which would rule men. Although Bellamy believed with James that once this state had been achieved these institutions would become unnecessary, he also believed that men could best exist in a socialist state—but one that would rule not men but production and distribution.

Bellamy did not envision the immediate coming of such an anarchical society; but he did believe that the moral life, the love of others, the educational opportunities, the lack of concern about economic problems, the increased leisure, and the spiritual growth made possible by it would eventually result in a great improvement upon even the ideal society which he had depicted in *Looking Backward*. The ideal state was, he wrote, "a single step in the infinite progression of humanity toward the divine" and men would so develop the Greater Self that the day would come when they would have discovered new truths about the infinite and when "spiritual forces" would "fully dominate all things." "Questions of physical power" would then "cease to be of any importance in human relations"; for the control and the leadership of humanity would be given to those who "partake most of the Spirit of the Greater Self"—"one of our names for the soul and for God."[58] And these men would never misuse their power for selfish ends; if they did, it would cease to be power. Like Emerson, Bellamy believed, therefore,

that men were perfectible; and, like James, he believed that
when they were sufficiently perfected they would be able to
live socially in a state of anarchy.

The ideal moral man of Bellamy was also the practical, speculative man of the Transcendentalists; for he, as Bellamy described him in *The Religion of Solidarity*, would be neither the
"Indian Buddhist in ecstatic contemplation seeking to merge
himself in God in disregard of his actual status as individual"
nor the "self-seeker in the insanity of individualism concentrating his being in microscopic activities (equally microscopic
whether they concern fagots or empires, since they are pursued in the spirit of individualism)." He would be "he whose
spirit dwells among the stars and in all time, but whose hands
are as deft with the most menial as with the mightiest tasks
through which this soul of solidarity can find expression; who
turns his hands with equal readiness to the founding of
empires and to the washing of beggars' feet, holding all tasks
in honor, since with him the infinite motive overshadows the
deed itself."

Besides the Transcendental movement—a compound itself of
the influence of German and English philosophers, Oriental
mysticism, Swedenborg, Plato, Plotinus, and Fénelon's Quiet-
ism—there were also the Hegelian and the social gospel movements in Bellamy's era. Walt Whitman saw in Hegel the "perfect philosophy" for his concept of the democratic development
of the city of friends; and William Torrey Harris, Denton J.
Snider, Bronson Alcott, and the Reverend Elisha Mulford also
promoted Hegel's ideas.

Harris and Snider, who had not only translated but studied
Hegel, founded their *Journal of Speculative Philosophy* in 1867
in St. Louis, Missouri. In the first issue in "To the Reader"
the editors wrote:

The national consciousness has moved forward during the last
few years. The idea underlying our form of government had
hitherto developed only one of its essential phases—that of brit-
tle individualism—in which national unity seemed an external
mechanism soon to be entirely dispensed with, and the enterprise of the private man or of the corporation substituted for it.
Now we have arrived at the consciousness of the other essential phase, and each individual recognizes his substantial side to
be the state as such. The freedom of the individual does not
consist in the more arbitrary, but in the realization of the rational connection which finds expression in established law.
That this new phase of national life demands to be digested

and comprehended, is a further occasion for the cultivation of the speculative.

Snider pointed out the dangers of monocracy to democracy since wealth was used to the detriment of others; and he saw the cure for the dangers of individual ownership to be civic ownership or state socialism which would express and be the final form of the will of the people—just as James and Bellamy saw it as the society which would permit internal unity based upon the brotherhood of man. Although Harris and Alcott organized the Concord Summer School of Philosophy (1877-1887) with the hope of bringing together New England Transcendentalism and the ideal of democratic socialism, they did not found a major school of thought. Indeed, after *Looking Backward* became popular, Harris attacked Bellamy's plan; for to Harris capitalism was no threat to the spiritual or moral life of man.[59]

This view of the effect of the industrial system was not shared by Hegelian Reverend Elisha Mulford, the friend of Frederick D. Maurice, the English Hegelian and Chartist. Mulford published a highly respected periodical, *The Nation,* and a book, *The Republic of God* (1881). In the latter—which contained a preface paying tribute to Hegel, Maurice, Stahl, and others—Mulford introduced the social gospel movement to America. In his book he presented the idea of the nation as a moral organism, the need of religion in secular reform, and the possibility of achieving the Kingdom of God on earth.

The efforts of Mulford, O. B. Frothingham, Josiah Strong, Edward Everett Hale, Washington Gladden, and Jesse Jones were important in the development of the social gospel movement in the United States. Though the conservative members did not advocate (like Jones for example) political socialism as the solution of the problems and threats of industrial capitalism, they did recognize the need of greater social and economic equality and of greater sympathy for the proletariat on the part of the church. They also recognized the role played by a poor environment in the development of depravity, and they encouraged consideration of the cooperative and profit-sharing plans which had been proposed as solutions to the economic injustices and problems of the period. Believing with William Blake that religion was politics and that politics was religion, they also sponsored the application of Christian principles to the material life of the nation.

Edward Bellamy was, as we have seen, a reader of the books written by those involved in the Chartist movement in England; and the importance he attached to their work is indicated by his editorial about Maurice, Kingsley, and MacLeod in the *Union*[60] and by his article about Thomas Cooper in the *New Nation*.[61] His reviews and articles of the 1870's also show that he had read Hale, Bushnell, Gladden, Frothingham, and Professor Crocker's *Theistic Conception of the World*. Of Crocker's book Bellamy wrote that it expressed the author's belief that the crowning achievement of men would be "the establishment of human government on the basis of liberty, equality, and human brotherhood."[62] When he reviewed Bishop Clarke's *The Dew of Youth*, Bellamy stated that the author laid down the true and Christian principles of trade and had pointed out that it was better to starve than to follow the immoral business practices of the day.[63]

That Bellamy had also read Hegel and Swedenborg is proved by an entry in his journal of the early 1870's in which he quoted Hegel,[64] and by his reviews in the *Union* of books about Swedenborg. In 1876 in a review of Theophilus Parson's *Religion and Philosophy of Swedenborg*, Bellamy not only recommended the book by the "distinguished writer upon jurisprudence" as being the "clearest and most fascinating" interpretation of Swedenborg by his "American followers"; but he also stated: "the chief essentials of Christianity seem to be included in Swedenborgianism, with the addition of a poetical and beautiful spiritual philosophy, belief in which is doubtless a consolation to many sensitive souls and could not possibly harm anyone."[65] In the same year, Bellamy also reviewed *Algatchie, Seen and Unseen*, which he proclaimed to be a presentation of the doctrine of Swedenborg in the guise of fiction,[66] and Wilkie Collins' *Two Destinies*, which illustrated "the Swedenborgian conception of love."[67]

Besides movements which sought to ameliorate the conditions resulting from the industrial, competitive system, there was also another—begun twenty-five years before the publication of *Looking Backward*—by the political economists who rejected the Adam Smith or Manchester School of economics which had upheld the laissez-faire doctrine with the argument that what the individual did for his own good could not but be beneficial to society. John Stuart Mill, whom Bellamy had read since his seventeenth year, and Bastiat, whom he also admired, had long since argued that there must be complete harmony of the interests of the individual and the community; and Mill had stressed not only the importance of economic equality but the utilitarianism of the Golden Rule as an ethical code. Richard Ely and Frank Lester Ward in the United States had seen the dangers of individualism; and they, like the social gospelers, had denounced the Manchester School and moved toward the acceptance of Christian precepts as a basis of economic life such as had been sponsored by such men as Professor Schmoller in Germany; De Lamennais in France; and Fawcett, McCulloch, Henry Sidgwick, and Sidney Webb in England.

These efforts to combine religion, economics, and politics were noted by Bellamy in his editorials and book reviews in the *Union* in the 1870's. In his articles Bellamy himself called for the application of Christian principles to the political and economic life of the nation, for, he said, people were acting like barbarians or gypsies rather than Christians. Bellamy's reviews also indicate that he had read the essays about political economy of Harriet Martineau and of Frederick Bastiat; he stated that these writers had performed the valuable service of making the people conversant with political economy. Among the other books dealing with this subject which Bellamy reviewed or mentioned were works by Jevons, Cairnes, John Stuart Mill, Washington Gladden, General F. A. Walker, and others. Of Gladden's *Working People and Their Employees* Bellamy wrote in 1876 that the author's "moral economy is as sound as his political economy. It is his theory that the two go together and that the one is to be interpreted by the other, and certainly the success he has met with in solving industrial problems by moral tests bear out the theory."[68]

Bellamy was also interested in another great intellectual and religious problem of his era—the reconciliation of religion with Darwin's theory of evolution. In 1873 he wrote that the aim of the true student should be to make the unity of science and religion manifest, for both were branches of science—if science recognized true wisdom and was inspired by the right motives, and if the elements of religion were correctly grasped. Both science and religion should have the same rank, and to find a way to this basis through "whatever jungle of physical or theological error" was the great necessity, he asserted, of modern thought.[69]

In his editorials and reviews Bellamy showed that he had read many books concerned with evolution and the scientific problems of his day written by such men as Darwin, Spencer, Huxley, and Tyndall. To readers who wished to become informed about the theory of evolution, he recommended Dr. M. E. Cazelle's *Outline of the Evolution Philosophy*.[70] Of the books which he reviewed which sought to reconcile the theory of evolution with religion were Asa Gray's *Darwiniana,* Professor Draper's *Religion and Science,* John Fiske's *The Unseen World and Other Essays,* Dawson's *The Origin of the World According to Revelation and Science,* and Alexander Winchell's *Reconciliation of Science and Religion.*

In his Utopian novels Bellamy differed from men of his day like W. G. Sumner who argued that Darwin's theory supported the doctrine of laissez-faire; for Bellamy, while accepting the theory of natural selection and of evolution, felt that, unless men exerted their intellects and wills to create an environment which would permit *the best to survive,* those who survived the fray of the competitive society would be the most ruthless, cunning, and amoral. Like Lester Frank Ward before him and Hegelian philosopher Josiah Royce after him, Bellamy considered economic competition to be not only wasteful but inhumane; for, instead of encouraging brotherly love, it necessitated internecine strife and a dependence on bread for survival which robbed man of all his dignity.

Believing that all men were part of the Absolute; that they should live in Christian brotherhood; and that, as an early journal entry of the 1870's testifies, they had the power of creators,[71] Bellamy sought to create an ideal society which would provide an environment in which men would be restored their dignity, their loyalty to one another, and their ability to direct evolutionary growth toward perfectibility—toward God. American, optimistic, perfectibilitarian Bellamy stated in one of his articles that scientific proof of the possibility of achieving the ideal man was to be found in Spencer who stated that he would ultimately develop.[72] The pronouncement should, wrote Bellamy, inspire the creation of an environment which would encourage not only the development of godhood in man but the best physical type of men.

Bellamy had not only read Spencer and John Stuart Mill but also Auguste Comte. Although he probably became acquainted with Comte during his self-organized reading course at Union College, his references to Comte and his reviews of writers who were popularizing his ideas attest to the fact that his interest in positivism was a lasting one. In the 1870's Bellamy wrote of Harriet Martineau's condensation of Comte's philosophy, of Elizabeth Dudley's articles on the ideal life and character of the positivist, and of Taine's notes on positivism. He also discussed the ideas about immortality expressed by the English positivist Frederick Harrison; and he extolled the virtues of

George Eliot's novels. In his editorials he made many references to Comte's philosophy, and in an unpublished manuscript entitled "Woman Worship" and a short story, "A Positive Romance" (1889), Bellamy discussed Comtean ideas.

Because of these evidences of Bellamy's long-lasting interest in Comte, there can be no doubt that positivism contributed to Bellamy's optimism about the use men could make of material progress, to the basic ideals of both Bellamy's *Religion of Solidarity* and his ideal society, and to his brilliant synthesis of ideas and practices of his time in the creation of his Utopia. Generally—and there is space for only a general discussion— Bellamy reflected Comte's desire to unite order with progress; to unify the past and the present into a harmonious whole; to direct all the social forces to one end—moral progress; and to subordinate all things to and establish all man-willed evolutionary progress upon the basic universal principle of love.

Comte wished to create a new religion for a harmonious society by retaining the good of the old and by ridding it of errors and of superstitions; he sought also to establish woman as the symbol of humanity. Bellamy—as a result of his reading of Comte, the biblical studies of such advanced scholars as Max Muller, Dr. Muir, and Whitney, and his close following of the religious movements of his day which fostered the placing of less emphasis upon creeds and theology—banished theology and institutionalized religion from his ideal society. He maintained, however, the Christian ethical code and philosophy of love, established brotherhood as the basic motivator toward and the principle of the new society, and expected men to continue to develop their spiritual force until it became the only significant power in the world. Like Comte, Bellamy regarded woman as the representative of humanity; and he described her as the centripetal force which developed the impersonal—unselfishness—in man which made solidarity and, therefore, true progress possible.

Like Comte, Bellamy searched for the simple uniting principle or system which would harmonize all facets of life—political, economic, social, intellectual, and spiritual—and to establish thereby a society which would ensure the perfectibility of men by solving the material problems which so preoccupied and so corrupted them. As he searched for the scientific solution which would leave no "unaccounted for residuum"—for, if it did, wrote Bellamy, it was "no solution"[73]—he found his basic principles of brotherly love, of the development of the impersonal, and of evolution in the intellectual environment which nourished him; and these he added to his political heritage from Jefferson and Locke.

Bellamy's synthesis of the intellectual preoccupations of his era with social criticisms and experimentations and with political and industrial achievements and difficulties, made *Looking Backward* the focus of nineteenth-century liberal thought. In all of his Utopian society Bellamy displayed, however, what Louis Hartz in *The Liberal Tradition* has described as "one of the secrets of the American character: a capacity to combine rock-ribbed traditionalism with high inventiveness, ancestor worship with ardent optimism." Bellamy also, as we have noted, considered himself an American conservative; and in doing so he illustrated the truth of Gunnar Myrdal's observation that though the American "is . . . conservative . . . the principles conserved are liberal and some, indeed, are radical."[74]

Because Bellamy was an American who carried his country's "democratic theology over from politics into economics," because he solved the problems of the industrial revolution and of individual enterprise in a fashion which would enable economic democracy to serve "humane culture," and because he blended so many "mental and spiritual resources," his *Looking Backward* was—asserted John Dewey—"one of the greatest modern syntheses of humane values."[75] Because of the moral values he stressed and the familiar ideas his work contained, *Looking Backward* became not only one of the most popular but one of the most internationally influential novels ever written by an American.

Although Edward Bellamy was an American nineteenth-century liberal, his ideas lived into the twentieth century. His powerful portrayal of an ideal society and trenchant criticisms of capitalism contributed to the spreading of socialist concepts and—startling as this may seem—the creation of the Russian Revolution which inaugurated a Marxist-inspired communist state.

# CHAPTER TWO

# A Little-Known Story:
# Bellamy in Russia

by

## ALEXANDER NIKOLJUKIN

THE STORY OF THE POPULARITY and influence of Edward Bellamy's
Utopian fiction in Russia is an interesting but little-known page
in the annals of Russo-American literary and social relationships
during the late nineteenth century. Although Bellamy's *Miss
Ludington's Sister* was published in a translated, condensed version as early as 1885, it had received little notice; and Bellamy's
name did not become a byword among Russian democratic and
socialist circles until *Looking Backward* had been translated.

## I  *Tolstoy, Translations, and Censors*

Significantly, the first translation of this famous Utopian
novel was made as a result of the interest it aroused in Leo
Tolstoy, who in 1889 had been given a first edition of the book
by Isabel F. Hapgood, the American author who frequently
visited Russia and who also translated Tolstoy's works into
English.[1] This copy of *Looking Backward*, which is preserved
in the library of Tolstoy's country estate in Yasnaya Polyana,
contains marginal notes in the famous author's writing which
indicate that he had read the novel very attentively. On June
30, 1889, Tolstoy wrote in his diary his impression of Bellamy's
novel: "An exceedingly remarkable book: it would be a good
idea to have it translated."[2]

Having formed this opinion, Tolstoy began late in the same
year to seek not only a suitable translator but also a publisher.
Among his letters to publishers is one addressed to A. S. Suvorin
in which Tolstoy wrote: "Have you heard about a book by

the American writer Bellamy called *Looking Backward?* It is
a remarkable book which enjoys great success and is at present
being translated into all European languages. I would advise
you to publish it; it is being translated by an acquaintance of
mine."[3]

What attracted Tolstoy most in *Looking Backward* was,
first and foremost, its scathing censure of the inhumanity of
capitalistic society; for, when he read the novel, he heavily
marked the section about Julian West's nightmare, in which
he returns to the squalor and human degradation of nineteenth-
century Boston's working-class district which he had left to visit
the contrastingly magnificent, luxurious home of his fiancée to
make a stirring speech about the future world of plenty which
would be sanctified by economic and social justice and maintained by brotherhood.[4]

Although *Looking Backward* also attracted Tolstoy because
of its affinity with the ideas of Christian socialism, Tolstoy's
own religious and patriarchal notions led him in his political,
religious, and philosophical writings to criticize—often contra-
dictorily—Bellamy's concepts of the future and of human progress. In a short book entitled *The Slavery of Our Times* (1900),
Tolstoy criticized Bellamy's plan because he himself believed
that technical progress and the socialization of all means of
production would not be able to solve the problems of economic
inequality. He rejected, therefore, Bellamy's picture of the future
in which, wrote Tolstoy, "the workers will all join unions and
associations, and cultivate solidarity among themselves by unions, strikes, and participation in Parliament, until they obtain
possession of all the means of production, as well as the land;
and then they will be so well fed, so well dressed, and enjoy
such amusements on holidays, that they will prefer life in town,
amid brick buildings and smoking chimneys to free village life
amid plants and domestic animals; and monotonous, bell-regu-
lated machine work to varied, healthy, and free agricultural
labor."[5]

These words indicate how Tolstoy thought the socialists—
both in Utopias such as that of Bellamy as well as in scientific
works—represented future economic conditions. To Tolstoy, only
moral and ethical growth could be of very much importance
in realizing an economic Utopia—and then it would be one
in which the citizens would prefer a country life. Despite his
differences with Bellamy, Tolstoy used Bellamy's denunciations
of man's inhumanity to man and his criticisms of capitalistic
exploitation to preach the need of moral self-perfection.

After the translation of *Looking Backward* appeared in 1889 and after the novel had also been published in an abridged translation in the journal *Knigy Nedely*, Russian society—because of the growing working-class movement and the increasing interest in socialist ideas—became so interested in Bellamy that other of his works were translated. In December, 1890, the newspaper *Russkiye Vedomosti* published a translation of "With the Eyes Shut," a Utopian short story which depicted the revolution made in society by what the world today would call tape-recording machinery. In January, 1891, the newspaper *Nedelya* published an abridged translation of Bellamy's article "What 'Nationalism' Means"; in June and July, 1891, the journal *Vsemirnaya Biblioteka* published complete translations of *Miss Ludington's Sister,* and, in 1893, of *Dr. Heidenhoff's Process.*

One of the most interesting and important publications during this period was an article by Bellamy which was written as a result of his direct contact with Russian journalists. Written for a charity collection published in Vologda for the benefit of peasants who had suffered deprivations as a result of crop failure, this article—dated March, 1892, and entitled "Some Account of the Propaganda Work in America Which Has Followed *Looking Backward*"—related for "Russians who have read" the Utopian novel, the "practical work which has resulted from it." In this article (which has been preserved in the Moscow Literary and Art Archives and which is published for the first time in English in the Appendix of this volume), Bellamy outlined the growth of the Bellamy Club movement, its basic principles, and the differences between Nationalism and Marxism.

The widespread interest in Bellamy also promoted the publications of other Utopian fiction which had been influenced by the writings of Bellamy. The first to be published was William Morris' *News from Nowhere* which appeared in part in translation in 1896 in the magazine *Russkaja Misl* but which was published in book form in 1906. Three others which were translated and published were: *L'anno 3000* by Italian Paolo Mantegazza in 1898; *Dans cent ans* by French scientist Charles Richet in 1893; and *Freiland: Ein sociale Zukunftsbild* by Theodor Hertzka in 1925.

All of these publications; the seven different translations of *Looking Backward* which appeared from 1889 to 1918; the translations into Georgian (1896), into Hebrew (1898), and into Lithuanian (1897-98) indicate the vast popularity of Edward

Bellamy in Russia. In fact, the growing interest in the 1890's in socialist literature and particularly in Bellamy's book made the tsarist censors anxious. Although the first publications of *Looking Backward* had encountered little opposition from the censors, the Moscow Censorship Committee banned on March 30, 1891, an article entitled "The Society to Be," which presented a brief account of the contents of *Looking Backward* and which had been intended for publication in the journal *Pomoshch Samoobrazovaniyu*. In 1899, the Moscow Censorship Committee once more showed concern about Bellamy's popularity; for it asked the Chief Press Department whether it would not be wise to ban the circulation of the book in public libraries and reading rooms.[6]

In 1897 when Bellamy's *Equality* was published, the London edition of the book was categorically banned by the Central Censorship Committee which labelled it as "not to be issued on individual demand even to persons trusted by the censors." The censor A. A. Annikov described the book as being "far removed from a harmless and safe Utopia."[7] As a result of this action and this judgment, *Equality* was not translated and published in Russia until ten years later—after the Revolution of 1905!

Because of this action of the censors, it is no wonder that the very first review of *Equality* which appeared in 1897 in Russia condemned the work because of its "institution of a crying injustice in the shape of complete equality of men who are capable only of kneeding dough with men who can invent the steam engine . . . and the abolition of private property, the main stimulus of life and work." To this reviewer, Bellamy's new social Utopia recalled the fearful Paris Commune: "Naïve humanity sometimes even believed these songs and entrusted men with the making of steam engines and the supervision of crews of workers, as, for instance, during the Paris Commune in 1871. . . ."[8]

The reaction in Russia in 1907 when *Equality* was first published was described in an article by the journalist A. N. Nikitin: "The benevolent dreams of *Looking Backward* about the peaceful evolution of capitalism have given way to a powerful phantasy about a great revolution which uproots, in the author's imagination, the capitalist order of the modern state and, on the latter's ruins, paints, in the novel *Equality*, a Utopia of a new universal social order based on the economic equality of all citizens without exception."[9]

Before *Equality* had been published in Russian, Chapter

XXIII, "The Parable of the Water Tank," was, however, circulated in Russia; and during and after the Revolution of 1905, the parable was exceedingly popular and ran in many editions before 1917. Separate editions of this anti-capitalistic allegory appeared not only in Russian but also in Lithuanian (1904), in Lettish (1905), in Georgian (1906), in Tartar (1906), in Hebrew (1906), in Byelorussian (1907), in Ukranian (1911), and in Slovenian (1919).

The total number of copies of *Looking Backward* published before 1917 was 50,000.[10] On the eve of World War I, according to Svyatlovsky in *The Russian Utopian Novel*, *Looking Backward* was popular with the readers of the working district of St. Petersburg.[11] During the first Soviet years, the novel, in the 1906 abridged edition of Nikolayev, was reprinted in 1917 and in 1918. "The Parable of the Water Tank" was, however, more widely circulated. In 1917, 85,000 copies were reprinted; in 1918, the total reached 200,000; and in 1919 and in 1922, new reprints were made.

## II  *Popularity among Workers, Students, Intellectuals*

As the history of the publication of the books of Bellamy indicates, Bellamy was extremely popular in Russian labor, revolutionary, democratic and socialistic, and student circles not only because of the author's ideas but because of the situation in Russia. The inflammatory conditions and the burning social questions which existed in Russia at the close of the nineteenth century—the development not only of capitalism but of the organized working-class movement and the impoverishment and oppression of the laborers and peasants—enhanced the importance of waging a social and political struggle. Russian conditions created, therefore, a situation conducive not only to increased popularity of socialist ideas but a great interest in the Utopian novel.

At this time, when the future of Russian society remained obscure, such works as *Looking Backward* provided a fictional picture of what the future might be. F. A. Afanasyev, worker and revolutionary, said in his speech given in 1891 at the *first secret May Day meeting* held by the workers of St. Petersburg: "I shall not paint you a picture of that better and just order; for, no matter how appealing, no one can be sure that with time men will not be able to think of a better future . . . also you may acquaint yourself in detail with that future by reading . . . Bellamy's novel *Looking Backward*."[12]

Bellamy's novel was not only mentioned in secret meetings,

however; for, by the 1890's, it had become popular in many
circles of Russian society—and it was particularly well known
by students and progressive youth. In 1891, *Rizhsky Vestnik*
stated the reasons it appealed to so many divergent groups:

> A most characteristic sign of the times is, perhaps, the great
> success of certain books on special problems. These books are
> not distinguished by the originality of the views developed by
> them—indeed, those views were put forward long before them
> by more serious and profound thinkers, but their books did
> not become so widely known at the time because their time
> had not yet come. These thinkers stood too high above the
> average level, were too far ahead for the mass to comprehend
> them and become imbued with their ideas. But as the decades
> go by and the course of social and historical process and its goal
> become clearer, writers of mediocre talent appear who speak
> of that goal in a language comprehensible to the mass of read-
> ers; the mass acclaims them because they give vocal expression
> to all which had pervaded its mind in vague forms. One such
> writer is the American Edward Bellamy.[13]

*Looking Backward* did more, however, than express the vague
thoughts and desires of the mass; it effectively spread socialistic
concepts and it also destroyed prejudice against socialism. In
1906, during the time of the First Revolution, M. I. Tugan-
Baranovsky, Russian bourgeois economist, wrote that Bellamy's
book "was more effective propaganda of the ideas of socialism
among the broad masses than any other book during the past
thirty years."[14] After explaining the profound impression the
book made upon the liberal intellectuals because of its dynamic,
easy-flowing style and its reformist attitudes, Tugan-Baranovsky stated that, in his opinion, *Looking Backward* had accomplished a great deal also in removing prejudices against socialism and, therefore, in promoting the growth on a worldwide
scale of the socialist movement.[15]

Among student circles, *Looking Backward* was also very popular. Maxim Gorky stated that all students were familiar with
Bellamy's ideas; and V. A. Selikhova testified that Bellamy was
popular on the eve of the Revolution of 1905 with the demo-
cratic-minded youth of the Urals and of western Siberia. The
effect of the Utopian novel upon students has been well described in the memoirs of veteran revolutionary S. I. Mitskevich,
who knew the "Last Mohicans" of the revolutionary *narodniki*
(populist) movements and the first Russian Marxists. In recalling his first acquaintance with *Looking Backward* while

in a free, student hostel (known as *Lyapinka*) in Moscow, Mitskevich wrote:

> In *Lyapinka*, I became acquainted with several interesting men
> —chiefly first-year students. . . . I remember Lozhkin, from
> Vyatka, a student of natural science. Together with him I
> read a novel by Bellamy called *Looking Backward*, the Rus-
> sian translation of which had then just appeared. The plot of
> that Utopian novel was laid in the year 2000 in North America,
> where the socialist order, vividly described in the book, had
> established itself. We thought that in all probability it might
> well prove to be so—that the socialist order would be first
> established in America, a leading industrial country, and that
> that would tell on the less developed countries. The novel had
> quite an invigorating effect upon us.[16]

*Looking Backward* became known far and wide in Russia not only among students and intellectuals but among the workers. During the early 1890's—as the well-known bibliographer N. A. Rubakin noted—the book was always in demand in the public library of Nizhny Novgorod.[17] According to P. I. Voyevodin, the book was popular among the workers of Yekaterinoslav (now Dniepropetrovsk) because of its political import. As has already been noted, it was mentioned in the first secret May Day meeting of workers in Petersburg in 1891; and K. A. Koshkin, a member of the Petersburg Soviet in 1905, related that the novel was read with interest during the first Russian revolution by the workers of the city and particularly by those at the Putilov Works, which was famous for its revolutionary tradi-tions. Koshkin recalled that the appealing portrayal of the radi-ant future and the social tendencies of Bellamy's Utopia won the hearts of the workers.

Further information about the effect of *Looking Backward* upon worker groups appeared in the 1930's in Soviet memoirs; but the most importance should be attached to the reminiscences of old worker propagandists of the Ivanovo-Voznesensk indus-trial district concerning the role the novel played in one of the first workers' unions in Russia.[18] M. A. Bagayev, member of the workers' circle formed in 1892 by F. A. Kondratyev (a propagandist of Marxism who was exiled to this area from St. Petersburg), recalled that Kondratyev left his pupils a small library on labor which included Pavlenkov's edition of *Looking Backward*. To this library were soon added N. G. Cherniskev-sky's banned novel *What Is To Be Done?*; R. Giovagnoli's *Spartaco*; and E. Voynich's *The Gadfly*—books which were also extremely popular with the progressive workers of those years.[19]

N. N. Kudryashev, another active member of the same circle
who was a laborer in a cotton-printing mill, recalled that *Looking Backward* was popular with the workers' union and that
in December, 1894, a bookshop, which actually belonged to
the town's social-democratic organization, was opened in Ivanovo-Voznesensk. "Through that shop we established new ties
—probed the workers who were attracted to reading books
and to public thought. The book was a wonderful means of
enlisting new members. . . ."[20] Because of this shop and particularly because of the influence of *Looking Backward,* the
organization secured one of its extremely valuable leaders:
A. A. Yevdokimov. After joining the local organization in 1894,
he soon became the secretary of the union and wrote its program entitled *The Theoretical Principles of the Working Class
Movement.*

Bellamy's novel also created a profound impression upon
another member of this same union, N. I. Makhov, who wrote
in his memoirs: "Having read Bellamy time and again, I
learned him almost by rote and kept holding forth everywhere on how well people will live in less than a hundred
years, deeply believing myself that everything would shape
out just as *Looking Backward* said it would."[21]

During the strike of the Ivanovo-Voznesensk weavers in 1895,
Makhov made a revolutionary speech before a crowd of two
thousand workers: "I spoke about the poverty of the workers
and their hungry and rightless life, about the starving countryside. . . . I spoke about the life of the workers and peasants
abroad and their struggles: about their strikes and the Chartist
movement. I spoke at especially great length about the future
social order . . . after E. Bellamy whose book *Looking Backward* I had learned by heart and was carrying everywhere in
my pockets."[22] Makhov recalled that there and then he had
"read a chapter or two from the book to the workers. The
next day everyone wanted to finish the book but, alas, that was
impossible,"[23] for that evening many of the strikers had been
arrested.

Among the famous Russian revolutionaries who read *Looking Backward* was Nadejda Konstantinova Krupskaya, the chief
assistant and then wife of Lenin and the life-long friend
of Clara Zetkin, the German translator of *Looking Backward.*
Both Clara Zetkin and Krupskaya worked for the emancipation
of women and wrote many articles to win their cause. After
the October Revolution, Krupskaya lectured, met personally
with women workers, served as a member of the Presidium of

the Supreme Soviet of the USSR, and was vice-commissar of
Public Instruction. In 1915 she published *Popular Education
and Democracy;* and six volumes of her pedagogic works are
circulating in the Soviet today.[24]

N. K. Krupskaya read *Looking Backward* in the 1890's when
she was a teacher in the Smolensky evening school for workers
in St. Petersburg, and years later she remembered: "Once Bellamy's *Looking Backward* was the craze. The book is full of
technology but it gives a barren picture of the future society
without any struggle or collective. When I first read the book
in the nineties, the future society portrayed by Bellamy seemed
to me more dull and tedious than the contemporary life in the
worker suburb of Petersburg where thousands of proletarians
were unanimously rising to the struggle against the vile exploitation and for the better life."[25]

But *Looking Backward* won the hearts of the workers because of the radiant future it so appealingly pictured and because of its political and social message. To these same laborers, however, the reformist illusions of Bellamy were alien, for
the Russian workers were aware that their road toward equality
and freedom lay through years of heavy struggle with the forces
of the past—through revolution. Bellamy appealed, however, to
intellectuals such as Tugan-Baranovsky because they sympathized with his reformist or evolutionary social and economic
views.

III  *Critical Patterns*

By 1890 the reviews of and articles about Bellamy's *Looking
Backward* showed definite patterns in critical attitudes: the
liberal bourgeoisie endeavored to use the novel as a pretext for
propaganda about bourgeois democratic reform; and the conservative, monarchist journalists attacked Bellamy's dream for
the future, for they believed that even the propagation of peaceful, evolutionary socialism constituted a threat to tsarism.

The liberal, bourgeois line of criticism was expressed more
completely than elsewhere in the article "A New Phantasy on
an Old Theme" by I. I. Yanzhul (1845-1914), the bourgeois
economist, who made a detailed comparison of Bellamy's economic Utopia with Thomas More's political one. Like other
Russian writers of his ilk before and after him,[26] Yanzhul considered the greatest weakness of both Utopians to be the lack
of clear, detailed plans for the achievement of the grandiose
social and political changes which were to be enjoyed by
humanity in an ideal state. In concluding his article, Yanzhul

stated: ". . . Bellamy's work possesses many qualities without which the new social novel could not have enjoyed the success described. From the point of view of form it is written in a lively and talented style, firing the imagination with its pleasant portrayal of the future and acquainting the reader with the economic aspect of it in an effortless manner, without boring or tiring him, while simultaneously heavily underscoring the shortcomings and vices of the present. These qualities chiefly determine the importance of this new work which has created such a stir. . . ."[27]

*Looking Backward* created, in fact, "such a stir" and evoked such favorable comments that—as has already been noted—the Moscow censors thought by 1899 that the book should be banned in public libraries and reading rooms, and early in the 1890's the outspoken enemies of socialism—the orthodox and patriotic champions of tsarism—pounced upon it. As a result, such monarchist journalists and sociologists as S. F. Sharapov (1855-1911), I. F. Romanov (1861-1913), and K. F. Golovin (K. Orlovsky, 1843-1913), attacked, criticized, or ridiculed Bellamy's ideas. In 1890 the clerical, Slavophile journal *Blagovest* published Sharapov's mud-slinging review; and in 1892 the printing house of the Ministry of Internal Affairs in St. Petersburg published Golovin's *Socialism as a Positive Teaching*.

## IV  Russian Books Inspired by Bellamy

Golovin himself pointed out in the preface that his book, inspired by *Looking Backward*, constituted a critical analysis of Bellamy's economic Utopia, which, though Bellamy was essentially a reformist, was conducive to the popularization of socialist ideas—a fact that could not be ignored or liked by the monarchists. Golovin was particularly critical of Bellamy's plan of economic equality for all; for Golovin considered economic inequality to be not only inevitable but also eternal. All attempts to overcome it would be doomed, he asserted, to utter failure because "the varying mental and physical traits within even a single family inevitably give rise to unequal proprietorship."[28] Furthermore, said Golovin, such a social, economic change could not be brought about by the increased economic production of society; for such development was a vision not likely to become reality.

He also scoffed at Bellamy's portrayal of a future, ideal state which would operate without police and without courts; and he derided Bellamy—as did Sharapov in his review—for pre-

senting the "fabulous amenities" of the year 2000 and particularly for portraying the "musical rooms"—rooms which today's
world recognizes as astute forecasts of radio and television.

I. F. Romanov, a monarchist journalist, published in 1891 in
Kiev under the pen name of "Rtsi," a short, political parody entitled *Sketches. An Evening of Black and White Magic (A Phantasy on the Theme of "Looking Backward")*. In this work, he
attacked not only Bellamy but also Leo Tolstoy; for he recalled
that the latter had helped Bellamy achieve popularity in Russia.

In *Sketches*, Julian West, the hero of *Looking Backward*, falls
into a lethargic sleep induced by the constant reading of news
items concerning the discovery of *bacillus kochii*. West awakens
three centuries later in the year 2200 in the apartment of Dr.
Kit, and, as he stares with disbelief at the geographical map on
the wall, Dr. Kit explains that there are now five great powers
in the world: the United Americas, the United European States
with their African and Australian possessions, the Council of
Orthodox Churches, India and China. The Council of Orthodox
Churches unites Russia, Serbia, Greece, Rumania, Abyssinia,
Japan, and Turkey. Rome has become the metropolis of the
European United States, and its supreme leaders are the Pope
of Rome and His Majesty Rothschild. Both the Pope and Rothschild live at sea with royal convoys surrounding their yachts
which are named, respectively, *Jesuita* and *Argentum*.

These two men rule almost the whole world; for the one,
Rothschild, owns Europe's gold; the second, the Pope, Europe's
souls. Both have enslaved men: "Rothschild enslaves mankind
by capitalizing on its wants and vices; the Pope enslaves mankind by capitalizing on the conscience of the believers and on
the mystical requirements of the human soul. Their aim as regards mankind is, however, one and the same: *Cadaver esto!*"[29]

Romanov was particularly incensed about Bellamy's forecast
that there would be no wars in the year 2000; for war to Romanov
—like economic inequality to Golovin—was an inevitable condition of humanity. After doing his utmost to depict the absurdity of Bellamy's ideal state and socialist conceptions, and after
asserting that disease—like war—would continue to plague the
citizens of even a Utopian society, Romanov—who ignored
Bellamy's plan for the storage of staples—resorted to drama-
tizing the threat to such a society of elemental calamities: "In
Russia, say, there has not been a drop of rain for three months.
The fields have been scorched by the sun. The harvest has
gone to the dogs. Gone is the back-breaking labor of an ideally

organized army of labor. What is to be done? How are clouds, poor roads, heavy rainfalls, and hail and frosts—not to mention all sorts of pestilential flies and worms—to be fought?"[30]

As might be expected, Romanov concluded his nihilistic views of social progress with a proclamation about the stability of— and his satisfaction with—the pillars of the world of the nine- teenth century: "We have had our fill of this evening of black and white magic. Let us go to bed firmly remembering that we are living in the year 1890 and that all is well and as it used to be."[31]

Besides Romanov's parody of *Looking Backward,* Bellamy's novel within little more than a decade after its translation also inspired two Russian Utopian novels which were aimed polem- ically at his work: Sharapov's *Fifty Years Later* (1902) and N. N. Shelonsky's *In the World of the Future* (1891). As late as 1927, V. D. Nikolsky's *A Thousand Years Hence* was inspired by Bellamy.

In *Fifty Years Later* Sharapov, who belonged to the same ideological group as Romanov, attempted to produce a polem- ical counterpart to Bellamy's Utopia—his own "fantastic politi- cal and social novel" about a Slavophile Utopia. In his foreword he stated: "The so-called novels of the future have, thanks to Bellamy, become a huge literary concern. Indeed, any pack of lies will go down if it is given this form, if only the narration is at all a lively one and the future depicted is better than the present. And since no one can possibly think of anything worse than the latter, it is remarkably easy to write in the vein of our Russian Jules Vernes and Flammarions.

"I too have been seized with the yearning to join their ranks —with, however, a commendable aim. I wished to show what would happen if Slavophile views would ascend to dominance among the public and in the ruling circles."[32]

Taking a page from Bellamy's book, Sharapov began his novel by having the hero become acquainted with an Indian scientist who puts him to sleep. After lying for fifty years in the cemetery of a Moscow monastery, the sleeper awakes in the year 2500 to behold a Russia which has realized the Slavophile dreams of the late nineteenth century. As might be expected because of Sharapov's autocratic, chauvinistic credo, Russia has remained a state of noblemen and landlords with the tsar at their head; even the old Russian boyars have been reinstated to their rights. In this monarchist Utopia, Sharapov regarded the historical development of Russia as a "harmonious blend of autocracy and self-government"—and the chief stimulus behind this development was the re-establishment of "our ancient clerical and communal order."

Because of his loyalty to neo-Slavophile views, Sharapov ignored technical and economic progress in his Utopia. Automobiles and bicycles are forbidden by the authorities because "society disintegrates as a result of speedy communications." He did, however, admit the possibility of some progress in publishing; for illustrations are telegraphed to the *Moskovskiye Vedomosti* which had survived the years. Sharapov also showed, as did Bellamy in *Looking Backward,* that money had been replaced by the check book. The purchase of goods was also effected in the manner suggested by Bellamy: an item selected in the hall of samples was ordered at the storehouse by telephone and paid for by check.

There can be no doubt that Sharapov employed certain elements of Bellamy's Utopia—such as those mentioned—in order to create an intriguing picture of a patched-up Russian autocracy; but his portrayal is intellectually unconvincing because he sought to combine the principle of autocracy with suffrage and self-government.[33] The absurdity of this attempt becomes apparent when the reader is told that the two highest legislative organs of the state—the Council of State and the Economic Council—are free to elaborate "opinions but that it is not compulsory for autocratic power" to accept them; in other words, these groups are consultative or deliberative groups and not truly legislative powers. All in all, it can only be said that Sharapov's Slavophile Utopia reflected the views of the most conservative section of Russian society which clung to the obsolete forms of the past and which could not, therefore, comprehend the future social development of a country entering a new, proletarian stage of the liberation movement.

Considerably greater interest was, and is, aroused in the reader by the fantastic *In the World of the Future* by N. N. Shelonsky which, published in 1891, was so popular that seven reprints were required. In his polemic, Shelonsky subjects Bellamy's socialism and the plan for the industrial army to severe —and unwarranted—criticism in the afterword of his novel; but Shelonsky undeniably created an original, sound science-fiction Utopian novel in which he portrayed the conquest of the North Pole and the development of science.

The heroes of his Utopia—Chebotaryov, the Russian orientalist and archaeologist; Markovic, a student of natural science; Yablonsky, his pupil who is an electrical engineer; and Jacques Leverrier, a French scientist and the relative of a famous astronomer—set forth in search of the treasure of the celebrated Indian fakir Daraainen, who had lived several centuries before Christ. On the island of the cave temple—Gharipuri in the Bay of Bombay—they find a stone inscribed with the last will and testament of the Indian, commanding that he be sought at the North Pole where he would bring life.

Soon after this discovery, a splendidly equipped aerial expedition embarks on a flight to the North Pole. The expedition employs the invention of Poyarkov, a young self-taught Russian scientist who—by the fission of complex chemical elements—has obtained colossal electrical power. When the group arrives at the North Pole, the expedition discovers an unknown continent with a temperate climate. Four members of the expedition—Yablonsky; Murray, the English geologist; Lecomb, the Frenchman; and Samoilov, the ship's boy—penetrate deep into the bowels of the earth to study its inner structure. During this investigation, the aircraft which had brought the men crashes with Poyarkov on board; the crash was caused by an explosion engineered by secret enemies—the railway tycoons of America and Germany who had seen in the aircraft a serious threat to their transportation systems!

After a long journey in subterranean caverns and many meetings with plesiosaurs and archaeoteryx, the underground travelers discover the tomb of Daraainen only to find him in a lethargic sleep. When they try to awaken him with a drug which they find in his tomb, they themselves fall into a thousand-year sleep. When they awaken and return to the earth's surface, they meet men of the twenty-ninth century living on the North Pole in a Russian town which has established a new way of life.

The future society which Shelonsky then portrays depends upon unprecedented technical progress and, at the same time, closeness to nature. Men of the twenty-ninth century so prize nature in its primordial state that they transform it only when necessary. Because of the practical application of new scientific discoveries and the use of solar and atomic energy,[34] mankind plays the role of master of nature:

> At one time man stood close to nature, but he was then wholly dependent on it. The struggle with nature and with his own kind made man the most miserable of creatures. His organism was maimed and deformed; its normal functions were distorted; and gradually man began to fight it—that is, to fight himself. The farther he disgressed from direct physical labor and contact with nature, the deeper were his forces involved in the fight against the deformed operation of his organism. Then

the first stage of his development began to seem attractive and desirable to him: in midstream he had spent his strength, and the very goal he was striving to reach vanished from his view. He was ready to stop. But happily and fortunately for him, that did not happen. Now he is once again near to nature; the issues of worldly life are once more clear and simple in his view, this time because all processes grew understandable to him and became his truth.[35]

In criticism of the urban Utopia of Looking Backward, Shelonsky depicted an anti-urbanistic state which glorified man's unity with nature. When the heroes visit the family of Nikolai Atos, he explains to them:

Our homes stand wide apart and are scattered over great areas. . . . We constantly see one another because distance means nothing to us. As for plants and factories—we have none. I recall that you needed factory production because man did not know how by himself to provide for himself. Therefore, men had to supply one another. . . . This resulted in inequality among people; some worked harder for others than they did for them. . . . Human happiness is unthinkable without independence, without full freedom. To achieve that, man must be self-sufficient; he ought to be able to produce for himself everything he needs without enlisting anyone's help. If he is helped, he is placed under an obligation; he is no longer free.[36]

As may be deducted from these statements, Shelonsky's conception of the ideal state is far from the cooperative society of Bellamy; in fact, its basic principles are antithetical, for they are that "each provides for himself"[37] and that no one is reliant upon the cooperation of others. To Shelonsky—as to Bellamy—"the ideal of human happiness is in free labor and independence" and the test of the social order is an absence of needy people. To Shelonsky, however, the division of labor in a cooperative society restricted individual liberty; and he sought the answer in the primitive concept of each man for himself—a concept which worked long, long ago but which can not work in today's highly organized, industrialized world.

Since Shelonsky was not much concerned with the economic aspects of the ideal state, he did not show in detail how the wants of all citizens were to be supplied. He was content to portray that vast technological and scientific progress easily guaranteed the satisfaction of all the economic requirements of the individual—and even provided him with a "chemical diet." He stressed, however, certain elements of the old Rus-

sian communal and patriarchal order—such as the paramount
role of the large family or of the clan several thousand people
strong.

Instead of focusing his attention upon economics and future
forms of government, Shelonsky concentrated upon future international society and politics. His world of the twenty-ninth
century is divided into two groups: the "civilized states,"
headed by France and Russia whose people have already
a century-old friendship behind them; and the "uncivilized
states," which, including England, have stopped developing.

England has lost all of her colonies and has preserved in
petrified form the ways of life which existed at the end of the
nineteenth century. The peoples of India had overthrown British
rule and won their national independence in the first half of
the twentieth century; and China's one-time backwardness and
stagnation have been followed by unheard-of progress. In contrast to China, the United States has had its development
checked by materialism and social antagonisms:

> All the talents of that people were spent on the solutions of
> questions of practical life. Even now you will find nowhere
> else such mammoth constructions as in America. But that coun-
> try is to this day rent asunder by internal conflicts. The Amer-
> icans will never be able to part with the traditions of the past:
> everything there is based on public participation. All their grand
> enterprises are public undertakings. They have public insti-
> tutions of every kind—public schools, libraries, public charity,
> and all this serves as a field for endless clashes and conflicts.
> Especially today the struggle for political determination is in
> full blast. No one can foresee what it will lead to.[38]

When Englishman Murray—one of the book's heroes—returns
from twenty-ninth-century Russia to England in the closing
episode of the book, Shelonsky—in a section analagous to Julian
West's nightmare visit to Boston of the nineteenth century in
*Looking Backward*—portrays satirically an English bourgeois
society which still worships Mammon although gold has lost
all meaning in the "civilized countries," and which still has
nineteenth-century cities. Although Moscow and Paris have
become, in the new era, cities studded with houses separated
by fields and gardens, London's thirty million citizens are
crammed in huge buildings which stand side by side. Murray
recalls that in the London of his own day luxury and squalor
had been close neighbors; and the slum scenes he sees remind

the reader of Bellamy's depiction of the Boston working-class district in the last chapter of *Looking Backward*.

Murray discovers that the whole of England has become one great factory city which floods the markets of Africa and Australia with its wares. Because of the savage competition and unemployment, human labor is the cheapest of commodities. Fabulous fortunes and horrible poverty, crises of overproduction, and all the other "blessings" of the capitalist system are depicted as present.

Despite their overproduction, the English live in a state of complete insularity and do not wish to have contacts with other European people—with the "civilized nations." During a war with France five hundred years before, the English had blown up a wonderful bridge which spanned the English Channel, and had also destroyed an underwater tunnel crossing it. The English, however, have an extremely aggressive attitude regarding the "civilized peoples": "Very soon we shall seize the lands of those barbarians. . . ! We need colonies. Besides we shall win new markets for our goods. If those savages will not buy from the English, we'll make them do it."[39]

Murray is treated with suspicion by his fellow countrymen and is declared to be an impostor. When he tries to call the press to his rescue, he discovers that it is in the hands of a gang of blackmailers. When he strives to induce the English to be friends with Russia and France and calls an anti-militaristic meeting, he fares little better. Although the meeting is attended by three million men, the public attitude is hostile. When he calls Russia and France the most civilized countries of the world, Murray is immediately surrounded by policemen. When he is accused of corrupting public morals and of being a paid hireling of the enemies of England, he discovers that, according to the new laws of the country, he, like all other accused ones, is to be tried in his absence. He also learns that after sentence has been passed, it can not be appealed—until after it has been executed! Murray is banished from England.

The war unleashed by England ends in a complete debacle of its armies and in the triumph of the forces of progress. Despite his differences with Bellamy, Shelonsky's novel also ends, therefore, on a note of optimistic faith in the powers of human reason and science to win a better world. His novel is an interesting example of literary, ideological polemics.

The Russian Utopias of the 1890's were obviously written for the Russian reader acquainted with *Looking Backward*. A comparative study of Bellamy's Utopia with these early Russian Utopias should focus attention, therefore, not only upon the points which compare with *Looking Backward* but also upon those which are contradictory. Since, however, these novels were written to refute Bellamy's major concepts, the contradictions are perhaps of greatest interest.

The most recent Russian novel to show the influence of Bellamy, *A Thousand Years Hence,* was written by V. D. Nikolsky and published in 1927. Although Nikolsky admits in the preface the influence of the famous American writer, his book is concerned with technical progress, atomic energy, space travel, and the creation of huge satellites of the earth; his novel therefore lacks Bellamy's broad consideration of social and economic problems.

## V   *Russian Writers Interested in Bellamy*

Besides the interest Bellamy evoked in Tolstoy for divergent reasons, he attracted the attention of some of Russia's foremost writers. In a letter to the publisher A. S. Suvorin, Anton Chekov wrote late in 1890: "A fragment from Bellamy's book I read while spending the night somewhere in Southern Sakhalin. In Petersburg, I hope to read the whole of it."[40]

V. G. Korolenko, an eminent Russian writer whose short stories were published in English in the United States from 1887 to 1925, stressed the social import of Bellamy's writings: "He is not an artist; but he, too, strives to create images and stir up emotion. The emotion of a man whose soul thirsts for a glimpse of the future. He does not yet know what shape it will assume; he paints it in a groping way, sometimes not painting but rather merely sketching it. . . ."[41]

Maxim Gorky also was interested in Bellamy; for, in 1902 in a letter to K. P. Pyatnitsky, he asked the latter to send him, among other books, five copies of *Looking Backward* for the town library of Arzamas.[42] In 1906 when visiting in the United States, he stated in a conversation with the literati of Philadelphia that American writers were appreciated in Russia: "We know more of your authors than you do of ours. *Uncle Tom's Cabin* is read in every part of the Empire; Edward Bellamy and his theories in *Looking Backward* are known to all the Russian students."[43] In the same year Gorky stated in *Appleton's Magazine* that the United States "is the country of Henry George, Bellamy, Jack London who gives his great talent to socialism. This is a good instance of the awakening of the

spirit of 'human life' in this young and vigorous country suffering with the gold fever."[44]

In conclusion, it should be noted that since the Russian Revolution several articles which have been published in Russia
about the Utopian novel have mentioned Bellamy and have
justly criticized his illusionary conception of a peaceful and
painless transition from capitalism to socialism and his effort
to stand above the class struggle. Bellamy's novel is regarded
today as the literary embodiment of bourgeois socialism; but
it is also esteemed because of its sharp criticism of capitalist
society and its artistic merits, as being the outstanding book
of American democratic literature of the past century.

Today, when Russians also recognize that the picture of
technical progress painted by Bellamy is no longer fantastic
but that his conception of the road to social-economic changes
was exceedingly naïve, Bellamy's Utopian fiction has lost some
of the attractiveness which in its day made it such a success
in the progressive circles of the Russian public. Despite this
present lack of interest in or fascination with Bellamy, it must
be recognized—as this study has pointed out—that his Utopian
novels played an important role in introducing people of all
circles to socialist ideas, in destroying the prejudices many
harbored against socialism, in inducing the dream of a changed
world, and in pointing out the inhumanity of capitalism. Bellamy's socialist vision therefore remains in the memory of the
Russian people as a striking page in the history of American
democratic heritage.

# CHAPTER THREE

# A British Sensation

By

## PETER MARSHALL

IN 1889 the famous American suffragette and teetotaler Frances E. Willard boasted to her friends and to reporters that she had been responsible for introducing Bellamy's *Looking Backward* to students at Oxford University[1] where—among other places—she had lectured. In the same year Helena Blavatsky encouraged her Theosophical Society members of England, Ireland, and the world to regard the Utopia as the outline of a state which would fulfill the dreams of her mystical followers in achieving a world of brotherhood and harmony; among the outstanding citizens of the British Isles who were associated with her group in one way or another were Oscar Wilde and his wife; Dr. Annie Besant, who was to lecture on Bellamy in London; George Bernard Shaw, the friend of Annie Besant and also a Fabian; William Butler Yeats, long well known for his Theosophical interests; George William ("A. E.") Russell, Irish poet and leader of the Theosophists, who told James Joyce, another socialist, that his interests were divided into three segments: economics, literature, and mysticism.[2]

In the 1930's, E. Sylvia Pankhurst described her liberal domestic background in *The Suffragette Movement*: "Discussions whirled about our young ears, mingling with our childish interests; the New *versus* the Old Trade Unionism, the socialism of various schools; the delightful prophecies of Kropotkin,* then at an early stage of his long exile here; the Socialist mag-

---

* Peter Kropotkin reviewed *Looking Backward* in Paris in "Le Vingtième Siècle," *La Révolte* (Nov. and Dec., 1889); he remarked that the novel, which had had a remarkable sale, had achieved many "conversions."—Editor.

azine *Today,* and the contributions therein of the much talked
of young man with sandy hair, the brilliant Bernard Shaw; Annie
Besant's *Link,* the Fabian essays, Bellamy's *Looking Backward*
and later Blatchford's *Merrie England. . . ."*[3]

In the 1940's when Paul Bellamy, the son of Edward and the
editor of the Cleveland *Plain Dealer* visited postwar England,
he was introduced to Prime Minister Clement Atlee who immediately remarked: "Bellamy, that's a good name. Are you related to Edward Bellamy?" When Paul replied that he was
the author's son, Atlee told him that *Looking Backward* was
one of the English Bibles and that the English socialist government was "a child of the Bellamy idea."[4]

Although these anecdotes indicate the possible breadth and
depth of the influence of Edward Bellamy in the British Isles
and the vastly complicated subject it is, this chapter must be
limited to a *coup d'oeil* of the sales of Bellamy's books in
England, of Bellamy followers, of a sketch of the changing
reactions toward him, and of his influence upon such personages as George Bernard Shaw, William Morris, and a few
others.

## I  *A Literary Sensation*

Although Bellamy's *Miss Ludington's Sister* and *Dr. Heidenhoff's Process* were published in Great Britain in 1884 by
David Douglas, an Edinburgh publisher who had been encouraged to publish the novels by William Dean Howells,[5] they
were seemingly not successful. *Looking Backward* first appeared in England in serial form from January to July, 1889,
in *Brotherhood,* a monthly magazine edited by J. Bruce Wallace, an Irish Congregational minister and social reformer.
Before the serialization had been completed, *Looking Backward* had, however, been published in May[6] by William Reeves,
who specialized in radical literature; Ebenezer Howard, the
famous town planner, later claimed that he had persuaded
Reeves to undertake the venture. Howard, who had received a
copy of the American edition, had been so impressed with the
message it contained about "a new civilisation based on service
to the community and not on self interest" that he had offered
to dispose personally of at least a hundred copies if Reeves
would print a British edition.[7]

Such a modest guarantee soon proved to have been unnecessary, for by the end of 1889 Reeves had issued seventeen
reprints of the book. In 1890 George Routledge issued an edition twice reprinted; and in 1891 Fredrick Warne marketed

yet another. As these facts indicate, the success of *Looking Backward* was sensational. The artist Henry Holiday, another Bellamy admirer, recalled how "piles of it were cleared off all the bookstalls every day";[8] and it has been estimated that over 40,000 copies were sold within a year of its publication.[9] By March, 1890, *The Review of Reviews*—though it complained that the Utopia was "as dull as ditchwater"[10]—reported that sales had already reached 100,000 copies. Furthermore, its message had penetrated the innermost circles of liberal politicians, for even the private secretary of Mr. Gladstone had read it.[11]

Because of this triumphant conquest of the British reading public, Bellamy's hitherto ignored earlier novels aroused general interest. In 1890 Ward Lock published *Six to One. A Nantucket Idyl;* and both Routledge and Reeves reissued *Dr. Heidenhoff's Process*, which Warne also reprinted in the following year, as well as a new edition of *Miss Ludington's Sister*. In 1890 Reeves commenced a series of popular editions entitled *The Bellamy Library* which comprised thirty-three volumes by 1902 and which ranged from works about the Salvation Army to Marxist tracts, from *Progress and Poverty* to *Songs of the Army of the Night* by the young radical poet Francis Adams. With the publication of *Equality* by William Heinemann in 1897, of *The Blindman's World* in 1898, and of *The Duke of Stockbridge* in 1901, the list of Bellamy publications in England was complete.

After the turn of the century, interest in Bellamy evidently declined rather sharply. Although Heinemann issued a popular edition of *Equality* in 1920 and the Guild of Youth and the Young Labour Library of the Independent Labour Party reprinted "The Parable of the Water Tank" in 1925, *Looking Backward* became the only Bellamy book for which there was a regular but modest demand. Routledge reprinted it in 1922; W. Foulsham in 1925, 1930, and 1945; and the last British imprint was that of Alvin Redman of 1948. At its peak, however, the popularity of *Looking Backward* was phenomenal: it has been estimated that—not counting the sales achieved by William Reeves—235,400 copies were sold between 1890 and 1935.[12]

## II  *Replies to Bellamy*

Imitations, elaborations, and criticisms naturally and rapidly added their weight to the impressions made by *Looking Backward*. English, American, and German continuations or counter-Utopias were published; and among those originally in English were many anonymous books such as *Julian West, My After-*

*dream* . . . (1900); *Atlantis A.D. 2050: Electrical Development at Atlantis* . . . (1890); *Looking Ahead . . . Not by the Author of Looking Backward* (1892); *Robinson Crusoe, Looking Upwards . . . The Up Grade from Henry George Past E. Bellamy* (1892); American Arthur D. Vinton's *Looking Farther Backward* (1890); and Sir Ebenezer Howard's *Garden Cities of To-morrow* (1898), which had first been published under the title of *To-morrow—a Peaceful Path to Real Reform.*

Criticisms were also provided by M. D. O'Brien in *Socialism Tested by Facts . . . Containing a Criticism of 'Looking Backward'* . . . (1892) and by George A. Sanders in *Reality . . . A Reply to E. Bellamy's 'Looking Backward' and 'Equality'* (1898). Egotistical and garrulous Thomas Reynolds, an ardent Bellamy fan, prepared *Preface and Notes . . . to Mr. E. Bellamy's . . . Book 'Looking Backward'* (1890); and he presented a copy of it to Prince Malcolm Khan, the Persian ambassador to the Court of Saint James. As Reynolds wrote to Bellamy, Prince Khan had at first been resistant to the ideas of the book; but he later admitted that he agreed with them and was "surprised that European statesmen ignored them." Prince Khan later became one of Persia's first socialists.[13]

None of these books is of particular interest or value—except as a reflection of the great Bellamy debate in England—and none certainly rivaled the popularity of *Looking Backward.* Although Holiday "rashly squandered" seven shillings on two refutations of *Looking Backward,* he claimed that he had never met anyone else who had read either of them—and that he saw no reason why anyone else should have done so.[14] As A. L. Morton indicated more recently in *The English Utopia,* these answers to the Bellamy menace to society "were ineffective and have passed today to the rubbish heaps of literature." Although Morton found *My Afterdream* amusing as the *reductio ad absurdum* of Bellamy's arguments about many things, he also admitted that these books were never serious criticisms of socialism but were valid ones because they waged war against "the bureaucratic distortions and the rigidly mechanical equalitarianism of Bellamy's Utopia, that is to say, of the most markedly non-Marxist aspects of this work."[15]

The debate about Bellamy assumed international aspects in England with the appearance almost immediately of Utopias which had been written either in reply to him or as a result of his popularity in other countries. These books were welcomed—as Marie Louise Berneri has stated in *Journey Through Utopia* —for Liberals and Conservatives must "have viewed with considerable alarm the popularity which the socialist utopias had been enjoying."[16] Among the books published were the anti-socialist German Utopias of Richard Michaelis, *A Sequel to Looking Backward or Looking Further Forward* (London, 1891); of Theodore Hertzka, *Freeland, A Social Anticipation* (London, 1891); and of Eugen Richter, *Pictures of the Socialistic Future* (London, 1893).

When Richter's attack upon the German Social Democrats and Bebel—with whom Bellamy was associated—appeared, the newspaper gave it a warm welcome. The *National Observer* advised that all working men "with a stiver to lose"—and also "many well-meaning busybodies that rank considerably higher" —should read it. The *Sydney Morning Herald* declared that it would be "a counter-irritant to the Bellamy remedies for Society, for it depicts the miseries of the socialistic regime and its final overthrow." The *Spectator* very soberly asserted that "there could be no other end to Socialism" than that which Richter had forecast: tyranny.[17]

The substantial and enduring effects which the great Bellamy debate had upon literature are found, however, in the works of William Morris, Oscar Wilde, and George Bernard Shaw; for both Wilde and Morris answered Bellamy in 1890 or 1891 and Shaw was to reveal indications—never acknowledged—of Bellamy's ideas in many of his speeches and in his plays. The first reaction came, however, from Morris who had become in 1883 an avowed socialist of the Marxist, philosophical anarchist type.

An early reader of *Looking Backward,* Morris had expressed his vigorous reaction to it to his friend Andreas Scheu: "I must surely write something as a counterblast to this."[18] The occasion for his first public pronouncement seems to have arisen at a meeting of the Hammersmith branch of the Socialist League. When Morris was requested to give a lecture on short notice, he declined because he did not have a new subject to offer; but, when the lecture secretary learned that he had recently read *Looking Backward* and suggested that he talk about it, Morris agreed.[19]

From this lecture probably emerged the review of *Looking Backward* published by Morris in June, 1889, in *The Commonweal* which he had founded and which he edited. Morris admitted in his article that "Socialists and non-Socialists have been so much impressed with the book that it" seemed that *The Commonweal* should notice it—and he then termed *Looking Backward* "a Utopia" which was dangerous for two reasons.

First of all, some would like the picture of the future which Bellamy delineated and would not see its "errors and fallacies" —in "which such a book *must* abound"—and it would "warp their efforts into futile directions." The second group which might be misled would be "enquirers or young Socialists" who, disliking Bellamy's society, would decide that they did not wish to promote socialistic concepts.

Morris then stated that Bellamy's "temperament may be called the unmixed modern one, unhistoric and unartistic; it makes its owner (if a socialist) perfectly satisfied with modern civilization, if only the injustice, misery and waste of class society could be got rid of; which half changes seems [sic] possible to him. The only ideal of life which such a man can see is that of the industrious *professional* middleclass man of today, purified from their crime of complicity with the monopolist class, and become independent instead of being, as they are now, parasitical. . . ."

After almost calling Bellamy the creator of a modified bourgeois society, Morris took an even clearer Marxist stand, for he denounced Bellamy for thinking that a new society could be the result of evolution rather than revolution: "It follows naturally from the author's satisfaction with the best part of modern life that he conceives of the change to Socialism as taking place without any breakdown of that life, or indeed disturbance of it, by means of the final development of the great private monopolies which are such a noteworthy feature of the present day. He supposes that these must necessarily be transformed into one great monopoly which will include the whole people and be worked for the benefit of the people. . . ."

Morris, who hated machinery and mass-produced items, and who was also opposed to systems then wrote:

The great change having thus peaceably and fatalistically taken place, the author has put forward his scheme of the organisation of life, which is organised with a vengeance. His scheme may be described as State Communism, worked by the vast extreme of national centralisation. The underlying vice in it is that the author cannot conceive, as aforesaid, anything else than the machinery of society, and that, doubtless naturally, he reads into the future of society, which he tells us is unwastefully conducted, that terror of starvation which is the necessary accompaniment of a society in which two-thirds or more of its labor-power *is* wasted: he *tells* us that every man is free to choose his own occupation and that work is no burden to anyone, the *impression* which he produces is that of a huge

standing army, tightly drilled, compelled by some mysterious fate
to unceasing anxiety for the production of wares to satisfy every
caprice, however wasteful and absurd, that may cast up among
them.

Completely misunderstanding Bellamy's moral and intellectual
objectives, Morris also charged that "a machine life" was the
best that Bellamy could invent for the world and that his only
idea "of making labour tolerable" was to "decrease the amount
of it by means of fresh and ever fresh developments of machinery. . . ." Morris declared that he did not think the future
would bring a "lessening of man's energy by the reduction of
labour to a minimum, but rather to a *reduction of pain* in
labour to a minimum. . . ." Because of this attitude, Morris felt
that Bellamy was unnecessarily worried about "seeking (with
obvious failure) some incentive to labour to replace the fear
of starvation, which is at present our only one, whereas it cannot be too often repeated that the true incentive to happy and
useful labour must be pleasure in the work itself. . . ." In this
last statement, Morris also completely overlooked Bellamy's
intent of having men do the work for which they were innately
suited and which they enjoyed.

Also ignoring Bellamy's emphasis upon brotherhood, a true
democracy, and development of personal individualism, Morris
then wrote:

> It is necessary to point out that there are some Socialists who
> do not think that the problem of the organisation of life and
> necessary labor can be dealt with by a huge centralisation,
> worked by a kind of magic for which no one feels himself
> responsible; that on the contrary it will be necessary for the unit
> of administration to be small enough for every citizen to feel
> himself responsible for its details, and be interested in them, that
> the individual man cannot shuffle off the business of life onto
> the shoulders of an abstraction called the State, but must deal
> with it in conscious association with each other. That variety
> of life is as much an aim of true Communism as equality of con-
> dition, and that nothing but a union of these two will bring
> about real freedom.

After criticizing what Morris interpreted as Bellamy's concept
that art was an adjunct of life and not the "necessary and indispensable instrument of human happiness," and after also declaring that the American's "ideas of life are curiously limited,"
Morris criticized him because he had no "idea beyond exist-

ence in a great city; his dwelling of man in the future is Boston
(U. S. A.) beautified."

Morris stressed his differences with Bellamy because of his
fear that the portrayals of the future society in *Looking Backward* would be generally accepted as those of socialists—and,
as A. L. Morton has stated in *The English Utopia*, there was
a "strong tendency" even in England, where socialism and Marxism had long been known, for Bellamy's picture of life under
socialism to be accepted as authoritative."[20] Morris made it
clear, however, that he did not wish to denigrate a book which
he agreed was "one to be read and considered seriously"; but
he also made it apparent that he did not wish it to be considered as "the Socialist bible of reconstruction."[21]

Morris' criticisms were reflected in his own picture of life
under communism which *Looking Backward* stimulated him to
write: *News from Nowhere.* His Utopia began to appear in
*The Commonweal* on January 11, 1890, and was published as
a book in 1891. Although J. W. Mackail wondered why Morris'
*News from Nowhere* had been translated "into French, German
and Italian, and has probably been more read in foreign countries than any of his more important works in prose or verse,"[22]
Mackail could not know that Morris' Utopia was usually translated after Bellamy had created a stir in these countries, as well
as in others, such as Russia.

As might be expected from the article in *The Commonweal*,
*News from Nowhere* reflected the criticism Morris had made
of Bellamy's socialism and also—as G. D. H. Cole has indicated
—the author's "expression of personal preference"[23] and interests. When Morris' hero William Guest awakens two hundred
years after he has gone to bed thinking of the days of bliss
and brotherhood following the revolution which he had discussed
with his comrades at the Hammersmith Socialist League, he
finds that London, as a result of a bloody uprising, has become
many villages separated by woodlands and flowers; instead of
Bellamy's centralized government, it is a world of agricultural-
industrial groups which are autonomous; in place of the military discipline of an industrial army, there is artistic work for
all when one wants it; instead of new inventions and factories,
machines have been permitted to rust away, for they did not
produce goods by art; instead of credit cards, there is no money;
instead of happiness which has resulted from progress, there is
a belief that felicity is not the result of either progress or abundance; and instead of the world of the twentieth century, the
society has many of the characteristics of the Middle Ages. As

this far from complete summary indicates, Morris' Utopia was the antithesis of Bellamy's.

In the United States, the critic of the Reverend Edward E. Hale's *Lend a Hand* considered Morris' Utopia inadequate to meet "great social problems";[24] and Bellamy himself wrote in the *New Nation* of February, 1891:

> Mr. Morris appears to belong to the school of anarchistic rather than to the state socialists. That is to say, he believes that the present system of private capitalism, once destroyed, voluntary coöperation, with little or no governmental administration, will be necessary to bring about the ideal social system. This is in strong contrast with the theory of nationalism which holds that no amount of moral excellence or good feeling on the part of a community will enable them to dispense with a great deal of system in order so to coordinate their efforts as to obtain the best economic results. In the sense of a force to restrain or punish, governmental administration may no doubt be dispensed with in proportion as a better social system shall be introduced; but in no degree will any degree of moral improvement lessen the necessity of a strictly economic administration for the directing of the productive and distributive machinery. This is a destination which anarchists too commonly overlook, when they argue against the necessity of government.[25]

Bellamy might have been more approving of Oscar Wilde's *The Soul of Man Under Socialism,* which created quite a sensation among the Oxford students and Wilde's aristocratic friends when it appeared in the *Fortnightly Review* of February, 1891. Wilde, who for some time had been a friend of Mrs. Annie Besant, Helena Blavatsky, and of other Theosophists, and who had attended Fabian meetings, had been present with his wife at the opening of the West End Restaurant for Working Girls in 1889. He had also attended a Fabian meeting in July, 1888, and had participated in the discussion following a paper "The Prospects of Art under Socialism" which had been presented by Walter Crane, the artist.[26] These incidents are cited to indicate that Wilde was friendly with people who were supporters of Bellamy's *Looking Backward,* interested in the cause, and certainly in a position to have been acquainted with Bellamy's famous book. It is more than likely, therefore, that instead of having written his famous essay because of a reaction to a Shavian lecture—as Hesketh Pearson has stated "may have been" the case—he wrote it as a result of Bellamy's Utopia.

In fact, an analysis of the ideas expressed by Wilde in *The*

*Soul of Man* indicates that he was not only taking a blow at the Webb group which deified the state,[27] but striking at or approving some of the ideas which Bellamy and Morris had presented. Like Bellamy, Wilde did not want industrial tyranny which might enslave the citizenry but an institution which was made *for* man; because of his desire for freedom for the artist and all others, Wilde advocated socialism because he felt it would contribute to the development of individualism. As did Bellamy, he wanted property abolished because it hampered and degraded the rich as well as the poor and because he thought starvation resulted in crime. Unlike Morris and like the American, Wilde thought that machinery should do all the tedious work; that the state should be in charge of production and distribution; and that both the machines and the state should be the servants of the citizens who would at last be free to enjoy cultivated leisure.

Such a state would permit the machines to produce the necessary and the artists to create the beautiful; but Wilde took great issue with Bellamy's plan to have the public judge the artist's work:

> . . . whenever a community or a government of any kind attempts to dictate to the artist what he is to do, art either entirely vanishes, or becomes stereotyped, or degenerates into a low and ignoble form of craft. *A work of art is the unique result of a unique temperament. Its beauty comes from the fact that the author is what he is. It has nothing to do with the fact that other people want what they want.* Indeed, the moment that an artist takes notice of what other people want, and tries to supply the demand, he ceases to be an artist and becomes a dull or an amusing craftsman, an honest or a dishonest tradesman. He has no further claim to be considered an artist. *Art is the most intense mode of individualism that the world has known.*[28]

Believing with Bellamy that technical progress could produce enough for everybody and that the state would equitably distribute it, Wilde wrote:

> The fact is, that civilization requires slaves. The Greeks were quite right there. Unless there are slaves to do the ugly, horrible, uninteresting work, culture and contemplation [two aspects which Bellamy had stressed as desirable] become almost impossible. Human slavery is wrong, insecure and demoralising. On mechanical slavery, on the slavery of the machine, the future of the world depends. And when scientific men are no longer called upon to go down to a depressing East-End and distribute bad cocoa and horse blankets to starving people, they will

have delightful leisure in which to devise wonderful and marvellous things for their own joy and the joy of everyone else.
There will be great storages of force for every city, and for
every house if required, and this force man will convert into
heat, light, or motion according to his needs [as Bellamy fore-
saw]. Is this Utopian? A map of the world that does not include
Utopia is not worth even glancing at, for it leaves out the one
country at which Humanity is always landing. And when Humanity lands there, it looks out, and, seeing a better country,
sets sail. Progress is the realisation of Utopia.[29]

Although Wilde makes no direct mention in *The Soul of Man*
of Bellamy or of his book, his reference to ideas which the
American had expressed and to Utopia when a book about one
was making a great sensation, would indicate that he had
him in mind. Indeed, as we shall see at the end of this chapter, no less a person than Shaw also used Bellamy's ideas—
and did so without specific credit to their source. In fact,
Shaw was to prove to be a greater supporter of the ideas of
Bellamy—and certainly a more popular one. For, if Wilde's
and Morris' replies to Bellamy received attention, Percival
Chubb believes that Bellamy's Utopia attracted more sympathy
and support than *News from Nowhere*.[30]

### III  *English Bellamyists*

The political situation in England contributed not only to
the favorable reaction toward Bellamy's Utopia but also led
to the immediate formation of Nationalist clubs. By 1889 British
politics had become distinguished for their ferocity and confusion; the Liberal party had split over the issue of Irish Home
Rule and the attempt of the Conservatives to pacify Ireland
was meeting with no success. Violence had entered the English
scene: November 13, 1887, was dubbed "Bloody Sunday" because violent clashes, involving troops, occurred at a meeting
in Trafalgar Square of the Social Democratic Federation which
had gathered there in defiance of a prohibition of the meeting
by the police. This event probably gave Morris the idea for
the portrayal of the uprising of the people in *News from Nowhere*.[31]

Economically, free trade was commencing to be undermined
by the steady development overseas of industry and of protective tariffs. Victorian industrial growth was slackening pace
at the same time that the demand of the working class for
a large share of the national income was voiced by unions in
which the unskilled laborers as well as the craftsmen were now

enrolled. The successful strike of the London dockers in 1889—
which had repercussions in New Zealand and Australia—directed the attention of the public toward labor problems to
a degree unparalleled in the previous half-century.

But other economic and social trends also revealed the problems and tensions of the era. Business began to organize on a
larger scale, and the small capitalist complained of unfair competition. Humanitarians investigated and demanded the redress
of urban social conditions; and socialist doctrines grew in prom-
inence and popularity. But whatever remedies might be propounded, it was clear to many that a view of Britain of the
later 1880's and early 1890's would provide little complacency
and certainty either in the present or for the future.

For all these reasons Bellamy's ideas found a receptive audience, and it was natural that the enthusiasm with which they
were adopted should lead to the formation of clubs for their
advancement. On July 3, 1890, twenty people met in London
to found the Nationalization of Labour Society. By October
the group was issuing its own magazine which appeared monthly
and sold for one penny—but which was also distributed free of
charge to the secretaries of union chapters all over Britain.[32]
This publication, the *Nationalization News,* announced on its
cover that it was "established to promote the system proposed
in *Looking Backward";* and the first number declared that the
aim of the society was to secure the nationalization of every
thing. It stated: "Stupendous as such aims may at first sight
appear, it is wonderful how soon the light of common sense,
when brought calmly to bear upon the question, reduces the
mountain of difficulty to a mere molehill, and when facts about
which there is and can be no dispute are brought to our aid, it
becomes evident that events are fast tending in the direction we
indicate. We have only to spread our sails and ride before the
breeze which is moving us slowly but surely toward the desired
haven."[33]

With this note of optimism the Society entered print; elected
John Orme, a dealer in photographic supplies, as president;
and Walter Godbold, a printer, as secretary. It enrolled in its
first three months two hundred and thirty members. During
this same period, the organization sold nearly three hundred
copies of *Looking Backward* and distributed 14,000 pamphlets
describing the objectives of the organization.

The Nationalist Society began to create branches in other
parts of England. In October a successful meeting was held
in Bath, a somewhat surprising location for a new radical move-

ment; but Orme noted that the members there were "suffering from the effect of combinations among large concerns, whose great resources and many shareholders attract the consumers and leave the small tradesmen out in the cold." In November a branch was also formed in South London at Walworth, and the December issue of the magazine announced this progress at the same time that it published the congratulations and approval of Bellamy. By the end of the first year, the membership exceeded four hundred; but the state of the treasury was reported to be "very low."

In February, 1891, a formal political program was announced. The Society had been established to "gradually, lawfully, and peacefully bring about a complete social Reformation"; and it sought to achieve this objective through the distribution of literature; the extension of state ownership over land, mines, and water; state management of public services, which included education and recreation; scientific supervision of agriculture; and the immediate establishment of cooperative agencies which would grow into "vast productive establishments" leading gradually into a national recognition of the Bellamy principle.

By March, although progress at Bath had halted, a new branch had been formed at Bradford; and Walworth claimed over eighty members. By the end of the first year, additional groups had been founded in North London and Southwark; and the total membership of five branches totaled five hundred and sixty members. In July, 1891, a Leeds branch was founded; and, in August, Pimlico became the fourth group in the London area. It was not, however, until autumn that an attempt was made to secure the support of the East End workers. In October, Sunday meetings were held in Victoria Park, Poplar, and the establishment of a local branch followed.

The movement was completely eclectic in the interest that it aroused, as a description of the formation of the Liverpool branch indicates. At the inaugural meeting in October "there were present Socialists, Trade Unionists, Co-operationists, Anti-Co-operationists, Good Templars, Theosophists, gentlemen holding important positions under Government, Traders, thus making in all a very sound representative meeting."

The initial enthusiasm which had carried the Society through its founding period soon began to flag; for in March, 1892, the general secretary of the Nationalists reminded the branches of the necessity of holding regular, frequent meetings. In May Orme announced that membership was now over twelve hundred, but he also wondered how many members were active and pointed out that the magazine was being published at the cost of an increasing deficit. In July the new president of the Nationalists, the Reverend Arthur Potter, admitted that "at this moment there seems to be a loss of active interest in the Society's welfare"; in the following month, the general secretary's report declared that only the Liverpool branch had done satisfactory or good work. By October, the financial deficit had reached forty pounds; and a letter from the North London branch secretary opened: "Now Sir, it seems to me that the great want in our Society is enthusiasm. . . ."

Although the publication of the organization survived until the end of the year of 1893, the general secretary continued to complain about the mounting deficit, the lack of funds, the imperfect communication between members, and the need of concerted action on the part of sympathizers. But no practical help was forthcoming, and in April, 1893, the executive committee agreed to the amalgamation of *Nationalization News* with J. B. Wallace's magazine, *Brotherhood*.

Lacking outstanding leaders and unable to secure financial support, the collapse of the Nationalists as an independent group was perhaps inevitable. Yet the fundamental failure which created its deficiencies was an inability to provide the movement with a distinctive policy. Furthermore, two attitudes became apparent which did not strengthen the prospects of attracting substantial popular support: one was the attitude toward radical groups and the other toward Utopian colonies.

A tendency to give attention to the establishment of Utopian colonies had indeed been apparent from the moment of the first issue of the *Nationalization News,* and this must have limited the appeal of the Nationalists to a handful of idealists. First of all, the magazine carried reports about the status of the North American Utopian colonies; frequent letters and accounts of visits kept members informed of the fortunes of the settlers at Kaweah and Topolobampo; and an attempt to create a similar community in England represented a natural development of this interest. The first proposal to the Society was made in July, 1891, by Walter Godbold, the general secretary, who was either ignorant of or indifferent to Bellamy's attitude toward such futile endeavors. In either case, Godbold declared: "We must at once commence the building up of a Co-operative Colony here in England. Immediately it is perceived that our Society intends carrying out such a practical scheme of social reform, we shall awaken an interest in the minds of thousands who are practically inclined, and it will mean a considerable addition to our numbers." Kaweah would, he thought, provide a good example for imitation. This colony, which had been founded in California in 1886, to establish the principles of Gronlund's *Co-operative Commonwealth*, attempted to entice Nationalists in the United States to join it; the Topolobampo Bay Colony in Mexico also advertised that it was seeking to fulfill Bellamy's dream.

No immediate response was noticeable to Godbold's declaration; but in February, 1892, the *Nationalization News* published a call, signed by Orme and J. B. Wallace, who had visited the American colonies, to those who might be "willing to abandon Capitalistic slavery for co-operative and meaningful work." They also argued that tempting though migration to Topolobampo might be, they surely preferred to begin the building of the cooperative commonwealth in England. A farm of about five hundred acres which would yield food, flax, and wool and which would have industries to consume its produce, would provide the basis for gradual expansion toward the new social order. Funds would, however, be required for the initial purchase; and, in order to make a beginning, a moderate rate of interest would be paid on loans.

In March a meeting appointed a committee to find a suitable tract of land for the "Home Integral Co-operative Colony." Its settlers would be paid, if practicable, at trade union rates, and they would work for forty-four hours a week. The profits, it was hopefully suggested, would be distributed in bonus payments, used for the creation of a fund for the sick and aged, and expended in making interest payments and in further expansion. The readers of *Brotherhood* and of *Nationalization News* were counted upon to provide over a thousand replies, but by August no more than a hundred and twenty had responded favorably.

The committee did not produce any concrete proposals until the beginning of 1893, and then it warned that capital of from two to three thousand pounds would be required. It also announced that land would be acquired and placed in the hands of trustees who would receive the rents and administer the financial affairs of the colony. The general management of the colony affairs would, however, be entrusted to a board elected by the adult residents, who would have one vote each. The colony was to be as near as possible to London and located on a railroad line; for such a location would persuade industrial concerns to move there from congested districts and would also supply the colony with "the combined advantages of town and country."

As the committee realized, this proposal did not create a fully cooperative colony, but its plan represented the maximum degree of agreement which could be achieved. Orme reported: "Our colony has for the last month been our main effort. We have held meetings twice every week, wherein every shade of opinion was expressed, from individualism to extreme communism, and it finally appearing that the only point on which all will agree was common ownership of land, the rents to be expended in such public works as are now paid out of rates, co-operation in other matters being left to voluntary associations. . . ."

Obviously, this solution fell far short of the Nationalist theory and could at best be considered a point of departure. And Orme admitted: "You will see that this is NOT a Bellamy society. It is simply, or at least, mainly concerned in acquiring land. It will lease its land to all who choose to apply for it, and therein we as a body of co-operators come in, and will be able fully to carry out the principles of Integral Co-operation as set forth in *Looking Backward*. . . ."

By April, 1893, a suitable site had been located near Hockley in Essex, and it was comprised of nine hundred acres of uncultivated land. Guarantees would have to be offered that three hundred acres would be immediately settled, and Orme announced that five acres would be rented at about two shillings and sixpence a week. He also warned, however, that much labor, six to eight pounds of capital per acre, and two years work without returns would be required; and the cost of buildings and three or four thousand pounds for roads and drainage would be needed. He did not expect more than thirty to forty families to start the enterprise, but he hoped that the remainder of the thousand members of the Society would subscribe at least two shillings and sixpence a month to assist in supporting the pioneers.

The financial burden evidently proved too great, for there is no indication that the colony ever became actuality. The shaping of the project, however, indicated a fundamental dilemma which faced the Nationalists. They had either to believe that the future would bring their revolution in its fullest extent or attempt a small beginning which, as Orme and the Kaweah Colony admitted,[34] did not constitute society as Bellamy envisaged it but might at most evolve toward it. To an extent, however, realism had bred Utopianism; but the consequence was a draining of Nationalist support toward the movement which had led to the establishment of numerous colonies at home and abroad during the last years of the nineteenth century; the inevitable result was a loss of interest among the more practical members of the Society.

The second tendency of the Society which also weakened its prospects was simultaneous but contrasting: it made a constant effort to support socialist and radical campaigns in British politics. Exclusiveness was frowned upon, and readers of *Nationalization News* were urged to attend courses of lectures given by J. A. Hobson, the author and economist, and by Beatrice Potter, who later became in 1892 Mrs. Sidney Webb. Moreover, the groups were asked to support Labour Churches; and Wallace's Brotherhood Church invited Tom Mann, leader of the dockers' strike, to speak; the Walworth branch arranged for a lecture by Keir Hardie, chairman of the Scottish Labour party and also the editor of *Labour Leader*.

The Nationalists also hailed radical pressures and incursions upon *laissez-faire* society as portents of the approaching triumph of Nationalism and suggested that they be supported because they were contributing to the battle which might win a victory over capitalism. The *Nationalization News* offered friendly commentaries about the progress of radical movements; for example, in November, 1891, it declared that "the effort now being made to form a Labour Party is one of the most encouraging signs of today, and should receive the combined support of all who have the interests of the toilers at heart." During 1892 Liberal or—when possible—Labour candidates were supported during the general election; and the victory of the Progressives at the election for the newly established London County Council was a delightful incident to the Nationalists.

Orme regarded the return of Gladstone on the Newcastle platform and the socialist activity of the campaign as a clear indication that the peaceful, constitutional revolution had commenced. He also saw that it offered his members and other possible supporters opportunity to make a political impression more immediately because of the established radical and socialist organizations. When Keir Hardie and friends succeeded in establishing the Independent Labour Party in 1893, the Nationalist reaction confirmed this situation; for, torn between alternatives, the British Nationalists either enlisted in the cause of communal idealism or played a modest role, like Orme and Godbold, in the new labor organization. As a result, the Nation-

alist movement vanished as an independent force in Great
Britain; and it did so before the publication of *Equality* in 1897.

## IV  *Among the Fabians*

Enthusiasm for *Looking Backward* was not confined to the
Nationalization of Labour Society; an enthusiastic reception
of this Utopia was evidenced by the Fellowship of the New
Life which had been founded in 1883 in a room in Chelsea,
London, by a group of young radicals who had listened to
Thomas Davidson, an American descendant of the Utopians of
Brook Farm and the Phalanstery, who wanted to find something "in the nature of a community of superior people with-
drawn from the world because of its wickedness, and showing
by example how a higher life might be led."[35]
As a result of the inspiration of Davidson, the Fellowship of
the New Life was founded with the objective of "cultivation
of a perfect character in each and all"; and its guiding principle
was "the subordination of material things to spiritual." These
elevated aims evidently caused some misgivings among the
more terrestial-minded of the founding members; for in January, 1884, they established the Fabian Society and adopted
the following motto: "For the right moment you must wait,
as Fabius did, most patiently, when warring against Hannibal,
though many censured his delays; but when the time comes
you must strike hard, as Fabius did, or your waiting will be
in vain and fruitless."[36]
Actually, the group comprising the Fellowship had from the
beginning been divided: some wanted only regeneration of the
individual; others maintained that the emphasis should be placed
upon social progress, sympathized with the work of the Social
Democratic Federation but did not wish to join it because it
ignored the ethical development necessary for a new society,
and also felt that the new order could be achieved immediately.
Since only a difference in emphasis had caused the rift in the
Fellowship, the members intermingled and played prominent
parts for a time in both the Fabian and the Fellowship clubs;
soon, however, little was to be found in common between the
two organizations.[37]
In 1889 the New Fellowship began the publication of its
own journal, *The Sower*, but quickly changed the title to *Seed-
Time* when it was discovered that another magazine already
bore the name first chosen. The first issue contained an account
of the growth of the Nationalist movement in the United States
and an enthusiastic review of *Looking Backward* by J. F.

Oakeshott, a stalwart of the Fellowship and for many years also a member of the Fabian Society Executive.

During the autumn of 1889 and the first quarter of 1890, the activities of the Fellowship centered around a careful study of Bellamy's ideas. In October, Oakeshott provided an introductory paper; in November, James Cash considered the form of the New Industrial Organization; and in December, A. J. Bywaters dealt with the system of distribution and exchange. Three more meetings followed in 1890 at which Rowland Estcourt considered the treatment of law and crime in *Looking Backward,* Alice Woods expanded its scanty references to education, and Edith Lees discussed the position of women. Miss Lees was honorary secretary of the Fellowship until December, 1891, when she was married to Havelock Ellis and was succeeded by J. Ramsay MacDonald, who joined the Labour Party in 1894, eventually became its leader, and even later organized the first labor ministry in the history of Britain.

The Fellowship's enthusiasm for Bellamy was seemingly not sustained, for though it continued to publish *Seed-Time* until 1898, no mention of Bellamy or of his books appeared after 1891. Attention had turned to Utopian settlements—to Hertzka's *Freiland* and the proposed colony in East Africa; to the progress of Topolobampo; and to the hopes of South American ventures. The Fellowship's intensive interest in Bellamy had, however, led to an earnest and perhaps influential consideration of his ideas.

The Fabians had in the meantime enlisted some of the most brilliant minds of England: Shaw had joined in 1884; Sidney Webb and Sidney Olivier in 1885; and among the other early joiners were: Percival Chubb, William Clarke, Graham Wallas, Annie Besant, H. W. Massingham, Hubert Bland, Edward R. Pease, and H. H. Champion. Others who joined somewhat later were H. G. Wells, Ramsay MacDonald, Pethick-Lawrence, Beatrice Potter Webb, Keir Hardie, G. D. H. Cole, and Sir Leo Chiozzo-Money.[38] As has already been noticed, this group —or many of its members—moved freely back and forth not only among the Fellowship but—as Sidney Webb pointed out in *Socialism In England*—participated "in nearly all reform movements, as well as by their works at the Universities and in the field of journalism and the teaching of Political Economy. It is not, however, a numerous body, and makes no attempt to increase its numbers beyond a convenient limit. Its influence on the Socialist movement has been marked by the present predominance of the ideas of gradual social evolution, and the importance of correct economic analysis."[39]

In 1889 Sidney Webb wrote in *Socialism in England* that the indication of the British interest in political economy "was increasing. The first edition of the English translation of Marx's 'Capital' . . . was soon exhausted, and more popular writings on economics now find a ready sale. Works like Gronlund's 'Co-operative Commonwealth' (Modern Press: 1s.) and Bellamy's 'Looking Backward' (Reeves: 1s., of this, over 40,000 have been sold in England, and 210,000 in America), are exercising a potent influence on public ideals and are but premature popularisations of the current economic views as to the future of society."[40]

Although Webb did not enthusiastically sponsor *Looking Backward*, Annie Besant was lecturing about Bellamy in London in 1892;[41] and William Clarke—who contributed in the famous *Fabian Essays*, edited by Shaw, the lecture and essay about the indications in industry which would lead to capitalism—visited the United States in 1893 and discussed with Mason Green and others on the American Nationalist Correspondence Committee the proposal that the Fabians and the Americans work together since their problems were the same.[42] In 1894 the Fabians were willing to have Bellamy write an essay-introduction to the *Fabian Essays*—and in it he pointed out his differences not only with socialism but with the Fabians: He sponsored economic equality and they did not.[43]

In fact, the only known member of the English Fabians who did sponsor economic equality was, as Harry W. Laidler stated in *A History of Socialist Thought*, George Bernard Shaw.[44] And that Shaw knew Bellamy is evident; for he remarked when he talked with Archibald Henderson that the Fabians had not considered the American too seriously: "We took it for granted . . . that we knew all about *Equality* and did not read it. We rather turned up our noses at Utopias as cheap stuff until Wells stood up for them; and by that time Bellamy was a back number. Later on, we found that we had underrated him, and that he had made many converts." Henderson then remarked —as another scholar was later to prove more specifically—that Shaw "followed in Bellamy's footsteps."[45]

Shaw's view of the attitude toward Bellamy was accurate; for, as the Fabian tactics were developed and as confidence in their ultimate success grew, their denunciations of Utopianism became vehement. A lecture delivered in 1894 by Sidney Webb brought the conflict into the open. He expounded his belief in the validity of gradual political reformation and denounced the errors of Insurrectionist and Utopian proposals for violent and total changes—although Bellamy had urged no violent change but had sponsored an evolutionary, peaceful, eventually total one.

The next two assaults had as their target *Brotherhood*, which just a few months before absorbed *Nationalization News*. Wallace, though described as "a comrade whom we all respect for sincerity and boundless energy," was quoted at length as one who evaded "such pettifogging work as slowly and with infinite difficulty building up a Municipal Works Department under the London County Council . . ." and preferred the glorious but impractical vision of a cooperative commonwealth which was to be created overnight.[46] Two years later Webb returned to this charge in another Fabian Tract which reprinted, with minor changes, an article which had first appeared in the *Economic Journal* of June, 1891. Webb declared: "Down to the present generation every aspirant after social reform, whether Socialist or Individualist, naturally embodied his ideas in a detailed plan for a new social order, from which all contemporary evils were eliminated. Bellamy is but a belated Cabet, Baboeuf, or Campanella. But modern Socialists have learnt [sic] the lesson of evolution better than their opponents, and it cannot be too often repeated that Socialism, to Socialists, is not a Utopia which they have invented, but a principle of social organization which they assert to have been discovered by the patient investigators into sociology whose labors have distinguished the present century. . . ."[47]

Almost simultaneously a report on Fabian policy presented to the International Socialist Workers and Trade Union Congress held in London in August, 1896, and drafted by Bernard Shaw, stated succinctly the attitude toward the founders of Utopian colonies: "The Fabian Society desires to offer to all projectors and founders of Utopian communities in South America, Africa, and other remote localities, its apologies for its impatience with such adventures. To such projectors, and all patrons of schemes for starting similar settlements and workshops at home, the Society announces emphatically that it does not believe in the establishment of Socialism by private enterprise. . . ."[48]

When *Equality* was published in England in 1897, its critical reception, which was "anything but gracious,"[49] confirmed the decline of Bellamy's reputation. Despite the condemnation of the book as a tiresome, economic tract, individual enthusiasm was not diminished. Henry Holiday read a paper about *Equality* to the Hampstead branch of the Fabian Society in January, 1898, but was compelled to record that *Looking Backward* was incomparably the more successful publication. He attributed its wider sale in part to its lower price of sixpence; *Equality* sold for six shillings.[50]

## V Changing Attitudes

Although this difference in cost might have limited sales, *Equality* undoubtedly suffered more from the transformation which had occurred in the political scene. By 1897 British radicalism had grown more mature, confident, and sophisticated than it had been a decade earlier; and its general indifference toward the sequel, which contrasted so greatly to the enormous enthusiasm which had greeted the appearance of *Looking Backward*, reflected not only the less immediate appeal of *Equality* but a decisive shift in the aims and interests of the labor movement.

Evidence of the decline of Bellamy's fame may be found in the replies to a questionnaire circulated by W. T. Stead in 1906 when the general election of that year returned fifty-one members of parliament as candidates of the Labour Representation Committee or by local agreements, as "Lib-Labs." Stead's poll of this new breed of politicians had the aim of discovering intellectual origins; and of the forty-five members who answered his request to name the books which had formed their convictions, only one—John Williams, a Welsh coal miner—mentioned Bellamy.[51] Further evidence of the neglect of Bellamy may be seen in the fact that Holiday, still convinced of Bellamy's significance, thought it necessary in 1914 to summarize *Looking Backward* in an appendix to his *Reminiscences* for the benefit of readers unfamiliar with its arguments. Twenty years earlier he would not have deemed this necessary.

More recent historians of political thought have been content with cursory, even contemptuous, assessments of Bellamy's contribution. G. D. H. Cole's judgment was: "Not an original thinker but only a populariser of other men's ideas."[52] Sir Alexander Gray was even less generous: "Bellamy's *Looking Backward* presents a rather vulgar and unattractive world of state socialism run mad."[53] Others have relegated the American to a disparaging footnote.

Historically, however, such verdicts are not only unfair but superficial. Although Bellamy's greatest moment of popularity

and influence may have been brief, its very intensity ensured
its importance. R. C. K. Ensor, who possessed great personal and
historical knowledge of the origins of the new radicalism, declared that "'out of Henry George by either Bellamy or Gronlund' was a true pedigree of the convictions held by nearly all
the leading propagandists who set socialism on its feet in Great
Britain between 1886 and 1900."[54] For some, acquaintance with
Bellamy's concepts at a crucial stage in their political education made an impression which remained perpetually vivid.
Josiah Wedgwood, later an unorthodox but highly respected
representative of labor in Parliament, declared that Bellamy
had made him a socialist. He had read Looking Backward,
when at the age of eighteen he had entered Armstrong's ship-
yards at Newcastle-on-Tyne, and he was directed by its arguments into radical politics.[55] Alfred Salter, another representative
in the Parliament, read the Utopian novel when he was seventeen; and he attributed to it his conversion to socialism.[56]

Furthermore, numerous fragmentary glimpses of the per-
meation of the labor movement can be obtained. Bradford
socialists in the 1890's sold Looking Backward from door to
door.[57] A meeting of the Manchester Labour Church in 1891
read the lesson from Bellamy.[58] "The Socialist Portrait Gallery"
offered pictures of Morris, Tolstoy, and Bellamy.[59] In the
provinces, devoted if little-known pioneers, such as the Reverend
H. Bodell Smith, Unitarian minister at Crewe and a member
of the Independent Labour Party, held classes for the workers
for the study of socialist literature, and at one of these Looking
Backward was the text.[60] As A. L. Morton stated in a letter
of February, 1957, to Sylvia E. Bowman, ". . . one has only
to talk to some of the old stagers in the Labour Movement
to realise how considerable [Bellamy's influence] was."[61]

Although only a handful of those influenced or converted by
Bellamy during the years can now be traced, many may have
assumed the vague outline of an uncle of G. K. Chesterton: "one
of those sensitive and conscientious men, very typical of the
modern world, who had the same scrupulous sense of the duty
of accepting new things, and sympathising with the young,
that older moralists may have had about preserving old things
and obeying the elders. I remember him assuring me quite
eagerly of the hopeful thoughts aroused in him by the optimistic
official prophecies of the book called Looking Backwards [sic];
a rather ironical title, seeing that the one thing forbidden to
such futurists was Looking Backwards. . . ."[62]

Although the enthusiasm for Bellamy did not last and although he proved a momentary excitement, many individuals struggled to keep his ideas alive in England. Henry Holiday remained constant in his admiration although he had first read *Looking Backward* against his will, at the urging of one of his art students. Reading the book proved to be an act of permanent conversion, for Holiday recalled: "On finishing the book I experienced a sensation unlike anything I had known before. It was the sense of a strong hope, of a gleam of light where all had been gloom, of a straight well-defined path where all had been groping in a dark tangle; a feeling of exaltation, and a consciousnessness that life offered something indeed worth living for. . . ."[63]

Like his art student before him, Holiday, converted, insisted that his friends share his experience. And among them were Professor Stuart, a prominent liberal educator; Russell Rea, a liberal businessman; G. F. Watts, an artist; all agreed that *Looking Backward* was a most remarkable book.[64] Because of his enthusiasm, Holiday began to correspond with Bellamy; and, when he visited the United States in 1890 to fulfill a number of commissions for stained glass windows, he stayed for four days in Chicopee Falls. The meeting of the two men was most successful, for an "absolute sympathy" was apparent. Holiday felt that he had never "formed so warm an affection for a man on so short an acquaintance as did [he] for Edward Bellamy."[65] Although Holiday—like Bellamy—later espoused the cause of dress reform, as well as other causes, his admiration and his convictions never deserted the cause of Nationalism.

Another convert to Bellamyism was Professor H. Stanley Jevons, the son of the more famous economist William Stanley Jevons and the author of *Essays on Economics* (1905) and *Money, Banking, and Exchange in India* (1922). Professor Jevons—who had taught economics at the University College of South Wales and Monmouthshire and at the University of Allahabad, India—published in 1933 *Economic Equality in the Co-operative Commonwealth*. In the preface of his book, Jevons stated:

> More's *Utopia* should be read by everyone, and the social writings of William Morris. For myself, however, I feel that I have gained more from Bellamy than from any single author. He deserves more attention from economists than he has received. The casting of his message in the form of a story, his acceptance of middle-class values—delight in the splendour of marble halls and the triumphs of mechanical devices—his industrial army, with its captains and lieutenants, are to many social

thinkers repulsive features of his scheme. Yet he had a remarkable prevision of the mechanical and electrical progress of the
twentieth century. . . . Perhaps in the social sphere his forecasts may not be less accurate. The economic system he outlines
does stand a rigid examination for workability in its essential
features.[66]

As may be deduced from this comment and from the title of
his volume, Professor Jevons sponsored a communist state like
Bellamy's; and he tried to foreshadow and describe a "society
of economic equality." He felt that "projects of economic equality must sooner or later become the subjects of research, propaganda, and controversy. . . ." Jevons made it quite clear, however, that his communism was not to be associated with "the
creed of the Communist Party of Russia, including class war
and the dictatorship of the proletariat."[67]

Much space has also been devoted to Bellamy in books about
the Utopian novel which have appeared in recent years. Ethel
Mannin in *Bread and Roses* (1944) mentions Bellamy frequently in her discussion of Utopian plans for a better world,
and she also seemingly adopted some of his concepts as her own
ideas. A. L. Morton in *The English Utopia* (1952) approaches
Bellamy with a socialist's criticism but admits that *Looking
Backward* had "seemed to many to point to a practical solution
of real problems."[68] To Morton, Utopias contributed much to
the modern concept of socialism; and, although he condemned
Bellamy with the criticisms used by William Morris, Morton
thinks that *Looking Backward* was the voice of the hopes and
aspirations of many people, as well as of the gentle Bellamy,
and that such books as *Nineteen Eighty-four* have expressed
the fears and warnings of the capitalistic writers.

In 1950 Marie Louise Berneri's *Journey Through Utopia* was
posthumously published, and Lewis Mumford deemed it to be
not only the superior of his own book but that of Hertzler. A
former editor of anarchist periodicals published in England,
Miss Berneri remarked in her study that she would be tempted
to call Bellamy "a prophet, rather than a Utopian, if he had
not been sadly mistaken in thinking that" the changes he depicted would "bring us happiness." Berneri's consideration of
Bellamy is prejudiced, however, by having tasted "the reality
of state control" under the Fascists of Italy and by her anarchist
associations; and she regards Bellamy as one who cleverly
sponsored state control of an authoritarian nature.[69] She thought
that one of his appeals was his "clear and practical approach

to economic problems" but that he consciously tried to appeal
to the middle class: "It is also obvious that the cultured classes
would not accept dictation in matters of taste or restriction in
what they considered to be their intellectual freedom, and
Bellamy ingeniously combined state control in matters of production and distribution with private initiative in literature and
art, and allowed a greater degree of independence to the liberal
professions than to the industrial workers."[70]

After summarizing Bellamy's ideal society, Miss Berneri remarked that "Bellamy's state socialism allows a greater degree
of personal freedom than most other Utopias based on the
same principles. But it is the freedom which might be granted
to soldiers once they have been conscripted; no provision is
made for 'conscientious objectors.'" She then remarked that
not only did every citizen have to respect a contract to work—
originally made by his forefathers—between himself and the
state, but that Bellamy envisioned the rule of what James
Burnham has called the "'managerial class'"[71] or of an "industrial aristocracy." To Miss Berneri, Bellamy had as much faith
in the "wisdom of experts and of the 'administration'" as he
had "confidence in technical progress."[72] His state is not
acceptable because "his rigid regimentation of men's lives takes
little note of the differences in the psychological make-up of
individuals."[73] Miss Berneri considered Morris' *News from
Nowhere* much more preferable than "the stifling atmospheres
of Cabet's and Bellamy's Utopias, with their complicated
bureaucratic machines run by an all-wise, pervading state."[74]
She admitted, however, that she could not deny that Bellamy
had found a solution.

Interest in Bellamy still exists in the British Isles; for C. E.
Ratcliffe contributes letters and news from England for the
*Equalitarian Bulletin* which has for many years been published
by Bellamyite Walter Nef of Los Angeles, California. Letters
from other areas of the British Commonwealth have also been
published frequently in this bulletin—as have some from Scot-
land and news of the Bellamy Association of Holland.

## VI  *Distinguished Converts*

Besides the many, many people of the socialist, labor, religious, and Fabian movements who were affected by Bellamy's
concepts, there are a few who deserve special mention—and one
of the most distinguished of these is Alfred Russell Wallace.
Best known as the propounder, with Darwin, of the theory of
evolution, Wallace had turned his attention to politics in the

1880's and had become, through the influence of Henry George, president of the Land Nationalisation League. Private ownership of land was initially his only objection to the existing economic system, for his reading of Mill and Spencer had convinced him of the necessity of individual competiton as a spur to progress. This belief persisted until 1889, when confidence in the practicability and necessity of socialism as the only means of advancing civilization became a permanent feature of his political creed.

Wallace later recounted the contribution Bellamy had made to this changed attitude:

> The book that thus changed my outlook on this question was Bellamy's *Looking Backward*. On a first meeting I was captivated by the wonderfully realistic style of the work, the extreme ingenuity of the conception, the absorbing interest of the story, and the logical power with which the possibility of such a state of society as that depicted was argued and its desirability enforced. Every sneer, every objection, every argument I had ever read against socialism was here met and shown to be absolutely trivial or altogether baseless, while the inevitable results of such a social state in giving to every human being the necessaries, the comforts, the harmless luxuries, and the highest refinements and social enjoyments of life were made equally clear. From this time I declared myself a socialist. . . .[75]

When Wallace read *Equality*, he was even more convinced. He had by the time of its publication read many more works about socialism, but Bellamy's last Utopia impressed him "as being the most complete and thoroughly reasoned exposition both of the philosophy and the constructive methods of socialism" that he had encountered; he regretted that "comparatively few, even of English socialists" were acquainted with its arguments.[76] In 1909 Wallace was still upholding the merits of *Equality*, and he gained, therefore, the gratitude of Andreas Scheu, the veteran socialist and friend of William Morris, who had found Bellamy's vision of the future in *Looking Backward* "so dry, so mechanical, so altogether American that my aesthetic sense revolted against it." Scheu was, however, more impressed with *Equality*.[77] Although Wallace's position in radical politics depended primarily upon his scientific reputation, he seemingly carried very little weight; and, although his views were indefatigably expressed, his belief in Bellamy served largely to emphasize his individualistic attitudes.

One of the most positive and permanent effects of Bellamy's writings is found in the work of Ebenezer Howard, who had been instrumental in getting *Looking Backward* published in England and who had initially "swallowed whole" its arguments. After discussing the book with friends, Howard recognized the dubiousness of the "assumption that such a tremendous change could be effected at once"; and his reaction was the development of a more manageable proposal which would test Bellamy's principles through the creation of an entirely new town. His concepts first found literary expression in *To-morrow* (1898), which is accepted today as a basic contribution toward the creation of the Garden City movement.[78]

Lewis Mumford has claimed for Howard the distinction of being "the first modern thinker about cities who had a sound sociological conception of the dynamics of rational urban growth,"[79] and the importance of *Looking Backward* as his point of intellectual departure has long been recognized. But Howard's connection with the Nationalist movement has not been traced although it proved decisive in the development of his thought. In February, 1893, when the plans for the Nationalist colony were nearing completion, the *Nationalization News* printed a summary of the proposals which Howard had submitted for its development. In it, he clearly outlined the basic principles which he enunciated five years later in *To-morrow*.

From this article it is possible to determine how Howard had already modified Bellamy to the extent of separating communal freehold from individual leasehold rights. No attempt was to be made to introduce Integral Co-operation; but leases would, where possible, be granted to those most likely to sympathize with such an end result, and land would not be disposed of without considering the use to which it would be put and the price it would bring. The mingling of agricultural and industrial employment, the creation of municipal facilities, the planning of communal services, the existence of a master plan of development, and the hope that the financial success of the project would lead ultimately to the extinction of landlords' rents and the municipalizing of capitalist undertakings, were prominent features of his scheme. Howard believed that it would thus prove possible to reconcile the need for a strong central executive and the retention of individual initiative. Furthermore, it would focus in one great movement the efforts of reformers of many types; and it would combine freedom and planning in harmonious unity. Although Howard's ideas were

not tested for another decade, the planning of this colony
formed a vital link in the development of a conception that
emerged at Letchworth Garden City, which exerted its influence throughout the world. As Harold Orlans has stated in
*Utopia Ltd.*, the Utopians had dreamed of escape from the evils
of the industrial city but "it remained for Ebenezer Howard to
formulate and demonstrate the idea of the garden city that had
increasing influence upon town planners in ensuing years, and
whose success was climaxed by the New Towns Act, 1946."[80]

An even more famous man whose ideas were influenced by
Bellamy was George Bernard Shaw, who—as has already been
noted—admitted that he had read Bellamy and changed his
mind about him. Although Henderson and Maurice Colbourne
pointed out in their biographies of Shaw that the Fabian and
playwright had followed in Bellamy's footsteps, the most detailed study of Bellamy's influence is to be found in Julian
Kaye's *Bernard Shaw and the Nineteenth-Century Tradition.*

Although Laidler had pointed out that Shaw was one of the
few who sponsored economic equality, he did not—as Kaye
does—attribute to Bellamy this principle which Shaw had proposed in *The Intelligent Woman's Guide*, in *Everybody's What's
What*, in the introduction to *Androcles and the Lion*,[81] and in
a speech he gave to the Political and Economic Circle which was
published in December, 1913, in *Metropolitan.*[82] In his speech
Shaw argued, in Bellamy terms, that "human equality" to him
meant "equality of income," "the only plan which has ever been
successful, the only plan which has ever been possible." In
pointing out the use of the plan in the pay of soldiers, etc.,
Shaw argued also in terms which Bellamy had employed; and
he also used the social-fund theory as support and the "old
mystic, religious" one as an argument that "all human souls are
of infinite value, and all infinites are equal." He also used
political, economic, and biological objections to economic inequality comparable to those Bellamy had presented; for Shaw
argued that plutocracy corrupted democracy, that it owned
the newspapers, and there was no "genuinely popular government in this country." Economically, inequality of income contributed to poverty, for "production is determined by purchasing power and always will be." Biologically, Shaw considered
economic equality essential to natural selection, to brotherhood,
to broad minds, and to a classless society.

Although Kaye remarked that Bellamy's greatest contribution to "Shavian economics" was the principle of economic
equality, he also demonstrated that Shaw had used Bellamy's

solution of the problem of getting the dirty work of the nation performed in *The Intelligent Woman's Guide;* had repeated the explanation the American had given in *Equality* of depressions in *The Intelligent Woman;* and had used the portrayal of the eventual fate of industrialized nations in the preface to *Man and Superman* (1903). Furthermore, Kaye maintains that Shaw used Bellamy's religious argument for equality of income in *Androcles and the Lion,* and that the playwright's concept of God as the Life-Force and Bellamy's of "the Greater Self" were comparable. Kaye also shows that Shaw used Bellamy's eugenic argument for equality of income in *The Revolutionist's Handbook* and in the preface to *Androcles and the Lion;* that he supported more passionately even than Bellamy the concept of the necessity of economic independence for women to free them from forced and incorrect marriages and from prostitution even in marriage in "The Economic Slavery of Women," *Man and Superman,* and in the preface to *Getting Married;* and that he also followed Bellamy "in demanding that the state protect the rights of children from the tyranny of their parents" in his remarks in the preface to *Misalliance.* All in all, many of the concepts which Bellamy had promoted were used by Shaw in his economic theories presented in his plays, in his prefaces, in his speeches; but he gave the American no credit for them.

Since another Irishman, George Russell, was not only associated with the Theosophists but with socialism, and since the ideas he advanced in his book *National Being* are quite comparable to those of Bellamy, the work of this economist, philosopher, editor, and poet should also be investigated. Russell wrote in *National Being:*

> It is not enough to organize farmers in a district for one purpose only—in a credit society, a dairy society, a fruit society, a bacon factory, or in a co-operative store. All these may be and must be beginnings; but if they do not develop and absorb all rural business into their organization they will have little effect on character. No true social organism will have been created. If people unite as consumers to buy together they only come into contact on this one point; there is no general identity of interest. If co-operative societies are specialized for this purpose or that—as in Great Britain or on the Continent—to a large extent the limitation of objects prevents a true social organism from being formed. The latter has a tremendous effect on human character. The specialized Society only develops economic efficiency. The evolution of humanity beyond its present level depends absolutely on its power to unite and create true social organisms.

In this one passage, the intent of Bellamy may be seen not only in the attitude toward the cooperative as a transition measure but toward the social organism, the effect of it upon human character, the evolution of humanity, and upon unity. As Nethercot stated in *The First Five Lives of Annie Besant,* Theosophy had had a strong appeal to both mystics and advanced thinkers; and he quotes Katharine Tynan as saying: ". . . all queer people, the Fenians and Socialists and Theosophists, and worst of all Papists."

During the period when Bellamy was a sensation in London, H. G. Wells arrived there to seek his fortune; became a member of the Fabian Society; and first won literary fame in 1895 with the publication of *The Time Machine.* Wells had been working for a long time on a story entitled "The Chronic Argonauts" before he arrived in London; and it may well be that Bellamy's success and popularity—rather than that of Jules Verne with whom some critics compared Wells at this time—was responsible for his recasting his work into *The Time Machine,* in which Wells took the reader on a journey through time and in which he also allegorically portrayed the social conflicts between capitalists and socialists which might lead to tragedy.[83]

In 1899 Wells published in book form *When the Sleeper Wakes,* a title which suggests immediately the experience of Julian West; but the novel had been serialized under a title even more suggestive of Bellamy: *The Year 2000.*[84] Like *The Time Machine,* the novel was concerned with portrayals of social changes; for in *When the Sleeper Wakes,* Wells' ambition had been to "paint a picture of the future, showing all the results of mechanization and the altered structure of society." His sleeper, who has been in a trance for two hundred years, wakens to find himself in a world "of material expansion" which contains many of the technical inventions Bellamy had conceived: enormous automatic restaurants have replaced family dining rooms; modern methods of heating and lighting are employed; airplanes provide rapid transportation, television enables people to witness the news; citizens with psychological problems are relieved of them with a treatment reminiscent of *Dr. Heidenhoff's Process;* and reading and writing have been replaced by mechanical devices. The sleeper does not find himself in an ideal world, however; it is one controlled by wealth; and, soon after his arrival in it, the workers revolt.

In *A Modern Utopia* (1905) Wells made some references to Bellamy, but the only extended discussion of him is in the following passage. However, it is one which shows why Bellamy might have attracted the famous English Utopian: "Plato commenced the Utopias without machinery . . . . it is only in the nineteenth century that Utopias appeared in which the fact is clearly recognized that the social fabric rests no longer upon human labour. It was, I believe, Cabet who first in a Utopian work insisted upon the escape of man from irksome labours through the use of machinery. He is the great primitive of modern Utopias, and Bellamy is his American equivalent."[85]

Although Wells knew Bellamy and may have been inspired by him to turn to this *genre* of fiction, A. L. Morton and Marie L. Berneri believe that the economic systems of his Utopia were derived from Hertzka's *Freeland* rather than from Bellamy. A. L. Morton remarked, however, that Wells, who regarded himself intermittently as a socialist, was one "derived from St. Simon, Comte, and Bellamy rather than from Marx and Morris."[86] Whatever the story of the relationship of Wells and Bellamy may someday prove to have been, Wells seemingly employed ideas and attitudes which he must have secured from the American Utopian; and, as Shaw remarked, Wells battled for recognition of the significance of the Utopians.

Because of the influence which Bellamy exerted upon these distinguished writers and social planners, he would merit a place in British social and literary histories. But Bellamy's influence was wider and more important than these facts indicate—although it is impossible to give a precise estimate of the extent of it. *Looking Backward* seemingly stimulated rather than created British socialism; and the date of its appearance explains its role. A decade earlier, Henry George had proved of greater significance, for his panacea had appeared at a time when the British movement was groping for inspiration. The immediate application of his land policy to Ireland and the great oratorical powers that he displayed during his extensive tours of the British Isles were important additional explanations of his popularity. By 1890 British socialism had acquired its first solid group of leaders—and many of them had been attracted to it by reading *Progress and Poverty.*

The task performed by Bellamy—and in particular by *Looking Backward*—was to bring about the conversion of the rank and file. For this purpose, Bellamy's writings were particularly effective because of their emphasis upon the refutation of two major intellectual obstacles to the advance of socialism. First of all, Bellamy convinced thousands that the growth of the state was not, as so many Victorians had believed, synonymous with the destruction of individual freedom, but an essential preliminary to its full development. Second, Bellamy's presentation of a peaceful, evolutionary achievement of the socialist state put to rest the spectre of mounting class warfare and hatred, which many had felt was the inevitable consequence of the spread of socialist ideas and which, after reading *Looking Backward*, they no longer linked with opposition to the established order. Bellamy represented, therefore, one of the most important influences through which the British labor movement reduced its intellectual dependence upon Marxism. His vision offered those who were fearful and opposed to the rigid dogmatism of the Social Democratic Federation saner proposals and a humanitarian dream which led them to harness their energies to radical politics and to avoid a prospect of hatred and violence. By contributing so largely to the creation of popular support for a labor party, Bellamy's Utopias made a full contribution to a revolution which—if it did not agree in every detail with his prophecies—was comprehensive; it was also as peaceful as he had wished it to be. As Oscar Wilde had observed, "Progress is the realization of Utopia"; and as R. C. K. Ensor indicated, the English socialist movement "from its start was Utopian and idealistic, not analytic":[87] it owed more to Henry George, Gronlund, and Bellamy than to Marx.[88]

CHAPTER FOUR

# The Australian Impact

By

## ROBIN GOLLAN

TO TRACE FULLY the continuing but now declining influence of Edward Bellamy's *Looking Backward* and *Equality* in Australia would be an interesting but tedious and difficult task best undertaken as a part of a broad history of Australian socialism. This study of the impact of Bellamy's ideas is limited, therefore, to his early influence upon Australian opinion in general and upon the Australian labor movement in particular.

*Looking Backward* first became widely known in Australia in 1890, one of the most critical years in the country's short history. Accepted as a book of revelation by the few, it colored the thought of many, for it became a primer of socialism and an inspiration to social reform. Although *Looking Backward* played an important role in the events of the critical year of 1890, it is today read most commonly by historians who are interested in recapturing the intellectual climate of the end of the last century; but there are still some people who consider it a serious contribution to the solution of contemporary political problems. Others who still read the book have been guided to it by those interested in socialism; and, even today when the book is out of print, as many as fifty people a year ask for it at the leading left-wing bookshop in Sydney. In the seventy years between its first appearance and today, *Looking Backward* has been one of the intellectual influences upon two generations of Australian socialists; *Equality,* launched when the tide of socialist enthusiasm was receding, was read but it never evoked the response that greeted Bellamy's earlier book.

Because Australia had an audience eager for the message *Looking Backward* contained, the book not only sold in large numbers but was used by influential journals which wished to filter its ideas to its readers. In no country in the world did

Bellamy's ideas fall on more fertile ground, because the book gave body and coherence to ideas that were already more than half formed in the minds of many Australians. To organizations —and particularly to the trade unions—*Looking Backward* was a justification of their short-term policies and their long-term aspirations.

Yet, at first glance, it may appear strange that Bellamy's Utopian novel struck such a responsive chord in Australia. Three million people who inhabited a vast continent politically divided into six colonies of Great Britain seemed scarcely to form the kind of community to which a book—written in the heat and smoke of an expanding industrial economy to advocate the socialist organization of industry—would be likely to appeal. But first impressions are misleading. In important respects Australian development in the second half of the nineteenth century was similar, of course on a much smaller scale, to that of the United States. Where it differed, the differences were of a type to make Bellamy's ideas even more acceptable than in their country of origin.

I  *A Climate for Bellamy's Ideas*

In the thirty years after 1860, the Australian economy expanded very rapidly. The national product, according to the best estimate made so far, grew at a rate almost double that of Britain and only slightly less than that of the United States.[1] This rapid, sustained expansion rested on the importation—primarily from Great Britain—of both human and financial resources. Immigration, together with a high rate of natural increase, swelled the population nearly four per cent annually— a rate much higher than that of the United States but one very much higher than that of Britain. Similarly the rate of capital investment was high; it was approximately the same as that of the United States and double that of Britain; but more than half of the new capital was imported.

In this importation of resources the government was deeply involved. Approximately half of the migrants who reached Australia did so with government assistance, and half of the overseas capital invested was on government account. Founded as a convict colony, Australian government from the beginning was centralized and positive. In the period of rapid expansion, governments continued to play a decisive part. Thus by 1890 the tradition of positive state action was firmly entrenched in Australia.

Just as important to this study as the scale and rate of expansion and the role played by the governments was the direction in which resources were channelled. The traditional picture of Australia of the nineteenth century is of a vast sheepwalk, with the whole economy dependent on the production and export of wool. Although wool was of great importance, emphasis upon it gives an unbalanced picture of the economy as a whole; for, during the decades from 1860 to 1890, its relative importance was declining.

In 1861 primary production was responsible for forty per cent of the net national product; but thirty years later it was down to thirty per cent. On the other hand the share of secondary industry rose from ten per cent in 1861 to twenty-five per cent thirty years later. The fact is, therefore, that Australian economic expansion, despite the importance of the wool export income, followed a pattern similar to that of other developing industrial societies. As N. G. Butlin, an economic historian, has stated, "Australian economic development is mainly a story of urbanization. The building of cities absorbed the greater part of Australian resources diverted to developmental purposes; the operation of enterprises in the towns employed most of the increasing population engaged in work."[2]

Although in 1861 more than half of the population of New South Wales lived in rural areas, thirty years later there were twice as many urban as rural dwellers. And of the urban population about half was concentrated in the major cities of Sydney, Melbourne, Brisbane, and Adelaide. For example, of the total Victoria population of about 1,100,000 in 1891, nearly half a million lived in Melbourne. In New South Wales, which had a comparable population, nearly 400,000 lived in Sydney. As T. A. Coghlen, a South Wales statistician has noted, "The progress of these cities has been extraordinary and has no parallel amongst the cities of the old world. Even in America the rise of the great cities has been accompanied by a somewhat corresponding increase in the rural population. In these colonies perhaps for the first time in the history of the world is seen the spectacle of magnificent cities growing with wonderful rapidity, and embracing within their limits one third of the population of the territory on which they depend."[3]

As might be expected, trade unions had grown with the cities. In the fifties, unions had been formed in the building trades and a number of other skilled occupations. Between 1860 and 1880 there was a gradual extension of unionism among skilled workers in the cities and also some organization among the less skilled. For example, coal miners formed unions in 1861; seamen and metal miners in the 1870's; but in the 1880's unionism extended very rapidly among unskilled workers in the cities and even among the rural workers. By 1890 probably twenty per cent of male wage and salary earners were members of unions.

Because relatively high real wages for skilled workers had been established during the gold rushes of the 1850's, the union policy tended to emphasize the retention of existing wage rates and to seek gains in the form of increased leisure and the improvement of working conditions. The eight-hour day became general in the building industry before 1860, and the central plank of the union platform from that time was the maintenance and extension of the principle of eight hours. By 1890 most skilled trades and not a few unskilled occupations worked an eight-hour day. Trade unions had made, therefore, the most of the thirty years of expansion—"a generation during which children grew to middle age without personal experience of economic depression."[4] As a result, relatively strong and confident unionists were looking for new fields to conquer.

This tendency was strengthened by the formation of unions among the rural workers who founded something unique in the Australian labor movement and who contributed most to the climate of opinion favorable to the reception of Bellamy's ideas. Despite the continuing attempt to settle the land with a yeomanry—the most popular political slogan of the nineteenth century—the land had in fact been settled, and then held against all attempts to break their grip, by pastoralists or squatters. Numerous land laws designed to open the land to small scale settlement had failed in their aim—particularly in New South Wales and Queensland—despite the general acceptance in parliaments and in political debate of the need to establish a small-holding farming class. The failure of the attempts to divide the land was due to the economic power held by the squatters, the suitability of the soil and climate for the production of wool and their unsuitability for agricultural purposes, and the expanding market for wool in Britain. As a result the large holding, operated either by resident owners or managed on behalf of powerful companies and worked by a small army of permanent employees and a larger group of seasonal workers, was the typical structure of the pastoral industry.

In the struggle for the land deep animosities were generated. Class war in the countryside is not an exaggerated description of the relations that existed, therefore, between squatters and the small farmer on the marginal land, the potential farmer, or the rural workers. When the bush workers formed unions in the 1880's, they brought to unionism the attitudes generated and consolidated by more than half a century of contests with employers.

The two major unions founded in the 1880's drew either all membership or part of it from bush workers. The Amalgamated Miners' Association (AMA)—many of whose members worked in small metal mines scattered throughout the country—grew between 1886 and 1893 from a mere handful of members to a large efficient union with more than twenty thousand members in all the colonies. Similarly the Amalgamated Shearers' Union (ASU), founded in 1886, had over twenty thousand members by 1890 in New South Wales, Victoria, and South Australia. In the north, the Queensland Shearers' Union, also formed in 1886, had by the end of the decade eight thousand members.

These new unions brought not only the strength of their numbers to the trade-union movement but also, more important, their expressed opinions about and their example of the doctrine of industrial solidarity. In contrast to the narrow sectionalism of the unions of skilled workers, the bush workers' unions had a gospel of massive organization and their emphasis was, therefore, on the *union movement* as against the *trades union*. This attitude strengthened a trend, already evident, towards giving greater authority to central trade union bodies; and it led in 1889 to the project, never fully implemented, for an Australian Labor Federation which would represent workers as a class not only in their industrial relations but in the political arena.

Aside from this movement toward solidarity, the bush worker occupied a key position in the growth of national self-consciousness. By 1890 Australia was ripe for nationhood, and it needed a type with which the nation could be identified. Europeans had inhabited the continent for a century and seven of every ten of its people had been born in Australia. The colonies, with the exception of Western Australia, had enjoyed colonial self-government for a generation and in that time progress had been remarkably fast. The establishment of a nation—to be achieved politically at the end of the century—implied greater independence from Britain and the assertion of distinctive national values.

The representative of these national values was the bushman. As Francis Adams acutely observed in the 1890's, "the one powerful and unique national type yet produced in Australia is . . . that of the Bushman. . . . It is in the ranks of the shearers, boundary riders, and general station hands, that the perfected sample must be sought, and it is the rapid thoroughness of the new social system . . . which has chiefly 'differentiated' him into this new species."[5] Although only a small minority of Australians were bushmen, most natives in 1890 were prepared to believe that the bushman represented the unique and distinctive *Australian;* and they shared in some degree his qualities.

Russell Ward in a recent study has demonstrated the deep influence of "up-country" life in moulding the national outlook. This influence, he has pointed out, was a continuous one which reached its apogee in the last decade of the nineteenth century: "The process by which the distinctive up-country ethos, in a rather romanticised form, passed into the keeping of the whole people was not simple, nor was it confined in time to the period discussed here. Indeed, we have attempted to underline the continuity of the influence exercised by bushmen, throughout the nineteenth century, on city folk and new chums. Yet, as has been often recognized, this process culminated in the period 1890-1900 and in the years immediately before and after that decade. Only then did the powerful current come to the surface of events, to dominate formal literature and to provide a native tradition for the new industrial trade union movement."[6]

This "up-country ethos" can be best found most clearly and fully depicted in the writings of Henry Lawson, Joseph Furphy,* and A. B. Paterson who in the nineties and the early years of the twentieth century laid the foundations of a distinctly national literature. In Paterson's ballads, in Lawson's verses and stories, and in Furphy's classic novel *Such Is Life,* the Australian bushman is portrayed as he was seen by the eyes of sensitive, imaginative writers. The outlook of their bushman was characterized by "a manly independence whose obverse side was a leveling, egalitarian collectivism, and whose sum was comprised in the concept of mateship."[7] Frontier conditions had put a premium upon independence; but because it was a "big man's" frontier, it also had imposed the need for cooperation among the "little men." In an essentially male nomadic community of workers, mateship met practical needs

---

* Professor Ian R. Maxwell of the Department of English of the University of Melbourne has stated that Bellamy's *Equality* was one of Furphy's favorite books.

According to Professor A. G. Mitchell, of the University of Sydney, Vance Palmer, an Australian novelist of standing, also wrote on the subject of Bellamy.—EDITOR

and was idealized into a primitive but almost religious article
of faith.

This ideal of mateship found in unionism an institutional form
of expression. In a well-known passage, the first president of
the Shearers' Union expressed this situation vividly in the
following statement: "Unionism came to the Australian bushman as a religion. It came bringing salvation from years of
tyranny. It had in it that feeling of mateship which he understood already, and which always characterised the action of one
'white man' to another. Unionism extended the idea, so a man's
character was gauged by whether he stood true to union rules
or 'scabbed' it on his fellows. The man who never went back
on the Union is honored today as no other is honored or respected. The man who fell once may be forgiven, but he is not
fully trusted. The lowest term of reproach is to call a man a
'scab'. . . . At many a country ball the girls have refused to
dance with them, the barmaids have refused them a drink,
and the waitresses a meal."[8]

For the bushmen the central argument of *Looking Backward*
of the virtue of cooperation was already an article of faith.
Bellamy's novel merely sanctified their ideal and delineated
its consequences if it could be universally applied.

II  *The* Bulletin's *View of Bellamy's Ideas*

Contributing not only to the power of the figure of the
bushman as a distinctive national type but also to the influence of radical nationalist opinion and to knowledge of Bellamy's *Looking Backward,* was the influential Sydney *Bulletin*
which, founded in 1880, was in 1890 a publication read throughout the continent. Its tremendous influence may be deduced
from the following comments. The *Times* stated that "it is hard
to overestimate the extent to which this journal modifies the
opinions (one might almost say the character) of its readers."[9]
A contemporary wrote that "the arrival of the *Bulletin* is an
event in coast towns from Darwin to Perth."[10] A visitor commented that "you meet with it everywhere; it is on the tables
of all the clubs and hotels, not of New South Wales alone,
but of all the Colonies, including New Zealand and Tasmania;
and if you go into the bushman's hut, there are a hundred
chances to one that you will find the latest number there."[11]

That the *Bulletin* was read by all classes is indicated by the
following statement of Francis Adams: "A back-block shearer
once said to me: 'If I'd only one sixpence left, I'd buy the
*Bulletin* with it.' The premier of a colony far distant from

Sydney . . . remarked to me: 'The *Bulletin?* Oh, yes! But does it sell much here? I can't tell you. Of course I read it myself!' "[12]

The source of the popularity of the *Bulletin* was its policy, and, for its time and place, its high literary standards which attracted the most able writers who, in turn, maintained the quality of the publication. Its policy was well defined as "Republicanism seasoned by Socialism, Fiscal Protection as a means to the first, and ruthless and unscrupulous satire of all authority as a means to the second. . . ."[13] Mateship was also the creed of the *Bulletin,* and it—above all other literary influences—made the bushman into the national archetype.

The remarkable practical evidence of the extent to which the concept of mateship—of cooperation—had seized the public imagination was the response to the appeal for financial assistance for the London dockworkers who were on strike in 1889: more than thirty thousand pounds was contributed to the cause by Australians. Strongly supporting the union, the *Bulletin* may have exaggerated (but not greatly) the public enthusiasm in the following description: "The trades-unions have voted away for the cause, funds which they themselves might require any day, parsons and priests have preached for it, atheistic, and other lecturers have lectured for it, prize fighters have bruised and been bruised for it, footballers have kicked and sweated for it, orators have orated, ladies have canvassed and lectured for it, horses are going to race for it, newsboys, folks living from hand to mouth have subscribed to it."[14] Even the wife of the governor of New South Wales, the leading pastoral firms, and the conservative newspapers made donations to the dock-workers' fund.

As might be expected, *Looking Backward* was first noticed by the *Bulletin* shortly after the dock strike of 1889. A letter to the editor and a full-scale review brought it to the notice of readers. The letter announced that the novel would "count against industrial slavery as 'Uncle Tom's Cabin' did against chattel slavery. . . . the time is at hand when Labour will ask for rights instead of concessions, as the fate of Bismarck's anti-socialist Bill the other day, the world's sympathy with Ireland and the dock slaves and other signs show clearly."[15]

Under the heading "The Latest Gilded Pill" the review, written by Francis Adams, advised those who wanted a book which treated in a popular manner the ideas advocated by the *Bulletin* to spend a shilling to purchase *Looking Backward.* Adams commented, however, that the book was less for the informed socialist than for the "social babe and suckling" who should be exposed to basic socialist concepts. He wrote: "If you have a friend and brother sailing o'er life's solemn main in an A-1 copper-bottom vessel, with chicken and champagne laid in copiously, and want to rouse in him some sense of sympathy and apprehension for all the poor, half-starved fellows in the rotten-timbered cockle-boats, warranted to secure the full insurance money in under three voyages, give him a copy of *Looking Backward*."[16]

Adams compared the Utopian novel's sentiment and the popularity of its style with Henry George's *Progress and Poverty*, and he anticipated that Bellamy's book would have influence similar to George's book, which had taken Australia by storm a few years earlier. Adams was, however, adversely critical of Bellamy's having placed the action of the story in the future; for he felt he had done so in order to escape the unpleasant task of describing the transition to the socialist state.

Adams also found Bellamy's religious views quite unacceptable; for, he wrote, "Religion is treated with the extremest gentleness. All the orthodox American and Bostonian Unitarian cant about 'The Creator,' and His benevolence and beneficence, and all that, flourishes here like a green bay-tree." Both Adams and the *Bulletin* were too irreverent to accept Bellamy's religious sentimentality—or that of his heroine who remarked that her grandmother had been in heaven for nearly a century. Adams, who found Julian's fiancée too pale for life, commented: "Girls who are the 'consummate flower' of A.D. 2000 are not likely to talk in quite that way, I fancy."

Adams' most substantial criticism was reserved for the idea that a socialist organization of society would overcome all the problems of the relationship between the sexes. To him Bellamy had simply taken as his model the "best specimens of the present leisured classes" and had then cast all his socialized characters in their mold. A little unkindly, but in language typical of the *Bulletin*, Adams concluded that Bellamy "is for the hightoned, cultchawed sow-ciety of Bawston, dontercherknow. 'Falsehood,' he says ingeniously, 'is not common between gentlemen and ladies, social equals.' To which one is tempted to reply in the language of Yankeeonia: 'Say, now, Bellamy old man, what are you giving us, anyway?' "

### III  *The* Worker's *Use of Bellamy*

While Adams was critical, the *Worker*, the journal of the associated workers of Queensland, swallowed whole the pure milk of Bellamy. This reaction to his ideas was doubtless due to the fact that the new trend of unionism towards greater unity of the trade-union movement was more marked in Queensland than in any of the other colonies because of numerous factors. Perhaps the most important of these was that the society was newer and that the "big man's frontier" was bigger than in the other colonies. The trade-union movement too was new and hence was less influenced by entrenched interest.

Significantly, it was from Queensland that the proposal came to attend an intercolonial trade-union conference in 1888 for the formation of a national, central trade-union group to represent the organized workers industrially and politically. Until the plan could be implemented nationally, it was put into effect in Queensland with the formation of the Australian Labour Federation which was intended to become the Queensland section when the organization became effective in other colonies. The political aims of the Federation were frankly socialist; for they included the nationalization of all sources of wealth and of all means of production and exchange, and "the reorganization of society on the above lines to be commenced at once and pursued uninterruptedly until social justice is fully secured to each and every citizen."[17]

In March, 1890, the Federation launched the *Worker* as a monthly—and later as a fortnightly—journal.* Beginning with an issue of fourteen thousand, twenty thousand copies of the *Worker* were soon circulating before the end of 1890. The *Worker* became not only the trade unionists' but also particularly the bushmen's "Bible"—and *Looking Backward*, the serialization of which began in the first issue, became their Pentateuch. In explaining the reason for publishing the Utopia, William Lane, the editor, quoted with approval a letter from a friend: "'How many times,' writes Mr. J. D. Fitzgerald, ex-president of the N. S. W. Typographical Association, 'have I felt at a loss to explain the working of a co-operative commonwealth. Now I have only to say, Read *Looking Backward*.'"

Serial publication was not, however, the only method by which Bellamy's ideas were spread.† *Looking Backward* was

---

* Stewart Grahame in *Where Socialism Failed* stated that Lane established *The Worker* as a cooperative journal.

† Both *Looking Backward* and *Equality* were published by the Socialist Labour Party of Australia. According to Lloyd Churchward, senior lecturer in the Department of Political Science of the University of Melbourne, the former novel was reprinted many, many times during a fifty-year period and reprinted as late as 1942. —EDITOR

also the first of a short list of books which were not only advertised but distributed by the *Worker;* the others were Gronlund's *Co-operative Commonwealth,* George's *Progress and Poverty,* and Oliver Shreiner's *Story of an African Farm.* These books were also carried by union organizers into the back country; and in May, 1890, a letter from the Aramac shearing shed in the remote interior noted that "already by the ready access to such books as *'Looking Backward'* (which I received from Mr. Casey in Barcaldine for general use) and other works of interest, the character of discussion has been much improved."[18]

Bellamy's ideas were also expounded in the columns written by William Lane, editor of the *Worker,* who was an idealistic journalist of great ability and who for a few years exercised a greater influence on the labor movement and opinion generally than perhaps any other person in Australian history. Well-read in all the socialist literature of his time, Lane knew Gronlund and quoted Marx—but he was saturated with Bellamy. To him Gronlund's " 'Co-operative Commonwealth' may be compared to an economic framework for Bellamy's romance of 'Looking Backward'. . . ."[19] Although Lane considered Marx's *Capital* a very important work, there were not only few copies of it in Queensland but its value was limited by the fact that "to the everyday man Marx is unreadable."[20]

To Lane, *Looking Backward* was readable by all; and, although he recognized that the ideas in it were not original, he referred to Bellamy as an inspired advocate of ideas that had been "the political aims of all progressive labour men since the Chartist time. . . ."[21] Bellamy's most distinctive quality to Lane was that more effectively than any one else he had detected the trend of his age and constructed not only an ideal but also a realizable future. Lane wrote: "He has seen the drift of our racial development, and has detected that a new order is rising, even while the old is passing, and from this he has woven a future so human and so practical and so possible that not one of all the millions who have read it but have felt that in the Bellamy 'state' they could be content."[22]

Lane accepted Bellamy as his master and translated him in terms that would conform with what he felt were the practical needs of Australia in 1890.* The extent to which Bellamy

---

* Lane advocated a "practical socialism," as he termed it, which demanded that all means of production be owned by the people and used and governed by them.—EDITOR

shaped Lane's propaganda—and through him the thought of
*Worker* readers—can be seen from an examination of the main
lines of the argument that Lane, as a good teacher, stated and
re-stated in the columns of his paper. As a trade-union journalist and as an inspirer of union organization, Lane argued—
though Bellamy would not have agreed with him*—that the
unions were already to an extent Bellamy 'states' in microcosm,
and that, to make Australia socialist, it was therefore only
necessary to extend the ideas and practices of unionism to the
whole of society. He wrote: "Socialism means the brotherhood
of man, the union of all for the securing of Social Justice.
Socialism is the natural sequence of unionism."[23] In a purple
passage, Lane also stated that "trade unionism, then is the
sword, Socialism the trowel—how long will men bless the
knife that inflicts the wound and curse the healing balm?"[24]

Lane's socialistic state was also Bellamy's; for, in his first
editorial which stated the *Worker's* aims, Lane wrote: "It
aims, as all thinking workers aim, at the securing of a happier
state of society, which, though not, perhaps, on the same
lines, is imbued with just the same spirit as that which imbues
society in Bellamy's 'Looking Backward.' "[25]

Like his master, Lane, the trade-union journalist, never tired
of reiterating the idea that employers too could be converted
to socialism. As evidence of this possibility he had the case
of "Hop Beer" Marchant, who was, as his sobriquet suggests,
a manufacturer of soft drinks. Lane announced that "Marchant,
one of Bellamy's converts to socialism, had offered the *Worker*
free machine room and free machine power whenever it feels
like getting its own press."[26] A little later he reported that
Marchant had, as a result of reading Bellamy, first tried profit
sharing as a solution but that he had become convinced that
"there is no way out but Socialism pure and simple and that
all other attempted remedies will only prolong and emphasise
the evil."[27] Lane was not too far wrong about the attitude of
employers, for during the Maritime Strike—the greatest indus-

---

* In *Looking Backward* Bellamy gave the labor unions no credit
for the achievement of the ideal state, but in *Equality* he stated
that the thousands of strikes sponsored by the unions had aroused
the world to an awareness of the industrial problem and had focused
its attention upon it. Bellamy, unlike Gronlund, did not believe the
union should rule the country; for he felt that, if the union did so,
the nation would have exchanged one selfish group—capitalists—for
another—labor.—EDITOR

trial upheaval in Australian history—some employers did take the side of the unions. Among these capitalists was, wrote Lane, "Marchant, the ablest capitalist in Brisbane, [who] boldly took the chair at a strike meeting; one Queen Street store keeper sent a five pound note to the Strike Fund; while here and there the touters for blacklegs to be driven like sheep to the wharves by their employers ran across business men who announced that they'd see them blanked first."[28]

Not only these examples of conversion to the cause of the worker but also ideas which Lane held in common with, or because of, Bellamy, made him optimistic. He believed that employers would see the errors of their ways because they too— as Bellamy argued—were victims of the competitive system. Lane wrote: "The employer too is caught in the machinery of production and the more he has the more he is caught."[29] Believing with Bellamy in a crude sort of determinism, Lane wrote that "humanly speaking, capitalists and wage-earners are all brothers; industrially speaking, they are necessarily forming inimical castes."[30] Lane also had the faith in the future and in the perfectibility of man which Bellamy had; for the editor of the *Worker* wrote that socialism would inaugurate "the brotherhood of man, the union of all for the securing of Social Justice."[31]

Belief in the essential dignity of labor and the degrading effects of the wage system was common to the *Worker* and to Bellamy. Marchant, echoing Bellamy, wrote that "to think that one man should have to depend on another for work, and only work when it pleases another, is monstrous, and unless things are re-arranged and adjusted and labour fully recognised as the most ennobling thing, I fear something serious will happen."[32] This concept of the dignity of labor was popular among the workers, and it had indeed been one of the basic attitudes of the Australian bush workers and one of the characteristics of the city artisans.[33] A bank manager testified to some of the more ludicrous forms that this aspect of Bellamy's influence took. He said that in the north of Queensland he had engaged a boat to land him from a steamer. But, he related, "I offered the boatman four half crowns and he refused; he said that to take money would render his service 'menial.' He had been reading Bellamy."[34]

Although the *Bulletin* had found Bellamy's ideas about the relationship of the sexes stuffy and naïve, William Lane did not share this attitude. His socialist society was one in which "men and women would be lovers all the time and in which the

little ones would be like flowers and in which every single one
would have leisure because we would all be industrious and
economise on work and not waste it as we do now."[35] Men
and women would be transformed, and socialism would mean
that "where every Jack has his Jill and every Jill her Jack
there is no room for lust."[36]

Although Lane was perhaps more optimistic than Bellamy
in his belief that the cooperative society would cure all that
he believed to be ill in it, he, like Bellamy, stressed that socialism was a movement for moral regeneration. In both Bellamy
and Lane this concept is central to their thought and is tinged
with a religious quality. In Lane's attitude, however, there was
less identification with any contemporary institutionalized religion. His religious zeal is more messianic and less contemplative,
but the incentive to reform is essentially religious. He wrote:
"The religious instinct is simply the burning faith that somehow
or somewhere there is something better ahead, not perhaps for
ourselves but for others, a faith that rises supreme in the hour
of deepest discouragement and moves the religious to keep
always pegging away."[37]

On some occasions Lane called upon Bellamy as support for
his religious inspiration, as in the following quotation: "If
Jesus is not with the Labour Movement, where is he? Is there
not in 'Looking Backward' the Christ-spirit breathing?. . . . To
care for the widow, to feed the orphan, to cherish the sick, to
see that none want—that is the inspiration of the socialistic desire, the duty of the ideal socialistic State. Is this with Jesus
or is it not?"[38]

In religious feeling and in moral aspirations, Lane, like Bellamy, saw the hope of mankind. Like Bellamy, he also believed that the capitalistic system forced men to deny both
Christ and ethical principles if they would eat and feed their
children. The only solution to Lane was expressed in the
following sentences: "We must take Socialism as our Religion,
and whether we are employed or employer, robbed or robber,
must do our utmost to end this industrial system which is
based on robbery and cemented with crime and sodden with
the blood and tears of untold millions of tortured lives."[39]

Throughout the vicissitudes of the labor movement's experience in 1890 to 1893, Lane continued to chant Bellamy's basic
tenets. His was a song of labor organization, of martyrdom, of
religious conviction, and of the ethical benefits of socialism.
Lane sought to convince the majority of people, whether employee or employer, that a cooperative society would be far

better in all respects than Australia's competitive capitalism of 1890.

In assessing the significance of the influence of William Lane and the *Worker* on opinion and upon political action, it must be concluded that it was for a short period very great. Lane's direct influence ceased when, in despair of realizing his objectives, he set off with a band of faithful followers to establish on a small scale in Paraguay the new cooperative society which he had failed to achieve in Australia. Although his South American colony was, as Stewart Grahame has pointed out in *Where Socialism Failed*, the result of his "perfect faith in the righteousness of his cause" and in the practicality of Bellamy's plan, the colony failed. Had Lane been a more profound student of Bellamy, he would have known that the American prophet did not advocate the founding of colonies; for Bellamy regarded them as doomed to failure because they had to be surrounded by a different type of society.

## IV   Effect of Bellamy's Influence

But Lane did not fail in preaching Bellamy's views, for they became formative influences in establishing the Australian Labour Party. They also, states Stewart Grahame, earned Lane recognition as a central figure in the development of the Australian socialist party. As Lane's biographer, Lloyd Ross has pointed out in *William Lane and the Australian Labor Movement*,[40] Bellamy through Lane, and Bellamy directly, deeply influenced the Labour Movement in all colonies in the course of the first full-scale industrial upheaval that beset Australian society: the Maritime Strike of 1890. The strike paralyzed the economy of eastern Australia for a month and, in its defeat, gave birth to the Australian Labour Party.

Since so much has been written about the Maritime Strike and its consequences, it will be dealt with only very generally in this study.[41] The strike itself was a clash on a broad front between organized workers and organized employers. There were side issues, but the central one in dispute was the "closed shop." The unions had reached a point in organization which enabled them in many important sectors of industry to insist that the union be recognized as the instrument for negotiating all the conditions of labor. The employers argued, however, for the right of "freedom of contract." As the dispute developed, it became a straight battle between capital and labor in which the unions articulated a vaguely conceived political objective—the reorganization of society. And although there was no con-

sensus about means or about objectives, reorganization meant
to the unions a change in the direction of socialism.

The manifesto issued by the shearers' union, which set the
tone of the contest, referred to the "reconstruction of society."
The meaning of this phrase was considered at length by a Royal
Commission established by the New South Wales Parliament
to investigate the causes of the strike. The strike leader, W. G.
Spence, testified that there was a widespread desire for fundamental social change. He said, "There is a widespread feeling
in favour of socialism, but men differ as to what it should be."[42]
He considered Bellamy's Utopia a pretty and inspiring but impractical idea—and he personally favored Henry George's pre-
scription. He lamented, however, that many unionists "have not
grasped the rent idea at all, and hence they talk about the 'reconstruction of society' without knowing the exact meaning of
the term." This lack of definiteness is not surprising since the
ideas of the leaders, including Spence, were anything but precise. However, most trade union and other witnesses questioned
about the feeling and aspirations of unionists agreed that there
was a general, if vague, desire for some kind of socialist reform.
The experience of the strike, combined with these vague ideas,
resulted in the decision to form a labor political party.

Before the Maritime Strike, moves had been made in this
direction by the unions, but the conservative craft unionists
had been reluctant to depart from the principle that unions
should be non-political institutions. At the end of the strike
which had polarized society and in which the actions of governments were interpreted by unionists as being in support of
capital, the opposition to the formation of a party was overcome. As a result of the New South Wales election of 1891,
the newly formed Labour Party held the balance of power. In
the other colonies labor parties were formed within a few years.

By 1910 the Labour Party was in power in the Commonwealth and also in the leading state of New South Wales. It had
been in office briefly in Queensland in 1899, the first Labour
government in the world, and it had also held office in the
Commonwealth for a few months in 1904. In and out of office
before 1910, the Labour Party had been a major factor in laying
the foundations of the welfare state, foundations sufficiently
impressive for Australia to be regarded as a "social laboratory"
whose experiments were worthy of the attention of scholars
and reformers from countries as diverse as the United States,
England, and France.[43]

The influence of Bellamy upon these developments has been

implied by what has already been written about his impact in
Australia. His *Looking Backward* was one of the intellectual
forces which contributed to the projection of a trade union
movement, operating in a climate of opinion which favored
reform, into political activity. But there any considerable influence by Bellamy ceased; for, after its formation, the Labour
Party's policy and practice were moulded more by parliamentary
pressures, by the need to win the votes of a majority of elec-
tors, and by the demands of the trade union movement for specific reforms than by any comprehensive ideological influences.
The party became one of social amelioration and of industrial
regulation rather than a force for fundamental reorganization
of society. In a sense this development conformed unwittingly
with Bellamy's ideas of how social change should occur, but
the policy was not directly influenced by his views. It was a
response to contemporary political realities rather than a tactic
to achieve long-term objectives. For an example, William Morris Hughes, one of the leaders of the early Labour Party and
Prime Minister during World War I, was inspired in his youth
by Bellamy; but, as a practical politician, he showed little of
the idealism which was Bellamy's most significant contribution
to political thought and action.

Furthermore, as the Labour Party became increasingly melior-
istic, it shed its left wing. Many of the more ardent spirits followed William Lane to Paraguay, where their hopes of creating
a Bellamy "state" collapsed with the failure of the "New Australia" colony.[44] Others devoted themselves to socialist organizations which, as they were alienated from the Labour Party,
became increasingly, in Bellamy's term—"followers of the red
flag." Working at first as ginger groups—doctrinaire socialist
groups—associated with the Labour Party, they became by the
end of the nineteenth century generally separate from it and
openly critical of what they regarded as its opportunism. For
these socialists, Marx, Hyndman, William Morris, and Kropotkin were the authorities.[45] Later they came under the influence of the American I. W. W.* and the diverse strains of

---

* Industrial Workers of the World was established in the United
States in 1905 and soon acquired the reputation of being both radical and lawless. The policy of the organization was militant industrial unionism; and, under the leadership of Big Bill Haywood and
Vincent St. John, the group—mostly of unskilled workers—advocated
the sabotage of industry by strikes and work stoppages and the
refusal to form any contract between employers and employees.
—EDITOR

thought which contributed to its theory and tactics. For them Bellamy was a dangerous narcotic who diverted attention from the need for the continuing struggle to overthrow the capitalist system.

The general influence of Bellamy's ideas in Australia was, in summary, that he made a major contribution to creating the climate of opinion which made possible the birth of the Labour Party. His influence then declined very rapidly when that party became less concerned with theories or Utopias and when the left-wing socialists found him a barrier to the achievement of their objectives. Nevertheless, Bellamy's books continue to be read by the "social babe and suckling" and to be used by such one-man political parties as L. G. De Garis of Victoria, Australia, who has made frequent mention of Bellamy's ideas in his publications trumpeting the cause of the Social Credit movement: *The Monthly Miracle, Outlook, Insight,* and in a series of pamphlets entitled generally "The Deathless Bomber." There is evidence, therefore, that at least until before and after World War II, *Looking Backward* and *Equality* were still capable of unfolding in the minds of young and old a vision of a more rational social order.

CHAPTER FIVE

# Canadian Reactions

By

## W. R. FRASER

IN A LETTER to Russian journalists in 1892, Edward Bellamy remarked that "although Nationalist agitation was" of "too recent origin to be much understood outside of the United States," it had a foothold in Canada "and in England."[1] In the 1930's Paul Bellamy was quoted as saying that his father had many, many followers in Canada,[2] and Mrs. Edward Bellamy claimed that the "Co-operative Commonwealth Party in Canada" was the "direct outgrowth of the seed which was planted by" her husband's Utopian novels.[3] As these comments indicate, Bellamy—the American prophet who proposed not a New Deal but a New Game—had an impact in Canada not only in the nineteenth century but during the depression of the 1930's.

## I  Publication, Reaction

Tracing the history of the publication of Bellamy's Utopian novels in Canada is almost as difficult as discovering indications of his influence. Dr. W. Kaye Lamb, director of the National Library at Ottawa, reported that only two of Bellamy's books bear Canadian imprints: Looking Backward[4] and Equality.[5] But he also commented that such an imprint did not necessarily mean that the books were published in Canada. On the other hand, Robert H. Blackburn, chief librarian of the University of Toronto, believes that Equality at least was printed and copyrighted in Canada.

Other evidence indicates that cheap editions of Bellamy's Utopias or excerpts from them were also circulated and published in Canada. The Chairman of the Vancouver Council of Social Engineers, Herbert D. Clark, stated in a letter of Sep-

137

tember 25, 1958, that ten or fifteen years ago the Co-operative
Commonwealth Federation—the socialist party of Canada—republished *Looking Backward* in a cheap, paper-covered edition.[6] Although no other evidence of this publication has been
located, another cheap edition circulated in British Columbia
before the Co-operative Commonwealth Federation was organized in 1932. In substantiation of this fact, Harold Winch, a
Vancouver socialist and member of the House of Commons,
wrote on April 7, 1959, from Ottawa: "After a passage of some
twenty-eight years, I cannot remember who published Edward
Bellamy's *Looking Backward,* of which I personally sold something of over two thousand copies. All I can tell you is that it
was a book with a soft cover. I am firmly of the conviction that
it was a Canadian publication. . . ."[7]

Douglas Carr, vice-president of Local 796, International
Union of Operating Engineers and a member of the Co-operative Commonwealth Federation, recalled in a letter that the
Ontario socialists had printed the "Parable of the Water Tank"
and had "widely circulated" it for propaganda purposes wherever the "C.C.F. sold its literature."[8]

Although it is impossible to relate with exactness where and
how Bellamy's novels were published, *Looking Backward,
Equality,* and Arthur Morgan's pioneer biography of Bellamy
were reviewed in Canada. In 1889 a critic who signed himself
J. A. M. published a review of *Looking Backward* in the *Knox
College Monthly.* After describing the plot and Bellamy's economic theories, he strongly recommended the Utopia to Christian ministers for summer reading . . . and he rated it even
above Mrs. Humphrey Ward's very popular *Robert Ellsmere!*
The review ended with the following comment: "What fools
and barbarians we shall appear to those, who from that brighter
day, will look backward upon the 19th century of the Christian
era."[9]

An appreciative but less enthusiastic review of Bellamy's
*Equality* was published in the *Canadian Magazine* by John A.
Cooper. Entitled "Bellamy and Howells," the article pointed out
that Howells—who had published his Utopian *Visitor from
Altruria*—was in ". . . a most complacent mood" but that Bellamy ". . . was much less complacent, and a much more dis-
gusted citizen of the country which is supposed to hate monarchy, aristocracy, and plutocracy. . . . A close study of Mr.
Bellamy's ideas of 'economic equality' may lead Canadians to
see more clearly the dangers of large financial accumula-
tions. . . ."[10]

In 1898 W. A. Douglas adversely criticized the ideology of *Equality*. In his article "Bellamy's Blunders," he stated in the preamble: "It is not to Bellamy's dream that we ought to object, but to his philosophy. In his description of our present social injustice, he is strong; but when he comes to the work of construction, to the methods of reform, then he is weak. . . . When he shows that society is divided into two parts, those who have secured a seat on the coach and those who must pull at the traces, no objection can be taken to the correctness of the description.

"To rectify this wrong, Bellamy proposes heroic measures; he would make the State supreme in everything. He would give the Government charge of all the machinery of production and exchange, and then he would have everyone receive an equal reward."

In the following three sections of the review—"Is Life the Basis of Property," "Bellamy and the Capitalist," and "An Equal Division of Wealth"—Douglas stated:

To justify this method of production and distribution, Bellamy assumes that life is the basis of property. But, in making this assumption, he overlooks the fact that property is of two utterly different species; firstly, there are the natural resources, the sunlight, the atmosphere, the land and the water, the minerals and other raw materials which man never produced and on which he has never expended any labor; and secondly, the houses, the clothing, the food, and other forms of wealth, the finished articles, that have been produced by industry. . . .

The great object of Bellamy's condemnation is the capitalist. But he never seems to notice that there are at least two ways in which a man may become a capitalist . . . the method of acquiring capital by honestly producing it, and the method of appropriating the product of other men's industry by means of some undue advantage. . . .

Bellamy insists strenuously on an equal division of wealth, and teaches that if we do not secure this equal division, then the men of greater wealth endanger the lives and liberties of those of less wealth. But here again, he overlooks the two uses to which wealth can be applied, or it might better be said, the use and abuse of wealth. A man may use his wealth to produce still further wealth, and thus add to the prosperity of the nation; or he may use his means to hold land in idleness, where it is much needed, contiguous to some great city. This is the misuse of wealth. . . .

Nothing is easier than the rectification of this wrong. Let us once learn to distinguish the right use of wealth from that which is injurious, and then so adjust our taxes as to encourage the beneficent and to take away all hope of profit from the injurious, and with this simple adjustment we will prevent any man using his wealth to the injury of his fellows. . . .[11]

In his last-quoted comments, Douglas was echoing one of Bellamy's rivals in radical economics—Henry George. Douglas overlooked, however, Bellamy's statements in the thirteenth chapter of *Equality* which portrayed the inadequacy of "the single tax" on land values and in which he argued that agrarian reform could not solve the problems of the industrial era. Furthermore, although Douglas described what he thought to be Bellamy's "blunders," he also evinced attitudes which many influential Canadians continued to have toward the American prophet. In assessing their attitudes, it is important to remember that Bellamy was not merely a socialist, but a most extreme socialist—comparable to Marx. But he was even more dangerous—or more usable—than Marx; for Bellamy could be understood by all and Marx could not!

In 1912 James Edward Le Rossignol observed in an article entitled "The March of Socialism" that "Socialism does not seem to thrive in Canada." He then avowed: "The weakest part of the Socialist program is the demand that all the means of production be owned and operated collectively, and neither Bellamy nor any other Socialist has been able to suggest a scheme by which production could be carried on as efficiently as under the regime of private property. . . ."[12]

In a review of Arthur E. Morgan's *Edward Bellamy*, Sylvia Thrupp commented in 1945:

Many were perhaps attracted by some inconsequential detail in his [Bellamy's] scheme rather than by the kind of regimentation—universal conscription for work under military discipline —that he advocated. I, for one, remember being enchanted by the prospect of unlimited supplies of beautiful paper clothes, to be discarded after a single wearing. The book undoubtedly owed much of its immediate popularity to the pains with which Bellamy dissociated his ideas from those of Europe-born socialism; he exalted nationalism and dismissed "reds" as mere troublemakers subsidized by the opponents of true reform. Scores of "nationalist" clubs sprang up, sponsored by well-to-do theosophists who liked the ethical tone of his writing; but when Bellamy sought to interest them in building a political movement they melted away. Was he then, as William Morris and other critics assumed, a mere shallow nonenity? Or was he a disquieting portent of latent middle-class leanings toward authoritarianism? The full length portrait that emerges from Arthur Morgan's careful study is of an oppressively serious and ambitious mind. A notebook filled at the age of thirteen contains an essay on usurpation that winds up with the stern conclusion, "Time cannot change evil to good, nor make a rightful inheritance out of a usurpation." Somehow Bellamy never outgrew the stiffness and naïveté of his precocious boyhood. . . . His knowledge of economics seems to have rested on a reading of Mills' *Political Economy* at the age of seventeen, but the construction of *Looking Backward* grew, as his biographer shows, out of a life-long if somewhat desultory struggle with arbitrary schemes for improving the world.[13]

## II  *The Socialists*

Crauford D. Goodwin, of the Assumption University of Windsor, Ontario, and the author of an unpublished doctoral dissertation *Canadian Economic Thought: 1814-1914*, has stated that the problems attacked by Henry George seemed of greater significance before 1914 than those which concerned Bellamy. Although as late as 1929 the people in Alberta were discussing the agrarian reform theories of Henry George, Bellamy had entered at least one home in the Milk River area by "the back door." A clergyman there possessed a much admired copy of Bernard Shaw's *The Intelligent Woman's Guide* which supports —without acknowledgment, of course—the American socialist's plan of economic equality for all citizens. For, as Maurice Colbourne made clear in *The Real Bernard Shaw* (1949), Shaw's theory of "a national dividend" was taken from Bellamy's *Equality*.[14]

Bellamy's ideas came more directly to Canada through the indefatigable efforts of the fascinating H. Gaylord Wilshire, who, born in Cincinnati, Ohio, had become interested in gold mining in California by 1884. In the years after 1884, Wilshire engaged in mercantile and stock-market enterprises; served as president of the Fullerton Land and Trust Company and of the Beaver National Bank of New York City; wrote *Socialism Inevitable* (1907); and ran for public offices in the United States and for parliament in both England and Canada. In 1923 Upton Sinclair listed Wilshire in *The Brass Check* as one of the millionnaire converts to socialism;[15] interestingly enough, both Sinclair and Wilshire had been fascinated by the ideas of *Looking Backward*.

During his amazing career, Wilshire had become a member of one of the many Bellamy clubs of California, and the Reverend Doctor Everett W. MacNair describes him in *Edward Bellamy and the Nationalist Movement, 1889-1894* (1957) as having been one of the most outstanding and worthy men capable of carrying on "Edward Bellamy's idealism and influence."[16] Wilshire traveled in the states from coast to coast delivering lectures for the Bellamy clubs; he wrote articles about trusts and monopolies for the *California Nationalist;* and he made in 1893 a study of trusts in England and in 1894 he ran for election to the English Parliament as a representative of the Social Democratic Federation of Manchester.

In 1902 Wilshire began the publication in Toronto of *Wilshire's Magazine,* which he had begun to publish in Los Angeles in 1900. In the first Canadian issue he described himself as "the Los Angeles animated fashion plate, socialist, 'hoot mon' golf player, bill board magnate, hiker and gentleman rancher" who was now "breaking out in a new spot."[17] In his magazine, which was "straightforward" and "a high-grade publication,"[18] Wilshire preached the same type of Bellamyite socialism that he had lectured about in the 1890's in the United States when he had stated to the Economic Club of Los Angeles that "overproduction arises because our productive capacity has been developed to the highest degree with labor-saving machinery operated by steam and electricity, while our consumptive capacity is crippled by the competitive wage system which limits the laborers who constitute the bulk of our consumers, to the mere necessities of life."[19] Convinced that a socialistic state was the inevitable answer to economic problems and that Bellamyism was the socialism he preferred, Wilshire spread Bellamy's ideas not only in the United States but in Canada in his popular, socialistic, muckraking publication.

But Bellamy's influence was also received directly from the reading of his books by Canadians. Although the present leader of the socialist party in Canada, M. J. Coldwell, has written that while "the plans he [Bellamy] had in mind have not been carried out in the manner his writings suggest, many of the ideas he enunciated have found fulfillment in both economic developments and social legislation";[20] the Canadian socialists owed much to the influence of the American Utopian. In fact, the material gathered about Bellamy's influence indicates that Mrs. Edward Bellamy was not amiss when she stated that her husband's books had contributed greatly to the socialist movement in Canada and to the founding of the Co-operative Commonwealth Party. Bellamy, as will be seen, had an impact upon such socialists as J. S. Woodsworth, M. J. Coldwell, H. Winch, J. W. A. Nicholson, F. M. Young, J. B. MacLachlan, F. W. Creen, W. E. Peirce, A. Andras, and many others who left no record behind them or who were not interviewed—or could not be.

Long before the socialists had a party, there was an active group of them in British Columbia early in the twentieth century. W. E. Peirce, one of them, stated that although he thought he was more influenced by Robert Blatchford's *Merrie England* (1894) than by *Looking Backward*, he remembered that Bellamy was highly "successful in convincing his readers not only of the reasonableness for changes in our society but also of their attractiveness and desirability."[21] Three members were elected from this early socialist group to the provincial legislature in 1907 and the first federal representative was elected in 1930.[22]

Peirce himself "once ran afoul of the Censor when" he was "publishing a small weekly newspaper" and spent three months in jail. Although he could not remember whether or not he had propagandized Bellamy's ideas in his publication, he did think that he had probably cited him in his propaganda lectures during his long career in which he ran unsuccessfully five times as a C.C.F. candidate (twice in the federal elections and thrice in the provincial ones).

Harold Winch, socialist member of the House of Commons, recalls in a letter that "the books by Edward Bellamy played a very significant role in British Columbia many years ago, especially the one entitled *Looking Backward*. When I first became actively interested in the political scene in 1931, approximately 2,000 copies of this book came into my possession. They were quite speedily disposed of in the course of my speaking engagements throughout the province. I was often told by people making application for membership in the C.C.F. that the clinching argument for doing so came about as a result of their reading this wonderful literary effort."[23]

The reminiscences of others also indicate the influence of Bellamy with groups and individuals. Mr. A. Andras, Director of Legislation of the powerful Canadian Labour Congress, recalls that the career of Stanley F. Knowles—long a stalwart of the socialist party and now vice-president of the Canadian Labour Congress—had been influenced by Bellamy. When Mr. Knowles read *Looking Backward* in the early 1930's, it helped him leave the Christian ministry for a venture in politics.

Mr. Andras also relates: "During the early 1930's a group of us belonged to a socialist youth organization in Montreal. It was a branch of the Young Peoples Socialist League which had its headquarters in the United States. I remember that we read Edward Bellamy and were much impressed with *Looking Backward* and its sequel *Equality*. I venture to say that other socialist groups in that period and others which were interested long before also read Bellamy and were influenced by him. Evidence of Bellamy's popularity is to be found in the fact, I think, that *Looking Backward* keeps cropping up in one edition or another on the bookshelves of virtually every secondhand store I have visited across Canada."[24]

In the Montreal of this period, it was "fashionable for nearly everyone to be at least faintly pink,"[25] but this statement could not be made of Quebec at large which never elected a socialist to either the provincial or the federal legislatures. Quebec's consistent trend has been to support capitalism, and this and its religious allegiances would not have made Bellamy's ideas popular.

In the Atlantic provinces, the influence of Bellamy was, however, recorded. The Reverend J. W. A. Nicholson, of the United Church of Canada, reported that religious groups often discussed Bellamy's ideas after *Looking Backward* was first published; but he also added that it would have been dangerous for the person who approved the book. In one of his letters Mr. Nicholson emphatically stated that *Looking Backward* had had an impact upon him. He had admired the book, he observed, and valued it "not for the novelty of its ideas but for the striking program picturing the desired process, the ideal realism of the economic system." After his retirement, Mr. Nicholson ran twice, but unsuccessfully, on the socialist party ticket.

Only one well-known Maritime radical, Mr. James B. MacLachlan, appeared to regard Bellamy highly. The Reverend F. M. Young, who has been active on behalf of socialism, feels, however, that "The Parable of the Water Tank" probably influenced a great many Maritimers who read this publication from *Equality* which was distributed by the socialists. Dr. Howard S. Ross, another but unrecognized 'radical' Nova Scotian, stated about 1950 that Bellamyism in its ultimate economic aspects was nearest to his preference which was Equitism—and Equitism, as will be seen in the next section of this chapter, had much in common with Bellamyism.

S. M. Lipset also recorded in his *Agrarian Socialism* the reaction to Bellamy of the farmers in Saskatchewan: "The first secretary of the Saskatchewan Grain Grower's Association (S.G.G.A.), Fred W. Green, had been a socialist in Lancastershire, England. He often used his regular column in the *Gra in Grower's Guide* to disseminate ideas on socialism without explicitly mentioning the word. Under his secretaryship, the S.G.G.A. distributed thousands of Bellamy's socialistic classics, *Looking Backward* and *Equality*. Many C.C.F. farmers cite these books as their first contact with socialistic ideas."[26]

Further indication of knowledge of Bellamy is found in J. S. Woodworth's comments in his foreword to *Social Planning for Canada*, which is often called the "Bible" of Canadian Socialists. Mr. Woodworth commented: "Socialist literature has been scarce in Canada and for most people, unconvincing. The idealized pictures of Morris and Bellamy and Wells, while stimulating our imaginations, carried with them a sense of unreality. . . ."[27]

As a result of the socialist activity in Canada—and of reading Bellamy's books—many groups, convinced that capitalism should be abolished and that an economy based on production for use rather than for profit should be substituted for it, met in August of 1932 at Calgary, Alberta, to organize the Co-operative Commonwealth Party. Professor F. R. Scott, one of the authors of *Social Planning for Canada*, observed: "The conference brought together, for the first time in Canadian history, Marxian socialists from British Columbia, men raised in the tradition of the British Labor movement, and the agrarian socialists. The delegates decided to form a new national political party to be known as the Co-operative Commonwealth Federation (C.C.F.). Its first national convention, meeting in Regina, in July, 1933, drew up a lengthy program that was a compromise between the Marxian socialists and the much more conservative farmer's representatives from Eastern Canada. Each provincial section of the party, however, was left free to interpret the program as it saw fit and to draw up its own provincial program."[28]

During 1944 this relatively new party won high distinction in the province of Saskatchewan by being *the first avowedly socialistic group of North America to be successful at the polls*. Professor Scott opined that this convention "marked a turning point in the history of the Saskatchewan farmer's movement as well as in the socialist movement across Canada."[29] Dr. Seymour M. Lipset, author of *Agrarian Socialism*, observed: "It is impossible to understand why an avowedly socialist party should have won a majority of votes among supposedly conservative farmers unless one recognizes how often the social and economic position of the American wheat-belt farmer, in the United States as in Canada, has made him the American radical."[30]

To one who viewed the citizens of Saskatchewan in the early 1930's their political reactions to their conditions would have posed no mystery. Already in the grip of the great economic depression, dust storms added to the ever-present misery of the people. With the sun shining, large areas of Saskatchewan looked like a desert; after a rain, the rough prairie roads were channels of mud into which trucks often sank to the axles. With the sun followed by wind, vast regions were so covered by dust that day became as night; and, no matter how secure the windows of a home might be, dust entered to cover everything.

Sometimes the farmers could not afford gasoline for their trucks and often their vehicles were horse-drawn—and the people in vicious criticism of the premier of the federal government called them "Bennett buggies." Although "government relief" meant something, many of the farmers felt that much more financial aid should have been provided them.

Sometimes trains had but one passenger car, and the tops of all the box-cars were covered by homeless men who traveled about the country in a desperate quest for work. When the train stopped, most of the travellers descended to the ground to stretch themselves and to walk about. When the indulgent conductor's "All aboard!" was heard, these men climbed back to the tops of the cars and continued their torturous journey.[31] The farmers who remembered vividly this period of Saskatchewan's history were ready to vote for a party that offered relief from such conditions.

As this recital of the accounts of individuals and of the founding of the Co-operative Commonwealth Federation indicates, reading Bellamy often led people—as Heywood Broun observed in his introduction to *Looking Backward*—to socialism. In Canada Bellamy's Utopian fiction was distributed and read; and it not only contributed to the formation of the socialist party but influenced many of its leaders. Canadian socialists have not, however, accepted either the socialism of Bellamy or of Marx; they strike a judicious, practical stand.

## III  *Other Influence*

In 1934 Stephen Leacock wrote to Mrs. Edward Bellamy: "I was a student in college at the time your husband's book came out and well remember the universal interest in it. . . . In my classes at McGill in political and social theories we use it as one of our chief books of reference, but we do not have any assigned compulsory text books."[32] He wrote later to Arthur Morgan that he was one of "the many people to whom

. . . *Looking Backward* came as a sort of illumination of the world that might be. I know now that humanity is not as yet fit to live in a Bellamy commonwealth, that old age is not as wise as he thought it or the instinct for work for all as strong as he imagined it. . . . But even if his Commonwealth is a soap bubble, at least it had in it those iridescent colors which will in some long day light up the world. *Looking Backward* made an impression on my mind never to be effaced."[33]

Since Leacock used Bellamy in his classes, many of his students may have been influenced by *Looking Backward*. Leacock himself became a Utopian novelist when he published *Afternoons in Utopia* (1932). He also wrote *Arcadian Adventures with the Idle Rich* (1914), *Moonbeams from the Larger Lunacy* (1915), *Frenzied Fiction* (1917), and *Elements of Political Science* (1906).

Dr. Howard Ross, a "radical" Nova Scotian, lived most of his life as a barrister in Montreal. Although his face suggested Santa Claus, he had a mind akin to that of Edward Bellamy or of Henry George. He admired Bellamy's broad vision but differed from him in respect to ultimate economics. Despite his admiration, Ross' ideas about economics were cautiously advanced as suggested reforms of capitalism; and his moral tone was such that it pleased Rotarians and many churchmen. But in spite of this, he was one of the great, though unacknowledged, socialists of Canada.

About 1950, Dr. Ross stated that Bellamyism in its ultimate economic aspects was nearest to that of his preference—Equitism. The founder of Equitism was Warren E. Brokaw of Del Rosa, California—the state noted for its Bellamyism. Like both Bellamy and Ross, Brokaw disliked the term "socialism" to describe his beliefs. Furthermore, Ross and Brokaw detested regimentation and feared that Bellamy's state would lead to it—and in their thinking they both erred because they did not clearly distinguish between political and economic, democratic and totalitarian socialism. Basically, Brokaw and Bellamy were akin; for Brokaw was asking with both Shaw and Bellamy the ultimate question: "How much for each?"

Brokaw, once a follower of Henry George, had left the doctrine of single tax for the far more sweeping one of what may be termed the "single price" on work. He believed that in the interests of human happiness nothing but work should have a price and that the price should be in terms of time. Surely Equitism, as he conceived it, meant economic socialism—although of a brash and Utopian nature. In 1950 Ross stated at a

Rotary Club meeting in Sherbrooke, P. Q., that ". . . equitism
. . . teaches that human work is the only suitable source of
ownership; that honest money can buy and sell nothing but
human work; that nothing but human work should have a
price; that the greatest mistake ever made by humanity was
the putting of a price on the natural resources of the world;
that the dollar (unit of account and exchange) should be
issued solely for and redeemed solely by one hour's adult
human work. . . ."[34]

In his book *Equitable Society and How to Create It* (1927),
which was, significantly enough, published by the Vanguard
Press that Upton Sinclair had been instrumental in founding,
and by the Equitist League, Brokaw wrote: "The thing that
oppresses is not land, nor money, nor machinery, nor competition, but the power of compelling tribute. . . ." Then in reference to Bellamy's ideas of the "social fund"—the resources of
wealth and of inventions which men through the ages had
created and which should, therefore, belong to the public—
Brokaw wrote: "This 'social fund' idea offers the newest principle of the new economy; that is, man is entitled not only to
his own product, but more. He is entitled to his share of the
produce of the social organism.

"This idea is based on a misconception of what constitutes
a product. . . . The excess yield of nature on one location to
equal effort on another is counted as the product of human
work, whereas it is the gift of nature. Our commodity currency
system puts a price on it and thus makes it appear as a product.
But a work-unit currency would not put any price on that part
contributed by nature, so that it would cheapen the result instead of creating a 'fund.'

". . . By our inequitable methods of exchange we are con-
tinually creating a fund and giving it to privileged classes.
Instead of tracing this to its source, Bellamy looks upon it as
a social fund to be distributed by public supervision."[35]

Brokaw's concept of "labor hours" as bearing on distributive
justice is not new, but he seems to have developed the idea
independently and to have given it a theoretical extension that
is unique. A labor-hour unit had failed, for example, in a limited but memorable test directed by Robert Owen in London,
England, in 1832. Be that as it may, Brokaw's writing and work
indicate a knowledge of Bellamy; but further research is needed
to prove the extent to which Brokaw was influenced by him.
Bellamy influenced directly and indirectly, however, Dr. Howard Ross.

Evidence of Bellamy's influence upon the social gospel movement also exists in Canada. A. B. Davies, Secretary of the Gospel Christian Association at Hamilton, Ontario, has written large numbers of pamphlets and articles about social affairs. "Christocracy," one of them, combines Bellamyism with trust in Providence. In his strenuous efforts to bring about fundamental economic reforms, Mr. Davies wrote many times to F. D. Roosevelt and MacKenzie King, whose replies were, however, non-committal.[36]

Although George Mooney described the effect of Bellamy on cooperative societies and the Social Credit Party in Quebec and in Canada at large as being no more than "peripheral," Mr. Mooney paid tribute in his definitive work *Co-operatives Today and Tomorrow* (1938) to Dr. Toyohiko Kagawa, as well as to many others. Kagawa, an authority on cooperatives, told Mrs. Marion Bellamy Earnshaw that he greatly admired Edward Bellamy and his books.[37] Although the influence of Bellamy may once more have been peripheral and indirect, the cooperative societies of Canada do not—as Bellamy did—strike at the basic roots of capitalism. Bellamy—as he stated in *Equality*—considered them, however, as one step of the transition period.

Edward Bellamy also "contributed" to my philosophical novel *A White Stone*. Although I thought of his theories frequently, I mentioned his name only once: "'. . . Shaw's rationalism led him to some dangerous extremes. Many of the socialists themselves have been horrified by the doctrine of absolutely equal income for every body.'

"'I have no doubt of that. None the less, I suppose that Shaw's outlook—or should I say Bellamy's?—is bound to survive as one of the possible theories of distributive justice.'"[38]

Besides mention of Bellamy in my novel, I also noted in a lecture before the Canadian Philosophical Association in 1958 at Edmonton, Alberta, that Bellamy's outlook—echoed by Bernard Shaw in *The Intelligent Woman's Guide*—offers one of the "ultimate" theories of socialism.[39] I also give every year in one of my courses at Sir George Williams University a lecture about Bellamy's speculative economics.

In summary, we may say that Edward Bellamy influenced many people in Canada through his Utopian novels and particularly *Looking Backward*. Except for "The Parable of the Water Tank," Bellamy's *Equality* does not seem to have been widely read; and yet this was his most significant contribution to the philosophy of economics. There was much discussion in Canada of Bellamy's books near the end of the nineteenth century, and his first Utopia was widely distributed and discussed in the 1930's before the founding of the Co-operative Commonwealth Party to whose founding he contributed. Although the socialists of Canada—and others—used him for propaganda and for inspiring people to believe in a better economic system, they did not and do not dream of attempting to fulfill his plan. They admit, however, that "many of the ideas he has enunciated have found fulfillment in both economic development and social legislation."

Bellamy belongs to the ages, but he still presents a challenge to modern thinkers. To many who have not studied Bellamy, this suggestion could mean a trip into science fiction and not an aspect of "the philosophy of social science." Yet, with all homage to analytical theorists, the time has surely come for a scrutiny of the most speculative social hypotheses. If this be metaphysics, it is yet the sort concerned with the luxury of survival and with the knowing, the enjoying, and the sharing of the world.

# CHAPTER SIX

# The German Acceptance and Reaction

By

## FRANZ X. RIEDERER

ALTHOUGH THE NAME OF Edward Bellamy means little to the average, younger German citizen of today, the older generation still remembers the popularity of Bellamy's *Looking Backward* and *Equality* when it hears their German titles: *Ein Rueckblick aus dem Jahre 2000, Alles verstaatlicht,* or *Gleichheit.* This is not, however, a remarkable reaction, for the reception of Bellamy's first Utopian novel in Germany was described in 1892 by Arthur von Kirchenheim in the following positive fashion: "Bellamy! Indeed, two or three years ago one could hear nothing else but Bellamy. In every railway compartment you could see somebody reading Reclam's Number 2661/2; the student read it during lectures instead of listening to an exegesis, interpretation or conjecture; and even the peasants studied this kind of national economy."[1] Bruno Schoenlank, the German correspondent for the *New Nation,* a reform publication which Bellamy published, had also reported this effect in "Socialism in Germany" in 1891; but he had also remarked that the working class studied the book, that women were enthusiastic about it, and that it reached an audience which could never be touched by Marx, Lassalle, or Engels. Socialists, however, saw the propaganda value of the book while recognizing that it was not the scientific socialism of Marx or Engels.[2]

The economic situation of Germany—as did that of the United States—contributed to the interest which all groups showed in *Looking Backward.* In the last quarter of the nineteenth century, Germany had changed from an agrarian economy to an industrial one; and it soon became evident that the political system was not adequate to care for all the resultant problems. When depression followed the panic of 1873, measures such as protective tariff laws tried to protect home industries, to limit competition, and generally to preserve the national welfare. To the working class, it seemed that the democratic movement which had destroyed feudalism and made capitalism possible had failed. By the last part of the nineteenth century the so-called average man had been reduced to the position of a wage slave who had no future but one of meagre existence, and by 1895 two-thirds of Germany's population was classified as proletariat. These workers—men, women, and children—lived in crowded quarters; they suffered from high rents; their employment was unstable; and, as a result, alcoholism, prostitution, and crime increased at a high rate.

As might be expected as a result of this condition, a party soon rose to fight the battle of the oppressed people—that of the Social Democrats. When Bismarck passed in 1878 the Laws of Exception against the socialists, he seemed only to strengthen the party. To win support from the people, the government passed social-reform laws to alleviate their plight. In this attempt, the government was moving toward "paternalism."

During this period of suffering and hardship but also of increased invention of means of production, many people began to question the hitherto accepted idea that poverty was part of the natural order. To them, it had become evident that modern technology, scientific cultivation, and modern transportation systems would easily and quickly provide "welfare for all." Yet despite all the abundance and all the ability to produce, poverty seemed to increase among the people while machinery rusted in shut-down factories and the market was so glutted with the necessities of life that grain rotted. Soon the question which touched a basic issue was formulated: If man could produce such abundance, why could it not be shared by all? As many Germans pondered this query, they also posed another question: Could the socialist program provide the answer to the problems of society? Because Bellamy's *Looking Backward* proposed an answer to both these inquiries and because it appeared in an era described by Werner Sombart in 1905 as one of changing ethical and economic concepts, it became so popular that multiple translations and editions of it appeared.

I  *Translations and Important Translators*

The first German translations of *Looking Backward* were published in 1889, but both editions of the book were incomplete. The one published late in the year by Ekstein Nachfolger of Berlin under the changed title of *Alles verstaatlicht* (Every-

thing Nationalized) was a hurried, inaccurate translation prepared by Georg Malkowsky who had also taken great liberties
with the text. He omitted the preface, first chapter, and many
paragraphs and sentences which he thought would be of little
interest to the German reader; and he also ended the novel
with Julian West's unhappy experiences when he returns to
the Boston of 1887. Although Malkowsky obviously thought
that omission of the re-awakening of West to learn that he is
still living in the year 2000 would force the reader back to the
misery of 1889, he served Bellamy and other translators no
good; for this German edition was translated into Polish. The
other edition issued during the same year and reprinted in
1893 was a digested version published under the title *Ein
sozialistischer Roman.* Edited by Max Schippel of the socialist
publishing house of *Verlag des 'Vorwaerts' Berliner Volksblatt,*[3]
this edition formed one of the volumes included in "The Berlin Workers Series."

As early as 1890, two famous publishers included *Looking
Backward* in their collections of famous novels. The English version of the book was published by Bernhard Tauchnitz, and a
new translation was issued by Phillip Reclam, Jr., of Leipzig
under the title *Ein Rueckblick aus dem Jahr 2000 auf 1887*
as one of the books in his very popular pocket-book series
*Universal Bibliothek.*[4] Although Tauchnitz was famous throughout Europe for publishing the works of the most prominent
English and American writers in their original language, Reclam
was just as well known in Germany for its series of over seven
thousand books selected from world literature.[5]

The translator of the Reclam edition, which was a fairly
accurate one and certainly the best translation yet made, was
Georg von Gizycki (1851-1895), a professor of philosophy at
the University of Berlin who taught what would today be called
"social sciences." He belonged to a party called *Nationallibera-
len,* which had broken with the Manchester School. Because it
believed socialist criticism was often justified, the group was
called socialistic. Von Gizycki belonged, therefore, to a group
which was also represented by Schmoller, Wagner, and Bren-
tano. Because of his attitude toward *laissez-faire,* it is not surprising that he stated in the preface to his translation that,
despite the criticism from conservatives and socialists, *Looking
Backward* contained "deep ethical truths."

In 1890 three other publishers also brought forth editions
of *Looking Backward.* The translation which Richard George
prepared for Otto Hendel was the first edition which contained

Bellamy's letter to the Boston *Transcript* and which did not
omit or distort the meaning of a single sentence. In his introductory note to the volume, George stated that the moral and
sociological progress depicted by Bellamy demanded "admiration and criticism as well." He admired the peaceful evolution
which was to lead to a better state, but he decried the fact
that Bellamy's book had been regarded as a parody of socialist
dreams. To George, the novel was also important as a mirror
which reflected not only the shortcomings of his day but also
a happier future.

The translation which Alexander Fleischmann made for Otto
Wigand in Leipzig was so literal that the style was impaired.
He also reduced the value of the book by omitting Bellamy's
criticism of the banking and monetary system of the nineteenth
century. Despite these blemishes, *Ein Rueckblick aus dem Jahr
2000 auf das Jahr 1887* was reprinted six times within the year.

One of the most popular editions of *Looking Backward* of
1890 was, however, that published by the famous socialist publishing house of J. H. W. Dietz in Stuttgart. Dietz, who had
been printer and editor of the socialist daily *Hamburger-
Altonaer Volksblatt,* had taken over in 1878 a cooperative printing house in Hamburg and had started an enterprise which
became the socialist publishing house. Aside from publishing
almost all of the works of such famous socialists as Marx and
Engels, it also issued the theoretical organ *Die Neue Zeit* and
Clara Zetkin's woman's paper *Die Gleichheit.* The firm, which
had moved from Hamburg to Stuttgart, became the property
in 1906 of the socialist party; and it merged in 1924 with
another socialist publishing house *Verlag des Vorwaerts.* Closed
by Hitler when he came into power in 1933, the publishing
house of Dietz was re-established in 1945 in East Berlin where
it is now the official publisher for the *Sozialistische Einheits-
partei Deutschlands,* the East German Communist Party.

This history of the publishing house of Dietz and the biography of the translator, Clara Zetkin, an ardent socialist, are of
interest as we consider the history of the 1890 edition of *Looking Backward.* In 1914, the book was reissued with an introduction by Clara Zetkin; and this edition was reprinted seven
times by 1922. In 1949, this translation was reissued with an
introduction by Dr. Hermann Duncker, who not only edited
the volume but added explanatory footnotes which explained
the historical background and which also cited references to
passages in the works of Engels and Lenin. As late as 1954,
the Zetkin translation was republished in East Berlin by Volk

and Welt, a publishing house founded in 1947, which, as its title implies, has the objective of bringing to the people the literature of the world.

The oft-reprinted translation which Clara Vitale Zetkin made of Bellamy's most famous novel is a complete version except for publication of the author's letter to the Boston *Transcript*. Clara Zetkin, a well-educated-for-her-time member of a German bourgeois revolutionary family, was well qualified to translate and edit a socialist German edition of *Looking Backward;* for, since 1878 when she had met Ossip Zetkin, a Russian political refugee whom she later married, she had been in close contact with socialist and revolutionary ideas and causes.

Introduced to the Socialist Party of Leipzig, Clara Zetkin—after a trip to Russia in 1878 and a few years of teaching—devoted herself to working for it. She moved to Zurich and later to Paris, where she joined Ossip Zetkin, who had had to leave Germany because of Bismarck's *Sozialistengesetz*, the anti-socialist laws. During their stay in Paris, both Clara and Ossip were very active in the political life of the circle of exiles and in the French socialist party. After Ossip died in 1889, Clara continued her political work and made her first contribution to the international working class movement by aiding in preparations for the founding congress of the Second Socialist International. One of the few women delegates to this congress, she met again her old friends from Germany—and among them were August Bebel and Wilhelm Liebknecht, the leaders of the German Socialist Party.

After the congress Clara Zetkin worked in Zurich; but in 1890—after Bismarck had resigned and the anti-socialist laws had been repealed—she returned to Germany where she worked for publisher J. H. W. Dietz. As her biographer has noted, ". . . she translated—as one of her first works in Germany—the then famous book of the American Bellamy, *Looking Backward*, which was enthusiastically read by the generation of socialists who lived before World War I."[6]

Clara Zetkin soon found a task more to her liking, for she was asked to head the editorial board of the recently founded *Dei Arbeiterin*, the publication of the socialist women's movement which sought to organize and inspire German females to fight with the Social Democrats for equality. In 1891, she founded *Die Gleichheit*, which not only became her voice as she struggled for the equality of women and for the acceptance of socialist ideals, but also the most important publication of the German and the international women's socialist movement. Besides doing this work, Clara Zetkin also became an indefatigable organizer, orator, and guide to and battler for the women of her day.

When the congress of the socialist party was held in Gotha in 1896, Clara became the first woman to exercise a responsible political function; and she was elected to the control commission of the German Socialist Party after the convention had accepted the demands of women which she had presented in a speech. In 1897 she attended the International Congress for the Protection of Workers in Zurich; and in 1910 she attended the second International Conference of Socialist Women in Copenhagen where she and the American representative suggested the formation of International Women's Day to symbolize their struggle for the right to vote.

Before World War I, Mrs. Zetkin worked not only for the international and domestic movement but for peace, for her main concern was the threat of an international war and the possibility of a split in the party. Having become a devoted Marxist, she strongly criticized the right wing of the German Socialist Party which seemingly deviated from the principles of the International. During World War I, the German Socialist Party did split; and the left formed the so-called Independent German Socialist Party. As a result, Mrs. Zetkin lost her position as the chief editor of the *Dei Gleichheit*. When the extreme leftist group of the party left the Independent German Socialists to form in 1917 the *Spartakusbund*, which became in 1918-1919 the Communist Party of Germany, Clara Zetkin became the editor of the women's section in its paper, *Leipziger Volkszeitung*.

In 1915 when she had attended the international women's peace conference held in Berne, Clara Zetkin had met Nadejda Konstantinova Krupskaya, Lenin's wife, who was to be a lifelong friend. The two women had many mutual interests, for Krupskaya was also a valiant fighter for women's rights and for peace. Like Zetkin, she had published such books as *The Woman Worker* (Geneva, 1901), and had founded the magazine *Rabotnitsa* (Woman Worker) in 1914.[7] Although Mrs. Zetkin became a member of the German parliament in 1920, her friendships and sympathies drew her more and more toward the Soviet brand of communism; she made many visits to Russia where she also formed a friendship with Lenin. Eventually, she headed the women's secretariat of the Third International.[8]

Although the last years of her life were spent almost entirely in the Soviet Union, she reached the final height of her political career when in 1932 she was elected senior president of the *Reichstag*. On August 30, Clara Zetkin, gravely ill and almost blind, rose to make her opening speech in which she called on the German people who loved peace to unite against the terrible danger which was confronting humanity. Aware of the fact that German militarism and Nazism were preparing for a second world war, Clara Zetkin made her last great plea for peace. Her address was considered a moral defeat for the Hitler party, which nonetheless came into power half a year later. After her address, Mrs. Zetkin returned to the Soviet Union where she died on June 18, 1933. She was burried in the Kremlin wall which faces the Red Square in Moscow.

When we consider the role which Mrs. Zetkin played in the socialist and Marxist parties, it is not surprising that her translation of *Looking Backward* was so often reprinted, for although the Marxists denounced Bellamy's view of the ideal world as unscientific, they did not hesitate to use it, as the story of Bellamy in Russia has proved or as the republication of *Looking Backward* in East Berlin indicates.

In 1891, the year after Clara Zetkin's edition appeared, a new translation of *Looking Backward* was made by Johannes Hoops, which was published by the *Bibliographische Institut* of Leipzig in *Meyers Volksbuecher*, a series of good books of low price. Dr. Hoops (1865-1949), a professor of English philology at the University of Heidelberg and a member of various academies of science, prepared by far the best literary translation of Bellamy's Utopia which appeared in Germany and also the most complete because it contained not only the Boston *Transcript* letter but also the quotation from Tennyson's "Locksley Hall."

In his introductory note to his edition, Dr. Hoops presented a short report about the attempt of the Bellamy clubs in the United States to spread and to realize the ideas of Bellamy; he then stated his opinion of *Looking Backward*, and in doing so made a most objective criticism of it. To the professor, *Looking Backward* was not only "a book written by the right man at the right time," but one which was significantly different from other socialist programs in that it presented a "positive . . . picture of the socialist future state." Although Hoops regarded the book as the result of many years of study and as having been written by a man able "to do justice to the demands of all classes and professions," he felt that it would not be read because of its aesthetic values but because of its socialist content. He remarked, however, that the novel would not have scored such success in circles "far from socialism" had the author not presented his material in such an interesting fashion.

Hoops asserted that Bellamy had, however, made some obvious errors. To him, they were "the same, which generally are inherent in the socialist doctrine; . . . socialists always consider human beings as ideal creatures." To Hoops, human laziness was a problem which should not be underestimated. Despite this common error, *Looking Backward* was of value because, opined Hoops, of its "noble and humanitarian spirit" and its "ennobling ethical effect."

Although there were reprints from 1891 to 1919 of other publications of *Looking Backward*, there was not a new edition until 1919 when one was issued in Munich by George Mueller as one of a series of Utopian novels. Though no translator is named, comparisons of this edition with earlier ones confirm not only that it was a new translation but that it was comparable in excellence to that of Richard George.

After World War II a new edition of *Looking Backward* was published in Switzerland, but circulated in Germany, by the Swiss publishers *Mensch und Arbeit* under the title *Erlebnisse im Jahre 2000* (Experiences in the Year 2000). Although no translator is mentioned, a comparison of texts indicates that the edition was based on the one prepared by Georg von Gizycki. As we have already noted, an edition prepared by Dr. Hermann Duncker appeared in 1949 in Germany and one in East Berlin was published in 1954.

Although there were many translations and editions of *Looking Backward*, there is only one known serialization:[9] that which appeared in 1889-1890 in the Vienna *Die Illustration*. Bellamy's *Forum* article "First Steps Toward Nationalism" (1890) was, however, published in *Nord und Sued* in 1894 with an introduction by Edward Bellamy, which has been published in English in the appendix of this volume.

Other of Bellamy's novels which were translated and published include two different editions (1890 and 1895) of *Dr. Heidenhoff's Process*, two (1890 and 1891) of *Miss Ludington's Sister*, and separate editions containing "An Echo of Antietam," "A Positive Romance," "With the Eyes Shut," "A Love Story Reversed," and "To Whom This May Come."

Despite the many editions of *Looking Backward* and the duplicate ones of Bellamy's earlier novels, only one of *Equality* was published in Germany because of the enforcement of a bilateral copyright agreement made between it and the United

States in 1892. Translated by M. Jacobi, who closely followed the original version, and published in 1898 in Stuttgart by *Deutsche Verlagsanstalt, Equality* was reprinted three times within the year. Its sale attested to the great, remaining interest in the ideas of Edward Bellamy.

## II  *Early Critical Reaction*

German critical reaction to Bellamy's two Utopian novels may be divided into two periods: the early, before 1900, in which he received attention in reviews, pamphlets, and an occasional history of Utopias; the later, after 1900, in which criticism appeared mainly in academic theses, prefaces to new editions of *Looking Backward,* and in histories of Utopian fiction. This division does not, of course, include the many Utopian novels which were written in Germany in response to Bellamy's novel, for consideration of this reaction to his impact is treated in the next section of this chapter.

According to German bibliographies, the first review of *Looking Backward* was that of "K." which appeared in June, 1889, in *Die Neue Zeit,* the monthly theoretical publication (from 1884 to 1911) of the Socialist Party. In his article, the reviewer made a distinction between two types of modern socialist Utopias. The one, he thought, originated from "the poetical desires of the working class" and the other from "the need of socialists belonging to higher levels of society who were trying to propagandize their ideas in their own circle."[10] To "K.," Bellamy and his book belonged in the second category.

Although "K." began his review with the denial that *Looking Backward* was a work of art, he later admitted that the literary method and the style had contributed to its success in the United States. He acknowledged that the novel had been particularly influential with the American public in general and with the laboring class in particular; and he ended his review with a full quotation of the famous analogy of the coach which, he remarked, was one of the best pictures in the book—but one which had not been printed in the German edition published in *Arbeiter Bibliothek.*[11] "K." absolutely rejected, however, Bellamy's view not only of socialism but of the role played by the proletariat in achieving the new society.

"K.'s" major criticism was, therefore, launched against Bellamy's picture of the society of the year 2000, his concept of how it was to be achieved, and his seeming ignorance of Marxism. Denying that Bellamy had drawn a vivid picture of a future state, he asserted: "Instead of giving us a picture of the life and activity of the new society into which Julian West has been transferred, the author keeps us in the house of Dr. Leete, where this man or his daughter reports what the new Boston looks like."[12]

More specifically, "K." took issue with Bellamy because contrasts between the city and the country, labor, and intelligence remained. He also thought that women had too privileged a position and that Bellamy had completely disregarded the "pedagogical, hygienic, and economic advantages of well-organized . . . children's work" as well as those of free medical service.[13] Furthermore, Bellamy's society did not appear as a socialist one after a hundred years had elapsed: it was, wrote "K.," one which could be immediately established by revolution! Because he considered peaceful, evolutionary achievement of an ideal society as impossible, "K." charged Bellamy with being uninformed about socialist literature and particularly about the contents of *Das Kapital.*

In keeping with his denunciation of peaceful evolution, "K." also accused Bellamy of lacking understanding of the role the workers' movements and of wanting, therefore, the cooperation of all classes in attaining the ideal state. The reviewer concluded that Bellamy had absolutely "no idea of the extremely deep gulf between the classes, the historical role of the class struggle, and its importance as a motive for social progress."[14] He did, however, offer Bellamy some excuse for his ignorance, for he remarked that Bellamy could only know the workers' movement superficially because of its lack of a strong organization in the United States.

He concluded that Bellamy's socialism was incomplete and naïve and that it occupied a middle position between that of the old Utopists and that of the modern scientific socialists. But, he admitted, its incompleteness might be of "symptomatic importance,"[15] so far as its propaganda value was concerned among the workers of the world. Among the laborers the book would be effective because of its criticism of existing society. In America, it would be effective because it would familiarize people with socialist ideas, and then they would certainly turn to better sources than *Looking Backward.* But as to the effect which Bellamy had hoped to make with his novel, he would— asserted "K."—fail: the workers would not be calmed by the book, the capitalists would not be less disgusting, and the middle class would not be enthusiastic about the future state.

In 1890 the Vienna monthly *Monatsschrift fuer christliche Social-Reform* published a short, unsigned review of *Looking*

*Backward* which, after reciting the wide distribution the novel had had, emphasized that its value was not in its fantastic picture of a future society but in its criticism of the contemporary scene. The reviewer considered Mr. West's description of his own circumstances in 1887—which he quoted in full—to be a fine satire of capital and interest; but he pointed out simultaneously that Bellamy did not really understand the temporarily quite successful struggle of the church against private enterprise, for he came from "North America, a state which came into existence when the Christian order was already breaking down."[16] Despite his critical comments, the reviewer highly recommended *Looking Backward.*

In 1891 the publishing house Reinhold Werther of Leipzig published a lecture, given to the *Deutsch-Sozialen Reform-Verein* (German Social Reform Club) by Hans Gustav Erdmannsdoerffer, which criticized *Looking Backward.* Although Erdmannsdoerffer spoke favorably of the novel because it had awakened an interest in social politics among those who had hitherto cared little about the subject, he also warned that the lucid and often poetic language of the book could be dangerous for the unsuspecting reader.

After reviewing the contents of the novel, Erdmannsdoerffer concentrated his critical comments upon the following characteristics of Bellamy's plan. First of all, the year 2000 would be too soon for society to achieve the sociological and technical standards which Bellamy forecast; such progress required a longer period to evolve. Second, he doubted that economic development would tend toward the formation of the large trusts and monopolies that Bellamy, with much exaggeration, had depicted. Furthermore, combination would certainly not occur in agricultural areas, for the trend there was toward the family unit. Third, he considered Bellamy's optimistic view of production as possible in cities and in large industries; but he also asserted that such production would not be possible among agriculturists because they would have to be tightly controlled by a central supervisor and they would also be dependent upon climatic conditions. Fourth, in speaking of the industrial army, the free selection of profession, and the allotment of working time according to difficulty, Erdmannsdoerffer's main objection was that Bellamy was overly optimistic about mankind. He also directed against Bellamy and his society another stock argument against socialism—the danger of overpopulation.

In his summation, Erdmannsdoerffer concluded: *"Es wird nicht sein"* (It will not come true). He added, however, that,

though achievement of Bellamy's plan had been proved un-
feasible, no one should believe that the society of the time
was wonderful or that it should remain as it was. He then
stated: "No, there are many things rotten in state and society,
trade and exchange, morals and customs. And it was Bellamy's
great merit to have pointed these out with burning letters.
But what we miss with him is the least shadow of an attempt
to carry out his work on the facts given."[17]

The most violent attack upon Bellamy's Utopian concepts
was also launched in 1891 in a pamphlet written by Dr. Heinrich Fraenkel entitled *Against Bellamy! A Refutation of the
Socialist Novel 'Looking Backward' and the Socialist Future
State in General.* His motto from *Hamlet* was, "Though this
be madness, yet there is method in it." Dr. Fraenkel, who reflected both the fashionable humanistic and the anti-socialist
views of his day, based his criticism upon Bellamy's desire
to improve the plight of the working class. Although Dr. Fraenkel did not lack a desire for social justice, he felt that Bellamy's
plan was insane. Because of his attitude, he criticized, one by
one, the labor system, the methods of exchange and the credit
cards, the forecasted cultural and religious development, the
equality of men and women, and the lack of control of the
birth rate.

Like Erdmannsdoerffer, Fraenkel believed that development
of the technical possibilities of the nineteenth century could
not be attained within a century. He was also sceptical of man's
moral improvement and, therefore, of his ability to create the
social atmosphere Bellamy had depicted and of his willingness
to do the unpleasant or dangerous tasks for the sake either of
the commonwealth or of shorter working hours. To Fraenkel,
men were motivated either by high wages or by a threat to
their existence. After posing a rhetorical question[18] as to
whether or not Bellamy himself believed men capable of such
development, Fraenkel asserted that Bellamy's system would
work only in a society comprised of ideal people.

Besides criticizing *Looking Backward,* Fraenkel violently attacked the German socialists for having written Bellamy's
ideas on their banners or for having gone even beyond that
action. He finally concluded that socialism could best be
halted and refuted by actions: by voluntary social reforms
and by laws which protected the interests of the workers.

In the same year Dr. J. Jastrow referred to *Looking Backward* in his review, published in the *Jahrbuch fuer Gesetz-*

*gebung, Verwaltung and Volkswirtschaft im Deutschen Reich,*
of the Utopian novel *Freiland* by Theodor Hertzka.[19] In referring to Bellamy's use of the comparison of individual umbrellas
to the fully covered and protected streets of the ideal state,
Jastrow stated that he thought it "the most important phrase
that the literature of the day had put forth in popularizing
an economic theorem."[20] He asserted, however, that, from an
over-all view, Hertzka's novel was a finer literary work than
Bellamy's.

When Dr. Friedrich Kleinwaechter, professor of political science at the University of Czernowitz, published *Die Staatsromane—Ein Beitrag zur Lehre vom Communismus und Socialismus* (1891), he wrote in the preface that one of his reasons
for writing his history of political Utopian fiction was "that in
the last months of 1889, rather simultaneously, two new political Utopian novels were published which belong by far to the
best ever written. These are Bellamy's *Looking Backward* and
Hertzka's *Freiland*."[21]

In his history, Kleinwaechter divided the "state novel" into
two categories: the political Utopian novels, such as Xenophon's
*Cyropaedia;* and the economic Utopian novels which he sub-
divided into socialist ones, such as Plato's *Laws* and Harrington's *Oceanus;* the communist ones, such as Plato's *Republic,*
More's *Utopia,* and Campanella's *City of the Sun;* and the semi-
communist Utopias, such as Bellamy's *Looking Backward.* He
stated that this listing of Bellamy's Utopia was justified because
Bellamy limited nationalization of property to the means of production and did not extend it to consumption as well. Bellamy
was, however, misunderstood by Professor Kleinwaechter; for
he definitely stated that all means of consumption and production were to be collectively owned.

After an extensive summary of the contents of *Looking Backward,* Kleinwaechter considered Bellamy's economic concept,
which he thought could be best described by the title of the
Malkowsky translation: *Everything Nationalized (Alles verstaatlicht).* Although he had very little space left for criticism after
his lengthy résumé, Kleinwaechter wondered—as had many of
Bellamy's readers—how the society of One Great Monopoly was
going to be achieved and whether the property of the stockholders would be confiscated or whether they would be com-
pensated for it. He also stated that, despite all of Bellamy's
endeavors to insure equality, a certain inequality remained.
His laborers were paid with shorter working hours when they

did hazardous or unpleasant tasks; to the professor, there was not much difference between higher wages and shorter working hours.[22]

Also in 1891 Dr. Richard Loewenthal published in Berlin a pamphlet entitled *Der Staat Bellamy's und seine Nachfolge* which incorporated some unusual criticism presented in the guise of a fantastic story. During a ride in an extraordinarily fancy airship, Dr. Loewenthal learned from an angel-like figure why Bellamy's state was doomed to fail and that only a new religion called *Cogitantenthum*, based on increased scientific knowledge, would overcome the pessimism of the late nineteenth century.

Dr. Loewenthal also criticized the regimentation and the role of women in Bellamy's ideal state. He expressed his attitude to the first with the statement that it would be wrong to convert mankind into a "huge flock of sheep"[23] in order to solve society's social problems. Toward the problem of women, whom Bellamy had portrayed as marrying only those who had acquitted themselves creditably as workers, he assumed an unusual attitude: the influence of the emancipated women would become so great that seeking their favor would be as corruptive as money had been in the old society. He stated that physical beauty would become the first quality necessary for advancement in the ranks of the industrial army. Furthermore, since marriage, because of women's financial independence, would no longer be contracted for economic reasons, physical defects would doom a person to celibacy.

In 1892 Carl Tiburtius published a booklet entitled *Bellamy als Lehrer* (The Teacher Bellamy) in which he emphasized that, although Bellamy's theory of communism did support the aim of the German socialists, he was not to be identified with them. Since the German critics were not able—as they would wish—to brush Bellamy's book aside with the statement that it was just another Utopian novel, they were forced to create a series of counter-Utopias. This method, thought Tiburtius, would result only in an unfavorable comparison of their efforts with Bellamy's "first-class piece of art."[24]

Although Tiburtius admitted the artistry of Bellamy's novel, he pessimistically took exception to many of his concepts. First of all, he did not believe that the world peace foreseen by Bellamy would be possible; but he added that the social idea of the International was an important move toward that goal. Second, he, like Fraenkel, believed that hunger was a better spur than personal ambition, and that one of the main obstacles to achieving a communist society would be laziness. Third, Tiburtius stated—like both Erdmannsdoerffer and Fraenkel—that, although Bellamy's system would be workable in large industries, it would fail with agriculture where dependency upon weather and daylight would never permit either regular working hours or sufficient control of the workers. Fourth, the technical development envisioned by Bellamy would not occur because the supply of coal, the main source of energy, would have so decreased by the year 2000 that instead of progress there would be technological regression. Fifth, Bellamy's plan for marriages based solely upon love and fitness and freed from economic ties or burdens would be disastrous, for it would lead to overpopulation. To Tiburtius, a communal society without any regulation of marriage by special licenses or some kind of *Codex Malthusianus* was doomed.

Relative to the possibility of establishing a communist society, Tiburtius assumed a different and rather interesting point of view. He did not accept Bellamy's peaceful evolution, for he thought that only a German emperor—who would have the confidence of the people and the military power—could introduce and establish such a system. Once established, whether it would be workable or not "no power and wisdom on the throne could guarantee."[25] Tiburtius also doubted whether Bellamy had such wisdom; for he remarked in his conclusion that, although readers could not learn from the American what the world of the year 2000 would be like, Bellamy served a valuable purpose in that he made them think about the future. He warmly recommended *Looking Backward* to young people in particular as a product of idealism from which they could learn about the equality of men.

In 1893 Moritz Brasch dealt with Bellamy's success in Germany and with his Utopian predecessors in an article in the quarterly *Deutsche Revue*.[26] After reviewing the books of the most well-known Utopists after Plato—More, Campanella, Francis Bacon, Harrington, Cabet, and others—Brasch concluded that readers should not take *Looking Backward,* a product of fantasy, too seriously; it would, he announced, be forgotten as soon as Cabet's *Voyage en Icarie*. Completely misjudging Bellamy's influence, he further advised that no one should seriously care about trying to refute Bellamy's theory; it would be demolished by satires and parodies.

In 1894 Franz Sintenis gave a series of literary lectures about Hermann Sudermann, Heinrich Seidel, Mark Twain, and Edward Bellamy which was published in Jurjew, Estonia. Sintenis stated that "in the long run America would not be able to do without academically educated men—nor could it struggle too long against that respect which piety and courtesy prescribe to educated people."[27] He then stated that America did have at present both these men, as well as this education, and that "we find both advantages united in Edward Bellamy."[28]

After illustrating the differences between Mark Twain and Bret Harte on the one hand and Edward Bellamy on the other, and after stating that the Utopian's *Dr. Heidenhoff's Process* and *Miss Ludington's Sister* were satisfying to him because of their "amiable naïveté," he emphasized that he doubted, however, that the achievement of the ideal society which Bellamy had portrayed in *Looking Backward* would satisfy even a small portion of humanity. He immediately added, however, that— because of the immense effect *Looking Backward* had had on both sides of the Atlantic—Bellamy could not have been too much of a dreamer. Bellamy must, he thought, "have expressed the desires of many people."[29] He then concluded his inter-pretation with the statement that "Mark Twain is a humorous mocker; Bellamy, a socialist enthusiast."[30]

When *Equality* was published in Germany, it was immedi-ately reviewed in the weekly *Die Neue Zeit* on February 5, 1898. The reviewer, a staff member named Julie Romm, con-sidered *Equality* to be an improvement over *Looking Backward* because of Bellamy's display of economic knowledge. To her, "the most interesting and most important facts of this new book are its economic explications, which, though sometimes a bit tiresome because of their longwindedness, are extremely clear and understandable and show a certain progress in Bellamy's theoretical development."[31]

Much less the aggressive, critical reviewer than that of *Look-ing Backward* had been, Romm made little criticism but gave an extensive, illustrated summation of *Equality*. She did criti-cize Bellamy's non-Marxist attitude toward the class struggle; but she believed that he was sympathetic with it because of the chapter "The Strikers." To her, Bellamy remained, how-ever, the ideologist who—despite his recognition of the unten-ability of capitalism—refused to see the economic necessity of revolution.

Warmly recommending the book, she also drew special at-tention to the now famous "Parable of the Water Tank" which she thought contained Bellamy's criticism of capitalism *in nuce* and which was "characteristic of his view in the good as well as in the bad sense."[32] She added, however, that as soon as

Bellamy left the field of economics he "sails without rudder and compass, driven by fancy and inclination and personal sympathies and antipathies on the boundless sea of Utopia."[33] In conclusion, Julie Romm remarked that she found it remarkable not only that Bellamy could be so optimistic about the future of mankind but that his honest nature could permit him to agree with the old prejudices about segregation. And with this remark, Miss Romm showed that she had either misinterpreted Bellamy or had not thoroughly digested what he meant; for Bellamy aired no racial or religious prejudices. He always made it quite clear that his ideal world was for people of all colors—and all sizes!

On December 4, 1897, the weekly literary magazine *Das Magazin fuer Litteratur* published a review of *Equality* by Ernesto Gagliardi.* To the reviewer, *Equality* was more a philosophical and political book than *Looking Backward,* but he treated it in an ironic manner. In reviewing its contents, Gagliardi pointed out that the difference between the new era and the nineteenth century was portrayed with drastic contrasts —and, of course, in favor of the new society. He also regarded as unbelievable and as fanciful Bellamy's forecasts that commodities would be made from paper or that women could be independent and yet charming.

After ironically comparing the new social order to a huge consumer cooperative, Gagliardi regretted that Bellamy had only superficially reported how the human being, with his complexities of good and evil, would fit into this new order. Gagliardi then launched further criticism with a series of questions: Would passion and vice cease to exist when poverty had been abolished? Would the possession of necessary items protect humanity against greediness for an abundance of luxuries? Would status seekers really cease to exist? In his conclusion, he reflected his negative attitude toward *Equality* with the following statement: "Perhaps Bellamy has left these questions and some others unanswered on purpose in order to present us a third book. God forbid."[34]

## III  Later Criticism

As has already been noted, the criticism in Germany after 1900 of Bellamy's Utopian fiction was confined for the most part to doctoral theses, prefaces to new editions of *Looking*

---

* Gagliardi was an Italian journalist; he is also discussed in Chapter XII.

*Backward,* or to histories of Utopian literature. The first thesis was that of Ottmar Weichmann: *Edward Bellamy's 'Ein Rueckblick aus dem Jahre 2000 auf 1887' im Zusammenhange mit den Staatsromanen der Vergangenheit* (1908). Although the announced purpose of the study was to show the relationship between Bellamy and earlier Utopists, Weichmann did little more than point out that Campanella could be regarded as a forerunner of Bellamy so far as government management of production and consumption was concerned; that a title similar to Bellamy's had first been used by an anonymous French author (Sebastien Mercier) for his book *L'an deux mille quatre cent quarante;* and that there were—to him!—similarities to be found in Varaisse's *Severambes,* where "production of goods is carried out by the state and every citizen receives his share of the food and other products for his work according to his needs" and Bellamy's equality of labor and of income.[35]

Instead of being a comparative study of ideas, Weichmann's study became nothing but a brief history of Utopian novels from Plato's *Republic* to Theodor Hertzka's *Freiland* (1889). Although he gave the most consideration to the contents of *Looking Backward* and *Freiland,* Weichmann made no contribution to knowledge; for he thought—as had earlier critics who assessed both books—that Hertzka's novel was more precise so far as economic theories were concerned and that there was no relationship between the two Utopian writers because Hertzka had rejected any type of communism in favor of co-operatives. The profundity of his study of *Looking Backward* may be judged by Weichmann's regret that Bellamy had omitted describing the economic and moral benefits to the individual inhabiting his moral industrial democracy.

In contrast to the superficial contents of Weichmann's thesis, that of Fritz Koch—*Bellamy's Zukunftsstaat* (1924)—contained not only a thorough analysis of *Looking Backward* but also some of the best German criticism of Bellamy's theories. Koch concluded that the two basic prerequisites of Bellamy's ideal state could not be confirmed: "Concentration of capital and enterprises will neither reach such dimensions that the future state will emerge from the present state all by itself—nor will the hope in the 'new people' be fulfilled. The facts employed to confirm these hopes are not satisfactory: Ambition is not a common feature of all people; patriotism does not occupy everybody at any time to such an extent that it could serve as a constant regulator of will-power."[36] The result of

Bellamy's state would, he thought, be worse than present conditions.

To secure justice, to achieve international peace, to improve morality, and to prevent bureaucracy in the future state, Bellamy provided equality—economic and political and social equality. But economic equality, thought Koch, could never be achieved with Bellamy's principles; for equal possibilities could not necessarily equalize individual needs. When seen from the viewpoint of different requirements, Bellamy's principle of equality became, therefore, inequality.

When Koch considered the earlier arguments made against Bellamy's ideal society, he agreed that, even if absolute equality could be maintained, Bellamy's state would be impossible to achieve. Destruction of family life and overpopulation would have disastrous influences upon the morality and economic welfare of the citizens; and the bureaucracy necessary to control the economy would further general corruption.

Koch also rejected Bellamy's arguments against the capitalistic system, for he reasoned that they were generalizations based upon features characteristic of only the earliest phases of capitalism. Koch also asserted that Bellamy's prophecy of an abundance for all resulted from his exaggerated estimate of the beneficent effect of centralization and from his unjustified assumption that hitherto unknown technical progress would occur in the future. Instead of the new society's stimulating technological development, Koch believed that its governmental system—bureaucracy—would halt progress. He also argued that, if Bellamy's state promised a decrease in non-productive labor (middlemen, lawyers, advertisers, and tax collectors), increased demands upon the government would require other employees who would not be productive. For all these reasons, Koch concluded that the efficiency of a collective state would lag behind that having free enterprise. He stated: "Abundance of goods, however, is the *conditio sine qua non* for Bellamy's ideal society. But as this cannot be fulfilled, Bellamy's state would be unable to survive. The sketch of his dreamland which he presents is the creation of an ingenious but fanciful head which omitted to consider realities sufficiently—it is, in other words, a Utopia."[37]

In 1929 Karl Sengfelder completed his dissertation *Utopische Erziehungsideale und praktische Schrulreformversuche der neuesten Zeit* (Utopian Ideals of Education and Latest Practical Education Reform Experiments) which consisted of two major divisions: (1) Utopian novels and social reform programs; and (2) the comparison between practical educational reforms and experiments and Utopian theories.* After presenting a historical review of Utopian educational ideals, during which he quoted the comments from *Looking Backward* relative to this subject, Sengfelder turned to a consideration of the realization in Germany of 1929 of the ideas expressed by Bellamy, Cabet, Hertzka, Fourier, and others. He thought that their suggestions about unity of academic and professional-vocational training, close contact to nature and agricultural work as a compensation for mental work, equal educational rights for women, increased facilities for adult education programs, and the stress upon better understanding of economics had already been implemented in various German experimental and ordinary schools. Sengfelder concluded, however, that the application of these ideas had not been due to the influence of Utopists but to that of theoretical pedagogues.

In 1926, 1936, and 1938 three other doctoral dissertations were devoted to a consideration of Edward Bellamy in respect to Utopian fiction, to German Utopias, or to the Utopian novels of William Morris. Two of these were written in Germany but the other, written in the United States, was concerned with Bellamy and the pre-World War I German Utopian fiction.

Dr. Karl Heisig's *Edward Bellamy und William Morris als Utopisten* contained, first, a definition of Utopian fiction; second, a review of the Utopian literature of Plato, More, and Campanella; third, a historical delineation of the economic, social and political development of nineteenth-century England; and fourth, an extensive analysis of Bellamy's *Looking Backward* and Morris' *A Dream of John Ball* and *News from Nowhere*. Heisig was particularly concerned with their concepts regarding dress, their criticism of the bourgeoisie, their reasons for and the form of their predicted societies, and their basic principles. After comparing the two systems, Dr. Heisig drew his conclusions—but this section of his thesis was lost from the only accessible extant copy.

Wolf-Dietrich Mueller's *Geschichte der Utopian-Romane der Weltliteratur* (History of Utopian Novels of World Literature) of 1938 briefly listed the contents of *Looking Backward* but merely repeated parts of Fritz Koch's criticism and referred

---

* In the United States, Gildo Masso's *Education in Utopia* was published in 1927; he also tried to determine to what extent the ideas of the Utopians had been employed.

to earlier criticisms and counter-Utopias. The pioneer study of the influence of Bellamy upon German Utopian novels is contained in a thesis written in the United States by Edwin M. J. Kretzman, *The Pre-War German Utopian Novel, 1890-1914* (1936), which presents an extensive examination of the social background which produced the German Utopian literature of the period; the impact of Bellamy in Germany upon Utopian fiction; and the fantastic, socialistic, anti-socialist, and technological Utopias published in Germany.

Though Kretzman praised Bellamy's "passionate sincerity and obvious humanitarianism,"[38] he was critical of his ideal society because ". . . the form in which Bellamy had depicted the socialist state of the future, . . . was not a happy prospect." To Kretzman, "Bellamy's government owned and operated state is only an anticipation of planned capitalism and has merely the virtue of being honest. Instead of having a *sub rosa* control of the government by certain economic groups under the pretense of democracy, the government has frankly and openly assumed control of all the economic functions and administers them through a bureaucracy which can become just as oppressive as the former state of affairs."[39] Kretzman admitted, however, that Bellamy had created a very important character for Utopian novels: that "of the passionate, sincere, well-intentioned reformer," Julian West. He added, however, that, in all the anti-Bellamy or anti-socialistic Utopias, Julian West "becomes the gullible dupe of people more clever and less scrupulous than he."[40]

Turning from the theses which Bellamy's ideas and popularity provoked to the prefaces issued in new editions of *Looking Backward,* that of Clara Zetkin in 1914 immediately attracts attention because it was written by a staunch Marxist socialist. After emphasizing that the background which produced *Looking Backward* also accounted for its "short period of popularity" in the 1890's, Clara Zetkin described the era: "Crises, epidemics of bankruptcy, years of strikes, demonstrations by the unemployed, and bloody clashes between exploiters and exploited made vast circles in the United States aware of the fact that there must be something to improve in the organization of labor. This knowledge found its expression in Bellamy's novel."

Bellamy was, however, to be considered a Utopian because he was a social inventor who intended his completely developed system "to create the new social order theoretically in advance." He was also not a scientific socialist because, declared Clara

Zetkin, he had not endeavored "to uncover those powers and laws in society which necessarily lead to higher forms of society." Although he had seen the tendencies which in a capitalistic society would, she admitted, prepare the way for nationalization of production, Bellamy had not seen "the human power [Marx's revolutionary proletariat] which knowingly and willingly must carry these tendencies to victory."

Just as she criticized Bellamy for not envisioning a revolution, so did she attack his Nationalist Party because it was neither the creation of nor the party of the proletariat. She thought, however, that the constitution of Bellamy's party was due to his lack of historical education as well as to the political backwardness, the splits, and the weaknesses of the American proletarian movement of his era. Despite her criticism, she concluded that the idea of the Nationalist Party was "the beginning of a socialist awakening and unification movement." Furthermore, although *Looking Backward* lacked the depth and the precision of scientific socialism, it was full of critical and fertile ideas about today's and tomorrow's society and could, therefore, "still . . . give much to the working masses."

Dr. Hermann Duncker, who wrote the introduction for the 1949 edition of Clara Zetkin's translation, was far more complimentary to Bellamy than many others had been. Although he regarded *Looking Backward* as a "socialist Utopia,"[41] its ideal society was based on tendencies toward technical progress and upon social-economic contradictions within the capitalistic system. Bellamy had not presented, however, a portrait of an early socialistic society but had described a completely developed one. His portrayal was important not because he had tried to present the solution to particular problems of life in a socialist society but because it might lend more flexibility to socialist fantasies.

The strongest and most valuable parts of *Looking Backward* were—as in all other socialist Utopias—the criticism of the contemporary situation and the description of the future. Bellamy had not, however, given his enthusiastic readers a plan for achieving the ideal society; but, asserted Duncker—who ignored or pretended ignorance of the delineation of the evolutionary process in *Equality*—the new order should be brought about by "a revolutionary uprising of the masses, which Bellamy had conceived in a kind of socialist people's front, but unfortunately had called the Nationalist Party."[42] Like Clara Zetkin, Duncker then assumed that Bellamy had doubtless favored evolutionary processes because he was not a student of Marx.

Duncker also thought it was interesting that Bellamy "during the last decade of his life, . . . worked hard to deepen his knowledge of socialism. One year before his death he published an extensive continuation of his Utopia with the title *Equality* in which we can find valuable additions concerning the solutions of the old problems of 1887."[43] Duncker asserted that he considered Bellamy no mere novelist who had occasionally produced socialist literature; he had been a conscientious, passionate socialist who had intended to give the greatest publicity possible to socialist ideas in his narratives. Duncker then declared that Bellamy was as little out of date in 1949 as he had ever been.

In 1920 and 1947 Bellamy was considered in two books about Utopian novels. Rudolf Blueher in his study of such fiction, which he considered to be a contribution to the history of socialism, presented not only a background sketch of the economic and political situation of nineteenth-century United States and England, but also a short history of *Looking Backward* and the Nationalist movement. He then presented an extensive analysis and criticism of Bellamy's ideas about a future society.

In his critical comments, Blueher attacked Bellamy for having completely disregarded the power of human traditions and habits. Although he considered Bellamy's society to be "state-organized communism"[44] which had developed from democratic principles and which guaranteed equality, the individual was forced into uniformity. Furthermore, continued Blueher, the people who were to dwell in Bellamy's ideal society would have to be devoid of all passions and weaknesses prevalent among his own contemporaries; if they were not, the system would fail. He reasoned, for example, that their greed for property might not be extinguished; for Bellamy had not realized that bartering of private possessions—all the citizens truly owned in the new society—might lead to the accumulation of "a fortune of goods"[45] and to a new plutocracy.

In considering the incentives for the workers to serve others unselfishly, Blueher posed this question: "Everybody is supposed to do his best; but who causes him to do it?"[46] Like other critics before him, Blueher wondered if replacing competition with desire for recognition and love of work would be sufficient motivation for the worker and for progress. He deemed Bellamy's plan of shorter hours for hazardous or unpleasant tasks to be dangerous because it not only would require an enormous labor force but would also draw intelligent people from needed professions. He also doubted that the morals of the workers would improve if they were under constant, mutual supervision and if other supervisors of production were the pillars supporting industrial democracy.

In Ernst Bloch's brief history of Utopias *Freiheit und Ordnung* (Freedom and Order) of 1947, Bellamy merited consideration in the chapter *"Zukunftsromane und Gesamtutopien nach Marx: Bellamy, William Morris, Carlyle, Henry George."* To Bloch, Bellamy had satisfied the demand for a picture of a future society, but he had presented one which had been rejected by the Marxists. In spite of this reaction, *Looking Backward* was, asserted Bloch, not so un-Marxist because Bellamy had dreamed of "a future as it might be if only the present tendencies (mechanization and concentration of capital) were developed."[47] Bloch finally concluded that Bellamy's Utopia was basically, however, the product of a capitalistic civilization and that, although the author sponsored the nationalization of private property, his plan would ameliorate the social problems but not change the basic pattern of life.

## IV  *Utopian Response*

Further criticism of Bellamy's Utopian society was presented in a flood of counter-Utopias which either satirized *Looking Backward* or presented alternate programs. Because of Bellamy's great popularity in Germany, some authors wrote Utopian novels which imitated his methods and his narrative; and others sought to benefit from his fame by coining titles which suggested a similarity to his first novel. There were also, however, four Utopian novels which sought to develop his plan. Since Bellamy's influence upon German Utopian literature extended from 1891 to 1919, it may be justly stated that his greatest *concrete* influence was upon literature.

The first critical reply to *Looking Backward* was that of Richard Michaelis, an American of German origin and editor of the daily Chicago *Freie Presse,* whose *Ein Blick in die Zukunft. Eine Antwort auf: Ein Rueckblick von Edward Bellamy* was published by Reclam in 1891 and in the United States as *Looking Further Forward* in 1890. To the American reviewer of *Lend A Hand* (1891), Michaelis' book was the "best considered reply" to Bellamy because the author had portrayed how the "terrible tyranny of what in Germany they call Bureaucracy" would be the great danger threatening the industrial army of the future state.[48]

After stating in his preface his objections to Bellamy's ideas of equality and after defending competition as the source of

the progress civilization had achieved, Michaelis summarized
the contents of *Looking Backward* and then began his narrative
with Julian West's initial lecture at Shawmut College, Boston.
Although West was complimentary about the progress he had
noted in the new society, he was surprised when his lecture
earned only restrained applause from his audience. Mr. Forrest, his demoted predecessor who had been the lecturer on
nineteenth-century literature and who in the novel is the spokesman for Michaelis, informs Julian that the audience had reacted
indifferently because of the shortcomings of the new society.

Mr. Forrest's historical research had led to the conclusion
that the new social order was not progress at all and that it
was by no means a solution of nineteenth-century problems.
His criticism and his conclusions are summarized in the following statement:

> I believe I have proved that our state with its institutions which
> presumably are based on the equality of all people is a failure,
> that inequality as founded by nature is not in many respects
> much more depressing than it was in your time, that nepotism
> and corruption grow as exuberantly today as 113 years ago,
> that personal freedom almost vanished completely and that in-
> tolerable slavery connected with cringing and servile obeisance
> toward superiors filled its place, that the members of the indus-
> trial army are exposed to the mercy of their officers, that those
> members of the "industrial army" who are regarded as enemies
> of the government are forced to lead a miserable life which
> may well be called a twenty-four-year hell on earth, and that
> the abolition of competition has caused a regression of intelli-
> gence as well as of national wealth. Indeed, the abolition of
> competition, the shortening of working years as well as working
> hours and the creation of numerous sinecures for lazy favorites
> and mistresses of the influential politicians made production
> decrease to such an extent, while the number of consumers was
> increasing constantly, that our average yearly income today is
> hardly bigger than that of an ordinary worker of your days.
> It allows us only a very moderate life. And there are no doubts,
> according to my opinion, that, if mankind continues to live
> under this system, it is bound to return to barbarism in a couple
> of centuries.[49]

Mr. Forrest then proceeds to express Michaelis' ideas about
the solution of the social problems, and his views undoubtedly
have certain similarities to German social developments of the
1880's. Mr. Forrest believes that there should be a semi-con-
trolled economic life which would include planned production

in order to prevent waste and nationalization of institutions
(such as the railroads, the postal system, and the telegraph)
which serve the public. He also advocates special laws to prevent accumulation of capital and land in the hands of the
few, and he suggests the establishment of producer and consumer cooperatives by private groups. Free competition and
freedom of the individual as guaranteed by the American Constitution are to be maintained in order to save mankind from
regressing to barbarism.

Although Michaelis had admitted in his preface that Bellamy's theory still was moderate in comparison to that of the
anarchists or the extreme communists—which are emphatically
rejected because they advocated free love and destruction of the
family—he included in his Utopia a radical or extreme communist party which might be compared today to that of China.
At the end of the novel, the radicals create a revolution during
which Mr. Forrest and Dr. Leete are killed. Julian West awakens in his bedroom under his house to find that he is still in
the year 1887 and that his experiences in the new world had
been but a nightmare.

Like Michaelis, Phillip Laicus (a pseudonym for Phillip Was-
serburg) published in 1891 his *Etwas spaeter! Fortsetzung von
Bellamy's Rueckblick aus dem Jahr 2000* because he objected
to a society "without God, without family . . . . without private
property"—and because he wished to express his own view of
a future state. To fulfill his purposes, Laicus further described
West's life in the ideal society as a husband and a lecturer in
Boston; as a member of a government mission sent to Cuba;
and, finally, as an observant information seeker in Germany.

Since Laicus was a devout Catholic who regarded marriage
as a hierarchical order which required the wife to be completely
subordinated to her husband, and since he associated Bellamy's
ideas with the atheistic, materialistic ones of the nineteenth-
century German socialist, he felt that the most vulnerable
part of Bellamy's society was that which concerned marriage
and family life. He regarded Bellamy's plan for marriages for
love and affection as a loose arrangement devoid of religious
or ethical standards which could be contracted or dissolved by
merely serving notice of intent. When Julian West awakened
after his hundred-year sleep, he thought he was in the heart
of a family which "presented nothing which would have contradicted" his inherited and instilled concepts; but "when Edith
blessed" him "with her hand," Julian West realized "that marriage here no longer has importance in the life of an individ-

ual. . . . Everything was so much . . . like living with a mistress."[50]

Although Laicus admitted that Bellamy's economic democracy might be successfully realized in North America, he denied that it could function in territories with a southern climate and population. He portrayed, therefore, the corruption and chaos which the change to the new society had created in Cuba because the white population continued to burden the Negroes with all the labor. Julian West was, therefore, sent to Cuba to deliver lectures to stimulate the people to work and to demonstrate the superiority of the new system.

When West learned about the social system of Germany and Edith learned about God from two Jesuits who were also visiting Cuba, he obtained permission to go to Germany to study the government that had been instituted when the people had revolted against the dictatorship of the proletariat which had existed there. The following explanation of the attitude of the Jesuits toward the socialist state are of interest: "Our former Social-Democrats had fallen into the error of believing that there was such a thing as an average man, and that there was a state of affairs most congenial to that person. Therefore, they wished to create the same happiness for all men—one with which everyone would have to be content." They further explained the attitude of the Catholic Church: "Worldly government is acceptable to God, but for the fulfillment of divine purposes. As long as it fulfills this function, every type of opposition is sin. But when the government demands wrongdoing, then disobedience becomes a duty; for if the governments base their authority upon God, then God is over and above all governments, and their power stops at that point where they begin to collide with the laws of God."

The future Germany that West sees—and as Laicus envisioned it—is a mixture of Catholicism and of liberal and socialist ideas. As might be expected, education and family life, which had been restored, are matters of the church and of individuals; but the state, headed by a five-man directorship, is the sole owner of the land of which it sells sections only for the building of houses. The basic industries are also nationalized; but small private industries, which supply luxury items, remain. Money still exists as a representation of "stored labor and as exchange media,"[51] but all investment is controlled by the state.

Conrad Wilbrandt's counter-Utopia *Des Herrn Friedrich Ost Erlebnisse in der Welt Bellamy's* (1891) was a general attack on the socialist view of a future state from the contemporary agricultural point of view and was not, as its title might suggest, a parody of *Looking Backward*. Wilbrandt's hero, Mr. Frederich Ost, an agricultural specialist, is buried alive by a method invented by Hindu fakirs. Because, for some unexplained reason, the witnesses who were to awaken him after a few weeks disappeared, Mr. Ost slept until October, 2001. He was then resuscitated and placed in a hospital in Berlin where he is cared for by Sister Martha, who becomes his guide, introduces him to the new socialist society, and aids him in finding a new existence.

When Ost has recuperated enough to read, he forms a picture from Martha's diary and periodicals of the new society. Because he had known of Bellamy's description of the blessed life of the year 2000, what he reads about the society of 2001 fills him with amazement, disappointment, and criticism. When he is released from the hospital and employed as an agricultural analyst by the ministry of the German chancellor, Ost gains authoritative knowledge of conditions from his conversations with the chief of the statistical bureau and from the chancellor himself—and both evince their deep concern about the future of the socialist, industrial society which had only been inaugurated by a government act of 1993 and which had neglected production of agricultural products. Their concern is justified; for failure of the experiment comes with the outbreak of war in Asia which closes the door to Germany's vital market for her industrial products.

Wilbrandt's completely negative reply to Bellamy is based on nineteenth-century economic assumptions. His attitude toward the contents of *Looking Backward* is exemplified by the remark attributed to the chief of the statistical bureau: "'There is hardly a nonsense Dr. Leete would not think of, Julian West would not believe, and Bellamy not write down.'"[52] Besides his criticism of Bellamy, Wilbrandt presented his own positive views about contemporary social problems in an appendix called "aphorisms on social questions."

Wilbrandt asserted that equality of income, of education, and of the sexes would, when combined with lack of family life and competition, result in stagnation, corruption, and failure. The battle for the personal advantage to be gained from easier tasks would create chaos, lack of production, and, therefore, a scarcity of consumer goods which would cause the breakdown of the socialist government. Fearing not only the role special interests would play but also a decay of idealism and ethical practices, Wilbrandt also feared that there would be a lack of balance of employment and of products. As a result, "the socialist state" would "not fail because there" would be "a shortage of labor but because there" would "be no work for all hands."[53]

Like Richard Michaelis and Phillip Laicus, Dr. Ernst Mueller began his counter-Utopia *Ein Rueckblick aus dem Jahre 2037 auf das Jahr 2000* (1891) by having Julian West, lecturer about nineteenth-century history, learn about the progress of the ideal society. Mueller depicted what the new society had become in thirty-seven years, and its development was comparable to the bureaucracy envisioned by Michaelis.

When West began his lectures about the nineteenth century, he soon realized that not everything which he said was tolerated by the educational administration. He discovered that everyone was closely supervised by the government authorities and that severe censorship existed. When he drew naïve parallels between the French Revolution and the change from capitalism to the new socialist order, his statements were misinterpreted as being critical of the new order and he was forced to cease giving lectures. Bewildered, West went to Washington to see the president, who also misunderstood him, considered him an enemy of the new society, but gave him another chance by giving him a position with the government.

West learned from the president that the intent of the new society—which Dr. Leete had convinced him was effective in securing justice and equality—did not harmonize with personal liberty and with freedom of speech. On the contrary, these liberties only hindered the fulfillment of the program which Bellamy had outlined; for, remarked the president, iron discipline, as well as patriotism, was necessary if the masses were to be kept together. The president admitted, however, that he could not express these ideas to the public; for the citizenry wished not only to live well but to enjoy the liberties it had fought to achieve. His major difficulty, therefore, was that he had to preserve the appearance of having a government based on the American Constitution. He remarked: "Personally I am fully convinced of the truth of the socialist gospel. I want that all should enjoy the fruits of this world. But do all, therefore, have to govern? No! The enemies of the socialist state in the nineteenth century were not so wrong when they called it a huge prison camp. Only when all are slaves can all be satisfied."[54]

When West assumed his new position as a government commissioner in a little town in the West, he gained a more detailed knowledge of the new society. First of all, his wife Edith not only did not anticipate leaving cosmopolitan Boston for provincial Ebertytown, but also had difficulties quitting her job. In Ebertytown, West came in contact with the highly corrupt bureaucracy. Although he tried to realize socialist ideals, he also had to fight not only corruption, but rebellion: and, when necessary, even he employed dictatorial methods to do so. His unsatisfactory position was suddenly ended, however, by the death of the president and by a revolution led by radical communists and anarchists. The liberal forces, supported by the masses who also desired a refined but free economy based on the slogan "to everybody the fruits of his own labor,"[55] finally won the battle for power.

Dr. Mueller fully misunderstood the issue and, therefore, the reason for *Looking Backward*. As a bourgeois property enthusiast, he regretted that in Bellamy's socialist society the virtue of thrift would be obsolete. Because he supported the middle-class family life with its bit-by-bit accumulation of property, he completely disregarded the existence of nineteenth-century socio-economic problems. He did not realize—or want to—that the vast majority of the proletariat had no opportunity to acquire by thrift the property which would enable it to be integrated into the middle class.

In 1893, Dr. Ferdinand Kemsies' *Socialistische und ethische Erziehung im Jahre 2000* employed Bellamy's setting, Julian West as a character, and socratic dialogue to present the arguments of West and Dr. Weiss. Kemsies explained his purpose in his preface: "In order to illustrate the political significance of the socialist and ethical demands and to emphasize their distinguishing features, it seemed wise to deal with the idea of a future communist society; Bellamy's conception of one was, therefore, used as typical." Although Kemsies demonstrated his ideas about ethical education, his book was far inferior to *Looking Backward* in both literary quality and sincerity of tone.

After giving Julian West a German background and education, Kemsies has Dr. Leete suggest that he go to Germany in the year 2001 to study the conditions there. Because he has not planned an itinerary and because he feels somewhat lost after his arrival, West pays a visit to his old high school where he meets Dr. Weiss, the headmaster. When West is surprised that so little has changed in Germany since his student days, Dr. Weiss explains that social change might not be so radical in Germany but that the ethical culture foundation of it was more apparent than in the United States. After devoting two chapters to arguments between West and Weiss about the relative merits of the two systems, the third chapter delineates the new educational system in Germany—one which keeps alive the old ideologies of national pride and of armament.

Dr. Weiss' criticism of Bellamy's ideal society is a repetition of the familiar anti-socialist arguments. He thought that a sudden change to the Bellamy system would result in cruel hardships and that such a change should not occur in Germany. He also doubted that industrial democracy would realize the concepts of liberty, equality, and fraternity; for these were to be achieved only by ethical means since they were ethical concepts. In Bellamy's America of 2000, these rights had only been achieved in theory, for in reality "their liberty is arbitrariness at the top and duress of a prison camp below. Their equality seems to be realized by the denomination 'worker,' but in reality it is nothing but the most eminent inequality. And their fraternity? Economic order is the substitute for that. Their fraternity is only a superficial one, hardly a legal one, and not at all an ethical one because personal freedom is suppressed."[56]

In order to avoid such shallow achievement and development, Dr. Weiss related how Germany—like Bellamy!—had chosen to initiate an ethical education of the people which would eventually cause the capitalists to give their means of production to the nation and thereby avoid any violence. But in the Kemsies system there would be family life as it had been known in the nineteenth century, and the state would not interfere in its affairs. Religion, which also played an important role in ethical education, was also to be wholly a private affair of his citizens. Kemsies' goal—like that of Bellamy, though he seemingly did not recognize a resemblance—was the ethical coordination of the freedom of the individual with the interest of the state.

In 1893 another reply to Bellamy was written by A. Reichardt in *Des Bellamy Zeitalter 2001-2010 Erfindungen, Entdeckungen und Begebnisse.* Reichardt's aim was to show that even in the best of socialist states the weaknesses, failings, and stupidities of the old society would not cease to exist; they would actually be magnified. He intended to fulfill his purpose by writing a satire of *Looking Backward;* but, in the classical sense, his continuation of Bellamy's novel is an attempt to carry the American's ideas *ad absurdum* by drawing partially fantastic and often dreadful pictures of a Utopian society. The end result of his attempt could not have been injurious to Bellamy's popularity because Reichardt's exaggerations were too pronounced and so clumsily presented that they could have affected only his own reputation.

In Reichardt's narrative Julian West no longer plays a major role; for he is overshadowed by a distant relative, Nepomuk West, who is the inventor of the fantastic technology of his era: moving pavements, ultrafast means of transportation, huge airships powered by solidified sun rays, and a weather regulation machine. Among the wild, fantastic inventions of the ideal society is also a method of disposing of the dead. To avoid any waste, the dead are converted into pressed furniture; but this invention is not too successful because it results in superstition and spiritualism. The state has also secretly introduced a new method of capital punishment: extermination in a "chemical bath."[57]

Julian West soon discovers that the happy society and ideal government described to him by Dr. Leete are in reality a police state and a dictatorship; the generals of the industrial army have formed a new oligarchy and have suppressed freedom of speech and all personal liberties. Because of their oppression, citizens had escaped from the ideal society to the West where they had established their own state based on private enterprise. Eventually bad harvests, strikes, and corruption within the higher ranks of the bureaucracy of the ideal state bring it to the brink of ruin, and a counter-revolution ends the Bellamy Age. A new constitution and an emperor of America establish "the peace and security of a monarchy" in the United States.[58]

Among the Germans who were inspired by Bellamy's popularity to write Utopian novels which imitated *Looking Backward* was the famous leader of the nineteenth-century pacifists, Bertha von Suttner, whose *Das Machinenalter,* published in 1889, used Bellamy's method of looking backward in order to launch a violent attack against the ideology and ways of life of her era. Her book consists of a series of lectures given in the late twentieth century about nineteenth-century politics, sociology, education, religion, the status of women, art and science, reform movements, and, in particular, pacifism. Although the author repeatedly pled for social justice, the emancipation of women, an international court of arbitration, pacifism, and altruism on a national basis, she was so carried away by her criticism that her book became neither a Utopian novel nor a manifestation of her program.

Although Emil Gregorovius did not deal with Bellamy's view of a future society in *Der Himmel auf Erden* (1892), he was

certainly influenced by Bellamy's literary methods and he may
have been inspired by the popularity of *Looking Backward*
to refute socialist ideals of a future state. In his preface—which
he pretended was written in 1912—Gregovorius stated that since
the socialist government of Germany from 1901 to 1912 had
ended, he wished to portray what had happened as a warning
to future generations.

Although Gregorovius presented no intelligent criticism of
a socialistic society, he certainly etched a picture of the revolution that had established the socialist government of 1901
which would warn and deter anyone. Having in mind the ex-
cesses of the French Revolution of 1789, Gregorovius depicted
how slaughter of the people had been necessary to establish
order. Although the socialists had tried to install a socialist
"heaven on earth," they had instead converted the whole nation
into a large prison camp disciplined by brutal force. Although
more concerned with portraying the inhumanities and injustices which occurred, Gregorovius was also occupied with some
of the failures of the system. In portraying the favoritism practiced in the factories, he showed how one man, because he
was desired by an undesirable woman and because he was
afraid he would lose his job if he refused her advances, was
forced to marry her. Women, discontented with their lot, attacked the children's home to repossess their children.

The dictatorship of the proletariat failed in the winter of
1912 because the workers, no longer driven by personal interest, decreased their production to such an extent that bankruptcy of the state occurred. Starvation and cold drove the
people to create a horrible revolution—one so horrible that
people committed suicide and resorted to cannibalism. Peace
and prosperity were regained with the restoration of a monarchial form of government.

A clumsy imitation of the fable employed by Bellamy in
*Looking Backward* appeared in *Auch ein Rueckblick aus dem
Jahr 2000*, an anonymous election pamphlet published in Dresden in 1898 to wage war against the "turnover tax." This municipal sales tax was paid on the total amount of annual business,
and the cities of administrative districts were permitted to determine whether or not it would be levied. In the pamphlet, the
hero, Herr Nord, fell asleep while studying the draft for such
a tax; and, in his dream, he awakened in the year 2000. After
regaining his physical strength, he is shown the disastrous
results the tax had had upon Dresden: the former capital of
Saxony had been changed into a small provincial town. In con-

trast, the nearby village of Mickten, which had not permitted the tax, had become one of the biggest, most prosperous cities of Germany. Fortunately, the fate of Dresden was only a dream; but whoever loved his city, warned the author, should vote for an opponent of the tax.

Theodor Herzl, an Austrian journalist and founder of Zionism, presented his concept of a future Jewish state in Palestine in a treatise *Der Judenstaat* (1896) and also in the Utopian *Altneuland* (1900). In this novel he emphasized that his Utopia had a more realistic basis than that of Bellamy; for the American had—like other Utopians—made the mistake of *petitio principii*. To Herzl, Bellamy had accepted as a principle "something which had to be first proved; that is, that people already possess that maturity and freedom of judgment which would be necessary to install a new society."[59]

Herzl's literary devices are, however, comparable to those of Bellamy; but his hero Dr. Friedrich Loewenberg of Vienna spends not a hundred years out of the world but, like Rip Van Winkle, only twenty. Furthermore, Dr. Loewenberg, has not been asleep; he, a desperate, unemployed, young Jewish intellectual, has joined Mr. Koenigshoff, a German-American millionnaire who hates mankind, on a lonely island. After two decades of exile, they decide to return to Europe to see what has been happening. When they enter the Mediterranean via Suez, they learn about the Jewish state which has been founded and which has flourished. They stop at Haifa, the trade center of the New Israel; and there Loewenberg is recognized by David Littwack, the son of a poor Jewish salesman whose family the doctor had once saved from misery. David Littwack then plays the role of Dr. Leete, for he introduces the two men "from the past" to the new life of the civilized world in general and to that of the Jews in particular. David's sister Mirjam assumes the role played by Edith Leete; and the economic manager-general of the new nation, Joseph Levy, gives a recorded speech which is the equivalent of the sermon of Dr. Barton in *Looking Backward*.

Little influence can be found, however, in *Altneuland* of Bellamy's economic system. The foundation of the Jewish state is described "as a co-operative, a huge co-operative, within which there exist various smaller co-operatives as the various tasks demand. And our congress is nothing else but the general meeting of the co-operative, which is called the New Society."[60] The New Society controls, however, the entire economic life and supervises the subsidiary co-operatives and the private enterprises which exist due to the principle of "co-existence of all ways and means."[61]

The general principles of the New Society are, however, comparable to those of Bellamy. First of all, the principle of evolution is stressed, for "the older order must not suddenly perish in order to make the new one possible . . . and an old society does not die for the reason of a new one arising."[62] Second, the New Society guarantees the equality of men and women, free education, health service, and protection against exploitation. Third, the labor force, which guarantees all social and public institutions, plays a role comparable to Bellamy's. Furthermore every citizen of the New Society spends a two-year term in public service, and he usually does so after his education has been completed.

Mention should also be made in this section of two other German imitators of Bellamy's Utopian fiction: Eugen Richter, member of the German Liberal Party and of the *Reichstag* and ardent foe of socialism; and Dr. Theodor Hertzka, Austrian economist. Richter, in his *Sozialdemokratische Zukunftsbilder* (1891), presented a satiric, sometimes ridiculous picture of the downfall of a socialistic society. When Edward Bellamy wrote about the book in *The New Nation* (1893), he remarked that though the novel had "been referred to as an answer to *Looking Backward* . . . it does not appear to be. Its perusal does not suggest that the writer knows anything of Nationalism. His satire seems indeed chiefly directed against the theories of the German socialists and especially those which Mr. Bebel has developed in his books."[63] To Bellamy—recorded Mason Green, his friend and fellow-worker, in an unpublished biography of the Utopian—Richter's " 'prophecy, like all anti-socialistic arguments, is, in the first analysis, insulting to humanity.' " Bellamy felt that Richter had crushed all the " 'finer instincts which determine personal friendships and make happy homes.' "[64]

Although Richter made no direct attack against Bellamy in his description of the development of the social-democratic police state which failed, he must also have had him, as well as Bebel, in mind; for, as will be seen, Bellamy was identified by all with him and with the German socialists. There is only one passage in the book which would indicate that Richter was familiar with Bellamy: the one in which his hero writes about the difficulties of the distribution of labor in the new society because of the socialist principle of freedom of choice of professions and then mentions Bellamy's proposal of varying working hours according to the difficulty of the task.[65] Richter also described, however, the miserable service offered by the communal restaurants which had been so glowingly portrayed in *Looking Backward.*

The very popular *Freeland: A Social Anticipation* (1890) by Hertzka presented, stated Bellamy in *The New Nation* (1891), "new contributions to the subject of the ideal industrial basis of a free society." Bellamy concluded, after a review of the most important new features of the Viennese economist's managed but basically capitalistic economy, that the scheme was not practical but the social criticism was good.[66]

Although Hertzka tried to dissociate himself and his book from Utopian writers who had proposed panaceas for all the sufferings of mankind, he admitted that, after much deliberation, he had decided to present his ideas in a fashion which would be vivid. At the risk, therefore, of being thought to be another romantic enthusiast or of being placed in the same category as More, Fourier, Cabet and others who had mistaken their own desires for sober reality, he had written a Utopian novel. Although he did not mention Bellamy, he must have had *Looking Backward* in mind; for it was, after all, the most popular Utopian novel of the period.

In his second Utopian novel *Entrueckt in die Zukunft, Sozialpolitischer Roman* (1895), Hertzka related the story of Jules who went to sleep, did not awaken until 2093, and who then heard the history of the world from a friend. Incorporated in this Utopian novel are other items typical of Bellamy: the hypnotic sleep of the hero, for so his sleep is later explained to Jules; his feeling that he has known before the girl he meets and loves; the spirit of universal cooperation; the many fantastic inventions; and the argument that changed conditions had led to a different expression of, but not to a changed, human nature. The economic order which Hertzka portrayed was, however, completely different from that of Bellamy; like that of *Freeland*, it is a Utopian capitalistic society. Furthermore, Hertzka portrayed how this social order had resulted from a revolution which had destroyed a socialistic state.

Because of the great popularity in Germany of Bellamy's Utopia, other Utopian novelists were, like Hellenbach, ascribed a relationship with it; or they actually tried to capitalize upon Bellamy's fame by coining titles which suggested his novel. Although L. B. Hellenbach's *Die Insel Mellonta* was commonly called a sister-book of *Looking Backward* in advertisements and catalogues mentioning it,[67] there was actually no relationship between the two Utopias. First of all, the German Utopia had been first published and revised in 1887. Since the 1896 or third edition of the book appeared three years after Hellenbach's decease, it is not likely that changes due to the influence of Bellamy had been made.[68] In the second place, Hellenbach's is a typical island Utopia based on ideas from sources explicitly mentioned in the book: Plato, Voltaire, Rousseau, and Charles Fourier.[69]

Wilhelm Schaefer wrote a satire of socialism and anarchism in *Aus einem anarchischen Idealstaat* (1906); and, as arbitrarily as he combined these two different "isms," so did he ignore the ideological differences of Bebel's *Die Frau und der Sozialismus* and Bellamy's *Looking Backward* by mentioning them together and by making no distinction between their ideas. Schaefer's criticism is presented by a globetrotter who had been shipwrecked in the South Seas and driven ashore to an island Utopia—the ideal anarchist state. During his visit on the island, the hero experienced socialist liberty, fraternity, and equality; but he decided that, compared to the capitalistic societies, the anarchist state had not fulfilled men's desire for these privileges. He also noted that culture, science, and morals were declining; that the economy was not productive; and that corruption in all spheres of social and governmental activity had contributed to the decline. Schaefer directly referred to Bellamy's analogy of the umbrella and the covered streets of his ideal society,[70] but he also extended its significance. His whole island was covered by canvas—which represented socialism—but it had become irreparably rotten and therefore ineffectual as early as 1906.[71]

In 1906 M. Pulvermann published a pamphlet entitled *Die Gleichheit des Zukunftsstaates* which, stated the cover in an obvious appeal to those acquainted with Bellamy, was "*nach dem Englischen bearbeitet.*" The hero of the story sleeps for two hundred years and awakens in a society which guarantees absolute equality. In his pessimistic picture of the society, Pulvermann included some exaggerated pictures of the superficial equality which existed; people, for example, were washed by the state in order to insure hygienic equality.

The magic term "2000" was also employed by Rosa Voigt for the title of her Utopian novel: *Anno Domini 2000* (1909). In this third-rate novel which has the form of a diary, Voigt recorded the gossip of a happy, middle-class, future society. In her pleas for equal rights for women and in her vision of centralized kitchens and household conveniences, Voigt reflects Bellamy's influence. She does not do so, however, in her praise for the German emperors nor in her picture of the improvement undergone by mankind as soon as alcohol had been prohibited.

Germanus (a pseudonym) also sought public attention by employing a reference to *Looking Backward* in his title *Die Soziale Entwicklung Deutschlands im 20 Jahrhundert* (1906). The society which he depicted in this Utopia is a Prussian-type bureaucracy which has half-nationalized industries and has established a maximum income for each citizen. Social life is organized by the bureaucracy which dictates even the most intimate of individual relations, for Germanus presents his method of artificial selection of the best for the improvement of the species. Bellamy, however, had supported Darwin's theory of natural selection as the best system for the mental and physical improvement of mankind. As may be deduced from this brief résumé, Germanus was highly critical of the Social Democrats; but, it should be added, he was just as much so about the Catholics and the liberal and conservative parties.

Among the many, many others who employed titles suggestive of *Looking Backward* for their Utopian fiction may be mentioned Michael George Conrad's *In Purpurner Finsternis, Roman-Improvisation aus dem dreissigsten Jahrhundert* (1895), which makes some satiric comments about equality and a mechanized and highly regimented society; Oscar Justinus' *In der Zehnmillionen Stadt* (1890) which attacks democracy and favors monarchy but contains many technical improvements; Fluerscheim's *Deutschland in Hundert Jahren* (1890) which derived its economic principles from *Bodenreformer* (a group which supported the ideas of Henry George) but which portrayed domestic inventions and an equal income comparable to Bellamy's; and F. E. Bilz' *In Hundert Jahren* (1907) and *Der Zukunftsstaat—Staatseinrichtungen im Jahre 2000* which show no influence of Bellamy's ideas.

Among the German Utopias published from 1891 to 1919 there were four which were pro-Bellamy in their attitudes; and some supported, enlarged upon, or combined Bellamy principles with Marxist ones. In 1891 Koehler's *Der Sozialdemokratische Staat* not only outlined the program of the Social Democrats, but presented a future state which would result from its fulfillment. Although Koehler denied any Utopian ambitions, he admitted the propaganda values of *Looking Backward*. He obviously borrowed, says Kretzman in his doctoral thesis, some features of his program from Bellamy's Utopia; and he justified doing so with these words: " 'No Social Democrat will object to ideal pictures of the future—the propaganda value of which cannot be doubted—which are clearly drawn and hung up at a sufficient distance to prevent their being desecrated. And we certainly can allow ourselves to copy as much of such pictures as we can use to advantage for our immediate ends and for practical programs."[72] Koehler's book was not a very successful nor constructive one; the reviewer of the *Die Neue Zeit* condemned it;[73] and, as we shall see, the Social Democrats denied it.

Hansel Truth's *Am Ende des Jahrtausends* (1891) is a fantastic Utopia which has a hero who falls asleep and dreams that he is living in the year 1999. He finds that many forecasts of Bellamy—television, radio, symphonies—have been fulfilled. The social organization is also similar to that of Bellamy: "All these industries are now in the hands of the state. In the city there are many warehouses where wares are stored: furniture, clocks, machines, foods of all kinds, and also the factories where the requirements for each day are prepared. This house is only one of many and I, like all citizens, am a worker in the service of the state which is the common householder of us all."[74] Furthermore, war has been abolished; women enjoy equal rights and privileges; Darwin's theory of evolution has been employed to perfect the human race; technological progress has contributed to the general welfare of the people: and an elderly, reactionary, ex-lawyer regrets the passing of the system which had enabled him to unravel legal entanglements.

Although Truth gives much attention to the social organization, he seems to rely upon technological progress as the source of the better world of the future. Even the development of *Voland,* an explosive, has abolished war and is employed peacefully as a source of power for all machinery. Although Truth emphasizes that much attention should also be given to economics, he himself is not much intrigued by the social struggle of his day although he devoted much space to its practical problems. As he stated, "In a realistic period the poets must either gaze forward or backward to find something which pleases their fancy."[75] As Kretzman has pointed out, Hansel Truth's main concern was to tell an intriguing, diverting story.[76]

In 1900 Martin Atlas' *Die Befreiung* not only repeated many of the inventions forecast by Bellamy but delineated how science could become the liberator of mankind. In his ideal technological Utopia, there is no economic scarcity and no war; both sexes enjoy economic, social, political and moral equality; the citizens practice eugenics and birth control; the administration is in the hands of the intellectual aristocracy; and the citizens—like those of Bellamy's short story "To Whom This May Come," which had been translated into German in 1894— can read one another's minds—an art which reveals all people's thoughts and insures the existence of a true democracy! Although competition, which had contributed so much to society, is not eliminated in this technological society, its dangers are minimized because of the credit given the citizens.

The following passage shows clearly the comparable views of Bellamy and Atlas of the nineteenth century:

> How could it be different in a society where the material well being of one was dependent upon the suffering of another? The same condition exists as in the animal world, where beasts of prey feed upon the flesh of other animals, and as long as a limited amount of supplies is present as a basis for the existence of mankind (the possession of which means everything that the world can offer) so long also will greed and avariciousness have a natural justification among men, and it will be the natural course of things that each is concerned with taking away the goods of the other, for there is no other possibility of getting ahead. Wherein is this society any better than an organization based upon the rights of booty and combat? One does not use naked swords here, but the cleverer and "gentler" weapons of the social struggle, no matter whether they be called trade, agriculture, industry, or stock-market, since it is either the avowed or concealed attempt of each to increase his well-being or to protect himself against the attacks of the other. Is it the peasant's fault that he envies the wealth and the luxuriousness of his master, when he himself has nothing? Can this landlord, in a world where every man's hand is turned against his neighbor, can he be blamed for exploiting the poverty of the peasant and making him labor for a wage that barely suffices to keep body and soul together? If he did not do it, he would soon be left behind in the ruthless struggle for material goods, and those who were less considerate and magnanimous than he would soon ruin him completely.[77]

Perhaps the most positive, interesting result of Bellamy's influence in Germany upon Utopian fiction is Heinrich Stroebel's *Die erste Milliarde der Zweiten Billion* of 1919, a book which marked the end of Bellamy's influence upon German literature. Stroebel—who was originally a Marxist socialist, a political journalist, a leader of the Social Democrats both before and after World War I, and a member of the *Reichstag*— seemingly found any party too narrow. After the defeat of imperialist, militarist Germany at the end of World War I

and after the subsequent socialist revolution at the beginning
of the Weimar Republic, Stroebel decided that the time had
arrived for the evolution Bellamy had so adequately described.[78]

A true believer in parliamentary democracy, Stroebel's thesis
in his Utopia was that contemporary democratic practices had
to be purified and extended; or, as he stated in words comparable to Bellamy's, the "democratization of democracy"[79]
had now to begin. The instrument he created to accomplish
this purpose was the *Bund Neue Menschheit*—the Federation
of New Mankind—which, like Bellamy's Nationalist group, was
to be above all political parties and was to unite all positive
democratic forces regardless of their original political or ideological concepts.[80] The program of the Federation—like that of
the Nationalists—was to be an educational one.

Although Stroebel's aim in his Utopia was to present the
program for his Federation of New Mankind, he also included
—as Bellamy did in *Equality*—comprehensive criticism of the
society of his day and particularly of bureaucracy, which he
considered dangerous in either a democratic or a socialist state.
The goals for which his Federation were to strive included
internal and external refinements of democracy, complete political and professional equality of men and women, and reform
of existing law and prison practices. The views Stroebel expressed about contemporary fashion and the treatment of prisoners are also quite like those of Bellamy.

Aside from these specific likenesses, it is impossible to say
that other ideas incorporated in Stroebel's Utopia came directly
from Bellamy; for, by the time Stroebel published his novel
in 1919, Bellamy's ideas and the general socialist demands of
various origins had become so amalgamated that it would not
be wise to attribute any of them to any particular source.
Despite this difficulty, Stroebel's *Die erste Milliarde der Zweiten
Billion* may be regarded as the most positive German reaction
to the Utopian novels of Edward Bellamy.

## V  *Influence on German Socialist Party*

The facts already presented about (1) the publication of
*Looking Backward* by socialist publishers with introductions
by socialist leaders, (2) the anti-socialist replies and criticism
of it, (3) the Marxist rejections of its picture of the future, (4)
the socialist improvisations upon it which lasted until 1919,
and (5) its popularity among all social classes of Germany
indicate that Bellamy's Utopia had an impact not only upon
the socialists but upon the middle class which was, for one

reason or another, intrigued by the socialist program. In considering the influence Bellamy had upon German socialists, it is necessary to review, first of all, their status at the time *Looking Backward* was published in Germany, their ambivalent attitude toward the book, and the use which the middle-class elements made of it.

When the first translation of Bellamy's famous Utopia appeared in 1889, the gulf between the bourgeoisie and the proletariat had never been deeper or wider. This breach had been created in part by the Laws of Exception. Passed by Bismarck after two attempts by anarchists to assassinate Emperor Wilhelm I, these laws had prohibited from 1878 to 1890 any political activity which furthered socialism, communism, or anarchism—"isms" which had been lumped together in order to strike at the socialist party.

As a result of the Laws of Exception, the socialist party presses were shut down; the party organizations were dissolved; the members of the party were imprisoned, persecuted, or exiled; and party activity was an underground one. Despite the suppression, it was during this period that August Bebel, the leader of the German socialists, wrote his well-known *Die Frau und der Sozialismus*, which was a classic exemplification of the Marxist thesis that only a socialist revolution could emancipate women. Secretly printed and distributed, this book —besides the classic ones of Marx and Engels—provided the only knowledge available to the opposition and to party members about the socialist concept of the future state. Although *Die Frau und der Sozialismus* was—like Marxism itself—a mixture of prophecy and science with the emphasis upon the former, the orthodox Marxist regarded the book as too Utopian.

Since the Laws of Exception had suppressed socialist publications, the appearance of *Looking Backward* in 1889 was welcomed with enthusiasm by both the proletariat and the bourgeoisie; everyone longed to know what society would be like after the *grosse Kladderadatsch*—the socialist revolution. Although *Die Neue Zeit*, the theoretical organ of the socialist party, had announced that the German socialists had nothing in common with Bellamy's ideology and had even labeled him a bourgeois, *Looking Backward* was regarded as a socialist document by all except orthodox Marxists. As a result of this attitude, the novel engendered two-fold reactions among both the socialists and the middle class. First, the majority of the bourgeoisie condemned Bellamy's ideal society with the oft-repeated words "a huge prison camp"; but, second, a great many others were influenced by it. Heinrich Fraenkel reported in the preface to his criticism of *Looking Backward:* "I know a number of cases in which people, who are far away from any inclination to fancy enthusiasms and who in particular were far from being socialists, were so enchanted by Bellamy's book that they—as one of them said—were shaken 'in their entire *Weltanschauung'* and converted all of a sudden to the socialist concept."[81]

The socialists, whose party had sponsored the publication of *Looking Backward* under the title *A Socialist Novel*, accepted it as a vehicle for propaganda and agitation but rejected its ideology. Bellamy's pictures of the injustices and inadequacies of capitalism were useful to socialist propagandists, but his plan for a peaceful evolution and not a proletarian revolution to attain the ideal society was unpalatable as anti-Marxist. Furthermore, his portrayal of a future society had to be considered as unscientific in accordance with the thesis expounded by Friedrich Engels in *Der Sozialismus von der Utopie zur Wissenschaft.*[82]

When the Laws of Exception lapsed after the death of Emperor Wilhelm I, the socialist party was freed from underground activity and enabled to continue theoretical argument. The topics of the day concerned changes in their program—and the old problem of the "future state" arose. Marxist ideology was, however, gaining power among the German socialists; and it influenced, therefore, the party attitude toward the formation of pictures of the society to be achieved. This Marxist attitude—as well as the problem presented by the question of the future society—was reflected in the closing speech of the party congress which met in October, 1890, to draft a new program. William Liebknecht, leading politician of the party, stated: "Those who want from us information about the 'Future State' should consider the fact that we lack any basis on which we could predict what a state or society, let me say in ten years —nay in one year—would look like. . . . Who would dare to predict what Germany will look like next year? People who ask such questions have no ideas of social problems, no idea of the organic process of the development of the society, and they prove themselves to have unscientific and unthinking minds."[83]

No less a person than Friedrich Engels then explained in *Die Neue Zeit* his reaction to portrayals of the future: "One of the most pleasant differences between the present and the pre-socialist way of thought of the great masses or partisans lies in the complete disappearance of Utopian concepts, the dreaming about the 'Future State.' Not only the new draft of the program is free from any trace of it, but also in our party press as well one would seek in vain for such thing. . . ."[84]

At the same time that Bellamy's popularity was increasing in Germany, the leadership of the party prepared for the death of any opposing socialist view by denouncing it in Marxist terms. When the party congress was held in 1891 at Erfurt, the socialists adopted the purely Marxist Erfurt Program which Karl Kautsky, soon to become the leading theoretician of the party, had outlined. As if in fear of temptation, the socialists then warred against any socialist ideas not consistent with this program; and the socialist reviewer of Koehler's *Der Sozialdemkratische Staat,* which had used the Erfurt Program as a basis for a portrayal of a Utopian society, denounced it! Being a German socialist meant being a Marxist; and being a Marxist meant rejection of all Utopian thought—of all projections of the future state.

Despite the rejection of Utopianism and Bellamy, the socialists continued to pretend that the right hand did not know what the left was doing. At the moment their leaders were denouncing all portrayals of the future, J. H. W. Dietz, the socialist publisher, issued a new edition in 1891 of *Looking Backward*—but one which contained a preface in which the anti-Marxist, ideological shortcomings of Bellamy were clearly stated. Furthermore, as Dr. Heinrich Fraenkel pointed out in his anti-Bellamy pamphlet of 1891, all socialist book dealers and all socialist agitators were promoting the book. To him it seemed that using *Looking Backward* had been effective in winning people to socialism.[85]

In the same year that the socialists were denouncing but republishing *Looking Backward,* a major attack against Bellamy was launched by August Bebel in the preface to the ninth but first legal edition of *Die Frau und der Sozialismus.* Since people associated the two portrayals of the future society, and since Mrs. John Shipley (pseudonym of Marie Brown) had published in New York in 1890 her pamphlet *The True Author of Looking Backward* in which she had attributed Bellamy's ideas to Bebel, August Bebel obviously thought that the time had come to dissociate himself from the American Utopian. Bebel stated that he might have influenced the ideas of Bellamy since the first edition of *Die Frau* had been published in 1879 and since it had appeared in English in 1885. He then asserted that the whole matter of influence or relationship was really insignificant because the evils of the bourgeois society were so obvious that any thoughtful man would conclude, after an analysis of them, that the logical solution was socialism. Bebel then wrote that

> . . . a more than very superficial accord between myself and Mr. Bellamy in the view of various things and certain criticisms cannot be found. Whoever reads or has read our two books and is able to judge them critically will find that Mr. Bellamy is a well-meaning bourgeois who, without any knowledge of the laws ruling society and merely from the point of view of humanity, has recognized, as a good observer, the monstrosities and contradictions of the bourgeois world and has portrayed a future social order in which bourgeois thoughts and bourgeois conceptions break through everywhere. Mr. Bellamy differs from the old Utopians in nothing but the fact that his descriptions bear the dressing of a modern world and that the sharp criticisms of the bourgeois society which marked the old Utopians is missing. . . . Mr. Bellamy is a Utopian and no socialist.

Bebel then remarked that he "would not have wasted a word" on *Looking Backward* "had it not also in Germany been related to my book and used against the Social Democrats."[86] He then called Bellamy's novel "sugar water" and emphasized that "we Social Democrats do not belong to the naïve ones *à la* Bellamy who think that only a decent, logical argument would be necessary to convince our opponents who defend the perversity of present-day social institutions."[87]

As Bebel had indicated in his denunciation of Bellamy's *Looking Backward*, he was concerned because the middle class, eager as the proletariat to discover something about the proposed socialist future, had read Bellamy, had identified him with the Social Democrats, and had then used *Looking Backward* as a basis of criticism of the socialist program. The fact that, despite all the denials of the socialist German leaders, *Looking Backward* continued to be associated with Bebel and German socialists and to be considered the most comprehensive statement of their aims was demonstrated even by the politically well-informed members of the *Reichstag*. When the Social Democrat deputies launched a cutting criticism of contemporary German society during the debate of January 31, 1893, about the budget for the Ministry of Interior Affairs, the deputies representing the National-Liberal Party and the Catholic Conservative Party replied by questioning the Social Democrats about their concept of the "Future State."

When August Bebel replied that the answer might be read in socialist literature, the next interrogator wanted to know in which book in particular this portrayal might be found;

and he then proceeded to enumerate not only Bebel's and
Koehler's books but also Bellamy's *Looking Backward*.[88] During
the widely publicized, four-day debate that ensued, the Social
Democrats were constantly heckled to take a stand about the
future of the social order which had been presented in *Looking
Backward*.[89] The socialists replied, however, from the strictly
Marxist viewpoint which permitted no concessions about forecasts of the future society. Their views were expressed by Wilhelm Liebknecht in his speech on February 7, 1893: "As far
as the 'Future State' is concerned, it is a matter of fantasy.
Everyone, without exception . . . has his future state, even if
one's ideal is situated mostly in the past. . . .

"The 'Future State' is in a certain respect an ideal; science
has nothing to do with it. Our party, the Social Democratic
Party, has never accepted the Utopia of a future state in its
program."[90]

On July 15, 1893, Karl Kautsky gave a clear picture of the
socialist idea of a future society in his letter to Franz Mehring,
a leading socialist politician and later the party historian: "In
my opinion only the Parliamentary Republic can be the soil
on which the dictatorship of the proletariat and the socialist
society may grow. This republic is the 'future state' for which
we must aim."[91] In the second part of his two-part pamphlet
*Die Soziale Revolution* which is sub-titled *Am Tage nach der
sozialen Revolution* (The Day after the Socialist Revolution),
Kautsky made it clear that his intent was not, as the title
might suggest, to present a Utopian picture but to outline what
would have to be done if and when the revolution predicted
by Marx occurred. He also made it quite clear that he considered the revolution to be a historical process and that it would
not be the task of the Social Democrats to "dream up recipes
for the kitchen of the future."[92]

But there were also socialists who did not agree with Kautsky
—and his antithesis was Eduard Bernstein (1850-1932) who,
during the period of enforcement of the Laws of Exception, had
been in exile in England. While living in London, he had established relationship with the Fabians—among whom Bellamy
was also popular—and had been impressed with their rational,
moral, educational program with which they hoped to prepare
for the gradual achievement of a better world for all levels of
society. As a result of the Fabian influence, Bernstein reviewed
Marxist doctrine with the eyes of a pragmatist; and he concluded that developments had not confirmed Marx's predictions.
Bernstein therefore decided that revision of Marx was neces-

sary, and Revisionism was born. In Bernstein's view, the method of the movement was to be everything; and he chose—like Bellamy and the Fabians—evolution and not revolution. When he expressed his view, the party rejected it, Kautsky banned him as a heretic, and Bebel supported the ban. Bernstein served, however, as a member of the *Reichstag* for eighteen years from 1902-1928; and, in 1916 when the Social Democrats split, he became a member of the Independent Socialists; in 1919 he rejoined the Majority Socialists. It was at this time that Stroebel's Marxist-Bellamy book was published which supported also the evolutionary process.

When Revisionism was born, the polemics against the Utopians recommenced. In 1908 the subject of Bellamy was no longer so insignificant as Bebel had deemed it in 1891. Not only did his influence have to be recognized and dealt with, but in the following quotation from the article *"Utopistische Ideen im modernen Sozialismus,"* written by Franz Laufkoetter and published in *Sozialistische Monatshefte,* the effect of his influence may be seen. Wrote Laufkoetter as he attempted to deal with Utopianism:

> The Utopians make things easy for themselves. In their heads they create a world and do not ask whether this magic world can be realized; they simply place it in front of us and demand that we believe in it; they describe a wonder land as being a reality, which exists, however, nowhere but in the fantasies of childish enthusiasts. . . . And this wonderful virgin land is created overnight. Julian West, the hero of Bellamy's *Looking Backward* goes to sleep in 1887 and awakes in the year 2000 in the new society. Are there not even among us numerous people who think that one is able to go to bed as a citizen of a capitalist state and arise as a citizen of a socialist state? . . .
>
> We cannot sleep into the socialist society, we must work our way into it; step by step at hard labor we must conquer every square foot of this virgin land. Therefore, it is not sufficient merely to destroy the old, out-lived society. Rather the main emphasis must be placed on construction. . . . Only a Utopian wants to destroy the capitalist society down to its roots, in order to build a new house on its ruins. The scientific, practical socialist tries—according to Karl Marx—to carry over the achievements of the capitalist era into socialism. . . .
>
> And after all, in reality, the future state will be quite different from that the Utopians describe. There also people will have to work hard in order to supply their increased needs. There will also be a compulsion to work and a control of efficiency.

We do not simply grow into socialism, as the Utopians think, but we must have proper human resources to ⌐ ⌐⌐ter the capitalist situation and form capitalism into a socialist society.[93]

An analysis of Laufkoetter's statements indicate that the socialists held mixed views about Marx—and confused concepts about Bellamy's ideas as to how the future state was to be attained. While still arguing from the Marxist point of view against Utopianism, the socialists seemed already to have abandoned the idea of revolution and to have accepted the Bellamy-Revisionist conception of evolutionary progression. Marxist ideology had become corrupted; and other factors—such as periods of economic prosperity—seemed either to weaken or to contradict one of Marx's theses. Despite the ban against Revisionism and perhaps because of the ambivalent attitude socialists had had toward *Looking Backward,* Bernstein's and Bellamy's basically reformist attitudes gained influence in the ideology and political practices of the Social Democrats.

After World War I and the revolution of 1918, the Social Democrats, the strongest party in Germany, took over the government. As it assumed the responsibility of governing, it gradually surrendered Marxist aims and used its power to alter society through specific legislative measures. Although Heinrich Stroebel's book attempted to combine Marxism and Bellamy in order to present a future objective for the socialists, the program adopted by the party congress at Heidelberg in 1925 almost abandoned completely the concept for a "future state." Bellamy, however, would have considered their step-by-step reform program as a means of evolving his ideal state.

During the period in which Hitler's *Nationalsozialistische Deutsche Arbeiterpartei* was rising to power, some Germans—usually socially inclined but anti-Marxist bourgeois—thought at first that the National-Socialist German Workers' Party would be a version of the American Nationalist movement as outlined by Bellamy since its program had certain superficial similarities to it. These comparable plans included the *Reichsarbeitsdienst,* the compulsory labor force which everyone had to join after his education had been completed; the *Volksgemeinschaft,* the formation of a classless society which combined the *arbeitsfront* (workers) and the *stirne und faust* (intellectuals and inventors); and the appeal for a unified, patriotic, collectivist society to solve the social problems which existed.

These similarities did the reputation of Bellamy irreparable harm because—as all the world knows—Nazi Germany had non-economic aims which were completely the reverse of Bellamy's and which created a world which would have made him shudder. The National-Socialists had a political, racial ideal to fulfill, and the German economy was only an instrument for its fulfillment. Although the means of production supposedly remained in private hands, the National-Socialists developed a dictatorship which completely abandoned freedom of employers and of employees. Although a superficial union of the nation for the solution of social problems was sought, it was not promoted by love but by hatred of a fellow man—the Hebrew— and it was devoid of humanitarianism and of the religious enthusiasm which Bellamy had advocated. Furthermore, the fanatical patriotism of the Nazis was to lead to world conquest by the superior race.

When the Nazis were defeated in World War II, the socialist party of Germany—which had been suppressed by the National-Socialists—faced new problems. The fall of Hitler's Germany was the end not only of Germany as a state but also of the idea of a "future society" in either the Marxist or the Utopian sense. The attitude of the resurrected Social Democratic Party about this concept was expressed by Dr. Kurt Schumacher, postwar leader of the socialists, at the party congress of May, 1946, at Hanover: "We cannot deal with the fantasies of a classless society, with a dreamed goal, if we do not know when and to what extent these things can be realized, but rather we have to deal positively with that which is necessary, and that is the democratic state with socialist content."[94]

In the preface of the 1947 edition of the Heidelberg program, the socialist aim of the postwar party was stated thusly: "Socialism is no longer a far-off goal. The German Social Democratic Party appeals for immediate socialist initiative concerning all practical problems in the state and in the economy."[95] When this statement was reviewed by the congress held in November, 1959, at Bad Godesberg, it was rephrased but its meaning was retained.[96]

The socialist party of West Germany has, therefore, become a social reform party which has surrendered not only its relationship to Marx but to Marxist ideology concerning the class struggle, the revolution of the proletariat, and the dictatorship of the proletariat.[97] As was stated in the program of the principles of the congress at Bad Godesberg, "The Social Democratic Party developed from a party of the working class to a party of the nation."[98] The basic values of today's Social Democrats are freedom, justice, and solidarity;[99] and the party aims to achieve a welfare state based upon democratic principles. The program of the Social Democrats is, therefore, quite com-parable to that of the British and Scandinavian socialists—and Edward Bellamy would view these aims and objectives as the evolutionary first steps toward his industrial democracy. But achievement of Bellamy's state is, of course, not the aim of the German socialists.

In fact, the Marxist and the Bellamy demand for a planned economy based on nationalization of industry has completely disappeared. Today's economic maxim is, instead, "Competition as much as possible—planning as much as necessary."[100] The government is expected to influence or control the national economy only through such methods as taxes, price control, public-work measures, trade and customs regulations, and so forth. Free choice of consumer goods, free selection of occu-pation, and freedom of initiative for private enterprise are important policies in this economically free, competitive society.

The only remnants of the old demand for nationalization or for the cooperative society which remain in West Germany are, first, the enterprises known as *Gemeinwirtschaft*—the pub-lic enterprises which, on a local or national level, are non-profit companies which serve the customer exclusively and which are expected to create a certain balance of economic power and prevent control of the market by giant private enterprises. Al-though the cooperative system exists to increase the efficiency of small agricultural holdings, the socialist concept of agricul-tural policy stresses the family unit. These two socialist policies are, however, completely divorced from Marxism; for the So-cial Democrats of Germany today, though founded in the past and maintaining a certain tradition, have severed all ideological ties with the nineteenth century. Devoted to practical politics, the socialist party of Western Germany has emerged ideologi-cally as a democratic party with social reform ambitions.

## VI  *Reactions of Other Groups, Individuals*

Although it has been noted that both the socialists and the anti-Bellamyites remarked that Bellamy had been very popular and even very effective among the laborers of Germany, it is impossible today to estimate his influence with the trade union groups. First of all, the trade unions were, during Bebel's time, officially independent but associated with various political par-ties. The *Freie Gewerkschaften* (Free Trade Unions) were as Marxist as the nineteenth-century Social Democrats; the Chris-tian trade unions were associated with the Catholic Conservatives; and the *Hirsch-Dunkerschen Gewerksvereine* (Liberal-National Trade Unions) were bourgeois-democratic. Because of their liaisons with these political parties, the unions were permitted no independent, ideological developments of their own.

Second, the fact that Bellamy had minimized in both *Looking Backward* and in *Equality* the role the workers were to play in achieving the future state did not win him favor with the German proletariat. In fact, a columnist of a German trade-union paper wrote as late as 1948 on the occasion of the sixtieth anniversary of the German edition of *Looking Backward* that the book was only "of documentary interest and without any practical meaning."[101] The article, which is highly critical of Bellamy for having neglected the revolutionary role of the trade unions, shows, however, that Bellamy's ideas were not only still remembered but alive enough to have to be considered. A thorough search through all the publications of the various trade unions might show, therefore, that Bellamy was used by these groups.

Bellamy had renounced the labor groups of his own country because of their narrow program, and he also had denounced the churchmen for their lack of support of Nationalism. What he had stated about both groups in the United States applied to the German Christian social movements. First of all, the churches regarded socialism as basically atheistic; and, second, both Catholics and Protestants regarded the achievement of a Paradise on earth as in direct conflict with the doctrine of original sin and with the Kingdom of Christ which is yet to come. Although their view that neither perfect justice nor perfect happiness can be attained in this world would have caused them to reject Bellamy, it did not make Christian social movements impossible. It did, however, limit their attention and their activities to amelioration of everyday problems; and it did cause them to disregard any other future goal than a heavenly one.

Among the social movements sponsored by religious groups was a unique one of the Catholics initiated by Adolf Kolping (1813-1865) and Bishop von Ketteler (1811-1877). The ideological background of this pre-Bellamy movement had been stated by the papal encyclicals, *Rerum Novarum* and *Quadragesimo Anno*, issued by Pope Leo XIII in 1819 and by Pope Pius XI in 1931, respectively. Although the Protestants also had an early pre-Bellamy movement called the *Innere Mission* which had been founded by Johann Heinrich Wichern (1808-1881), it was based on the idea of Christian charity and did not preclude social reform. Closer to Bellamy—but with the Protestant restrictions mentioned earlier in this discussion—were the movements started by Adolf Stoecker and Friedrich Naumann.

Adolf Stoecker (1835-1909), a Berlin court preacher, was not only influenced by state-socialist ideas but he propagated a Christian socialist kindgdom. His movement was directed mainly against the contemporary German Socialist Party; but his ideas had very little influence on the German workers. He had more success among the middle class with his *Berliner Bewegung*, a movement which was anti-Semitic because Stoecker regarded the Hebrews as the center of liberalism. Since his *Bewegung* was geared to suit his own personality and ideas, his movements disappeared shortly after his death.

A colleague of Stoecker, Friedrich Naumann (1860-1919) came into contact with the social problems via the Wichern movement; and he founded his *National-Sozialen Verein* in 1896. The program of the National-Social Federation aimed to reform the state and economy on democratic principles (an idea he shared with Bellamy) and to win the cooperation of the workers in order to create a socialist monarchy. Although Naumann was a staunch critic of the Manchester School, he was also a supporter of a strong state; for he believed that welfare measures could be forthcoming only from the economy made possible by such a government. When his party movement failed, Naumann joined the liberals and lived as a writer in Berlin. After World War I, he was again active politically during the Weimar Republic. Although his ideas of Christian socialism never became reality, he exercised considerable influence upon younger Germans through his publications *Die Hilfe* (1895) and *Die Zeit* (1896-1897; 1901-1903) and his book *Mitteleuropa* (1915) in which he set forth a plan for a German central-European empire.

Comparable to Naumann from the standpoint of their socialist aims, Dr. Joseph R. Von Neupauer's *Der Kollektivismus und die soziale Monarchie* (1909) and Berthold Otto's *Der Zukunftsstaat als sozialistische Monarchie* (1910) also supported the formation of a socialist monarchy. Having nothing in common with Bellamy's concepts, the authors developed their theses as Bellamy had because he had made forecasts of future states popular.

Among others who seemingly reacted to the ideas of Edward Bellamy should be mentioned Dr. Rudolph Broda and Josef

Popper-Lynkeus. Although Arthur Morgan stated in *Edward Bellamy* (1944) that Broda had read *Looking Backward* as a young man and had been so influenced that it had "started him on an interesting career," Morgan gave no source for his statement—and no confirmation of it has been found.[102] An investigation of Broda's *Die Kulturaufgaben des Jahrhunderts* (1914), of his organization of young liberals of Europe which was called "The League for the Organization of Progress," and of his publication *Records of Progress* shows, however, that Broda had ideas which were comparable to Bellamy's.

"The League"—founded in 1910 in Paris and containing among its members such men as Eduard Benes, Emile Vanderveld, Ramsay MacDonald, Aristide Briand, and Karl Renner[103]—had as its aim a human progress which was to be achieved by a non-political, international cultural party. Like Bellamy, Broda argued against affiliation with either the socialists or non-socialists; for he desired to remain free of the struggle between parties. He wrote: "Therefore, the League declines to take a stand for the antithesis of the individualist or of the socialist orders of economy because—since the differences between the classes connected with these groups are too strong—a voice, which is based on biological principles far from everyday life, would not be heard in the noise of the day."[104]

In his program, Broda demanded—no matter what the form of government—absolute freedom of thought for all individuals and a nationalized and planned economy which would improve the condition of the working classes. Broda's social aim originated not from a desire for social justice based on equality of man but from an urge to increase the health and nobility of the human race. Although Bellamy also wished to achieve the mental and physical perfection of man, he also desired economic and educational equality which would, he hoped, lead to social equality. Contrary to Bellamy, Broda did not plead for absolute equality; he wanted equality in legal and educational areas; but he also intended that special support be given to the elite who would take control of the higher positions and responsibilities of society. Bellamy also felt that the "natural aristocrats" should rule the future state, but he planned that they would rise through the ranks to prove their merit and then be given the education they merited.

Strong similarities also exist in the desire of both Broda and Bellamy to renounce the Marxist idea of class struggle and to require cooperation of all groups on an international basis, to use education to improve mankind, to make women social and political equals, to settle international affairs with an international court of arbitration, to support scientific research, and to plan programs for the improvement of the health and heredity of the human race. Yet despite these similarities, no proof exists—or has been located—that Broda was inspired by Bellamy; and, because these ideas were so commonly discussed and demanded, the influence may not have been a direct one.

Josef Popper-Lynkeus' plan for the solution of social problems had some resemblance also to the ideas of Bellamy; for he maintained that the state should provide a minimum living for each citizen and guarantee thereby social equality for all. To provide the necessary wealth of the nation, he created in *Die Allegemeine Naehrpflicht* (The Common Duty of Nutrition), which was published posthumously in 1923, the *Naehrarmee*—the army of nutrition—which was to produce and distribute everything necessary for a decent existence: food, clothing, furniture, houses, medical service, and a small amount of money for cultural expenses but not for exchange of commodities. The state controlled all basic industries including agriculture, the post office, and railroads. Apart from the nationalized enterprises, there would also exist private enterprises which would employ those who had completed or had not yet begun the thirteen-year period of service in the industrial army and which would produce items not provided by the state and not widely demanded. In his Utopia, Popper-Lynkeus sought a compromise between socialist ideas and capitalist institutions; and he tried to consider the equality of man and the demands of the individual.

After World War II, an attempt was made to revive the ideas of Popper-Lynkeus. In 1948, B. Kalkum presented them in a booklet entitled *Utopia 2048*. In it, a summary of Popper-Lynkeus' *Die Allegemeine Naehrpflicht* was presented in the form of a radio address delivered by the president of the German state in the year 2048. It is also a tribute to Bellamy that the revival took a Utopian form and that it made use of the famous year 2000.

Further evidence of the recent remembrance of Bellamy's great Utopian novel occurred as late as November, 1958, in a discussion, sponsored by a university group of the *Katholische Akademie,* about equality and inequality. Professor C. Korth mentioned the social status of Bellamy's Dr. Leete as the possible future one of physicians in society.[105]

VII  *An Estimate*

Although the political and literary influence exerted by Bellamy in Germany has waned, mention of "the year 2000" or of the title of one of his books still evokes response from the older generations. Because of his tremendous popularity with all levels of nineteenth-century society, because he was to provoke so many Utopian and political replies to his ideas, and because he was "used" by both the socialists and the middle class to achieve diverse objectives, it is impossible to assess accurately his influence in Germany. It may be said with certainty that the middle class employed him to circumvent or to argue against the socialists; that some middle-class people were converted to socialistic ideas by him; and that both of these facts probably prevented the more liberal bourgeois groups from adopting or featuring any of his concepts as part of their social programs.

On the other hand, the socialists published him and used him because he was good propaganda and inspirational material; but they also denounced him as a Utopian. Because they were too handicapped by their own ideological loyalties—first to Lassalle and later to Marx—they could not accept nor adopt openly his ideas. How much Bellamy contributed, however, to the general political climate, to the policies of Revisionism, and to the modern moderate goals of the socialists can not be stated. Certainly the policies which the Social Democrats sponsor today are more like his concepts and those of the English and Scandinavian socialists—among whom he was also popular— than those of Marx. Whatever the amount of Bellamy's lasting influence, it may with certainty and justice be stated that few American novelists have so deeply or for so long affected another culture, have been so frequently published and republished, or have been used by such diverse groups. And it should not be ignored that one of the most recent publications of *Looking Backward* was in East Berlin. Although denounced by Marxists as Utopian, Bellamy is still being employed for educational, inspirational purposes.

# CHAPTER SEVEN

# The Bellamy Association of Holland

By

## K. ZYLSTRA and J. BOGAARD

ALTHOUGH Bellamy societies or clubs mushroomed in the United States in the late 1880's and 1890's and although new groups were formed there during the depression period of the 1930's, the largest Bellamy association in existence today is to be found in Holland; but in the 1930's clubs also existed in such widely separated areas as the Dutch East Indies, South Africa, Belgium, and New Zealand. To understand the extent and the character of the influence exerted by Bellamy's *Looking Backward* and *Equality* in The Netherlands, a short description of the pattern of its public life and history is not amiss.

About 1500, the European cultural pattern of the Middle Ages, which for several centuries had been the unifying factor of European public life, seemed to have outgrown its usefulness and therefore began to dissolve. The Renaissance, with its freedom of aesthetic expression but frequent lack of morals, had made its appearance in Italy; and in northern Europe, religious life, with its stress on morals but frequent lack of aesthetic appreciation, began to free itself from Catholic domination. In the so-called Religious Wars, the Dutch people played a prominent role; and the Republic of the United Netherlands was the political result. Although Protestantism of the Calvinistic denomination was the leading cult, tolerance was practiced as much as circumstances permitted. In many respects the Netherlands were in those days an example of freedom and tolerance for the whole world.

The consequences of the French Revolution caused the Dutch Republic to disappear from the scene. After some years of French occupation and influence, the fall of Napoleon enabled the establishment of a constitutional monarchy, the present kingdom of the Netherlands. Following the British example, political parties—called liberals and conservatives—made their entry into parliamentary life. In the social and economic areas, the individualistic point of view ruled.

In the last half of the nineteenth century the character of the political life of Holland gradually changed. The conservatives as a distinct group disappeared. The Liberals—first represented by the *Liberale Partij* which later divided into the more democratic *Vryzinnig Democratische Partij* and into the more conservative *Vryheidsbond,* and then united as the *Volkspartij voor Vryheid en Democratie*—found two religious groups opposed to them. The Protestant group was represented by the dogmatic *Anti-Revolutionaire Partij* and by the more tolerant *Christ.- Historische Unie;* the Catholic group maintained its unity first as *Rooms-Katholieke Staats-Partij* and later as the *Katholieke Volks Partij.* Each of these groups had its own program which dealt with the cultural, social, political, and economic life of the nation—but from, of course, its own point of view.

Towards the end of the nineteenth century the socialists entered politics as the *Sociaal Democratische Arbeiders Partij.* At first a very small group, the party gradually grew; and this growth was at the expense of the liberals whose influence in public life declined. At this time everyone who wanted a radical change in the existing social and economic order—changes which would improve the living and working conditions of the lower classes of society—was likely to be dubbed a socialist.

The Dutch socialist party actually followed the example of the German socialists and adopted Marxist doctrines. There were, however, exceptions such as the anarchists, who formed their own short-lived groups. Oddly enough, however, the larger the leading socialist party became—the *Sociaal Democratische Arbeiders Partij*—the more its faith in Marxism declined. After World War II, during which the party had been dissolved by the Nazis, a new socialist political party—*Partij van de Arbeid*—was formed in 1946 which maintained only a few remnants of Marxism, and these in diluted form. But all the time there were socialists, members of the leading Dutch political group, who—like Frank Van der Goes—could combine Marxist radicalism with admiration for the concepts of Edward Bellamy. Although these socialists did not form a distinct group in the party, they no doubt—because of their position and their literary ability—inevitably influenced it and those who read their articles.

I  *Socialist Translators of Bellamy*

Although Bellamy did not wish to be associated with the
word "socialism" because he considered it to be indicative of
one-sided class interests and because his economic aims were
all-inclusive and his moral principles more profound, it is
understandable that—conditions being what they were—*Looking
Backward* was translated into the Dutch language by a socialist
writer as soon as it became known in Holland in 1889. Frank
Van der Goes (1859-1939), the translator, was well known in
progressive literary circles for his articles in the *Nieuwe Gids,*
a progressive literary journal. Significantly, he became in about
1890 one of the founders and theoretical leaders of the new
socialist movement in the Netherlands. In 1891, he was the
Dutch delegate to the Second International Congress at Brussels; in 1896, he founded the *De Nieuwe Tijd;* and from 1912-
1925, he was the foreign editor of the leading socialist daily
*Het Volk.* Although Van der Goes was a Marxist and although
his independent spirit brought him into conflict with the conventions of his time, he was respected for his upright character
and admired for his brilliant writing.

Van der Goes' translation of *Looking Backward* was published as *Het Jaar 2000* in 1890 by S. L. Van Looy, regular
publishers of Amsterdam. In his preface to the second edition,
Van der Goes wrote:

> It matters little what people say of propaganda literature; the im-
> portant thing is that they read it. That people have read *Looking
> Backward* is undoubted, for the first edition of 1,500 copies was
> sold in eight months. No other socialist book of its size has been
> distributed in Holland in the same quantity. One can say that
> the publication of Bellamy in Dutch has been a useful enterprise.
>
> If Bellamy had meant only a nice story or a wonderful tale,
> the great amount of economy would have made his book a fail-
> ure. Economy is so preponderant in it that evidently he has
> written the book just for that reason. That a work so prosaic
> in this respect could become popular in Holland should have the
> great, pleasant significance of success for all friends of socialism.
> This little book contains more wisdom and truth than all the
> Dutch scientific economy taught in many and extensive works
> from Vissering to Pierson.
>
> Respectable people who are not familiar with the character
> of socialism have criticized *Looking Backward* because they
> could not find in it all their general ideals about life. They con-
> sidered this to be a shortcoming of the author. In my opinion
> it is a merit of Bellamy that he, knowing himself to be only an
> economist, did not try to become a poet or a philosopher. All

the rest of his book has been added only for the sake of read-
ability.

It is economy which he asks to submit to judgment. And just
as little as socialist economy pretends to have found a solution
for all the riddles of life (which some people are inclined to
offer to each other for solution) but only pretends to be a scientific answer of the simple question of how to obtain a livelihood, just as little should one expect *Looking Backward* to be
a complete philosophy. People who ascribe to Bellamy narrow-
mindedness in literature and religion will not be contradicted
by me. I maintain only that he should not be judged with regard
to these matters.

After the publication of *Looking Backward* by Van Looy
in 1890, the rights to the book were sold to Cohen Brothers
of Amsterdam which republished the Van der Goes translation
in 1919. In 1930 Cohen Brothers published a new translation
of the novel by Henri Polak (1868-1943), a Dutch socialist
political leader. Polak, who had begun his career as a diamond
worker, became the founder of the *Algemeene Nederlandsche
Diamantwerkers-Bond*, a labor union which became the nucleus
of the modern trade-union movement in the Netherlands. For
many years Polak served as president of the World-Union of
Diamond Workers; and from 1913 to 1937 he was a socialist
member of Parliament. He not only contributed important
articles to the socialist daily *Het Volk* but he also became in
1932 a member of the staff of the Municipal University of
Amsterdam.

Before World War II, *Looking Backward* was republished
by an unknown translator in 1935 by *Bibliotheek voor Ontwikkeling en Ontspanning* of Zandvoort, and issued in 1937 in
Esperanto under the title *Rigardante Malantauen* by Cohen
Brothers. Since some of the Dutch members of the Bellamy
Association were and are students and promotors of the artificial international language, they—C. Oderkerk, a school
teacher, and others—started an organization devoted to Bellamy propaganda in Esperanto. Through the literature they
published and through letters exchanged with other students
of Esperanto, the Holland Esperantists aroused interest in
Bellamy in people in other countries.

*Equality*, which had first been published in 1897 by A.
Abrams of The Hague, was published again in 1933 by Cohen
Brothers for whom Henri Nolles—a teacher, an artistic pro-
motor, and a member of the Bellamy Association—prepared the
translation.

During World War II, the records of the Cohen Brothers were destroyed by the Nazis, and the members of the firm were liquidated in concentration camps. When the war had ended, the Bellamy Association of Holland published a new edition of *Looking Backward* in 1950 and reprinted it in 1951. It had also reissued *Equality* in 1946, but the book had been published by Phoenix, regular publishers of Bussum.

## II  *Bellamy Association Founded 1932*

Idealistic admirers of Bellamy who were affiliated with no political parties decided in 1932, when the world-wide economic depression began to affect the Netherlands and resulted in an alarming growth of the unemployed, to formulate a non-political propagandist Bellamy association. P. J. Burgers, an accountant for Studebaker Motors, took the initiative; and a meeting was held in The Hague which was attended by M. H. Van der Styl, also an accountant for Studebaker; F. Onnen, an academic engineer; Mrs. A. Nolles-Heuff; and Miss J. Andriessen. The group chose the name of *Internationale Vereniging Bellamy*. Mrs. Heuff became president of the organization, and, when she resigned, Dr. P. Yssel de Schepper accepted the presidency which he held until 1941.

The new Bellamy movement soon found adherents everywhere —everywhere in the Netherlands and, as we shall see, in Dutch settlements abroad. By 1940 the association had over 10,000 members who were distributed among 110 local Bellamy clubs in such towns and villages as Aalsmeer, Abbenbroek, Akkrum, Alkmaar, Almelo, Amersfoort, Amsterdam, At. Annaparochie, Apeldoorn, Appelscha, Arnhem, Baarn, Beetgumermolen, Bergen NH., Berkhout, Berlicum, Beverwijk, Bilthoven, Blaricum, Bloemendaal, Bussum, Castricum, and Cornjum. Clubs also existed in Delft, Deventer, Dordrecht, Drachten, Enschede, Franeker, Giekerk, Gorinchem, Groningen, Grouw, Den Haag, Haarlem, Hardagarijp, Harlingen, Heereveen, Hengelo, Hensbroek, Hilversum, Hoofddorp, Hoogeveen, Hoorn, and Huizen NH. Other towns having clubs—to mention only a few more—were Jelsum, Koog a/d Zaan, Laren, Leeuwarden, Leiden, Maassluis, Minnertsga, Nijhhorne, Nijmegen, Oosterwolde, St. Pancras, Rauwerd, Ried, Roden, Roordahuizen, Rotterdam, Schellinkhout, Sneek, Stiens, Ureterp, Utrecht, Velsen, Vlissingen, Wormerveer, IJmuiden, Zaandam, and Zwanenburg.

As may be deduced from the number of Bellamy clubs that were formed, the association did a tremendous amount of propaganda work through lectures and publications. Bellamy lecturers traveled all over the country, and often large meetings were organized in different towns and sections. Well known among these lecturers were Mrs. A. Heuff, the first president, who talked about ethical subjects; M. H. Van der Styl, economic ones; J. Bogaard, social and economic problems; C. Oderkerk, popular religious subjects; Dr. P. Yssel de Schepper, second president, ethical topics; and J. Horsmeier, Jr., third president, and J. Dik, president of the 1950's, who discussed ethical, social, and economic matters. Besides these popular lecturers, there were also members of local clubs who covered the towns and districts in their vicinities.

The Bellamy Association not only issued copies of *Looking Backward* and of *Equality* in issues of 5,000 or more, but it also published countless pamphlets and booklets which found such ready sale that some were reprinted several times in quantities of 10,000. Some of the titles were: *The Solution of the Crises, Lasting Welfare, Welfare for All, Principles of the Bellamy Idea, Economic Equality, The Profit System, The Bellamy System, et cetera.* The bi-monthly periodical of the Association, the *Bellamy Nieuws* had a circulation of 30,000; but, when a particularly important issue was published, the circulation often increased two or three times. When the Germans occupied the Netherlands during World War II, the group not only had to stop all activity but had all of its records destroyed by the Nazis.

III  *Postwar Bellamy Association*

When the war in Europe ended in 1945, the resurrection of the Bellamy Association started gradually with J. Horsmeier, Jr., as president; for Dr. Yssel de Schepper, the pre-war president, had died in 1943. Since most of the association's records had been destroyed and since the restoration of the communication system of the country took some time, the reorganization was not an easy task.

While the central and western parts of the Netherlands were still occupied, members of the Bellamy Association of the northern sector organized the Netherlands Bellamy Party in July, 1945, with the intent of making it a political action group. The founders of this party were Mrs. A. Heuff, Henri Nolles, Mrs. F. M. Wolfson, Derksen-Staats, P. J. Kremers, and Mr. E. B. Van der Muijzenberg; and they issued a proclamation of their intent to become political without "acting politically"; that is, the group had no intention of maneuvering and compromising in the typical political fashion. The aim of the group was not "to vote for palliatives. Only one aim we have to keep in view, and that is abolishing the profit system and introducing economic equality for everybody, as mentioned by Edward Bellamy in his books." Although the Bellamy political party found supporters in the rest of the country, its participation in parliamentary elections was not successful and the movement soon faded away.

But the non-political Bellamy Association of Holland today still has a membership of nearly two thousand people; it holds rallies and programs in various parts of the country; it publishes not only Bellamy's books—as has been noted—but also propaganda material in the form of leaflets, pamphlets, and a newspaper *Bellamy*, the official organ of the association, which has now been published for twenty-seven years.

One of the most interesting issues of *Bellamy* is the one of March 22, 1950, which celebrated the hundredth anniversary of Edward Bellamy's birth. In this commemorative publication articles were contributed by Mrs. Emma Sanderson Bellamy, the widow of Edward; by Paul Bellamy, his son; by Mrs. Marion Bellamy Earnshaw, his daughter; by Arthur E. Morgan, author of the first biography of Bellamy; by Norman Thomas, famous leader of American socialists; and by Adolf A. Berle, Jr., Assistant Secretary of State during the Franklin Roosevelt administration. Norman Thomas wrote on March 4, 1950, from San Francisco: "I am one of thousands upon thousands of men and women in America and Europe who first was awakened to an interest in socialism by reading Edward Bellamy. He left behind him no organized political party and no democratic program for achieving his good society. But the ferment of his vision and hope still works in the world. Of that fact the existence of your society and your plans to celebrate Bellamy's 100th birthday give proof."

Adolf Berle, Jr., wrote on March 6, 1950, from New York:

Let me offer my greetings and best wishes on the occasion of your celebration of the 100th birthday of Edward Bellamy.

Bellamy was perhaps the most distinguished exponent of the Utopian school of thought in the United States. His ideas have entered in large measure into the thinking of our people, influencing great groups who do not realize how much his writing has shaped their thought.

Fundamentally Bellamy hoped to turn the resources of the rising mechanical developments so that they should be the servants of society rather than its masters. In that case, he thought, friendship between man and man, and between peoples and peoples, could become the principal concern of the human race.

In 1952 the Bellamy Association organized a large meeting at Whitsuntide in the public flower auction hall of Aalsmeer, the international flower center. Nearly two thousand members, supporters, and foreign guests attended. The mayor of Aalsmeer made the opening speech, and he was then followed by Jacques Duboin of Paris, France, who is the founder and president of the *Mouvement Français pour l'Abondance* and the editor of the organization's weekly periodical *La Grande Relève*, which serialized in 1955 and 1956 *Looking Backward*. According to Duboin, his movement was inspired by the reading of Edward Bellamy's novels.

The *Mouvement Français* is a French non-political organization with a membership of over ten thousand members which propagates economic, social, and moral ideas in many respects similar to those of Edward Bellamy. Like Bellamy and the Holland Association, the French group has the final goal of welfare for all in the form of a distributive economy based on equality. Although the main argument of the propaganda of the Dutch Bellamy movement has generally been ethical and its appeal has been to the moral conscience of the Dutch people, the French movement has always stressed logical argument with potential material abundance resulting from modern scientific methods and with mass production as its starting point.

Although the Bellamy Association continues its educational program today in the Netherlands, the members of the group are disappointed in the results of their dissemination of the ideas of Edward Bellamy. To them, the war seems to have destroyed not only the pre-war idealism of the older generations but also the interest of the younger generation in social and economic ideals.

## IV  *Socialist Reactions to Bellamy*

From the time Bellamy's books were made available in Holland, they were also well received by the socialists; for they must have been considered a welcome, enriching addition to the stock of social Utopian thought. Although the Marxist theory still was believed to be the scientific basis and method of socialism, socialists who could not completely agree with the class conflict theory and with the concept of the revolutionary achievement of a better world were glad to have a modern Utopia which appealed to higher and more humane, rational principles.

The reactions of different Dutch groups—socialists, Catholics,

Protestants, and liberals—to the ideas and books of Edward
Bellamy were pronounced during the period from 1932 to 1940
when his ideas claimed the most attention in the Netherlands.
The characteristic attitude of the socialists was voiced in an
article in their leading daily *Het Volk* of June 5, 1935, in which
the booklet *The Bellamy System,* written by K. Zylstra and
published by the Bellamy Association, was discussed. From this
review-essay, an interesting view of the past influence of Bellamy and of the attitude of the socialists of the 1930's toward
him and his influence may be gleaned.

The *Het Volk* article reads:

> One of the most remarkable phenomena of the economic de-
> pression is the revival of the ideas of Bellamy. When fifty years
> ago in intellectual circles a growing interest for socialism started
> to awake, the books of Bellamy, *Looking Backward* and *Equal-
> ity,* formed the issue of the contest between supporters and
> opponents. That issue proved to be exactly the wrong one at
> that time; and the fairy-tale of equality, which in later time
> has so often been attributed to socialists, perhaps had its origin
> in the discussion of the books of Bellamy. Even though that dis-
> cussion in the *Nieuwe Gids* was by such a distinguished charac-
> ter as that of Frank Van der Goes.
>
> The idea of orderly planning had at that time, at least for
> literary intellectuals of the *Nieuwe Gids,* evidently not so much
> attractive power.
>
> Now we are writing in 1935—fifty years later. At present the
> call for orderly planning, for a Plan, is stronger than ever all
> over the world. Bellamy is risen from the dead and is wor-
> shipped anew as a prophet, as the bringer of the only solu-
> tion, just as ardently . . . as until some years ago Henry George
> was worshipped in the circles of land nationalizers.
>
> Mr. K. Zylstra, who already has edited a booklet that aimed
> to be a plea for Bellamy's economic equality, has at present de-
> sired to demonstrate the practical efficiency of the Bellamy sys-
> tem. "Bellamy," writes Mr. Zylstra, "gave his ideas the form of
> a story. This seemed to him more attractive. Now, however, the
> time has come to deal with the practical form of the Bellamy
> ideas, his system, in a more judicious manner."
>
> Mr. Zylstra has tried to gratify the understandable desire for
> orderly planning in more objectively inclined and business-like
> natures by a logical and systematic explanation in which literal
> quotations from both famous books have been provided with
> short elucidations and "translations."
>
> "Like bringing together the dispersed bricks of a box of bricks,
> I have," says Mr. Zylstra, "brought together the most impor-
> tant parts from both books of Bellamy which have to do with

the system as a logical whole and have thus presented the system in a clear, comprehensible form. It is Bellamy himself, so to say, who is speaking.

"I am convinced," writes Mr. Zylstra, "that what will happen to you will be what happened to me, and you will come to the surprising discovery that, no matter how often you have read the books of Bellamy, there still remains something which has before been overlooked and that new perspectives, formerly not sufficiently noticed, will become apparent."

After remarking that Mr. Zylstra's booklet would "render good services as propaganda for the Bellamy Association," the writer of the article remarked that he questioned whether or not the energy expended by him might not have been "better placed somewhere else." After again recalling the wasted expenditure of energy of the followers of Henry George, the reviewer then cleverly stated: "Or rather: for us it is no question. For finally we read in the above booklet of the Bellamy Association: 'Order has to be created. It is waiting for creators. One of these you can be if you are willing. Order has to rest on a sound, reliable plan. The plan is there. It is there in headlines which, of course, are capable of extension! the Plan of Bellamy.'

"Then we think: yes, our own socialist Plan of Labor is necessary—extremely necessary."

In 1952 the socialist broadcasting system—V.A.R.A.—asked Sam de Wolff, a contemporary of Van der Goes and a prominent Dutch socialist, to broadcast a portrayal of Edward Bellamy. De Wolff, who studied first at the University of Amsterdam and then in England, became a member of a radical group of socialists—the *Sociaal Democratische Partij*. During his long career, he has also written such books as *The Crisis* (1932), *The Heroic Life and Doctrines of Karl Marx* (1933), and *History of the Jews* (1946).

During his long political career until his retirement at the age of eighty, de Wolff was often at odds with his socialist party in which he played a more theoretical than practical role. An orthodox Marxist, he was at the same time an admirer of Bellamy. This seeming contradiction may be explained by the fact that he saw in the economic principles of both Marx and Bellamy a scientific basis and a goal which permitted no compromise. For this reason, de Wolff could not agree with the political compromises of his party which, to increase its membership in parliament, often followed the line of least resistance.

Although many prominent Dutch socialists have always been receptive to Bellamy's ideas, a review of *Het Jaar 2000* published February 24, 1951, in *De Vlam*, the independent socialist newspaper of Amsterdam, is particularly interesting because of the attitude evinced toward Bellamy:

> It is more than twenty years ago that I read the translation of Henri Polak of *Looking Backward*. At that time it made a great impression on me, not because I had or have no objections against its contents, but because it gives a picture of a socialist society. In fact, Bellamy belongs to the Utopians one should have read to form some kind of idea of a concrete structure of socialist society.
>
> That time I lent my copy to Dr. P. Yssel de Schepper after we had had a discussion about the way we socialists pictured a future society. Several years ago at a chance meeting, Dr. Yssel de Schepper told me that the book had been a turning point in his life. In the years before the war he had become a fervent promoter of the Bellamy movement and even its president. *Looking Backward* is a story with many explanations of the social system—as the writer saw it. As a novel, it is moderate; as an exposition of social possibilities, interesting. It belongs to the books one should have read as a socialist.
>
> Moreover it has been better and more fluently written than *Equality*, its sequel. Nevertheless, I wish to all young socialists the patience required to read both books. They will gain by it, which cannot be said of very many books. The Bellamy movement has, therefore, done good work to publish *Looking Backward* again in a good translation. An index makes reading more easy. One should read it, critically read it; but anyhow read it.

From these articles and from the De Wolff broadcast, it may be deduced that the books of Bellamy and the propaganda of the Bellamy Association have not been without influence upon the Dutch socialists. The main contention and the major criticism to be discovered are that propaganda without political organization or action was a waste of time and energy. Furthermore, the ending of the article in *Het Volk* was an invitation to the members and supporters of Bellamy, who had no political affiliation, to join the ranks of the socialists and work for a plan.

But the strength and the influence of the Bellamy Association propaganda have rested in its theoretical and non-political character which has enabled it to popularize the ideas of Bellamy by presenting them to the Dutch people from a many-sided, unprejudiced, non-political point of view. Whether due to the influence of the Dutch association or to the concurrent influence of the English Labor Party—which also at one time made wide use of the ideas of Bellamy—the socialist party of the Netherlands has, since World War II, not only changed its name but also its tactics and slogans. Imitating the English, it adopted the name of *Partij van de Arbeid* (Labor Party); and its slogans of irreconcilable class conflict were practically placed on a shelf—as were its animosities toward both Catholicism and Protestantism.

Indeed, the recent slogans and accomplishments of the *Partij van de Arbeid* are typical Bellamy slogans and measures. Among the key words of the new party are the Bellamy slogans "a rightful part of the national wealth for all" and "social insurance for all from the cradle to the grave." Furthermore, the new Labor Party has succeeded in having several progressive social laws passed by the Dutch Parliament—and the socialists may have been aided in forming the necessary majority to pass them because Bellamy's ideas did not remain without influence among other groups represented in the legislature. In 1956 the General Old Age Law was, for example, accepted by the Parliament; as a result, an equal national old-age pension has been granted since 1957 to every person older than sixty-five, regardless of any other source of income.

In summation, it may be stated that whatever the reason Dutch socialists were attracted to Bellamy, there can be no doubt that he influenced such leaders as Frank Van der Goes, Sam de Wolff, Henri Polak, and J. de Kadt. Athough many other socialists doubtless found a place for Bellamy's novels in their libraries, very little mention of the name of Bellamy is to be found in socialist literature; and one can not, therefore, escape the impression that socialist leaders did not wish to admit that in many cases Bellamy had been their source of inspiration, of their information, and of their modified programs. They feared, no doubt, that this admission might mark them as Utopian socialists—a term and a group so despised by the fanatical Marxists.

This conclusion is strengthened by an article of February 11, 1953, published in Amsterdam in *Parool,* an important, popular semi-socialist daily newspaper. In this article J. de Kadt, one of the leading socialists members of the Dutch Parliament, commented on a book entitled *Socialist Documents of a Century,* which was compiled by Professor W. Banning and Professor J. Barents and published by *De Arbeiderspers* of Amsterdam. De Kadt criticized the fact that the Communist *Manifesto* of Marx occupied twenty pages of the book and that Bellamy

7

## EDWARD BELLAMY ABROAD

was not even mentioned. De Kadt then wrote: "With all respect for the *Manifesto*, why should one forget that Bellamy's *Looking Backward* probably has had as much influence on the formation of ideas of the socialist masses in the Netherlands as Marx or Lassalle?"

### V  *Liberal, Protestant, Catholic Reaction*

To understand the full significance of the influence which Bellamy must have had, it is necessary to comprehend political-religious groups of the Netherlands. The growth and consolidation of the *Sociaal Democratische Arbeiders Partij* finally caused the whole of Dutch public life to be formed, influenced, and, in a certain degree, controlled by four major social groups: the Protestant, the Catholic, the socialist, and the liberal. Each segment has its own ideology about cultural, social, political, and economic matters. The Catholics and the Protestants have their own churches and schools; and all groups have at present their own daily newspapers and broadcasting systems. There are also three leading unions with a total membership of nearly a million; the socialists have *Nederlands Vak Verbond* (N.V.V.); the Catholics, *Katholieke Arbeiders Bond* (K.A.B.); and the Protestants, *Christelyk Nationaal Vakverbond* (C.N.V.). In matters of common interest, these groups cooperate to some extent; but religious or political disputes from time to time alienate them.

Each group gives its members its own directives and answers about questions of common or public interest. Once having become a member of a political party, most people remain with the party for life; but there are, of course, many who are not members of any political party. As none of the four groups seems to be able to obtain a clear majority at elections, proportional representation in parliament was introduced some forty years ago. This system means that the numbers of the members in Parliament of the different parties are in the same proportion as the votes cast by each group in the whole country at general elections. A government is formed, therefore, by a temporary coalition of parties.

The relative advantage of this division of the Dutch people into distinct ideological groups is that new ideas accepted by the leadership of a group may soon become common property of the whole group and meet practically no mental or moral resistance from it. The disadvantage of this ideological division is that new ideas accepted—but as a rule one-sidedly interpreted—by one group are usually rejected by the other groups which do not even take the time and thought necessary to objectively appraise them.

The fact that Bellamy was more or less adopted by the socialists Van der Goes, Polak, de Kadt, and others, would have made him acceptable to other members of their group—but unacceptable to other parties. But, of course, numerous people not belonging to any political party also read the books of Bellamy and on many of them the ethical insight, the economic logic, and the moral conviction of Bellamy made a strong, lasting impression. This was, for example, the case with Dr. P. Yssel de Schepper, a retired judge and the chairman of the International Order of Odd Fellows of the Netherlands, who became president of the Bellamy Association.

Among the liberals of Holland, who—as has been previously noted—lost their power to the socialists but who in recent years have been regaining strength, the ideas of Bellamy have been ignored. To them, Bellamy is a socialist—and he is, therefore, to be rejected. Their attitude is understandable since the liberals are the defenders of the system of private enterprise. As such, they are opposed to any laws which would interfere with it; and they also have little sympathy for social measures— one of the reasons they lost power.

The arguments of the Protestant Calvinists today are theoretically exactly as Bellamy described those of Christian institutions as being in "The Book of the Blind" in *Equality* and in his articles. Although many ministers of the United States supported Bellamy's ideas, many clerics and many Christian laymen found nothing of the message of Christ in his books. Bellamy lambasted the churches for not recognizing the message of love and religious emotion and motivation which were basic elements of his ideal state; and he announced that, because the churchmen had been so blind, they had forfeited their right to respect and, eventually, the institutionalized religion which had permitted the clerics to be controlled by the wealthy elements of their congregations. Despite the institutional attitude of the Dutch Protestant group, Bellamy actually has appealed successfully to many church members and also to those who belong to the Protestant labor union.

When *Looking Backward* was published in 1950, *De Jonge Kerk* (Amsterdam), which is a Protestant monthly for young people, surprisingly enough published a comment about the novel but not, as might be expected, a very enthusiastic one. The review stated: "Bellamy's *Looking Backward* gives a picture of the America of the year 2000, in which the competitive

struggle and the individual accumulation of wealth—typical of
the America of the time of Bellamy, about 1880—have disappeared. A new form of government has come; the state owns all
national resources. Because Bellamy presented his ideas in the
form of a novel, his book has found very many readers. The
doctrine of Bellamy has features which remind one strongly
of communism."

Although the Catholics seldom mention Bellamy's name in
print or in public, the objection of the church was expressed in a
booklet of more than sixty pages entitled *De Bellamy Beweging*
(Bellamy Movement). This publication, issued by Paul Brand's
Publishing Company of Hilversum in 1939, was one of the
series entitled *Non-Catholic Wisdom of Life*. The principal
author of the booklet was Professor J. H. Niekel, a Catholic
priest; but the material dealing with economic theory was
prepared by Dr. E. A. V. Vermaas.

Although the authors express their appreciation for the purpose of Bellamy—welfare for all—and for the unselfish devotion
and efforts of his followers, they criticize the fashion the disciples and Bellamy himself sought to reach his goal. Where
Bellamy maintains that all means of production and distribution
should belong to the community and that private ownership
for profits is not only morally but economically wrong, Professor
Niekel asserts—on the basis of Catholic clerical authority which
is quoted—that only the misuse is wrong and that, to improve
the present conditions, energy should be directed to restrain-
ing misusage. Where Bellamy considers a sound democracy of,
by, and for the people to be the only form of government which
is morally acceptable, Professor Niekel asserts that democracy
is just a matter of political expediency and not of ethical principle. The general opinion of Professor Niekel is that, although
the final or ideal goal of Bellamy may be termed praiseworthy,
his methods of achieving welfare for all are not.

In the second section of the booklet Dr. Vermaas presents
a critical analysis of the economic ideas of Bellamy and concludes that some are contradictory and are not in accord with
the logic of economic science. Despite the divergence of principles and despite the approach from the Catholic point of
view, the argument is maintained in a friendly tone throughout
the booklet. A more recent expression of the Catholic attitude is
found in a review of *Het Jaar 2000* which appeared in the
Catholic *Gelderlander-Noordooster* of Nymegen on January 25,
1951: "Edward Bellamy wrote *Looking Backward,* published
as *Jaar 2000* by the Central Administration Bellamy in Ede.

That the eleventh edition could appear pleads more for the curiosity than for the sense of discrimination of the Dutch reader."

## VI  Recent, Independent Reviews

Review copies of *Het Jaar 2000* were sent to a number of newspapers, but most of them printed only a short notice mentioning the title and the publishers. The following comments, gleaned primarily from the independent provincial papers and from periodicals, reflect a less biased summation than the organization publications. They also express opinions about the timely qualities of Bellamy's Utopia, about the need for change in the socio-economic order and for idealism, and about the Bellamy Association.

The independent *Zandoortse Courant* review of December 20, 1950, remarked that *Het Jaar 2000* was "the title of the eleventh Dutch edition of *Looking Backward*" and that the review was to be "a general comment . . . fitting for a newspaper that asks the attention of the readers for ideas and movements of which people in our country talk." After commenting that people do talk about the Bellamy movement in Holland, the review states that

> . . . the Bellamy Association is still holding its own, although we have the impression it is not so large as before the war. This we regret in a certain sense, for there are always people who are more susceptible to this kind of propaganda than to party politics, at least in the beginning.
>
> As for ourselves, we cannot be fascinated by the Bellamy movement, which we find too sterile. Talking about politics and not participating in politics cannot be satisfying in the long run and may easily lead to zealotry.
>
> As to the ideas of Bellamy, we are quite willing to admit we have not the slightest objection if they should become reality tomorrow. But that we said forty years ago when we wrote our first comment about *Looking Backward*. We believe, however, just now as little as then in a sudden social change from today to tomorrow. Nevertheless, we sympathize with the Bellamy Association because it is attracting only people who really have the best intentions with regard to their fellowmen and its form of society. That is already much in the present egoistic world.

The *Nieuwe Noordhollandse Courant* of Alkmaar stated in January 26, 1951:

> Of course it may be assumed that the well-known book of Edward Bellamy, *Looking Backward*, is generally known; but that

everybody has read it is another point. This opportunity is here
again because a new, complete translation has appeared. . . .
We can say we have again read this book with as much interest as we read it years ago for the first time. "Is this book still
of present interest?" the publisher asks himself. Quite certainly
—and we suppose that in a time such as ours great interest for
it exists. Anyhow, it is a book overflowing with love of one's
neighbor, and it is a boon to everybody who reads it.

To the reviewer of the *Nieuwsblad voor Zuidholland en
Utrecht* (Schoonhoven) of February 28, 1951, the Bellamy Association's edition promised—because of its index and footnotes
—to provoke "fruitful discussions about Bellamy's ideal society
as he saw it." He then remarked that "it is sometimes astonishing to hear that even in leading socialist circles the Bellamy
principle is evaded or even denied." To the reviewer, the ideal
society depicted was "logically constructed . . . human and
honest" but "attainable only by an idealistic humanity."
He then remarked that little idealism seemed to exist in the
world of 1951 and that "it is, therefore, warming to see that
in this country there can be found money and energy to publish
anew a purely idealistic book of which it may easily be said
that it is old and well-known." After commenting about Bellamy's cleverness in presenting his portrayal of the ideal society
not "as a scientific work or as a collection of theses" but in the
"form of a fascinating story which is still readable," he stated
that he hoped the book would be widely read.
The reviewer of the *Delftsche Courant* (Delft) of July 21,
1951, flatly announced that *Looking Backward* "deserves all
attention" because of the general uncertainty which existed in
the world. Specifically, the book needed to be read because
the "present economic system is compelling more than ever before consideration of drastic improvements. The great merit of
Bellamy is that he has shown a road to it which he has moulded
in a somewhat romantic style. But, because of the difficulties
governments and nations have at present to contend with, this
American author deserves consideration. His book may perhaps
serve as a guide."

## VII  *Professional Literary Reactions*
The mention of Bellamy in serious and fictional Dutch literature needs to be fully investigated, but such research would
be the long work of a painstaking scholar because of the decades of popularity and influence of Bellamy in Holland. The
following comments about Bellamy show, however, one area

that needs to be studied and also the divergent attitudes toward Bellamy's Utopias—a difference of opinion which has been reflected in estimates of his work since his books were first published.

Among the Dutch authors who may have been influenced by Bellamy is Frederik van Eeden (1860-1932), the Dutch poet, novelist, playwright, neurologist, and idealist. The founder of the cooperative agricultural colony of "Walden," which failed, Van Eeden was also the author of a work often classified as a Utopian novel *De Kleine Johannes* (Little Johnny) which he published in three parts from 1886 to 1906. Van Eeden was also one of the co-founders of *De Nieuwe Gids,* for which Van der Goes wrote articles; the author of the psychological novel *The Deeps of Deliverance* (1900); and of satirical, sociological plays.

Van Eeden wrote in 1890 the following tribute to Edward Bellamy:

> A little book by an American seems to play in our days a part that was played by *Uncle Tom's Cabin* in the days of anti-slavery. I mean *Looking Backward* . . . an excellent book . . . clear, simple, and it hits. It will have more effect on the changing of contemporary morals than a thousand speeches which affirm those convinced in their opinion but which discourage those who vacillate. Bellamy's world—the world after a hundred years—is impossibly perfect, impossibly good, and impossibly dull. But that does not matter; we know it and we do not bother about a correct plan for the future.
>
> But Bellamy had the intention of showing us the world in which we live from a height from which we could have a free view of the life in our time. This height is a construction in outline but still obtainable by our thoughts. His criticism of our society is clear and penetrating. Irrefutable is Bellamy's thesis, the principal thesis of the book: We human beings are supreme on earth and the earth is bountiful enough. If only one individual suffers, this is the fault of men and not an inevitable destiny.

A far less complimentary view of Bellamy was written in *The Socialists* (1901) by H. P. G. Quak (1834-1917), a former student of law who became in 1863 the secretary of the Dutch railways, in 1877 the secretary of the Bank of the Netherlands, and in 1885 a professor of politics in Amsterdam. In the seventh chapter of his book which is concerned with North American socialists, Quak reviewed the life of Bellamy and the impact of his trip to Europe which seemingly opened his eyes to the

sharp contrasts of wealth and poverty and which inspired him
to try to do something about the sad plight of the world.
After stating that Bellamy's answer to the problem was *Looking Backward,* after paying tribute to Bellamy's vision of the
development of electricity and other modern conveniences, he
described his Utopian novel as childlike and banal. He also
asserted that, when Bellamy died in 1898, his novel had already
been forgotten by his rich countrymen and country and that
his name was mentioned only during carnival amusements.
Quak then related that, in 1899 during the Mardi Gras, Mrs.
Stuyvesant-Fish had given a *bal-a-l'envers* (Looking Backward)
at which the gay guests had worn their masks on the backs of
their heads and their wigs on their faces. In his examination
of the contents of *Looking Backward,* Professor Quak takes
a quite cynical approach—one typical of the Dutch intellectuals
of the time, who had a mortal fear of any idea which suggested
socialism.

Of more interest is the comment of Professor Fred L. Polak
in *De Toekomst is Verleden Tijd* (The Future Is the Past
Tense) which, published in 1955 by De Haan of Utrecht, not
only considers many Utopian novels but also the Utopian vision
as a dynamic influence upon cultural development. According
to Polak, the future is determined by the inspired, visionary
thinkers' hypothetical portrayals of what the future—projected
from the seeds of the present—could be. Because the Utopian
presents a totally changed world but one within human and
reasonable possibilities, he may inspire human beings to exert
themselves to attain the ideal goal; and what the Utopians have
dreamed or predicted may afterwards become actual history.

In his book Professor Polak gives Bellamy a place among
E. Renan, G. B. Shaw, W. O. Stapledon, H. G. Wells, and Walter
Rathenau in his chapter which considers the Utopia from the
nineteenth to the twentieth century. After a general description
of Bellamy and mention of the Dutch Association, Professor
Polak favorably compares Bellamy to other Utopians and then
comments that Bellamy has been at present underrated. The most
striking feature to Professor Polak of Bellamy's Utopias is not his
humanitarian idealism, his many striking anticipations of future
events, his bravery in daring to give a picture of the Marxian
Utopian world without class struggle, his involuntary contribution to conventional socialism, but his visionary looking backward from an imaginary future. Professor Polak then states
that despite all of Bellamy's theoretical economic defects, he

made history by helping to determine the future course of events.

Although it would be dangerous and impossible to determine what the exact extent of Bellamy's influence in Holland has been, it may in conclusion be deduced from what has been stated in this chapter that Bellamy inspired many people to study socialism; that he caused many to take an active role in educating people about a world that could exist if men were humane, religious, and determined; that he without doubt influenced some areas of Dutch literature; and that he, because of the sanity and humanity of his concepts, succeeded in modifying the views of some Dutch Marxists.

Although Bellamy's books and ideas still live in Holland, many indications point to the lack of interest—if not of belief— of the general public in a radical solution of the economic and social problems. Although these problems have not been solved, the challenge of the present seems to be that the public *must* find a sound, efficient, democratic solution to national and international social and economic problems. Because the search for the key must be continued and the answer found, it is not yet improbable that the radical ideas of Bellamy may have to be considered as logical and not Utopian suggestions for the formation of what he called a positive democracy—a democracy based upon universally accepted and practical principles of ethical morality, technical efficiency, and sound economy.

CHAPTER EIGHT

# Bellamy Societies of Indonesia, South Africa, and New Zealand

By

HERBERT ROTH*

## I *Indonesia*

ACTIVITY in spreading the ideas of Edward Bellamy was not confined by the Dutch to the Netherlands; for in the 1930's the Dutch East Indies (now Indonesia) had Bellamy clubs in such different towns as Batavia (now Djakarta), Bandoeng, Cheribon, Semarang, Djocja, Madioen, Batoe, Malang, Soerabaja, Pasoeroean, Medan, Kotaradja, Solo, and Blitar,[1] Palemban, Makassar.[2] One of these groups, probably that of Batavia, prepared and published its own Dutch translation of *Looking Backward*. The groups also published for almost five years (1935-1940) a newspaper entitled *De Uitweg, Officieel Orgaan der Internationale Vereniging 'Bellamy.'* Its headquarters were in Bellamy Huis, 21 Logeweg, Bandoeng, Java, and the editor of the publication was R. Neil Williams.

Although these societies were the result of the fact that many Dutchmen occupied positions in the colonial government, in commerce, in industry, and in other enterprises in this area and that they had become acquainted with the Bellamy movement during their frequent visits to the Netherlands, the clubs were not limited to Dutch members: many natives who spoke or read the Dutch language were also affiliated with them. Furthermore, although the East Indian groups had some intercourse with one another and with those in the homeland, they did not

---

* Mr. Roth prepared only the material about New Zealand; but, since it comprises the majority of pages in this chapter, his name is cited here.

create an integrated organization nor did they form a part of the Bellamy Assocation of the Netherlands.[3]

Because the Japanese during World War II occupied the Dutch Indian colonies, exiled the Dutch, and destroyed or lost the records of the Bellamy clubs, only a few tokens of their activity remain. Among the papers of the late Mrs. Edward Bellamy of Springfield, Massachusetts, there is a telegram which relates that the "first Bellamy congress" was held in Java on July 26, 1935."[4] When Mrs. R. W. Hughes of Kuala Lumpur, Malay, visited the United States in 1939, she visited the Bellamy family in Springfield;[5] and, after her return to Java, she wrote about her hospitable reception to R. Neil Williams, editor of *De Uitweg*, a member of the board of directors of the Bellamy Association of Java, and an engineer by profession.

In a letter to Mrs. Edward Bellamy of September 26, 1939, Williams wrote:

> You possibly do not realize the extreme veneration with which all those who have read Edward Bellamy's books look upon him and upon every detail connected with his work which they can get to know about. Of course his immediate family had undoubtedly a great share in his life and work and the ups and downs connected with it.
>
> It is not just hero-worship that has led us to print our Java paper *De Uitweg* (which means the Way Out), but a wish to bring nearer to our readers the personality of your great husband. We know that in doing so we are fulfilling one of the dearest wishes of our members to whom until now the name Bellamy stands for all that is sensible and ethical in life, but to whom the personality of the philosopher Bellamy was a blank page.
>
> This is a War number [a copy of the paper obviously accompanied the letter] and at this time it is well to hold before our followers the fact that Edward Bellamy was not just a mythical personage, but a flesh and blood human being gifted with a super-intelligent mind, whose genius would certainly have proved more conclusively than our feeble efforts are able to, that this terrible war is but the consequence of not following Bellamy's principles.
>
> We hope that the war may bring millions to realize in which direction their only salvation lies, but we would of course rather have seen this realization come through evolution than through revolution, which is war.[6]

Although it is impossible to assess the possible influence of the Indonesian Bellamy societies upon the populace, it is significant that natives were permitted to join them. A photograph sent to Mrs. Edward Bellamy shows a classroom and native teachers—and on the wall are two sketches: one of them is of Edward Bellamy and the other represents with a modern building the new world he had foretold.

## II  *Bellamy League of South Africa*

The Dutch translation of *Looking Backward,* which was published in Amsterdam in 1906 by Cohen, was also distributed in South Africa—but the name of a South African publisher appears on the title page below that of the Dutch publisher.[7] Copies in English of both *Equality* and *Looking Backward* were also always stocked by Anderson's Bookshop and by the Vanguard Booksellers of Johannesburg—and this was no doubt due to the fact that a Bellamy organization had been formed as early as 1932 in South Africa with headquarters in this city.[8] Knowledge of Bellamy in this area of the world must be attributed to three converging influences: that of the Dutch and the English settlers and that of the South African Theosophical Society.

The constitution of the South African Section of the International Bellamy League and other of the League's publications, found in the files of Mrs. Edward Bellamy and of her daughter Mrs. Marion Bellamy Earnshaw, indicate that the constitution was drawn in the year 1932. A telegram from Fred. W. Bell, chairman of the league which had headquarters at Hamilton House, Rissik and Kerk Streets, Johannesburg, informed Mrs. Bellamy on October 14, 1933, that leagues had been established not only in Johannesburg but also in Capetown, Durban, Port Elizabeth, East London, Benoni, and Krugersdorp. He added that "interest [is] deepening."[9]

The aim of the South African League as expressed in its publications and its constitution was "propagation of the general ideas contained in the books *Looking Backward* and *Equality* . . . and the dissemination of writings contained in these works, and also the performance of whatever may be considered conducive to the attainment of the state of affairs and conditions of life, generally, depicted in these books."

In Article 3 of its constitution, the South African League expressed the determination to "be strictly non-party in the political sense, non-racial, non-sectarian, but widely humanitarian. Its aim shall be, broadly, in accord with the principles and general ideas laid down by Bellamy in his books. . . . Although non-political in the party sense, nevertheless, the influence of the League may be extended to induce any or all parties or people to work in the direction of the attainment of its declared Object, but, as a body, the League shall remain strictly independent of other bodies political or otherwise." In keeping with this general intent of broad, inclusive humanitarianism, it is interesting to note, in view of the present chaotic conflict, that all members were expected to establish "the greatest harmony" and that there was to be also a "total absence of provincial or other jealousies."[10]

Because of the lapse of time, the lack of bibliographies and indexes covering material before 1940,[11] the inaccessibility of South Africa, and the inability to secure someone in the area who would do the research work, very little more can be related about this Bellamy League. Clippings from the file of Mrs. Edward Bellamy indicate, however, that the group was not idle; for the book page of the Capetown, Africa, *Cape Argus* of November 17, 1934, carried a long article with the subtitle "What Do You Know about Edward Bellamy?" After relating that "the work of Edward Bellamy has recently begun to attract as much attention or even more attention than it did during his lifetime," that a Bellamy League existed in South Africa, and that Fousham had just published a new edition of *Looking Backward*, the author reviewed Bellamy's life and then commented that "though an advanced thinker, he was in many ways strongly conservative. But being a thinker and possessing in many respects an extraordinary gift of prophecy, he saw that the economic and financial sides of our social structure could not long endure. And not only that, but he clearly visualized and foretold the present disruption which is taking place."

At the end of the article, the reviewer stated: "the main interest of Bellamy's work lies in the plan which he provided for a healthier, happier and more stable order of things. He believed that there is enough in the world to supply the needs of all, food, clothing, and shelter, as well as the good things of life which people might reasonably need or want to enjoy.

"He believed that these desirable things should be within the reach of all, and as you read his books you may well wonder why this is not so. In an age of philosophical and practical experiment such as the present, men might do worse than go back and have a look at Bellamy."[12]

When the thirty-sixth anniversary of the death of Edward Bellamy approached, Fred Bell, chairman of the league, prepared an address to deliver over the African Broadcasting Company because he had learned that the "National Broadcast in the United States" planned on May 22, 1934, to present a pro-

gram about Bellamy and that his widow and his son, the late
Paul Bellamy, editor of the Cleveland *Plain Dealer,* were to be
speakers. Although the secretary of the network wrote to Mr.
Bell that "in the opinion of the Directors it [his speech] has
been found unsuitable for broadcasting," the address was printed
by the League in a four-page, tabloid-size pamphlet.

In the opening paragraph, Bell remarked: "A book written
in 1886, together with its sequel published about ten years later,
will, I believe, be found in the future to have influenced social
life and conditions to a greater extent than any other for the
last few hundred years. I speak of *Looking Backward* and . . .
*Equality* by Edward Bellamy." After a brief review of Bellamy's
life, books, and message, Bell indicated not only his being in
close touch with Americans who were then speaking about
Bellamy—Principal Rollo G. Reynolds of Horace Mann School
of New York City and the Reverend John Haynes Holmes—
whom he quoted, but also the reasons Bellamy appealed to him.

To Bell, Bellamy had comprehended and dealt with all the
reforms the world needed in his books—and had done so more
sanely and logically than others. Understanding Bellamy more
than many others who wrote or spoke about him, Bell realized
that he had merely tried to indicate the solution and that he
had intended for others to work out the details which would
have to be adapted to "time and circumstances." To Bell, Bellamy was "a latter-day guide" to the solution of the problems
of war, of birth control, of the competitive system, of education for the use of leisure, and of evolutionary and legal change
of any existing system. To Bell, the future of the world was
some form of fulfillment of the vision which Bellamy had
presented.[13]

The only other located mention of Bellamy in South Africa is
in *The Link,* the publication of the Theosophical Society of
South Africa. In the issue of April-May, 1942, Bellamy's system
is suggested as the solution for the general reconstruction of
society after the end of the war—and *Looking Backward* is
mentioned as being a detailed explanation of the way in which
social and economic reforms could be achieved. To substanti-
ate the suggestion that Bellamy be consulted, the author of the
article reminded his readers that H. P. Blavatsky, the founder of
the Theosophical Society, had stated that "Bellamy's ideas were
in line with the future race"; and he also suggested that "anyone interested should write to our great Bellamy expert, Mr.
T. F. Day . . . Johannesburg." The existence of a Theosophical

Society in South Africa is important; for this organization—whose story is more completely related in Chapter XIV—had promoted Bellamy since 1889.

## III  New Zealand

Edward Bellamy was also popular and influential in New Zealand in two highly significant periods: in 1889-90, when, toward the end of a long depression, a liberal government was elected; and in the 1930's when, in the wake of another depression, the first labor government came to power. During these two periods the works by Bellamy which were reprinted in New Zealand included *Looking Backward* (1890) and *The Parable of the Water Tank* (1932). There is no doubt that Bellamy's ideas contributed materially to the ferment of radicalism which was so noticeable both in the 1890's and in the 1930's. In the latter period an organization of Bellamy supporters was established in New Zealand which existed for almost nineteen years; but it was in 1889-90 that Bellamy's influence in New Zealand reached its peak.

## IV  The Nineteenth Century

"In 1889," wrote William Pember Reeves, a future minister of the government, "everyone was reading collectivist tracts and listening to altruistic sermons."[1] A "wave of socialistic feeling," as he called it, swept over New Zealand. Under the impact of the successful London dockers' strike, trade unions in New Zealand more than quadrupled their membership within a year. Reeves himself, under the pseudonym "Pharos," wrote a series of articles on "Communism and Socialism, their Dreams, their Experiments, their Aims, their Influence" for the *Lyttelton Times,* a Christchurch daily paper. Among the writers he selected for detailed treatment was Edward Bellamy.

*Looking Backward,* wrote Reeves, was a remarkable feat by a writer hitherto unknown. "Pithy, clear, forcible, it possesses the true eloquence—that which springs from intense conviction, based on study and thought. Every page tells us how well Mr. Bellamy has brooded over, mastered, and digested the creed of Socialism. He knows it so thoroughly that he can condense without being dull, and argue at red heat without straying from or losing a single point."[2] To readers who might object that Utopias were impractical, Reeves replied: "It is from the contemplation of such ideals that the 'divine discontent' with society as it is, which is the hall-mark of European civilization, springs. Upon this discontent, all reform, all improvement, all that unwearying struggle upward to a brighter and better day are founded."[3]

Reeves called *Looking Backward* "the book of the day." In the previous two or three years, he estimated, the novel had been read by something approaching two million people in the United States and the British Empire. Nobody knows, even approximately, how many people in New Zealand read Bellamy's book, but the demand for it, in 1890, was phenomenal. "Sold out again of *Looking Backward*," announced bookseller W. Wildman in the *Auckland Star* of April 19. "Fresh supply of 500 copies will be here in a few days."[4] A week later, on April 26, the *Auckland Star* reported: "Bellamy's little brochure is just now the rage of the hour and we are afraid to mention how many of the various editions we are told have been circulated in Auckland alone."[5]

From Christchurch, a correspondent in the *New Zealand Tablet* reported on May 30: "For some weeks past the first query on the lips of every second person whom one met in the street or elsewhere was 'Have you read *Looking Backward?*' Then, without waiting for an answer, the querist would proceed to expatiate upon the merits of the book—'Grand book that; will cause a revolution in society. Bellamy's the man to paint the future. Another book like that and poverty and oppression will be wiped out.' "[6]

*Looking Backward* was reprinted in Christchurch by the firm of Whitcombe & Tombs. In Dunedin, it was published by James Horsburgh, with a cover proclaiming: "The Novel of the Day." These local editions merely filled the gaps between the arrival of shipments from overseas. In the Dunedin *Evening Star* of April 17, 1890, Joseph Braithwaite, of Braithwaite's Book Arcade, announced: "I have sold about 5,000 copies of this marvellous Socialistic book since I reviewed it in the *Star* about six months ago."[7] Another thousand copies from England were due to arrive at Braithwaite's on April 23. They sold out within two days; but, fortunately, another thousand copies were expected on April 30.

Last year, recalled a Dunedin newspaper in November, 1891, everybody was reading *Looking Backward*. What did New Zealanders think of it? Maurice W. Richmond, a Wellington lawyer, was cautiously sympathetic in a detailed review which he contributed to the *Monthly Review*. He expressed his personal belief that Bellamy had rightly judged the tendency of the times and that cooperation had to replace the present chaos of competition. "In New Zealand," wrote Richmond, "we may look upon ourselves as some steps in advance of the rest of the world in the right direction. Not only are our railways, telegraphs, and telephones in the hands of the Government, but we have a Government Life Insurance Department; and State Farms, and also, it may be said, compulsory national insurance are within the range of practical politics. It is to be hoped that relief from financial pressure may shortly enable us to feel a freedom in dealing with these and other matters, which perhaps does not at present exist. Meanwhile, the circulation of Mr. Bellamy's book throughout the country should do something to make it more easy to deal with them with the largeness of spirit which they require."[8]

William F. Kitchen, the editor of the radical monthly *Zealandia*, was carried away with enthusiasm. "This is an excellent book," he told his readers. "It is one of the very few modern works that it is a positive moral duty for all who profess to be thinking beings, or to have the slightest regard for their fellow creatures, to read. . . . It is an appeal to brains and hearts, and readers must be possessed of both to appreciate it at its full value. . . . It is an earnest, serious endeavour to solve the difficulties attending social progress." Bellamy, wrote Kitchen, had made an indelible impression on him; and the only weakness he could find in the book was the description of the means by which the good end was to be attained; it would involve a lengthy Purgatory before Paradise was reached. "No one can read *Looking Backward*," he concluded, "and not be lifted out of self, and made to feel there are higher ends in life than grasping selfishly at the goods of others, or striving to see how comfortably one can live at the expense of others' misery."[9]

There was, of course, also much criticism of Bellamy's ideas. In Auckland, W. Wildman reprinted in a pamphlet an article published by Professor F. A. Walker in the *Atlantic Monthly: Mr. Bellamy and the New Nationalist Party. A Criticism of the Views contained in Looking Backward*. In Dunedin, the Reverend A. R. Fitchett, preaching in All Saints', said that all attempts to reconstruct society were doomed to failure because it was against human nature to expect the rich to surrender their wealth voluntarily; but, neither was it right, he hastened to add, to despoil the rich by force. Similar sentiments were expressed by the Christchurch correspondent of the Catholic *New Zealand Tablet* who called Bellamy's ideas utterly impracticable, useless, and politically and philosophically unsound. The poor, he wrote, would always be with us; poverty could be ameliorated but not abolished; the best that could be done for humanity was "to make the chains chafe a little less painfully upon each other's limbs."[10]

This outburst drew an indignant reply from J. C. of Waitahuna who thought the Christchurch correspondent was one of those who viewed *Looking Backward* from the top of the coach. "If they came down from the top of the coach it would be easier to pull along," he wrote. "It would be easier still if they took to pulling at the rope." And J. C. concluded his letter: "I am of the opinion that Bellamy's pamphlet is something like what discovered gravitation. It set the people a thinking which will be a benefit to the world, but a calamity to the present occupiers of the coach."[11]

No clubs of Bellamy supporters were formed in the nineteenth century in New Zealand. Henry George, whose book *Progress and Poverty* was also widely read in the late 1880's, was more fortunate. An Anti-Poverty Society, founded in Auckland in December, 1887, gained the support of some wealthy local businessmen. When the ship which took Henry George to Australia stopped at Auckland on March 1, 1890, he was welcomed by a representative delegation of local radical organizations, which was led by Sir George Grey, New Zealand's elder statesman, who had accepted the presidency of the Anti-Poverty Society. Henry George's ideas predominated among the Knights of Labor who flourished in many parts of New Zealand in the early 1890's. When the Knights became settled on the land, however, they forsook their radicalism; and the single-tax movement became confined to Auckland and a few other centers. Although it has continued in existence in New Zealand to the present day, it has never again been so influential as it was in the 1890's.

Bellamy's popularity also suffered an eclipse after the defeat of the Maritime Strike late in 1890. Before the strike Bellamy had appealed to more radical spirits than Henry George, and *Looking Backward* had been the inspiration of the workers of New Zealand who were seeking the "emancipation of Labor." They had no clear ideas of how to achieve this aim; but it was widely believed that, by organizing trade unions and associations, labor would become so overwhelmingly strong that the rich would give up all thought of resistance and would of their own free will join in building the new society. In the first half of 1890, hardly a day passed without the formation of some trade union. Oystermen at the Bluff and gum diggers in the far North, farm laborers in the backblocks, servant girls, and staid public servants all formed their unions and associations; and the joke was current that only the grave diggers had refused to join the movement because there were already enough openings in their trade.

Locally the unions combined into Trades and Labor Councils. Nationally they formed federations, and some of them were affiliated with Australian organizations. The most important of these national federations—the seamen, miners, watersiders and railwaymen—joined together in a Maritime Council which, in turn, became affiliated with the Maritime Council of Australia. By August, 1890, the New Zealand Maritime Council claimed that it spoke for 20,000 workers, while another 40,000 were in unions outside the Council. One in every eleven New Zealanders was then an organized trade unionist.

The employers, too, were marshalling their forces. The inevitable trial of strength came late in August, 1890, with the outbreak of a Maritime Strike in Australia which quickly spread to New Zealand. The daily press, which had been fairly sympathetic to trade unionism earlier that year, now turned against the strikers. Bellamy was widely blamed for the prevalent unrest. "This bundle of fallacies," wrote the Napier monthly *Typo* with reference to *Looking Backward,* "circulated, as it has been, by tens of thousands—is an exciting factor in the present ceaseless revolt. . . . It is quoted by the leaders of the movement as their text-book." At a unionist meeting in Wellington, according to *Typo,* a Mr. Cliffe had predicted that the Bellamy paradise would be realized not in the year 2000 but "within fifty years." John A. Millar, the leader of the strike, had told a meeting at Oamaru that he believed that the outcome of the present dispute would be a great, grand commonwealth where all would be employed and paid by the state.[12]

The Maritime Strike ended in defeat for the unionists. The Maritime Council disappeared and so did most of the newly-founded trade unions, whether affiliated with the Council or not. Socialist ideas and the labor movement suffered a severe setback, and Bellamy went down with them. "The maritime strike of 1890," wrote Reeves, "dissipated many bright visions of peaceful cooperation between Labor and middle-class altruism. Many who had toyed with socialism, many who were not insincere in their friendship for Unionism, shrank from allies whose war upon 'free' labor had consequences disturbing to industry and disastrous to themselves."[13]

Defeated in the economic struggle, the workers of New Zealand gave their votes to the Liberal Party which won the elec-

tions of December, 1890, and assumed power the following
January. Unlike Australia, no Labor Party was then formed in
New Zealand though half a dozen manual workers were among
the newly elected members of Parliament. The new government
which was led by John Ballance and which included Reeves as
Minister of Education and later of Labor, introduced far-reaching progressive legislation which its conservative opponents
promptly denounced as Bellamyism and socialism. "If they are
not checked in their mad career, they will at last arrive at the
mad doctrine propounded by Bellamy," cried a member of
Parliament in 1892.[14] Nothing could have been further from
the truth. Even Reeves, the most radical and intellectual member of the new cabinet, was only a very mild, Fabian socialist;
and Ballance, the new Premier, had expressed his lack of faith
in Bellamy's ideas in an article "The Altruistic State," which
he had contributed to the *Monthly Review* of April, 1890.

Unlike most critics of Bellamy, Ballance did not believe that
human nature could not be changed, but he thought Bellamy
was too impatient: it would take not a hundred but thrice a
hundred years to reach the dawn of the new age. "It is amusing," he wrote, "to find people forming clubs to promote Utopia. Their energies will only be wasted or pernicious."[15] Furthermore, wrote Ballance, the way to bring about the new order
was individualism—and not socialism: "The Individualist, who
lops off the rotten branch which obstructs the growth of the
tree, who strikes down abuses, and who puts his hand to every
reform which seems good and desirable, is a more practical and
useful worker in the field than the Socialist who demands a
brand new state of the Utopian order fresh and complete from
the brain of Zeus."[16]

This statement of belief expressed admirably the pragmatic
approach to social problems which the liberal government was
to follow in the years to come. If it is not quite correct to speak
of New Zealand's "Socialism without Doctrines," the fact remains that the new government was never tied to any particular
doctrine or blueprint for the future. Bellamy and the other radical and socialist writers whose works had circulated so widely
in 1889-90 were now dismissed as impractical dreamers. But
*Looking Backward,* more than any other single book, prepared
the ground in New Zealand for the enormous expansion of the
powers of the state which occurred in the liberal era.

In the late nineties the first socialist propaganda societies
were formed in New Zealand. Two British Labor leaders, Ben
Tillett and Tom Mann, came on lecture tours; and, in 1901,

a socialist party was formed, largely by recent British immigrants. These new groups comprised followers of all schools of socialist thought which were then active in Britain. Among them were Fabians and Independent Labor Party members, adherents of the labor churches, and supporters of the Social Democratic Federation. Soon, however, Marxist influence gained the upper hand in the New Zealand Socialist Party while I.W.W. ideas strongly influenced the New Zealand Federation of Labor. Bellamy was little heard of in this period, but his works continued to circulate. In Christchurch, for instance, lived a retired Canadian businessman, Mr. T. J. McBride, who spent hundreds of pounds importing socialist books and pamphlets from Britain and the United States. With fine impartiality he allowed socialist groups of all factions to distribute these among their followers.

Among those who came under McBride's influence was a young man named David Low. One day, in 1908, or thereabouts, McBride asked Low to come to his house to do a drawing of him. Almost fifty years later, Low, now a world-famous cartoonist, recalled the incident in his autobiography: "He received me kindly and we sat in his beautiful garden while I drew him. This wise, if somewhat forbidding old gentleman, touched off by something I had said, began to talk quietly of the possible beauties of living, the ideal organization of the state and the ultimate triumph of wisdom. He took the world view, moving outside our locality, past New Zealand, beyond the British Empire to the wide horizons of the human race. Secure in his fine house, he rejected the glib assumption of the permanence of social inequality. We sat constructing and reconstructing societies, finding the true balance of order and liberty for the betterment of the lot of mankind. I had read some of this before, but it was new to hear it spoken by a rich and successful businessman. The sun was shining, the garden was green, the sky was blue—all that was needed was a fig-tree and we might have been Aristotle and a pupil. When at last I got up to leave, he went to his library and brought to me, as a parting gift to an attentive listener, a copy of Bellamy's *Looking Backward.*"

"I never saw him again," continued Low, "but I still have his book. . . . He little recked of the seed he planted that day. Before that my political ideas had been disconnected. After it, they began to take shape and relationship. *Looking Backward* led to a course of New Worlds—Plato's *Republic,* Butler's *Erewhon,* Wells's *The Sleeper Awakes,* which I balanced with a

good go at Burke, and just to counterbalance Burke, Tom Payne
and William Morris."[17]

## V  *The Bellamy Ban; Clubs of 1930's*

In 1912, the liberal government was defeated in Parliament
and a conservative administration took over. Soon afterwards
the leftist forces solved their differences and combined in a
new labor party. In the general elections of 1919, the New Zealand Labor Party obtained almost a quarter of the total vote.
Clubs for the study of Marxism were formed in a number of
places and the first writings of Lenin reached New Zealand.
Caught up in the widespread enthusiasm for things Russian,
leaders of the Labor Party expressed their hope that the social
revolution would triumph throughout Europe; and the party's
national journal even toyed with the idea of affiliation with the
Third International. The conservative government went to extreme lengths in an effort to keep New Zealand insulated
against such heady ideas. "Undesirable immigrants" were deported while "undesirable" publications were seized by the
custom authorities. Stringent war emergency regulations were
kept in force long after World War I had ended and were
used to harass left-wing opposition.

Lists of banned publications were published from time to
time in the *New Zealand Gazette*. At first these lists were confined to Communist and I.W.W. publications; but on March
17, 1932, Edward Bellamy joined the censored company of
Bukharin, Radek, Trotsky, and Zinoviev. *The Parable of the
Water Tank*, published by the Workers Bookshop in Sydney,
was declared to be a document which incited, encouraged, or
advocated violence, lawlessness, or disorder, or expressed a
seditious intention.

Two months earlier, the unemployed had rioted in Dunedin.
In April, 1932, new and more serious riots occurred in Auckland and again in Dunedin. In May it was Wellington's turn to
see thousands of starving men engage in an orgy of window-
smashing. Neither repressive legislation introduced by a fright-
ened government nor the harsh sentences meted out by the
courts could suppress the mounting discontent with the existing social order.

Again, as in the earlier depression of the 1880's, the people
of New Zealand sought to find in books the answer to the
problem of starvation in the midst of plenty. Marxist and
Social Credit ideas predominated, but Bellamy, too, had his
followers. The banning of the *Parable of the Water Tank*

served to draw attention to its author. Local reprints of the *Parable* appeared and were passed from hand to hand among the unemployed; and Bellamy's longer works—*Looking Backward* and *Equality*—also found many new readers.

Among those who read, or rather reread, *Looking Backward* in 1932, was Alexander Scott, the president of the New Economics Research Association. A native of Glasgow, Scott had lived in the United States for some years before World War I. Active in the Socialist Party there, he was editor of the *Weekly Issue*, a socialist paper published in Paterson, New Jersey. At the time of the textile workers' strike of 1913, Scott attacked the local police for their brutal handling of the strikers and was convicted and jailed. He was freed on appeal after widespread protests—including one from Upton Sinclair.

After serving in the British forces during the war, Scott in 1919 became active in ex-servicemen's organizations and edited a soldiers' journal, *The New World*, in Glasgow. One of the British delegates to a congress in Geneva which formed the Ex-Servicemen's International, Scott was elected treasurer; and Henri Barbusse became secretary. In 1922, Scott came to live in New Zealand. He worked as a journalist but took little part in politics, apart from trying to interest school committees in dental services and in the state's supplying school requisites. During the depression years Scott formed the New Economics Research Association which propounded ideas of monetary reform similar to the Douglas Social Credit schemes. He had known of Bellamy and had read *Looking Backward;* but, on rereading the book in 1932, he was most deeply impressed and became, in his own words, "fanatical" about Bellamy.

When Scott wrote in May, 1933, to Upton Sinclair, he remarked in his letter that "this depression is the world-wide social revolution which Bellamy predicted." He also suggested that *Looking Backward* be made into a film, for, "read in the light of present-day events, it is a wonderful book." Upton Sinclair gave Scott's letter to a Hollywood film agency which had been trying for some time to raise the money for a film version of *Looking Backward*. On September 27, 1933, Scott published two full-length articles about Edward Bellamy on the front page in the most prominent position of the New Zealand *Worker*. In the two-column, full-length article entitled "Bellamy's 'Looking Backward,' " Scott pointed out that Bellamy's Utopian novel was "a book to be read now. It is an inspiring book and, therefore, a book for these times when inspiration is so much needed. But there are other reasons why this book is a book for the present time. The change-over from the old order to the new planned economy, as predicted by Edward Bellamy, should be taking place. Is it taking place? Is the complete revolution to be a bloodless one? Will the year 2000 A. D. be anything like Bellamy's prediction or will it be better than Bellamy ever conceived?" After stating that the book "provokes sober thought, stirs the imagination, and, in a wholesome manner, the emotions," Scott devoted the rest of his article to excerpts from *Looking Backward* and appended his own timely comments.[18]

In the other two-column article entitled " 'Looking Backward'/Bellamy's Famous Book/No Funds Obtainable for Film Version/Banker-controlled Companies Decline Production," Scott stated that he had published in 1932 a "review of 'Looking Backward' which was not published as intended, but that in it he had wondered why the book had never been filmed. In his 1933 article, he published letters he had exchanged about the possibility of making such a film with Upton Sinclair, Howard Scott (leader of the Technocrats), and Gordon Rigby of a Hollywood film agency. Rigby's letter of August 7, 1933, stated that he and his partner, Mr. William Morris, Jr., had for seven months been trying to "see his [Bellamy's] philosophy translated to the screen" but with little success. Rigby pointed out that the producers were not exactly hide bound; but that they were "merely puppets in the hands of powerful Wall Street bankers," that no help could be expected from the "banker-controlled producers," and that raising money for an independent venture seemed "next to impossible."

Rigby asserted that this statement was not surmise; for he had "covered the continent" in an effort to secure money but that, though "there are thousands who share your desire to see Bellamy on the screen, to the end that a better and more equitable social structure shall be achieved," these were people without money. Rigby pointed out that he was still trying to fulfill his dream of a film which would not ignore "the social aspect" of *Looking Backward;* for he was convinced that "a sincere picture" would "beat all known box-office figures."

To support his statements, he stated that "Paul Bellamy, son of the author, tells me that over four million copies have been sold in English alone. There are about a million members of various Bellamy societies in America and Canada. The book is today a best seller." He also wrote that he had "been assured of the cooperation of the scores of the finest minds in the country should we succeed in raising the moneys necessary to pro-

duce the picture. Howard Scott, Dr. Graham Laing, Upton
Sinclair, Stuart Chase, Heywood Broun, Lawrence Stillings, and
other well-known writers, educators, and scientists have assured
us of their cooperation."[19] The copy of a letter of January 12,
1936, from Scott to Rigby in the Bellamy files indicated that
Scott was still interested in the film and that he thought that
the New Zealand Labor Party, which was then in control of
the government, might help. He also announced that he intended to keep publishing articles in *The Standard*, the official
labor newspaper, and that he also was preparing a series of
lectures about Bellamy to broadcast.[20]

On March 27, 1934, Scott thanked Mrs. Bellamy for sending
him a pamphlet about the New York Edward Bellamy Association and announced once again that he intended to establish
a Bellamy society in New Zealand. In this letter Scott stated
his opinion of Bellamy: "Of all the Utopias that have been
written, I think there can be no shadow of doubt that Bellamy's
is the best of all. It does inspire and purify and give hope, and
that is what humanity needs most at the present time. If I were
a millionaire, I would have *Looking Backward* screened. . . ."

In his postscript to this letter, Scott also stated his assessment
of—and perhaps his attraction to—Bellamy: "The Bellamy Plan
is the purest of pure socialism. It is Utopian socialism and
therefore more practical and scientific than what was a while
back called 'practical' or 'scientific' socialism. The fact that
the term 'socialism' (or 'communism') has been misused and
misunderstood and abused does not for me alter its true significance. It is a beautiful word. However, it may be just as
well to drop the term for the time being. But I must confess
that I don't like to see Bellamyists denying socialism and radicalism and making an appeal to popular 'patriotism.' "[21]

On April 3, 1935, W. H. Williamson of Auckland wrote to
Upton Sinclair—who obviously mailed the letter to Mrs. Bellamy—that he wanted to republish *Looking Backward* in New
Zealand because of the growing demand for the book and
because it was not available. Scott enclosed a clipping for
Upton Sinclair, and requested that he reply to this now-lost
article through his *Epic News*. Scott also suggested that Sinclair and his group in California "link up in some way with
us, as there are thousands of supporters who admire *your attitude*."[22] Sinclair, who had very early in his life been influenced
by Bellamy's books, had been a Democratic candidate for the
governorship of the state of California; and he had run on a
public-works platform with a "production for use" program

which would "end poverty in California"—hence the use of the word "E. P. I. C."

Mrs. Bellamy sent Scott an autographed copy of *Equality*, which contained pasted-in paper bearing the author's signature. This gesture was much appreciated by Scott who proudly displayed the volume to his audiences when he lectured about Bellamy's "immortal ideas" while his plans to form a Bellamy Society in New Zealand waited. 1935 was election year and Scott, a member of the Labor Party, threw himself wholeheartedly into the campaign to elect a labor government. In letters to the press Scott urged all "social reconstructionists"—Social Crediters, Bellamyists, land and monetary reformers, and genuine communists—to join forces in support of the Labor Party. Labor, he wrote in the *New Zealand Worker*, was pledged to abolish poverty in New Zealand. This was "the best and the biggest thing any party could do. And to exercise such a mandate without fear or favour is the natural task of a government of genuine social reconstructionists."[23]

The Labor Party won the elections. In an atmosphere similar to that of 1890—a severe economic depression, social unrest, and a ferment of radical ideas—the people of New Zealand gave the party an impressive majority in the new Parliament. Michael Joseph Savage, an ex-brewery worker from Auckland, became New Zealand's first labor prime minister. Scott and his fellow thinkers on the left were full of enthusiasm; the millennium, they thought, was just around the corner.

Lecturing on Bellamy at a public meeting in Kilbirnie, Wellington, in December, 1935, Scott claimed that most of the members of the new government drew their inspiration from Edward Bellamy. They were idealists, they had a goal to aim for and a clear vision of better days. "Think what that means to New Zealand," he cried, "and think what it may mean (who knows?) to the whole world!"[24] The Hon. R. Semple, Minister of Public Works, who was present at Scott's lecture, spoke briefly on the work of the new administration. Two other ministers, Walter Nash and Peter Fraser, sent their apologies. Mrs. Bellamy, when she read Scott's address, expressed her pleasure that Bellamy's ideas had contributed so much towards the birth of a labor government in New Zealand. "Long may it live to serve the people of your country," she wrote to Scott, "and may you live to keep it true to the ideals which brought it into being and which now are the life of its success."[25]

Mr. W. J. Green, the editor of the Labor Party's weekly journal, was sympathetic to Bellamy's ideas. With his assistance

Scott arranged for *Looking Backward* to be serialized in the *Standard* between January and July, 1936. A radio talk on Bellamy which Scott submitted to the broadcasting authorities was accepted as part of a series of talks on "Modern Utopias." On March 18, 1936, Scott inserted a notice in the *Standard* asking all Bellamy enthusiasts to communicate with him with a view to forming a society in New Zealand. Replies were received from many parts of the country and the inaugural meeting was held in Wellington on July 9. Though attended by only six people, it was described in the minutes as "marked by enthusiasm, unanimity and purpose." Those present decided to form an "Edward Bellamy Society of New Zealand" and to elect a committee; it included Mrs. Emma Bellamy as patron and Scott as president. The Labor Party's *Standard* was adopted as the official organ of the society.

The aims and objectives of the Bellamy Society were defined as: "(1) To disseminate the principles enunciated by Edward Bellamy as being the permanent remedy for the social and economic evils inherent in the capitalist system, now in process of transition to socialism. (2) To encourage the reading and intelligent discussion of Edward Bellamy's books—*Looking Backward* and *Equality*—(both books and especially the latter) to the end that the people of this Dominion may better understand and appreciate the political, social and economic changes that are taking place in this Dominion and throughout the world, and the still greater changes yet to come. (3) To work in the closest harmony with the Labor Movement and the Labor Government of New Zealand in furtherance of the ideals which we hold in common."[26]

The remaining points dealt with contact with Bellamy societies in other countries, the production of a Bellamy film, the importation of moderately-priced editions of Bellamy's books, and the establishment of a cooperative Bellamy Publishing Society. When the society was incorporated in November, 1936, these objectives were significantly altered. In point one the reference to the capitalist system and to the transition to socialism was cut; and the second and third points were omitted altogether.

Although the social composition of the new society was mixed, it was predominately middle-class. Of the sixteen members who signed the application for registration, three were journalists, two were teachers, one a company director, and one a member of Parliament. Only two of them could be described as well-known—W. J. Lyon, the newly elected M.P. for Waitemata;

and Professor Von Zedlitz, whose dismissal from Victoria University College, forced by the government in 1915, had just been atoned for by his appointment as Professor Emeritus.

Between 1936 and 1938, when the Bellamy Society was most active, attendance at its regular monthly meetings rarely exceeded a dozen members. The total membership in Wellington was in the vicinity of fifty but the work of the society was carried on by a few stalwarts: Scott, who was indefatigable in his exertions for the cause; L. Waddell; J. Rough; W. H. Scammell, a retired teacher who was appointed secretary-treasurer in December, 1936; C. R. C. Robieson; and W. O. Beere. Robieson, a company director, had been head of the Department of Industries and Commerce. Beere was a surveyor. Both men had collaborated with Scott in the New Economic Research Association and had followed him into the Bellamy Society.

Though small in numbers, the Bellamy Society made its voice heard. The editor of the *Standard* had become a member, and news items about the society's activities were prominently displayed in his journal. Besides regular "Bellamy Society Notes," the *Standard* published articles and book reviews by Scott, and among these is one recommending to readers H. Stanley Jevons *Economic Equality*, in which a tribute was paid to Bellamy. When Scott gave his radio talk, "The Immortal Bellamy," the paper printed it in full. Reprints of this address, given over Station 2YA, Wellington, on September 10, 1936, were also distributed by the society. On March 26, 1937 —Bellamy's birthday—another Scott broadcast was presented which was also issued in pamphlet form in an edition of 5,000 copies. It was widely distributed to teachers and ministers of religion.

Great efforts were made to see that Bellamy's books were freely available in New Zealand. The society wrote to the ministers of the government concerned to ask that copies be placed in prison libraries and public works camps (these requests were granted); and it sought to gain the approval of the Minister of Education for the use of Bellamy's works as textbooks in schools, teachers' training colleges, and universities (these requests were met with evasive answers). The society also arranged for the importation of cheap editions of Bellamy's works, particularly *Equality*.

In August, 1936, the Society sent a questionnaire to all labor members of Parliament, asking them whether they had read Bellamy's works and to what extent they had been influenced

by them. Bellamy, wrote Mr. Lyons, had consolidated his socialist outlook; and he added: *"The Parable of the Water Tank* has
been my platform standby for years."[27] Dr. D. G. McMillan,
representative for Dunedin West, replied: "Hearty congratulations on an effort to revive the socialist outlook. Organized
socialism in New Zealand is dead at the very time when it
should be most active. Anything I can do for you I will be
pleased to."[28] The Prime Minister wrote: "The book *Equality*
is one which, in my opinion, should be read by all."[29]

Only two members of Parliament joined the Bellamy Society
in 1936—Lyon and H. E. Herring—but a note in the society's
minutes, possibly based on the returns to the questionnaire, lists
an additional seven labor members as "Bellamyists in Government": J. Thorn, C. Carr, E. J. Howard, C. M. Williams, W.
Lee Martin, A. S. Richards, and Dr. D. G. McMillan. Mrs.
Catherine Stewart, who was elected to Parliament in 1938,
joined the Bellamy Society in that year.

Efforts to form branches of the society outside Wellington
were largely unsuccessful. The printed *Constitution* of November, 1936, lists foundation members from Kaitaia in the far
north to Shag Point and Otautau in the south, but only in Auckland and Christchurch were there sufficient numbers to make
branches possible. The most active Christchurch member was
Mr. L. B. Freeman, a solicitor. Several times the formation
of a Christchurch branch was announced as imminent in the
*Standard,* but it somehow never came to pass. In Auckland,
on the other hand, a branch was formed on April 15, 1937,
with Mr. S. Oldfield as president and Mr. J. Kay as secretary-
treasurer. In Kaitaia, Mr. A. E. Hollay called, on his own initiative, a public meeting in 1940 and formed a Bellamy Club
which held meetings for a year. This group had no connection
with the Wellington society which by then was all but defunct.

Through Mrs. Bellamy, Scott learned of the existence of an
International Bellamy Association, with headquarters in Holland. Letters were exchanged and news of New Zealand activities appeared in the *Bellamy Nieuws,* while the *Standard* reprinted the latest reports from Holland. Scott also maintained
contact with Bellamy groups in Indonesia and with American
organizations such as the Commonwealth Federation of Colorado.

The Bellamy Society's major activity of the year 1938 was
the appearance of Scott and W. O. Beere before the Parliamentary National Health and Superannuation Committee. The
labor government had published proposals for a far-reaching

social security scheme and a Select Committee of the House of Representatives had been appointed to examine these proposals and to hear evidence from interested individuals and organizations. The representatives of the Bellamy Society appeared before this committee on April 26, 1938. While congratulating the government, Scott suggested that more money should be spent on the scheme. "Superannuation," he said, "should not be paid as a compassionate allowance, but as a right. It should be payable to every citizen on a basis of strict equality, irrespective of need or income. Normally, age and term of residence should be the only qualifications." Scott urged the government to proclaim a declaration of human rights; for every New Zealander should be entitled by right or by law to a living or a share in the country's wealth. He should be entitled to employment which would enable him to work for a living. He should have access to land or other means of producing a livelihood. Every citizen, man, woman and child, should have a share in the social heritage—an equal share eventually, but, to start with, a share. "The first step in the restoration of that social heritage to the people as a whole should be the absolute right of every citizen to receive a social dividend when he or she has reached the age of 60 years. . . . The second step should be the establishment of a social dividend for children, or Motherhood endowment."[30]

Scott was closely questioned by members of the committee, among them the Prime Minister, Mr. Savage, and the Minister of Finance, Mr. Nash. "I should like to go all the distance you have spoken of," Mr. Savage told him, "but we shall get there all right. There is no need to worry on that score."[31] The committee approved the government's proposals but added a recommendation in line with Scott's submissions that "immediately the procedure for the social security proposals has been instituted, the Government should consider the extension of the scheme to provide a gradual increase in allowable income until universal superannuation is realized."[32] As will be seen, these reforms were realized.

By 1938, enthusiasm for Bellamy seems to have waned. Nothing further was heard of the Auckland branch of the Bellamy Association and it seems, therefore, to have ceased to function. The "Bellamy Society Notes" continued to appear weekly in the *Standard*, but they consisted mostly of extracts from *Equality* and announcements of the society's monthly meetings. Lack of funds precluded the publication of another pamphlet; but

Scott, now employed by the Broadcasting Service, used his position to propagate the ideas of the American prophet.

## VI  *The Radio Scripts*

In a letter to Mrs. Bellamy dated April 17, 1938, Scott not only outlined his plans for such broadcasts but told of receiving a full-length stage play based on *Looking Backward* which had been sent to him by a correspondent in Sydney, Australia, who called herself "Tory Bic" and who came from Canada. Scott announced that he intended to deliver a broadcast lecture about Bellamy on the anniversary of his death and to accompany it with musical interludes. He also revealed that he broadcasted a radio program "Musical Memories" every other Sunday afternoon from Wellington and that he always managed to "get a bit of propaganda into these musical talks."[33]

Included in the material in the file of the late Mrs. Bellamy and of her daughter Mrs. Marion Bellamy· Earnshaw are three radio scripts which give a clear picture of the type of propaganda which Scott presented. One of them—undated—is entitled "Talk on Social Justice" but a notation in Scott's handwriting states that the broadcast was "over 2ZA Wellington" and that it was relayed "to 1ZB, Auckland; 3ZB, Christchurch; and 4ZB, Dunedin." In the opening lines of the script, Scott stated that he was speaking under the auspices of "The Crusade for Social Justice," which he identified as "the name of an organization with headquarters in Auckland."

During the broadcast he spoke about the need for ideals; their importance in the formation of the future, when they became reality; and the contrast idealism formed with the "spirit of self-satisfaction, self-advancement at the expense of others," with "the lust for power manifested by certain individuals, groups and nations," and with "cynical acceptance of evils, social injustice, unemployment, poverty, and so on, as necessary evils." After pointing out that no social evils were necessary, Scott attacked "the *laissez-faire* attitude" and the "armed hooliganism of reactionary dictatorships." He affirmed that there was still idealism in the world but that it might, indeed, be responsible for—or an excuse for—"the springing up of a counter-growth, maleficent, anti-social, poisonous species of weed that will attempt but will not succeed in strangling the flowers of idealism—social justice."

Turning to a discussion of lust for power and self-advancement, Scott stated that these—personal and national—were expressions of the desire for security "for self, for family, for class interests, for a national group. . . . It is striving for partial social justice which after all means social injustice." To him, "there is no personal security except in social security. There can be no personal justice in social injustice. . . . There is no security in selfishness." And then, as might be expected, Scott introduced the author of *Looking Backward* and *Equality*.

After quoting from Bellamy about the impossibility of finding personal security so long as social insecurity exists and after equating Bellamy's concepts with the message of Christ, Scott stated: "I believe he [Bellamy] has done more than any one man to advance the ideal of social justice and the fundamentals of the message of Christ, which, according to Bellamy, is one and the same thing, equality." After showing how many of the prophecies of Bellamy had come true, Scott then cited Bellamy's statements in *Equality* about the religious crusade which would secure social and economic security for all men.[34]

The two talks which Scott prepared for the celebration on May 22, 1938, of the fortieth anniversary of Bellamy's death are explicit examples of the type of material which he gave to the listeners of the New Zealand radio stations and of the clarity with which he presented the basic ideas of Bellamy's Utopian novels. In the script entitled "The Prophet is Not Dead," Scott presented a program with music from Sullivan and from Grieg about which he had written to Mrs. Bellamy. A fifteen-minute broadcast, it was geared to capture the fancy of the audience; for the emphasis was upon Bellamy as a prophet who had foretold many developments which had been accomplished by the 1930's:

> Over fifty years ago Edward Bellamy predicted and accurately described radio broadcasting as we now know it, and even better than we know it. We can get some new ideas about broadcasting from his books—written fifty years ago, mind. Bellamy also predicted and described television over forty years ago in his last book *Equality*—real television as it will come. He describes theatre-going by radio and television and envisages a trip around the world from an arm-chair, by means of television. To get a better appreciation of what this means it is only necessary to remind ourselves that the first crude broadcasting was done in 1920 and that what we now understand as broadcasting is not much more than about ten years old. And Bellamy gave us an accurate description of it over fifty years ago.
>
> Bellamy prophesied with amazing accuracy the mechanical and electrical devices that have come to us only in recent years

and also the social and economic changes through which the world is passing today. Let us look at some of Bellamy's prophesies in the realm of invention and also in the realm of human events. Bellamy—fifty years ago, mark you—predicted the passing of the horse and the coming of the motor car and smooth roads. He visualized the passenger aeroplane—air cars that could hover and rise and descend vertically. That is yet to come, and it will come. And his pen pictures of radio and television are arresting.

His list of predictions is a large one and includes: Airships, radio, television, electric cooking and heating, dictaphone, counting and bookkeeping machines, invisible lighting systems, the electric eye, production of cold from heat and heat from cold, artificial silks and cloth of all sorts from vegetable fibres, paper clothing, dishes, footwear, etc. ("making paper as hard as steel"), seamless clothing, utilization of the tides for power, heating, etc., phonographic writing. With regard to this latter item, Bellamy prophesies that handwriting will in time become almost a lost art, and already there are definite indications that he is right.

After relating that Bellamy in both *Looking Backward* and *Equality* had told the story of a rich young man who had slept until the year 2000, Scott remarked that Bellamy, in telling the story of what his hero left behind when he fell asleep and of what he saw when he awakened, "traverses every phase of social and economic life—life as we know it today." Scott then pasted in the script the following printed clipping from what must have been an article by him; for, in other sections of his script, he had always been very careful to state sources. This clipping reads:

Scientists and economists, too, are "discovering" Edward Bellamy. The once-belittled Utopian, the "impractical visionary," is proving after all to be more practical, more scientific than the self-styled practical or scientific socialist economists of thirty, forty, or fifty years ago. And certainly Bellamy is years ahead of the most up-to-date of the orthodox-economists of the present day. And for that matter he is still ahead of most of the so-called new school.

Edward Bellamy's writings have stood the test of time—a very severe test throughout the period in man's history when more changes have taken place than in any other similar period. I refer to the last thirty or forty years. Edward Bellamy s writings are better understood—more understandable—today than when they were first published. They will be still better understood and appreciated ten years hence, and by the year 2000

A.D., I venture to predict, Edward Bellamy will be looked upon as the world's greatest teacher and prophet. The idealism that Bellamy inspires is deep-seated, fundamental, permanent. Thousands of men and women in all walks of life in this little Dominion, and many millions of people throughout the world have received from Edward Bellamy's writing the inspiration for their life's work—or dreams—their hopes of a better, freer, happier world, a world in which the milk of human kindness will flow more generously, more naturally.

These people believe, with Edward Bellamy, in his words: "What the divines and philosophers of the old world never would have believed, that human nature in its essential qualities was good, not bad, that men by their natural intention and structure are generous, not selfish; pitiful, not cruel; sympathetic, not arrogant; God-like in aspirations, instinct with divine impulses of tenderness and self-sacrifice, images of God indeed, not the travesties upon Him they had seemed."[35]

In the radio script entitled "Two 'Books of the Age' as well as 'Books of the Moment'" Scott devoted his time on the network to a serious consideration of Bellamy's ideas as the solution of world problems. After briefly relating his life and death, his intent in his Utopian romances, his prophetic vision in describing the inventions and conveniences listed in Scott's other speech, Scott gave the following appraisal of Bellamy's two books.

These two works of Edward Bellamy, from some points of view, may be regarded not only as books of the moment, but as books of the age. And if it be thought in saying this that I am making an extravagant claim I would ask my hearers a single question. I would ask whether if two books presented a social and economic plan capable of accomplishment, which might be adopted, and under which almost all the evils from which the world is at present suffering would be alleviated, would they not merit the designation of "books of the age?" Under the Bellamy Scheme international wars would be ended—their root-causes having been removed; unemployment would have ceased; there would be no poverty or material distress amongst individuals or classes; and sordid elements that tincture and befoul the thoughts and dealings of people under the competitive profit-system would be eliminated; racial, and even religious, antagonism would be eased, if not removed, their causes too having disappeared.

The professions would be purified, the question of material gain no longer being a consideration. The aged, infirm, and children would no longer suffer hunger or want. I do not ask my hearers, on my word alone, to believe that all these things could be brought about. But I ask them to read, and study, the books, and then to ask themselves whether my claim be true. . . .

At this point in the speech, Scott turned from a consideration of Bellamy and his novels to a summation of his ideas. Because of the excellence and the appeal in the 1930's of his summary, the following extract from the script is quoted:

Bellamy believed, as is now proved, that there is enough in the world to supply the needs of all—food, clothing, and shelter; as well as the good things of life that people might reasonably need, or want to enjoy. He believed that these desirable things should be within the reach of all. He believed that science, inventions and machinery would not only enable all to be supplied with the good and necessary things, but that they could be produced, distributed and enjoyed without the necessity of grinding toil on the part of the masses, or the soul-wearing anxieties so often endured by business and professional classes. And that all should be given the opportunity, and leisure, to dwell upon and realize the purpose of existence. Machinery, he considered, should spell leisure and freedom from drudgery, not unemployment. And believing these things, he set himself the task of showing how all this might be brought about, not by upsetting everything, or by bloody revolution, but by merely utilizing, sensibly, reasonably and justly, for the benefit of all, what is at hand and what has been accomplished. He showed how, in the process, none need be dispossessed of what is their due. He did not want to rob the rich to enrich the poor. Nor did he advocate reducing everyone to a dead level of equality, or of mediocrity. He aimed at unity, but unity through diversity, not uniformity.

The main features of Bellamy's plan, worked out in detail in his books, are these. All land would belong to the State. And it should be so, for, in reality, God Almighty is the only Landlord. The State would only hold land as the Trustee for the benefit of all living at present on earth, and for posterity. Therefore land could not be alienated. Yet people might fully enjoy and occupy land, and have its use under leasehold title, provided they paid the dues to the State for such right. The means for the payment of such dues, and indeed for all else, would be furnished to all by the State, as will be indicated later. Incidentally, this payment for leasehold use of land would be the only tax. For the State would give dividends and benefits to its members rather than, as now, burdening them with taxes. The State would assume responsibility for production. And in return for supplying its members with the results of production (for the State would be the sole supplier of goods and services), it would receive payment for what was supplied, very much as at present, from the wherewithal to make such purchases, which would be given to all adults annually till death. In return for this guaranteed income all capable of service would render it to the State till middle life was reached.

The question is asked, "Where is all the money to come from to do all this?" Here we come to an important point requiring attention. In the plan Bellamy depicts there would be no "money" in the sense we ordinarily regard it. What we might call "money of account" would be furnished to all adults in the shape of a handsome income, or credit, given annually till death. The value of such money would remain constant, and could not be halved as the pound sterling was during the war, or rendered worthless as the German Mark was about the same time, or largely diminished as in the case of the Franc about nine years later. Nor could such money be saved. There would be no necessity for saving or hoarding. All would always have sufficient, and their future needs guaranteed.

This individual yearly income given for life to each adult, male or female, would be their share of the Total National Annual Income. Bellamy carefully estimated that this in the United States would be four thousand dollars, or, at the old rate of exchange, about 800 odd. Production there could be easily multiplied twenty times over. In other parts of the world much the same applies, so individual incomes could be easily increased, if necessary, by merely "speeding-up" production. But with prices about half [the] present ruling rates, incomes would be amply sufficient.

After quoting from *Looking Backward* the passage in which Bellamy insisted that the possession of money was no indication of a rightful title to it and that a society based upon buying and selling was "essentially anti-social in all its tendencies" because it was an "education in self-seeking at the expense of others," Scott devoted himself to a description of the service the Bellamy state would require of all its citizens. He said:

The books fully explain how the money-system would work, and how the "money" or credit would be given to all adults for service. Each would serve according to his, or her, capacity and endowments. People would "carry on" much as at present, only they would work systematically under a co-operative system of production for use and for general distribution, instead of under a happy-go-lucky cut-throat competitive scheme of production for individual profit, and for exportation.

The true welfare of a nation is not measured by what it produces (or exports) but by what it consumes. And working thus for the general good and the welfare of all, individual incentive would not be diminished, the spirit of emulation would still remain. Effort indeed should, and possibly would, be greater in the mass working for their own interests instead of for others. Individual initiative and emulation would not be smothered, but instead of trying to get the better of our neighbor, we should be striving to excel in laudable pursuits, and in our service to the State. The holding of personal effects would still obtain, but such possessions would not, as now, be held precariously and insecurely, but security for the same, and for leasehold possession of our dwelling places, as desired, would be safeguarded and guaranteed for life.

It might be thought that all this is too good to be true. There are millions, however, who consider such ideas as Bellamy put forward as practicable and practical, as well as desirable. Their number is rapidly increasing, and this, it might be remarked, is brought about more by existing unsatisfactory conditions and by circumstances, and the glaring failure of the present "system" to "deliver the goods," than by the preaching of enthusiasts. It is, however, noteworthy that an ever-growing number of level-headed thinkers espouse the cause put forward by Bellamy.

To prove his last point, Scott—like Fred. Bell of South Africa —mentioned the radio address of Principal Rollo G. Reynolds, of the Horace Mann School, New York, which had been delivered on February 11, 1938. According to Scott, Reynolds had not only praised Bellamy and his ideas but had ended with the "following passage—'Edward Bellamy dreamed of a land where want in the midst of plenty was unknown—a land where citizens lived full, rich and happy lives. Such a land is still a dream, but it is in reach of reality. If there is any goal to which the Public School should dedicate itself, it is so to teach its children that this dream may come true.'"

Like Bell, Scott also cited the address given by the Reverend John Haynes Holmes and entitled "Four Reforms Which Would Save the World." In his summation of this address, Scott wrote in his script: "Mr. Holmes describes as his 'first reform' the Nationalization of Land as advocated by Henry George in his book *Progress and Poverty*. This he calls his foundation on which he wishes to erect the Bellamy edifice. He appears to have forgotten that Bellamy himself started with this same foundation. Mr. Holmes' 'second reform' is the whole social structure envisaged by Bellamy, which he unreservedly recommends. Indeed he goes so far as to say, 'As surely as *Progress and Poverty* is the Old Testament of our American social Bible, so surely is *Looking Backward* the New. The two books fit

together perfectly as the two parts of a completed whole.' "
Of Mr. Holmes' third reform, birth control, Scott—like Bell also
—opined that Bellamy had dealt with this subject more com-
prehensively and more clearly in *Equality* than had Mr. Holmes.

Of the fourth reform, the abolition of war, Scott said: "In a
Bellamy world the root-causes of war would no longer exist.
They are all to be found in the competitive profit system em-
bedded in the realms of finance and economics. They comprise
economic rivalries, trade jealousies and hostile tariffs, as well
as the financial obligations and considerations arising out of
such matters. The point I would here make is that all the
reforms even such a publicist as Mr. Holmes considered necessary were fully comprehended and dealt with by Mr. Bellamy. . . ."

Before concluding, Scott stressed the point that Bellamy "was
essentially a torch-bearer, one who lit and indicated the way.
One whose finger directly points to a bright and clear path
towards sunnier heights from a world in gloom." Scott then
emphasized that Bellamy's general principles and plans needed
to be studied, for "details will have to be adapted to time and
circumstances while the structure is being raised." He also
asserted that Bellamy did not believe in political parties because "parties imply disunion. The part can never attain to
the unity of the whole. His idea was to help humanity as a
whole. And so it is with the International League that bears
his name." The objectives of the Bellamy Society of New Zealand were then briefly stated.

In the last section of his broadcast, Scott also declared that
the change to the Bellamy plan was to be effected "in a comparatively peaceful manner." He then quoted Mrs. Edward
Bellamy who, "writing last December said,—'Mr. Bellamy always
warned against action that was not the result of careful preparation, and reiterated again and again that he was an evolutionist, not a revolutionist, and that he did not advocate the pulling
down of one brick in the old structure until a new and better
one was ready to be put into its place.' "

Scott concluded: "Many others there be who though they
share Bellamy's ideas, and also believe that the impending
change can be brought about in a constitutional manner yet
fear that the change is not nigh. They ask, 'How can it be
brought about?' I would reply—'We may make of this world
what we will, first by having a Vision, then uniting to accomplish it.' We must first realize that the patient is ill, then know
the cause. Then the remedy. Then apply it." According to Scott,

Bellamy had diagnosed the disease, stated the remedy, and described how it should be applied.[36]

When Scott reported to Mrs. Bellamy on June 1, 1938, he stated that his broadcasts had been very well received and he then added that "we are always spreading the light."[37] He had also stated in his letter of April 9, 1937, that progress was being made in spreading the ideas of Bellamy; that the demand for his books was increasing; and that the "weekly notes in the *Standard*" were "having a distinct influence on the Labor Movement here. More and more people are realizing that membership in the Labor Party is not enough."[38]

## VII  *Bellamy's Contribution*

Despite the efforts and the optimism of Scott, the days of the popularity of Bellamy's ideas were drawing to a close by 1939. At the monthly meeting of the Bellamy Society of April 26, 1939, the secretary, W. H. Scammell, announced that he felt he was wasting his time and offered to resign. He was, however, prevailed upon to retain his office. The society won, however, a small, delayed victory when the annual conference of the Labor Party that year approved a remit, submitted by the party's Gisborne branch, that Bellamy's books and similar works be included in school libraries and courses of English literature.

In the Labor Party, at that time, a split was developing between the followers of Mr. John A. Lee, M. P. for Grey Lynn, and the more financially orthodox leaders of the party; Lee had the support of the money reformers. At a meeting of the Bellamy Society, on August 30, a motion was put forward that the society congratulate Mr. Lee for his able speeches in Parliament. This was amended, however, and the society decided to congratulate the Prime Minister on the able speeches made by members of his party, without singling out any individual for praise.

In September, 1939, at the first meeting following the outbreak of war, Scammell finally resigned as secretary. The publication of the "Bellamy Society Notes" in the *Standard* ceased. Only two poorly attended meetings were held in 1940; and on September 17, 1941, Scott called another to decide whether the society should be reconstructed or ended. Nine people attended, but only three were members of the society. Scott and the secretary offered to resign if anyone else wished to take office and put new life into the society, but there was no response. A second meeting, held on September 30, was attended by eight people. After Scott moved that the society be wound up but could not find a seconder, it was decided to adjourn for six months and to leave it to the president and secretary to call the next meeting.

This next meeting was never held. The Edward Bellamy Society ceased to function, although it remained formally registered. Scott himself was transferred to Palmerston North, where he managed the local radio station. "The Bellamy Society has gone into recess," he wrote Mrs. Bellamy in August, 1943; and he added his explanation for the lack of progress in New Zealand: "The New Zealand Labor Government has moved away from the true socialist conception of things. It's nothing but compromise after compromise until now the Labor Government is not much better than any capitalist government. . . . The Bellamy (or true socialist) technique is to build a new system and not control the old one."[39]

Scott, in fact, shared the views of John A. Lee who had been expelled from the Labor Party in 1940 and had formed his own Democratic Labor Party. Under the pseudonym of "Peter Peregrin," Scott contributed regularly to *John A. Lee's Weekly.* When he returned to Wellington after World War II, he devoted his energies to the consumer cooperative movement in the new state housing areas in the Hutt Valley. They presented, he claimed, "some similarity to the Bellamy transition stage wherein public service stores and warehouses are established and operated on a co-operative, non-profit basis in competition with, or rather independent of existing establishments of private enterprise operating on a profit basis."[40]

In Napier, Mr. A. E. Hollay, who had gone there to live, formed a Bellamy group in 1945 by calling a public meeting. Regular meetings were held in large tearooms until, in Mr. Hollay's own words, "a strong section of communists joined up and started to preach the doctrine that nothing could be done through orthodox legislation, and direct action would have to be resorted to. This did not please me or most of the members, so I went into recess and have not been able to get going again."[41]

The Wellington Bellamy Society was not revived after the war. When the last secretary, James Rough, died in September, 1954, Scott consulted with the surviving members of the executive committee and they decided to de-register the Society. This deregistration became effective on April 17, 1955.

Although formally in existence for almost nineteen years, the Bellamy Society was active only between 1936 and 1941. Its

FIGURE 1. "One of the most interesting issues of *Bellamy* is the one of March 22, 1950, which celebrated the hundredth anniversary of Edward Bellamy's birth." In that issue, this woodcut by a Dutch artist was published on the front page.

Officieel sociaal-economisch orgaan van de Internationale Vereniging Bellamy   11e Jaargang No. 6
22 Maart 1950

**BELLAMY**

Abonnementsprijs ƒ 2,50 per jaar   Verschijnt elke 14 dagen   Prijs 10 cent
Redactie: Terraweg 68, Santpoort-Dorp   Redactie-secretariaat: Caninefatenstraat 13, Haarlem-N., Tel. 25361
Administratie: Stichting Centr. Adm. Bellamy, Stationsweg 89, Ede, Tel. 8113, Postgiro 136123

## KORTE LEVENSBESCHRIJVING VAN
# EDWARD BELLAMY

Edward Bellamy werd geboren op 26 Maart 1850 te Chicopee Falls, toen een plaats van 8000 inwoners, nu een voorstad van Springfield in het Westen van de Amerikaanse staat Massachusetts (Indiaanse naam, die betekent „land der blauwe heuvelen"). De bevolking van deze staat bestond uit verschillende kleine gemeenschappen, die zeer democratisch waren aangelegd en geen dwang van buiten dulden. Toen de dertien Amerikaanse koloniën zich noodgedwongen aaneensloten tot een unie, de Verenigde Staten, die doet denken aan de Unie van Utrecht in de Nederlandse geschiedenis, had zich het karakter dezer kolonies, die nu staten werden, reeds gevormd. Behalve als geboorteplaats van Edward Bellamy is Chicopee bekend door de grote bronzen deuren van het gebouw der volksvertegenwoordiging te Washington, het nationale Capitool, die in Chicopee gegoten zijn.

Het geslacht Bellamy behoort tot de eerste kolonisten der Verenigde Staten. Reeds in 1650 worden de voorvaderen van Edward Bellamy in Amerika vermeld. Een van hen was gehuwd met Francis Sherman, van de familie van Roger Sherman, een der ondertekenaars van de vermaarde Onafhankelijkheids-Verklaring. Het geslacht Bellamy leverde verschillende predikanten op. De vader van Edward Bellamy, Rufus Bellamy, was doopsgezind predikant in Chicopee Falls vanaf 1848, waar hij 34 jaren het ambt waarnam. De moeder van Edward Bellamy was dochter van een doopsgezind predikant. Edward's vader was een zeer goedhartig mens, die de gewoonte had, om hem na een huwelijk door de bruidegom gegeven gebruikelijke geldgeschenk, in de meeste gevallen de bruid weder in de hand te drukken als bescheiden bijdrage voor het nieuwe huisgezin.

Edward Bellamy had drie broeders, twee oudere en een jongere. De oudste stierf plotseling op 25 jarige leeftijd gedurende een reis in het Zuiden van Frankrijk. De band tussen de broeders was altijd zeer innig en sterker dan men gewoonlijk tussen broers aantreft. De zorgen van de moeder van Edward Bellamy kwam door haar bezwekt met Wiliam Packer van Brooklyn tot grote welstand. Packer overleed in 1850 en liet groot vermogen aan zijn weduwe na, de bijzonder gehecht was aan haar zuster's familie. Dit verklaart de grote zorgen aan de opvoeding der broeders besteed en de voor hun stand zeer kostbare buitenlandse reizen. Toen hij eventueel volwassen was, kon mets Edward Bellamy mede bewegen, geldelijke hulp te aanvaarden.

Tien jaar oud, gaf hij reeds uitdrukking aan zijn groeiende belangstelling voor een „werkkring", dat hij later de hoekstenen noemde van zijn maatschappelijk stelsel. Hij bewonderde militaire „organisatie" in het algemeen en oriende van een militaire loopbaan voor zichzelf. Die droom werd op zijn 18de levensjaar verstoord, doordat hij werd afgekeurd voor de militaire academie der Verenigde Staten in West Point.

In 1868 waren de families Bellamy en Packer samen op reis in Europa. Edward bleef in Amerika en zette zijn studie voort. De plotselinge dood van zijn oudste broeder Packer (naar de achternaam van zijn oom genoemd) en de sterke aandrang van zijn familie be-

wogen Edward zijn studie in Amerika tijdelijk te laten rusten en ook naar Europa te gaan met zijn neef William. Beide jongelui zetten hun studie voort in Dresden, leerden Duits en andere talen, en interesseerden zich voor Europese toestanden. Een in de nalatenschap van Edward Bellamy gevonden schrift van een verhaal doet vermoeden, dat zij ook enige dagen aan de Hollandse kust hebben vertoefd. Zij brachten ruim een jaar in Europa door.

Toen Edward Bellamy in Duitsland was, vocht Karl Marx met Bakounin en Proudhon in de Eerste Internationale om de beginselen der maatschappelijke revolutie. Zonder twijfel was later in Amerika Edward Bellamy niet onbeïnvloed door het Marxisme, van Europa overgebracht. Maar afschoon dit zijn diepe bewogenheid en geweldige staatskracht gegeven zou hebben, verwierp hij het. Hij zag verder dan zijn tijdgenoten hen verloop van de maatschappelijke strijd. Hij deed daarom doelbewust afstand van de tijdelijke tactische voordelen, die het ontketenen der lagere mens-lijke hartstochten en het in werking stellen der lagere menselijke drijfveren hem ongetwijfeld opgeleverd zouden hebben.

Edward Bellamy was zich terdege bewust van de klassenstrijd. Als eerlijk mens erkende hij dan ook het bestaan ervan. Maar als wijs mens met een diep inzicht in het maatschappelijk gebeuren, erkende hij niet de politieke, maar niet de economische noodzaak ervan. Zijn streven was niet een tijdelijk onderdrukte klasse aan de macht te helpen, maar rechtvaardigheid te doen zegevieren. Hij wist te wel, dat door machtsverovering de onderdrukte klasse van vroeger de onderdrukkende klasse van later kon worden. Hiervan aan wilde hij beslist niet medewerken. Zijn streven was niet enkel een onderdrukte klasse tijdelijk te helpen, maar de gehele mensheid metterdaad voor altijd.

Hij bouwde daarom zijn leer en zijn arbeid niet op de werking der lagere menselijke drijfveren, die als onvermijdelijk gevolg der maatschappelijke ontwikkeling ten slotte toch met meer technisch bruikbaar zijn en dan automatisch uitgeschakeld worden. Maar op de hogere scheppende drijfveren, die in later leven van de mens aanwezig zijn of waren en slechts wachten om zich te ontwikkelen in het grote maatschappelijk gebeuren. Zodra de lagere menselijke drijfveren als hoerwinde en doorslag revende maatschappelijke factoren zijn uitgespeeld en de hogere vanzelf aan bod. De economische leer van Bellamy is dan ook de enige duurzame uitweg voor de mensheid.

In Dresden bezocht Edward Bellamy de grote door de staat geëxploiteerde porceleinfabrieken, die aat een werkgelegenheid bood, ongetwijfeld was dit van invloed op zijn latere gedachtenontwikkeling. Het meeste en pijnlijkste troffen hem echter de Europese maatschappelijke tegenstellingen, die uit economische oorzaken ontstonden, het gehele maatschappelijke leven ontwrichten en ongezond maakten.

In Amerika teruggekeerd, beëindigde hij met succes zijn rechtskundige studie, was twee jaren op een advocatenkantoor werkzaam en werd niet tot de rechtsbank toegelaten. Het beroep van advocaat ging hem echter steeds meer tegenstaan, naar mate hij zich bewust werd, dat oneerlijheid en strijd tussen de mensen zijn voornaamste bronnen van inkomsten moesten zijn.

Het duurde niet lang of hij gaf zijn advocatenpraktijk voor goed op en werd redactioneel medewerker aan de New York Evening Post in 1871 en daarna van de Springfield Daily Union in 1872, waar hij enige jaren bleef.

In 1875 vond een gebeurtenis plaats, die geheel afgezien van enige betekenis van de zijde van Edward Bellamy, later van het grootste belang voor hem was. De Theosofische Vereniging werd door Mevr. Blavatsky in New York georganiseerd. Maar later aanbevelen werd van het boek van Bellamy van groot belang voor zijn beweging toen deze opkwam.

In 1878 publiceerde Edward Bellamy zijn eerste novelle, die later door andere gevolgd werd; en door een bijzondere stijl en een ongewone inhoud zeer opviel. In 1880 werd door Edward Bellamy en zijn broeder Charles de driewekelijkse „Penny News" (in het leven geroepen, die spoedig een zeer grote oplage bereikte. Later werd het de „Springfield Daily News".

De zoon heeft steeds zijn vader innig lief gehad en geëerd als een groot schrijver. Maar het rotsvaste geloof in een schone toekomst der mensheid, zoals zijn vader die mit zijn geestenoog zag, was blijkbaar een onoverdraagbare gave van Edward Bellamy zelf. Paul Bellamy was van 1923-34 president van de Amerikaanse vereniging van dagblad-redacteuren. Is directeur en mede-eigenaar van de grote Associated Press, en heeft ere-doctoraten van drie verschillende Amerikaanse universiteiten. Is redacteur van de „Cleveland Plain Dealer", het grootste morgenblad in de staat Ohio.

In 1885 werd een dochter, Marion, geboren. Deze gebeurtenis deed de concrete belangstelling van Edward Bellamy verder groeien in een wereld, die zijn kinderen moesten erven en in hun bijzondere trok het vrouwenvraagstuk zijn aandacht.

In de winter van 1886 zette Edward Bellamy zich aan zijn schrijftafel neer, met het vaste voornemen, een boek te schrijven, dat zijn lang gekoesterde, steeds ontwikkelende en aan slotte rijp geworden gedachten over een nieuwe maatschappelijk stelsel zou openbaren. Teruggetrok uit het jaar 2000" het nieuw verspreiden. In 1887 was hij persoonlijk in Januari 1888 kwam „Terugblik uit het jaar 2000" uit, en eerst uit. Einde 1888 waren er nog geen 10.000 ex. In Amerika verkocht. In de volgende jaren echter de afzet echter snel, en toen waren er eerste millioen bereikt.

De geweldige oplaag, die zijn boek in „Nationalismaakte leidde tot het ontstaan van de „Nationalisticsche beweging". Een van de eerste clubs was in Boston. Vanaf Mei 1888 verscheen het tijdschrift „The Nationalist". Het theosofische tijdschrift „The Path" in Amerika begon het boek van Bellamy warm aan te bevelen. Het Londense theosofische tijdschrift „Lucifer" volgde het voorbeeld. Het optiewekkende boek „The Key to Theosophy" van Mevr. Blavatsky kwam uit en bevatte aanbeveling In 1890 waren er in Californië alleen over de 60 Nationalistische clubs en in geheel Amerika wellicht tien maal zoveel. De Nationalisten leer klinkt het woord „nationalistisch" in verband met de Bellamy-beweging in later jaren, vond de huidige tijdsgeschiedenis nog vreemd in de zeer huidige tijdsgeest nog vreemd. En in geheel Amerika wellicht tien maal zoveel. Vergeten moet echter niet worden dat wij toen in 1886 beleven. Toen had trouwens het woord „communisme" een andere klank dan nu. Verder mag niet uit het oog worden verloren, dat het begrip „nationaal" het woord zelf nog niet dezelfde betekenis heeft in Amerika en in Europa niet de tijd van Bellamy. Voor Voor de Amerikanen in de tijd van Edward Bellamy vertolkte het woord „nationaal" de werkelijke ontwikkeling der 48 afzonderlijke en nauw zelfstandige staten met hun eigen belangen te een geheel wikkelde staten met hun eigen belangen te een geheel met gemeenschappelijke belangen. Een vervuld begrip dan In het Europa van onze tijd vooral is het woord „nationaal" een verengend begrip geworden, omdat het nationaal te nauw verbonden is aan de continentale Europese verwikkelingen.

## HERDENKINGSNUMMER
Edward Bellamy, auteur van „Looking Backward" en „Equality",
werd op 26 Maart 1850 geboren te Chicopee Falls

**Fraternal Greetings**
to
Family of Edward Bellamy
Springfield (Mass.)
Cleveland (Ohio)

**Edward Bellamy Centenary**
Los Angeles (Cal.)

**Dr. Arthur E. Morgan**
Yellow Springs (Ohio)

**and all other friends**
in the U.S.A.

In 1882 huwde hij Emma Augusta Sanderson, 11 jaren zijn jongere. In 1884 werd een zoon, Paul Bellamy geboren. Volgens Bellamy had deze gebeurtenis wel „te maken met het verschijnen van zijn liverdblad." Voorzien, zei hij, had hij de gewoonte over maatschappelijke vraagstukken te denken als een bedachtdrang. Toen hij evenwel ging denken over een wereld, waarin zijn eigen kinderen zouden moeten leren, begonnen al deze vraagstukken in eens uiterst concreet en praktisch voor hem te worden.

FIGURE 2.   "In this *Bellamy* commemorative issue articles were contributed by Mrs. Emma Sanderson Bellamy, the widow of Edward; by Paul Bellamy, his son; by Mrs. Marion Bellamy Earnshaw, his daughter; by Arthur E. Morgan, author of the first biography of Bellamy; by Norman Thomas, famous leader of American socialism; and by Adolf A. Berle, Jr., Assistant Secretary of State during the Franklin D. Roosevelt administration."

FIGURE 3. "But the non-political Bellamy Association of Holland today still has a membership of nearly two thousand people; it holds rallies and programs in various parts of the country; it publishes not only Bellamy's books . . . but also propaganda material in the form of leaflets, pamphlets and the newspaper *Bellamy.*" Among such material is *De Oplossing der Crisis,* the cover of which is pictured above.

# DE UITWEG

niet leden . . . f 1.50 per jaar
Nederland . . . . f 1.75 „ „
losse nummers . . . . f 0.15

No. 8
4e. Jaargang
MAANDBLAD
OCTOBER 1938.

Officieel Orgaan der Internationale Vereniging „Bellamy"
Centrale voor Nederlandsch-Indië

Redactie : Bellamy Huis. Logeweg 21/Tel. 1421/Bandoeng
Administratie : Tampomaslaan 12/Tel. 2327/Bandoeng.

## The
# EDWARD BELLAMY
## ASSOCIATION OF NEW YORK

*( formerly The Edward Bellamy Group of Brooklyn )*

### P. O. BOX 484
### GRAND CENTRAL ANNEX
### New York, N. Y.

---

#### Executive Committee

Sol Kashins, Chairman     George A. Kahn, Treasurer
Lou Kashins, Secretary     Leon Seltzer, Counsel

#### Honorary Members

Heywood Broun     Henry Neumann
John Dewey     Eliot White
Harry Elmer Barnes     Roger N. Baldwin
Mrs. Edward Bellamy

---

### PURPOSE

The Edward Bellamy Association of New York is a non-partisan and non-commercial organization devoted to achieving a social and economic system as advocated by Edward Bellamy in his "Looking Backward" and "Equality".

### PREAMBLE

There is no longer any doubt that something is radically wrong with our present social and economic system. As a result, innumerable remedies are being offered to increase consumption, and buying power, redistribute wealth, etc., and the depression-weary public snatches hopefully at them like the proverbially drowning man clutches at a straw. In his despair, there is but one thought in the drowning man's mind: to be saved. Finally a ship appears and rescues him. What joy and relief! But, after a brief period, during which his harrowing experience is all but forgotten, he discovers to his horror that the rescue ship is leaking. Suddenly the machinery breaks down and the boat sinks,—he is again drowning.

. . . . . .

This illustrates exactly the problem we have been contending with during the past fifty years. We have apparently been "saved" time and again from recurring periods of drowning or depression only to find that our rescue ships or so-called eras of prosperity quickly foundered.

---

## The EDWARD BELLAMY
## SOCIETY (N.Z.)
### (Incorporated)
#### G.P.O. Box 1305, Wellington (New Zealand).

Patron: Mrs. EMMA S. BELLAMY,
Springfield, Mass., U.S.A.

OFFICERS:
President: Mr ALEXANDER SCOTT.
Vice-Presidents: Prof. G. W. VON ZEDLITZ,
Mr. C. R. C. ROBIESON.

Executive Committee: Messrs. WYNFORD O. BEERE, J. W. TASKER, L. WADDEL, J. C. TURNER, J. A. ROUGH and E. A. DAHL.

Secretary: Mr. JAMES ROUGH.

Treasurer: Mr. E. A. DAHL.

---

## Constitution and Rules

1. The name of the Society shall be THE EDWARD BELLAMY SOCIETY, N.Z. (Incorporated).

SECTION 1.—OBJECTS.
2. The objects for which the Society is established are:—

(a) To disseminate the principles enunciated by Edward Bellamy as being a permanent cure for existing social and economic ills.

(b) To maintain contact with Bellamy Societies throughout the world and to foster world-wide fellowship therewith.

(c) To use all possible power and influence to ensure film productions, honestly and effectively portraying the principles and conditions set out in Bellamy's books.

(d) To arrange for delivery of lectures and the production of articles, pamphlets and other printed matter for educational purposes, and to secure the printing and distributing of moderately priced editions of Bellamy's books, and more particularly, if and when considered desirable, to establish a Bellamy Publishing Society (co-operative), and to take any other steps whatsoever that in the opinion of the Executive Council may appear desirable to further the objects of the Society and to further any other objects which, in the opinion of the Executive Council, may appear expedient and which are not inconsistent with the objects of the Society herein set out.

---

FIGURE 4. During the 1930's not only was there a revival of interest in Bellamy in the United States, where clubs were once again formed as they had been in the 1880's, but there were also Bellamy Leagues founded in Java, where *De Uitweg* was published as the official newspaper; in New Zealand, where the Bellamy Society was incorporated in Wellington but had many branches; and in South Africa.

FIGURE 5. The official insignia of the Netherlands Bellamy Association is the picture of the globe.

FIGURE 6. Alexander Scott played an important role in the Bellamy Society of New Zealand as a writer, lecturer, and radio speaker. In "December, 1935, Scott claimed that most of the members of the new government drew their inspiration from Edward Bellamy."

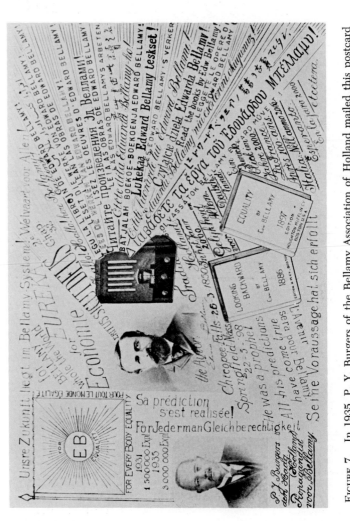

Figure 7. In 1935, P. Y. Burgers of the Bellamy Association of Holland mailed this postcard to members of all the governments of the world as his Christmas greeting and as a means of calling attention to the ideas of the American Utopian.

FIGURE 8. "Although it is impossible to assess the possible influence of the Indonesian Bellamy societies upon the populace, it is significant that natives were permitted to join them. A photograph sent to Mrs. Edward Bellamy shows a classroom and native teachers—and on the wall are two sketches; one of them is of Edward Bellamy and the other represents with a modern building the new world he had foretold."

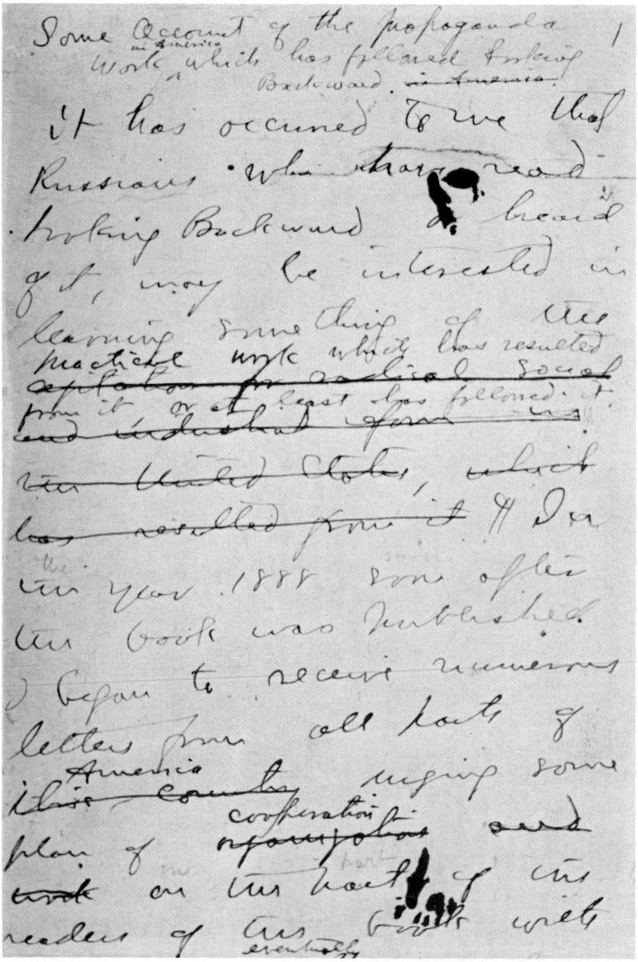
Some Account of the propaganda 1
Work in America which has followed Looking Backward.
It has occurred to me that Russians who have read Looking Backward or heard of it, may be interested in learning something of the practical work which has resulted from it or at least has followed it. In the year 1888 soon after the book was published I began to receive numerous letters from all parts of America urging some plan of cooperation on the part of the readers of the book with

FIGURE 9. "One of the most interesting and important publications during this period was an article by Bellamy which was written as a result of his direct contact with Russian journalists. Written for a charity collection published in Vologda for the benefit of peasants who had suffered deprivations as a result of crop failure, this article—dated March, 1892, and entitled 'Some Account of the Propaganda Work in America Which Has Followed *Looking Backward*'—related for 'Russians who have read' the Utopian novel the 'practical work which has resulted from it.' In this article (which has been preserved in the Moscow Literary and Art Archives and which is published for the first time in English in the 'Appendix' of this volume), Bellamy outlined the growth of the Bellamy Club movement, its basic principles, and the differences between Nationalism and Marxism."

EDVARD BELLAMY

# VUONNA
# ◇ 2000 ◇

SUOMENTANUT

J. K. KARI

◆

TOINEN PAINOS

◇ ◇

HELSINKI
TYÖVÄEN SANOMALEHTI OSAKEYHTIÖ

FIGURE 10.   In Finland ". . . after the Russian Revolution of 1905, a
re-issue of *Vuonna 2000* was needed; and it appeared in 1907 with
Kari's preface and in bright red covers. On the front cover was a picture showing a factory-lined street which was crammed with workers
marching with hands uplifted toward the rising sun. Needless to
say, *Vuonna 2000* was widely read among the working classes, and
it did not fail to have an impact upon its readers."

FIGURE 11. *Cien Años Después* "was published in Spanish in Genoa, Italy, by editor Carlos Maucci." This edition was widely circulated in South America.

# Das Programm der Nationalisten.

Von

## Edward Bellamy.*)

— Chicopee-Falls (Massachusetts). —

### I.

Die Veröffentlichung des folgenden Artikels in „Nord und Süd" giebt mir die willkommene Gelegenheit, den deutschen Lesern meines „Rückblicks" einige Worte über die Bewegung zur Einführung eines von Grund aus neuen Wirthschaftssystems zu sagen, welche in den Vereinigten Staaaten herbeizuführen jenes Buch beigetragen hat. Der Socialismus ist in Europa etwas Altes, aber in Amerika etwas Neues. Seit dem Beginn der modernen demokratischen und humanitären Bewegung hat in der alten Welt das Schauspiel des wirthschaftlichen Elends der Massen den Geist wohlmeinender und denkender Personen dazu bestimmt, über mögliche sociale Neuordnungen nachzusinnen, welche die allgemeine Wohlfahrt wirksam befördern würden. In den Vereinigten Staaten ist es ganz anders gewesen. Dank der Größe unseres noch nicht occupirten Continents, unserer ungeheueren materiellen Hilfsquellen und unserer relativ schwachen Bevölkerung hat es in unserem Volke bis ganz neuerdings wenig andauerndes oder weit ausgedehntes wirthschaftliches Elend gegeben. Jeder, der stark und bereit zum Arbeiten war, war bisher, allgemein zu reden, wohl in der Lage, sich einen guten Lebensunterhalt zu erwerben. Infolgedessen hatten socialistische Ideen absolut keinen Boden in diesem Lande. Nationalökonomische Gelehrte und einige Gruppen europäischer Einwanderer in unseren großen Städten wußten etwas vom Socialismus; aber das Volk im Allgemeinen wußte weder etwas von der Sache, noch wollte es etwas davon wissen.

*) Autorisirte Uebersetzung von Georg von Gizycki=Berlin.

FIGURE 12. In Germany, in 1892, Arthur von Kirchenheim stated: "Bellamy! Indeed, two or three years ago one could hear nothing else but Bellamy." In 1894, Bellamy's article, "First Steps toward Nationalism," translated by Professor von Gizycki, was published in *Nord und Süd*.

influence on New Zealand public opinion was slight compared with the impact made by *Looking Backward* in 1890, but it was not negligible. Despite its small membership, the society did reach a wider audience through its publications, regular notes in the *Standard*, and radio broadcasts. If Bellamy's writings, in the eighteen-nineties, prepared the ground for New Zealand's emergence as "the birthplace of the Twentieth Century,"[42] the Bellamy Society, in the thirties, helped push the country farther along the road to the Welfare State.

Because of persistent prodding from the left-wing, certain basic principles have become accepted as part of the New Zealand way of life: that every New Zealander is entitled to full employment (New Zealand, alone among western countries, has had virtually no unemployment for over twenty years); that he is entitled to his own home; to free education and health services; to motherhood endowments and universal superannuation; and to numerous other state-supplied benefits.

Mr. Scott, however, is fully aware of the fact that these ideals have not been reached in every case and that New Zealand is still far away from Bellamy's vision of the perfect society. "Economic equality as Bellamy visualized it," he writes, "could not operate alongside wages, profit, usury, land speculation, the buying and selling of houses, insurance racketeering, individual inheritance, etc. Property rights are ever so much more protected than human rights. New Zealand may be a bit less crude in its class distinctions in a social sense, but money talks here as loudly as anywhere else, if not more so."[43]

# CHAPTER NINE

# A Contribution to Scandinavian Socialism

By

## LARS AHNEBRINK

THE SCANDINAVIAN REACTION to the ideas of Bellamy is intimately connected with the emergence and growth of socialism in Denmark, Sweden, Norway, and Finland. To relate a detailed history of his vast and complicated influence in these countries is beyond the scope of this chapter; it will unfortunately be necessary, therefore, to indicate the most essential features of Bellamy's history and impact; but it is hoped that doing so will encourage other scholars to make more detailed studies of the reactions (1) of the socialist, liberal, and conservative publications, (2) of the socialists, and (3) of the Utopian novelists of Scandinavia after 1889 to the ideas of the great American Utopian novelist and socialist.

From Germany, socialist ideas spread to the Nordic countries where they were gradually adopted, first by labor organizations. As early as 1871 a Danish section of the First International was established; called Den internationale Arbejderforening for Denmark, it was directed by L. Pio, H. Brix and P. Geleff. In 1878 Socialdemokratisk Forbund was founded, and in 1884 this party was able to secure two seats in the Folketing; but, in 1909, it had twenty-four of the one hundred and fourteen seats.

In Norway a social-democratic association was founded in Oslo in 1885 by Chr. K. Knudsen, and in 1887 Det norske arbeiderparti was inaugurated. In 1903 the party won four seats in the Storting; but, by 1912, the party had secured 26 per cent of the votes and twenty-four seats. During the 1880's there also existed a number of social-democratic associations in Sweden, and in 1889 the *Sveriges social-demokratiska arbetarparti* was founded. In 1902, this group won four seats in the *Riksdag;* in 1905, fifteen; and in 1908, thirty-six. The first socialist representative to be elected to the *Riksdag* was Hjalmar Branting, who was elected to the Lower House in 1890, who was the most important figure in the rise and development of the Swedish labor party, and who eventually became prime minister. By 1926, the Social Democrats had become the largest single party in Sweden.

In Finland the *Socialdemokratiska parti* was founded in 1899, but it did not play a very important role in politics until after the Russian revolution of 1905 because the Finns suffered a series of persecutions which decreased the party's membership. By 1907 the party won, however, its first large representation of eighty seats—nine held by women—of the two hundred in the national house of representatives. In fact, the Finnish socialist party became the first in the world to have a majority of seats.

As this survey indicates, the ground was prepared for the reception of Bellamy's socialist *Looking Backward* when it first appeared in Scandinavian translation in 1889. In fact, the atmosphere was more than favorable; for the debate for and against socialism ran high and the socialists were making good headway. Many of Scandinavia's foremost writers and critics— Ibsen and Bjørnson in Norway, Brandes in Denmark, and August Strindberg in Sweden—were greatly stimulated by the social issues of the day; and the public itself was greedy for solutions to the eternal problems of equality, freedom, and brotherhood. The era was indeed concerned with dreams of the future—and even Hjalmar Branting wrote in 1887 an article entitled "En svensk utopist."[1]

## I  *Denmark*

Because of its geographical position, Denmark has been as a rule the first of the Nordic countries to be influenced by new ideas and particularly by those of the Continent. The socialist movement, as we have noted, first took root in Denmark, and it appeared there before other Scandinavian countries were fully aware of the implications of socialistic doctrines. Because of its location, Denmark also became the first country in the Nordic area to respond to the popularity of Bellamy.

As early as 1888 the Danish periodical *Illustert Tidende* began to serialize Bellamy's *En Kaerlighedshistorie,*[2] and in 1889 the first Danish translation of *Looking Backward* appeared under the title of *Anno 2000-1889;* the translation had been prepared by Fr. Winkel Horn (1845-1898), a Danish critic and translator who based his translation on the sixteenth American edition.[3] The response of the Danes to Bellamy's Utopian dream seems to have been more than favorable, and the novel had many admirers in literary and political circles. During the nineties, the debate for and against the Future Socialist State (*Fremtidsstaten*) was particularly lively in Denmark; and the names of Bebel, Eugen Richter, Henry George, and Edward Bellamy were frequently referred to in this discussion. A question of first importance was "*When* would the *Fremtidsstat* become a reality? Would it be in the year 2000 as Bellamy had predicted?"[4]

A long article by the Danish minister and translator U. Birkedal (1852-1931) entitled "Utopier og Virkelighed" in *Dansk Tidskrift,* presented a survey of Utopian writings from Plato to Bellamy—but four pages were devoted to a summary of the leading ideas of *Looking Backward.* Evidently himself a Utopian socialist, Birkedal stressed the important role which Utopias had played in the struggle for human rights; and, seemingly, socialism had become to him the new religion of the world which provided a new faith and a new hope for millions of workers. He concluded his article, which was favorable to Bellamy, with the following optimistic statement about *Looking Backward:* "A Utopia, of course, but the kind that makes King Mammon tremble on his throne. Yet his power is a terrible reality at the end of this century and seems more tyrannical than ever before. *Seems,* it is true, for the night is always darkest immediately before dawn."[5]

Because of Bellamy's early recognition in Denmark—and doubtless his popularity—the lesser known *Miss Ludington's Sister* (1884) was published in translation in 1891 as *Frøken Ludington's Søster,* and it was the only Scandinavian publication of this novel. Although *Miss Ludington's Sister* was quickly and deservedly forgotten, *Looking Backward* made its way into wider and wider circles of readers: the Utopia was, however, most enthusiastically received by the working classes of Denmark. A new edition of the book, entitled *Om 100 Aar,* was published in Aarhus in 1901; but it had originally been serialized in *Landarbejderen* (The Farm Worker). Although Bellamy's reputation suffered an eclipse during the two world wars, *Looking Backward* was retranslated by Eiler Jørgensen and republished in 1946 under the title *Tilbageblik Aar 2000.*

Although it is doubtful that *Equality* was ever translated in its entirety into a Scandinavian language, a twenty-two page pamphlet in Danish entitled *Lighed* was published in Copenhagen in 1905 as one of a series by the Copenhagen Socialist Youth Clubs' Publishing House; the translation was prepared by John Packness. *Lighed* contains the first chapter of *Equality* called "En skarp Forhørsdommer" (a sharp cross-examiner) and according to a note on page four, the next pamphlet was to contain Chapter II of *Equality*—"Hvorfor Revolutionen ikke kon for" (why the revolution did not come earlier)—and also Chapter III—"Jeg faar en Aktie i Landet" (I acquire a stake in the country).

The pamphlet also included the preface of *Equality*—with the exception of the first paragraph—and it included quotations from Rousseau, John Packness, Makato, and Bellamy.[6] The one from Rousseau read: "The fruits of the soil belong to everyone, the soil to no one." Because of this quotation, it seems probable that the publication was intended for circulation among the Danish working classes who would have most appreciated such a declaration.

## II  *Norway*

Bellamy seems to have played a less important role in Norway than in Denmark,[7] but he stimulated the socialist movement and caused some debate in the early 1890's. Although there seemingly was no translation in Norway of Bellamy's major works,[8] the Danish translations were easily accessible to Norwegian readers; furthermore, *Looking Backward* had been immediately translated and printed in the United States in Norwegian by Houghton Mifflin.[9] According to Professor Sigmund Skaard, a typewritten master's thesis about Bellamy was presented about 1950 by A. H. Hansen.[10]

The widely circulated Norwegian review *Kringsjaa*, which was a non-political periodical of general interest, devoted much attention to social, political, and cultural contemporary problems. The journal was ably edited by an idealistic Unitarian minister, H. Tambs Lyche, who had spent from 1880 to 1892 in the United States. Naturally, he gave much attention to the United States and to American writing in his magazine as an attempt, perhaps, to correct the false picture of the country given by the Norwegian writer Knut Hamsun, who had published in 1889 a mischievous attack on the United States in *Fra det moderne Amerikas Aandsliv*.

*Kringsjaa* carried in the issue of March 17, 1894, a description of American life on the western frontier—"Fra det fjerne

Vesten"—and also published eight illustrations. Two pages of this number were also devoted to Mark Twain, who, with Bret Harte, was said to be the best-known American author in Europe. In this same issue Bellamy was introduced to the readers of *Kringsjaa* by one of his own articles entitled "Det nationalistiske program,"[11] which had been taken from *The Forum*. A footnote stated that Bellamy was the author of the well-known socialist novel *Et tilbageblik* and the leader of the Nationalist movement in the United States. This movement, the readers were told, had most of its adherents among the well-to-do classes in the New England states and had found many spokesmen among community and church leaders.

Bellamy argued in his article that the Nationalist movement in the United States grew out of the changing conditions which had affected American life in the 1870's, 1880's, and 1890's. The rise of American industrialism and the formation of enormous trusts had enslaved large groups of the population; and, among these, the farmers and the workers had suffered the most. The Nationalist movement, which advocated economic democracy, desired to rid the country of the tyrannical power of the wealthy industrialists and to apply the democratic principle to the production and distribution of wealth; for in 1890, 71 per cent of the nation's entire wealth was owned by only 9 per cent of the population. As transitional steps and as a rectification of some of the existing conditions, Bellamy wanted to nationalize the railroads; the communication system; and gas, water, and electric supply companies, etc. He also argued that, to help the unemployed, the government should—and would, if nationalized—guarantee work for everyone. He then stated that the Nationalists dreamed of an age when total equality would be achieved, when everyone could do the work for which he was best qualified, and when each would receive his share of the wealth of the nation.

Such words were sweet music to the ears of the Norwegian radicals, who were embittered by existing economic conditions. A month after Bellamy's article was published, another appeared in the same magazine which discussed the Fabian Society of England and once again referred to the American Nationalist movement.[12] The magazine also published a poll it had taken among its readers to determine the most popular authors; and it indicates that Bellamy was not a household name in Norway at this time, for Bjørnson's *Stories* headed the list and Ibsen's *Per Gynt* was second.[13] Of the non-Scandinavian writers, Dickens was eighth; Shakespeare, twelfth; and Tolstoy, thirteenth; the only American mentioned among them was Harriet Beecher Stowe, who ranked thirty-eighth.

But in the 1890's socialism and Utopian projects were much debated in Norwegian periodicals and newspapers.[14] Reports were published about the socialist movements in Germany, Russia, England, and France; Hertzka's *Freiland* was translated into Norwegian in 1894—as were the *Fabian Essays on Socialism*. Reports also appeared about the California socialist colony of Altruria, about the New Harmony experiment in Indiana, and about the Norwegian socialist colony New Hardanger, which was located in the state of Washington.[15]

When Bellamy died in 1898, his death was duly mentioned by the press; but his impact seemed to have waned. One critic remarked that eight and nine years ago Bellamy's name was on everybody's lips and his book *Looking Backward* was "read everywhere and in every language." The novel was remembered by the writer as one which presented a vivid description of the wonderful life which could result from the realization of socialist ideas.[16]

In the twentieth century, Norwegians seem to have largely forgotten Bellamy, although a thesis was written about him. Recent encyclopedias devote a short paragraph to him stressing the influence of *Looking Backward* upon socialism.[17] The leftist *Arbeidernes Leksikon* of 1932 presents a brief analysis of *Looking Backward* and then concludes rather critically but in true Marxian terms: "Bellamy is a true Utopian writer." The article also states that his ideas were nothing but the result of his imagination, that he had no understanding of the forces underlying history, and that he certainly did not understand "the revolutionary part played by the working classes."[18]

Although it is beyond the scope of this chapter to state whether or not Bellamy had any influence upon creative writers in Norway, it is interesting to note that the Danish critic Georg Brandes wrote in his review of Ibsen's *Hedda Gabler* that the play's prophetic book of author Løvborg was "sheer Bellamy, or whatever his name is."[19] It is also safe to say, however, that radical writers like Bjørnson and—as indicated—Ibsen, must have been familiar with Bellamy's ideas, which had won world renown. Bellamy's *Looking Backward* must be considered, therefore, as one of the factors which stimulated socialism in Norway; but his influence there was of less importance when compared to that of his fellow-countryman Henry George, whose impact upon Norwegian life and thinking was considerably greater. Not only were some of George's works translated

into Norwegian but the Norweigian Henry George movement
published a periodical entitled *Retfaerd.*

### III  *Sweden*

*Looking Backward* first appeared in Sweden in 1889, and it
was published then in both book and serial form. Under the
title *En blick tillbaka från året 2000 till 1887,* it was serialized
from July 23, 1889, until May 29, 1890, in *Arbetet,* the Swedish
labor paper of Malmo. The notice accompanying the first installment stated that the Utopia had caused a great sensation
in America and that it had helped to make socialism known
among readers who were not particularly interested in studying scholarly, socialist publications. The editor of the labor
newspaper at this time was Axel Danielsson, who later wrote a
short story "Framlingen" (The Stranger) which was more or
less directly influenced by Bellamy. In this story, the hero
makes an imaginary visit to a society in which the new socialist
order has been successfully introduced.

The translator of the edition of *Looking Backward* which
was published under the title of *En återblick* by Looström
and Company[20] in Stockholm in 1889 was Gustaf Steffen
(1864-1929), a noted political scientist and sociologist; he—
according to Ake Lilliestam in *Gustaf Steffen* (1960)—adopted
Bellamy's idea of simplicity of private life and luxurious public
life, for he advocated the spending of surplus wealth or production for the embellishment of cities and for organized public
entertainment.

Since the day *Looking Backward* was first published in
Sweden, it has been kept alive; but in the 1890's it was—reported
Carl Anderson in *The Swedish Acceptance of American Literature* (1957)—read extensively by Swedes regardless of party
lines.[21] The socialist press complained, however, that the price
of three Swedish crowns[22]—about seventy-five cents—was beyond the means of the workers and that consequently only the
upper classes could afford to buy the revolutionary book. In
comparison to the reception of the book in Denmark among the
laboring classes, Bellamy's Utopia was seemingly more widely
read in Sweden by the upper classes.

The second novel by Bellamy which was published in Swedish was *Doktor Heidenhoffs upptäckt,* which was also translated by Steffen and published by Looström in 1890. This novel
seems to have caused little stir and to have been soon forgotten.
Bellamy's novels appeared at a time of considerable social upheaval, for the era was marked by prolonged periods of unem-

ployment, by strikes arranged by the growing socialist movement, and by socialist demonstrations and the emergence of
the labor press—*Social-Demokraten* (1885), *Arbetet* (1887),
and *Ny Tid* (1892).[23] This situation explains—if the difference
in literary quality would not—the reason *Dr. Heidenhoff's Process*
was practically ignored but why *Looking Backward* was immediately hailed as an imaginative, Utopian-socialist novel of
great interest.

The critics had, however, many reservations despite the novel's easy and fluent style; they opined that the ideas of the
Utopia were not particularly original and they remarked that
the book market abounded with similar expositions of the
glories of the future society. One critic asked how it would be
possible to maintain equal rights in regard to enjoyment and
have free choice of the means of doing so when, for example,
some individuals—in this case the reviewer—had an absorbing
passion for truffles?[24]

Another critical voice came also from *Ute och Hemma,* a
periodical devoted to contemporary cultural life. This writer
stated: "As regards Bellamy's dream, it is to be feared that it
will always remain a Utopia, unless the essence of human
nature is changed. His ideal is pure communism and arouses
as such invincible objections."[25] A similar doubt about the possibility of so changing human nature that it could adjust to
Bellamy's ideal society—or even create it—was also voiced by
the critic in *Svensk Tidskrift.* He pointed out that Bellamy's
society was already perfected in *Looking Backward* and that
the citizens had had time to realize the principles upon which
they had agreed as the foundation of the new state. But, in
view of human limitations, he thought not only that the whole
picture was fantastic but that it would have been more natural
if the hero had awakened at the end of the twenty-first or the
twenty-second century. Nonetheless, he recommended the "interesting book" to anybody who wanted a brief insight into
one aspect of modern socialism.

This article in *Svensk Tidskrift,* entitled "Moderna Utopier
och framtidstankar," is interesting because of its discussion of
other Utopian novels; but the popularity of Bellamy's *Looking
Backward* may be deduced from the fact that five pages of
the article were devoted to it. Although not recognized as such,
the other Utopian novels discussed were in one way or another
associated with the international fame which *Looking Backward* had won or with a criticism of its ideas. One of the Utopias mentioned was Ignatius Donnelly's *Caesar's Column,* which

had been translated and published in Sweden in 1891 under the title *Varldens undergang*. To the reviewer, Donnelly's book was an anti-Utopia; Bellamy was proclaimed the prophet of optimism in the field of socialism, and Donnelly the apostle of pessimism. The critic obviously had not studied Donnelly's book very carefully; for, instead of being anti-Bellamy, Donnelly portrayed in his book what would undoubtedly happen in the plutocratic-ridden United States if the people did not heed Bellamy's plan. The Swedish critic may, however, be forgiven his error; for the same one was made more recently by an American writer who described the book as "different from other Utopias," because, although it portrayed "a utopia in a remote spot of Africa, the main story portrayed a sadistic anti-utopia arrived at, as it were, by standing Bellamy on his head."[26] The Swedish critic was, however, correct when he remarked that Donnelly described a world divided between the rich and the proletariat; for the American had shown how this division and conflict had evoked a revolution of the people.

Among the other Utopian novels discussed was I. Thiusen's *En framtidsblick,* published in Sweden in 1892. This novel, really written by Professor John Macnie of the University of North Dakota, had been published about four years before Bellamy's novel appeared; when *Looking Backward* was published, many reviewers stated that Macnie's *The Diothas*—the American title—reminded them of *Looking Backward* because of the similarities of the plots; the Swedish critic felt, however, that *The Diothas* was "a most odd fantasy" and that its author had tackled an impossible problem and had, therefore, failed to solve it. The other books discussed—which were also published in Swedish—were anti-Bellamy books which had been written in Germany and in France. One of them, E. Gregorius' *Ett himmelrike pa jorden* (Sw. 1892), was influenced in literary matters by Bellamy's *Looking Backward;* and it may have been inspired by the necessity of refuting Bellamy's ideas—so popular in Germany—as well as those of the German socialists. The other book, that of Professor Charles Richet—published in Sweden in 1893 as *Om Hundra ar*—had been first published in France.

None of these books found favor with the critic because each had ignored the question of religion. He remarked that, although both Bellamy and Donnelly had included sermons in their Utopias, they were nothing more than commendations of the new society. Furthermore, no gratitude had been expressed to those generations who were responsible for all the beneficial

changes which had occurred. The critic found Bellamy's Dr.
Barton's sermon particularly and sadly lacking in religious feeling; and he remarked that it did not give honor to God for
the good fortune of the new society.[27]

In 1895 Hertzka's *En resa till Friland* was published, and the
translator G. H:son-Holmberg said in the introduction that
*Looking Backward* was the most "interesting" of the Utopian
novels which had appeared in Swedish translation. Bellamy's
novel had created a sect, he stated, but not one of enthusiasts
of art but of reformers of society. In an article published in the
distinguished, cultural, and non-political *Ord och Bild* and
written by Otto v. Zweigbergk (1863-1935), a journalist who
was also the editor of the liberal *Dagens Nyheter*, the author
was also complimentary to *Looking Backward;* he called it
the most famous *statsroman* of modern socialism.

Zweigbergk devoted considerable attention to *En återblick*
in his article "Den sociala frågan i den moderna litteraturen,"
for he also discussed Richter's *Socialdemokratiska framtidsbilder*,
Donnelly's novel, Zola's *Germinal*, Per Sivle's *Strejk* and Paul
Gohre's *Tre manader som fabriksarbetare*.[28] To Zweigbergk, Bellamy's starting point had been Rousseau; for, like him, the American believed that human nature was basically good and that,
if the bad influences which contaminated human nature were
removed, man's innate good impulses would reign supreme and
create happiness and bliss the world around. The blight which
had to be removed was, of course, the capitalistic state which
Bellamy had portrayed as the root of all evil.

Although Zweigbergk praised Bellamy for his ardent belief in
his cause and for his great imaginative power, he also asserted
that Bellamy had a deplorable gap in his presentation: he had
not told his readers how the great social changes—at which
they were so amazed—had been achieved. Zweigbergk then
remarked that the same criticism could, of course, be trained
at the other socialist writers who had described the earthly
paradise which was due to arrive when the socialist system had
been introduced. No one was inclined, however, to explain
why human faults and passions would not have to be considered
as a problem under the socialist system. Zweigbergk admitted,
however, that because of *Looking Backward's* appeal to the
imagination, it was much easier and a greater pleasure to read
than a brochure on Marx's theory of value. *En återblick* was,
he concluded, not only an excellent piece of propaganda but
also a best seller which had stimulated a new literary *genre:*
the Utopian novel.[29]

When we consider the reaction of the labor press to *Looking Backward*, we find much less criticism than in the large, well-established journals; the labor publications seemingly accepted Bellamy's doctrines. One reason for this favorable attitude was the fact that—as Zweigbergk had suggested—the book was being used as a propaganda weapon of first importance against the capitalistic system.[30] The popularity of the Utopia may be illustrated by the fact that the Stockholm library of the Labor Party owned no less than four copies of *En återblick* and that only Strindberg could rival Bellamy. In this library there was no more than one copy of any other book by popular American authors: those represented were Aldrich, Mark Twain, Eggleston, Bret Harte, Simms, and Harriet Beecher Stowe.

In order to spread Bellamy's gospel among the working classes, the Social-Democrats decided to make a new translation[31] of *Looking Backward* and to distribute it widely in the form of pamphlets which could be sold very cheaply.[32] Their idea was not a new one; for in 1891 the *Utilistiska propagandans skrifter* had issued a four-page pamphlet, entitled "Det nya samhallet" by Bellamy, which had sold for two öre a copy, or seventy-five copies for one crown. In simple, direct prose the pamphlet enumerated some of the reasons the older order was a failure —labor and class problems and the feminine question; and it had set out the glories of the new system—cooperative work, no war, equal rights, no unemployment, education for all, and a democratic government.

The Social-Democrats persisted with their plans to publish *Looking Backward;* and, when the Christmas issue of *Brand,* a radical periodical, appeared with gaudy pink covers, it carried a half-page advertisement of the new, cheap edition of *Ar 2000.* The advertisement made the extravagant claim that in two months this remarkable Utopia had sold 3,150,000 copies in England and America; and it ascribed the reason for its popularity to the fact that "this book is the most valuable, the most interesting and the most thrilling Utopian novel ever to be published." It also stated that in every country where the book had been published newspapers of every persuasion had praised it for its extraordinary subject matter, its remarkable enthusiasm, and the masterful style which made it so readable. In America Bellamy had become the most popular author—with the exception of the well-known humorist Mark Twain, who held his own. Furthermore, the new translation was considered as a worthy companion volume to Peter Kropotkin's *Kampen för brödet.*[33]

The advertisement also explained that *Looking Backward* was to be published in twenty pamphlets which would sell for ten öre each. Sales agents who were to receive the first pamphlet free of charge, would earn a 30 per cent commission—or three öre—for each pamphlet sold. On such favorable conditions, it was hoped that every energetic person in the villages would be eager to get subscriptions and to make some extra money. Specimen copies were also available. The advertisement then concluded: "Go forward at once and get subscribers. Go to your friends, your workshops, and your factories, to meetings and public places, and get subscribers. In so doing you will spread in ever-widening circles our ideas of deliverance and contribute to creating among our people an eagerness to work for the great and beautiful future aims of socialism."[34]

To boost the new translation of *Looking Backward*, Brand published the following year an article illustrated with a large photograph of Bellamy. In the article—which was written by Karl Börjesson, a socialist, a partner of the Björck and Börjesson publishing house, and in 1892 the founder of the Stockholm Social-Democratic Youth Club—the author asserted that Bellamy's *Looking Backward* "Had been more influential than any other book in the propagation of socialist ideas." In an alluring, romantic style adorned with noble and beautiful language, the Utopia described the coming and the advantages of the new socialist society and compared the ideal order with the old one which had been characterized by private ownership, exploitation, and brutal competition.

Börjesson then described the book as being simply "the saga of a race which grows in power and understanding of itself and its strength, which arranges its exterior social conditions in such a way that they will not be able to disturb the good cooperation, the altruistic emotions and the joy of life, which always must be held in respect in an advancing society." He hoped, therefore, that the new edition of the book would be as great a success as the first one had been; and he was certain that those who had already read "this sublime novel about an earthly paradise should read it again, or more correctly, they couldn't help rereading the novel."

Börjesson included a sketch of Bellamy's life and work; and in it he asserted that Bellamy should be remembered because he had given himself wholly to the socialist cause. Furthermore, thousands of readers ought to be grateful to him for the beautiful pictures which his masterly narrative art had evoked —pictures which had aroused enthusiasm for the new social ideas and given the battle summons to the people "tormented

by the polluted air of the old class-society. . . ." He also announced that plans were being made for the publication of
*Equality* in pamphlet form after *År 2000* had been completely
published.[35]

The same issue containing Börjesson's article also carried a
large advertisement about *År 2000*. It read: "Among the workers
of all countries this book has been adopted as a gospel of the
future; and we hope that also the Swedish workers, thanks
to this edition, will understand and appreciate the glorious
views of the future which the author shows us." The advertisement, dated March, 1899, reported also that the book would
consist of sixteen pamphlets which would be sold at ten öre
each and that one pamphlet would appear each week beginning on April 1, 1899; the first pamphlet had already appeared.[36] In a later issue of *Brand* another advertisement stated
that the novel would be published in fifteen or sixteen pamphlets and that "every man and woman ought to procure this
extraordinary, well-written and thrilling Utopian novel."[37]

Today only the first published pamphlet could be located; and
it is impossible to state whether the plans of publishing and
distributing *År 2000* in fifteen, sixteen, or twenty pamphlets
was ever realized. Certainly *Equality* never appeared in Swedish; but a small section of it, *Vattentornet* (The Parable of
the Water Tank) was published by Klasskampens Förlag in
Karlstad in 1918. This thirteen-page pamphlet was evidently
used by the local labor organizations to stir the workers to
make a continued struggle for their cause and their ideals.

The need of the socialists for a cheap edition of *Looking
Backward* was obviously great, for in 1901 a new edition, translated presumably by Anna Godecke,* was published in Stockholm as a *Folkupplaga* (people's edition); in red covers, it
sold for the reasonable price of seventy-five öre. On March 29,
1901, Anna Godecke wrote a long letter to the Social-Democratic
Party Committee in which she complained that she had received no payment for her translation.[38]

Only five years passed before another cheap edition (*Svensk
billighetsupplaga*) appeared in unobtrusive grey covers as the
second volume in the series *Berömda Böcker* (Famous Books)
published by Björck and Börjesson of Stockholm. The first

---

* Anna Godecke was presumably a radical and a socialist; she
was the daughter of a famous educator P. A. Godecke (1840-1890),
who was a conservative idealist.

book was Bertha von Suttner's *Ned med vapnen.** Other books in the series included ones by Dumas, Hugo, Balzac, Zola, Dickens, Conan Doyle, Kipling, Poe, Mark Twain, Dostoevsky, Ibsen, and Heine.

In 1910 Bellamy was discussed in an article published in *Stormlockan,* a publication founded in 1908 by the Stockholm Social-Democratic Youth Clubs but since 1921 a communist paper. In the article entitled "Utopier," the writer—who might have already acquired some Marxist views—declared that Bellamy's Utopia was too unreal. He also wondered if such a state of absolute harmony would not be somewhat vapid and boring. Furthermore, he remarked that "we could not recognize ourselves, our passions, our weaknesses and our strengths in Bellamy's people of the year 2000."[39]

After World War I, there was again a demand for a new edition of *En återblick;* and it appeared in 1919 as Number 82 in the series *Berömda Böcker* of Björck and Börjesson, publishers. The spelling of this edition was modernized; and a symbolic, new cover was designed. The *Social-Demokraten* reviewed the book with Anatole France's *På den vita stenen;* and, without knowing that the French novel had been written because of the influence of Bellamy, the critic opined that "both of these books are worthy of notice." He then remarked that Bellamy's book had been received with enthusiasm when it had first appeared but that now it was largely forgotten. Furthermore, although it was not so witty nor so imaginative as William Morris' *Nytt fran en ny varld* (*News from Nowhere*), its plan for a new society was worthy of consideration. On the whole, however, the labor critic considered *Looking Backward* an interesting experiment in socialist thought but one which lacked significance for the present era. His verdict indicates that the original enthusiasm had subsided, that the message of the Utopia no longer spoke to responsive hearts, that it had already performed its duty and was now to be remembered only as a literary curiosity.

But Bellamy's book is still kept alive in Sweden. It was men-

---

* Bertha von Suttner, née Countess Kinsky, was an Austrian writer (1843-1914) who worked for the peace movement in Germany and Austria, who published the pacifist periodical *Die Waffen Nieder* (1892-99), and who was awarded the Nobel Peace Prize in 1905. The work upon which the Swedish translation was based was *Die Waffen nieder* (1889); she also wrote *Martha's Kinder* (1903).

tioned several times in Professor H. W. Donner's *Introduction to Utopia,* which is primarily concerned with Thomas More's contribution to socialistic thought. In January, 1960, *Looking Backward* was used to introduce a series of literary essays about Utopian novels in Sweden's largest liberal daily, *Dagens Nyheter.* Dr. Olof Lagercrantz, a literary critic and the writer of the article, maintained that Bellamy's sociological gospel is on the whole forgotten but that *Looking Backward* still has value as a work of literature and that its historical importance is beyond dispute. He also wrote: "Bellamy's earthly paradise was founded on the quality of pity. He was one of the forerunners of those who in the world of reality tried to establish a new social order."[40]

## IV  *Finland*

Socialism appeared later in Finland than in the other Scandinavian countries, for it was not until after 1900 that the democratization of political and social life in Finland gained momentum.[41] It was natural, therefore, that the impact of Bellamy was not felt until this period, although mention of him had been made in the nineteenth century. The literary and cultural periodical published in Helsinki and called in Swedish *Finsk Tidskrift* devoted a page to a review of the Swedish translation of *Dr. Heidenhoff's Process* in 1890. The reviewer, V. Hermanson, remarked that Bellamy had "surprised and delighted the thinking public with his social novel *En återblick.*" He regarded the new novel—called a "psychological short story"—as an important book which was "stamped with the sound spirit of Anglo-Americanism." Furthermore, he thought that *Dr. Heidenhoff* formed a healthy contrast to the cheap French books about adultery and vivisection which were flooding the market. He took some issue with the theme of the novel which, he stated, was the power that the past exerted upon our minds; Dr. Heidenhoff's discovery consisted in finding the means to rid the mind of painful memories—and his remedy was oblivion, which the critic felt to be merely an easy substitute for fulfilling one's duty. He also opined that Bellamy's style was often heavy and that sometimes his meaning was obscure because of the inability of the Swedish translator to "express clearly Bellamy's thought."[42]

Another reviewer of *Finsk Tidskrift* in an article about Donnelly's *Världens undergång* stated that most European critics claimed—and rightly—that Bellamy's *År 2000* was of superior artistic value.[43] In 1898 C. Enckell made an interesting comparison of *Looking Backward* and Benjamin Kidd's *Den sociala utvecklingen*. He saw Bellamy's book as "a poet's vision"—as an idealized picture of a phase of human development.[44]

Such early comments were, however, comparatively rare in the literary periodicals of the 1890's in Finland; for Bellamy was not recognized as a force in the socialist movement until 1902 when the first Finnish translation appeared. Translator, J. K. Kari, based his translation—*Vuonna 2000*—upon a German edition; significantly, the book was published in ten pamphlets at a very low price in Helsinki by a labor organization. Kari, Bellamy's translator, played an important role in the development of Finnish socialism. A teacher, customs official, and a journalist, he became the secretary of the labor trade union at Abo (Turku); and in 1899 he was appointed the first secretary of the Finnish Labor Party. In 1900 he studied the labor organizations of Germany and Scandinavia; in 1904-5 he was a member of the Parliament; and, during the Great Strike of 1905, he was a member of the temporary Finnish government. Kari became the first Finnish socialist to have a seat in the Senate of the government, and as a politician he played a leading part in the development and the strengthening of socialism in his country. Besides his translation of *Looking Backward*, he also translated other socialist works into Finnish; he was also a contributor to the labor publications.

In his preface to his edition of *Looking Backward*, which is dated Turku (Abo), March 4, 1902, Kari stressed the popularity of the book in America and in England. He stated that during the first two years after its appearance it had sold more than 300,000 copies in the United States and that during the same period more than twenty editions had appeared in England. Kari remarked that the novel threw a sharp light on existing social conditions whose injustices were innumerable, and he hoped that Bellamy's readable and interesting description—with its profound ethical teachings—would be an eye-opener to many readers. Kari concluded his preface by saying that the influence of *Looking Backward* had been greater, more varied, and more profitable than had been previously believed.

Five years later, after the Russian Revolution of 1905, a reissue of *Vuonna 2000* was needed, and it appeared in 1907 with Kari's preface and in bright red covers. On the front cover was a picture showing a factory-lined street which was crammed with workers marching with hands uplifted toward the rising sun. Needless to say, *Vuonna 2000* was widely read among the working classes;[45] and it did not fail to have an impact upon its readers.

The only book-size edition of *Equality* in translation was published in Finland under the title *Yhdenvertaisuus;* it was first published in Hancock, Michigan, in 1905-1906 by what would seemingly have been radical Finns living in the United States. In 1906 *Equality* was published in Tampere (Tammersfors), and was issued by the workers' own publishing firm.

## V  *The Influence of Bellamy*

As this recital of Bellamy in Scandinavia indicates, his greatest popularity was in the 1890's and in the first decade of the twentieth century. If we are to accept the remarks of the socialist leaders of the time, his book was recognized as a powerful force in making people aware of the injustices of the social order, in informing them about the concepts of socialism, and in stirring them to battle for their rights. From the facts which have been gathered, *Looking Backward* seems to have been read by all levels of society, to have been promoted particularly by the socialist and labor leaders who wanted to educate the Scandinavian masses, to have provoked a great debate, to have inspired the publication of many anti-Bellamy Utopian novels of other countries which were influenced in one way or another by his most famous novel.

As the reviews indicate, the Scandinavians did not accept Bellamy's doctrines uncritically, for they were prone to judge his Utopian society by comparing it with others, and later radical reviewers were to gaze upon his Utopia through eyes prejudiced with Marxian attitudes. But on the whole, the reaction of the Scandinavian people to Bellamy was a sane and balanced one; there were no frantic enthusiasts who preached that Bellamy was the new messiah; there was no violent opposition to his ideas; and there were no Bellamy societies or clubs founded for the propagation of his ideas. The temperate reaction of Scandinavian critics may be accounted for by the fact that labor conditions in the Nordic countries in the 1880's and the 1890's were not so aggravating as they were in other areas of the world. Furthermore, the gulf between the rich and the poor was certainly not so apparent, so alarming, nor so oppressive as it was in Germany, England, and Russia—or even the United States.

More specifically, Bellamy seems to have influenced such socialist leaders of the Scandinavian countries as Gustaf Steffen; Axel Danielsson,[46] who not only serialized *Looking Backward* but also occasionally discussed it in *Arbetet,* lectured about it, and wrote a Utopian sketch in the Bellamy vein; John Alexander, who considered the Utopia a socialist text; and J. K. Kari. H. Branting, the famous Swedish socialist leader, does not mention Bellamy, but two of his leading articles published in the *Social-Demokraten* seemingly refer indirectly to the American. An unsigned article—probably written by Branting who was editor of the *Social-Demokraten*—stated in 1898 that Bellamy's ideas as they had been expressed in *Looking Backward* were well known "to most of our readers. The book . . . undoubtedly stimulated thought and provided us with new ideas about our modern capitalistic society."[47]

Aside from the Utopian story of Danielsson, further investigation should be made—as has been indicated in the beginning of this chapter—of all the Utopian novels written in the Scandinavian countries since 1889. It may be stated here, however, that two sketches which appeared in Sweden may have been influenced in one fashion or another by Bellamy. One of them was written by C. O. Berg; entitled "Efteråt" (Afterwards), it waged war against the socialist future state; the other by Quercus was called "Om hundra år"; this pro-socialist sketch appeared in the Stockholm *Social-Demokraten* of January 5, 1889.[48]

Whatever future researchers who go through the labor, liberal, and conservative publications of the Scandinavian countries may discover about Bellamy's impact, it is certain that Bellamy played his major role in educating the people about socialism almost a half a century ago. Today his name and his most famous book are still alive in Scandinavia, but it cannot be stated that he is generally spoken about or read. Neglect of Bellamy today is symbolic of an era to which the future can be anything but a socialist paradise or a Utopian dreamworld.

# CHAPTER TEN

# Changing French Attitudes

By

## GEORGE LEVIN

IN 1888, when *Looking Backward* was creating in the United States a sensation which was rapidly spreading to European countries, France had been a republic for two decades; and it seemed that, despite some opposition, she would remain one for an even longer time. The liberal and socialistic tendencies of the period are represented today by the still remembered names of Jean Jaures, Leon Gambetta, Jules Guesde, and Jules Valles; and the strong desire of the people for more liberty and equality was reflected in the newspapers of the era. Because France enjoyed a more liberal form of government and greater liberty than other European countries, Bellamy's *Looking Backward* and the socialist cause itself were not so popular as in other nations; for, as Michel Savigny has indicated in *The Socialist Movement in American and Germany*, the repression of the socialists in Germany contributed to their success.

Another important factor which influenced the reception of Bellamy's Utopia was the attitude of many French writers toward the United States. As Professor Arnavon has related in *Les Lettres Américaines devant la Critique Française* (1951), many French critics of the late nineteenth century thought that the center of the world existed in certain Parisian circles and salons, and they were biased by their chauvinism, by their class consciousness, by their political or religious ideas, by their pseudo-classic taste. As a result, they smiled with "protective condescension upon Whitman or Mark Twain," they never truly understood the democracy of the frontier, and they mistreated or misjudged many writers—and among these was

276

"the moderate socialist Edward Bellamy." Among the critics
who are belabored by Arnavon for their narrow, prejudiced
views is Thérèse Bentzon, who wrote—as we shall see—several
articles about Bellamy from 1885 to 1897.[1]

Another circumstance which may have affected the French
reception of Bellamy was the prevalence of many of the ideas
he expressed. As has been pointed out in Chapter I in this
volume and in *Le Dévelopment des Idées d'Edouard Bellamy*
by Sylvia E. Bowman, Bellamy's major principles and many
of the details of his plan had much in common with famous
French thinkers such as Morelly, Cabet, Proudhon, Fénelon,
St. Simon, Comte, Blanc, and others. Because of the similarity
with ideas familiar to the French intellectuals and social reformers and because Bellamy presented his theses in the form
of fiction, his Utopia would have been regarded not only as a
synthesis of ideas but as a work not to be considered so seriously as the non-fiction of the French writers or even of the
American Henry George.

But these situations and these French attitudes do not mean
that Bellamy was ignored in France, for several editions of
*Looking Backward* were published from 1891 to 1939. Furthermore, the critical reactions to Bellamy's concepts were not relegated only to introductions of these volumes; they appeared
also in periodicals, studies by economists and politicians, and
doctoral theses. As we review the reactions to the novels of
Bellamy we find that during the decades that have passed
since the first publication of *Looking Backward* in France, the
attitudes toward the famous Utopist have undergone a marked
change. Moreover, we also discover that his influence resulted
in French literary works and that his ideas are popular even
today among several organizations.

## I  *Translations*

Bellamy was known in France long before *Looking Backward*
made him famous, for *Miss Ludington's Sister* had been reviewed in 1885 in *La Revue des Deux-Mondes* by no less a
person than Thérèse Bentzon, who was in charge of reviews of
American books. A prolific novelist and a friend of George
Sand, Thérèse Bentzon had been introduced by the more famous
novelist to Buloz, the editor of the review; and, during her years
of contributing to *La Revue*, she introduced to the French
reader such famous American writers as Mark Twain, Henry
James, and Walt Whitman. In her article, which included
*Miss Ludington's Sister*, she had, however, done little more

than classify the book as a romance about immortality and
summarize its contents.[2]

*Miss Ludington's Sister* was translated and published in
France in 1891—the same year which witnessed two different
translations of *Looking Backward*. One of them was made by
Viscount Gaetan Combes de Lestrade for publisher Guillaumin
and the other by Paul Rey for E. Dentu. The edition of *Miss
Ludington's Sister* contained an introduction by Thérèse Bentzon in which she showed her preference for imaginative novels,
declared that she was attracted by the element of mystery and
horror introduced by the use of spiritualism, and, though not
overly enthusiastic about the novel, congratulated Bellamy upon
"having found this rare bird: a new topic."[3] As we shall see,
she was less enthusiastic about *Looking Backward*.

Other editions of *Looking Backward* were published in France
in 1893, 1898, and 1939. The edition of 1893 published by
Flammarion was prepared by Mrs. A. Berry, who adapted the
novel and presented, therefore, a much weakened version of
the original. In 1898 Flammarion published a new edition translated by Mrs. Poynter-Redfern; and in 1939 the 1891 translation
of Paul Rey was republished with an introduction by E. Charpentier. Aside from these appearances in book form, the famous
Utopia was also serialized in a Paris publication in 1955.

The popularity of *Looking Backward* in France is not only
indicated by the number of editions which appeared but by
the translation of two other Utopian novels which were welcomed by those who were opposed to socialism. Eugen Richter's *Where Does Socialism Lead?* was published in 1892 with
a preface by Paul Leroy-Beaulieu, who made his position about
socialism quite clear with the following remark: "There is no
common way possible with socialism; the only thing to do is
reject it. . . . Socialism is like morphine." Besides Richter's
attack upon Bebel and the German Social Democrats—with
whom Bellamy was associated—Theodor Hertzka's well-known
*Freiland* appeared in 1894 under the title *Un voyage à Terre-
Libre*. In the introduction to the Austrian economist's Utopia,
de Wyzewa recognized that it had not been inspired by Bellamy, Marx, or Proudhon from the standpoint of principles but
by "Adam Smith, Bentham, and H. Spencer."

II   *Critical Reactions*

As we review the introductions to the different editions of
*Looking Backward*, we discover that their authors maintained
divergent attitudes toward it. One of the most interesting of

these is the preface of Viscount Combes de Lestrade, an engineer, a member of the Philological Institute of Florence, the translator of Paolo Mantegazza's *Physiology of Pleasure* (1886) and of F. H. Giddings' *Principles of Sociology* (1897), and the author of studies such as *Economical and Social Aspects of Russia at the Beginning of Nicholas II's Reign* (1896) and *Contemporary Political Law* (1897).[4]

In his assessment of Bellamy, Combes de Lestrade frankly announced not only that the American was a communist but that his Utopia was "of all communist books . . . I have happened to read . . . the most dangerous." Admitting that the novel had made a "very strong impression" upon him, he asserted that its danger lay in its artistry of presenting ideas. But of these Combes de Lestrade remarked: ". . . the book does not contain any fundamental ideas which are new. It is a mixture of Fourier, Proudhon, and Marx which he presents to his readers. But whereas these writers are only accessible to those whose previous studies would prevent contamination, Mr. Bellamy has given an easy and pleasant form to his ideas . . ." which would make him understandable to all. Combes de Lestrade then asserted that to translate the book and "go no farther would seem to me an incomplete task. I think it is a wise thing to have tried to show how specious Bellamy's arguments are and how mere common sense easily pulls apart his brilliant sophisms in spite of the great talent which makes them dangerous."

In order, therefore, to destroy the impact of the artistry and talent of Bellamy, and to mitigate the influence upon those who could easily comprehend it but not the works of Marx or Proudhon, Combes des Lestrade took great care to refute Bellamy's concepts and arguments with long, detailed comments and refutations.

In the course of his edition, Combes de Lestrade discussed most of the aspects of the New World depicted by Bellamy and opposed the following ones with vigor. First of all, he argued that the opinion of other writers about interest and profit should be consulted; and he did not find it at all difficult to quote a great many who had proved that they were not only legitimate but necessary. Second, he argued that those who sat on top of the coach had earned their seats—or their ancestors had—and that these passengers were essential: they not only rode but pushed the coach! Third, Combes de Lestrade considered *Looking Backward* to be a typically American product; and he argued that industrialization had not yet brought to

European countries the extremes and "many of the evils which, if we are to believe Bellamy, afflict the Americans. . . . In other times, this book would have been welcome, but it comes when all Utopias are accepted as achievable."

Fourth, although Combes de Lestrade agreed that concentration of capital had many advantages, he absolutely refused to consider those which One Great Monopoly might provide. To him, the collective state would represent the "establishment" of a "social regime" which would be harmful to the preservation of individual tastes and preferences. In his fifth major argument, Combes de Lestrade also questioned how Bellamy's one great monopoly could be achieved in a world radically opposed to monopolies; he thought, therefore, that it would be a very difficult if not impossible task to make people realize that combination was the right path to the Golden Age.

Sixth, Combes de Lestrade argued that Bellamy had confused the organization of labor with social organization, and he felt that these were completely different. In relationship to the problems of the new society, Combes de Lestrade discussed at some length the problems of good and evil and of moral values, and aired his own view that complete social change could not bring a transformation of the human heart, passions, or desires. He believed that people would not cease to cheat, to look after their personal interests, or to commit crimes against one another. Furthermore, he felt that society needed to be protected against criminals and that treating malefactors as sick people would not be sufficient protection nor adequate in ending the evil which existed in the world.

Seventh, Combes de Lestrade argued that the suppression of money would entail more disadvantages than advantages, and also asserted that economic equality could not be maintained. He remarked that Bellamy's permitting personal possessions to be inherited would endanger such equality because people could amass a fortune in goods. Furthermore, equal incomes for all would be "iniquitous"; it would "be the ruin not only of all progress but the immediate ruination of the generation which adopted" such a plan. When he considered Bellamy's argument for economic equality, Combes de Lestrade displayed, however, a weakness which nearly placed him on Bellamy's side. For, after he posed the question of how society could judge whether or not a man had done his best, he remarked that "Only God can judge of merit."

At the end of his edition of *Looking Backward*, Combes de Lestrade admitted that the social problems confronting the world were real and difficult ones, that the world was changing rapidly, and that the workers' conditions had to be improved. To him, the solution was not Bellamy's radically changed society but cooperation and associations which would provide profit-sharing and share-holding and which would give the laborers access to property. He admitted that his plan for amelioration would not usher in the Golden Age, but he asserted that it would result in a definite improvement of existing conditions. Furthermore, he suggested that the motto of the people should be "Work, Thrift, Will."

In contrast to Combes de Lestrade, Paul Rey[5]—a poet, a composer, and a specialist in the *la langue d'oc*, the language formerly spoken in the southwestern part of France—seemed to be content with merely translating it. The edition which he had prepared appeared, however, with an introduction written by Theodore Reinach (1860-1928), a professor of numismatics at the Collège de France and the author of books about ancient history, archaeology, and numismatics.

Reinach's introduction is much more reserved and objective than that of Combes de Lestrade—and it indicates also the effect *Looking Backward* had upon him. After reviewing the success of *Looking Backward* in Great Britain and the United States where the book had already sold "400,000 copies," its publication by Tauchnitz, and its translation into German and Italian, he remarked that Thérèse Bentzon had presented an analysis of the Utopia in *La Revue des Deux Mondes*. Reinach then opined that the great success of *Looking Backward* could not be attributed solely to the artistry of the Utopia—remarkable as it was in many respects—for its attraction and its popularity resided also in the ideas of the book, the pleasing *"passions,"* and the plans which it contained.

In assessing the fiction of Bellamy, Reinach astutely indicated that his two preceding romances—*Dr. Heidenhoff's Process* and *Miss Ludington's Sister*—had won the attention of the public because they had been concerned with the discoveries or the illusions of science; Bellamy was, therefore, to be considered as a writer of romantic fiction whose intent was to present a lesson, a dream, or a fantasy. For the most part, his novels were intended—like the dialogues of Plato—to serve the purpose of popularizing actual and interesting, false or true ideas which were the momentary concern of physiologists, of the spiritualists, and of the socialists. Bellamy was, therefore, to be classified as *"un romancier à theses"* and, as such, *"Looking Backward est son Utopie."*

In his review of the derivation of the term "Utopia," Reinach
pointed out that Bellamy's method of portrayal of the future
world differed from those of his predecessors: instead of leading the readers into the imaginary land, island, planet, or Golden
Age, Bellamy used the device, which might have been suggested
by Irving's Rip Van Winkle or by Edmond About's *l'Homme
à l'oreille cassée*, of transporting his hero through time by means
of a hypnotic sleep. Reinach believed that the book should have
been entitled *Looking Forward* since it described the society
of the future; and he also objected to the distracting love story,
although he admitted that, without it, the reader might have
been bored by the great abundance of technical details which
Bellamy's didactic novel contained.

After summarizing the basic principles and details of Bellamy's ideal society, Reinach remarked that the Utopian had
not demolished—as he had so many things—either religion or
family life. He then declared that Bellamy was a true Anglo-
Saxon because he could picture a radically altered society without riches and poverty, without a stock exchange, without
policemen, and even without a piano—but not one which lacked
"*le sweet home*" or the sermon on Sunday morning! He also
warned the reader that one of the values of the Utopia was
that one who was dissatisfied with Bellamy's plan could imagine his own and that the debate about the American's society
should rest upon the principles which he supported. And the
most important of these was whether or not the future society
was to be one of liberty or of slavery.

To Reinach, several questions posed themselves: he wondered if human nature, as it actually was, would be sufficiently
capable of working for honor and recognition and not for personal interest; if individualism might not disappear as a result
of the uniformity of the mediocrity and golden platitudes of
official art. The answers to the complex problems might be
found, thought Reinach, by considering whether or not it would
be better to have the type of society Bellamy depicted, or
whether such a society would truly be developed.

Admitting that the society of the 1890's was not satisfactory
because of its misery and vices, and observing that he thought
Bellamy had painted a somewhat black but not wholly false
picture of it with his analogy of the coach and its riders and
drawers, Reinach asked where the remedy of such situations
could be found. To have all the people of the world ride the
coach would either arrest it or cause a breakdown; to harness
everyone to it would leave none to enjoy the beauties of the

countryside! Seemingly, all one could do would be to repair the route and to multiply moments of respite for the drawers.

Reinach remarked that Morelly and Rousseau had preached the return to the state of nature as the solution to social ills but, to Reinach, suppressing civilization and diminishing the enjoyments of humanity would be to lower its degree of perfection without increasing individual enjoyments. To him, the Russian thinkers—such as Tolstoy—who followed the thinking of Rousseau in this respect but who were strongly Christian in their attitudes, did not recoil from these possible effects. In contrast to the Russians, the Americans pretended to conserve and even to increase the precious heritages of civilization; but, as in the case of Bellamy, the end result was the construction of a society of deadly uniformity, regimentation, and hierarchical arrangement; in fact, it was an America strangely comparable to the social order of China. To Reinach, the life, the progress, and the liberty dear to European minds fashioned by the Greeks, the Renaissance, and the French Revolution were lacking in the ideal society of Bellamy; as a result, life in that society would be mortally boring—unless one were a grocer or a salesboy!

But despite his criticism of Bellamy and of American aspirations, Reinach admitted that the ideal society depicted by the Utopian was not only possible but probable. Certain indications—some menacing and others encouraging—led him to believe that modern societies were tending toward the levelling not only of conditions but of intelligence. Warning that appearances to the contrary—as exemplified by the increasing inequality of riches—might be misleading, Reinach stated that such concentration, as Bellamy had forecast, might make it possible for the state to assume control. Furthermore, there were other significant symptoms which indicated that already *"bellamisme"* was in action: the expansion of education, which was becoming more and more utilitarian, the progress of applied science, the triumph of comfort and of inexpensive luxury and art, the means of transportation, and universal suffrage were all indicative that the dream of Bellamy was not so far from reality as it might at first seem. In fact, concluded Reinach, almost all the uglinesses of the future society were already present—and the present lacked only its beauties: reconciliation of classes, perpetual peace, abolition of crime, the reign of justice, and the humanity and unselfishness which flourished in all hearts in the year 2000. Reinach hoped that the beauties of Bellamy's prediction would not be the last to arrive!

Other critics of the 1890's were more hostile to Bellamy's ideas than Reinach—and they were also more skeptical and reluctant to accept "a peaceful acceptance of an inevitable transformation" of society. Among those evincing hostility was Thérèse Bentzon who criticized both *Looking Backward* and *Equality* from an aesthetic rather than an economic viewpoint, and in doing so was representative of an attitude fairly common in her era. She was also a representation, as Professor Arnavon has indicated, of a supercilious attitude toward Bellamy; for, adopting a bantering tone, she disguised with a smile her quite evident lack of sympathy for socialism in general and for Bellamy in particular. In her articles about *Looking Backward* and *Equality*—a book never published in France—she pointed out the Anglo-Saxon naïvetés and the biazarre features of the future society.[6]

Although Miss Bentzon had been attracted by the imagination of *Miss Ludington's Sister* and had complimented Bellamy for finding new topics to write about, she assumed a completely different attitude and tone when she approached his Utopias. Although she still liked some literary qualities which she found in Bellamy—his clever use of paradox and his ingenuity in popularizing or vulgarizing ideas—she asserted that his aptitude for finding new, disquieting subjects had become in *Looking Backward* "his dangerous mania to strike the public's imagination." Miss Bentzon's ill humor with the American was the result of her dissatisfaction with the Golden Age which he presented; for to her, his ideal society was too industrial, too common, and too unromantic. She missed the romance, the knightly feats, and the sound of the drum on the battlefield. She opined, therefore, that "one hundred years would not be sufficient to change our young men's conception of service and cause them to prefer the profits of the office-boy to the perils of the soldier's life."[7]

Furthermore, Miss Bentzon—like Reinach—considered Bellamy as representative of the American school of thought, and his ideal society as the outgrowth of the United States of the nineteenth century. She remarked: "We have no desire to imitate America in everything."[8] The only entertaining or amusing aspect of *Looking Backward* to this French critic of American literature was the fact that Julian West awakened to find himself in the nineteenth century; and she hoped that his doing so indicated that Bellamy did not regard too seriously his own panaceas!

When Miss Bentzon criticized *Equality* in 1897 in an article entitled "Communism in American Fiction," she found—as did many other critics—that Bellamy had erred in writing a sequel; for "continued books are never worth anything." Although she remarked that "the whole thing is difficult to swallow," she was obviously intrigued by certain aspects of the novel; for she gave particular, favorable mention to the chapter on women and remarked that she appreciated their emancipation. Of the chapter about religion, she stated that in it she saw the tendencies of an élite American society—particularly of the feminine élite —to express itself through active, organized charity. Miss Bentzon—who had visited some of the Utopian and communist settlements of the United States—asserted that the Shakers were more representative of communism than the chimerical world of Bellamy.[9]

Several anonymous lines also appeared in 1906 in *Le Mercure*, which indicate that the interest in Bellamy was not dead. The author—who may have been Davray or Gourmont—advanced the idea that the American Utopian might have been inspired by an eighteenth-century Utopia of Mercier: *l'An deux mille quatre cent quarante*. In any case, wrote Professor Arnavon in 1951, the success of Bellamy in France was not a result of his artistry as a romancer but attributable to the fact that he was a social reformer who had passionately criticized the American dogma of free enterprise. Professor Arnavon also indicated that this interest paved the way for—or explained—the interest which the French were to show many years later in the American novel of social criticism.[10]

Among the Catholic critics Bellamy was not popular; in fact, hostility toward his Utopian world was quite evident and the reasons not difficult to discover since too many aspects of his society were in direct conflict with Catholic tenets. Materialism could not be accepted by the church, and as Pope Leo III's encyclical "On the Condition of Labor" of May, 1891, indicated, the church might encourage new mental attitudes among the possessors and the privileged but it certainly did not advocate nor condone any drastic change: ". . . They [the socialists] are emphatically unjust because they would rob the lawful possessor, bring the State into a sphere which is not its own, and cause complete confusion in the community."

Catholic writers did not think that human nature could be changed to the extent that Bellamy had described in *Looking Backward* nor did they believe that "all obstacles could be removed, all opposition suppressed, all pain and poverty annihilated, and all passions subdued." To them such an accomplishment presupposed that "Nature was changed, that Providence itself is in the service of all these dreamers—in other words, all is the dream of fatuity and the Utopia of sensual imagination."[11]

In a Jesuit publication of 1895, the following comment was made by Father Fristot in the article *"Le Rêve collectiviste"*: "This alluring prospect [socialism] has taken shape in the American novel entitled *Looking Backward* by Ed. Bellamy. This system . . . is not new . . . but the book is written by an alert pen. What becomes of the family, this primordial institution? The author . . . shirks the difficulty. Is there a place for religion in this new humanity?" Like Reinach and many others, Father Fristot—misunderstanding Bellamy's ethical objectives—thought that "men would quickly tire of an existence which contained only mechanical pleasure and which did not care for moral good."[12] Although Father Fristot was aware of the evils of the epoch, he could not accept Bellamy's ideal society; but, mild and fair in his attitude, he very logically questioned the efficiency and the efficacy of the proposed remedies.

Among the socialists, the attitude toward *Looking Backward* was somewhat different from that of the Catholic Church; but their attitude could not be called enthusiastic; after all, Bellamy was a Utopian! In 1898, Jean Jaures—one of the most colorful and important socialist leaders of France, a powerful member of the Chamber of Deputies, a former professor of philosophy, and the co-founder with Briand and the editor of *L'Humanité*—remarked that he considered *Looking Backward* to be an "American masterpiece" which did "wonders toward dissipating hostility and ignorance against our ideas."[13]

Baron Emile de Laveleye, the Belgian economist, wrote in an article in *La Revue Socialiste* of July, 1890, that he found the book "well composed and well written" and greatly appreciated the scientific aspects which had been entirely lacking in previous books about model societies. But he objected—as a student of the technicalities of socialism—to the distribution of functions and of products. He also thought that Bellamy had retained in his society two motives belonging to pre-socialist times: "Mr. Bellamy does not abandon the two powerful motives of human actions: effort and reward. But . . . honor cannot become a reason for work, cannot become the motive power of industry. It can make a hero—not a worker." He also felt that Bellamy was too radical; for he not only espoused socialism but pure communism, and because of this extension, his ideal society "raises invincible objections." De Laveleye also did not believe that the human heart could be so completely transformed as Bellamy indicated it could; and he was, therefore, convinced that Bellamy's dream would ever remain a Utopia.

The critical article which appeared in *La Revue des Revues* in 1890 presented *Looking Backward* with objectivity, but also quoted extracts from Emile de Laveleye's comments.[14] The article also cited passages from an article written by Bellamy for *The North American Review*. These are particularly interesting because his suggestions about the reform of schools, allowances, nationalization, and social insurance correspond almost exactly with reforms which have been accomplished in the past fifteen years in France and many other European countries.

Another article in *Revue britannique*[15] reproduced extracts from Reinach's introduction, but two other articles published in May, 1890, in *La Nouvelle Revue*[16] and in *Le Correspondant*, made no mention of Bellamy but praised the popular Henry George. This omission of the more radical Bellamy is of interest, for it might indicate that George was better known or more favored; it might also be an indication that such writers as the Marquise de San Carlos Pedroso, author of the article in *La Revue Nouvelle*, did not wish to call attention to the American or that she did not consider his concepts seriously because they had—unlike those of George—been presented in the form of fiction. Certainly this attitude was shared by F. Grenard who in 1899 reviewed Bentzon's *Choses et Gens d'Amerique*—a compilation containing several articles and "Communism in America." Grenard assessed the last-mentioned article as "a clear and superficial analysis of *Equality*" which he termed "a clear and superficial book by E. Bellamy, this Jules Verne of socialism."[17]

Although Combes de Lestrade considered *Looking Backward* the most dangerous book about communism which he had read, and although Reinach thought it contained a portrayal of a probable future society, other writers of reviews and introductions seemed to feel that the life Bellamy described would be boring or that it was too extravagant to appeal to many logical French minds. When we turn to the introduction written in 1939 by E. Charpentier, we find the novel described, however, as one that had exercised and continued to exercise a considerable influence; and Charpentier stated that when, several months ago, an English list of fifty of the most important and influential books published in the last one hundred years had been compiled as the result of a survey, the books of Bellamy had been cited. Charpentier described the reaction in France toward the nineteenth-century editions as having been one of "lively curiosity," and he recalled that Reinach had classified the book as a Utopia which belonged with the work of More, Campanella, Harrington, and Cabet.

Although Charpentier conceded that Reinach's classification had been correct, he wondered if presenting the book in that fashion in 1939 would not lessen the significance it had attained because of the transformation of the structures of societies and because of the economic evolution which had occurred since 1887, and particularly since World War I. Although he warned the reader to remember that the novel had been written in the nineteenth century, he asserted not only that its interest had not declined but that its ideas were being supported by a whole school of economists. In the United States, the left-wing economists of the Democratic Party and the technocrats were all writing about the "production for use"—production for the consumer—and, in France, Jacques Duboin was the best-known representative of the theory of the economy of abundance. These economists not only supported but echoed the ideas of Bellamy who had spoken of the evolution of the ideal state as a means of providing not only plenty for all but as a necessary rectification of the immoralities and injustices of the capitalistic system.

Charpentier also pointed out that while technical progress had increased production and wealth, it had also brought in its wake unemployment, a lack of profit, and the progressive ruin not only of the possessors but of the state. As a result, everyone realized that the evolution of the political, economic state foreseen by Bellamy was inevitable; and even the rich were not so concerned with trying to salvage their wealth as with saving their social positions. Because of the inevitability of the future industrial democracy, Charpentier felt that *Looking Backward* was a good book to help people realize that present forms of government were inadequate and out of date in an industrial, technological age and one which would encourage them to anticipate, reflect about, and accept peacefully the inescapable transformation which was coming.

## III  *Reactions of Specialists*

Reactions to Bellamy's *Looking Backward* were not confined, however, to reviews and introductions; for a number of books published between 1890 and 1960 express favorable or unfavorable reactions to his ideas. But it should also be recognized when we consider these criticisms that Bellamy stood in a rather uncomfortable position between two conflicting groups: one sponsored violent revolution and the dictatorship of the proletariat; the other, expressed by liberalism, advocated commutative justice. For the hardened Marxists, Bellamy was not only too mild but also an evolutionary and not a revolutionary socialist; for the liberals, his world prefigured the end of liberty, the deadly monotony of the machine age, and an era of little initiative and of less intelligence.

The liberal attitude was reflected in 1899 by Joseph Perrot in his book *Nos Utopies politiques et socialistes devant le sens commun* (Our political and socialistic Utopias before common sense). Perrot, who titled himself "a disciple of Proudhon," disagreed with authoritarian socialism and announced that "the communist idea has no other reason for existence today than the criticism of the mistakes of 'bourgeois' economy." To Perrot, Bellamy's ideal state was not only "impossible to achieve" but would also be "the end of all liberty, the new reign of pure authority, the return of barbarism." As might be expected, he preferred not "distributive justice" but "commutative justice."

In 1892 Charles Richet—a professor of the University of Paris, a physiologist who also studied psychical phenomena, and a future Nobel prize winner—published *Dans Cent Ans* (A hundred years hence) which was without doubt written and titled as it was because of the popularity of Bellamy, but which is included in this section because it is less a novel than a "scientific guess" about the future state of the world. In the appendix of his book Richet mentioned *Looking Backward* as "a book . . . recently published in America in the form of a novel. . . ." Bellamy, he wrote, "gives no detail but the social organization of labor." The book "is a sort of rather ponderous socialist Utopia, and it is difficult to understand its considerable success."

In *Dans Cent Ans* Richet evidenced his desire to establish in a future world a balance between material improvement and a higher moral doctrine; but he also refused to lull himself with the idea that men would be happier in such a state, for he remarked that they would not. Among the guesses which Richet made about the future and which he based on statistics, past evolution, and other scientific methods, are some of interest today. After citing the population of the most important countries, he forecast that in 1992 the United States would have four hundred million people; Russia, three hundred and forty million;

and France, fifty million. He also prophesied that methods of war would become so efficient that warfare would eventually become impossible; but, envisioned Richet, the world would ruin itself for many years with an armed peace.

Thirty-eight years after he published *Dans Cents Ans*, Richet once more attacked Bellamy and communism in *L'Age d'Or et l'Age de l'Or* (The golden age and the age of gold). Although many of his ideas were similar to those he had expressed in *Dans Cent Ans*, Richet in his later book was more violent in his criticisms and attitudes toward communism of any kind. He wrote: "This absolute equality is pure fancy. . . . It would be the death of individuals. . . ." He insisted upon the preeminence of the élite, and he imagined the future superman who would be the result of evolution.

Maurice Block (1816-1901)—an economist who had served in the ministry of agriculture, who had written several books, and who was a regular contributor to the *Journal des Economistes*—agreed not only with Combes de Lestrade but with Charles Richet in his attitude toward Bellamy's Utopia. In his article "*Revue des principales publications économiques de l'étranger*" which he published in January, 1890, in *Le Journal des Economistes*, Block summarized the article which had been published by N. P. Gilman in the *Quarterly Journal of Economics* in 1889 in which the American economist had scathingly dismissed Bellamy's forecast of the disappearance of the power of the state, the supreme position of the federal government, and the abolition of private property. Gilman, who gave little consideration to the problems of his era, summarily dismissed Bellamy as an imaginative writer who did not realize that "the cornerstone of American freedom—the American State—will shipwreck every Utopia that strikes it."

Block's attitude toward Bellamy reflected Gilman's; but he also evinced surprise that any American would have expressed the ideas found in *Looking Backward*. For, wrote Block, "what must surprise every reasonable man is that in the free and progressive America, in a people which likes wealth and 'go ahead' . . . which is not afraid of risk . . . there could be found men consenting to submit themselves to other men in order to obtain—at the best—their daily bread." Like Gilman, Block also thought that since Bellamy had not explained how the ideal state could be achieved, he could, "explaining nothing, . . . envision anything."

In 1891 when Block published *Les Suites d'une Grève* (The

aftermath of a strike), he indicated that he—like his French contemporaries—favored neither socialism nor communism as the solution of the economic problems but cooperatives and consumer unions. Although he made no direct mention of Bellamy, he seemed to be striking at *Looking Backward* when he wrote: "Numerous Utopias have been published in the course of centuries. In almost all of them, methods are proposed to procure equal joys for men who are essentially unequal not only in their abilities but in their moral qualities. The failure of such ridiculous fancies can be easily understood."

Professor Charles Secrétan reacted promptly to Bellamy's *Looking Backward* with the publication of *Mon Utopie* (1892). Secrétan had already published in 1889 *Etudes Sociales*, and his *Mon Utopie*—a long series of essays and lectures which completely reveal his attitudes—was not only a continuation of the earlier work but a most important part of his *Nouvelles Etudes Morales et Sociales*. Although Secrétan did not directly mention Bellamy, internal evidence in his book indicates a striking relationship to *Looking Backward*. In the first pages, there are indications that Secrétan intended to follow the plan of the American Utopia in the section entitled *"Gillette ou le Problème économique."* The author falls asleep after a long walk in the hills of western Switzerland and dreams that he awakens many years later. In his dream, he meets a man who relates to him the transformations which have occurred in the world: People share their time between physical and intellectual occupations; everybody works; idlers have practically disappeared; and people labor only six hours a day to supply all that is needed.

The new man also explains how the transformation had occured. Communism had been considered as the solution; but, since it meant a war of extermination, it had not been very attractive. When a majority which had favored the proletariat had been elected because of universal suffrage and had experimented with collectivism in a limited district of Switzerland, the attempt had "been a complete failure, because it was impossible to keep and renew capital." It had finally been agreed, therefore, that capital could be found only in private fortunes; that, although people lived on their incomes from rent and interest, they also found management of their estates very serious work; and that land had been repurchased by the state—for Secrétan makes a distinction between private and land property. Although collectivism had been rejected, the state had become an "association of associations"; for "all the workers of a

mine 'or a factory are more or less the co-proprietors. . . ." As in
*Looking Backward,* the will of the people had finally prevailed;
and it had done so peacefully because of universal suffrage.

Warfare has been avoided because "the humble men" in all
countries refused to indulge in it; the people are happy in the
new state because more and more workers achieve property and
independence; idleness is condemned by public opinion; but the
capitalists "are considered as useful citizens and as the bene-
factors of their country." Since manual laborers are as well—if
not better paid—than the intellectuals, class distinctions have disappeared. Luxurious living has been minimized—not by taxes
but by education of the people.

In the second and the third parts of *Mon Utopie,* Secrétan
became less speculative and philosophical. In *"Turin"* he considered the position of women in a changing world, and he
concluded that their role should become more important and
entail more freedom for them. In *"La Montagne Ste. Genevieve"*
Secrétan stressed that religious need is the very root of every
man's being; and for this reason Secrétan was violently opposed
to socialism or communism.

In fact, his spiritual qualities and his own faith not only pervade the pages of his works but influence his attitudes. Secrétan
believed strongly in the primacy of the individual and in his
relationship to God as the means of salvation and the attainment of brotherhood. To him, "even if everything went the way
the collectivists hope, this organization implies such despotism,
lowers the initiative and the responsibility of the individual to
such an extent . . . that it would infallibly bring about the
degradation of humanity."

Furthermore, Secrétan could not accept equality; for he believed it to be unnatural. Believing that Nature and God had
practically the same meaning and that God had given his message of charity to the world, Secrétan argued that inequality
was natural and that the duty of the Christian and the aim of
nature was the achievement of solidarity by having the strong
help the poor and the rich give to the poor. Because of his attitude, Secrétan—like Combes de Lestrade—had very little respect for those who wished to impose equality. To him, "the
mob of levellers, literate or illiterate, and these philanthropists
on foot who see a personal offense in the circulation of coaches"
were not inspired by lofty ideals but by envy.

In a later book, *La Philosophie de la Liberté,* Secrétan expressed additional ideas about the future of society: "The
church of tomorrow will be based upon love, on liberty, on the

full accomplishment of the individuality. . . . The true society will not be established without great struggles and much suffering. . . . There will ever be laws and judges. There will ever be a 'thine' and 'mine.' These warrants of social peace and individual development cannot disappear, but more and more voluntary association will take the place of the state in economic matters as in the spiritual field."

Although Secrétan—a liberal—strongly insisted upon the maintenance of the right to own property because "everyone is the owner of his work because he is the possessor of his own being," and although he was firmly convinced that the "role of the state is not production but protection," many of the details of his social planning are quite comparable to those of Bellamy. As we compare and contrast the work of the two men, we find in them also the same strong, sincere, religious desire to ameliorate conditions and to raise mankind to a higher intellectual and spiritual level. Although Secrétan might not have agreed with Bellamy because he did not fully understand the religious fervor and motivation which had prompted the American, he and Bellamy were also not very far apart when they hoped that man, through love and through brotherhood, would not only discover solidarity but a better world.

In 1928 Professor Charles Gide, the author of a volume about political economy, published a new book entitled *Les Colonies Communistes et Cooperatives* in which he remarked that he was excluding all discussion of Utopian literature because it "is extremely dull and monotonous, right down from More's book, which has set the standard for the rest, and not excepting even those, like Bellamy's, which have had enormous popular success. It is strange that the imagination should prove so feeble in calling up the vision of a new economy and that even Mr. Wells' fancy, that soars so boldly in its journey to the moon and its flight into past ages, should become so poor and trivial in its descriptions of the New Utopia."

## IV  *Utopian Repercussions*

Although Bellamy was not regarded with very much favor by the economists, the socialists, or the politicians, he was more warmly received by the novelists who—unlike Charles Gide—responded to the appeal of his imaginative power. Among these was Anatole France (1844-1924), the novelist, poet, critic, and playwright who has long been regarded as one of the world's famous satirists and who was rewarded the Nobel prize for literature in 1921.

France's *Sur la Pierre blanche* (On the white stone) indicates not only the specific influence of Bellamy's program but France's disagreement with it in some respects. First of all, the hero of his socialistic Utopia—like that of Bellamy—goes to sleep and awakens in the year 2270 to discover a world that has formed a European federation. In his description of social and economic conditions, France also followed Bellamy's program: Money has been replaced by bonds; machines do the work; there are no longer tribunals, trade and armies; and everyone has an intellectual and manual occupation. One of the basic principles of the new society is the lack of individual property —except for personal possessions—and every one is entitled to the fruits of his own labor; for, as France stated, "We have not established equality. We have given a decent life to everybody." With the bonds—which represent so many hours of work —the people buy the products of the nation; but, because they also barter the bonds, rich and poor still exist.

In his description of the creation of his collective state, France was also influenced by Bellamy. Capitalism, which had created a state within a state, had paved the way for the assumption of power by the workers. He also criticized capitalism as being disorderly and wasteful, and indicated the role that science would play in making the agricultural and industrial wealth and abundance of the collective state possible. His attitude toward religion is also extremely liberal; he could not refrain from a prick at Catholicism: "There is still a Pope; he is Pius XXV, dyer, via dell'Orso, Roma."

*La Cité future, essai d'une utopie scientifique* (The city of tomorrow, an essay in scientific Utopia) by Ernest Tarbouriech displays even more clearly than Anatole France's Utopia the influence of Bellamy, but like France, Tarbouriech agreed and disagreed with the American. In the first pages of his book published in 1902, Tarbouriech made reference to *Looking Backward* and also defended himself for using the Utopian form: "I shall not tell a love story between a man of the capitalistic hell and a woman of the new paradise. My work, like that of Deslinières . . . despite a more serious, less picturesque appearance than *Looking Backward, News from Nowhere,* and *Freiland,* deserves the name of Utopia, just as well as the books of Bellamy, Morris, and Hertzka."

In *La Cité future,* Tarbouriech, as the title suggests, portrayed the collectivist metropolis. As in *Looking Backward,* the citizens have credit cards which they spend as they like, and many, many other aspects of the detailed portrayal are comparable to

those of Bellamy. The one point about which Tarbouriech disagrees with Bellamy, and in doing so indicates just how much
he had both *Looking Backward* and *Equality* in mind, is about
active service and the age of retirement. Tarbouriech remarks
that there are "two systems. One, presented by Bellamy, consists in fixing retirement as early as possible, at 45, for instance.
I think it is preferable to delay retirement until a more advanced age—fifty or sixty." Tarbouriech also wished his citizens to have a manual and an intellectual occupation and to
have them simultaneously and, not like Bellamy, "in succession."

Although Alain Le Drimeur's *La Cité future* was published
in 1890, just two years after the appearance of *Looking Backward*, it bears no striking resemblance to it except for the
fact that it is a Utopia which pretends to have been written
"at the beginning of the XXIst century." In style the book is
more comparable to that of Jules Verne, for the author gives
much importance to descriptive details. Furthermore, he chiefly
opposes the aristocratic life and supports sound republicanism.

*La Société Idéale* (1896) by Adrien Foray is, however, much
closer to the depiction of Bellamy than that of *La Cité future*.
In his Utopia, Foray presents a semi-collective system in which
everything affecting the welfare of all is held in common. The
future society which Foray envisions is, however, basically
Catholic and aristocratic, for the élite—the priests, the wise
men, and the nobles—give their time and intelligence to the
direction of the other classes, and all are ruled by a King-Pope.
Although the citizens possess a credit card, the commodities
which they purchase have been ordered by the priests and it
is also one of them who deducts what the citizen has spent from
the credit card. Furthermore, as might be deduced, Foray does
not believe that perfect equality is possible; he wrote: "The
wise men did not want an equality dreamed of but never
achieved." The same attitude toward the élite had also been
reflected in *l'Elite* by Paul Radiot, an engineer, who violently
favored a modern feudal state which would be reorganized by
a regeneration of the élite. Because he considered the rest of
humanity as being no better than cattle, we may assume that
Radiot considered himself one of the élite.

Reflections of Bellamy are also discovered in Emile Masson's
*l'Utopie des Iles bienheureuses* (The Utopia of the blessed
isles) which is colored with aestheticism, spangled with rare
words, and suffused with a lofty ideal of love and self-renun-
ciation. To Masson, as to Bellamy, the moral atmosphere of
the ideal society is as important as material welfare in con-

tributing to the happiness of the citizenry. Moreover, no one
owns anything, everyone is fond of work, and love is free. Vice
and crime are also regarded as in the ancient saying, which
Bellamy himself might have quoted: "No one is voluntarily
wicked or sick."

*Utopies de Justice,* which was published anonymously in
1898,[18] is an example of what may happen when an author
does not comprehend the difference between a general transformation and minute changes: the results may be ridiculous
or hilarious or both. Like Bellamy, the author replaced military
service with a "year in the service of the state to enable the
latter to build railways, roads, and canals. . . ." But after such
a reasonable proposition, he then suggested that, since the number of clerks would be multiplied *ad infinitum,* "the public
will no longer have to queue up in front of the windows. . . ."
and that "when a train stops, the doors will be cleaned before
the passengers get off. . . ."

Another French Utopia, *Pour un monde nouveau* (For a new
world), which was published in 1937 by Fernand Robert, may
also have been influenced by Bellamy's Utopias. Although the
novel lacks the precision and vigor of Bellamy's *Looking Backward,* its author insists upon non-opposition, non-violence, non-
possession, and equal rights for all.[19]

## V  The Twentieth-Century Theses

Although Bellamy was most commented upon, criticized, or
imitated in the decade following the publication of *Looking
Backward* in France, the attitude toward his Utopias changed
during the twentieth century. As has already been remarked in
the discussion of the introduction for *Looking Backward,* which
was written by Charpentier in 1939, the general attitude toward
him became one of greater understanding and, therefore, of
greater appreciation of his concepts. These attitudes are also
reflected in doctoral dissertations which have mentioned his
works.

The first of these—*Le Communisme au Nouveau Monde*
(Communism in the New World)—indicates that in the year
1900 not very much could be located about Bellamy, for
François Sagot, the author, quotes Bellamy but does not seem
to have been able to consult other materials. In fact, he wrote:
"Due to a lack of documents, we have not been able to give
more space to the communist attempts of Henry George and
Edward Bellamy; as a matter of fact, they do not appear to
have been successful."

The situation had seemingly changed by 1942; for Victor Dupont was able in *L'Utopie et le Roman utopique dans la litterature anglaise* (The Utopia and the Utopian novel in English literature) to devote nearly fifty pages to Bellamy and his influence. Because of his removal from the time in which Bellamy's ideas had been so debated and because of the events which had since transpired, Dupont's estimate of Bellamy is objective and balanced.

Although Dupont considers Bellamy's literary qualities to be as worthy of comment as Combes de Lestrade and Thérèse Bentzon had in the nineteenth century, the style and the fiction are not the valuable qualities with which he is concerned. Dupont does observe, however, that Bellamy's qualities as a writer are those of a propagandist and a preacher and that the less the Utopian was concerned with the problem of expression, the more vigorously did he express himself. Dupont is most favorably impressed, however, by the simplicity and logic with which Bellamy presented his ideas to his reader, by the "communicative warm feelings of" his pages, by the "unexpected blending of simplicity and emotion . . . which almost becomes dramatically symbolical" and which sometimes has the effect of biblical denunciations or evangelical allegories.

Dupont, who considered the very literary qualities he extolled as an accessory only for the sociological study which Bellamy presented, remarked that *Looking Backward* was "the expression of a generous individuality, of a clear bold mind. . . ." He admitted, however, that he felt that Bellamy saw his new world with American eyes; for ". . . after all, he dreams of rebuilding the world on the model of an American general store. . . ." To Dupont, this influence is, however, not reprehensible but quite natural, for all are influenced by their environment.

Unlike many other critics, the external aspects of Bellamy's work and his plan do not mislead nor confuse Dupont; for he perceived what many divines had not: Bellamy was "in reality . . . inspired by a lofty and pure ideal; believing in God, he never loses sight of human values. . . ." In his conclusion, Dupont evidenced the change in attitude which had occurred in France toward Bellamy, and also his own: "Bellamy is great in that he appears at the same time as an enthusiastic and convincing propagandist of order and as the apostle of a transformed humanism."

After World War II, Professor Raymond Ruyer presented an objective appraisal in his thesis presented at the University of

Nancy and published in 1950: *L'Utopie et les Utopies*. Like
Dupont, he felt that the fiction and the techniques of Bellamy
were somewhat primitive but that the merits of *Looking Backward* were its simplicity and clarity. He also remarked, however,
that Bellamy had, like St. Simon, the gift of well-turned sentences and of striking images. As an example of the latter,
Ruyer cited the statement of Dr. Leete that the covered streets
of Boston protected all citizens from rain but in the nineteenth
century each had had to protect himself with his own umbrella.
Ruyer remarked that the comparison is so seductive that one
forgets for the moment that the individual umbrella has its
merits when one is in the country!

Ruyer regarded Bellamy's socialism as having been "strongly
inspired by Marx" but he also pointed out that, although capitalism itself had prepared for and rendered inevitable the revolution, it was not a bloody but a peaceful one which had no
dictatorship during the period of transition; that no one class
was the victor; and that certainly the atmosphere of the society
of the year 2000 was not proletarian but bourgeois—that of a
cultivated, free, and distinguished middle class.

After discussing the organization of the labor corps and of the
basis of economic equality, Ruyer turned to the problem of motivation of the worker; he remarked that Bellamy *"dans un sens
très adlérien"* remarked that desire for money had in the past
been really the yen for power, for social position, and for a
reputation of success and of ability. After outlining the credit-
card system, the lack of money, the typical Utopian horror of
Bellamy of buying and selling, and the method of determining
production of material in the ideal state, Ruyer remarked
that one of the most interesting aspects of *Looking Backward*
was its plan for production. He wrote: "The production is not
directed, as in many socialist systems (in Rodbertus, among
others), by a vague 'social need,' which it is impossible to
define. . . ." Ruyer also remarked that the needs of the populace—or its desires about the goods to be produced—were determined not by the rich but by all the citizens who had equal
purchasing power.

Ruyer then outlined the fashion in which economic equality
and the industrial army had not only solved the problems of
the nation but eventually resulted in wealth. After discussing
the nobility with which the national riches were employed
to secure an equal education for all until the age of twenty,
and to insure the early retirement from labor of all citizens,
Ruyer then remarked—as few besides Dupont had—that it was

after retirement that Bellamy intended the true tasks to commence and envisioned a world freed from materialistic cares
in which man could accomplish his evolution and return to
God through the realization of the ideal.

In his summation Ruyer pointed out that ingenious and lucid
as Bellamy was, his plan presented some weaknesses not only
to the economists but to those who—during the years of World
War II—had known totalitarianism, ration cards, and inflation.
First of all, Bellamy had a strong tendency to present brilliant
comparisons for reasons; he had little or nothing to say about
agricultural problems; his credit cards were nothing short of
being a very bad money and not a perfection of it; and his
condemnation of exchange was close to being absurd. Ruyer
opined that in the year 2000 there would be created within a
few hours, or even minutes, not only money but a black market.

Ruyer felt, however, that Bellamy contrasted favorably with
"the satanic anarchists" who declared with Bakunin that " 'all
discourse about the future is criminal, for it hinders pure destruction and halts the course of the revolution.' " Furthermore,
Bellamy contrasted favorably to the Marxists; wrote Ruyer:
"The pacifist Marxism of Bellamy is perhaps more logical than
the Marxian war of the classes"; for, if the end of capitalism
was an evolutionary certainty, there seemed no logical need of
violence.

Bellamy was, however, to be considered as very American in
many ways: his work was filled with faith, generosity, and practicality; with solicitude for humanity and for high production;
with a desire for equality, a horror of the social parasite, and a
sincere love of liberty. Ruyer pointed out that to the European
the industrial army of Bellamy suggested regimentation and
brutalization, but he suggested that it should be considered
"*en style américain*"—for the American army was one without
military tradition and was always a dynamic and improvised
one! Furthermore, a great deal of real liberty existed in Bellamy's egalitarian ideal society which was a type of "*fordisme
socialiste*" that did not end in a grotesque "best of all possible
worlds." In any case, Bellamy's industrial and urban Utopia was
much better in portraying and giving a knowledge of the
future than was the artisan Arcadia of William Morris.

The only French thesis devoted wholly to Bellamy was presented by Sylvia E. Bowman in 1952 at the Sorbonne. In *Le
Dévelopment des Idées d'Edouard Bellamy* the concepts of the
American are placed against the background of those of German, French, English, American, and classical Utopian writers;

of those of social thinkers and reformers who preceded him; and of the various movements of his era with which Bellamy was conversant and which he had written about in editorials and book reviews before he published *Looking Backward* and *Equality*. Professor Bowman's eight-hundred page manuscript is, therefore, an intensive study of the genesis of the ideas of the great American Utopian, as well as a study in comparative literature.

## VI   *Influence upon French Organizations*

Although we have already observed that the socialists of the nineteenth century did not consider Bellamy's *Looking Backward* with much favor, we should also note that Paul Louis, author of a history of socialism in France published in 1950 and of *150 ans de pensée socialiste,* commented in the latter in his chapter "The Utopians" that Bellamy, whom he classified with Morris for some peculiar reason, was like the Englishman in that both were not to be highly considered. For "both their conceptions have nothing to do with scientific facts . . . the society which will be built by socialism will depend for the whole of its structure on the economic status and program accomplished by the world at the time of its achievement. . . ." Although his criticism is Marxist and although like the Marxists he considered both Utopians to have been inspired by "the elementary principle of socialism" as it appeared in their time and when they "had no example under their eyes," Louis—like Jaures in the nineteenth century—insisted that both books had historical value; and he admitted that they had contributed to the spreading of socialist concepts.

Many people in France today would differ with Paul Louis, however, for they—like Charpentier—feel that the concepts of Bellamy are not only of historical importance but of social import now. Among these is Jacques Duboin, who was mentioned by Charpentier in his introduction to the 1939 edition of *Looking Backward* as the most noted exponent of the society of abundance in France. Duboin—a former secretary of state in the Briand-Caillaux ministry before World War I and a representative to the French Assembly for many years—founded the *Mouvement français pour l'Abondance* in 1932;[20] today the organization has ten thousand members and publishes a weekly newspaper *La Grande Relève des Hommes par la Science.* Duboin is the author of such booklets as the following: *Reflexions d'un Français moyen* (1923), with a preface by Henry de Jouvenal, the editor of *Le Matin,* a senator, and the French delegate to the League of Nations; *Nous faisons fausse route* (1932), with a preface by Joseph Caillaux, a former minister of finance and a premier of France (1911-1912); *La Grande Rèleve des hommes par la machine* (1932); *La Grande Révolution qui vient* (1934) which was seized by the Nazis during their occupation of France in World War II; *Egalité économique* (1938); *Demain ou le Socialisme de l'abondance* (1940); *Economie distributive* (1946); and *Les Hommes Sont-ils Naturellement Méchants?* (1947).

Duboin, who is today an alert and dynamic individual in his eighties, maintains a close contact with the Bellamy Association of Holland; and he publishes regularly a column in *La Grande Relève* called *"Chez les Bellamistes"* which not only reports the activities of the association in the Netherlands but presents extracts of articles published by the newspaper of this society. Several years ago when Duboin attended a convention in Holland of the Bellamy Association, he remarked that reading the books of Edward Bellamy had influenced him in founding his movement. The reflection of the ideas of Bellamy are to be found not only in the booklets written by Duboin but also in *La Grande Relève* which serialized *Looking Backward* in its issues beginning on March 5, 1955.

Jacques Duboin thinks today that Bellamy was a very bright Utopian who correctly anticipated many future developments but who could not have foreseen in his day the extraordinary development of abundance for all which science has made possible, despite the fact that Bellamy argued that such progress would be possible. Further evidence of the wisdom of Bellamy is to be found in the program of the Movement for Abundance which has as its credo "Ever-increasing production because of scientific development will always provide a plentitude for all." Because science and technology will eventually permit mankind to enjoy leisure and because this enjoyment of life will not be possible until the obsolete economic system of "wages-profits-and prices" is changed, Duboin and his followers advocate a larger gathering of the means of production and distribution into the hands of the state, which can then enforce distributive justice, wipe out the misery and starvation which exist in the world, and inaugurate rational planning. Like Bellamy, Jacques Duboin thinks that violence is not necessary to achieve this industrial and economic democracy; for both time and events are concurring to destroy the capitalistic system. He believes today that mankind has but to wait—and push the wheel when it can.

The Movement for Abundance has had an ideological influence upon other organizations, or they closely parallel its ideas. One of these is the *Cercle Civique Vosgien* (Vosgian Civic Club),[21] which also tends toward collectivism. At the meeting at which the constitution of the club was presented, Pierre-Louis Maître gave a lecture which was significantly entitled *"Utopie d'hier, Réalité de demain"* (Utopia of yesterday . . . reality of tomorrow).

Another organization which sponsors dissemination of the ideas of Bellamy and those of Duboin's Movement for Abundance is a group of Esperantists[22] which is also closely associated or in contact with the members of the Bellamy Association of Holland which had published *Looking Backward* in this artificial language. Henri Cottereau, the present secretary of the *Bellami-Abundo Frakcio* (Bellamy-Abundance Section) writes that the group was founded by the Esperantists of the Bellamy Association of Holland and of the Movement for Abundance in France at the twenty-seventh annual convention in Nancy in August of 1954 of the *Sennacieca Asocio Tutmonds* (Mondial A-National Association), the section of the universal organization which believes that Esperanto should be used to promote political objectives.

The aims of the section, formed in 1954, are to (1) make Esperanto known among the groups interested in abundance, a distributive economy, and economic equality; and (2) to make the theories of these movements known among people who are interested in Esperanto and to encourage members to study such ideas. Beginning in January, 1955, the section began to publish in Esperanto a bi-monthly bulletin entitled *Liberigo de Mizero* (Liberation from Misery) which is widely distributed and which may be consulted at the Esperantist Museum in Vienna. The bulletin serialized in 1958 the Esperanto translation of *Looking Backward*[23] and has published many articles about the ideas of Bellamy. Furthermore, members of the French organization have published articles about Bellamy and the Movement for Abundance in such publications of the Esperantists as *Sennaiulo, Vegetarano,* and others;[24] and it also circulates two pamphlets to those who indicate interest in the ideas of the organization: "Liberation from Fear and Misery" and "Economic Facts in Twenty-eight Pictures." Since this publication circulates in Italy, England, France, Germany, Holland, and other countries, the work it has done in promoting the theories of Bellamy can not be estimated—nor can that of *La Grande Relève.*

Other French groups which have been in contact with the Bellamy Association because of their interest in Bellamy's ideas have been cited by M. Hoogeven, the member of the association who is the correspondent for France, Belgium, and French Canada. Besides the exchange with the Duboin group, there has been one with the *Fédération abondanciste révolutionnaire* of Paris which publishes *Agir;*[25] with *Groupes d'Action pour l'Economie distributive* of Paris[26] which publishes *Réagir;* and with *Mouvement pour l'Egalité économique*[27] of Toulouse which publishes *Lyg* and which has also had several of its articles published not only in the publication of the Bellamy Association of Holland but in that of the French Esperantists. The ideas of these groups are in most instances comparable to those of Duboin's Movement for Abundance; but some of them desire to begin action with the poorest classes of society.

A more recently organized group which has contacted the Bellamy Association of Holland is *Temps Nouveaux,* which was formed when three other French societies merged: *Les Amis du Droit* (The friends of law); *Les Clubs de l'Amitié* (The friendship clubs); and *Centre Français d'Etudes et de Liaison* (French center of studies and coordination), another organization for those who hold positions of responsibility in the country.[28]

This short survey of the vast subject of Bellamy in France— a study which does not pretend to be complete but which may open the way for future research[29]—shows that the change of attitude which has occurred in France since *Looking Backward* was first published there has on the whole been in Bellamy's favor. From the first, his literary qualities were recognized by all who read him and by such different reviewers as Viscount Combes de Lestrade, de Laveleye, Thérèse Bentzon, Professor Ruyer, and Professor Dupont; for each praised the vigor and simplicity of his style, the gripping power of his imagery, and his sincerity and his faith.

Because he used the Utopian novel to promulgate his ideas, he was considered by the stern theoreticians of socialism, by economists, by sociologists, and by politicians to have been— in the vulgar sense of the word—"Utopian." He was less popular and also given less serious consideration than Henry George because he was a novelist, but, as such, he was also powerful —as Jaures declared—in winning converts to socialism. Among the socialists he was not, however, considered with any great enthusiasm although even today they regard his book as being of historical importance; among the liberals, he was attacked as a very dangerous dreamer; among the anarchists (such as Severine, Jean Grave, and others) he was ignored—and this was also the reaction of the pacifists and the atheists.

Despite the variety of attitudes which have been shown Bellamy since 1890, the fact remains that his ideas have remained alive in France for seventy years and that they are still being given serious consideration by many groups of people. This changed attitude and interest of the present must be considered as the result of a world which has seen many of Bellamy's hopes and plans realized; as Charpentier and Ruyer pointed out, many economists have been sponsoring ideas which Bellamy made popular in the nineteenth century, and his concept of the peaceful evolution of society has its appeal to the non-Marxists who realize, however, that starvation in the midst of abundance should not be tolerated. Certainly it is not too much to say of Bellamy that his plea for justice struck deep echoes in French hearts and his efforts to create a rational world have eventually appeared not so Utopian to French minds after all!

# CHAPTER ELEVEN

# The Catholic, Liberal Attacks in Belgium

By

## PIERRE MICHEL

IN THE DECADE in which Bellamy's *Looking Backward* was being written and read, a climax was reached in the political history of Belgium. From 1830–the year Belgium became independent –until 1885, two parties had reigned without any difficulty: the conservative Catholic and the Liberal parties. Although the former remained traditional, regional, and Christian in its ideals, the latter had by 1885 undergone a democratic evolution and –in opposition to the Catholic group–had begun to look with favor upon social reform measures. But little progress was made in ameliorating the conditions of the workingman until after April 5, 1885, when the turning point in the political-economic affairs of Belgium was marked by the founding in Brussels of the Labor party,[1] which decades later openly called itself the Socialist party.

Although liberal economist E. Pirmez had stated that there "was no complaint from the laboring class,"[2] the proletariat had in fact long been unhappy because of its precarious working conditions. The laborer received little protection from social legislation, his working environment was often revolting, his unemployment was frequent, his income was very low, and his salary was frequently paid not in hard-earned money but partly in tickets which were to be exchanged for the necessities of life in the factory shops. Because of these circumstances and this exploitation, the workers seethed secretly; then they began to organize; and, with the founding of the Labor party, they campaigned vigorously for privileges which they would once not even have dared dream about enjoying.

The aim of the Labor party when it was founded was primarily to improve the socio-economic conditions of the proletariat through legislation. To achieve such reform measures, the party battled for universal suffrage in order to have the lower classes represented in Parliament; and it encouraged also the establishment of cooperatives so that commodities might be more cheaply provided or purchased. As a result of the strikes, riots, and protests of the Social War of 1886[3] and of political action, the Belgian worker was liberated from complete dependence upon his employer. Further improvements in his general condition were made when restricted suffrage laws were passed; the ticket system was abolished; new school laws made education obligatory; and wages rose and working hours decreased.

Since Belgians were dreaming of and achieving a better life in the 1880's and were prepared to be receptive to new theories, their socialist leaders and writers—De Paepe, Volders, Anseele, Bertrand, Vandervelde, Destrée, De Brouckère, and Huysmans —not only studied and accepted Marx's theories but also those of such famous collectivtsts as Saint-Simon, Colins, Fourier, Proudhon, Lassalle, Schaeffle, and Bebel, whom they often mentioned in their lectures and in their writings. Oddly enough they also wrote about ideas or theories similar to Bellamy's,[4] but they never mentioned him and they never listed his works in their most extensive bibliographies.

Although the famous editor, writer, and government official Camille Huysmans stated in a letter in 1958 that he had "often spoken of Bellamy and of his books from the platform before World War I"[5] and that some of his theories had made understanding of Marx easier, this statement and the publication of *Looking Backward* in Flemish by a socialist group in 1909 form almost the sole proof offered by the socialists that Bellamy's famous Utopia was read. The evidence that he was well-known and perhaps even considered dangerous is not to be discovered in socialist publications; it is found in the attacks which the literary critics and the Catholics and the Liberals made against *Looking Backward,* of which the French editions of 1890 (translated by Paul Rey) and 1891 (translated by Vicomte Combes de Lestrade) were circulating in French Belgium; in the Flemish sector, the edition prepared by Frank Van der Goes of The Netherlands was reviewed.

## I   *The Literary Critics*

In fact, the general attitude of the literary critics who reviewed *Looking Backward* would not have been conducive to considering the novel seriously. They admitted that it was a fine, fanciful work of art; but they dismissed Bellamy's ideas as not being feasible, although they were humanitarian. S. Merlino, who published a review in 1891 in *La Société Nouvelle,* published both in Paris and in Brussels, and the three reviewers who published in the Flemish publications of Ghent and Antwerp all shared this view in differing degrees. Merlino, in his highly critical consideration of *Looking Backward,* admitted that Bellamy had fulfilled his aim of portraying what the future of society might be and that it was the realm of the artist— not of the *scientist,* who carefully tested his hypotheses—to try to solve with intuition and imagination the problems of civilization.

Merlino thought, however, that Bellamy's novel had been included in Guillaumin's "Bibliothèque des Economistes" because the publisher wished to exploit the novel's popularity. For Merlino considered Bellamy merely a "bourgeois who was writing for other bourgeois"—and as one who was extremely capable of doing so because he knew their hearts and their languages. Although he admitted that Bellamy was well-intentioned and honest, he also thought he used the rhetoric of the sentimental, amateur philanthropist and that he was resoundingly materialistic.

Merlino condemned *Looking Backward* because the author pointed out that the industrial world of the nineteenth century did not know how to produce wealth but that the ideal state did. He also disliked Bellamy's having minimized the role of the legislature, his routine acceptance of a president of a nation, his expectation that the new nation would develop imperceptibly from individual trusts to one Giant Monopoly, his retaining divisions between manual and intellectual labor, his belief in God, his status quo of the family, his lack of recognition of the change the new era would bring in education and art, and his use of the absurd and tyrannical military system as the basis for his industrial organization. Regimentation and obligatory service were, stated Merlino, poor solutions for socio-economic problems.

Merlino had nothing but praise and admiration, however, for the artistry with which Bellamy depicted nineteenth-century society. He remarked that his view was not only truthful but skillfully presented in a fashion which led to a climax. He particularly admired the struggle of Julian West to adapt to the new society and Bellamy's use of the nightmare in which Julian returns to nineteenth-century Boston. This technique, wrote Merlino, made the reader realize what the illusion created by the book had meant to him and regret his loss. In another article of the same year in which Merlino considered Morris' *News from Nowhere,* he commented again upon the dramatic and psychological interest of Julian's struggle to adapt himself to the new life. Remarking again that Bellamy was "a bourgeois" but one who had been more or less converted to socialism, Merlino stated that, in estimating the two Utopias, *Looking Backward* had more dramatic intensity and interest than that of Morris, whom he considered to be an anarchist.

Wattez, in his estimate—published in *Nederlandsche Dichten Kunsthalle* (1891-92)—was even more concerned with the literary merits of *Looking Backward* than with its ideas. He admired the persuasive skill with which Bellamy presented his ideas and his ability to refute arguments before the reader could voice them. As a result, Bellamy's theories were presented in a manner which made them appear feasible. Furthermore, he was not a revolutionary; no bearer of the "red flag," Bellamy had his heroes speak harshly of those who were "reds."

Wattez doubted, however, that Bellamy's novel would find many readers among Europeans who were keen on love stories; for in Bellamy's book they would find reason replacing romance. He praised the Utopia, however, for its colorful and original language, the power of the last chapters, the wonderful sermon which indicated that religion still existed in a reformed world, and the dream of Julian West which gave evidence also of "a literary talent of first quality and of a very original mind." Although Wattez stated that he did not intend to judge if there was anything besides a Utopia in *Looking Backward* and that he also was not advertising the "new gospel," he felt that as a literary critic he could with impunity rank *Looking Backward* with the moving *Uncle Tom's Cabin* and with the masterly *Havelaar* by Multatuli (Edward Douwes Dekker).

Although Henrik de Marez, in his review of 1891 for the *Nederlandsch Museum* (Ghent) of Frank Van der Goes' translation of *Looking Backward,* also considered it to be "a product of fancy," he opined that it was a noble one because it aimed at forcing consideration of the horrible situation of the greatest part of humanity. To him the outstanding features were "the few lines" with which the author had presented nineteenth-century society "with a realistic truth which makes us shiver." One of the unusual features of his review was that Marez recognized, as few had, that Bellamy had applied Darwin's theory of evolution to society but had intended "the continuous choice of the good and the rejection of the bad" to aid in the creation of a relatively perfect society.

After explaining that Bellamy's perfected state was a collective one in which everyone worked for everyone, he remarked that few people realized what a relief it would be for men not to be humiliated by accepting alms. Unlike Merlino, Marez felt that Bellamy had written some wonderful pages in defense of humanitarianism—and had done so without bombast and hyperbole, but with simple reasoning and style. Marez criticized Bellamy's plan for artists; for he felt that if the public taste had to judge their creations, the best might not be subsidized by their income and thus freed to continue their work. Marez stated that "artists and writers who reap the greatest public success are not always the best."

In 1892, Jef van de Venne published in the *Nederlandsch Museum* an article in which he assessed three novels by Bellamy: *Dr. Heidenhoff's Process, Miss Ludington's Sister,* and *Looking Backward.* After a short introduction about former Utopias, van de Venne posed this question: "Would there still be interest in . . . abstract buildings made of cards which vanish and crumble down under the softest breath of reality?" In his reply, he asserted that Bellamy, "the daring American, shows experimentally that . . . 'impossible' was a vain word. He builds stone on stone on the basis of a few unstable guesses . . . and he raises monuments from which, pure and clear as sunlight, shine the loftiest ethical notions. . . ." To him Bellamy's strength and the popularity of his Utopia were due to his ability to "build systems, to give them life, and to carve them into the memory by framing them with wonderful and supernatural circumstances as if they were one with nature."

After discussing the success of *Looking Backward* in the United States and in Germany, and after surveying the legends of characters who go to sleep and awaken, he cited Dr. Heinrich Fraenkel's *Gegen Bellamy* (1891) and said that he agreed with the motto the German had printed above his pamphlet: "*Hat's auch Methode, bleibt es doch ein Wahnsinn.*" Van de Venne stated that he agreed with Dr. Fraenkel that "though it is based on Method, it remains Madness." Although he agreed with this writer who made one of the most antisocialist attacks upon Bellamy, van de Venne carefully quoted the good comments which had been made about the book in Germany. He then stated his own detailed observations and opinion: Bellamy's system of work and retribution would not be workable; his labor force would result in iron discipline, corruption, servitude, and sycophancy; his government would become a bureaucracy; and universities would lose their value: on their gates would be written: "Genius prohibited." All in all, he considered Bellamy an optimist, for he announced a peaceful forthcoming "social revolution, which is a subject about which all hearts and minds were concerned." Others, however, did not think that it would be peaceful.

In his discussion of *Dr. Heidenhoff's Process*, van de Venne stated that the book was typically American because it evinced "love of nature, an impulse for spiritual and physical activity, and boldness in the relations between the two sexes, which purify" the reader. To him, the novel was masterfully done, and it impressed the reader with its freshness and its purity. Of its theme, van de Venne stated that "with no memory, there is no pain, no remorse, no mischief, no stain. The biggest rascal is innocent in his new right as soon as his memory is dead." He obviously missed the point that Bellamy was trying to make: only religious persons have a sensitive conscience and are destroyed by sin; and Dr. Heidenhoff's electric shock was to save them from dying—figuratively or literally—as a result of their sense of guilt.

Van de Venne considered *Miss Ludington's Sister*—as did Sylvia Bowman in *The Year 2000*—to be the twin of Theophile Gautier's *Spirite;* but he felt that most readers would soon tire of the maddening conversations of Paul and Miss Ludington. After commenting about the use of the theme of the different stages of the development of man's personality and after relating the story—which he thought Bellamy intended to use to show that "the pure ideal is a mere bubble blown from the soap of hypothesis and based on eccentricities"—van de Venne made no further critical comments about the novel. In these comments, he had, however, stressed that the ideal was a bubble!

From the attitudes of these critics and from the attacks made by the Catholics and the Liberals, it may be deduced that the socialists preferred to remain silent about Bellamy because their opponents found it too easy to find defects in his ideal society or in his ideas. Because they were so easily ridiculed, the socialists did not wish to be associated with them publicly. In fact, almost before the socialists could have openly used Bellamy's famous Utopia or cite arguments from it, the Catholics and Liberals sought to discredit any new argument their socialist opponents might use by associating them with the ridicule hurled at Bellamy.

## II  *The Liberal Attack*

In 1890 Baron Emile de Laveleye (1822-1892)—the economist and author of *Le Socialisme Contemporain* (1881) and of
*Elements d'Economie Politique* (1882)—published his article
"Deux Utopies Nouvelles" in *Revue de Belgique*. This article
was also reprinted in February of the same year in *Littell's
Living Age* and in the March issue of the *Contemporary Review*\* in the United States where his criticisms were widely
quoted by American critics of Bellamy's ideal society. In 1893,
de Laveleye's critical comments were also published as a separate chapter in a book by P. Geiregat[6]—a book which was a
peculiar compilation.

In his foreword, Geiregat stated: "Social problems are now
much debated; attention is called to them in books, newspapers,
legislative assemblies, in addresses, in political meetings . . .
'Where are we going?' is a question which every thinker puts
to himself. . . . That is what the astonishing success of Edward
Bellamy's *Looking Backward* may be attributed to. . . . We
have summed up all the main elements [of his work], but have
retained everything that belongs to the actual building and
functioning of the new society which he imagined."[7]

After stating that his book should be useful to those who had
not the time or the opportunity to read *Looking Backward*,
Geiregat presented an objective compilation of Bellamy's ideas.
The reader of the summation of *Looking Backward* is, therefore, shocked when he turns to the chapter by de Laveleye,
which contains nothing but adverse criticism and complete
rejection of the ideas which Geiregat had so carefully presented.

De Laveleye is, however, somewhat ambivalent in his attitudes towards Utopias and toward Bellamy's plan. First of all,
he seemingly has no objections to a Utopian society nor to
some of Bellamy's major goals. He states in speaking of Professor Charles Secrétan's *Mon Utopie*—which had also been

---

\* Bellamy—who was interested in the critical comments about his
novel because they could contribute to ideas for the future society—
mentioned de Laveleye's article in his own "What Nationalism
Means" in the *Contemporary Review* of July, 1890. He remarked
that, though he should be gratified that de Laveleye had "lumped"
him with Plato, he was not pleased to be part of the "composite
photograph" of other Utopians because he could not "detect any
trace of . . . [his] own features or expression" in de Laveleye's
depiction.—EDITOR

critical of Bellamy—that "the nationalization of land, or rather its being put to the use of the community, does not seem to raise any great difficulty."[8] He also declares that he hopes "with Charles Secrétan that, thanks to education and to slowly acquired experience, the working classes will succeed in acquiring the qualities necessary for the management of industrial affairs without being obliged to depend on the intervention of capitalists; from that moment on, the social transformation will be achieved peacefully and ineluctably like any previous economic change."[9]

Although de Laveleye is aware that the "goods of this world are not distributed in accordance with justice" and that "something must be done in order to increase the portion of those who work"[10] and are responsible for the production of wealth, he calls Dupont-White, an advocate of social reform,* a prophet,[11] while he denounces Bellamy's society as a dream, which it will always remain "unless the human heart changes completely. His ideal is pure communism and, as such, it meets with irrefutable objections."[12] Although de Laveleye admitted later that he was an admirer of the Inca social organization, he immediately explained that it was "not exactly communist"; for in that state "every family reaped for itself the harvest of its piece of land."[13]

Because of this attitude, de Laveleye denounced Bellamy's distribution of wealth as being nothing short of "communism"[14] —and did not recognize that Bellamy's plan of economic equality outdid the Marxist distribution according to need! De Laveleye argued not only that Bellamy's system would be unfair but that a poor worker could not be rejected, "for rejection would be equivalent to a death sentence."[15] Like Secrétan and many other of Bellamy's critics, de Laveleye also doubted that there would be sufficient incentive for the worker to produce; for "honor can make somebody a hero, but not a worker."[16]

Like Secrétan, de Laveleye also had some specific criticisms of Bellamy's plan for the distribution of work. He asserted that arranging the hours to be worked in accordance with the difficulty or danger of the task was senseless. First of all, "it is obvious that everybody would choose the most pleasant jobs and that the unpleasant ones would not be accepted."[17] Furthermore, if the laborers worked shorter hours at noisome tasks,

---

* Dupont-White was the *nom de plume* of Mme. Sadi Carnot, the wife of the President of the French Republic, who translated the works of Mill into French.

one would need, for example, "a whole army of stokers aboard" a ship.[18]

De Laveleye could admire Secrétan, Dupont-White, or the Inca collectivist society, but he could not accept Bellamy. He undoubtedly could not do so because, as he asserted time and again, Bellamy was a "communist"; to him, the American had merely incorporated in his novel Louis Blanc's *L'Organization du Travail* (1840). As Van Kalken has pointed out in *Histoire de Belgique*, the fear of communism—of the "reds" and their violence—made people hesitant to accept even the most modest proposals;[19] and it must have been fear of Bellamy as such that led liberal-minded de Laveleye to take the ambivalent attitude he did. He could accept the Utopia of Secrétan, but not that of Bellamy because it was too "communistic"—too uncompromising and progressive.

## III   *The Catholic Ridicule*

Knowing the attitude of the Catholic Church toward any attempt to establish a paradise on earth and toward atheistic communism, it is not surprising to discover that more material is available about Bellamy—despite the Christian bases of his society—from Catholic writers. Their numerous attacks would not have been made unless Bellamy was being read—as one critic suggested—by "the workers."[20] The clever, antagonistic, Catholic criticisms of Bellamy were, however, aimed also at the Belgian socialists; for the church wished to ridicule and discourage them.

One of the moderate critics of *Looking Backward* was Jean Halleux who, in "La Société de l'Avenir d'après Bellamy" of 1892, began by praising Bellamy, by treating his ideas objectively, and then ended by ridiculing him. Halleux stated of *Looking Backward* that "a literary form has never been better adapted to the explanation of a collectivist theory."[21] The concepts were also so concretely and clearly presented that they could be understood by everyone; before Bellamy, collectivist writers had presented abstract theories which were incomprehensible to the masses. He then wrote: "Even now, what the public has heard of socialism is little more than criticisms inspired by hatred, and certain claims which have only a more or less remote connection with its basic dogmas."[22]

After objectively defining collectivism as Bellamy portrayed it as "an economic reform . . . which . . . [consisted] mainly in the concentration of all the capital in the state, and in the organization by the state of production and distribution of wealth," Halleux then presented four objections to Bellamy's plan—and did so without attacking either socialism or collectivism. First of all, he felt that Bellamy's state could not be attained without a revolution. Second, the system would be incompatible with individual freedom. Third, the citizens would not work efficiently. Fourth, Bellamy's theory of work was based upon a false concept of salary, for payment "was no reward of the worker's merit" but "merely a value which the worker" obtained "in exchange for a value which his work had procured to somebody."[23] Halleux then concluded his objections with the comment that "fundamentally the state will be the absolute master. Besides, without this absolutism, what would become of discipline, which is the indispensable condition for the existence of so complex an organization? Collectivism would soon stop being a social regime and would result in disorder and anarchy."[24]

In the pages following Halleux's analysis and criticism, material—seemingly not from his pen—was presented which purported to be from clippings dated October 16, 2001, from a newspaper called *Reverse the Engine—The Organ of a Few Men of Common Sense.* Mr. George Kaiser, who had found the clippings, refused to disclose how he had done so; the editor obligingly explained, however, that he surmised that Kaiser had discovered the newspaper "thanks to a process similar to that which Mr. Bellamy used to discover Mr. Julian West's journal."[25] The extracts from the newspaper portray the "practical difficulties in achieving Mr. Bellamy's" ideal state and they "support, therefore, the excellent arguments presented by Mr. Halleux." After reading the ironic, exaggerated, and often ludicrous arguments presented by Kaiser, one easily understands why the Belgian socialists did not care to be associated with Bellamy: they would seemingly have been united with the ridiculous.

Kaiser's criticism not only lambasted specific concepts of Bellamy but attempted to show their inevitable results. First of all, the ideal state resulted in an increase in alcoholism because the people sought either escape or solace from the monotonous life created by an absence of competition. Since the citizens could no longer accumulate private property for the benefit of their heirs, they lost interest in production. Because all artists and writers were controlled by the government, they lost interest in creation; and the arts either remained static or degenerated. Because the doctors worked in shifts like the factory workers and because they refused to work after hours, the people who needed a doctor often did not obtain one. Since complete equality meant the disappearance of all segregation and discrimination among the races, a thorough integration was supposed to take place between all peoples. In a public speech Mr. Monic, a famous anthropologist of the year 2001, deplored that variations still existed; but he then explained a system which would produce men who would be alike: they would have apple-green complexions, snub noses, and bandy legs.[27]

Kaiser's exaggerated comments did not consider seriously either the concepts or the arguments Bellamy had presented. Bellamy had portrayed the ethical and intellectual benefits which only an economically non-competitive society—for competition for recognition still existed in the army of workers— would provide; and he had hoped that such an environment would encourage the development of mentally, physically, and morally improved citizens. He had also tried to free art from government censorship and to provide an educational system which would enable all people to develop latent interests and abilities in every realm of interest. Believing that each individual should develop his individuality, Bellamy tried to prevent conformity and regimentation; and he had recognized that all men were not and never could be equal—except politically and economically. But, in all fairness to Mr. Kaiser, one must recognize that, had he tried to be just to Mr. Bellamy, he could not have presented a ridiculous picture of the results of his plan for an improved society.

Count Emeric du Chastel presented his criticism of Bellamy's and of Eugen Richter's Utopias in 1894 in the *Revue Générale* with a serialized article entitled "Deux Romans à propos du Socialisme." Du Chastel began his review by appearing to be favorable toward all schemes which might remedy the evils of the social order. He wrote: "The exaggerated monopolizing of riches by the bankers on the one hand and the ever-increasing pauperism of starvelings on the other hand offer such a disheartening spectacle that we would enthusiastically greet the beginning of new times and this [Bellamy's] attempt at a social overthrow if it only had any chance of being successful."[28]

As may be expected from the last part of this statement, du Chastel then developed his argument that Bellamy's system, which he termed that of "a socialist of the uncompromising collectivist school," could "never be put into practice. . . . For Mr. Bellamy, in spite of his obvious good intentions, his wonderful talent, and the care he took to answer all objections carefully, to provide against all eventualities, to foresee all the

difficulties of his system, has forgotten a most important thing:
to tell us how to change *human nature!*"[29] Although du Chastel
admitted that this was the only serious objection he could make
to Bellamy's ideal society, he argued that it alone undermined
—and would undermine—his whole plan.

He concluded his discussion of Bellamy by stating that no
matter how clever Bellamy might be, he was after all "absurd—
unfortunately—because of the eternal egoism of the 'human
beast' " who was "undeniably the stupidest of all beasts when its
interest is at stake."[30] The cleverness of du Chastel is evident:
he wanted to remedy society; he wished sincerely to consider
Bellamy's plan; but he had to reject it because Bellamy had not
recognized—despite his astuteness—that man is incapable of
either achieving or dwelling in such a society because of his
egoism and selfish stupidity.

In the second part of his article, du Chastel presented a summary and criticism of Richter's *Sozial-demokratische Zukunftsbilder frei nach Bebel* which he considered the "opposite view
and a victorious refutation of Mr. Bellamy's book."[31] Although
Richter's book had been presented in Utopian style as a result
of Bellamy's widespread popularity, it was a specific answer
not to Bellamy but to Bebel and the German socialists. Du
Chastel probably recognized this fact—just as he doubtlessly
knew that by identifying Bellamy with the German socialist,
he was also associating the Belgian socialists with him—and
demolishing all of them.

In 1895, the *Comité de Propagande de la Presse Catholique*
published a series entitled *Bibliotheque de Propaganda Antisocialiste;* and among these publications there were two which
attacked Bellamy. In *Le Socialisme au Pouvoir* by Richter,
which bore the subtitle *Application à notre Pays,* the contents
of Emeric du Chastel's summation of Richter's criticism is almost literally reprinted. Author A. Baisir, however, had adapted
the criticism so that it applied directly to Belgium and Brussels.
The aim of the pamphlet was definitely political, for the following statement was made in the foreword: "Let us hope that,
after reading these instructive and amusing pages, many workers
who have been attracted by socialist Utopias will open their
eyes to truth and will give up their sad mistakes." The author
then used the books of both Bellamy and Richter to ridicule the
Belgian socialists.

In the same year Bellamy was also used by the same organization as a means of sharply attacking the socialists in a pam-

phlet entitled *Het Jaar 2000, de Socialisten in Werking, door Ed. Bellamy*. In this publication the author stated that *Vooruit*, the official organ of the Belgian Labor Party, had printed that "they [The Catholics] say that our principles are illusions. But a well-known American writer, Ed. Bellamy, has recently published a work—*Looking Backward*—in which he leads the reader to a society where our doctrine is at work; and that proves sufficiently that the desires of the socialists can be achieved very easily."[32] This statement obviously afforded the Catholics another desired opportunity to deal a deadly blow to their political adversaries by concentrating upon the weakest points of Bellamy's theories.

Although the tone of the attack has changed from one of playful irony to spitefulness, the arguments presented are the same as those used by previous critics. The reader of this pamphlet feels that he is observing a political battle—and he realizes that the conservative critics had an easier task than the socialists who supported Bellamy. It is always easier to shatter than to defend something which exists only on paper.

## IV  *Bellamy Societies in Belgium*

Although a widely read Flemish translation of *Looking Backward—Honderd Jaar Later*—was published in 1909 in Ghent by Volksdrukkerij, a cooperative society founded around 1885 by Ghent socialists,[33] little mention is found of Bellamy in any Belgian publications after 1910. This lack of concern with the ideas of the Utopian, however, is easily explained by the change of policy of the Belgian Labor party. Before World War I, it had turned from its primary aim—collectivism—to fight stubbornly for universal suffrage. The socialists had realized that if they wished to take practical but legal, evolutionary steps toward achieving state socialism, they first had to get the right to the vote and then to establish a majority in Parliament. Their last action toward the achievement of this goal was a general strike in 1913 which spread over the whole country; but they did not win unrestricted suffrage until 1919.

During the war all ideologies and theories were submerged by the conflict; but, after World War I, the Socialist party gained considerable strength. From having, in 1902, only thirty-four seats of a total of one hundred and sixty-six in the House of Representatives, the Socialists had, in 1919, seventy seats of one hundred and eighty-six. Although the Socialists had by then become the second largest party in Belgium and now openly called itself "socialist," no mention of Bellamy is to be found in any of its publications. This is not strange; for, as Van Kalken has stated, all the leaders "did not trust the infallibility of the Marxist theories" and "the young members had plans, 'hard and new.'" They had given up the idea of the future collective state—whether of the Bellamy or the Marxist variety—and "they were concentrating their efforts on the nationalization of a few basic industries and on the management of the economy of the country by the state."[34] Despite the fact that the Socialists remain the second largest party in Belgium, their advance was halted during the years after World War I.

Although the Socialist party had little reason to discuss Utopian theories after World War I, one Bellamy society was formed in Belgium in the 1930's. According to the list of societies of the world given on the back page of the October, 1938, issue of the Bandoeng, Java, *De Uitweg*—the official publication of the Bellamy league of the Dutch East Indies—Belgian Bellamyites lived in Ghent and in Antwerp.[35] Information gleaned from former members of the Ghent association[36] and from the minutes of their meetings, reveals that the society was founded a year later as a result of communication with the Holland Bellamy Association and of the members' interest in socialist ideas and in Esperanto.

After reading the books of Edward Bellamy, a few people decided to found a Bellamy club; and the Ghent group officially organized on September 17, 1939, elected officers, and then drafted a circular letter which not only announced the intent of the group but invited others to join the organization. The aim of the Ghent association, as recorded in its minutes, was threefold: (1) *"to propagate the ideas* presented in Bellamy's two books to *all the members* of the population; (2) to make evident to all the economic cause of the chaotic situation of the moment; and (3) to enlist the interest of people in Bellamy's ideas."[37]

The letter which the group drafted for circulation read as follows:

> In the present state of chaos, despair and disorder, it is definitely necessary to help suffering humanity to come out of chaos and to show it the way to peace and well-being.
> All those who know and understand Bellamy's ideas long for them to be put into practice, for they know that Bellamy can and must bring the solution.
> So far there has not been any nucleus in Belgium for people

to work actively to spread this movement; that is why a few Bellamyites have decided to found a group where such work will be possible.

But many people may wonder, is it really necessary to found a new group? Just now, in these times of war?

Yes, right now, because the world is more than ever feeling the need for help, because it is now more than ever necessary to point out to suffering mankind that the present crippled economy alone is responsible for the current misery and to show it where the solution lies and how all may help to build a new world.[38]

Since the Belgian association could rely only upon membership fees and contributions from members to finance its propaganda work, it appealed to Holland for material to distribute. The Dutch Bellamy group sent pamphlets, leaflets, large numbers of its newspaper, *Bellamy Nieuws*,[39] and several copies of *Looking Backward*. Despite its use of the Dutch material, of publications in Esperanto, of the personal contacts and the circular letters, the Belgian group never had more than seventy members. At the beginning these people represented all classes of society and all political ideologies. The club had, however, advertised Bellamy's ideas primarily among teachers, students, and lawyers.

When the last meetings of the Belgian Bellamy Association were held, differences of opinion about the purpose of the group became evident. Some took a stand for a far-flung superficial propaganda effort which would draw new members to the association. Others, including the president, preferred to restrict activity to the study of Bellamy because they felt that most members were not sufficiently acquainted with his theories. As a result, information or study meetings were arranged.

Besides the different points of view about the purpose of the association, further difficulties arose because of the pre-World War II Belgian political situation. One member, who received strong support, stated that he would resign from the association if the committee admitted members of the *Vlaams National Verbond* or *Dinazo Party*—parties which were later to collaborate with the Nazis—or of the Communist party, because these parties advocated violence and dictatorships. Although it was finally agreed that only "true genuine Bellamyites" would be accepted as members, one of the members, Mr. Arpad Lodor, admitted that several members later joined the German National Socialist party because it sponsored equal rights for all, but that they had deserted the Nazis when they perceived the real use they were making of the theories which had attracted them to Bellamy and then to the National Socialists.

Although the Bellamy Belgian Association was never formally dissolved, it no longer holds meetings; and its efforts to revive interest in Bellamy were fruitless. According to the surviving members who were interviewed, their movement failed because the economic situation in Belgium was so good that people felt no crying need for change and were not ready for a collectivist society. Furthermore, the socialists of Belgium had not only forgotten Bellamy but had never regained interest in him. In the opinion of Mrs. Sweemer, whose husband is a socialist member of the House of Representatives, the socialists have changed so much that they today assume a capitalist attitude toward their cooperative societies. The Belgian organization also failed because of lack of financial aid for educational and propaganda purposes and because its action was not practical but educational. Although their attempt to popularize Bellamy's ideas was futile, the members interviewed still believe that there will ultimately be a slow, evolutionary realization of Bellamy's theories; and they cite such trends as nationalization of industries and increased democratization of all phases of public life to support their belief.

Besides the Bellamy Association, other evidence of Bellamy's influence appeared in three articles in the Flemish newspaper *De Dag*, in October, 1939. In these, "Argus" (the pseudonym for a journalist named Baert who wrote about political, economic affairs) investigated the disturbing international events, their causes, and their cure. His conclusion was that the "present economic situation had to be completely changed,"[40] that the conflict that was just beginning would ruin everything, and that mankind would then have the opportunity to begin anew—to build a new world. To Argus, the blueprint for the new society had already been drawn by Bellamy, whose "plan might have looked Utopian at one time but was extremely practical now."[41]

Argus then printed fourteen main points of Bellamy's theories; on the whole, he considered the principles he recapitulated to be "sound, healthy, logical and realistic."[42] The translation of the fourteen points follows:

> 1. The welfare of the community is the welfare of the individual. There is no welfare in a nation so long as it is not shared equally by everybody.

2. The means of the welfare of the nation must be placed in the hands of the government of the nation. Those means should not be placed in the hands of the people or organizations who may consider them as ways of increasing their own earnings or possessions.

3. The main source of welfare is work. The community has a right to use all possibilities of work for its members. The heads of the community must organize all work opportunities for the welfare of everybody.

4. No individual has exclusive rights. Everybody has duties to fulfill in the community. Everybody has to work; nobody may be denied the right of participation in working and producing.

5. The woman has the same rights and duties as a man. Work in the household is useful to the community and is, therefore, to be considered similar to any other work.

6. It is the duty of the fittest and strongest to perform better and to assume greater responsibilities than those who are physically or mentally weak. Whoever neglects his duty is in the wrong. Participation in providing the welfare of all is equal for all.

7. The difficulty of work does not determine wages, but will be reflected in the duration of the task.

8. Participation in the welfare of the community is the inalienable right of every member of the nation for his whole life.

9. Every individual will have a wide opportunity to develop his talents so they may be useful to the community.

10. Since the machine is a very important means of production and since other machinery is necessary for the distribution of goods, all machinery should belong to the community. If increased technological development makes production and distribution easier, working hours will be shortened. Man is, therefore, not to be in any case a slave of machinery.

11. The government is to distribute the products of the national industries in stores where every member of the community can get the necessary goods in accordance to his right to participation in production.

12. Everybody is free to use his income according to his own tastes and choice. Demand will rule production; but purchasing, though it will have a certain limitation, will be strictly a personal matter.

13. In order to obtain the necessary raw materials from foreign countries, the government will determine the production

of material for exchange with other nations. The government will control all exports and imports.

14. Every religious belief and ethical action will be granted complete freedom of expression.

Although no trace of Argus' having belonged to the Belgian Bellamy Association can be found, the principles which he enumerated are comparable to those listed on a sheet issued a month earlier by the Bellamy Association in Harlem, Holland, and entitled in translation, "Bases of a New Society." The only differences which exist in Argus' list and that of the Holland Bellamy Association are ones of wording in a few instances, the grouping of some points together, and his addition of those sentences that express the ideas that man is not to be a slave of machinery and that national stores will distribute products. Although these ideas are not listed by the Bellamy Association, they might have been, for they were both concepts of Bellamy. Their inclusion indicates, therefore, that Argus was familiar with the original source of these principles.

Although a translation of *"La Parabole du Réservoir d'Eau"* from *Equality* was published in Brussels in 1946, it seemingly did not become well-known—at least, the members of the Belgian Bellamy Association were surprised to learn of its publication. Although efforts were made to find out why "Pensée et Action" edited and published this selection—famous for its attack upon capitalism—at the instigation of Hem Day, they proved fruitless.

Although Bellamy is mentioned in the *Short History of Anglo-American Utopian Novels* by J. Hubaux, late honorary professor of the University of Liège, and although many other people are, as he was, readers of the Parisian publication *La Grande Relève*, which advocates a type of economic equality and frequently mentions Bellamy or prints articles about him, there is little mention in Belgium today of the name or of the books of Edward Bellamy. Although most libraries contain none of his books, an investigation brought forth an interesting reply from a librarian in Verviers, who wrote that his professional experiences have enabled him "to be certain of one thing: there is still today a sort of oral and freemasonic transmission of the virtues of Bellamy's book. People who otherwise read nothing, regularly ask for *Looking Backward*—and they take it away beaming. They belong, roughly speaking, to the same category of readers as the spiritualists and the followers of theosophies."[43]

In conclusion, the nebulous evidence from 1890 to 1960 indicates that Bellamy was—and is—read in Belgium; but the true story of *why* remains a mystery. Because of the attacks of the Catholic and Liberal writers upon him and his ideas, because they associated him with the German and Belgian socialists, and because of the few direct statements about the enemy being assaulted, we may safely surmise that Bellamy— though he was ignored in the official publications of the social- ist party—was being read and used by the members of this group. Had this not been the case, the opponents of the social- ists would not so much as have mentioned the American Uto- pian; they would not have wanted to call attention to his works.

# CHAPTER TWELVE

# The Italian Controversy

By

## GUIDO FINK

DURING THE LIFETIME OF Edward Bellamy, Italy—after centuries of division and subjection to foreign masters or despots dependent upon them—became a nation. In 1860, Camillo Cavour, the brilliant politician and the prime minister of Savoy, partially realized the dreams and ambitions of Guiseppe Mazzini and his band of *Giovane Italia* (Young Italy), of the *Risorgimento*, of the *Carbonari*, and of the Italian people, by establishing the Italian nation under the leadership of the northern Italian state of Piedmont. The people of the neighboring states soon expelled their foreign princes, and Garibaldi, famous Italian patriot, led forces into southern Italy and soon conquered the territory of the southern peninsula which he ceded to the king of Piedmont. Although Italy still did not include Venice—controlled by Austria—or Rome—ruled by the Pope—it was proclaimed a nation in 1861. In 1866, Italy obtained Venice; and in 1870 the unification of Italy was completed when the Italian troops moved into Rome. The long dream of the Italian people was then fulfilled, for Rome became the capital of the nation, which was—to the great unhappiness of some republicans—a constitutional monarchy.

Until the death of Cavour in 1861, the Parliament of the young nation had been a homogeneous, united group; after his passing, the Parliament, modeled on that of France, was divided into the Left and Right wings. From 1860 until 1876, the Right was in power and had the task of destroying the last partisan bands which had supported the Bourbons or the Pope and of trying to solve the problems posed by lack of schools and a system of communication, underdevelopment and poverty, and oppressive taxation. Although the Rightest bureaucracy accomplished comparatively little, the members of the Left did no better; they had seemingly exhausted themselves fighting for political independence.

In 1876, Agostino Depretis, a member of the Leftists, became a prime minister known for his policy of "transformism" and for the reforms and improvements he inaugurated. From 1887 to 1896 Leftist Francesco Crispi was prime minister (except for a brief interlude in 1892); he tried to solve the most urgent social problems and the misery of the South with violent, repressive measures against the uprisings of the people and with the bloody attempt to conquer Abyssinia to establish colonies.

Opposition against both the Right and the Left was expressed by the *Estrema Sinistra* (Extreme Left) both in the Parliament and all over the country. The *Estrema Sinistra* was comprised of the *Radicali* (Radicals), who were led by the popular poet and politician Felice Cavallotti; by some socialists; and by some of Giuseppe Mazzini's disciples who, under the leadership of Bertani, had deserted the great republican and, unlike him, were willing to accept the monarchy if it were democratic. No Catholics joined this group or any other political party, for the Pope, irritated by the loss of Rome, had decreed that Catholics were not to participate in the political life of Italy.

The members of the *Estrema Sinistra* were strongly opposed to the alliance with the Austrian empire, to bureaucracy, to the incorrect distribution of taxes, and to the policy of the government of "transformism"—a method which sought to form alliances with all groups, Right or Left, and which led to an Italian limbo of middle-of-the-road policies and ideas. The *Estrema Sinistra* was well organized in Milan where it published many newspapers. Among these was the Republican *L'Italia del Popolo*, which was edited by Dario Papa (1846-1897), a journalist and a follower of Mazzini.

Although the members of the *Estrema Sinistra* were not Marxists, some seemed to have been influenced by the anarchic theories of Bakunin. Although the first Marxist party—the *Partito Socialista Italiano*—was founded in Genoa in 1892, Marx's doctrines were known in Italy before that time. They had been spread by Labriola; in the environs of Reggio Emilia in the north of Italy, by Camillo Prampolini (1859-1930); and in the Polesine, the poorest area of the plains of the Po River, by Badaloni. Prampolini, the son of a family of political moderates who enjoyed comfortable circumstances, had turned to socialism because of his philanthropic, humanitarian spirit. He won the name of "the apostle" because he visited the poorest peasants and helped the poverty-stricken villagers establish cooperatives as a means of combating their misery; even today Italian peasants keep his portrait among their holy images. Besides this work, Prampolini began the publication of the newspaper *La Giustizia* in which he intended to publicize the ideas of Marx. In reality, however, his newspaper was the sponsor of a humanitarian type of socialism.

In Milan—the first city to be highly industrialized—some intellectuals seemed to have been influenced by Marxism; among these were Claudio Treves, Anna Kulisciov, and Filippo Turati. Turati (1857-1932) was a lawyer who—having observed the persecution by the government of the small group of intellectuals and laborers who had started a party called *Partito Operaio* (Labor Party)—had joined the group and eventually persuaded it to merge with the Italian Socialist party. Although Turati never became a true Marxist, he was affected by Marx's ideas. The founder in 1890 of the socialist magazine *Critica Sociale* (or *Cuore e Critica*), he later became responsible for the appointment in 1912 of Mussolini to the editorship of *L'Avanti*, the official organ of the Italian Socialist party.

From 1890 to 1900 there were several popular riots in Italy which were not started by either the socialists or the *Estrema Sinistra,* but which, once begun, were supported by them. The police suppressed the rioters with arms, and the Leftist publications were suppressed. After the turn of the century, King Vittorio Emanuele III and Prime Minister Giovanni Giolitti tried to help the poorest people with reform measures. By this time, the Italian socialists had concluded that riots and revolutions were ineffective, and they sought to obtain concessions and reforms from the government by pacific methods. Rioting continued, however, in the countryside; and the landowners, who distrusted a government they considered too advanced, organized armed bands which spread terror among the peasants. This movement was the precursor to fascism which, thanks to the weakness of the democrats, was to give Italy twenty years of dictatorship.[1]

## I  *The First Editions*

As might be expected from this recital of Italian political history, *Looking Backward* was first published in Milan's *L'Italia del Popolo*. On June 7-8, 1890, the first issue of the paper edited by Dario Papa carried the first installment of *The Mystery of the Cab* by Fergus Hume and a bold advertisement of another novel which was to be serialized: *"The Man Aged 133*—a novel entirely different from any other—dedicated to those who study important social questions."

The lengthy, anonymous article which followed this announcement related the success of the novel in the United States, England, and Germany; described briefly some of its contents; and then declared: "We had better say at once that what we like most in this novel is the way it denounces the injustices and disorders of our present time; this we like more than the descriptions of an imaginary society exempt from such evils." And with this remark the unknown author evinced the attitude which was to be that of the Italian extremists and of the socialists: they were to accept Bellamy's criticism of capitalism but not his ideal society.

After making this comment and after then stating that Bellamy's skill of invention had contributed to the success of the novel, the author quoted in full the famous analogy of the coach. He then commented that "this symphonic passage in the novel is masterly, in our opinion, and we think the readers will guess from it the trend of the whole novel. Other books describing future events have been written before, such as *Abracadabra* by Ghislanzoni, among the lighter literature; or, in a more serious strain and with a social purpose, *The Coming Race* by Bulwer. But the one we are discussing, which we will translate—summarizing some passages—for the benefit of the readers of *L'Italia del Popolo* is far more up to date. It has been literally written yesterday in the land of progressive ideas and modern development. We are certain that this novel will start discussion and awaken curiosity."

The June 8-9 issue carried a large advertisement on the front page: "THE NOVEL OF SOCIAL PROBLEMS! Today a new serial story begins on the third page . . ." The third page was filled with an awkward, abridged translation of *Looking Backward;* the preface was condensed to a few lines and some characters were omitted. In the second installment the title was altered to *The Man Aged 143.* Reduced to thirty-three chapters, *Looking Backward* ran in the paper until the July 11-12, 1890, issue.

The only notice given the publication of the novel was a *saluto*—a warm welcome to Bellamy's Utopia—which appeared in Turati's *Cuore e Critica* (which became the *Critica Sociale*) on June 20, 1890. But within a year, *Looking Backward* had achieved such literary fame that two different translations were published in Milan. The first satisfactory edition was that translated by Pietro Mazzoni, who had written to Edward Bellamy from London on July 21, 1890, that he was translating *Looking Backward* and that he wished Bellamy to state that his translation was the version approved by the author because there had been so many pirated editions of the book. He then stated that *L'Italia del Popolo* had cleverly adapted the work but "with the only purpose of suiting the taste of the lady readers rather than to give due relief to the more serious part" of it. He also informed Bellamy that another Italian was making a translation of the novel from a German edition;[2] this was the translation made by Oberosler.

When Max Kantorowicz of Milan published Oberosler's translation under the title *La vita sociale nel 2000*, he included in it a so-called social-economic dictionary which is really more like an analytical essay. It gives a "résumé of the plan for the nationalization of property as expounded in this work"; but, in doing so, it also expresses some generally socialistic but equivocal defenses and apologies. The writer of the summary, who may have been Oberosler, stated that, though *Looking Backward* had created "opposition from some readers," they had "had to withdraw with blunted swords" because Bellamy's conclusions were established too firmly to be uprooted easily. After stating that the plot was of little interest—"inventiveness, high-lights or bewildering effects" were lacking—the writer then asserted that "the intrinsic value of the work and the fundamental idea it contains" were the plea and the plan, respectively, for "a radical and forceful change in the present social order."

Turning to an explanation of Bellamy's attitude toward capitalism and change, the writer then stated that Bellamy "does not rail against capitalism; his aim is not to reduce it by force as some impatient people would suggest. His methods are peaceful, and it is with convincing arguments and sensible reasoning that he carries his point. He does not advocate robbery; his motto is not 'it is theft to inherit'; but he does demand that capital be used within legal limits, so to speak, for industry and national production."

In comparing Bellamy to the anarchists and the socialists who "want some kind of retaliation" and who desire "capital to be used for industries in a way that would, however, only tend to reduce and weaken the power of capital itself," the writer explained that "the real socialists, as seen by the author of this novel, aim at rendering capital productive." After explaining the principles which should guide the nationalization of property and that it would be imposed by degrees by giving power to the cooperative organizations, the writer concluded: "Some people might say that we wish to praise the author and his novel, but it would be an error to think so. Our sole aim has been to develop, so to speak, the more striking ideas to be found in the book, emphasizing its moral and highly humanitarian aspects . . . . and we close this argument with the hope that these principles will be duly meditated and eventually fully applied for the benefit of mankind, and for the definitive solution of the social problem."

Although the Kantorowicz edition was mentioned for many years in the propaganda leaflets of the socialist libraries, and although *Critica Sociale* offered the book to its subscribers for seventy-five *centesimi*, when the publisher's price was two lire, it was a very imperfect edition. Although the publisher announced that it was a translation of the 330th American edition, it was, as Mazzoni had told Bellamy, translated from a German text.

When Treves published the Mazzoni translation under the title *Nell'anno 2000. Racconto Americano*, the advertisements heralding the appearance of the novel were misleading. Although Bellamy had seemingly granted Mazzoni the right to state that his was the authorized edition, the publisher's statement gave the impression that Bellamy himself had asked that the translation be made by his "personal friend" Mazzoni. Despite—or because of—this misrepresentation, the Mazzoni edition was very successful; and by 1898 *Nell'anno* had reached its thirteenth edition.

In the "Publisher's Foreword"—which is dated Milan, November, 1890—an interesting point of view is revealed. It contrasts to the conservative socialistic interpretation of the "summary" in the Kantorowicz edition, because it depicts the attitude of the more liberal middle-class citizens towards Bellamy's novel: "The book we present to the public has had a brilliant success, first in America, then in England, and now also in Germany. It will be a success in Italy too. It will not reach the 335,000 copies of the Boston edition, nor the 100,000 copies of the English edition, nor shall we see Bellamyistic or Nationalistic societies emerging, but here too . . . discussions have started and are carried on with spirit everywhere."

After a short description of the plot of *Looking Backward* and after a reminder of previously published famous Utopias, the publisher then flatly announced that Bellamy's theories were superior to those of other Utopian writers and that his novel abounded with concrete examples and lacked foolish particulars. The writer then faced in the following passages of the foreword the objections which might arise to Bellamy's concepts:

> Is there much difference between money and the credit book? But let us not argue about the beautiful Utopia. It has been said that Bellamy's novel is not a novel nor even a work of art, but that it is only a dissertation. Were it our intention to criticize the book, we would say, however, that the author is far from successful when he insists in his efforts to entertain his readers with impressive incidents. The merit of his work lies in the fact that the book is good propaganda, supremely and deeply socialistic; and yet it neither provokes nor disgusts the upper classes. . . . and it is due to the gentle folk that this book, written for the poor, has been such a success.
>
> A French novelist would have amused his readers without convincing anyone; a French socialist would have cursed and inveighed to such an extent that no one could have digested his book. The novelty of Bellamy's point of view and his skill consist in his serene and peaceful tone, which captivates all readers. Bellamy's paradise may seem rather dull to the frivolous, but it must seem beautiful to the legions of unfortunate people who live from hand to mouth.

Two objections were then cited to Bellamy's plan. First, the author of the foreword argued that it would not be possible to achieve such a radical social transformation by means of the peaceful evolutionary process which Bellamy advocated. Second, he presented a criticism of Bellamy's optimistic view of human nature: "Bellamy, in common with all socialists, forgets what human nature is like. Let us admit that his beautiful dream comes true . . . but what about human passions? The author has forgotten nothing—except the feelings of men and women. His house of cards would be demolished in less than a month." Although the foreword is concluded with praise for the charity and the religious sentiment which made the book "likeable," it also reveals a light-hearted, superficial, and cynical attitude—one which was to appear in almost all the non-propaganda essays about *Looking Backward*.

## II  *Critical Reactions*

Turning from the publishers' forewords to the critical reactions to *Looking Backward,* one finds a varied attitude. First of all, no mention of the Utopia was made in the Catholic publications *L'Osservatore Romano* and *Civiltà Cattolica*. The Leftist papers evinced interest for a short time during which they propagandized the novel, recommended it to readers and to socialist libraries or clubs, and offered it free to new subscribers. In considering the socialist reaction to the Utopia, the fact that the socialists had not yet formulated a party and that they were regarded with hostility because of their support of the riots of the early 1890's must be remembered. The Conservative publications pretended at first to ignore the book; then they sought to minimize its importance.

Oddly enough, however, the most important critical comments about *Looking Backward* were contributed by the scholars and journalists of the Right wing and of the moderate parties. Although they all seemed to agree that the novel had no artistic value—which seems curious, for the opposite view would have been more just—they accepted some of its points but, of course, with many reservations. The authors of the most interesting essays about *Looking Backward* were Gaetano Negri who wrote in the newspaper *La Perseveranza* (December, 1890); Giovanni Boglietti, in *Nuova Antologia* (August, 1890); Ernesto Gagliardi, in the *Corriere della Sera* (October, 1890); and Bartolo Federici, in *Pensiero Italiano* (February, 1891).

An analysis of their articles shows that all of them considered Bellamy a Utopian, a "communist," and an American—and by "American" they meant a simple, ingenuous person. Their remarks smack, therefore, of a sense of superiority; their tone is indulgent but friendly. Although they made no attempt to conceal their dislike of Bellamy's ideas, they admitted admiration for his constructive artistry. An excellent example of their attitude is the following statement of Boglietti: "Bellamy's dream is not new; in fact, it is as old as Adam! However, his book is colorful and vivid, and the genial style makes amends for the stale ideas." Furthermore, all these critics echoed the same argument: no matter how perfect Bellamy's ideal society might be, human nature could not be adapted to it.

In the critical assessment which Boglietti published in *Nuova Antologia*, he both praised and disparaged Bellamy's Utopia. First of all, he placed it on a higher literary level than More's *Utopia* or Campanella's *La Città del Sole*. Then in summarizing the plot, he interpolated disparaging remarks. When, for example, he described Julian West's hypnotic sleep, he wrote: "Those who do not admit the physical possibility of such a feat should protest to Bellamy; it is none of my business!"

After quoting the French economist, statesman, and author Maurice Block, who had written about Bellamy in the *Journal des Economistes*, Boglietti maintained that "no revolution will ever cancel love of self and individualism from the human heart; Bellamy's mistake, and that of all the communists who preceded him, consists in the belief that the woes of society derive from and are caused by political and social institutions; the industrial revolution, as he imagines it, would destroy the effects of the Revolution of 1776, which emancipated the Americans politically and accustomed them to free and boundless use of their individual liberty."

After relating—in a fashion indicating that he probably wore a simpering smile while doing so—that he had seen "some American ladies with copies of *Looking Backward* in their hands" in the streets of Italian cities and that they were seeking "proselytes for their American novelist," Boglietti asserted that he doubted their sincerity and then proceeded to use them as an example of the fact that human nature did not change. He wrote: "These young women of America who are so much in love with the new gospel of social equality, would be ready to commit forgery to marry a marquis . . . so strong is the force of ambition, love of self and the desire to outdo others, the reaction of human nature to the artificial creations of our intellect."

In his long eighteen-page essay, Boglietti often assumed a somewhat hypocritical attitude and presented some pseudo-critical comments—both of which are exemplified in the following statement: "I have no intention of making fun of Bellamy's book; it would indeed be a misplaced and poor joke. Every effort made to mitigate the sufferings of humanity are sacred to me. . . . But . . . is this the best way to alleviate them? What is the use to represent to the poor an ideal condition of life which they cannot attain? Would it not be much more reasonable and to the purpose to recognize what cannot be altered in human nature and the constitution of society itself, and be satisfied with a slow but sure progress in accordance with them?"

A more broad-minded, honest approach to *Looking Backward* than Boglietti's apprehensive, hypocritical one was evinced by Ernesto Gagliardi, the correspondent for the Milanese *Corriere della Sera* in Berlin.* In his correspondence from Berlin which appeared on the front page of the October 17-18 issue of the moderate paper for which he wrote, Gagliardi stated that *Looking Backward* had not only had an enormous success in Ger-

---

* Gagliardi also wrote a review years later, published in Germany, of Bellamy's *Equality;* for a summation, see Chapter VI.—EDITOR

many but that "there are competent people who consider it even more important than *Uncle Tom's Cabin.*"

Obviously ignorant of the Italian translations which had appeared, Gagliardi then admitted that he himself had been bored by the catechismal, heavy tone of *Looking Backward.* After discussing the plot with interest and insight, he concluded: "Although the author's Utopia is too good to be true, the story deserves to be read with attention and discussed. We live in an epoch in which everything is possible, where legislation for the workers and the multiplying of scientific and technical inventions justify the most ambitious dreams. In the United States eccentric and philanthropic people abound. Here, we think they are a bit mad; but in America their eccentricities are easily accepted by the general public; even the most sceptical people respect them."

A more interesting article about *Looking Backward*—and one which created quite a furor—appeared in the Christmas supplement of the December 25, 1890, issue of the Milan conservative daily *La Perseveranza.* The essay, which filled seven and a half columns, was written by Senator Gaetano Negri, former mayor of Milan, a member of the Right wing, and a man whom the Milanese had nicknamed "the crafty philosopher." After making a minute analysis of *Looking Backward,* Negri declared that "artistically it is of little value; neither the episodes, nor the characters are interesting. The short love story included by the author does not impress us. . . ." But, admitted Negri, "it was not the author's intention to write a novel, but to depict a socialistic organization. He has achieved something of outstanding ability and constructive power, and his ideas *seem* real and feasible. Hence the success of the book, which is actually more responsible for the spreading of socialistic principles, than any sort of treatise. . . ."

Negri then expressed an exceedingly enlightened, comprehending assessment of socialism:

Actually, socialism is the outcome of the revolt of the people against the countless miseries which afflict modern society. It springs from the desire of a more equitable repartition of the riches of the world and the sense of revolt roused by the sight of injustice and the incomprehensible difference in the destinies of human beings. Never before have the conspicuous characteristics of socialism appeared more clearly than in this book. We usually associate socialism with anarchy, irreligion, atheism, plundering, and massacre. Well now, here is a book which might represent the catechism of socialistic doctrines; yet this book is serene, peaceful, full of hope and faith in the power of ideas. It does not deny Christianity; on the contrary, it clings to it; and it asserts truthfully that socialism is the actual result of the teachings of Our Lord, its Divine Founder.

Although Negri praised *Looking Backward,* he also evinced scepticism about achievement of such an ideal society because of the imperfections of mankind; smiled ironically at Bellamy's plan for complete economic equality; claimed that he was the defender of the right of the individual person against what he viewed to be Bellamy's cult of the Nation; and indicated that a world federation would be improbable so long as cannibals existed in Africa and South America. Negri was not, however, wholly pessimistic; for he—unlike Boglietti—assumed a positive attitude by mentioning the British Trade Union and by speaking of reform.

The immediate reaction of the socialist *La Giustizia* was twofold. First of all, the famous paper edited by "apostle" Camillo Prampolini published on the front page of the January 11, 1891, issue a long, full-page, eulogistic article entitled, "The Socialistic Confessions of a New Conservative Senator." The paper proclaimed that "the new Senator and former Mayor of Milan, Gaetano Negri, has published in the very moderate paper *Perseveranza,* a lengthy and important review of Bellamy's famous socialistic novel . . . with assertions which we consider a new triumph of our party, a new evidence of the truth of our ideas." The *Giustizia* promised, however, that it would answer in following issues the adverse comments which the senator had made about *Looking Backward* and socialism.

In the following three issues of *Giustizia,* the editor fulfilled his promise. Although the polemic which appeared in the paper sought to propagandize *Looking Backward* and to demolish the adverse comments of Negri, it also gave the socialistic *Giustizia* an opportunity to attack certain bourgeois conceptions such as the too frequently repeated refrain that human nature could not be changed—at least for the better—and then to expound upon other matters. The socialist writer of *Giustizia,* in reply to Negri's comments about economic equality, showed that he was willing to sacrifice some of Bellamy's concepts— and this is not startling, for the socialists had never gone so far as to demand absolute economic equality. Relative to this controversial subject, the anonymous author stated: "Certain peculiarities of the novel do not shake the foundations of social-

ism, from which they are entirely independent; to actuate socialism, it is not at all necessary to have absolute equality of
distribution, which *ad abundantiam* Bellamy advocates in his
novel." He also stated that freedom of the individual did not
exist so long as people lived in the deepest misery and ignorance; and he pointed out rather astutely that history showed
that cannibals or backward nations had progressed before—and
that progress could be made to achieve the world which would
be ready for world federation.

The controversy between Negri—who ignored the attacks—
and *Giustizia* echoed not only over the whole of Italy but in
other countries; and it marked without any doubt the moment
of the greatest popularity of *Looking Backward* with the press
and with the public. Evidence of the reaction in Germany in
the December 30, 1890, *Berliner Volksblatt* appears in a letter
a German reader of the paper purportedly wrote to the *L'Italia
del Popolo*—and the word "purportedly" is consciously used to
suggest that the letter might have been prepared in the office
of the newspaper in order to provide an opportunity for it to
enter the fray.

In any case the following letter addressed to the editor appeared in the January 4-5, 1891, issue:

> In the *Berliner Volksblatt* of December 30th, there is a corre-
> spondence from Milan, containing also this passage: "The ig-
> norance of the meaning of social problems . . . has spread
> enormously in Italy, even among the most cultured persons.
>
> "In these days a learned gentleman and a clever writer,
> former Mayor of Milan . . . in his long review of Bellamy's novel
> *The Year 2000*, which appeared in the conservative daily *La
> Perseveranza*, exposed about socialism and social economy some
> theories that actually made us shudder, so obsolete and ante-
> diluvian they are."
>
> A review cannot be reviewed with more impressive words,
> but I will be very glad if somebody will try to elucidate and to
> explain with substantiating evidence the deep ignorance of this
> gentleman who reviewed Bellamy's novel.

The letter was signed N. Hulss. Needless to say, the *L'Italia del
Popolo* obliged with an article entitled "Negri the Philosopher"
in which it also proudly related that it had been the discoverer
of Bellamy.

Further reaction to the Negri affair was reflected in the
*Pensiero Italiano* of Milan, an ambitious and important review

which published articles by men of culture of all parties. In its issue of February, 1891, an editorial note about the "Negri incident" appeared beside a long review of *Looking Backward* by Bartolo Federici. Although the tone of his essay is a severe, satirical one, the study it presented of Bellamy's Utopia is the most serious, disinterested, and thorough one which Italy produced.

Like others before him, Federici asserted that the novel was "not worth much, artistically"—but, to him, its major defect was one of logic. If Bellamy assumed that the addresses West presented to the students of Shawmut College were for their advancement and erudition, then he should have had West lecture about the nineteenth century and not about the renovated society of the year 2000 which they already knew! He then stated:

> This logical absurdity is apparent in the sermon preached by Mr. Barton which, in itself, is one of the finest things in the book—as is Julian West's final dream. But what is, after all, the picture representing the ideal new world. . . ? Dr. Leete, his wife and his daughter all seem to be people without any occupation, without friends or contacts with social life, people living on the outskirts, so to speak, of society. The whole framework of the novel is centered around a long conversation between those three characters: the doctor, Edith and Julian . . . the wife of the doctor appears only as a fleeting shadow in the background of the scene. The author keeps us all the while on the threshold of his world of which he summarily describes the most recent institutions in their structure and regulation. But we are not told how these organizations and principles function in social life, not even during the three moments when Julian steps over the threshold . . . and the town is dead, cold and empty like Pompei.

Federici's criticism of the political and social aspect of the Utopia are more general, but he posed problems which Bellamy sought to answer in *Equality*. Wrote Federici:

> The old formula was liberty and individualism; the new formula is collectivism and association. This sounds all right, . . . but does not the actual application of this formula represent an excessive reaction of collectivism against the exaggeration we have reached in individualism? Is it not, in other words, a far-off state of affairs instead of an actual condition? Does it not represent an artificial setting? Are we not entitled to think that human nature, so slow in adapting itself to any sort of change, might not submit to those new formulas—nor reach their realization by spontaneous evolution?

The immediate reaction to *Looking Backward* does not extend beyond these criticisms of the early 1890's—at least so far as the press was concerned. In May, 1891, *Giustizia* had promised its readers that it would "soon" dedicate space and attention to the refutation of Bellamy which had been presented by Combes de Lestrade—the translator of an edition of *Looking Backward* published in Paris in 1891. This promise, however, was not fulfilled.

The *Giustizia* had carried the following story, however, in January, 1891, which indicates that Dario Papa had obviously corresponded with Bellamy and knew of his intention to publish *The New Nation:*

> Edward Bellamy has made a large amount of money with his novel; in America and Europe, millions of copies have already been sold: this fact alone should suffice to show what an enormous power the socialistic ideas have acquired in the minds of civilized people. Bellamy will, within the current month, become the founder of a paper in New York and Boston, which will forward the radical, social and industrial reform. Dario Papa will be the correspondent of this new paper for Italy. Bellamy does not ask for news from his correspondents; he only requires facts and information regarding the development of the social situation in Italy. Anyone who can impart such information should get in touch with Dario Papa, Milan. . . .

Dario Papa had at this time retired from the editorship of *L'Italia del Popolo* because of poor health, and whether or not he contributed articles to Bellamy's *New Nation* is not known. As stated in this article, Bellamy's publication was begun in this year; and its columns did contain news—according to Sylvia E. Bowman's *The Year 2000* (1958)—about social reform progress from John Orme of England and from Bruno Schoenlank of Germany.*

### III  *Utopian, Other Responses*

In 1897 when *Equality* was on sale in the United States and when its translation in other languages was being advertised around the world, a well-known Italian physician, pathologist,

---

* Bellamy stated in the January 31, 1891, issue of *The New Nation* that he had arranged for letters from Berlin, Paris, Milan, Amsterdam and England to be published in his journal in order to tell people what was going on in the rest of the world. No letters from Dario Papa or from Paris and Amsterdam were published. —EDITOR

and writer published the Utopian novel *L'anno 3000*. The author, Paolo Mantegazza (1831-1910), had traveled widely in Europe and South America; and he eventually occupied a chair in the University of Pavia and later in Florence. His most famous works, aside from his Utopian novel were: *Fisiologia dell'Amore, Fisiologia del piacere, Fisiologia dell'odio, Fisiologia della donna,* and *Un giorno a Madera* (a novel). As might be expected from this short biographical sketch of Mantegazza and the title of his Utopia, his novel not only indicates the author's interest in science and his awareness of the popularity of Bellamy's picture of the year 2000, but also presents his critical answer to it, his analysis of the different types of socialism, and his own enthusiastically portrayed future society.

Paolo and Maria, the central characters of *L'anno 3000,* leave Rome, the capital of the United States of Europe, for Andropolis, the capital of the Planetary United States, where, after a preliminary examination by the biological Senate, they are granted authorization to celebrate a "fertile marriage" after six years of enjoying a free-love match. They are granted this privilege because Paolo has invented a thought-reading machine.

In Andropolis the visitors learn that the country had had "an ill-fated experiment of collectivism" which had cost civilization the loss of a century of progress. Decentralization of the government had finally occurred, and society had returned to rugged individualism and to family life.[3] Paolo and Maria find, therefore, a social and economic system which is typically capitalistic. They also see many modern, wonderful inventions; and they observe that the people only work six hours a day and never at night. They see a number of poor people huddled together in the galleries of Panopticon Theatre;[4] they see justice openly administered by citizens to a thief; they witness the disposal—with the mother's consent—of a baby declared unfit for life; and they discover that cremation is one of the rites for the dead.

After their tour of Andropolis, Paolo and Maria visit Ceylon, which is also called the Island of Experiments, where all the old forms of government are exhibited. In Tyrannopolis,[5] the two tourists are really shocked and dismayed by the cruelty of Nicolas II, who wantonly kills his subjects. In the land of the Egalitarians, however, they laugh uproariously at the people who believed that they had solved the problem of human happiness by giving absolute equality to everybody with regard to the rights and duties of man. In this exhibit, the people are all dressed alike and distinction between the sexes can be made only by hearing voices. People have no individual names but they are identified by numbers. Eating, drinking, sleeping, and love-making are not only done in a prescribed fashion but at the sound of a bell.[6] "With socialism," wrote Mantegazza, "the state has become a sort of gigantic tumor spreading over everything. Its sacred aim and intention is to distribute to all an equal amount of blood and life; but this repartition is made by human beings influenced by their passions, although they may be good and intelligent."[7]

His comments about the three different types of socialism are also of interest—interesting enough to quote in full:

> In the first category he [the Italian writer to whom he ascribed this material] placed the scientific socialists. It is true it wasn't very pure science, and yet they exhibited a serious, systematic, and dignified methodology. These socialists predicted the exact day, hour, and minute of the next social revolution and the bankruptcy of the bourgeoisie. Their discoveries were not lacking in extraordinary discrepancies. Whether one worked much or not at all, whether it rained or stormed, they saw nothing else in the world except damned Capital at one end and the God Mars, the great forerunner of Turati, at the other.
>
> Then there were the literary socialists: any man of talent, a few mediocre persons, and behind them the infinite horde of authors betrayed by fate, who saw in socialism a revenge for the lack of recognition of their genius, who conceived of socialism as a holy crusade to prevent the tyranny of capitalism from clipping the wings of the untrammeled flight of thought. They dreamed of happier days in which the dirty greed of publishers would no longer hinder their attempts, and this dream elevated them, and caused the tenderest and strongest strings of their hearts to resound. The literary socialist was an enthusiastic, but personally very harmless creature, who was convinced to the point of absurdity of the validity of his own ideas.
>
> In the third category . . . [were] the academic socialists. These were terribly learned people who plunged with heroic courage into the great sea of laws and judicial institutions in order to find the infallible recipe by which the sad word "suffering" might be obliterated from the human vocabulary. Their speculative work had unconsciously removed them from the world of the living and transported them to a realm where they recognized only one divinity: the Law. The Law comprehended all things, dared all things, and was capable of all things. There was no natural requirement of man which they deemed worthy of consideration. With the blithest insouciance they perfected all man's attributes, and transformed them to fit into their own systems. Beside the masters, the serious workers,

and those deceived by their own good faith, the superficial followers made their appearance. These latter proposed the most
exaggerated nonsense.[8]

The world of the future of Mantegazza is not one of social
reform; it is a fantastic world of scientific invention which he
ironically calls "admirable and progressive"—and agreed with
Giacomo Leopardi's *La Ginestra* by so phrasing his estimate.
Mantegazza also enjoys jabbing or joking at Marx, clerical
leaders, Filippo Turati, and Gabriele D'Annunzio. He also indirectly criticizes Julian West for being so respectful of all he
sees in the civilization of the year 2000, for Paolo and Maria—
and especially Maria—are the incarnation of eternal scepticism
or *italicum acetum*. When Paolo tries to persuade his wife to
use the *ecstasyometer* to measure her emotional reactions when
she watches a play at the Panopticon Theatre, Maria wearily
replies: ". . . It is too complicated, too artificial. You wear the
magic cap; as for myself, I will be satisfied with my own senses
this evening in the way God intends me to use them."[9]

Mantegazza lacks the sincerity, the humane sensibility, and
the contagious enthusiasm of Bellamy.* When *L'anno 3000* is
compared with *Looking Backward,* it becomes evident also
that Mantegazza—despite his vaunted infatuation with individual liberty and his arguments against collectivism—is much
less democratic than Bellamy. *Looking Backward* was the expression of a free, advanced nation on its way to progress;
*L'anno 3000* actually is a forecast of the authoritative government of Crispi with its repressive measures of 1898, and even
of fascism. It was not mere chance that the Planetary United
States, which represents all the countries of the universe, is
governed—according to Mantegazza—by a sole and absolute
ruler, the *Pancrate,* who rules only, however, for one year.
It was not unintentional either that towards the end of the
novel, Paolo is victorious in a pseudo-scientific tournament
over the foreign scientists John Newton and Charles Copernic;
for this smacks of the *ante-litteram* fascism. Furthermore, Paolo
offers the *Pancrate* the patent for the *psychoscope*—the mind-
reading instrument which would be most useful to dictators.

The only other known Utopian literary reaction to Bellamy's
*Looking Backward* was published in 1914; and it—*Un sogno—*

---

* Reference to the chapters about Bellamy in Germany and in
Russia will show that Mantegazza's novel was translated in these
countries because of the influence of the American Utopian.—EDITOR

was a pamphlet of ten pages written by Andrea Costa (1851-1910), the socialist leader and the publisher of the revolutionary magazines *Fascio operaio* (1871) and *Il Martello* (1874). Originally a convert to the anarchical theories of Bakunin, Costa, after being convicted as an anarchist and spending from 1874 to 1876 in prison, fled to Paris. There he met Anna Kulisciov, the socialist leader, and became a socialist; when he announced his change of convictions in a letter to Italy, it created enormous interest. When Costa returned to Milan, he started in 1880 a magazine entitled *Rivista Internazionale del Socialismo*. In 1882, he was the first socialist elected to the Italian Parliament; in 1892, he was one of the sponsors of the meeting in Genoa where the Italian Socialist party was organized; and in 1898, after the riots in Milan, he was imprisoned again but soon freed.

Although Costa does not mention Bellamy in his major speeches or essays, his *Un sogno* indicates that he was well acquainted with *Looking Backward*. In *Un Sogno* the author has a dream in which he is carried into the future and in which he sees that his own town—Imolo, near Bologna—has been transformed. All the inhabitants are happy and no social differences exist. Their improved condition has resulted, however, not from Bellamy's peaceful evolutionary process but from violent, worldwide revolution. At the end of the pamphlet, the author wakens to discover that all has been a dream. Filled with despair, he sees that the people of Imolo are still divided into the categories of rich and poor; he hopes, however, that eventually his dream will become true.

Two other books more seriously concerned with Bellamy's ideas were also published in Italy: *Pro e Contro il Socialismo* (1897) and *L'Utopia Collettivista, o La Crisi del Socialismo Scientifico* (1898). Both of these were published in Milan and both were written by Francesco Saverio Merlino, a famous anarchist who had been a follower of Malatesta. After twenty years of being an anarchist, Merlino quarreled in 1897 with Malatesta over the latter's refusal to accept the principle of democratic elections. Although Merlino then became a socialist, he never actually joined the socialist party; he remained all of his life something between a socialist and an anarchist. Before he died in Rome in 1930, Merlino had ceased his political work because of the accession to power of the Fascists. He had, however, in 1925, attacked them in his courageous pamphlet *Fascismo e Democrazia*. A prolific writer and a well-educated man (he had been a lawyer), Merlino published many works both in Paris and in Italy; from 1877 to 1897, he wrote propaganda for the anarchists; from 1897 until his death, he popularized socialistic theories.

The first article which Merlino wrote about Bellamy appeared not in Italy but in France and Belgium in *La Société Nouvelle* in August, 1891; it was written, therefore, long before his break with Malatesta and his partial conversion to socialism. As has been noted in Chapter XII, Merlino treated Bellamy as an imaginative artist, a writer of the bourgeois who knew how to appeal to his own, as a devastating critic of capitalistic nine-teenth-century society, and as one who had unwittingly ab-sorbed and employed anarchist ideas at the very moment he criticized them.

In *Pro e Contro il Socialismo* and *L'Utopia Collettivista*, Mer-lino's purpose seemed to be to reconcile all vaguely leftist or progressive parties by smoothing out their differences—actually their outstanding characteristics—in order to place all on the side of humanitarianism. His method of accomplishing his aim was overly simple; for he considered all the tendencies of the Marxist scientific socialism and of the anarchists separately and then proceeded to destroy their distinctive features, often with superficial or abstract arguments. In the end, he left noth-ing except the fact that all the parties concerned had had the same origin. In this study, the main interest lies in what Mer-lino had to say six and seven years after the publication of his first article about Bellamy's theories.

In *Pro e Contro il Socialismo*, Merlino stated that "everytime the democratic socialists have attempted to give a concrete form to their vague ideals (as in Bellamy's novel) they have inevitably drifted into a kind of state socialism."[10] In Chapter III of *Utopia Collettivista* in which he criticized this "state socialism," Merlino attacked not only Bellamy but Bebel, the author of *Woman and Socialism:*

> This system presupposes the complete dedication of the indi-
> vidual to the state . . . and his acceptance of the regulations
> imposed by the administration for production, of the purchas-
> ing value it decrees for products, of the occupations assigned
> to him, . . . But, supposing that the collective state could not,
> or would not, provide for the needs of the individual, or that
> the individual were not content with the occupation offered
> him, and refused to cede the proceeds of his labors to the
> collective state at the conditions decreed by the state, and neg-
> lected to look after the things he was allowed to use tem-
> porarily, would the collective state compel him to do so? If so,

it would drift into despotism; if not, the situation would degenerate into anarchy. . . . One cannot understand what the International Council could do to have tariff prices respected, unless it were able to hypnotize all the inhabitants of the globe. . . .[11]

Private enterprise, argued Merlino, would reappear because the collective state would not produce rare or valuable objects which could not be easily sold. Furthermore, land and capital would have to be leased to private people who would naturally endeavor to obtain the best land or to find work in the best localities. Workers would not be so free as they were in 1898 and they would not be able to select their own masters. Moreover, they would, as workers for the state, be deprived of their right to strike. Finally, prices and the evaluation of goods should not be fixed by a Central Administration but regulated according to demand, competition, market value, and purchasing power. The administration would inevitably make mistakes—and it would not be constantly under control of the citizenry just because, as Bellamy had stated in *Equality*, the telephone would make national elections easy and speedy.

Merlino then stated what he felt the end result would be: "As if there were no other difficulties for people to understand each other than those overcome by the telephone! The trouble is that for all the universal vote and the eligibility, responsibility, and revocability of the public officials, it would not be possible to chain the public administration down to the will of the people because these expedients would be annulled by the enormous economic power of the administration itself. Democracy is defeated by the very essence of collectivism."[12]

It is astonishing not only that Merlino quoted from the text of *Equality* but that he could ignore the answers Bellamy gave to some of his questions not only in his last Utopia but in *Looking Backward*. Merlino called the first Utopia *Looking Forward* —and this is not the only inexactitude in his books. His most appreciated work is, however, *Pro e Contro il Socialismo*.

The reaction of the orthodox socialists to Merlino's theories was not slow in coming; it appeared with the signature of a young man who was a relentless Marxist destined to become one of the leading figures in Italian politics, although in quite another area of action: Ivanoe Bonomi. The young Italian's reply to Merlino appeared in two installments in *La Critica Sociale* in the March 16 and April issues of 1898 under the title: "Due libri sul socialismo di S. Merlino"—"Two books on Socialism

by S. Merlino." Bonomi opposed the vague socialism of Merlino
—in which "a pinch of every drug can be mixed"—to historical
materialism, which had "banished the ideas of absolute justice
and progress on which Utopian socialism was founded and replaced it with the reality of social forces; as a conception for
the future, Marxism had the triumph of the proletariat. . . ."

Bonomi did not take the trouble to re-evaluate Bellamy or to
counter Merlino's criticisms of him. On the contrary, he associated him with Merlino: "Merlino has assembled the opinions of
various schools: collectivists, communists, mutualists; he has
ransacked Bellamy's novels and Bebel's *Woman* to discover
the modality of collectivistic socialism which he wanted to
fight. Then he exclaims triumphantly: 'But this is not socialism!'
Of course it was not! It was Bellamyism, Bebelism, only personal views and nothing more. . . . When he asserts that the
collectivism of Bebel and Bellamy and other writers is not
socialism, he is quite right, but not when he criticizes these
theories and takes 'the shadows for the concrete bodies.' . . . History is history, and not what Bellamy or Merlino would like it to
be." As may be observed from the quotation and from the gist of
his statements, Bonomi knew not only Dante's *Purgatory*[13] but
Marx's attitude about forecasts of the future: they were not to
be accepted as scientific if they were not his own. For this reason, Bebel was no doubt classified with Bellamy; for he had
forecast the freedom of women as a result of the socialist revolution.

## III  Equality *Published*

It is a curious coincidence that on the inside of the cover of
Merlino's *L'Utopia Collettivista* an advertisement stated that
*Nell'anno 2000* had sold thirteen thousand copies. At the bottom
of the notice appeared the announcement that *Eguaglianza—
Equality*—was soon to be published. In 1898, the year of Bellamy's death, the publishing house of Sandron of Palermo—
which was famous for having published the forbidden patriotic
books of Mazzini and others—issued a two-volume edition of
*Equality*. A second edition appeared in 1908.

*Equality* did not have either the success or the publicity
which *Looking Backward* achieved in Italy. Neither Bellamy's
death nor his last Utopia received much space in the newspapers of 1898, for they were full of the contradictory reports
about the notorious Dreyfus affair and of articles about the
Spanish-American War. A few days before Bellamy's death,
another event occurred which affected the reception of *Equal-*

*ity:* a famous popular demonstration had taken place in Milan, and the slogan of the people had been "Bread and Work." The demonstrators were ruthlessly quelled by the cannons of General Bava Beccaris; many socialists were arrested, hastily condemned, and given heavy sentences; and almost all the socialist papers were forced to stop publication. Only *L'Avanti!*—the organ of the Italian Socialist party published in Rome since 1896 —was able to salute the memory of Edward Bellamy. The article written in tribute to him declared that his death was a "loss for the socialists all over the world." *L'Avanti* also announced the publication of *Equality* and added that this volume showed "how thoroughly he had continued to study the new doctrines" and that his last book presented more penetrating "criticism of the contemporary world."[14]

The conservative *Corriere della Sera* published a long obituary in a flourishing style which was signed by Giovanni Borelli.* The eulogistic, hypocritical but often astute article described Bellamy as "the greatest constructor of optimistic figments in these troubled times" and as "one of the greatest seducers of the soul of the masses. . . ." Borelli then continued:

> Like God . . . having to create the world, he began with a terrestial paradise. . . Doubtlessly, this is, and was enough to dazzle the two halves of mankind: the one . . . which is really unfortunate. . . ; and the other which wishes to be unfortunate at all costs and, having drained all the moral and intellectual poisons, gives itself wholeheartedly to the devastating effects of polyglot narcotics. This is how Bellamy has triumphantly wandered all over the world. The man and the author deserved it; he belonged to the innumerable legion of evangelists, but he had a vigorous fundamental background, possessed of the most intimate geniality: the capacity to make his intuitions appear likely. . . . He dressed the wounds of suffering humanity. . . ; he was the soul of socialism galvanized by art. In the Marxist congregation, he was often taken for an amateur. A clever and also a useful one (more so than the unreadable and unintelligible book of Karl Marx, *Das Kapital*), but also a mischievous

---

* Borelli, born in 1867, was of a noble family which had given many patriots to the Risorgimento. In 1898, he quit the staff of the conservative *Corriere* and founded his own magazine, *L'idea liberale*, and a political movement—the *Movimento dei Giovani Liberali*. His ideals were nationalistic, monarchical, and conservative; but he was a violent enemy of Catholicism. He frequently debated with the socialist leaders at public and labor meetings; these debates aroused great interest.

and dangerous one. Of the socialistic preachings, Bellamy had in fact imagined a real application in future times; and it did not suit the Marxists to ratify the romantic elucidations of the American writer.[15]

Borelli defined Bellamy as a "conjurer of socialism" and then exclaimed: "God forbid that I should take Bellamy's defense— even after his death. His books have spread too much evil, and I cannot defend him in Milan and in this paper. . . . To admire the American author's faith and his noble ideals is a fine thing, but to keep cool and wide awake in the face of the floods of sentimentality, while our country and civilization are experiencing such sad days, is even better. . . ."

## IV  The Marked Copy of the Revolutionaries

Although Italy kept a "cool head," discounted the flood of sentimentalities—as Mr. Borelli had recommended—and continued to ignore publicly the work of Bellamy, there were "hotheads" who did not do so. One of the most interesting indications that Looking Backward was not only read but seriously thought about, is a marked copy of the ninth edition of the Mazzoni translation Nel l'anno 2000, which was found in the Communal Ariostea Library of Ferrara. The whole volume is defaced by marginal notes in ink and in pencil; the flyleaves at the front and back are covered with comments; and the text is underscored and commented upon.

Interestingly, these critical comments and reactions are not the work of one person but of five or six men whose notes are signed and dated. One note bears the name of Vittorio Bertoni with the date 1913; another, undated, is signed Vittorio Trevisani; and another, also of the year 1913, bears the signature of G. Vignocchi. The last-mentioned reader wrote: "Wonderful book, truthful and just, showing Bellamy's understanding in the way he suggests and sustains abolition of today's labor conditions and the substitution of a more efficacious and practical method."

Arrigo Bonfiglioli, a more enthusiastic admirer and a better scholar, wrote: "Comrade Bellamy, I cannot tell you how impressed I was when I read your book. Without doubt this work is a most convincing and efficacious demonstration, setting forth the need for a new social order to substitute the barbaric capitalistic methods of our day. I am convinced that modern labor conditions are inhuman and cruel, because they exploit women and children. Also that the realization of this so-called Utopia is not so distant as one might think, and as some people would like to believe. In fact, I think that if socialism were practiced in the manner you propose, it might bring about a golden age. Socialism is the sun of the future. Hurray for Socialism!"

An analysis of the markings in the book indicate that Bellamy's readers of Ferrara considered his book to be a text rather than a novel. Their frequent underlinings bring out salient points which are important in Bellamy's plan; words such as "mesmerism" and "congregational" are explained in footnotes; and the ideas of Bellamy, as Dr. Leete explains them to Julian West, are annotated with references to precise statements made in other books by Ferrero, Reclus, and Cathrein. Because Bellamy was influenced by the ideas of Auguste Comte, it is interesting to note that Guglielmo Ferrero (1871-1942) was an Italian historian and a positivist in his sociological theories who wrote an important Roman history called *Grandezza e Decadenza di Roma* (1901-1907). Jean Jacques Elisee Reclus (1830-1905) was a famous French anarchist who took an active part in the revolution of 1848 and in the struggles of the commune of 1870; he published while in exile in Switzerland, *Histoire d'une Montagne, L'Homme et la Terre,* and eighteen volumes of a universal geography. Viktor Cathrein (1845-1931) was a German Jesuit whose essay about socialism—*Der Sozialismus, eine Untersuchung seiner brundlagen und Durchfürbarkeit* (1890)—was published in all languages.

Other readers who read the marked copy often showed decided disagreement, not only with Bellamy but with the annotators. One unnamed critic condemned all of the writers with marginal notes couched in coarse language and with epithets of dubious taste. Another, also unnamed, expressed his rebellion against the "exaggerated optimism" of the author. At the end of Chapter XVIII he wrote: "Verbally it is easy to solve the most difficult problems, but it is in practice that difficult obstacles arise." Seemingly impressed by the hint that lawyers would be abolished, he was not convinced by the statements about love and marriage: "Here the disparities appear! Women will give precedence to great men, either on account of their genius or their physical beauty; these two classes will prevail over the others where men are concerned." In a serious strain, he posed the question: "What about prostitution?"

A third ironical, anonymous reader scattered his remarks here and there: "Mr. West is very simple-minded!" When he read about the future world federation which Bellamy thought to be the last hope of humanity, he remarked: "With the Hottentots in it?" He also became involved in a written argument

with the more enthusiastic Arrigo Bonfiglioli. Where the abolition of servants is discussed in Chapter XI, the anonymous
reader remarked: "Who, for instance, will serve at table?" Bonfiglioli retorted: "Those who are going to eat." To their comments, another anonymous reader appended the note: "This is
most inconvenient." When the protests of the workers of the
nineteenth century are described in Chapter XXII, Bonfiglioli
called the attention of the incredulous readers to the disorders
which had occurred in May, 1898, in Milan when the people had
cried "Bread and Work."

The intent in this study is not to overestimate the value of
the annotations of the men who curiously addressed Bellamy as
"comrade." The real worth of the notes they made is that they
indicate not only that Bellamy's Utopia was being seriously
studied by men interested in social questions before World
War I, but also that no accurate assessment of Bellamy's influence among the people could ever be found in libraries and
archives. To have truly investigated his influence in Italy, research should have been done among the old socialists and
anarchists and reformers who lived at the close of the last century. Unfortunately, this was impossible—no one can move
backward in time to speak with the dead.

Other evidence indicates, however, that Bellamy remained
popular with the old socialists of Italy. In the summer of 1960,
when an interview was held with Antonio Giolitti, member of
the Italian Parliament, and the son of the famous prime minister of the first decade of the twentieth century, a young member
of the Parliament who had introduced the researcher to Giolitti
was startled when he heard the name Bellamy. He then said
that when he was a little boy he remembered hearing the older
socialists of his town—Reggio Emilia, the birthplace of Camillo
Prampolini and one of the most socialistic towns in Italy—mention "the great Bellamy"; but, mispronouncing his name, they
had called him Bel-Ami. Since this young man—Venerio Cattani
—was born only thirty-one years ago, his memory would indicate that Bellamy was still being discussed in the early 1930's
by the socialists.

V  Later Mention; Edition of 1957

After World War I other Bonfigliolis may have continued to
read Bellamy's L'anno 2000 and Eguaglianza in libraries while
Italy drifted into its own brand of nationalism—a form of government of which Edward Bellamy would certainly not have
approved. Fascism was, however, also heralded by a literary

movement in which *La Nave* of D'Annunzio and the novels of Alfredo Oriani played an important role—as did the declarations of the Futurist poets, such as Marinetti. Also important in the growth of fascism were the publications of Maurice Barrés (1862-1923), who tried to inspire the French to a new nationalistic spirit, and of Charles Maurras (1868-1952), who—under the influence of Anatole France, Auguste Comte, and Barrés—was converted to nationalism. Among the Fascists were disillusioned ex-revolutionaries, Catholics who wished to restore the power of both the throne and the altar, and financiers and munition makers. Fascism led not only to the war in Libya—regarded by the Barrés and Maurras as a "blood bath" and as the "hygiene of the world"—but to dictatorship.

The attitude of the nationalists or Fascists toward Bellamy was clearly expressed by Carlo Curcio in *Miti della Politica* (1940); "Utopias, especially when someone wants to put them in practice, are a terrible and dangerous aberration of the mind; for they presume to be able to impose an absolute perfection in political and social life, a perfection which neither God nor human nature has given to man. What Mussolini said in 1922 is indeed very true: 'The perfect regimen exists only in books written by philosophers. . . .' "[16]

"However, during the second half of the nineteenth century . . . , the theories and practices of Utopia were destined, if not to disappear completely (there was Weitling's *Evangelium des Armen Sunders*, 1884; there were Wells' and Bellamy's plans for the future, and so on) to be considered as a mere literary exercise without . . . any political importance. . . ."[17]

Other mention was made of Bellamy by Benedetto Croce in his *Storia d'Italia, 1871-1915* (1928), in which he lamented that Italy had had no "Dante of Socialism." He then stated that "Italian socialists, youthful, gay and overconfident, wrote down their theories . . . working in the present, their eyes directed toward a near and happy future: they had no dreams but the plain, prosaic, exact and well calculated Utopias contrived by a Morris or a Bellamy."[18]

In the Italian histories of American literature, Bellamy is mentioned only in Carlo Izzo's *Storia della Letteratura Nord-Americana* (1959). After a brief summation of Bellamy's life and writings, Izzo points out that *Looking Backward* was "welcomed with hearty interest and enthusiasm" in the United States, that it refused Marxism as an "international and revolutionary idea," and that it may have had some influence upon Mark Twain's *A Connecticut Yankee in King Arthur's Court.*

In the most important Italian encyclopedia—Treccani's—Bellamy is not mentioned; but he is mentioned in the small, older encyclopedias of Hoepli or Garzanti, and in Bompiani's *Dizionario degli autori e delle opere.*

Despite this lack of mention of Bellamy or his novels, *Looking Backward* was published in 1957 by a publishing house in Turin in its series of books called "The Great Foreign Authors." The translation by Evi Malagoli is a faithful rendition of *Looking Backward* but the text has in places been modernized. Published under the title *Guardando Indietro*—a literal translation of the American one—the book also contains a ten-page introduction written by the translator in which she places the novel and its author in their proper milieu, mentions the formation of Bellamy clubs in the United States, and discusses some of Bellamy's ideology.

*Guardando Indietro* did not evoke much response either in political or academic circles, although the latter are usually responsive when a classical work has been reissued. Some papers and magazines, such as *Vivi tra i vivi* of Rome and the *Corriere di Catania,* published what appear to have been the publisher's notice of release. Sketchy reviews appeared only in the periodical *Leggere* of Rome and in the daily *Gazzetta Padana* of Ferrara. The anonymous reviewer of the daily Ferrara paper noted that ". . . in these times of interplanetary fantasy, the book appears to be unexpectedly modern. . . . Maybe the style in which the book is written does not entirely satisfy those who prefer brilliant narratives and descriptions in vivid colors; but the novel actually has a quite different aim from that of being artistic. . . ."[19]

The reviewer "D. C." of the *Leggere* approached *Looking Backward* as if it were an archeological discovery of an Egyptian papyrus of the Second Dynasty: "This novel . . . dates. . . . Much water has flowed under the bridges and the value of the book, to say the least, is questionable. It certainly represents an interesting historical document depicting the fashion, culture, and ideas of that epoch . . . but considered from an aesthetic and more generally literary point of view, it is doubtful whether it still holds its fascination and freshness. . . . We think today that, even in America, this book is considered a quaint one. . . ."[20]

So, although Bellamy's *Looking Backward* is either regarded as a historical document or is forgotten in Italy today, this is a not too surprising result of the general situation. Although contemporary American authors are popular with the reading public, the "discovery of America" which meant so much to

Italian intellectuals during the interim between two wars has rarely extended into the American literary past. Although it is painful to admit it, the names of Thoreau, Emerson, Hawthorne, and Melville are less well-known to the average Italian reader than those of John Steinbeck, John Dos Passos, or even Erskine Caldwell.

Although, as has already been indicated, it is impossible to evaluate today the influence Bellamy had among the people who read his books or among the socialists, it is evident from the research work that has been done that very few novelists of past generations—or even contemporary ones—ever received so much notice from the press as Bellamy did. Editorials and leading articles appeared in the most important daily papers, and reviews thirty pages long were published in the most authoritative periodicals.

Although Bellamy was one of the most discussed writers of his day in Italy—in the sense of space and attention given him— he was also abused and misunderstood. The conservative press tried to minimize the social significance of his work; the Leftists used his book as a weapon against capitalism but distrusted the positive ideas which Bellamy had to offer. Yet, when a comparison of what was written about Bellamy by the press is made with the amazing public success and sale of *Looking Backward* in the last decade of the nineteenth century, it becomes evident that the sincere, fervid plea he made for a more humane world had a universal appeal for the Italian middle class and the common people. They realized that he expressed their needs and encouraged their hopes—needs and aspirations which were to be forgotten for a long time, or, what is worse, betrayed.

# CHAPTER THIRTEEN

# In Other European Countries

BESIDES THE COUNTRIES which have been considered in separate chapters, other European nations, which are now associated with the Soviet Union or which are—like Spain and Portugal—dictatorships, published Bellamy's Utopian fiction and some of his other novels. Although the complete history of Bellamy's popularity and influence in these areas can not be related today—for obvious reasons—what can be narrated indicates that he was first translated in many of these countries by the first prominent socialist leaders of the nineteenth century; that he reappeared in print in many of them after the successful Russian Revolution of 1917; that he was without doubt used by the communists of Spain in the 1930's; and that, because of the fear of Marxism and of Russia, he was unpopular in Switzerland in 1947.

## I Poland

From 1890 to 1955, the fiction of Edward Bellamy was published, written about, or studied in Poland. Six editions of *Looking Backward* were published in Polish or in Poland: in 1890, two appeared almost simultaneously with the permission of the government censors in Krakow and in Warsaw; one was printed in Paris and another in Geneva in a series called the Workers' Library; and in 1905 and 1906 a Hebrew translation was published and then reprinted in Warsaw by "Progres." Selections from *Looking Backward* were also published in 1890 in *Prawda.*

Interestingly enough, two other novels of Bellamy were also translated. *Miss Ludington's Sister* was published in 1891; and *Dr. Heidenhoff's Process* was first serialized in *Glos* before it appeared in book form in 1891. "With the Eyes Shut" was a two-installment serial published in 1891 in the Warsaw *Przeglad Tygodniowy,* which presented the short story as a selection from Bellamy's most famous story of the future, *Looking Backward.*

As we shall see, further mention of Bellamy's books—so far as could be discovered—was reserved for the era which was to find Poland a Communist state.

When the editions of *Looking Backward* were published in Warsaw and Krakow by different translators, Warsaw's *Prawda* published a review of them by Piet Zyg. The translations by J. K. Potocki and K. O. R. were compared, and Zyg's verdict was that the former work had maintained more closely both the style and content of the original. Although the K. O. R. edition must have been prepared from the bastardized German socialist edition of Malkowsky, the Polish translator explained in his introduction that he had tried to give "harmony" and liveliness to the novel by cutting it, that he had summarized the analogy of the coach but omitted the first chapter, that he had also deleted the one in which Julian awakens from his nightmare to find himself returned to the world of the year 2000, and that he had discarded the unkind comments Bellamy had made about the role of the workers in creating the new world because they were "far from the historical truth." All these changes, wrote K. O. R., also made the novel more realistic; for the reader realized that the ideal society was only a dream and that he still lived in the 1890's.

Despite the translator's explanation of his omissions, Zyg stated that such deletions did not permit the reader to know the convictions and the ideas of the American writer who appealed to the good hearts of the middle class. But K. O. R. had remarked in his introduction that the middle class had widely criticized *Looking Backward* because of its plan of collective ownership and that the socialists had also done so because of Bellamy's not having attributed the birth of the new society to the worker party movements. These comments by K. O. R. probably led Zyg to conclude that, although the deletions might make the book more interesting, he thought that the translator was seeking to fulfill some purpose of his own. From the comments made by K. O. R. and from the omissions he made, he must have conciously followed the line of Malkowsky, who had translated the book for use by the German socialists.

The most interesting essay about Bellamy appeared also in *Prawda* in 1890 under the title "Nationalist League Agitation." Written by K. R. Zywicki, it stated that though Bellamy had written a novel in which he, like Jules Verne, sought to look into the future, he had based it on an underlying "scientific idea" which he then dressed in the form of fiction. That Bellamy had been right in giving a fictional picture of his scientific concepts could not be doubted; for, noted Zywicki, his book had sold many, many more copies than Gronlund's *Co-operative Commonwealth.*

After presenting what he called "the skeleton" of Bellamy's ideas and system, Zywicki discussed the influence of the novel, the formation of Bellamy clubs in the United States, the publication of *The Nationalist,* and the adverse criticisms of N. P. Gilman in "Edward Bellamy and Nationalism in the United States," which had been published in the *Quarterly Journal of Economics;* of Emile de Laveleye's "Deux Utopies Nouvelles" (1890), and of Russian I. I. Yanzhul's "A New Phantasy on an Old Theme." Zywicki commented that though Bellamy's ideas had been compared by some of these critics to those of More and Campanella, the comparison was inaccurate: they should be related instead with futures portrayed in the works of Rodbertus and Gronlund. As a result, Zywicki asserted that Bellamy's Utopia was not "an ideal dream" but "a deep synthesis of the present." To him, Bellamy was as scientific as Gronlund, who also had formed his work on a scientific basis, had invented a socialistic structure from what existed in the present society, and had then developed it to cover all human needs. To him, "in Bellamy or Gronlund, if we discard the details of everyday life, we will find the legal and political but democratic answer to the problems created by the industrial revolution and its means of production."

After summarizing the picture Bellamy had presented of the nineteenth-century society and industry of the United States, Zywicki commented that he had shown that there was no place for small factories, small businesses, or little railroads. All these had been gathered into monopolies which set prices and forced the small owner to combine or to perish. To Zywicki, to turn backward from such capitalistic development was impossible— and, furthermore, it would halt progress. He observed that Bellamy showed how one monopoly could be formed from the many huge ones without any violence.

Then he wrote: "Bellamy doesn't follow the true Utopian line, for his ideal state is the result of a concrete situation—that of his own. From this present, he creates the future—and it is based on his analysis of the present situation. He may be wrong in his attitude, which was unknown to Thomas More and other former dreamers. Of course, in making this statement, we have in mind only the general scheme and not the details." He remarked, however, that his article was supposed to be concerned not with criticism of Bellamy but with his popularity.

In speaking of Bellamy's popularity, Zywicki remarked that despite its wide scope, it would not be too serious. "In this instance, the author follows the Utopists because he wants to convert the masses of people—regardless of their lives and their class tendency—by appealing not to their interests but to their problems, for he thinks only of the future. In this way, he hopes to catch the interest of the educated intellectuals. Instead of an analysis of the present time, we see only the future. Anyway, we think that it is proper to let readers know about the book and so we are publishing two excerpts." The two excerpts were, however, the innocuous selections from *Looking Backward* which described shops and restaurants.

In the three other reviews which could be located in the files of Polish publications, the writers agreed for the most part with Zyg that the K. O. R. translation was misleading because it could not be truly representative of the thoughts of the American writer who had been unfairly treated. Some of the critical comments which were made are, however, of interest.

The reviewer of *Przeglad Tygodniowy* (The Weekly Review) disliked (1) having capital concentrated in the hands of the state while "an unaltered social system remained"; (2) having compulsory labor compared to military service; (3) thinking that labor would be motivated by being not man's duty but his right and his honor; and (4) using the term "price" in a Utopian society. He ended his review with the comment that just as people "had previously needed prejudices and superstitions, they now desired a Utopia, which expressed to them their own ideas."

In the article published in *Przeglad Polski* (The Polish Review), the writer stated: *Looking Backward* "is in novel form; but, because of its contents, it may be classed among works which popularize science. The problem of modern times which stirs up the most passion is political economy. The book presents a vision of the political system of the future, which reminds one of the program of the Socialists, and particularly that of the Communists. Mr. Bellamy's optimism makes him believe that economic development will heal man's psychological and physiological shortcomings. The removal of the 'struggle for existence' from human relations will cause a perfect intellectual and physical development." The reviewer then stated that, for himself, he did not desire a perfected humanity; for he believed that imperfections contributed to progress.

The author of the review in *Biblioteka Warszawska* (The Warsaw Library) agreed with Zyg that Bellamy appealed in his Utopia to the "philanthropy and the kind hearts of the bourgeoisie," but he called attention to the fact that the American "forgot to some extent the material interests of various social classes." Although he assessed Bellamy as "a writer not devoid of wit, one with a fertile imagination, but one without much knowledge of physiology and psychology," the reviewer concluded that the values of *Looking Backward* were that it pointed out that the Golden Age was in the future; that it satirically elucidated the situation of nineteenth-century economic conditions; and that it contained Mr. Barton's sermon to which 150,000 people had listened on the telephone.

Although Zywicki opined in *Prawda* that *Looking Backward* would appeal to the educated intellectual, he obviously did not know that the translator of the edition published in Warsaw in 1890 was not only an intellectual but would be "one of the ideological creators of modern Polish democracy."[1] Josef Karol Potocki (1854-1898) had graduated from the University of Warsaw and had begun his literary career in 1880 with the publication of literary articles and poetry which he published under a pseudonym. After teaching in private schools, he began to write for *Prawda* and for other journals articles which indicated his independent, militant attitude toward the existing social and political order.

As is indicated by one of his many pseudonyms, Potocki had advanced ideas; for he borrowed for one of his noms de plume the name of a young woman revolutionary worker of the first Polish proletarian socialist party who had been arrested in 1886 and deported to Russia, where she died. Potocki himself saw the future of Poland as one of democratization of culture; and he spread ideas which were anti-czarist, anti-landowner, and pro-independence in the publication *Glos*, which he not only founded but which today is considered to be a journal which played a significant role in spreading democratic thought in Poland.[2]

When Potocki took part in a manifestation in honor of Kilinski, a revolutionary leader, he was imprisoned and sent to Odessa. When he returned to Poland in 1897, he was physically and mentally a broken man; but he was not too destroyed to be prevented from resuming his battle against cooperative, peaceful attitudes toward the Russian czars. He published a series of illegal pamphlets; and, in 1898, he published illegally and secretly *Walka*, a newspaper which sponsored a radical patriotic policy. As a result of his attitudes, Potocki was caught between two strong parties: the National Democrats and the Polish Socialist party. Attacked by both groups, he lost his influence upon his former comrades and youthful followers; and he retreated to his home where he lived in poverty. In 1898, he mysteriously disappeared.

Although an advertisement in *Glos* after the publication of *Looking Backward* mentioned that the edition had reached its third printing,[3] no other mention could be found of Bellamy until 1950. In that year, Professor Stanislaw Helsztynski—a member of the Polish Academy and the chairman of the Department of English of the University of Warsaw until he was replaced by Professor Margaret Schlauch, formerly of New York University—published the first chapter of *Looking Backward* in an anthology which he prepared for secondary-school English students.

When asked how he became acquainted with Bellamy, Professor Helsztynski related that, before leaving burning Warsaw in 1947 to seek a hiding place, he had "stolen" the only book in English from the library of the friend from whose house he was fleeing the city. When he was safely hidden from his enemies, Professor Helsztynski opened for the first time the famous 1890 Tauchnitz edition of *Looking Backward*. During his exile from Warsaw, the well-known scholar and novelist read and pondered Bellamy's message; and he remarked that his picture of the future *somewhat* prepared him for the world he was to know after the war.

Under the direction of Professor Helsztynski, a student of the University of Warsaw wrote for his master's degree a thesis entitled *Henry George and Edward Bellamy, Two Anti-Capitalistic American Writers* (1955). The author, Henryk W. Pać, now prominent among the Communists in Poland, wrote in the foreword: "It may seem rather odd at first glance to artificially connect Henry George and Edward Bellamy in one thesis in an attempt to draw comparisons. The thesis aims, therefore, at showing that what the two authors had in common was their profound interest in social problems and anxiety about the future of man and civilization, which under Capitalism grew increasingly corrupt and degenerate." As this statement indicates, the attitude of Pać toward his subject is Marxist—and so, as we shall note, were his criticisms. He felt, however, that "both George and Bellamy were aware of the social evil around them, exposed and condemned it, and, each in his own way, proposed to eliminate it. Leaving the practical aspects of these proposals aside, their services to the degraded and oppressed will be, none-the-less, noteworthy."[4]

After portraying the background of depression, panics, and

labor movements which had preceded or been coincidental with these publications, Pać considered the "fallacious" but progressive ideas of George and then of Bellamy. He remarked—as had many nineteenth-century Marxists—that *Looking Backward* was worth reading because "apart from . . . Bellamy's Utopian and fallacious conception of the improvement of the capitalist social order in general, the author wrote many a passage of acute and damaging criticism of the society, the capitalistic system and its effects." Although Pać considered Bellamy's program to be a "radical one," he also condemned him because he was "unable to imagine the way of life in socialist society except by the middle-class standards of 1886 in Boston."[5]

To Pać, *Looking Backward* could be dismissed as an artistic or literary achievement but could not be ignored as a novel presenting a picture of a "socialist social order" or as a devastating depiction of the degeneration of the capitalistic society. To him, as to one of the nineteenth-century reviewers of Poland, it was important that Bellamy portrayed the Golden Age as being in the future; but "the essential thing about . . . [his] Utopian view of socialist society is that there is no exploitation of man by man." Furthermore, "the humanitarian character of the socialist society is expressed in the care that the society takes of all the insane, deaf-and-dumb, lame or blind."[6]

Because Bellamy had been "progressive and bold" in his program for the future, he had aimed at "a fraternal basis of industry and an equality of right and advantages for all" and had perceived that nationalization was the only answer. Pać then remarked: "It is clear from these quotations that Bellamy was aware of the social evil growing in the body of capitalist society. Nonetheless he failed to perceive that though the small tradesmen are oppressed by monopolies, yet they join monoplies to oppress and exploit the workers. Only an uncompromising class struggle against exploiters can bring about some essential change. This, the author failed to notice, and his proposal is only a Utopian one."[7]

As indicated by this quotation, Bellamy's major defects lay in his attitudes towards class warfare, evolution and not revolution, and his attitude toward the workers. Pać thought that one of the major blemishes of the American's concept of the socialist society was "his way of bringing it to life." Pać felt that his "Utopian conception" in this instance could be "accounted for by the fact that he approached social questions not from the standpoint of the Marxist class struggle but as a bourgeois liberal. In his attitude toward private property he was a radical reformer. In the practical aspects of his theories, Bellamy was a Utopian writer. But his scheme of life within the socialist society indicates that he was at the same time a conservative bourgeois.[8]

"Though Bellamy criticized capitalism, this was not because it was an unjust social order but because monopoly capital threatened thousands of small capitalists and the entire middle class. . . ." Pać then stated that Bellamy admitted "there can be seen a distinct division of capitalist society into classes of poor and rich, educated and ignorant. But this contains nothing of the Marxist idea of antagonistic classes. There is evidence that Bellamy did not even suspect a class struggle. All the more so, he did not realize that the only victor in the class struggle can be the working class. Bellamy's ignorance of this fact accounts for his mistaken belief that any change of the capitalist industrial and social system to a higher ethical level and for the more efficient production of wealth was recognized as being in the interest not of one class but equally of all classes. . . . Only a person who did not understand the proletariat and its motives, who had nothing in common with workers, could assume that revolution can be carried out with the consent of 'all classes'. . . ."[9] It was impossible to be otherwise than derisive, remarked Pać, "about Bellamy's notion that the Revolution would be carried out, not merely with the consent of the capitalist class, but on their initiation."[10] To Pać, therefore, the concept of a peacefully evolving new form of society was "only a fairy tale fit for children. . . ."[11]

Like many other Marxists before and after him, Pać was also incensed about Bellamy's comments about the "followers of the red flag." Not only, recorded the Polish student, had Bellamy dubbed them such with disdain, but he had also shown that they "had nothing to do with putting Bellamy's Utopian socialism into being but hindered it. This nonsensical stuff about the working class and the deliberate underestimation of the force and capabilities of workers reflected the fears of the possessing classes faced with the growing militancy of American workingmen toward the end of the Nineteenth Century." In considering Bellamy's statement that the "red flag" followers might have been hired by the capitalists to intimidate people, Pać asserted that it proved "that though hostile to the big monopolies, Bellamy did not have any sympathy with the militant working class. On the contrary, he was the spokesman of the middle-class, the parasitical part of the capitalist society."[12]

Pać also felt that Bellamy's conception of work and production suggested that he "did not understand the differences between work in a capitalist factory and work under socialism or communism. While in the former work is a curse, so to say, in the latter it means something other than mere exertion."[13] After quoting Morris to the effect that work would be a pleasure and after stating that Bellamy worried about incentives, Paĉ then aired his views about what he considered Bellamy's odd attitude toward the political rights of the workers.

He remarked that, "when reading the novel and comparing Bellamy's scheme with life," it became evident that Bellamy's treatment of the workers relegated them to "only . . . tiny parts . . . in the tremendous machine of the industrial army. They have to work and that is all. To ensure efficient work, they are refused political rights which socialism grants to all. They cannot vote and elect their top-rank officers and the president himself. This is to safeguard the operation of the whole industrial army. Voting rights for workers 'would be perilous to the discipline.' This is no argument at all, but, still, it was often used to supply a reason for depriving the oppressed of the chance to decide for themselves. Bellamy's world was, once again, planned very closely after the pattern of capitalism."[14]

In his final, general assessment of George and Bellamy, Paĉ made the following observations:

> Their greatest merit is, beyond doubt, the unmasking of some, if not all, the defects of capitalism and a thorough criticism of them.
> Henry George exposed and condemned the injustice of private property of land and proposed a solution to it. Edward Bellamy was also emphatic that capitalism is a degenerate social order. But contrary to George, he sought for the causes of the misery of the widest masses of population in the realm of industry. Bellamy was also convinced that the cause lies in the private ownership of the means of production. Hence his condemnation of the system which permits exploitation of man by man. Leaving the Utopian, fallacious character of his solution aside, it must be stressed that Bellamy proved that a communist order of society is not only realizable but also inevitable as the only consistent next step in the evolution of society.
> Being aware of both the evil and its correct solution, he failed to point out this solution other than in an Utopian way. Claiming that competition eliminated, monopoly capitalism will automatically and painlessly give place to communism, the author does not have any room for a revolutionary action of the working class. On the contrary, he regards the capitalist classes as the makers of social justice. And this is against facts.[15]

Ironic or debatable as some of Pać's critical comments about Bellamy may be in his not too penetrating or brilliant thesis, they are interesting because they not only reflect the attitude of a modern Marxist but also indicate that there has been little change in the Marxist criticism of Bellamy since the nineteenth century. Though both socialists and Marxists were intrigued by him and translated him in Poland as elsewhere, they were enthusiastic only about his analysis and his denunciation of the ills of capitalism, for they were incensed that he did not sponsor a violent proletarian revolution. It was mainly for this reason that they considered him "unscientific."

## II Czechoslovakia

Looking Backward was not only published in three different editions in Czechoslovakia but serialized; and Equality was on sale in Prague as early as 1898. The first appearance of Looking Backward was in serial form in 1890 in the workingman's daily Hlas Národa (The Voice of the Nation), published by the National Printing House and Publishers, which had been established in Prague in 1889 for the publication of the newspaper and of political and fictional books.

Before the serial began in the issue of January 21, 1890, the novel was announced in an article which stated in the headline that Bellamy's Looking Backward had been translated by K. Sobicka, the nom de plume of Václav Beneš Šumavský (1850-1934), a journalist, author of poems and short stories, and a member not only of the administrative staff of Hlas Národa but also the chief editor of the daily paper Národní Politika (National Politics). Šumavský's translation was also used in an undated edition and for the 1890 one published by the National Printing House and Publishers.

In the article announcing the commencement of the serial, the unknown author—who may have been Šumavský—declared in no uncertain terms that Looking Backward not only considered "the burning questions of today of employers and workers, capital and labor, but also solved them." He then stated that in Bellamy's ideal state there was "no more poverty, no more hunger. There is also no longer the problem of how one could conquer another; for the Utopia demonstrates how all people can use their power or force for the good of all. As a result, there is no more fight for existence, no more sordid conniving between individual groups and the government. . . ."

After pointing out that man lived with his fellows in equality —socially and economically—the author of the announcement article then assured his readers that Bellamy had not, however, sought to "solve the question of a beautiful paradise" on earth by presenting the reader with a fairy tale; he had based his story and his ideal state upon "the ground of serious economic studies." He then wrote: "At the same time the novel has solid moral foundations and has nothing in common with the criminal intentions of the revolutionary elements of today."

The anonymous author admitted that, though the book contained only a dream of what the solution of the social questions of the time might be, it was "a very educating and amusing" Utopia; for Bellamy wrote "quite deeply, interestingly, and in detail about the miracles of technique of the twentieth century, about art, about the feminine question, and about numerous other problems which are basic to human welfare." After stating that the book would give "extraordinary pleasure to those seeking serious reading material," he then assured all his readers that the story not only was not neglected but was told in a "really masterful" manner which "maintained the reader's attention in an extraordinary fashion from beginning to end." The article closed with a comment about the "great sensation" the book had created "in the United States" and with the prophecy that it "would also be warmly welcomed" in Czechoslovakia where it would "find many readers."

Although no record of the popularity of the serial or of the two editions of the Sobicka translations could be found, the indication that *Looking Backward* was warmly accepted by Czech readers exists in the fact that another edition appeared in 1893. Its editor and translator was Dr. František Bačkovský (1854-1906), a former professor who had deserted teaching to devote himself to his bookstore and to the publication of literary reviews—which failed—and of Czech classics and books for the laboring class of Czechoslovakia which at this time was fed a diet of cheap novels and calendars. In the memorial collection in honor of Dr. Bačkovský—*Vzpominkovÿ Sborńik* (1928)—he was honored as having been one who had won a permanent niche in his country for giving culture to the workers.[16]

Although Bačkovský's bookstore in Prague was noted for having the largest collection of Czech books in the city and as being a gathering place of writers and journalists, it soon became also a place watched by the police. For Dr. Bačkovský, who wanted to help the oppressed and whose desire was "to give part of his heart to everybody,"[17] was reproached publicly by the press for having become a social democratic specialist among the booksellers, for recommending on his book covers other publications for social democratic libraries, and for publishing books which were one-sided.

Dr. Bačkovský soon had established, however, a widespread acquaintance with the workers' circles and with their mushrooming cultural libraries; for the 1890's—when he began publishing —were known as the era of democratic activities. His books for workers were circulated in Bohemia, Moravia, Silesia, and Vienna;[18] and they had a tremendous influence upon the formation of the Czech workers' attitudes.[19] A greater idealist than businessman—although he was one of the first to use advertising in various publications to promote the sale of books— Dr. Bačkovský was soon warned by the government that he might lose his publishing house because of his social democratic interests and work.

In 1894—one year after his publication of *Looking Backward* —Dr. Bačkovský withdrew from the publishing business in order to save his bookstore.[20] In 1906, ill in health, he committed suicide; but he is still remembered as a man "who worked with one hand while he fought with the other"[21] and as a "heroic,"[22] "rare man"[23] who followed his aim against the current, who believed his work would not be in vain, who refused to acknowledge the hard facts of practical existence,[24] and who used his knowledge and culture to give cheap editions to the people.[25] Of him it was said: "What he had in his heart was on his tongue."[26]

Another indication of the popularity of *Looking Backward* in Czechoslovakia was the publication in translation of Eugen Richter's attack upon Bebel and the German social democrats: *Sozialdemokratische Zukunftsbilder* (1891). The editor's note recalled the publication of *Looking Backward* in the daily *Hlas Národa* in 1890 and then explained that the novel had "attained such great circulation over all the world—as few literary works do—that it had given impulse to so many essays, pamphlets, parodies and travesties, and critical analyses that they formed a body of literature themselves." He then explained that Richter, leader of the German liberals, had published a book in which "he used Bellamy's form" to describe a socialist democratic state of the future—and to attack the ideas of Bebel and "the ideals of Bellamy."

The author of the Introduction then stated that the book by Richter was being published because—despite Richter's "satire, irony, derision, exaggeration, and mockery . . . at such things which competent experts treat in earnest and objective essays"

—his work "is, nevertheless, instructive and informative about socialist theories and criticisms of them"; and it is such "not only for those who have read Bellamy's book but for everybody. For this reason, we decided to acquaint the readers of *Hlas Národa* who know Bellamy's book with the sharp answer Eugen Richter gives Bellamy."

In 1898 *Equality* was published by The Labor Printing House, the publishers of the Czech Social Democrats and, therefore, of the daily *Pravo Lidu* (The Rights of the People), of workmen's magazines, and of other types of social democratic and political literature. The translator and editor of the volume was Jaroslav Jirousek, a Czech journalist and editor who was well known for his translations of English and French novels.

Notices of the publication of *Equality* appeared in the April and May, 1898, issues of *Pravo Lidu,* and they declared that this sequel of *Looking Backward* was a "still more detailed, and in more interesting form, picture of the future society" and that it was "warmly recommended." The second notice called not only for the attention of those interested in "the picture of the future socialist society" but also asked "comrades to support this purely labor enterprise" by stating that such a request was really unnecessary. The announced price—or its equivalent—was fifteen cents!

Although three editions of *Looking Backward* and one of *Equality* appeared in Czechoslovakia, critical comments about them were apparently limited to a series of three articles entitled "Moderni Utopie Socialni" which appeared in *Cas* in 1890 and to notices of the death of Bellamy in 1898. In the first of the three articles which appeared in *Cas,* the author, after defining a Utopian novel, stated that the genre appealed to people who desired a better world but not to the middle class which did not approve of some of the pictures of the possible future. After demonstrating that many forecasts by Utopians had become reality, the writer opined that the role of the Utopian of 1890 was more difficult than it had been in the time of More because people were not only more critical and prudent, but also less likely to share with their ancestors their naïve faith in prophets and prophecies. The people of 1890 had, however, lost neither their hope nor their desire for a better world; but they were more realistic and skeptical. Furthermore, they wanted a better, more just economic system; and evidence of this desire was to be found in the popularity of the slogans of the socialists and communists.

After relating the tremendous success of *Looking Backward*

and after quoting from De Laveleye's recital of the growth of the Nationalist movement in the United States, the author asserted that Bellamy had borrowed his ideas from Marx by way of Lawrence Gronlund's *Co-operative Commonwealth*. To prove his assertion, he cited the Russian article by I. I. Yanzhul, who had demonstrated that Bellamy had repeated the ideas of Gronlund but had added details from Marx.

In the second article, Bellamy was cited as being optimistic; but he was excused for this characteristic because he came from a country which had accomplished much in a little over a century. After declaring that Bellamy was a convert to Marxism, the writer pointed out that the biggest change Bellamy contemplated was an economic one which sought to eradicate economic disparities and, therefore, other inequalities. Although the author agreed with Bellamy that civilization could not go backward and had to go forward, he did not advocate the overthrow of either capitalism or monarchism; but he admitted that both had brought unhappiness, as well as adventure, to the world. Since centralization had seemingly increased the riches of the world, the need in 1890 was to use capital's centralized advantages and rid it of its faults.

The Czech writer then returned to the "Americanism" of Bellamy because of his lack of fear of an industrial army; for the United States had none—or one of only 30,000 soldiers. He also remarked that at the time Bellamy created a state which would destroy militarism, he had also provided for an industrial army which would include all workers—and that he intended for all to be both masters and workers!

After commenting that Bellamy, who owed his concepts to Comte and to Spencer, depended upon evolution and not revolution, that his ideal government was only an economic organization, that only economics and not human nature had to change to achieve his ideal state, the article then presented a digest of the basic principles of Bellamy's Utopia. The closing comment about the state was that it was well constructed for the most part but that it would be more suitable for Europe than for the United States; for the latter was already democratic, had very few servants, had made more progress in the emancipation of women, and had advanced more with technical processes.

In the last article in *Cas*, Bellamy's picture was pronounced to be too rosy. First of all, it was difficult to understand how a state monopoly would bring—or insure—greater production of wealth. Second, Bellamy had stressed economics and organization and had forgotten two important items: religion and morality. Like Hegel, Bellamy was so impressed with the importance of his economic concepts that he had forgotten that man may not be so altruistic or so tolerant religiously and that the public may not be so responsible. After making clear that Bellamy's one-sided Utopia did not contain his ideal, the writer stated that *Looking Backward* was successful and that he recommended it to all readers because it "presented information about social questions in an agreeable form."

When Bellamy died in the year that Czechoslovakia witnessed the publication of *Equality*, notices of his death were published in both *Hlas Národa* (May 25, 1898) and *Pravo Lidu* (No. 145, 1898). The obituary in *Hlas Národa* took obvious pride in announcing that *Looking Backward* had been published in serial form in its columns; and the article in the other social democratic publication also reviewed the history of the publication of the books of "one of the most interesting literary personages of our century, the poet of the socialist future, whose name is also popular in our country."

After stating that *Looking Backward* had been published "in all languages of educated peoples" and that it had "created a great sensation and had spread over the English-speaking world," the article in *Pravo Lidu* declared that Bellamy's Utopias had

> . . . met the desires of all who wished to have a certain concrete picture of the future. He tried to describe a socialist order of society with all the details. He thought it would be bad to ignore such an important factor as human imagination; and poetical spirits always like to deal with serious topics—but readers must remember that what they read is a poetical creation and that reality may not necessarily follow the outline presented. A great part of the readers do not keep this in mind; they take the poetic description for poetic reality. The pictures in their minds about the future are there; but it is a future which nobody can know—or foretell.

After having complimented Bellamy and after denouncing him as "poetical," the writer of *Pravo Lidu* then discussed scientific socialism:

> . . . the followers of scientific socialism declare at every opportunity that they have nothing in common with similar Utopias; and they are reserved about the provocations of adversaries who want, or demand, them to give a detailed picture of the future socialist state. And they do not venture on the field of mere

combinations which could be easily refuted in this or that point. Scientific socialism describes with great certainty the tendency of evolution of economic forms; it describes the modern private capitalistic way of production, criticizes it, and shows that it bears in itself the elements leading to a change of society into collectivism or, in other words, socialization of the means of production. Scientific socialism is directed by proofs which it gives about the laws of economic evolution. To go past these laws and the concrete facts, to venture into the realm of fantasy—this is not the task of scientific socialism. It is necessary to say this so that we may form a correct opinion about Bellamy's book.

After establishing the fact that Bellamy was presumably frowned upon by the Marxists, the journalist then stated that the best part of Bellamy's *Looking Backward* had been not the picture of the socialist state, mentioned earlier in the articles as having been so gratifying, but his "criticism of the social order of today . . . thousands of readers were stimulated by it to study socialism more closely. In this sense the novel is an excellent literary means of socialist propaganda."

After reviewing Bellamy's activities with his periodical *The New Nation* and the formation of the Nationalist clubs in the United States, the author of the article stated that Bellamy's "literary and practical activity evoke a greater position" and that the clubs had without doubt "helped very much in expounding socialist ideas in" their native country. After recalling that many polemical literary works had been directed against Bellamy, the publication of *Equality*—"which deserves the greatest possible circulation"—was announced. After asserting that *Equality* showed Bellamy's "great talent as a writer," the author of the "tribute" to Bellamy stated: "We social democrats lose in him a faithful and indefatigible follower of the great, common socialist idea and an excellent literary talent."

## III *Jugoslavia*

Because the country now known as Jugoslavia is presently in the process of preparing a complete bibliography of material published in periodicals and newspapers, and because many files of such publications were destroyed during wars, gathering complete information about Bellamy's impact in Serbia and Croatia is nearly impossible. But from 1894 until 1910 his works were published; and as late as 1934 he was attacked by a Catholic writer. Although there is no proof that Bellamy was being read at this time by the communists—or used by them—

this adverse article would indicate that such was the case.

As might be expected, the first publications about and of *Looking Backward* appeared in *Zanatliski savey*—the organ of the Serbian handcraft and workers union—which had begun publication in 1892 and which reported upon economic and literary and political subjects. A very progressive newspaper for its time, it was greatly influenced by Svetoza Markovic, one of Serbia's most important and prominent socialists, and by Vasa Pelagic, the chief writer about economics. The newspaper was strongly opposed to the reign of King Milan, but it changed its attitude toward the government when King Alexander gave a representative of the handcraftsmen the position of minister of economics. This newspaper also published the news of the progress of the International Workers' movements and it discussed the effects on the home markets—and consequently upon the craftsmen—of imported items.

The first article about *Looking Backward* appeared in March, 1894, and it was written by no less a person than Zivojin Balugdzic (1868-1941), who at the time was associated with a socialist publication and who was to become a famous diplomat and member of the court. After studying law in Belgrade and Geneva, Balugdzic began his newspaper career in 1894 as a member of the editorial staff of the socialist papers *Socijal-Demokrat* and *Narodni prijatelj* (The People's Friend). After writing his article about Bellamy, he interestingly enough wrote another that may have been influenced by Bellamy's ideas which are suggested even by the title: "Destroy the Court." As a result of this publication, Balugdzic had to flee from his country to escape trial; he lived in Geneva and Munich as a reporter for foreign papers.

In 1903, after the change of dynasties, Balugdzic returned to Serbia where he became the secretary of King Peter and chief of the press bureau. After 1906, he served in the diplomatic corps as the secretary of the embassy in Istanbul, was consul in Skopje, general consul in Salonica, and later an ambassador in Athens, Rome, and Berlin. By the end of his long career, he was known as an adviser and then as a minister of the court, as the personal friend of King Alexander, and as a contributor of articles about Balkan and European problems in *The Serbian Literary Journal* and in the Belgrade *Politika*.

In his 1894 article about *Looking Backward,* Balugdzic compared it to the Utopias of More and Campanella, related that it had made many enemies and aroused much adverse criticism, and then stated: "I think it is wrong to consider this work a

mere picture of the future. As stated in its title, the book criticizes what actually exists. Bellamy uses his Utopia only to expose clearly how the society in which we live is not moral."
After commenting upon the criticism of nineteenth-century society as a good socialist of the time would have been expected
to do, Balugdzic then quoted some excerpts to prove his point.

A few issues later, an article signed "B. M." announced the
forthcoming publication of selections from *Looking Backward*
and gave a biographical sketch of Bellamy's life. According to
the author, who also translated the excerpts from the novel,
Bellamy had "become famous in Europe for his socialistic
novel"; had been widely translated on the continent; and had
also been greatly criticized by his enemies—Fränkel, Wilbrandt,
Müller—who had hoped to expose his wickedness as a communist. After quoting Michaelis' statement that Bellamy and his
followers should follow the example of the Amana Society and
found a settlement to prove how much humanity could be perfected, "B. M." stated: "We think that in [Bellamy's] work there
are many deep ethical truths and, at the same time, many real
criticisms; therefore, we are of the opinion that he must not
be considered a Utopian. . . ." and that his "ideas must not be
considered as Utopist." The excerpts appeared in four issues
only of the paper.

In December, 1901, *Trgovinski glasnik* (Trade Herald) also
published selections from *Looking Backward*. This newspaper
was one of the leading Serbian publications, for it sought to
cover not only domestic but foreign economic and commercial
problems. Not too conservative in its editorial policies, it was
popular among the progressive youths of Belgrade. The translation of *Looking Backward* was prepared by Hajim S. Davico
(1854-1940), a literary critic and reviewer who wrote for many
Serbian literary publications, was the author of many articles
about economics, and was one of the early Jewish socialists.

The third serialization appeared in *Radnicke novine* in issues
appearing from August, 1908, to September, 1909. This newspaper was the official publication of the Social-Democratic
Party and of the Main Workers' Union; and after 1925 it became the chief publication of the socialist party of Jugoslavia.
The socialists responsible for the publication of the book had
evidently obtained, by one means or another, the German edition prepared by Malkowsky which had been published in
1889; for the serialization ended in *Radnicke novine* in the
middle of Chapter XXVII. Malkowsky, who had taken great
liberties with Bellamy's book, had omitted Chapter I and had

ended the narrative with Julian West's awakening from his dream of the year 2000 to find himself back in the horrible Boston of 1887.

In 1910, *Radnicke novine* published extracts also from *Equality*; and the selections chosen were entitled Chapter XXV, which appeared in three issues, and Chapter XXXIII. Since Chapter XXV was a short one about the role of unions in creating the ideal state, the material following it about foreign commerce, the fallacies of the profit system, and the hostility of vested interests toward progress and invention seem to have been included. Chapter XXXIII was concerned with a view of how the people held the reins after the evolutionary process had been completed, how economic equality had been instigated, and how war and the old type of patriotism had disappeared.

It was not until 1903 that a complete edition of *Looking Backward* was published in Croatia in Zagreb under the title of *U godini 2000. Osvrt na godinu 1887.* In the unsigned introduction, the author mentioned the success of *Looking Backward* and then mentioned that it, like the novels of Jules Verne, transported the reader into a future society—a "world so magnificent and perfect that even the most daring socialist dreamers could not invent one like it." The qualities of the ideal society which aroused both admiration and criticism were not, however, its depiction of scientific and mechanical progress but its portrayal of man's moral and social progress. Among the excellent strides that had been made, the author listed so many items that he almost presented a résumé of *Looking Backward.* He remarked that a peaceful revolution had ended the competitive society and the unprofitable wastes of that capitalistic system; that words like "poor" and "rich" had become meaningless, for everyone had an equal income from the wealth provided by the ideal state; that all had to work in the labor force; that war no longer existed; that woman's position had been raised; that marriages were now made because of love and sympathy; that disease and crime had almost disappeared; and that greed and egoism had also been almost eradicated.

In his concluding paragraph, the author of the introduction remarked:

> These are the general situations in the year 2000 which are so interesting and so beneficent that no modern man dares imagine their existence in even the most distant future. It is no wonder, therefore, that some people have thought Bellamy's work to be a parody of the socialistic dreams of the future. But for all its

fantastic exaggeration, this book has great moral value. As in a mirror, we see the ugly characteristics of our time contrasted with a happy future. We learn how much ugliness and hideousness exist in our social life and how far we are from the Christian ideal. . . . In closing, we wish to draw everyone's attention to the author's appendix in which he denies the imputation that his aim was to ridicule socialistic teachings.

The appendix was, of course, Bellamy's famous letter to the Boston *Transcript* in which he asserted that his novel, "although in form a fanciful romance, is intended in all seriousness, as a forecast, in accordance with the principles of evolution, of the next stage in the industrial and social development of humanity, especially in this country; and no part of it is believed by the author to be better supported by the indications of probability than the implied prediction that the dawn of the new era is already near at hand and that the full day will swiftly follow." Since Bellamy argued that his Utopia was to be accepted as a picture of a more than possible society, the writer of the Croatian edition was without doubt consciously contradicting his own statement in the first part of the Introduction to the effect that no man could dream of such a future; he was also indicating that the book was a socialistic one; and that it should be taken seriously.

The only other article concerned with Bellamy's ideal state which could be located was "According to Bellamy's Recipe." Published in June, 1934, in *Hrvatska straza*, its author, Petar Grgec, was the most prominent writer of the Croatian ultra-Catholic intellectual group. Although he had published a series in *Hrvatska straza* about Utopian novels, the article about Bellamy is less philosophical and far more political than the others. To Grgec, Bellamy not only presented the "heart of the communist program but proved the unrealizability of the communist Utopia." Although he admitted that poets and writers performed an important role by inspiring humanity, Grgec thought they should not pretend to be leaders; for people of another kind should assume this position: those who pondered more calmly and seriously and who, if they perfected a program after long and mature consideration, "would provide a more powerful stimulus to progress than any hymn, short story, novel, or drama."

He then stated that if one read the scientific Marxists, their program of the future might seem at first to be the product of such serious consideration. But, further contemplation soon showed that Marx and Engels—as well as their anti-materialistic

predecessor Plato—had presented programs which were the
result of their imagination. To Grgec, Bellamy was also one
who falsified nature and people in order to prove that his social
reform was a simple, possible affair.

His most interesting statement is, however, that "the American socialist . . . is up to the present day the favorite reading
of the Marxist proselytes. The highest Marxist critics sometimes
renounce him because he is, they say, too naïve and sentimental.
There is, however," asserted Grgec, in the kindest statement
he made about Bellamy, "much more frankness and sagacity
in his explanation than in the theories of the modern communist demolishers. Their goal is the same as his, to be sure, but
they are careful not to expose to criticism the . . . patterns of
the [future] communist society. Present communist writers prefer describing negative types of society to unveiling their own
positive ideal. But their ideal is still that which Bebel tried to
present in his seemingly scientific work *The Woman* and
which tendentious storyteller Bellamy depicts in his book *Looking Backward.*"

After treating Bellamy as the Belgian liberals and Catholics
and the German anti-socialists had long before, Grgec then summarized the plot of *Looking Backward* and the basic principles
of the new society. Then he stated:

> Serious people should laugh at this novel when they have read
> it through. It is child's play to say: "Why, it's very simple."
> But in real life, we can see that these simplicities are very in-
> tricate. We can see today the communists at work in Russia.
> They have at their disposal inexhaustible resources of natural
> wealth, technical progress . . . but, alas, the people are not
> happy. Bolsheviks have brought about such tyranny as is un-
> known to living memories and have made for themselves many
> external enemies. It is questionable whether Russia will emerge
> from future chaos as an integral state or will be divided among
> known and unknown nations and governments. In spite of this,
> Marxian followers dream according to Bellamy's recipe but
> claim that it is unlike their eccentric combinations.

Grgec then referred to German Michaelis' reply to Bellamy—
*Looking Forward*—which, he thought, showed fairly well the
weaknesses of Bellamy's vision. Michaelis had shown in his
Utopian novel that there was no freedom; that all goods had
been communized; that there was no family life; that only
those who toadied to officials received promotions or good positions; that corruption and prostitution flourished; and that inequities and revolutionary tendencies had not been extermi-

nated. When the counter-revolution arrived, Dr. Leete was killed; and Julian West awakened to find that his vision had been only a dream. "He thanks God that he is living in the nineteenth century and not in a communist state."

Grgec then concluded: "Michaelis could not find more appalling colors to represent the bad characteristics of communism and its propagators. Antagonists of communism have, however, much more efficient means today with which to struggle against this Utopia and to disillusion all who believe that they would establish a paradise on earth if they used Bellamy's recipe. Reforms should be carried out—and more radical reforms than those suggested by Michaelis' cooperative society—but communism is an impossible and a pernicious Utopia."

As this spirited attack upon *Looking Backward* indicates, Bellamy's Utopian novel must have been popular once more and it must also have been in use by the Marxists. As Branko Hanz of the University Library of Zagreb has stated in a letter, it is possible that other publications about Bellamy appeared during this era or that fragments from his Utopias had been published in some of the left-wing newspapers. Since these newspapers were burned by the police or destroyed during World War II, most of them are very rare and some of them cannot be found at all.

## IV *Hungary*

Although an American could not enter Hungary in 1958 and 1959 to search for the reactions of the liberal or the conservative press to *Looking Backward,* the report prepared by the reference department of the national library in Budapest indicates that the Utopia enjoyed a long period of popularity—and, perhaps, influence. From 1891 to 1920, six editions of it appeared; in 1898 two of Bellamy's earlier novels—*Dr. Heidenhoff's Process* and *Miss Ludington's Sister*—were published; and in 1919 "The Parable of the Water Tank" was in circulation. Four of the editions of *Looking Backward* were issued by Franklin Publishing House, which, founded in 1873, was noted for its publication of Hungarian classics and for its inexpensive series of books.

Although the Franklin Publishing House was neither socialist nor Marxist in its editorial policy, the publisher of the two editions of 1895 of *Looking Backward*—one complete, the other a digest—was a socialist. Although publisher and bookseller Károly Rozsnyai was first known in Budapest for publishing for the lower classes such cheap booklets as *The Tales of*

*Venus: Naughty Stories,* he became a publisher of political books. In his series *Forradalmi konyvtar* (Revolutionary Library) were included such items as *Utmutato a szocialista irodalomba* (A Guide to Socialistic Literature); Victor Hugo's parliamentary speech of July 17, 1851, about the revolution and the republic and against the monarchy; Jules Michelet's *A no, a csalad* (The Woman and the Family); and *Mumka vagy anarchia* (Work or Anarchy).

The famous "Parable of the Water Tank" was published in Budapest by the Russians* and by the Socialist-Communist party of Hungary in 1919—a period when the Hungarian Soviet Republic was in power and when several pamphlets of political, economic, cultural, and scientific nature were published not only in Hungarian but in the languages also of the national minorities. "The Parable," printed at the *Voros ujsag nyomda* (Red Newspaper Press), which was also the publisher of the party newspaper, was one of a series of books entitled *Kommunista konyvtar* (Communist Library). Authors of the other booklets published in it were by Marx, Engels, Bogdanov, Bukharin, Lenin and by Hungarians Béla Kun and Ervin Szabo.

The history of the publication of these two editions of *Looking Backward* and of "The Parable" indicates that Bellamy was used by both socialists and Marxists—and other evidence exists to support this deduction. One valuable indication of the importance of *Looking Backward* in furthering the cause of the communists was its mention in a list of books compiled by József Madzsar, a leading socialist, which bore the title in English of "A Model Booklist for Municipal Public Libraries." The municipal library of Budapest—organized by Marxist historian and sociologist Ervin Szabo on the pattern of the American, German, and English libraries which sought to make books available to the proletariat—had become the veritable stronghold of the socialist movement. In all the editions of the model booklist of 1892, *Looking Backward* is described as "a very important book."

Another bibliographical guide to socialist literature—*Utmutato a szocialista irodalomba*—compiled by Ignac Rozsa and published in 1919 in Rozsynai's Revolutionary Library Series, also gives attention to Bellamy. Under "Writers of Utopias and Communistic Attempts," the following appears: "9. Edward Bellamy, b. 1850. His work: *Looking Backward 2000-1887.*" In the volume entitled *The Pioneers of Socialism,* Bellamy is

---

* The Russian edition of the "Parable" lists no publisher or printer.

mentioned in the chapter "American Socialists": "The majority
of the communist attempts took place in America. Here were
founded the communist clubs and workers' unions by Weitling,
[Joseph] Weydemeyer, etc. They contributed to the foundation
of the International Workers Unions too. The most remarkable
among the Americans were H. George . . . and E. Bellamy.
Bellamy's work: *Ein Ruckblick aus dem Jahre 2000* was published also in Hungarian, translated by Daniel Radvanyi."

Further proof of the use of Bellamy for propaganda purposes
is supplied by the abridged edition of *Looking Backward* published in 1895. In this thirty-two-page book, the story has been
almost completely omitted and only the political and economic
material retained. The comments about the text of the book are
somewhat arbitrary; for example, the publisher's footnote on the
third page states: "Bellamy's novel explains the difference between the circumstances created by the capitalistic mode of
production and the circumstances after the cessation of the
antagonism between capital and labor."

The table of contents—printed on the cover and on the title
page—shows a definite slanting for the purpose of propaganda:

1. The income of the capitalists in the nineteenth century
   consists of the expropriated income of the work of others . 3

2. The strikes were the workers' natural protestation against
   this expropriation; the workers were not enemies of the
   civilization ....................................... 5

3. The natural consequence of the increasing accumulation
   of capital was the passing of the instruments of production into the hands of the people ................. 9

4. In the socialist society, crime, law courts, penitentiary
   and government, in its actual meaning, fade away .... 13

5. The socialist economic system means a raise in the standard of living and is a contrast to capitalism ......... 17

6. Socialism and the emancipation of women ............ 23

7. Socialism and moral progress ..................... 28

Although the complete story of Bellamy's influence among
socialists cannot be related until much more research work is
done in Hungary, it is possible to record his influence upon one
Hungarian writer: Gaspar Kubowich (1852-190?), a village
postmaster and notary whose literary activities were not too
significant. In 1886 he had published a pamphlet *Tarsadalmunk
problemai es azok megoldasi modja* (The Problems of Our

Society and the Method of Their Solution). In 1890 he published *A mumkaskerdes memoranduma* (Memorandum of the Labor Question); and on the title page he wrote: "Bellamy's *Looking Backward* sold more than 100,000 copies in the United States. In this book Bellamy enumerates ideas showing a way out of economic crisis and over-indebtedness. Why should we sleep without dreaming when even in the United States, where crisis and over-indebtedness are unknown, people jump at saving ideas."

On the fifteenth page of his pamphlet, Kubowich stated: "Bellamy expounds his ideas in the form of a dream. He had to express himself cautiously because he felt himself threatened by the police of the usurious capitalists. But everybody who knows the difference between reality and imaginary dreams, knows also that Julian West is not a mere fantastic figure of the future, as for instance is the flying hero of Jokai's *A jovo szazad regenye* [The Novel of the Next Century, which is a fantastic picture of future technical achievements]. In Bellamy's novel, Julian West is a self-conscious economist, who lives among and expresses himself in parables."

In this pamphlet of 1890, Kubowich propounded a socialistic system of his own. He advocated that the state be the merchant for all agricultural products and that it increase the price of agricultural products and raise the rate of all the indirect revenues of the state. Kubowich argued that there was no antagonism between the capitalists and the proletariats; but he thought that capitalists, who were deficient in funds, hindered the development of the national economy. In his nationalization of distribution and in his suggestion that the state might be able to promote development with its funds, Kubowich indicated the impact of Bellamy's ideas.

Among the translators of Bellamy's works, Gyula Csernyei, who translated the 1892 edition of *Looking Backward,* was born in 1834 in Varanno in the city of Zemplen. A teacher, he later was a clerk of the court of justice of Kassa and Szeged and of the land registration office. He wrote many articles about political, social, economic, pedagogic, and literary subjects; and he published one book *A kozeppont* (The Central Point) in 1885 which is concerned with the connection between education and labor and in which he proved himself a follower of Rousseau and also a proponent of vocational education.

"A. S."—Sandor Adorjan—was a well-known translator between 1891-1930 who translated not only Bellamy's *Miss Ludington's Sister* but the works of Conan Doyle, Anthony Hope,

Jack London, F. H. Burnett, and others. Adorjan had been a student at the medical school and at the University of Technical Sciences in Budapest; and he later traveled widely in such countries as Germany, France, Egypt, Palestine, Greece, and Turkey. He later became the editor of the newspaper *Magyar Nemzet* but after the dissolution of the *Orszagos Szabadelyu Part* (National Liberal Party) he retired from journalism and politics. He later became an official of the Hungarian State Railways.

Dezso Naray, the translator of *Dr. Heidenhoff's Process*, did not publish or translate anything but this book. The novel was published in a series entitled *A nagyvilagbol* (Out of This World), which contained the works of Anthony Hope, Sienkiewicz, Jules Lermina, Charles Nodier, and others. Since *Dr. Heidenhoff's Process* related how an electrical shock treatment could cure those depressed by a sense of guilt, it is understandable why it would appear in this series and also why it was published under the title *A csdadoktor* (The Miraculous Healer).

The publication of *Dr. Heidenhoff's Process* and *Miss Ludington's Sister* would indicate that Bellamy was extremely popular in Hungary and that publishers who had not issued his famous *Looking Backward* were, in all probability, interested in exploiting the fame of the Utopian. All the evidence which can be presented at this time about the popularity and influence of *Looking Backward* would indicate that the socialists must have found him very useful for propaganda and recruitment purposes—and this for a quarter of a century!

## V   Bulgaria and Rumania

Much future work needs to be done to unearth the true story of Edward Bellamy in Bulgaria, for the material that is known indicates that such a search would bear fruit. First of all, three different translations of *Looking Backward* were published in this tiny country in 1892, 1900, and 1934. The first of these was prepared from a Russian translation of *Looking Backward* by the Bulgarian socialist Konstantin T. Bozveliev; and it was printed in Russia in 1892. This edition was reprinted, however, in Sofia as late as 1921.

Of the two other translations of Bellamy's famous Utopian novel, one, published in 1934, is only a fragment. The four-hundred-page edition of *Looking Backward* of 1900, prepared by Ilija S. Jovcev, is a literary curiosity. Taking the greatest liberty with the book, Jovcev added not only Bulgarian names and places but also political, economic, cultural events and personalities; he rendered the novel hardly recognizable.

Evidence which indicates that Bellamy was popular in Bulgaria for a long period is found in the fact that one of the novels of his cousin Francis Bellamy, a leader of the social gospel movement, was also published in 1898; Michaelis' Utopian novel, which was critical of Bellamy, was published in 1893. Articles about Bellamy appeared in 1898, the year of his death, and in 1925. One of his short stories was published in 1919. Furthermore, the acting director of the National Library of Sofia who supplied this information remarked that Bellamy was "a well-known Utopian writer" and that he had been a "valiant socialist-utopist, the fighter for a better future society."

Two editions of *Looking Backward* appeared in Rumania, one in 1891 and another as late as 1920. The first translation was a complete one but its translator is unknown. The second is an abridged edition which bore on the cover and on the title page the words "novel" and "historical fantasy." Despite these terms to describe the contents of the Utopia, the work was published by the socialists.

## VI  *Spain, Portugal*

Although one edition of *Looking Backward* was published in Portugal in 1891, several editions were published in Spain or in Spanish. *El año 2000*, translated by Ricardo Francia and illustrated by Pedraza, was published in Madrid but no date was recorded. Another undated edition—*Cien años despues*—was also published in Barcelona in a series entitled "The Great Novelists"; and another, bearing the same title, was published in Spanish in Genoa, Italy, by editor Carlos Maucci. Illustrated with bizarre pictures and containing a cover which showed the fetters of man being broken, this edition also contained even more unusual notes in the back about geographical, botanical, and sociological matters. Since this paperback book also printed a preface written by "Teodoro Reinach," the translation was obviously made from the French edition of 1890.

Editor Maucci seemingly specialized in publishing books which concerned occultism, anti-Catholicism, and social criticism. In his list of novels in the back of his edition of *Looking Backward*, he listed nine books by Zola, and among them were *La Terre* (La Tierra) and *Germinal;* three books by Eugene Sue; and the following suggestive titles: Jean Meslier, *La religión natural* and *Dios y el buen sentido;* Baldino Feddernoli, *Amores y orgias de los Papas;* Andrés A. Lutscher, *La piedra filosofal;* a collection by various authors entitled *La revolución intelectual;* Demófilo Italico, *Los misterios del Vaticano;* Ferreal, *Los mistérios de la inquisición de Espana;* and R. Verea, *La razón y la fé (Religión universal).* It is also interesting to note that on the title page four agencies of the company are listed: Buenos Aires, Mexico, Havana, and Caracas.

The two dated editions of *Looking Backward* were published in 1905 and 1939. The one of 1905, translated by José Esteban Aranguren, was published in Barcelona; the paperback edition of 1939, published by Cosmos of Valencia, cited no translator. This edition was not listed by the National Library of Madrid, and the only known copy is in the Institute of Social History in Amsterdam.

Many exiles from Spain now living in Paris stated that Bellamy had been popular among the Catalonians in particular in the days preceding and during the Civil War of the 1930's—and it need not be said which political group favored his ideas. Furthermore, Juan R. Parellada, cultural attaché of the Spanish Embassy in Washington stated in a letter of 1957, that "Utopian literature has had much development in Spain."

So evidence exists which would indicate that at some future date some student of political ideas or of comparative literature might profitably trace the story of Bellamy in Spain—and perhaps in the other Spanish-speaking nations. Although inquiries were sent to these countries, they were either ignored or answered with statements about the primitive condition of their bibliographies. The only evidence that indicates that Bellamy was known by a few people in Uruguay is found in letters received by the late Mrs. Edward Bellamy. In April, 1934, she received a letter from Alvaro A. Araujo of Montevideo who wrote that he had recently obtained a Spanish translation of *Looking Backward* and that it had aroused his interest. He had then read in the March, 1934, issue of the *Theosophist* of India an article entitled "The World Economic Crisis and a Way Out" which mentioned the International Bellamy League. Mr. Araujo requested—because of his interest in promoting better conditions and also brotherhood—that Mrs. Bellamy send him material about Bellamy for publication in his new magazine *Gnosis* which he had recently begun to publish. The magazine would, he wrote, "deal only with the possibilities of uniting knowledge with spirit, thus producing Wisdom."

A letter of November 15, 1937, from the president and the secretary of the "Asociacion Cristiana de Jovenes" of Montevideo indicated that Mr. Araujo had maintained an interest in Bellamy; for he had left for the library of the association an issue of the *Bellamy-News* which Mrs. Bellamy had sent him. The letter from the organization stated that it would be glad to receive the *Bellamy-News* and "any other printed matter that refers to Bellamy Plan for Social Work." The letter also stated that the membership of the group was three thousand strong and that its library was a very good one.

## VII  *Switzerland*

Although no edition of *Looking Backward* was published in Switzerland until 1947, the Swiss of the nineteenth century undoubtedly read the German, French, or Italian translations of it. According to the report of Dr. Werner Bleuler of the University of Zurich, interviews with older people revealed that most of them had either heard of or had read the book; and in most instances they had read the German edition of 1889. Furthermore, Professor Charles Secrétan of the University of Lausanne in *Mon Utopie* presented a criticism of Bellamy's book—and one which was widely quoted. Dr. Bleuler remarked, however, that the reaction of the Swiss in general to Bellamy's concepts seemed to be—unlike that of the Germans—that they were impractical and fantastic.

Although cultural ties with Germany were very strong prior to World War I, the Swiss tended to develop after it their own cultural and literary patterns. Although there was a need for idealism which might have favored a Bellamy revival in Switzerland during the 1920's, the only known indication of an attempt to familiarize the Swiss with his ideas occurred in one large factory: the owners distributed several hundred copies of the German edition of 1889 among the workers.

After World War II, Mr. Werner Reist—publisher and novelist*—published the first and only Swiss edition of *Looking Backward: Erlebniss im Jahr 2000*. He relates that he did so because of his duty to "bring out worthwhile books and make a success of them" and because he himself had read and reread Bellamy and had liked him "because of the love he manifests for humanity, because of the lucidity and originality of his writing, and because of his visionary conception of a future

---

* During the Hitler era, Mr. Reist wrote a successful novel *Menschen und Maschinen*, which was confiscated by the Gestapo in Germany but which was republished in serial form in 1953 in a workers' publication. He has also written such works as *Anarkali, Ege in Indien,* and *Herrlich ist die Welt.* Dr. Bleuler, who talked with him, described him as being a "Bellamy specialist."

society." Although Mr. Reist admitted that his estimate of the American Utopian had nothing to do with whether or not "such a society shall become possible," he remarked that "we like flowers for their beauty and perfume and not because we think they would make good food for us."

Commercially, the 1947 edition of *Looking Backward* was a failure, although the book received some critical attention, and although it was serialized in two newspapers. The *Anzeiger aus dem Bezirk Affoltern*—owned and edited by Dr. Jacob Weiss, a former judge of the circuit court—published the novel because Judge Weiss had become interested in it while printing it for Reist. *Looking Backward* was also serialized in *Merkur* of Zurich, edited by Mr. William Naegeli; a weekly publication, it has a circulation of about 16,000.

Although attempts were made to popularize and to sell the Swiss edition, most of the three thousand copies of *Erlebniss im Jahr 2000* were sold at ruinous prices to second-hand book stores. Shortly after the sale had been made, a German publisher who wrote to Mr. Reist asking for more copies of the book had to be referred to the Zurich shops which eventually sold all of them to Western Germany. This edition is, therefore, out of print in Switzerland today; but not because—stressed Dr. Bleuler—of the interest of the Swiss.

In considering the reasons for the lack of Swiss enthusiasm for Bellamy in 1947 and the subsequent commercial failure of *Erlebniss im Jahr 2000*, Dr. Bleuler and Mr. Reist presented some conflicting views. To Mr. Reist the publication failed because "the illusions of Marxism had spread" and become deeply imbedded. Since "the spirit of Bellamy may, in my opinion, be said to be diametrically the opposite of Marx," this difference could explain the lack of appeal of *Looking Backward*.

Dr. Bleuler believed that the lack of success was due not only to the Swiss aversion for anything which they deem impractical or unrealizable but also to their having begun to realize "the true nature of communism. Their disappointment was such as to render a book like Bellamy's taboo at once. Whoever published or read such a book was regarded a communist; it was a kind of 'McCarthyism.'" Dr. Bleuler also reported that the factory which had once evinced interest in *Looking Backward* was not only no longer interested in 1947 in the novel but politely refused to remember the distribution of it some twenty-five years earlier. Furthermore, the reviewers universally dismissed it as *eine liebenswurdige Utopie:* as "very amiable, very nice, very fanciful—but altogether unlikely to ever be put into practice." In summary, wrote Dr. Bleuler, the general attitude was: "Why should I read a book whose ideas are unrealizable and, therefore, uninteresting—and particularly if doing so is likely to classify me as a communist."

After considering the reasons presented by Dr. Bleuler for the failure of *Erlebniss im Jahr 2000*, Mr. Reist conceded that fear might have dictated the attitude of many Swiss or German readers at this time because Stalin had begun to disclose his true colors as "an enemy of humanity and a destroyer of free society. Although Bellamy advocates what in essence is a form of ideal communism, there was a great fear of being mistaken as an advocate or friend of Russian or Soviet communism. So the ideal good had to shrink into hiding before the danger of being misunderstood as the maximum of iniquity."

Whatever the reason for the unsuccessful—in Switzerland—edition of *Looking Backward,* Mr. Reist is still certain that Bellamy has a positive message to give to the world. He wrote:

> Marxism is the secret destroyer of Christianity because with its class warfare, its communism, its use of brute forces and its atheism, it has for one long century aimed at what is now manifesting itself . . . as the enslavement of all humanity. Bellamy, on the other hand, based his social and economic order on the noble thoughts and universal love which are the essence of the Christian religion. Whether his visions will ever become facts I do not presume to foretell—but nobody can fail to note how far we have gone toward them not only in technical developments, but above all in the shortening of working hours, in the fast advancing equality of social standing and income. (With this comment, I do not mean to express any opinion as to the ultimate desirability of such things.)
>
> Looking at the world in a realistic way, I find that there is one fundamental point on which all efforts for world peace and for a turning away from the frightening materialism of our days will always founder and suffer shipwreck: the lack of knowledge about the status, the life-purpose, and the essence of what man in reality is.
>
> . . . . There is hardly a university, a college, or other institution of learning, there is hardly a commercial or industrial enterprise of any size anywhere in the world without a series of laboratories, professorships, and experimental facilities in order to work for and achieve "Progress." And by this word is meant a better knowledge of the essence of matter, of material elements, of material forces, and of the behavior of such elements and forces under any and all imaginable circumstances, stresses,

and services. The results are at present shown by atomic energy, electronics, automation. Atomic fission and fusion may do to our good old earth what rats and termites used to do to our wooden bungalows—but with rather frightening consequences.

So while we get to know a lot—or lots—about those things which draw man away from the soil from which his sustenance used to come . . . man is losing his foothold on the earth and is sort of hanging in space and losing his bearings; we discover that we can no longer take man for granted. And we suddenly ask ourselves "what is man"; we find no convincing answer other than the ones given in the Bible. These would be sufficient if people were Christians—but who is? Look at politics!

Out of this situation arises the need for at least one research institution of post-graduate standard and national or universal standing whose only purpose would be the study of spiritual man. In the midst of widening technical horizons, we need to attempt giving real answers to such questions as: "What is man in reality? Why and how does he think? What makes him intelligent? What is truth, spirit, soul? What is good or evil?

Bellamy in his explanation of education and professional training assumes that men have absorbed the essence of Christianity, respect the laws given by it, and aspire for fuller spiritualization. He does not state this explicitly, but he takes it for granted—and with this his whole system begins to be Utopian. We need, however, a scientific definition of man; and I propose that the national institute make a study of man as a spiritual being and of all forces, purposes, aims and destinations pertaining to him and to his highest aspirations. . . .

Bellamy has abolished the love of money as a senseless folly. In our times the love of money has unfortunately become the mainspring of nearly all activities in commerce as well as in sport, in arts, etc. But this is not the time to complain, but to look beyond such shortcomings into the possibilities of remedy. Such remedies will be found through the scientific study of man. One of the main results I can visualize in the early stages of the career of the Institute will be the re-establishment of proper standing for all the forces of good—which today all too often have to submit to the rule of forceful politics and the might of the strong. Even that alone will already give to the Institute a rapidly growing moral recognition in all circles; it will become an outstanding moral power.

Mr. Reist, who had discussed the necessity of the scientific definition of man with members of the board of the Swiss Electrotechnical Society, was asked by the president of the association to outline his ideas for publication. His paper was published in 1959 in the highly respected journal of the association and he reported that it attracted "considerable attention." He also wrote that

> . . . at first most people express incredulity and surprise at the project. But such surprise is quickly dissolved when we realize that the very thing has been done for many decades, *but in the negative* by the adherents of Marxism. They have studied man in order to find out his weaknesses so as to undo him; they have indoctrinated the results of their studies with iron discipline into armies of agents—and the result is a measure of success, which today is reaching out for full world domination, for the annihilation of liberty, human rights and dignity, and everything that pertains to man and his noble destiny.
>
> So we do need an Institute for re-establishing knowledge of and faith in sound moral standards, spiritual advancement, and increasing liberty in the midst of a world that begins to provide for man's needs at very little cost to the individual. Without such an Institute, we shall remain subject to power-politics even in the smallest communities—and we shall never overcome the universal defeatism with regard to expressing fuller manhood, liberty, nobility, and finally, world peace.

# CHAPTER FOURTEEN

# The Theosophical Society; The Orient

THE STORY OF THE IMPACT in the Orient of Bellamy's Utopian novels remains incomplete. Because of the political impasse between the United States and China, it was impossible to secure any cooperation in tracing the influence of Bellamy among the Chinese; but certain facts are cited. The record of Bellamy in Japan dates not only from the nineteenth century but extends into the present; for *Looking Backward,* as we shall see, is being read there now in a new edition published after World War II. And in India, the record contains many unresolved problems but also fascinating aspects. Among these is the Theosophical Society.

## I  *India and Theosophists of the World*

Because of the multiple influences of British culture, Theosophy, and socialism in India, *Looking Backward* was "promoted" by many different groups and had, so far as could be discovered, not only many legends associated with its history but several facts. One of the most interesting of these is that the Theosophical Society—founded in New York in 1875 by Colonel Henry Steele Olcott and Mme. H. P. Blavatsky—has had its world headquarters in India since 1879, has interested many of India's leaders, and has retained an interest in Bellamy since *Looking Backward* first appeared. This lasting interest of the society in the novel must be attributed to the recommendation of it by its fabulous co-founder Helena Blavatsky (1831-1891) and perhaps also to that of her successor as leader of the Theosophists, the no less interesting Dr. Annie Besant (1847-1933), who once lectured about Bellamy in England.[1]

Helena Blavatsky wrote in the "Bible" of the society, *The Key to Theosophy* (1889; 1939): "The organization of society, depicted by Edward Bellamy, in his magnificent work *Looking Backward,* admirably represents the Theosophical idea of what should be the first great step toward the full realization of universal brotherhood. The state of things he depicts falls short of perfection, because selfishness still exists and operates in the hearts of men. But in the main, selfishness and individualism have been overcome by the feeling of solidarity and mutual brotherhood; and the scheme of life there described reduces the causes tending to create and foster selfishness to a minimum." After stating that, as a Theosophist, she would take part in an effort to realize such an ideal society, Madam Blavatsky then related that the Bellamy clubs of the United States were coming to the fore and that these clubs and this party were started in the first instance by Theosophists. One of the first, the Nationalist Club of Boston, Mass., has Theosophists for President [George Ayers] and Secretary [George Ransom Bridge], and the majority of its executives belong to the T. S. In the constitution of all their clubs and of the party they are forming, the influence of Theosophy and of the Society is plain, for they all take as their basis, their first and fundamental principle, the Brotherhood of Humanity as taught by Theosophy."*

Although Arthur Morgan stated in *Edward Bellamy* (1944) that the Theosophists had aided in the formation of the clubs, and also asserted that they had soon lost interest in the Bellamy movement when it began to have political aspirations or to support the People's Party,[2] my own research and that of Reverend Dr. Everett MacNair, as recorded in his published doctoral dissertation *Edward Bellamy and the Nationalist Movement* (1957),[3] prove that the Theosophists remained active in the group into the 1890's. Publications of the Theosophists indicate that the interest or awareness of Bellamy's ideas lived even longer—and not only in the United States, but in other countries of the world besides India.

As we follow in chronological order the mention of Bellamy in Theosophical publications, we find that he has been mentioned throughout the years. In February, 1889, Walter Q. Judge,

---

* Other members of the Theosophical Society who were active in the first Boston Nationalist Club were Henry Willard Austin, Arthur B. Griggs, John S. Cobb, and Sylvester Baxter. According to the memories of the garrulous and not too reliable, senile Cyrus Field Willard, which are quoted in Morgan's *Edward Bellamy* (1944), he and four other Theosophists comprised five of the committee of seven who drafted the "Nationalist Declaration of Principles." The others were Baxter, Austin, Ayers, and Griggs. According to the memories of Abbott E. Clark, who is also quoted by Morgan, the Theosophical societies of California in the 1890's were instrumental in the formation of the many Bellamy clubs of that state.

editor of the American Theosophical publication the *Path*, wrote to Bellamy that "Nationalism . . . is . . . founded on the principle of Universal Brotherhood. I thus conceive of it as closely linked to Theosophy, and a desirable means whereby Theosophists may assist in the ethical advancement of the race, substituting brotherhood and cooperation for competition, and do good work on the practical plane. Hence I desire to popularize Nationalism showing it in the above fraternal light. . . ."[4] Although Judge requested that Bellamy write an article for *The Path*, none was published by him. The March issue of the journal carried, however, a strong endorsement of *Looking Backward*; the one in October was less favorable.[5]

The July, 1889, issue of the London *Lucifer*, edited by Blavatsky, contained the following article:

Edward Bellamy's remarkable romance, *Looking Backward*, has started in America a movement that bids fair to become of considerable importance. Men and women touched with "the enthusiasm of humanity," and feeling a sense of personal shame for the inhumanity of our present social system, have been fired by the beauty of the Socialist Utopia to make an effort toward bringing it about; and they are gathering themselves into "Nationalist Clubs" to work for its realization. The name "Nationalist" is ill chosen, connoting as it does in the minds of most the separateness of the different nations rather than the internationality of the Socialist ideal; but it is used, not to mark off peoples from each other, but to indicate the breaking down of the narrower barriers of class and the nationalization of the land and capital now held as private property. The central idea of the movement, as expressed in the constitution of the Boston Nationalist Club, is "The Nationalization of industry and the promotion of the Brotherhood of Humanity."

The Boston Club has established *The Nationalist* as its organ, and starts its career with articles from the pens of Edward Bellamy himself, Col. T. Wentworth Higginson, H. Willard Austin, J. Ransom Bridge, Cyrus Field Willard, and others, and among those who promise contributions are Mrs. Helen Campbell, author of the "Prisoners of Poverty," Laurence Gronlund, the well-known Socialist, Rabbi Schindler and Thaddeus Wakeman. In the opening number Edward Bellamy tells how he came to write "Looking Backward" starting with the idea of "a fairy tale of social felicity" and transmuting it into the "vehicle of a definite scheme of industrial organization." We notice with interest that three of the writers in this first issue belong to the Theosophical Brotherhood, a sign that the American brethren mean to work, as well as speak, for the Brotherhood of Humanity. . . .

In 1890, a long article, " 'Looking Backward' and the Socialist Movement," written by E. Douglas Fawcett, was published in the June issue of *The Theosophist,* published in Bombay and later in Adyar by Madam Blavatsky. After commenting that the spread of socialism was "not alone among the masses" but among "thinkers of unquestioned depth and candour" in Germany, Italy, France, England, and the United States, and after reviewing the history of Utopias and of the "creeds rejoicing in the generic name of Socialism," Fawcett discussed in particular the scientific socialism of St. Simon, who drew "up a scheme applicable not only to isolated groups of men but to the social organism at large," and the followers of Marx, Bebel, and a hundred other notables who were primarily concerned with pointing out the defects of capitalism, with awakening the masses, and not with "formulating paper schemes of legislation which cannot have more than a provisional value relative to immediate economic data." After suggesting that much comfort "has resulted to the working classes as a whole from the great march of politics, enterprise and discovery characteristic of the last two centuries in Europe," Fawcett then remarked that "it is equally true that much remains to be done before a healthy social organism can be expected to put in an appearance."

Turning to Bellamy, he classified him as a constitution-building socialist and—despite the name of Nationalism—as one "of the advanced communistic school." *Looking Backward,* which "embodies a very graceful attempt to formulate a sound working scheme for the administration of the future plan for a Socialist state," resembled, remarked Fawcett, Fourierism in its "treatment of the distribution of tasks and professions" and St. Simonism in the picture of the much talked-about industrial army—but here the resemblance to these two ended although correspondences to other writers might have been mentioned.

Before turning to a survey of *Looking Backward,* Fawcett listed "the main defects of the modern social fabric which appeal so strongly to the sympathies of these reformers"—and in doing so he almost condensed those of Bellamy. Fawcett wrote:

> Needless to say the social fabric is what is known as Western civilization, the only sphere in which the dream of socialism admits of any practical realisation. Socialism, if its investure of the state with enormously extended functions is to succeed, presupposes an educated and all-influential democracy, a general spirit of official integrity, an already highly organized state of

the national industries, and the possession of very large resources in the background. Obviously, therefore, such a momentous step as the nationalisation of Land and Capital is not within the bare horizon of practical politics outside Europe and America. So far, so good. Premising my analysis with this reservation, I may sum up the main points of the socialist indictment against the rule of Capital as follows:

(1) The "humiliating dependence" of the worker on a superior—often a most galling and ignoble yoke, (2) The enormous waste of wealth caused by the faulty competitive methods for the distribution of produce, (3) The "horde of idlers"—landlords, capitalists and otherwise—who at present prey like parasites on the common stock; men, the large majority of whom neither toil nor spin but cleverly "exploit" the worker, (4) The terrible drudgery incidental to the carrying on of the existing civilisation—a drudgery the brunt of which is borne by a despised and brutalised proletariat, (5) The stigma attaching to honest manual and domestic labour, the compensation for which is miserably inadequate to the outlay in the shape of effort, (6) The relegation of the dreariest, most repulsive and worst paid classes of task to one particular stratum of humanity; a practice highly illustrative of the manner in which the best dishes in the feast of life are reserved for the favoured few.

"These six heads," continued Fawcett, "appear . . . to constitute useful enough signposts for directing attention to the various points in the fascinating romance of Bellamy." While relating the story of Julian West, he compared the passage in which West describes the idleness of the rich and burdens of the poor to Zola's *Germinal*, from which he quoted a paragraph; he then compared this to the famous analogy of the coach which he also cited in full. In his review of the new economic system, Fawcett remarked that Bellamy's description of the transition from corporations and trusts to the socialist state had real force; but he doubted that "any such kid-gloved constitutional termination to the long standing feud between employer and employed" would be possible. "Legislative enactments, or the special decrees of National Conventions, would in any case leave a very large, desperate and determined minority to be dealt with. That these millions of men, rich in every resource, knit together by the firmest ties of self-interest, and long prepared for all attempts at what they would naturally consider their 'spoliation,' would tamely submit to socialism is a mere chimera of the optimist. Of a surety, if the socialist regime is ever inaugurated, its baptism will be in the blood of frenzied parties."

After summarizing Bellamy's plan for the industrial army and stating that the "very dangerous tasks, be it noted, are speedily executed if the administration labels them as 'extra-hazardous' owing to the greed of the young men for honour," Fawcett opined that "evidently the socialist state must not ignore the weak side of human nature." He also criticized the equal income of the citizens; for, though "abstractly speaking," the plan was moral and "plausible enough reasoning," he could not believe that

> . . . the average energetic and enterprising man will rest content with this ideal sort of return on his labour. Human nature manifests not only a rational but an emotional element—"justice" being a very fluctuating ideal fashioned by the latter and susceptible of a gradual but relatively slow evolution. And if it is supposed that the temperament of the physical man, stamped as it is with the impress of aeons of individualist striving, can be moulded into so pure a moral tone by the year 2000 A. D., a very grave error is committed. It is scarcely necessary to add that this part of Mr. Bellamy's scheme is but an incorporation of the familiar *communistic* doctrine of Louis Blanc, Owen, and other extremists.
>
> The national spirit essential to the success of any such practice would have to be very considerable. In this connection it is worth noting that "history bears witness to the success with which large bodies of human beings may be trained to feel the public interest their own. And no soil could be more favourable to the growth of such a feeling than a Communist association, since all the ambition, and the bodily and mental activity which are now exerted in the pursuit of separate and self-regarding interests, would require another sphere of employment and would naturally find it in the pursuit of the natural benefit of the community." (Mill). Difficulties, it is obvious, might arise at any time owing to the presence of a large malcontent element led by ambitious men and fostered by secret association, and might render the working of the social machinery very laboured. All would then depend on the mental and moral endowments of the official classes in general.

After remarking that readers interested in other aspects of Bellamy's book would have to read it themselves, Fawcett presented the following assessment:

> The merits of "Looking Backward" are so patent as to require little or no indication. It cannot be said to have burst like a novel stroke of genius on the world, seeing that its ideas of an organized industrial army and of a thorough-going communistic Socialism, were already familiar enough. But its really admirable grasp of detail, and forcible presentation of an Economic

issue in a lucid and popular garb, stamp it as a work of signal ability and usefulness. Defects in its exposition there certainly are. The question of Population—that burning topic of socialist and economic discussions generally—is ignored in a manner which detracts in no small measure from the comprehensiveness of the administrative scheme. Utopian, moreover, to a degree is the moral atmosphere of the so miraculously re-organised United States; no provision having been made for the necessary vicious and selfish elements, that Ahriman of individual "vileness," which runs *pari passu* with the Ormuzd of individual "virtue" in any progressive civilization. And—the really vicious element apart—it is not stated how far the communistic form of politics can itself rest permanent. Many students of sociology hold and hope that the "coming slavery" of communism will at best herald the realisation of the Anarchist programme, and it is certainly difficult to see at what point in this vista of Utopian reforms Innovation is to give up the ghost. The omnipotent demo-cratic state is susceptible of many highly deplorable develop-ments, some of which are almost sure sooner or later to super-vene. In concluding the paper, let me impress on the attention of my more conservative readers the three "broad and simple" rules laid down by John Ruskin in his "Stones of Venice." Were they observed, they would go far to lift the workman from his present monotonous level:—1. Never encourage the manufac-ture of any article not absolutely necessary, in the production of which *Invention* has no share. 2. Never demand an exact finish for its own sake, but only for some practical or noble end. 3. Never encourage imitation or copying of any kind, except for the sake of preserving a record of great works.

Although the London *Theosophical Review,* edited by Annie Besant, mentioned Bellamy's attempt to reconstruct society in an article, "The Wise Way," in 1905-6, *The Path,* also published in London under the editorship of D. N. Dunlop, mentioned Bellamy in its issue of March, 1913, under the title of "Reflections and Refractions": "Edward Bellamy, William Morris, H. G. Wells and many others have from time to time put before us visions of a future state which quicken the imagination to some extent: and probably even before Plato's *Republic* there were many other Utopias presented to the human mind to stimulate the 'seed of perfection' nestling in the heart of man. The latest de-scription of the ideal community I have read is Mr. Leadbeater's sketch of the early beginnings of the Sixth Root Race Colony to be started in about 700 years hence somewhere on the Pacific Coast."

In June, 1919, an article by James Taylor, entitled "Looking Backward" appeared in *The Messenger,* the official publication of the American Theosophical Society. After remarking that most people felt their era to be a bewildering one because "the old social and economic structures which have lasted for centuries are crumbling to pieces and no definite new ones have yet emerged with sufficient clearness to show in what forms the life of the new age will be ensouled," and because there was "the usual clouding of wisdom by 'a multitude of councellors' [sic] who are presenting for acceptance all kinds of schemes . . . guaranteed to cure all the social and economic ills" but which were most "obviously produced at the moment to meet a momentary need," Taylor paid the following tribute to Bellamy:

> Amidst all this clamour and uncertainty, it is refreshing to turn away from the turmoil of the present and seek guidance from one of the most powerful and virile thinkers that this continent has produced—Edward Bellamy, and who in his remarkable book, "Looking Backward," has foreseen with prophetic insight the conditions that exist today, and as a result of profound study shows the way whereby mankind may rise out of present conditions into a higher and simpler and nobler state of life. In this remarkable book a glimpse may be had of a more perfect society toward which mankind is steadily tending, and an examination of the conceptions which it embodies will visualize in many minds the main principles and ideals which will actuate the age.

*Looking Backward,* described Taylor, presented an "outline, in the form of a novel, of an ideal state wherein the principles of brotherhood of souls are carried out to the very highest degree, where in fact a brotherhood of souls would be possible and where the divine faculties in man could find their fullest expression." After reciting statistics about the sale of the novel, Taylor optimistically stated that not only had "this great popularity showed that even then [in the nineteenth century] it struck a responsive chord and proved by its great success that the world is ripe for its reception and in some measure ready for the embodiment of the ideal it contains. The enormous influence it has since exerted on thousands of minds may very possibly have largely contributed to set in operation many of the forces that are now making for a reconstruction of society on an altruistic basis." Taylor then declared that there was—according to booksellers and librarians—an increased demand for the book which indicated "a great recurrence of interest in the reconstruction schemes which it outlines."

After quoting Madam Blavatsky's recommendation of *Looking*

*Backward in Key to Theosophy,* Taylor referred the readers to the book with assurance that her endorsement of it would make them regard it "with more than usual interest" and make them feel "that added authority has been given to his conceptions." In fact, the aim of the article, bluntly stated Taylor, was not to describe the novel but to "direct the attention of readers to the book itself so that they may glimpse a vision of the high ideals which it holds up as possible for attainment of the race."

Taylor was not content to halt with his recommendation, however, for he continued to discuss Bellamy's concepts:

Bellamy's State may be said to be the ideal State as far as mankind at present can see. It is founded on the theory that things material have a spiritual basis and that the soul in man is more important than his body; that spiritual values are the true aim in life, and that reconstruction, like all other things, will only be true and permanent in so far as it approximates to spiritual ideals. It entirely reverses our present standard of values, whereby we judge of the greatness of a nation by its Banking and Clearing House Returns, its imports and exports, its bales of cotton manufactures, etc., and places the national greatness on the health, the moral welfare and the high intellectual standards of its citizens. It holds that the physical and material needs of all men are approximately the same, differing only in detail, and that the needs of the highest and the lowest can best be met by consolidating all the natural resources of the State and allowing each individual to share in the joint product of these resources on the one basis, to which no exception can be taken—the basis of their common humanity. When these physical needs have been met, individual men will be free to cultivate their higher natures, intellectually, morally and spiritually, for it is evident that the time has now come in the evolutionary development of the race when it is no longer possible to continue a system that demands that nine-tenths of the citizens of each country should devote three-fourths of their time to their purely physical requirements.

After this interpretation of the basic aims of *Looking Backward*—which far surpasses that of Alfred Kazin and of Lewis Mumford, both of whom regarded Bellamy as essentially a materialist—Taylor pointed out just as astutely that Bellamy's Utopian scheme differed from others because of "its definite idea of industrial organization on a national basis" and because of "the equality of allotment to all persons of the products of industry, or the public income, on the same ground that men share equally in the free gifts of nature, such as air and water; it being absolutely impossible to determine any equitable ratio between individual industrial efforts and individual shares in industrial products on a graded basis.

> Bellamy regarded equality in material well-being as essential to the true spiritual development of the race, or, in other words, he maintains that the ethics of the Sermon on the Mount are the only sound and, in the last analysis, the only possible economic basis on which a State can be built. These ethics are not only of the highest moral and religious import but are also the soundest business principles and the one foundation on which a lasting system of political economy can be built.

After stating that Bellamy was "an artist and a poet as well as a great political economist" and that *Looking Backward* had "a very high place among the great novels of the last century," Taylor considered why Bellamy appealed to the Theosophists— or should. First of all, like "all idealists, he intuitively glimpses many Theosophical truths. He recognizes the unerring operations of the law of cause and effect and in one place his heroine expresses a belief in Reincarnation. In the same way he talks of the 'Evolutionary Journey of Mankind' and refers to what Theosophists would call 'the path of return,' by saying that the return of God is twofold: First, the return of the individual, and second, the return of the race." Taylor admitted, however, that not all Theosophists would accept the book; but reading it would "have a lasting effect for it is charged with that spiritual vitality which stirs into activity the noblest in the reader."

In considering the effect of *Looking Backward*, Taylor quoted a "recent writer" who had remarked that "in many instances it has aroused those who were quite satisfied with the present order of things to a burning zeal for improvement." Taylor asserted that "no one could possibly come into contact with its transcendent beauty and remain quite the same person afterwards" but he also felt that other benefits were to be derived from it. Anyone reading the book would "acquire a knowledge of some of the fundamental conditions of Social Government and Economics which are basic in their constitution and nature, and that in itself is of enormous importance at the present time." For the Theosophists, having these "fundamentals before them" would enable them to "hold their balance amidst the many conflicting schemes of reform offered for their acceptance" and help them "more intelligently to throw their weight in favour of all influences that are clearly making for a truer realization of a brotherhood of souls and for a higher and fuller expression of the divine powers in man."

Taylor stated that to many readers

. . . the scheme is too ideal for the present time, too impossible of attainment—that something more "practical" is needed and that, of course, means something more sordid. In an age of compromise like the present, when the highest is usually sacrificed to the lower, and when expediency is the watchword, the higher ideals are usually lost sight of and less altruistic ones take their place. This is very disappointing so far as ideals go because just as ideals decline, so will attainments decline in like proportion. Emerson's advice in regard to "hitching our wagon to a star" is absolutely necessary for, unless the very highest is visualized, there will be a corresponding loss in practical results. In fact, if all material things have a spiritual basis, then the idealistic is the only reality because it is the nearest in the heart of things and if put into operation would run more smoothly and be of more permanence than any less ideal scheme, for the nearer we approach to the Ideal, to the archetypal, the more permanent do our intuitions become, and difficulties are experienced just in so far as we fail to reproduce archetypal forms. What the world needs at the present time then is more Idealism and the way to attain it expressed in clear mental forms; and Theosophists are pre-eminently capable of giving a lead in in that direction. For by "peopling the magnetic field" with reconstruction forms of this kind they will exert an enormous influence on public opinion, and prepare for a great revolutionary step forward.

In the two closing paragraphs of his article, Taylor once more pointed out the pertinence of Bellamy's ideas to those of Theosophists and then defended his author's concepts.

To the Theosophists as such, whose one "Credo" is the Brotherhood of man, "Looking Backward" is an exceedingly interesting and important contribution to a difficult subject. It is the most successful attempt to apply in the field of economics the spiritual law, that all men are brothers, the children of one common father. It clearly establishes beyond argument and doubt that the same laws and feelings should pervade the state as permeate the life of a family. It agrees with Mrs. Besant that the very word "Brotherhood" implies an identity of blood and interests but not of ability and from that foundation principle builds the whole social and economic structure.

We have in the private family individuals of all ages, with different temperaments and ideals, yet are not all the essentials of life held in common? If any difference at all is made is it not the youngest and weakest who receive most of the benefits and do not the older and stronger delight in sacrificing for them?

As we gain in spiritual insight we will see that the same law that now rules in the family must ultimately rule in that larger family—the nation—and finally throughout the whole of mankind. Towards the realization of such an ideal consummation, Edward Bellamy's book will have played an important part.

In December, 1923, a letter to the editor—J. Krishnamurti, head of the Order of the Star in the East—in the *Herald of the Star* read:

> With reference to Major Galloway's excellent article in the August issue entitled "If the Atom is Exploded," I have recently read a very interesting book, wherein the hero in the year 2000 is awakened from a trance to find the Industrial Problem has been solved while he slept. Everyone is employed on the work to which he or she is most suited, no wages are given, but every person has a credit card for the same value, so no one is richer than another, and no snobbishness exists. In fact it appears to be Utopia, and not an impossible one I think, if we take Major Galloway's advice and get a "move on." The title of the book is "Looking Backward, 2000-1887" by Edward Bellamy.
>
> I am sure members will enjoy it, and will afterwards read Major Galloway's article, and start thinking and I hope acting. [Signed] A Member.

In the 1938-39 volume of the *Canadian Theosophist*, the official publication of the country's Theosophical Society, reference was made to the recently republished *Key to Theosophy* of H. P. Blavatsky at a time when there had been, as noted in the Canadian chapter, revival of Bellamyism in Canada. After stating that H. P. Blavatsky had "spoken very highly of this book, and of the Nationalist Clubs—one of which was established in Toronto, most of the founders being members of the Toronto Theosophical Society," the author commented that the book presented "a state of society that has taken the first great step towards the full realization of universal brotherhood."

In considering equality, the writer stated: "long before Bellamy's time 'Equality' was the magic word that would bring well being to all. In due time it became clear that there was no such thing as equality in Nature. The cry was changed to 'Equality of Opportunity.' But this too is elusive. For the ability of men to meet their brothers on equal terms is rendered impossible by all the difference of soul age that is inevitable and unavoidable." Although the writer ignored that Bellamy did not expect men to be or think themselves equal in soul capacity or sensitivity, the author did not condemn Bellamy completely;

for he felt that seers like Henry George and Bellamy—as well as occultism—had shown that man is not helpless in solving "the problem of increasing poverty that automatically goes hand in hand with growing wealth rendered possible by cheap power and scientific research." In the end of the article, the author recommended *Looking Backward* by once more quoting Blavatsky's statement that it was a "magnificent work" and that it "should be the first great step toward the full realization of Universal Brotherhood."

The April-May issue of 1942 of *The Link,* the publication of the South African Theosophical Society, carried an article considering the reconstruction of the world after the end of the war. The author stated: "Another point is that it is my firm belief that no general reconstruction of the world after the war is possible unless the whole control of money is placed in the hands of the Government of the post-war world. The Bellamy system explains very fully and concisely how this can be done, and his book 'Looking Backward' gives every detail and explains every possible eventuality in such a clear manner that it should recommend itself strongly to all advocates of social and financial reforms. The financial reform of the world's monetary system should, I think, be the very first factor in all world problems of reconstruction." After once more quoting Blavatsky to the effect that "Bellamy's ideas were in line with the future race," the author referred anyone interested to write to "our great Bellamy expert, Mr. T. F. Day, Box 7060, Johannesburg."

As late as 1950 *The Aryan Path,* published in Bombay, India, under the editorship of Sophia Wadia, celebrated the centenary of the birth of Edward Bellamy by publishing an obviously requested article about her father by Mrs. Marion Bellamy Earnshaw. In the editor's note to the article, Sophia Wadia wrote:

> . . . this year marks the centenary of the birth of the eminent American thinker and lover of justice and of humankind, Edward Bellamy. The centenary has been observed in more than one country. The Internationale Vereeniging Bellamy at Ede, Holland, has brought out a memorial issue of their monthly paper, with contributions by Mr. Bellamy's wife, son, and daughter and by Dr. Arthur E. Morgan, his appreciative biographer. American libraries have arranged memorial exhibits and in Los Angeles a centenary dinner was arranged, with a tableau of Mr. Bellamy's famous "Parable of the Water Tank," and the launching on the same occasion of a Bellamy Foundation for the propagation of his gospel of Equality. A film of *Looking Back-*

*ward* is reported to be planned. It is hopeful that many today are
reading his message and considering sympathetically the scheme
of economic and social organization which he worked out with
so much earnest and self-sacrificing zeal; because its implemen-
tation would be a long step towards the full realization of universal brotherhood.

After thanking Mrs. Earnshaw for writing the article for *The
Aryan Path,* Sophia Wadia ended her introduction with the
following: "We take the occasion to express our own high
appreciation of the nobility of the ideals and life of Edward
Bellamy."

Although these articles are interesting because they indicate the
lasting interest in Bellamy and the reasons for it of the Theosophists, they are more important because they show that articles
about Bellamy were accessible to many Indians interested in
the society. Furthermore, Sophia Wadia, editor of *The Aryan
Path,* the monthly publication of the Indian Institute of World
Culture at Bangalore of which she is also president, and of
*P. E. N.,* the monthly bulletin of the All-India Centre, stated
in a letter of September 15, 1959, that nearly three decades
ago many articles about Bellamy appeared in some of the Indian
journals in English and in others in the Indian dialects.

According to Madam Wadia, who herself became interested
in Bellamy in 1923 when she read Blavatsky's *Key to Theosophy,*
the Theosophists took the initiative in popularizing the teachings
of Bellamy. Hindi and Sindhi versions of *Looking Backward*
were prepared for publication; and articles about him were published in two other English journals of the organization in India
besides *The Theosophist of Adyar: The Indian Theosophist of
Varanasi,* and *The Young Builder of Karachi* (now West Pakistan). One ardent Theosophist of the Adyar school, Professor
Jethmal Parsram Gulrajani, of Hyderabad, Sindh (now in West
Pakistan), not only wrote articles in Sindhi in his publication
*Hindrasi* about Bellamy but attempted to put into practice some
of the principles enunciated by the Utopian. When the professor
and his family migrated from Hyderabad to India, they were
forced to leave all publications and papers behind them; and
the professor died in 1948.

Professor D. V. K. Raghavachari reported in a letter of April
23, 1959, that Sophia Wadia had told him that the Young Radicals of India during the 1920's were interested in Bellamy and
in Carpenter, both of whom were known by Gandhi—as were the
Theosophists. In fact, both Gandhi and Nehru were interested

by Theosophy and both famous leaders of the Indian people when they were studying in England frequented circles interested in the ideas of the American Utopian.

In the very early 1890's when Bellamy was popular among the Fabians, the Theosophists, and the suffragettes, Gandhi, not yet twenty-one, had already met both Dr. Annie Besant and Helena Blavatsky; he had been introduced to them by two bachelor brothers who were also Theosophists. Professor Arthur H. Nethercot indicates in his excellent *The First Five Lives of Annie Besant* (1960) that Gandhi "felt himself unworthy to touch" the garments of either the founder of the Theosophical society or of her dynamic convert who later became a leader of the organization.[6] Although Gandhi never became a Theosophist, he did read Blavatsky's *Key to Theosophy*, which stimulated his interest in Hinduism and rid him of the Christian concept that it was "rife with superstition."[7] As Nethercot points out, Gandhi always retained a respect for Theosophy "as being Hinduism at its best" and as a preachment of the "brotherhood of man."[8] When Gandhi became a powerful leader many years after his sojourn in England, he was impressed when he discovered that in the beginning "the top Congressmen were Theosophists."

When Gandhi wrote that he had many political differences with Dr. Annie Besant but that his "veneration for her did not suffer abasement,"[9] he might well have been discussing his attitude toward Bellamy. Although future research work should be done to locate the references which Sophia Wadia reported Gandhi had made in his publication, Shri Pyarelal, the secretary of the director of Gandhi Sanghralaya, wrote in a letter of April 2, 1960, that Gandhi's "difference with Bellamy's views . . . was confined to the Western craze for mechanization of life."[10] According to Pyarelal, Gandhi was referring to Bellamy and to this difference of opinion with him when he wrote in his banned book *Hind Swaraj* or *Indian Home Rule*—material first published in his weekly *Indian Opinion* in 1909—the following:

It has been stated that, as men progress, they shall be able to travel in airships and reach any part of the world in a few hours. Men will not need the use of their hands and feet. They will press a button, and they will have their clothing by their side. They will press another button, and they will have their newspaper. A third, and a motorcar will be in waiting for them. They will have a variety of delicately dished up food. Everything will be done by machinery. . . . There are now diseases of which people never dreamt before, and an army of doctors

is engaged in finding out their cures, and so hospitals have increased. This is a test of civilization. . . . Formerly, people had
two or three meals consisting of home-made bread and vege-
tables; now, they require something to eat every two hours so
that they have hardly leisure for anything else. What more
need I say? . . . . Civilization seeks to increase bodily comforts,
and it fails miserably even in doing so. . . . This civilization is
irreligion, and it has taken such a hold on the people in Europe
that those who are in it appear to be half mad. They lack real
physical strength or courage. They keep up their energy by
intoxication. They can hardly be happy in solitude. Women,
who should be the queens of households, wander in the streets
or they slave away in factories. For the sake of a pittance, half
a million women in England alone are labouring under trying
circumstances in factories or similar institutions. This awful fact
is one of the causes of the daily growing suffragette movement.
This civilization is such that one has only to be patient and it
will be self-destroyed . . . civilization is not an incurable disease, but it should never be forgotten that the English people
are at present afflicted by it.

Sophia Wadia* stated in a letter of September 15, 1959, that
she had been told that Gandhi's colleague, the late Mr. Mash-
ruwala, had made a special study of Bellamy's principles. Further research needs to be done to determine whether Gandhi's
ideas of non-violence, of universal brotherhood, and of unselfish
service were influenced not only by Thoreau but by Bellamy,
Theosophy, and his own native religion. Certainly Gandhi recognized that many of the top leaders of the National Congress
were Theosophists; and Professor Nethercote relates in *The First
Five Lives of Annie Besant*[11] that many prominent Hindus
and Brahmins joined the Theosophical Society in the days when
Bellamy's ideas were being propagandized by it. Among those
were A. O. Hume, the leader and chairman of the Indian
National Congress; Damodar K. Mavalankar; and A. P. Sinnett,
editor of the Allahabad *Pioneer*. A future study of the lives of
these men and of those Gandhi referred to so vaguely *might*
uncover interesting information about the impact Bellamy made
upon them.

---

* Sophia Wadia's statements should be considered seriously; for, as
Professor Ragavachari stated in his letter of September 29, 1959, "she
belongs to the generation of Indian intellectuals who had actively
participated both in the Theosophical and the Nationalist movements.
She knows Prime Minister Nehru and the rest of the Socialist and
non-Socialist leaders personally, and they have a great regard for her."

Among the members of the Theosophical Society not listed by Nethercot is a name famous the world round—Nehru. In his book *Toward Freedom* (1941), Nehru related how, when he was eleven years old, he had an English tutor named Ferdinand T. Brooks, who stimulated his interest in books and in science. As a result of Brook's guidance, Nehru became a member of the Theosophical Society at thirteen.[12] After studying at Harrow and Trinity College, Cambridge, Nehru went to London to study law; there he became "vaguely attracted to the Fabians and socialistic ideas" and was particularly interested in the woman's suffrage movement.[13] Nehru was, therefore, conversant with three groups who were vitally interested in Bellamy.

Although nothing can definitely be stated about whether or not he was acquainted with Bellamy's ideas, a review of the changing attitudes of Nehru indicate that he well might have been—or that he may have been influenced not only by current events but by members of the National Planning Committee or other Indian leaders to change his concepts. According to Sophia Wadia in her letter of September 15, 1959, she was told that "Shriman Narayan, at present a member of the Planning Commission, also had studied Bellamy." A letter to the Indian Government brought forth a denial; but this does not necessarily indicate that Wadia's information was incorrect; for few governments would wish to be considered as having been influenced by a Utopian or as having implemented his concepts.*

As we review the changing concepts of Nehru and the objectives of the Indian government of today, it becomes apparent that both are quite comparable to ideas and objectives Bellamy entertained. In 1926, Nehru had a broad knowledge of communism; in 1936, he studied Marx and Engels but disliked their and Russia's oppressive and violent measures; and he recognized that, although socialism might be the answer to India's problems, it had to be adjusted to fit the needs of the country. In the 1940's, shocked by the opportunism and the imperialism of the Marx-

---

* In substantiation of this statement is a letter from the U.S.S.R. Embassy of the United States dated July 26, 1934, to Mrs. Edward Bellamy who had written on December 3, 1933, to enquire about her husband's influence. The letter to her stated that the Soviet Society for Cultural Relations had determined that "no editions of Mr. Bellamy's books have appeared in his country since the October revolution of 1917" and that the translation made before the war had been out of print "for about twenty years."

ists, he rejected Marxist communism. In 1935, Nehru had, however, espoused the idea of the class struggle; but, by 1955, he sponsored national unity and emphasized that the common interests of all classes were to be considered in the development of the resources of his country. In 1935, he had also believed that socialism could never be successfully implemented through democratic processes because capitalistic interests would prevent its development; by 1955, he believed that the socialist state had to be attained through democratic processes and that this, in fact, was the "only way to build up a socialist state on a firm foundation." Nehru viewed the parliamentary system as the best one to provide action for such a development.

When we review his attitudes toward Western democracy and Eastern communism and the objectives of the Indian government, further resemblances to Bellamy become noticeable. First of all, Nehru made it clear in *The Discovery of India* that "all the evils of a purely political democracy are evident in the U. S. A.; the evils of the lack of political democracy are present in the U.S.S.R."[14] Furthermore he believed—reports Donald Smith in *Nehru and Democracy*—that capitalism stimulated greed for private profit and that it had to be destroyed "in order to develop new and more desirable habits and ways of thinking."[15] Furthermore, to Nehru the cooperative effort required by collectivism was more "fully in harmony with old Indian social conceptions, which were all based on the idea of the group."[16]

When Nehru defined democracy, as reported in Norman Cousins' *Talk with Nehru,* he stated: "I would say that democracy is not only political, not only economic, but something of the mind, as everything is ultimately something of the mind. It involves equality of opportunity to all people, as far as possible, in the political and economic domain. It involves the freedom of the individual to grow and to make the best of his capacities and ability. It involves a certain tolerance of others and even of others' opinions when they differ from yours. It involves a certain contemplative tendency and a certain inquisitive search for truth—and for, let us say, the right."[17]

Nehru's aspirations became, therefore, the attainment of an *economic democracy* to be achieved through economic and social equality and through a slow transition toward state ownership of the means of production. Nehru's objective, adopted by the Congress Working Committee as its economic program, became, recorded Smith in *Nehru and Democracy,* "the establishment of a 'Welfare State' wherein there is economic democracy, a national minimum standard in respect to the essentials of physical and social well-being, a rise in the standards of living of the people, full employment, elimination of exploitation, the progressive narrowing down of disparities in income and wealth, so that there may be equality of opportunity to all for self-development and the growth of personality."[18] Nehru also stated in his radio address of December 31, 1952, that he was striving for a fundamental change in the social-economic structure: "We have to aim deliberatley at a social philosophy which seeks a fundamental transformation of this structure; at a society which is not dominated by the urge for private profit and by individual greed and in which there is fair distribution of political and economic power."[19]

Whether or not the ideas of Bellamy influenced Nehru or others of his planning commission, his objectives are in keeping with those of the American Utopian. Although the possibility of the influence of Bellamy upon Nehru is today purely speculative, the influence of the author of *Looking Backward* upon some other prominent Indian leaders is ascertainable. M. Pratap, now a member of the Indian Parliament, reported in his letter of December 6, 1958, that "in 1908, a great reader of books, Sardar Jugendra Singh told me that my views were similar to [those of] the author of *Looking Backward*. I got the book and I was thrilled to see that indeed we were thinking alike. It must have further influenced me. Sardar Jugendra Singh later became a minister of Punjab under the British." Mr. Pratap further stated that he himself had left India in 1914; had sought the aid of the German Kaiser, the Sultan of Turkey, and the Amir of Afghanistan in an attempt to free India before World War I; and that, after it, he had sought the aid in 1919 of Lenin. Pratap is the author of *The Book of the Religion of Love* and the publisher of *World Federation*, which he began publishing in Berlin in 1929.

Sibnarayan Ray, a well-known Indian leader and writer, wrote in his letter of September 28, 1956, that one book in Bengali had been inspired by Bellamy's *Looking Backward*. The author of *Anāgata Sudiner Tarey* (For The Happy Days Not Yet Arrived) was Mr. Hemchandra Kanungo, a "leading figure in the Bengal Revolutionary Movement of the first decade of the present century," who had been sent to Paris to learn the techniques of the secret revolutionary societies. After he had learned the art of making bombs and using explosives, he returned to Bengal only to be exiled by the British to the Andamans. He related in the Introduction to his book that while there, he was given a copy of *Looking Backward* by a British soldier; he read the book, which made a profound impression upon him and lead him to read *Equality*.

As a result, Mr. Kanungo dropped his close connections with the anarchists and Communists of Paris, and wrote his book of some two hundred and twenty-six pages, which is an exposition of the ideas of Bellamy in the form of a long dialogue between a man and a woman. *Anāgata* was written after Kanungo's return from the Andamans; it was published in 1946 before the author's death by Professor B. N. Banerji, Renaissance Publishers, 15, Bankim Chatterjee Street, Calcutta-12. Although Sibnarayan Ray stated that he did not know whether the book had "any great influence in Bengal," he could report that "Socialist ideas have been quite strong with our intellectuals from the beginning of the present century." Professor Ragavachari also reported in his letter of June 24, 1957, that—according to a Bengali colleague, Dr. Ila Sen, with whom he was discussing the work of Kanungo—Duggirala Gopalakrishnayya of Chirala was, like Kanungo, interested in the work of Bellamy.

Although this material about Bellamy in India is in part speculative, it also indicates that future research may discover that Bellamy played an important role in the formation of Indian aspirations and political-economic objectives if the following areas are fully investigated: the political ideas of the politicians converted to Theosophy; the parallels with Bellamy that exist in the socio-economic thinking of such Indian thinkers as Tilak, Gokhale, M. N. Roy, Narain, Ashok Mehta, Chintamani, Ranade, and others; and the lives and influence of others mentioned in this study as having been ascertainably influenced by Bellamy. At this moment all that can be said with certainty is that many Indian leaders were acquainted with his ideas and that many of them played important roles in Indian history.

*Looking Backward* would have appealed to them for the same reason it appealed to Theosophists: it sponsored universal brotherhood and unity; it emphasized the spiritual and intellectual development of humanity; it taught peaceful evolution and not revolution; and it taught that men of the right spirit might create a better world. As S. Radhakrishnan remarked in "The Culture of India," "Perfection can be achieved only through self-conquest, through courage and austerity, through unity and brotherhood in life." In fact, if Indians had been able to read Bellamy's *Religion of Solidarity*, they would have accepted him as a brother in spirit—as indeed he was both because of his view of man's relationship to man, God, and to dogmatic

religious beliefs, and because of his emphasis upon the importance of the spiritual life if development of any kind were
to be achieved.

## II  *China and Japan*

The first translation into Chinese of *Looking Backward* was
made by Timothy Richard, the novel appearing in abridged
form under the title (translated into English) of *Awakening
100 Years After.* Published in Shanghai in 1893 by the Society
for the Diffusion of Christian and General Knowledge, which
later became the Christian Literary Society, reprints of the
book appeared as late as 1920. Because of the current political
situation, it was impossible to get further information about
Bellamy in China; but an interesting story about his influence
upon the early revolutionary leaders of the Chinese may someday be related by future researchers.

The story of Bellamy in Japan, however, is more complete.
According to Iyoji Aono, associate librarian of the University
of Tokyo, and Shiro Sugai, director of the reference division
of the National Diet Library, three editions of *Looking Backward* were published in Japan in 1903, 1904, and 1953. Professor
Masaki Yamamoto of Meiji University's English Department,
the most recent translator of *Looking Backward,* related in a
report that the first edition of 1903 appeared under the title:
*The Society One Hundred Years Hence.* Translated by Hirogoro
Hirai, an enlightened liberal who suggested in his postscript
to the book that Bellamy's ideas were "very remarkable and
enlightening for liberal-thinking intellectuals," the novel was
published by Kesei-sha, a progressive publishing house whose
name in translation means "awakening, enlightening." This publisher also released books about democracy, socialism, syndi-
calism, anarchism, and comparable subjects.

Since industrialism and capitalism were still in an early stage
in Japan in 1903, and since class-consciousness among the laborers was not acute and was very slow to awaken, Professor
Yamamoto doubts that the first edition of *Looking Backward*
had a very large following in the rather limited reading circles
of the day. The translation itself was not a very good one, but
it may have found an audience among the intellectual, liberal,
middle class which was "imitative, amateurish, and embryonic"
in its advanced ideas.

The second edition of *Looking Backward,* published under the
translated title of *The New Society One Hundred Years Hence,*
in 1904, was translated by Kosen Sakai, one of the pioneer so-

cialists of Japan. Although he abridged the book, he was obviously eager to use it for socialistic propaganda purposes. The publisher of the pamphlet of some thirty pages was the Heiminsha Press, which professed to publish books about democratic processes and governments for the enlightenment of the people. *Looking Backward* appeared in its "Commoner's Library Series," and the publisher reduced the already low price of the books in it in order to sell Kosen Sakai's booklet in "lump purchases." The book, reports Professor Yamamoto, was widely read by those either vaguely or professedly interested in socialism.

Although these editions without doubt attracted the interest of the earlier socialists and even contributed to attracting others to socialism, later socialists turned to Marxism in its radical or revised form; as a result, they gave little attention to Edward Bellamy's famous Utopian novel. Finally the government became so alarmed by the gradual increase of foreign social and political concepts and movements that it suppressed all books about Marxism, socialism, anarchism, or radicalism of any kind— and this ban included Bellamy's *Looking Backward*.

Professor Yamamoto received his copy of *Looking Backward* from an American in Luzon; this secondhand Modern Library edition served as the text which he used for his complete edition of *Looking Backward*, published in 1953 by Iwanami Press, which does not follow any party line but is "definitely progressive and democratic" in its editorial policy. Professor Yamamoto stated that he translated the novel because he "took a fancy" to it "as a Utopian romance . . . [which tended] to kindle in youthful minds a yearning for a better world to live in. . . ." Therefore, he did not, he writes, translate *Looking Backward* because it was a "document of socialist propaganda."

Published immediately after the censorship was abolished, *Looking Backward* had sold three thousand copies by 1958; and, since the reviews of the work were favorable, there was a prospect that more reprints would be made and sold. Professor Yamamoto uses the book in his college classes; and he reported also that "some study groups are reading" it but that "neither political parties nor labor movement groups are reading it systematically."

In the postscript to his edition of *Looking Backward*, which Professor Yamamoto kindly translated, he indicates first of all that Utopian romances are certain to have many "enthusiastic readers" and that

. . . the mind without any kind of Utopia is as a rule rather less sensible of the immediate realities of life and accordingly commits blunder after blunder because it drifts with the superficial currents of the time. Most thoughtful people have a Utopia —whether of their own creating or of their borrowing from others, whether relatively well systematized or relatively loosely coordinated—but, at any rate, their own Utopia.

A Utopia is born from the experience and judgment of the realities of life as an ideal opposed to the follies and irrationalities of the real life. So a man with a Utopia in his mind has acute insight and appreciation of the realities of life, and his emotions and feelings are at once deep and ardent. All of these constitute part of the motive power of innovation and reconstruction.

But one may say, on the other hand, that Utopians are apt to indulge in the dreams of their self-made Utopias; to escape from real life; and, consequently, to thwart, through their self-righteousness, general innovations.

A Utopia is an ideal born as an antithesis to the follies and irrationalities of actual life, but once it has been born it begins to develop as an ideology independent of the movements of actual life and ends in consolidating itself as a world with a system that is complete and perfect in itself—and which leaves an ever-widening gulf between itself and the actual world.

Utopians sharpen their observation and judgment of the actual life from their Utopian point of view, but the object—the people—to whom the Utopians can hope to appeal is limited; the world at large—the proper object to which the Utopians want to appeal—is beyond their reach; and the leading or ruling classes are naturally hostile to them and, as a rule, use every means to counter-attack or persecute them.

Accordingly most Utopians give up the immediate direct appeal to the present world; console themselves by being absorbed in the dream of their own Utopia; and entrust the hope of realization to the posterity through their present—however small in number—followers and sympathizers.

Several notable works of Utopian literature since the *Utopia* of More are part of the results of these circumstances. All the genuine men of letters are more or less Utopian, who may or may not write their own Utopian romances, but do observe and criticize the society and men of their time from the view point of their own Utopia and then write their novels and romances with their Utopian enthusiasm.

Society, however conservative it may be, will change more or less steadily. Various changes in economy, culture, and politics are affected through the advances of science and the conditions of production; and the organizations, formerly thought to be Utopian, become realized. So the relative progressive radicalism of each Utopia will change in contrast with the progress of ages.

Thus Utopias, unless they are constantly revised and reconstructed, are exposed to the danger of becoming supporting props for the conservatives or the reactionaries. And a large number of Utopians are apt to overlook the significance of their Utopias' relationship to the times, to hold one of the notable Utopias as the Golden Rule, to be intoxicated by it, and to escape from the realities into self-righteousness. All of us who love Utopias must be aware of these points.

After stating the facts about the publication of *Looking Backward*, its popularity in the United States, the atmosphere of discussion and conflict which produced it, and the complimentary statements made about it by Howells, Frances Willard—the American suffragette leader—and E. C. Stedman, Professor Yamamoto then speculated that Bellamy had probably come in contact with the ideas of Marx when he studied in Germany; he also stated that Bellamy had said in the article in *The Nationalist* of May, 1889, that he had begun his novel as a novel of social felicity and not as a serious contribution to the social reform movement.

Professor Yamamoto then wrote:

A feature, which is common to the Utopian romances of all time and which makes the romances fantastic or Utopian, is the fact that they fail to give any convincing comment as to how and through what process the ideal conditions of the new society have been achieved. In this respect, *Looking Backward* is almost the one exception. The idea, the way, and the process that led to the new order of society are stated pretty clearly in this book. According to Dr. Leete, the followers of the red flag—who waved the red flag and talked about burning, sacking, and blowing people up—had nothing to do with the establishment of the new order of things, except to hinder it. The labor parties, as such, never could have accomplished anything on a large or permanent scale. For purposes of national scope, their basis as merely class organizations was too narrow. It was not until a rearrangement of the industrial and social system on a higher ethical basis and for the more efficient production of wealth was recognized as the interest not of one class but equally of all classes—rich and poor, cultured and ignorant, old and young, weak and strong, men and women—that there was any prospect that it would be achieved. Then the national party arose to carry it out by political methods. It probably took that name because its aim was to nationalize the functions of production and dis-

tribution. . . . The most patriotic of all possible parties, it sought
to justify patriotism and raise it from an instinct to a rational
devotion by making the native land truly a fatherland.

To wait for the consent of all would seem to the impatient
a long postponement of the millenium; yet the postponement,
Bellamy argued, need not be long. The over-reaching greed of
private capitalism was daily hastening it. The new order must
come about speedily as a necessary consequence of two forces:
the compulsion of economic fact and the stimulus of new ideas.
Readers may differ on this point. I offer this translation for
the readers to make their decisions.

Aside from the interest of the early socialist leader, Kosen
Sakai, and of the liberal Hirogoro Hirai, Bellamy is known to
have interested the famous Japanese social reformer and evan-
gelist, Toyohiko Kagawa (1888-1960). The latter, on one of the
four visits he made to the United States, visited Mrs. Marion
Bellamy Earnshaw, the daughter of Edward Bellamy, to talk
with her about her father whom he said had interested and
influenced him. Kagawa, the son of a nobleman and a concu-
bine, was converted to Christianity by a Presbyterian mission-
ary when he was fifteen. He studied for several years at Princeton University where he earned three degrees. After his return
to his native country, he became a powerful influence in Japanese life. He traveled the length of Japan organizing cooperatives and labor unions, and achieved a worldwide reputation
as a specialist on the cooperative movement. Kagawa also organized over two hundred and fifty churches in Japan; but he
identified himself with no particular denomination and, as
soon as a church was organized, he found a good leader to
whom he could relinquish it. After 1927 his power in Japan
was somewhat diminished because he had criticized his country for its war with China. Later, however, he supported the
war against the United States. After the end of World War II,
Kagawa continued his work among the masses of Japan despite
the opposition of the Communists. He believed that work
among the nation's farmers gave him the best opportunity to
preach the gospel for moral reform.

The story of Bellamy in Japan is an old one; but it is also
one for which a new chapter may eventually be written. If Professor Yamamoto and—as he indicated in his letter—other professors of Japan, who are notably liberal or left-wing, are using
*Looking Backward* in their classes, many of the already radical
students who will be the future leaders of Japan are being

exposed to a book which has been considered by many practiced revolutionaries and propagandists to be a powerful critique of capitalism and a successful converter to socialism of all
varieties. Since Japanese youth is restive and radical and many
Japanese—because of their war guilt—feel a desire to be closely
associated with Red China, pondering over *Looking Backward*
could encourage them to use their parliamentary processes to
achieve a better order—or it could promote in them a greater
drift toward Marxism and China.

# CHAPTER FIFTEEN

# Patterns of Criticism, Influence, Future Research

AS WE SURVEY the criticism, the influence, and the use of Bellamy's Utopian fiction around the world and in the United States, we find not only that certain patterns exist but also that those of the nineteenth century were often broken in the twentieth. The industrial, political, and governmental changes and experiences which occurred after Bellamy's Utopias were published must be considered in assessing not only the early but the later critical evaluations—and so must many comments which have been made about some of his concepts.

## I  *American and Foreign Criticism*

Because a detailed summation of the many foreign and American criticisms would consume too many pages, this discussion must be limited to a consideration of only the broad, general, but important basic criticisms which were leveled at Bellamy's ideal state—criticisms he studied with interest because they might contribute ideas to the ideal society which he had considered by no means static and which he himself developed at the same time that he answered his critics in *Equality*. Among the major concerns of the critics were: the role of the government, the regimentation of the citizenry, the plan for achieving the ideal state, technological development, economic equality and the motivation of the worker, and the religious characteristics of the ideal society.

When *Looking Backward* was written, Bellamy had intended to present a plan for an industrial democracy which would destroy plutocracy, restore the truly democratic voice of the people and preserve the liberty, the freedom, and the pursuit of happiness granted by the Constitution, the Declaration of Independence, and the political system which had evolved from them. Although some Germans and Russians thought that Bellamy's government should be replaced by a monarchial form

which would provide the military power necessary to implement
his plan, most American and foreign critics charged him with
attempting to dispossess people of their political rights, their
individuality, and their initiative.

First of all, A. D. Vinton,[1] L. Gronlund,[2] and General F. A.
Walker[3] asserted that Bellamy was advocating a militaristic
government as was also feared by some of the French and Polish
critics; W. L. Garrison,[4] Joel Benton,[5] and Spencer[6] all asserted
that his centralized system would lead to "tyranny, absolute and
unqualified"; and de Laveleye and Americans alike suggested
that his paternalistic state would resemble that of the Incas;[7]
others like William Morris and Henry George denounced a centralized collective government; the first preferred the small
communal unit and no system,[8] and the second stated that turning back to the "socialism of the tribal state" would be retro-
gression and that anything which savored of "regulation and
restriction" was bad; furthermore, George opined "that *laissez-
faire* (in its full true meaning) opens the way to realization of
the noble dreams of socialism"—if, of course, the single-tax
were applied to land.[9]

Although many of the German and French critics realized that
capitalism needed some governmental control because of the
great differences in existing economic conditions, American
W. L. Garrison, a firm believer in Darwin's theory of the survival of the fittest, felt that laissez-faire was the only answer
to the existing problems; he aired his views about government
interference in the following terms: whenever governments
"have undertaken to meddle with industrial functions, disaster
has followed. The clumsy feet of legislation mark a pathway
of woe. In despotic governments the people have been impov-
erished and fertile fields forced into sterility. In partial repub-
lics—for no real republic has yet ever existed—the governing
power has acted on crude and havoc-making theories of commerce and finance. . . ." Garrison doubted that One Great
Monopoly would flourish as well as the business combinations
had; for he wondered if the people would elect the best; if the
ability to run Bellamy's government existed; and, if it did,
whether men possessing it would be contented to accept an
equal income.[10]

Nineteenth-century critics such as Loewenthal and Blueher
of Germany and Combes de Lestrade and Reinach of France
feared with L. Gronlund, Walker, and Garrison that the industrial army would so regiment the lives of people that they
would become "like a flock of sheep" or that they would lose

all sense of initiative, responsibility, and ambition; but some of the European critics were prone to excuse Bellamy on the grounds that, as an American, he did not really know what militarism entailed. Other critics such as Lane and Marchant of Australia felt that men would be freed of unemployment, from the indignity of wages, and from the dependence upon another man for the right to earn bread.

Closely associated with the criticism of the industrial army and equality of income was the problem of whether men would work for honor or recognition—if this could reasonably be expected of humanity. William T. Harris and Garrison[11] argued that men only worked for personal interest and private gain; and such Europeans as Tiburtius, Fraenkel, and others asserted that only the threat of starvation kept them at their tasks. Because only ideal men could be expected to work for the reasons Bellamy had established, Koch of Germany argued that production would fall far short of that of a competitive society and that wealth would never result from the collective ownership of production and distribution.

Three of the greatest arguments which centered around Bellamy's plan were, therefore, concerned with the questions of whether or not human nature could be changed; whether collectivism would work; and whether technological progress and abundance would result. In respect to the problem of human nature Fraenkel, Gagliardi, Secrétan, and Blueher of Europe and Walker, G. Smith, and Maher of the United States—to cite only a few—declared that human nature could not be so changed and that greed, vice, passions, laziness, and self-interest were so inherent in man that Bellamy's system would fail. To Maher[12] and Smith[13] this problem posed one of the weakest points of Bellamy's program; for, since all workers enjoyed economic equality, they felt that, their needs supplied, they would not work; others argued that they could only be stimulated to do the "dirty work" of the nation if they were starving. Some felt that, if men could not have the hope of amassing a fortune, they would rapidly lose not only interest but individuality.

Some who considered the problem of human nature were more optimistic or romantic; they—like William Lane, Max Georgii, and Richard Ely[14]—believed that experiments in cooperative enterprises and in profit-sharing had proved that men, as Georgii wrote, needed only "humane environment to bring out their best qualities" and that this truth had been noted when he had toured the factory of the cooperative society of Ghent. There he had seen men interested personally in the work entrusted to them; and he remarked that their absorbing concern contrasted with the indifference of the wage slaves of other factories.[15] Astute Annie Besant also pointed out that under socialism men would have to work if they intended to enjoy the comforts and necessities they wished;[16] and Shaw argued with statistics that the system of distribution as it existed did not encourage exertion because too much of the profit went to the owner or the middleman.[17] Furthermore, C. R. Henderson suggested to those who thought that competition was necessary to spur men to endeavor that it still existed in a modified form in Bellamy's plan; it had been harnessed, however, to provide recognition for those who served the good of all.[18]

Positive and negative attitudes were also assumed toward the question of the success of collective ownership of production and distribution and toward the technological developments which would provide the world of abundance which Bellamy had predicted. Some of the Russians were inspired with hope because America was already advanced industrially; Tolstoy, Gandhi, and Morris refused the concept of development of the machine age; but Reinach felt that such development was already under way. Fraenkel and Tiburtius bluntly stated that such technological progress was impossible; and they and Wilbrandt and Erdsmanndoerffer also argued that neither the collective nor the technological development depicted would succeed with agriculture. Others doubted that men would be as inventive, that the bureaucracy would sponsor use of inventions, or that even with scientific and technological development the unmotivated workers would be productive enough to insure abundance. Some of the counter-Utopias portrayed the failure of the industrial state, a revolution created by the starving people of the collective order, and a happy return to the competitive society.

Critics such as Marie A. Brown, who charged Bellamy with taking his ideas from Bebel, agreed that when men worked for themselves they would be interested in doing whatever they did to the best of their abilities and in improving the methods and the machinery of production. She forecast that "the ambition of inventors and discoverers will be stimulated to the highest degree, each will endeavor to outdo his fellow in propositions and ideas."[19] Others like Lane and Wilde agreed that machinery should be used to free men; and Nationalist Henry Austin pointed out in a pamphlet that every facet of the state would encourage men to develop their abilities and to be honored for their contributions to progress.[20] He and Lane also argued that, since men relied upon knowledge and inventions of the past for the ideas which they developed in new forms, economic equality was the only fair return; as we have noted, Shaw agreed with them.

Perhaps the most amusing of all the arguments which centered around the problem of economic equality was its effect upon women. Although Shaw and Frances Willard agreed that women should be freed from economic subservience to their husbands and from marriages for economic reasons which interfered with the law of natural selection, many men and women were vociferous in the international debate which occurred about the deleterious effects such economic independence would have. Adams of Australia remarked it would not solve the sex problem; Dr. Loewenthal stated that women, economically freed, would become a corruptive influence greater than money had been; and he remarked that physically handicapped men would probably never find a wife! Gagliardi asserted that he did not believe that women could be both independent and charming; Laicus felt the wife should be completely subordinated to her husband; and American Caroline Corbin argued that women did not want the advantages depicted for them: they wished to stay at home, to be intuitive guides and helpmates of their husbands, and to be supported by them.[21]

Although Lane of Australia was glowing in his remarks about the charm marriage and children would have in Bellamy's world of economic equality, other critics were fearful that lack of financial responsibility would result in disastrous increase of population. American Malthusians argued that economic equality would destroy responsibility for children and thereby decrease the prudence which helped control the birth rate, would increase the tendency to contract early marriages, and would provide such a life of ease and well-being that people would live longer. Tiburtius and Dr. Koch of Germany argued, for example, that birth control would be necessary to check the growth of the population; and Atlas also sponsored a system of eugenics. Other Malthusians, who had absolutely no belief in the promised technological and scientific progress and inventiveness which were to increase the production of all source materials, were, of course, certain that catastrophe would result if Bellamy's state were implemented.

Almost as ludicrous as the international debate about women was the one about the religion, or lack of it, in *Looking Backward*. Although the novel is suffused with the idea of brotherly love and although the sermon by the Reverend Barton indicates how the ideal state is the fulfillment of Christian concepts, Catholics and many Protestants the world over were emphatically divided regarding the ideal society. To Lane of Australia, the religious motivation was apparent and satisfactory; to Francis Adams, there was too much of it; to a Swedish critic, there was no religion in the book; to Laicus, of Germany, it was not only a society without God but one which had tried to establish a paradise on earth.

In America, Anna L. Dawes published an article in which she charged that Bellamy was "anti-Christ" in his philosophy, for his Utopia did not contain the Christian concept that sorrow, pain, and darkness were the "necessary conditions of moral growth." Furthermore, he portrayed that happiness and virtue resulted from material surroundings; and this improvement she discounted because what was good for the body was not always good for the soul. Moreover, Buddha, Christ, and Mahomet had lived hard lives without comforts, and had been virtuous men. Bellamy could not, asserted Anna Dawes, be a believer in God since he sought the equalization of material conditions. Furthermore, he was not even a good Darwinian for his plan was contrary to the rule of the survival of the fittest which permitted the strongest to survive in physical evolution, in social evolution, and in the Christian state. It was, therefore, neither Christian nor scientific to have the strong help the weak.[22]

If this article made Bellamy's blood boil—as his friend Mason Green reported it did—he could not have been soothed by articles by William Higgs, Michael Maher, and A. G. Sedgwick[23] which stated that *Looking Backward* was opposed to Christianity because Christ had stated the "poor would always be with us" and because God had commanded that man must forever earn his bread by the sweat of his brow. Bellamy was, perhaps, gratified by the reactions—as we shall see—of some of the ministers and economists and by that of Frances Willard, who proclaimed that *Looking Backward* would bring the common people back to the church and that it might result in a "practical working plan" for Christianity—in people's talking less about their religion and living it instead.[24]

As Bellamy once stated, what he had included in *Looking Backward* was seemingly less important than what he had omitted, and among these conscious omissions was a plan for the achievement of the ideal state. Those who were inspired by *Looking Backward* desired to know how to reach the ideal state; others, averse to it, declared, like Henry George, that

Bellamy had not delineated the steps necessary to achieve it because none could be given for reaching "a mere place in the clouds";[25] and other Americans remarked that, had Bellamy outlined his procedure, it would have "scared his ladies so much that they'd have read no farther."[26] Comparable comments were made by Russian, Australian, and German critics; but to some such as Bloch and Lane the evolutionary development from the trends of the time seemed sufficient.

To the Marxists, the indications of the method to achieve the ideal state were sufficient to arouse violent criticism; for, as Zetkin and others asserted, the capitalists would not peacefully surrender to the One Great Monopoly and the only route to the ideal state was through revolution—and this meant an uprising of the masses. To them, it seemed that Bellamy was naïve, and worse: he was a middle-class citizen who sought to preserve— as Pać and others indicated—middle-class standards and values. They not only disagreed with him, but they feared that he would have a narcotic effect which would make people wonder why there should be a revolution if they could achieve the ideal society by peaceful, legal, evolutionary methods. Furthermore, as Marie A. Brown noted, Bellamy had said nothing about the expiration of religion; and he seemingly did not consider the church to be the chief master of the race nor to realize that it and the state combined held men and women in poverty and subjection. To her, he—unlike Bebel—was foolish for not recognizing that to leave the church was folly or that it had played an important role in the subjugation of women.[27] Moreover, the Marxists objected violently to a delineation of the future of society, to the lack of credit Bellamy gave the proletariat in achieving the ideal state, and to his statement that the red-flag wavers had indeed hindered its arrival; and they insisted—because he disagreed with Marx—that he was unscientific and Utopian. However, as we shall see, they not only recognized his power but used him; and later they were to find that his positive picture had modified even the "scientific" Marxists.

## II   Nineteenth- and Twentieth-Century Replies

Because of the criticisms and demands for answers to many of the widely discussed problems presented by *Looking Backward*, Bellamy very soon realized that he was obliged to answer not only his critics but his interrogators; he soon began to do so in *The New Nation* and in other publications, and, finally, he presented his last will and testament to the political, economic world in *Equality*. Although this sequel was considered

dull and uninteresting by many of his literary critics—and justly
so—*Equality* indicated Bellamy's economic and political growth;
and this fact was recognized by Julie Romm of Germany, Professor Fraser of Canada, Shaw of England, by the Russian
censors who banned it, and by the people of New Zealand who
imported it to help answer the questions of the 1930's.

Many of the arguments which Bellamy had read and then
answered in sundry articles were also considered in *Equality;*
and among these was the question of the militarism, totalitarianism, and regimentation of his ideal society. He presented in detail not only his portrayal of the development of democracy—
which has been reviewed in Chapter I of this book—but he made
it quite clear that all the democratic documents and democratic
procedures of the United States stood between his state and the
military, totalitarian one of his critics. He asserted that his state
could only be the outgrowth of a democracy, and that, to have
a true democracy, economic equality had to support equality
of opportunity, equality before the law, and equality for the
pursuit of happiness—no matter how different that pursuit
might be.

But no matter what the structure or the safeguards, Bellamy
constantly argued that only the eternal vigilance of the citizenry
could safeguard a nation's liberties. And in relationship to this
point, he asserted that, since the citizens of the ideal society
would be better educated and more interested in the affairs
of the nation because they had such a great stake in them,
they would be more alert than most had been in safeguarding
their freedom. Even if a plutocracy existed which could assume
the powers of the government and use them for its own devi-
ous purposes, the people would now be too alert to be victimized
once more by leaving their political and economic welfare in
the hands of "irresponsible persons with hostile interests." And
to the charge that his government was paternalistic, Bellamy
replied that the paternalism of the plutocrats—whom he termed
"fathers" who had mistreated their step-children—had promoted
the creation of the new government; and that it, being of the
people, could not be paternalistic to them. The new relationship
was *fraternalism.*

As Mason Green stated, some of the critics believed that
"only a thin wall of paper" separated Bellamyism from Marxism
but "upon that thin wall are written the whole federal constitution and provision for orderly amendments. Bellamy placed
the commonwealth of his dreams down on American soil without disturbing the political structure of the republic."[28] To John

Dewey, as to Mason Green, there was no doubt in the 1930's of Bellamy's democratic zeal—as there was to be to Italian Marie L. Berneri in 1950 and even to Canadian Sylvia Thrupp in the 1940's, who regarded Bellamy as a representative of the middle-class trend toward authoritarianism. To Dewey, Bellamy was distinguished by "the clear ardor with which he grasped the *human* meaning of democracy as an idea of equality and liberty. No one has carried through the idea that equality is obtainable only by complete equality of income more fully than Bellamy. Again, what distinguished him is that he derives his zeal and his insight from devotion to the American ideal of democracy."[29]

More recently, H. A. Meyers stated that "in spite of his faults as an extremist and doctrinaire" Bellamy won "the honors of the controversy over economic liberty and equality." He then remarked: "His was the voice of the future. He has even provided us with a striking phrase to describe the new economic ideal which is slowly winning its place as part of the meaning of American democracy." Like Jacques Duboin of France, Meyers believes that the future will see even the American people expand their belief of the present that "all are entitled to the necessities of life—to adequate food, clothing, housing, and medical care. Indeed, from the events of the past fifty years one may venture to predict the idea of economic justice is likely to prevail in America. As time goes on, the new ideal will tend more and more toward economic equality. But it will never" reach the extreme which Bellamy predicted, although Duboin of France thinks it will.[30]

Closely associated with the charges of trying to establish a totalitarian government were those claiming that Bellamy's ideal society, and his industrial army in particular, would result in regimentation. When Bellamy answered his critics about the necessity of governing the labor force of the nation so as to get the work done and to regulate production in accordance with the needs of the consumers, he not only pointed out that some regimentation would always be necessary but that it existed in capitalistic society. And his words recall the pictures of such a society as those presented today by Pierre Boulle in his entertaining novel *S. O. P. H. I. A.* (1959) and by William Whyte in *The Organization Man* (1956).

First of all, Bellamy informed General Walker and others in an article in the *North American Review* that they had confused an analogous term—"industrial army"—with the military system, but that he had indeed meant that all people would serve in the labor force to protect or serve others just as they did in the army. He then presented—as did Mason Green in an article in the *New Englander*[31]—facts about the numbers of men who were already employed in the post-office and other branches of the government; although they were seemingly happy working for some "socialized" government services, the employees also had to work: necessity required that they do so.[32] Bellamy pointed out, however, that under Nationalism men would be given the tasks which they were most innately fitted to do— and he forecast what is today popularly known as the "guidance program." Other advantages would be that all would have equal opportunities to develop their admittedly unequal abilities; that they would be able to change positions because of the labor exchange bureau; that, because of their training and their job mobility, they could easily be switched to another task if technological progress made the old one obsolete; that they had many safeguards to protect them from despotic superiors; and that they would not suffer the demoralizing relationship of master and servant which had existed to the intellectual and moral detriment of both parties in the nineteenth century. He then affirmed in an article of 1893 that the "root of the evil of the whole present economic system is that men take advantage of the needs of their fellowmen to use them for their selfish ends, which is offensive to the dignity of human nature and can never be right.

"It is wrong," he wrote, "whatever be the name of the system or the device used, and equally so whether the compulsion be hunger or direct coercion, that one human being should be used for the convenience or advantage of another, save out of love, and therefore the only plan worthy of humanity by which the world's work can be done is by the cooperation of equals for the service of the whole. This and nothing less is the meaning of the brotherhood of man, and those who do not mean as much have no right to take the words on their lips."[33]

In his "Talks on Nationalism," Bellamy wrote in *The New Nation* in 1891 that he could not understand what liberties his program deprived people of except "the precious liberty of loafing." He then argued:

> Assuming that it is right to require a man to work, is it a loss of liberty to guarantee him the opportunity to work at what he likes best and can do best? Is it tyranny to insure him promotion, leadership and honor in precise proportion to his achievements? Is it a curtailment of his liberty to make him absolutely

free of dependence upon the favor of any individual or community for his livelihood by giving him the constitutional pledge of the nation for it? Is it oppressive to guarantee him against loss of income in old age, and absolute security as to the welfare of his wife and children after he is gone? If to do all these things for a man means to take away his liberties and tyrannize over him, we had better get a new dictionary for the definitions in the old ones are evidently all wrong.[34]

Bellamy also made it quite clear in articles and in *Equality* that his *secondary* aim had been to supply the material needs of the nation; and for this—as he answered Morris—some systematic procedure and some regimentation were necessary. He asserted always, however, that his *primary* intent was to provide a society which would free man not only from the the immoral practices forced upon him by competition but from concern about his material welfare so he could devote himself to intellectual and moral development.[35] As has been stated in *The Year 2000: A Critical Biography of Edward Bellamy,* he believed that if material progress did not bring inward peace and enlargement of the souls and intellects of men and that if it did not develop in them a more constant sense of sympathy with others, the technological developments he foresaw would become the dangerous enslavers and playthings of a soul-less humanity. He hoped, therefore, that providing men with leisure, the financial security and an ethical environment would enable them to develop their best and fullest individualities, to perfect themselves, and to return to God.[36]

William James, in his essay "The Moral Equivalent of War," presented—as Arthur Morgan pointed out—one of the strongest arguments for the industrial army; he wrote:

If . . . there were, instead of military conscription a conscription of the whole youthful population to form for a certain number of years a part of the army enlisted against *Nature,* the injustice would tend to be evened out, and numerous other goods to the commonwealth would follow. The military ideal of hardihood and discipline would be wrought into the growing fibre of the people; no one would remain blind as the luxurious classes are now blind, to man's real relations to the globe he lives on, and to the permanently sour and hard foundations of his higher life. To coal and iron mines, to freight trains, to fishing fleets in December, to dishwashing . . . would our gilded youths be drafted off, according to their choice, to get the childishness knocked out of them, and to come back into society with healthier sympathies and soberer ideas.[37]

Although this passage may remind many educators of the effect they have seen the military services of the present have upon youths of the nation, it should also remind them of the New Deal "C.C.C. camps" for the unemployed youths of the nation which did so much to help them maintain morale during the Depression and which, like the industrial armies of unemployed older workers and artists, enabled necessary work to be done for the good of the nation while avoiding for all the stigma of accepting charity.

Many years after his friend William James had stated his attitude toward an industrial army, John Dewey wrote his opinion of Bellamy's so-called regimentation:

> I wish that those who conceive that the abolition of private capital and of energy expended for profit signify complete regimenting of life and the abolition also of all personal choice and all emulation, would read with an open mind Bellamy's picture of a socialized economy. It is not merely that he exposes with extraordinary vigor and clarity the restriction upon liberty that the present system imposes but that he pictures how socialized industry and finance would release and further all those personal and private types of choice of occupation and use of leisure that men and women actually most prize today. His picture of a reign of brotherly love may be overdrawn. But the same can not be said of his account of freedom in personal life outside of the imperative demand for the amount of work necessary to provide for the upkeep of social capital. In an incidental chapter on the present servility to fashion he brings out the underlying principle. "Equality creates an atmosphere which kills imitation, and is pregnant with originality, for everyone acts for himself, having nothing to gain by imitating any one else. It is the present system that promotes uniformity, standardization and regimentation."[38]

Dewey, like his admired Bellamy, would have told Vance Packard, the author of the *Status Seekers*, that the answer to the problem with which he is concerned is to give everybody an equal income; with the knowledge that each had equal wealth, argued Bellamy, no status would be achieved through ownership of anything, and no hypocrisy associated with the purchase of status symbols as so often exists among people who seek to appear either rich or successful by purchasing things they can ill afford.[39]

Bellamy's concepts of human nature and of the motivations of the workers which were so widely criticized in the nineteenth century have also been more or less vindicated by twentieth-century specialists. Bellamy, who had never believed that human nature was wholly evil, had also never insisted that it was wholly good; he was, like many other humanists—such as Paul Elmer More and Thornton Wilder today—quite aware of the duality of man. He did, however, think that man was capable of developing the good in him if he lived in a society which would emphasize moral behavior rather than cunning, deceit, and craft; and, although he did not, as he wrote, intend to change human nature, he hoped to promote the best expression of it and to channel the vanity of men, their selfishness, and their pride in such a way that they could satisfy these characteristics while laboring for the good of all. Bellamy also argued that men did not necessarily strive to earn money for the sake of obtaining wealth: they wished the expression of self, the recognition, the power, the accomplishment, and the security which it gave them. Recognizing the power of emulation and of competition, he also employed these to increase the benefits which would be shared by all.[40]

Because of his view of humanity, Bellamy planned that the incentives which would motivate the workers of the new state would not only be economic equality but selection and assignment of work they were capable of doing in such a way as to insure not only pleasure but possibility of success. To stimulate further their success, he planned a system of recognition for all, promotion on the basis of merit, training to insure job mobility, and discipline for the slackers in the form of group disapproval. He also provided in *Looking Backward* that the disabled would be employed for the sake of their morale and their contribution; and in *Equality* in particular he insisted that women be granted not only equality of income but equal rights to work, to be promoted, and to hold any merited position of importance.[41]

Today such surveys of the desires of workers as that of Rensis Likert—"Motivation: The Core of Management," published in 1953 by the American Management Association of New York City— indicate that Bellamy's view was extremely modern. Likert, the director of the Institute for Social Research of the University of Michigan, reports that production was high among groups that had pride in their work, that people worked hardest when they were understood by their supervisors, and that they desired recognition.[42]

Furthermore, F. C. Minaker, a well-known writer about business administration, has stated that there are two types of wages: money and mental. He remarked that most administrators believe that men work mostly for money and more money; but a ten-year study conducted by Elmer Roper showed that workers had only four desires—and all of these are classified as mental wages. They wanted, first, security or the "right to work continuously at reasonably good wages"; second, "a chance to advance"; third, recognition; and fourth, a feeling that their "jobs contribute something important to human welfare and happiness."[43]

A United States Chamber of Commerce release of February 24, 1957, indicated that twenty-four companies surveyed showed that supervisors thought men wanted, first of all, money; second, job security; and third, promotion and growth within the company. The survey of employees indicated, however, that the workers wanted, first, full appreciation of the work they did; second, a feeling that they were "in" on things; third, sympathetic help with personal problems; fourth, job security; fifth, good wages; sixth, work that would keep them interested; seventh, promotion and growth within the company; eighth, personal loyalty to them; ninth, good working conditions; and tenth, tactful disciplining. Interestingly, the human factors—such as feeling a part of something, sympathetic help and understanding, and recognition and appreciation of the work done—were listed last by the supervisors or managers. If we are to accept these reports which have already had an effect upon management methods in the United States, Bellamy was in advance of his era when he recognized that human characteristics had to be recognized, human needs to be fulfilled, and that morale—the zest to accomplish anything—could only be developed in a positive, constructive way by supplying these needs.[44]

If Bellamy was singularly astute in his recognition of the need of men for security, appreciation, and a sense of accomplishment and contribution, he was just as perceptive of their need for development of intellectual and spiritual resources and their desire for identity. Today hundreds of articles, serious studies, and novels reflect the loss of identity of the modern man of the urban, technological, scientific world of mass production; they also reflect his insecurity, his fear, and his resentment of the Frankensteins—as Bellamy conceived the inventions of modernity—which minimize man's sense of accomplishment, creativity, or contribution and which also threaten destruction of civilization. Man also feels lost because of complicated problems which appear insoluble; he is ever more ready to delegate his power of decision-making to some one else, or to conform in his private life to the demands of suburbia.

Instead of having brought the comfort and the intellectual and social advancement which Comte, Bellamy, and Thomas Huxley dreamed science and technology would supply humanity, they brought instead the fearful possibility of *1984,* or of the era which C. Wright Mills calls that of "The Cheerful Robot." As he points out in "On Reason and Freedom" in *Identity and Anxiety* (1960), the society in which the "cheerful robot" appears is the "antithesis of the free society." Mills warns that all should be concerned because maintenance of democracy is at stake: we cannot maintain it if men feel alienated, apathetic, or indecisive. Mills also wonders if the age of technology has has not contributed to the deterioration of "the human mind as a social fact" since those who use devices do not understand them and since those who produce them understand nothing else! Admitting that he does not know the answers to the problems created by mass production, Mills fears, however, that men may abdicate and permit an élite to make their decisions[45]— and where these might lead is a moot but dangerous question.

The answer to Mills and the vindication of Bellamy's concern about the development of man's individuality and of his faith in the ability of humanity to create a better world by adapting to a changed environment may be deduced from Dr. Bruno Bettelheim's *The Informed Heart: Autonomy in a Mass Age* (1960). Although Dr. Bettelheim's purpose was not to tell men what to do but to relate what happened and why in Hitler's Germany, he hoped that his analysis would help others decide "what reshaping of their personalities they wish to effect to better meet the moral and emotional requirements for withstanding the pressures of a mass society; or to put it differently, how to inform the heart in the service of autonomy."[46] But as we follow the observations of and conclusions about what developed, we are convinced that Dr. Bettelheim is as concerned as Bellamy was about certain positive values.

Dr. Bettelheim learned from his experiences in a German concentration camp and from his adjustment to society in America that human behavior could be radically changed by its environment and that he had himself gone too far in thinking that a change in man alone could create one in society. Since he thinks that we can no longer "see personality change as proceeding independent from the social context" and that we may see more radical changes such as that wrought in China amid a people frozen in traditional patterns, Dr. Bettelheim thinks that it is imperative that we have a better understanding of the influence of environment and be better prepared also to protect men through education and development to combat environment's potentially destructive influence. Dr. Bettelheim also asserts that man must be "better equipped to change society so that it will not be an obstacle to living the good life, but a setting that facilitates and encourages it." In other words, man must not only live such a life but engender in each generation the concept of the "good society for himself and all others."

As Dr. Bettelheim reviews the life of the Germans both in and out of prison camp, he indicates the roles played by fear, anxiety, and insecurity and by the surrender of identity, responsibility, and autonomy—all of which created apathy, rationalization, and degeneration. Dr. Bettelheim indicates throughout his book that men who had pride in their work and self-respect because of a sense of values, who had interests which could be preserved, who had deep emotional or religious ties, and who had a greater understanding of and ability to analyze life, were those who were able to preserve their rationality and influence their own fate.[48]

What Dr. Bettelheim has to say about mass society and the slow inroads Hitlerism made upon Germany is applicable also to the world of technology in which men today are losing their autonomy and their sense of identity, are ridden with anxiety and fears, and are likely to become the slaves of the machines or of the society they created to free them. Dr. Bettelheim indicates, however, that 1984 does not have to be the inevitable result; for he believes that man can reshape his personality so he can modify society into one that is not only human but conducive to true democracy "based on individual autonomy and responsibility."[49] Such a society, says Dr. Bettelheim, has to offer "meaningful human relations, satisfying living conditions, and significant goals." It also has to strike a balance among human aspirations, society's rightful demands, and man's nature—there must be no submission to any one of them.[50] His challenge and his hope is, therefore, that men will create an age of "reason and humanity." But to fulfill this hope and this challenge "heart and reason can no longer be kept in their separate places." And he states that work, art, family, and society can no longer develop in isolation; the heart must invade reason and reason must give way to "the informed heart."[51]

When we turn from Dr. Bettelheim's book to Alfred Cobban's In Search of Humanity, to Reinhold Niebuhr's Moral Man and Immoral Society, and to Ortega y Gasset's The Revolt of the Masses, we find comparable answers to the problem which confronts our age of pessimism and anxiety. First of all, Reinhold Niebuhr feels that part of the tragedy of today is man's "inability to conform its collective life to its individual ideals"; in other words, man is moral and society is immoral.[52] Ortega y Gasset asserts that—though we live in a time when man is lord of all things and when he believes himself capable of creating anything—he "does not know what to create," "he is not lord of himself," he is lost in the midst of abundance, and his world drifts—just as the worst of worlds have.[53] Alfred Cobban believes that only a return to ethical and rational discussion and decision about the social ends we desire can save our civilization; we must not only find a sense of direction and have a purpose but we must also make a "positive effort to counter current evils." He suggests that, as we do so, we remember that human behavior "has been altered in the past and therefore presumably can be altered again."[54]

As Cobban indicates, human nature—which he terms an elusive thing—has many ingredients shared by all people; but, as Bettelheim has also demonstrated, man's reactions may be determined by his environment—and the good society should be so arranged that it will provide the comforts of civilization but at the same time secure for each citizen the "maximum possible of human satisfactions." The solution is to be found "only by opposing inner to outer freedom; emotional freedom to the freedom to . . . discharge aggression."[55] Furthermore, to insure that man will have these human satisfactions, Bettelheim argues that it will become essential—as more and more leisure results from technological improvements and invention—that he develop significant interests which will occupy him, give him inner resources, and preserve his individuality when mere earning of a living for himself and family has become less meaningful and less of an occupation.[56]

Although these writers of today have vindicated Bellamy's recognition of the flexibility of human behavior and of the need for individuals to develop their intellectual and spiritual resources, they have also stressed independently his concepts of the need for moral, ethical motivation of men and for the definition of the ends of society so that men may constructively achieve them. Furthermore, they have also indicated that Bellamy was wise in sponsoring not a specific brand of religion but only a humanitarian one based on the love advocated by Christ, although this quality of his religion led his contemporaries to criticize him. Bellamy, who was conscious of the division of society wrought by warring and jealous creeds, believed that such conflicts destroyed brotherly love; this fact has been stressed by Cobban who also pointed out, however, that men have discovered today that it is possible to live peacefully in a society comprising many different beliefs. Dr. Bettelheim also indicates that the men of strong religious conviction were more capable of preserving their integrity but that those of narrow creeds became angered and quarrelsome when their credos were questioned.[57] Furthermore, the trend today in the Protestant churches is to minimize the differences of interpretation and to emphasize the social gospel of love. Only fundamentalists would present the religious arguments of the nineteenth-century critics in opposition to Bellamy's concept of the role religion should play in the social and political life of the nation. Some would, however, war against his collective state despite the Christian basis which he provided as one of its cornerstones; the Catholics, for instance, have consistently done so.

Furthermore, since most of the writers cited have recognized that we cannot in the future avoid a more powerful state, their comments about our necessary concern with the individual, with social and political results, and with humane ethical concepts become more and more important. Others, such as Wilhelm Roepke, for example, in *A Humane Economy: The Social Framework of the Free Market* (1960), believe that the Western world is headed for some form of mass or collective society. Roepke—with nostalgia for the past—pleads for the creation of a state which will take human needs and satisfactions into account. He is fearful that a centralized government may, like that of Russia, be unconcerned with its inhumanity; and he advocates preservation of the individual and his soul. Like Dr. Bettelheim, Roepke sees similarities and dangers to both not only in the free world, but in the slave one. Furthermore, A. A. Berle, Jr., in a review of W. W. Rostow's *The Stages of Economic Growth: A Non-Communist Manifesto*, shows that while Rostow and Marx agree that society evolves from an economic point of view, Rostow denies that humanity is necessarily dominated or motivated by desire for economic change. Although Rostow considered other motivations as outside his subject, Berle himself thinks that "the why, the moral or emotional imperatives which cause society to pass from one stage to another" are "determinative, or at least more dynamic than strictly economic considerations."[58]

Although there is little doubt expressed in any of these books that man has achieved the world of affluence or of abundance because of the technological development and inventiveness that most nineteenth-century critics distrusted or questioned when Bellamy forecast it, the Malthusians of today still argue that an increasing population and longevity may lead to starvation; and one prominent scientist—Julian Huxley—advocates birth control as a means of halting population growth and disaster. Other scientists and economists feel, however, that man's inventiveness and his discovery of new resources will always be able to supply his needs. Furthermore, a report published a few years ago about the decrease in the population growth of Puerto Rico when educational and cultural levels had risen may also indicate that Bellamy was not too far wrong when he argued in *Equality* that the birth rate decreased as the educated and the cultivated peoples of the world increased.

But the production of truly educated and cultivated people is threatened today by the fears and anxieties of men who are involved in a scientific armament race which forces nations to place emphasis upon scientific subjects and not equally upon the liberal arts. Furthermore, there is recognition of the fact that the poor, women, and Negroes are often barred by economic reasons or by prejudices from obtaining the education which they could absorb; and, if women and Negroes do obtain it, from finding an equal opportunity to practice their professions or vocations according to their merit; these statements are substantiated in the following books or reports: Theodore Caplow and Reece J. McGee, *The Academic Marketplace* (1958); *The NEA Higher Education Research Report* (1959); and the Department of Labor's *Handbook on Women Workers* (1958) and *Manpower Challenge of the 1960's.* Such deterrents to national growth, progress, safety, and the fulfillment of American principles are recognized by the President's Commission on National Goals report (1960); for it states that prejudice and discrimination—as Bellamy had pointed out—are "economically wasteful, and in many respects dangerous." It stresses that equal opportunities for all must prevail; and it also emphasizes that "our society must stimulate and support richer cultural achievement" and that posterity will judge American civilization not only on the basis of its scientific achievements but by its contributions to literature and the other arts.

Although Bellamy's critics scoffed when he advocated a world government as the ultimate social ideal, and regulation of international trade as an economic necessity, the world of today is rapidly realizing that it needs to arm the world court at Geneva with respect and legality, to give the United Nations a constitution and executive powers, and to prepare to solve the problems of the atomic and space ages with these international organizations which could legally and not militarily solve the complex problems of today and tomorrow. Bellamy's critics who asked him what he would do with the Hottentots and other Africans would without doubt be surprised or amazed if they could see the government of Nigeria and the role played by the United Nations in the Congo in 1960 or previously in other areas of the troubled world. Furthermore, as Shaw was one of the first to recognize, Bellamy's portrayal in *Equality* of the industrialized nations who depended upon world trade for their prosperity can easily become more meaningful to the twentieth century, in which formerly backward nations are rapidly being developed and in which the Eastern and the Western worlds are struggling for the possession of trade and of economic areas. Just as many have recognized the benefits to be derived from other areas of specializations, so must nations eventually realize that they must find some method of insuring exchange which will permit countries to produce the products they can most economically and readily produce. A free *world* trade would have many benefits to all peoples of all nations; perhaps the world will, like units of it, one day recognize the benefits of planned production and distribution.

As we view some of the current reactions to the problems which Bellamy faced and to the answers which he presented to them, we can easily realize why Charpentier, Duboin, Professor Fraser, and Dr. Duncker have suggested that he is as relevant to the twentieth century as he was to the nineteenth—perhaps even more so because he considered problems and solutions which are more understandable to our era than to his own. Long a student of humanity, Bellamy proved not only in *Looking Backward* and in *Equality* that he understood the motivations and needs of men, for his greatly neglected novel *Dr. Heidenhoff's Process* sustains a thesis which has also been recognized as sound by the well-known psychologist O. Hobart Mowrer and by such a famous psychotherapist as Albert Ellis. In this novel, Bellamy studied the effect of sin upon a religious, tender conscience; portrayed the insidious, destructive power of guilt; and evolved a method of shock treatment to relieve and to restore the stricken person to a useful life. As both Mowrer and Ellis have pointed out, this reaction of man must be taken into account, as well as the necessity of Freudian insight; and Ellis stated that the guiltier a person feels, the less likely is his chance of becoming "a happy, healthy, or law-abiding citizen. His sense of sin will literally drive him away from not doing wrong and toward doing it."[59]

## III Patterns of Influence, Future Research

As we consider the advanced concepts and the positive values which Bellamy presented as essentials of his ideal society, it is not difficult to understand why *Looking Backward* appealed to many intelligent, well-educated people around the world who were seeking answers to nineteenth-century problems; it is also not difficult to understand why the liberals, the monarchists, the religious, the Marxists, and the conservatives attacked him: he was opposed to their particular interests or he was too advanced for them to comprehend. Had *Equality* appeared at the moment of deepest intensity of the great Bellamy debate, Bellamy's influence might have been even greater. For in this sequel Bellamy outlined the full effects of economic equality; answered his critics with almost unanswerable arguments; depicted the route to the ideal state; argued for the institution of recall, referendum, and initiative; related clearly the role religion would play in the formation and maintenance of the new society; and ruthlessly portrayed the wastes and dangers of individual enterprise. But though *Equality* was more or less ignored, it too played its role; for, as we have noted, the "Parable of the Water Tank" was one of the most widely circulated and devastating criticisms of capitalism.

The international debate and controversy which arose because of Bellamy's books popularized his ideas; and it is today possible to state that they were effective in creating both at home and abroad a sizeable library of international literature, Utopian and otherwise; in acquainting many people with socialist concepts and in converting others to them; in creating a dream and an inspiration of a better future for humanity; and in influencing the growth of Marxism and—paradoxically—its modification.

As we survey Bellamy's influence, we discover many similar reactions in areas influenced by him. First of all, *Looking Backward* spurred the writing in the United States of countless Utopian novels by such men as William Dean Howells, Ignatius Donnelly, and Rabbi Solomon Schindler—to mention only the best known of the nearly one hundred replies published across the nation. His ideas also stimulated such writers as Upton Sinclair, William Allen White, Mark Twain, Robert Herrick, Ida Tarbell, Vida Scudder, S. Anderson, William Vaughn Moody, and countless others who wrote socialistic, muckraking, or Populist fiction, non-fiction, and poetry. In Europe, Bellamy appealed to such writers as Russell, Shaw, Van Eeden, Tolstoy,

Wilde, Wells, Gorky, France, and Chekhov; in Australia, he influenced Joseph Furphy and Vance Palmer. Further research needs to be conducted about the influence Bellamy had upon these and possibly other foreign writers; and an interesting story might be related if someone made a thorough study of Utopian novels written in all countries of the world after *Looking Backward* became famous. We have noticed that these were multitudinous in Germany and that others were written in France, Italy, England, and other countries; but those of Spain, the Balkans, and other areas need to be fully investigated.

Aside from his influence upon literature, Bellamy intrigued the early socialists in many, many countries; for in Poland, in Rumania, in Holland, and in Jugoslavia his works were translated by men who were to play important roles in the development of social democratic parties and of Marxism. In the United States, Bellamy was the inspiration of such men as Thorstein Veblen, Eugene Debs, Norman Thomas, and Professor Daniel De Leon; and, as we study the drift of many members of Bellamy clubs in the United States into more radical organizations, we find that they were so tainted with Bellamyism that they invariably created difficulties because they would not accept the Marxist concept of class conflict or of a bloody revolution. As social scientist and student of communism, Louis Boudin remarked in his address at a Marxist convention in the 1930's, the only really native American socialist movement was that of the Nationalists of which "Bellamy was the leading spirit"—and that "notwithstanding the fact that the social movement became officially Marxian about the time [*Looking Backward*] . . . was written, and remained so . . . this Utopian attitude inherited from . . . [Bellamy] and his co-workers in the Nationalist movement has been an influential factor in retarding the growth of our movement during its entire existence of some forty-odd years. The history of this Utopianism of our movement has never been told. When it is told, it will form an interesting story, and to many a surprising one. For this ideology influenced people whom no one would ordinarily suspect of being subject to its influence." As Boudin has indicated, and as *Bellamy at Home: A Study of Literary, Political and Religious Influence* will prove, Bellamy's impact in the United States was paradoxical.

Bellamy not only removed prejudice about socialism in his own country as he did in Germany, England, and Russia, but he also made it popular once again among the intellectuals and the middle class, among the farmers and the industrial workers. Just as Bellamy's influence was not limited to the nineteenth century abroad, so was it in the United States. For, as Henry S. Commager has stated in *The American Mind* (1950), the People's Party platform affected liberal thinking and legislation even up to the present; and William Dean Howells remarked that Bellamy virtually founded this party. Furthermore, a study of the people who were instrumental in promoting the concepts of the New Deal—as listed and discussed in Schlesinger's *The Crisis of the Old Order*—will show that many were associated with Bellamy's Nationalist movement. Furthermore, the Townsendites and the Technocrats owed their ideas to Bellamy; and many of the New Deal innovations had been popularized by Bellamy long before they became a part of the American way of life.

Although the story of Bellamy's tremendous ideological influence in the United States will be related in *Bellamy at Home*, some student of the history of political ideas should thoroughly investigate the role which Bellamy played in modifying the ideas of such leaders abroad as Van der Goes, de Kadt, and others such as Eduard Bernstein who played important roles around the world as revisionists of Marxism. For as has been noted throughout *Bellamy Abroad*, the influence of the American socialist in European and other countries was also paradoxical: it created interest in socialism and it led many people to Marxism; but it also became such a threat that the Marxists had to denounce and dissociate themselves from Bellamy's portrayal of a future state because its influence was too powerful. Although the Marxists are still using his Utopias or sections of them as inspiring, easily comprehended instruction about the collective state and about the sins and wastes of capitalism, they are also careful to stress his negative values and not his positive ones; and they call him unscientific because he disagrees with Marx's most negative principles.

Further research should also be conducted about Bellamy's influence upon political and economic theory in European nations. Although he was attacked in his own country by Sumner and Walker, who believed in laissez-faire, he was also regarded favorably by Richard Ely, John R. Commons, and Thorsten Veblen. Bellamy was esteemed by Ely because he denounced the brutalities of rugged individualism and because he envisioned an economic system with an ethical foundation; he inspired Veblen to become interested in his life's work, and his plan of marketing and distribution is close to Bellamy's; Professor John Commons used Bellamy in his classes when he was head of the Department of Political Economy and Social Sciences at Indiana University, and he even had Bellamy judge an essay contest in 1894. Commons later founded a group of Christian Socialists at Indiana University, and was a follower of Ely and Bellamy in advocating ethical economics.[60] Abroad Professor von Gizycki, who was highly critical of the Manchester School, translated Bellamy's book; and, although economists such as Block attacked him, others—like the German and later like Professor Stanley Jevons and Jacques Duboin—must have been affected by him. Since Bellamy was and still is discussed in the classrooms of Europe and of the Orient, his influence in changing concepts about capitalism must have been—must be—tremendous.

Another story which should someday be related is the effect that Bellamy may have had abroad upon the social gospel and the Christian socialist movement. In the United States, he was welcomed by many of the followers of Kingsley and Maurice; and such men as the Reverend Francis Bellamy, Herbert W. Gleason, Rabbi Solomon Schindler, Alexander Kent, W. D. P. Bliss, the Reverend Franklin Monroe Sprague, Bishop Huntington, and many others not only belonged to Nationalist clubs but helped to found the Christian Socialist movement which, as Quint observes in *The Forging of American Socialism*, helped to keep the ideas of Bellamy alive in the United States,[61] although some members could not accept his complete program. In 1891 Bishop Huntington declared to the Working Women's League in Ithaca, New York:

> It is high time for the church to preach and for mankind to believe that a Heavenly order of society is not to be postponed to a future world, but is to be set up here on the earth in that faith which proclaims, "One is your master, even Christ, and all ye are brethren." A competition which swells a large fortune in one man's hands by wearing down to the edge of famine the nerves and fingers of fifty women with fatherless children, sewing sixteen hours a day for forty cents, getting eighty cents for the making of a lady's cloak which the employer sells for $18, or fifty cents for making a dozen pairs of trousers . . . is not a competition for Christians to be proud of, and in Christ's name I repudiate it as infidelity to God and abomination to man.[62]

Such remarks must have cheered Bellamy who had—as we have noted—been attacked by the more orthodox; and he must also have been pleased by the reports sent to him by Orme of England about the interest of many ministers there in his plan for a better world. Although *Bellamy Abroad* records the consistent denunciation of the Catholics and a divided attitude among the Protestants of the world, certainly many ministers must have been impressed by the spiritual, religious import of Bellamy's message.

Study should also be made of the use of his Utopias by the suffragettes, for ardent Frances Willard lectured for years about Bellamy wherever she appeared, and other suffragette leaders such as Mary A. Livermore and Abby Morton Diaz were pleased with *Looking Backward* and even more so with *Equality*. In Europe, Sylvia Pankhurst of England mentioned him, Annie Besant lectured about him, Clara Zetkin translated him, and Lenin's wife read him. Since all of these women were leaders of the suffragettes, their publications and their letters should be studied for information about their use of Bellamy.

Another interesting aspect of the influence of Bellamy which needs to be further investigated is the role he played among the early Zionist leaders both in the United States and in Europe. In Europe Theodore Herzl surprised everyone who knew him by the radical change which suddenly occurred in him enabling him to write *Der Judenstaat*—a work which greatly stimulated the Zionist movement, outlined the salvation of "The Society of Jews" by technology and an industrial army,[63] and frequently speaks in terms which are pure Bellamyisms. As noted in Chapter VI, Herzl's *Altneuland* showed further evidence of the influence of the American Utopian.

When Herzl succeeded in founding the European Zionist movement, he asked Rabbi Henry Pereira Mendes of New York City to organize the American Jews. Mendes became one of the first Zionists in the United States, and he was elected vice-president of the Federation of American Zionists and a member of the Actions Committee of the World Zionist Organization at the Second Zionist Congress in Vienna (1898) and in Basel (1899). Mendes, who also helped found the Montefiore Hospital and the Jewish Theological Seminary of America, also published in 1900 an anonymous Utopian novel entitled *Looking Ahead*, which has been called a "remarkable study in anticipations." In May, 1954, Dr. G. Kressel published in *Davar* (Tel-Aviv) an article in which he showed the influence of Bellamy upon this Utopian novel.

Another noted Jewish radical leader, Rabbi Solomon Schindler of Boston, was so impressed with *Looking Backward* that he arranged with Bellamy to be its first translator into German and in 1894 published *Young West: A Sequel to Edward*

*Bellamy's Celebrated Novel, Looking Backward* in which he
outlined an educational system. Furthermore, Rabbi Samuel
Freuder of San Francisco resigned from his synagogue to devote himself to "preaching to both Jew and Gentile the gospel
of Nationalism."[64] As we have noted, early Jewish liberals or
socialists of Europe were responsible for translating or publiciz-
ing *Looking Backward* in their countries; and three Hebrew
editions of it were published from 1898 to 1903 in Poland and
Russia. Because of the novel's wide influence upon Jewish Zionists and radical leaders, an investigation might reveal that it
not only inspired them but contributed to the plan of the present communist state of Israel.

Another religious group which played a powerful role in
the dissemination of the ideas of Bellamy was, as we have suggested in Chapter XIV, the Theosophical Society. Since this
organization has groups in many, many other countries besides
those mentioned in this study, further research might show that
its approval of Bellamy's Utopia led many people to socialism
of one type or another. Certainly a fertile field of investigation
would be the role Theosophy played in introducing the ideas
of Bellamy to the early leaders and revolutionaries of India.

When men have achieved a world of peace, studies should
also be made of the role Bellamy's ideas played in Spain, in
Hungary, in Rumania, in Albania, and in China; furthermore,
since some of the publications by Bellamy which appeared in
the Balkan countries were printed in Russia, future investigation
should be made not only of the wide use made of Bellamy by the
Marxists, but of his reported popularity in Georgia and the possibility of his influence upon the people of this region—from
whence came Stalin—and upon other prominent Russian leaders.

As this survey of the international pattern of influence and of
future research that must be done before the complete story of
the impact of Edward Bellamy can be told shows, Bellamy was,
if not the greatest literary artist the United States produced,
certainly its most influential one from the ideological standpoint. Although *Looking Backward* has been condemned and
praised as a work of art, its artistry was sufficient to present a
message about the future which inspired and moved the hearts
and minds of men. Although *Equality* should be considered as
a very poor pseudo-novel, the "Parable of the Water Tank" is
a masterful and moving allegory in biblical style; and the political, economic arguments of the novel should not be disregarded,
for they are Bellamy's most significant ones.

Although Edward Bellamy was rarely mentioned in American literary histories before 1920, assessments of him began to appear after the revival of his books during the Great Depression. He has been recognized, therefore, by Russell Blankenship, Walter Fuller Taylor, Oscar Cargill, and many other American literary scholars as a writer who gave impetus to a spate of Utopian novels and to the writing of revolt literature. In most studies of reform movements and of political ideas, he has merely been mentioned as the writer of a popular Utopia imitated by Ignatius Donnelly;[65] as a "genteel Utopian" who had more appeal for native Americans than Marx's "analysis of the class struggle";[66] as one of the group of intellectuals—who are named without any order—who insisted that laissez-faire capitalism had "betrayed the original meaning of the American Revolution";[67] or as one whose book *might* have arrived on the desk of Eugene Debs and reinforced his ideas that the ballot could usher in the Golden Age.[68]

Although the literary historians have been more generous in their mention of Bellamy than the writers of histories about communism and socialism, this fact is understandable: Bellamy was dubbed *Utopian* and *unscientific*—and dismissed rather too readily. As Martin Buber asserts in *Paths in Utopia,* Marx and Engels first called everyone *Utopian* who had not been able to study the development of industry; later, however, their term became "the most potent missile in the fight of Marxism against non-Marxian socialism." They did not care to consider objectively counter-arguments or proposals; and they always found "science and truth absolutely and exclusively" in their so-called scientific interpretation and "utopianism and delusion" in any rival camp. Buber then declared that to be *Utopian* today means to be "out of step with modern economic development" as seen by the Marxists;[69] Buber argues, however, that "if socialism is to emerge from the blind-alley into which it has strayed," the word *Utopian* "must be cracked open and examined for its true content."[70]

As Charpentier of France argued in his introduction to *Looking Backward* in 1939, Bellamy should no longer be judged a mere *Utopian*. He must, as Walter Taylor asserted in *A Literary History of the United States,* be considered "in the words Goethe once applied to Carlyle" as "first of all, a moral force." He must also be reconsidered as the spokesman who was the focus of "nineteenth-century liberalism in America,"[71] who played a tremendous role in influencing the ideological development of many important leaders and artists and in creating the socialistic world in which capitalism is now struggling to survive. As John Dewey remarked, Bellamy's power was his lack of bitterness, his constructiveness, his "atmosphere of hope," his fulfillment of the democratic ideal, and his dream of the "psychological emancipation" of man which concerns all men today. By the year 2000, Bellamy may indeed be recognized as The Great American Prophet (the appellation Dewey gave him) and the author of a novel which was, in fact, the *Uncle Tom's Cabin* of capitalism.

# Some Account of the Propaganda Work in America Which Has Followed *Looking Backward*

By

EDWARD BELLAMY

March, 1892

It has occurred to me that Russians who have read *Looking Backward,* or heard of it, may be interested in learning something of the practical work which has resulted from it, or at least has followed it. In the year 1888, soon after the book was published, I began to receive numerous letters from all parts of America urging some plan of cooperation on the part of the readers of the book with their eventually bringing about the industrial reorganization of the country substantially upon the lines which it laid down. As my own motive in writing the book was entirely practical, it may easily be supposed that I was exceedingly glad to fall in with this suggestion. The work proposed was indeed a vast one but that was only a reason for losing no time in undertaking it.

The first of the proposed organizations for practical work was effected in Boston in December, 1888. Similar societies sprang up almost simultaneously in all parts of the country, presently aggregating some one hundred and fifty so-called clubs. The formation of these organizations was entirely spontaneous, and there has been little or no attempt to organize them under any central control. The following Declaration of Principles put forth by the original society or club in Boston has, however, been generally adopted by the societies subsequently formed.*

---

* Appended to the MS is the title page of *The Nationalist* (April, 1891) with the "Declaration" printed on the other side.

The name popularly given to the social and industrial doctrines of *Looking Backward,* when proposed as a practical program, was Nationalism; the associations formed to propagate
the doctrine were called Nationalist clubs and those in sympathy with the doctrine were known as Nationalists. Some explanation of the significance of this terminology will throw light
upon the general character and purposes of the movement. The
reason why a new name seemed necessary in order to distinguish the doctrine of the Nationalists from those of the various
sects included under the generic term of socialists was that the
new doctrine was characterized by several principles not known
to be all held by any other school of social reformers. There
were indeed some other social reform sects which held one or
two of the peculiar principles of Nationalism but it was not
known that there was any which held all of them.

The first of these principles is that which suggests the name
of Nationalist; namely, that the industries of every state should
be nationalized. Now all socialists believe that industry should
be socialized, that is, managed collectively, but to socialize an
industry is not necessarily to nationalize it. An industry may be
socialized by placing it in the hands of associations of workingmen, either within national lines or on an international basis
that disregards and tends to obliterate national distinctions. To
believe ever so strongly in a socialized or collective conduct
of industry is not, therefore, by logical consequence to be in
sympathy with Nationalism. The Nationalist not only believes
in socialized industries but that its socialization should be on
the already established lines of the national organism in its
various grades of the municipal, the state (or departmental),
and of the general administrations. According to the Nationalist
the solution of the industrial question will result strictly from
the evolution into industry of the national idea which is that of
a collective administration of the common affairs of citizens in
the equal interest of all.

The second distinctive feature of Nationalism is a corollary
from the first; namely, the economic equality of all citizens,
women sharing equally with men in the product of the national
industries. All sects of social reformers propose great ameliora-
tions in the general lot and a greater equality in human conditions, but it is not known that there is any which commits itself
to the principle of complete economic equality to all with anything like the explicitness with which Nationalism does. The
formula of Nationalism is economic equality under an equal

law of service. This is merely the industrial and economic application of the law of military service and the right of military
protection as they are already recognized in all civilized nations.
Not all persons are equally able to render military service, but
the right of military protection is equally enjoyed by all women
as well as men, exempts as well as recruits. So it is likewise
with all public expenditures and indeed with all public functions of every sort, which are for the equal benefit of all although
some pay taxes and some do not. Here again Nationalism is
seen to be but the more perfect evolution of the national idea—
merely the extension to industry and general economics of a
principle already realized in the political, judicial, and military
functions of the nation.

Another distinctive principle of Nationalism is its rejection
of the principle of many other socialist schools that the propaganda of social reform should consist in the appeal chiefly or
exclusively to the proletariat or labouring class. It knows no class
feeling or class war, but appeals equally to all classes to join
hands in abolishing class. It is a national not a class movement.

While the spirit of the nationalist agitation is strongly patriotic, it should not be inferred that it is in any way opposed
to international sympathy. On the contrary it is believed that its
program points are the surest and straightest way by which an
international or world-union can be reached. Let once ten
nations be organized on a basis of industrial nationalism, or
even a few of them, and the very next step will be toward international federation.

The composition of the Nationalist clubs, in accordance with
the sentiment of the doctrine, has been made up of all classes
in the community, workingmen, business and professional men
and clergymen acting in cordial association. Several journals
and magazines published by the clubs or by sympathizers have
aided the educational work. The most important of these was
*The Nationalist,* a monthly magazine published for two years
by the Nationalist Educational Association of Boston and succeeded in 1891 by *The New Nation,* a weekly periodical published in Boston, of which I am editor.

The program of the Nationalists has from the first been a
double one. On the one hand they have devoted their efforts
to convincing the world theoretically of the beauty and feasible-
ness of an ultimate ideal of a fraternal order of society based
upon a national organization of industry for the equal benefit
of all. At the same time they have in the practical plane of leg-

islation and politics pushed a group of measures, as immediately practicable first steps in the direction of their ultimate end, which is the universal guarantee of employment according to gifts [innate abilities] and universal maintenance on the basis of equality. This practical program of first steps has consisted in the advocacy before municipal councils, state legislatures, and the national Congress, of the substitution of public municipal or national conduct of businesses at cost for the existing system of management by private corporations or individuals animated by the motive of profit. They have thus definitively advocated the management by municipalities of all public or quasi-public services such as water-works, lighting, street car and local transit systems, dock-yards, coal-yards, *etc.* They have also advocated the national ownership and operation of the telegraph, telephone, railroad, banking, and monetary systems, as well as exclusive national management of the coal-mining business and forest lands. They also advocate taking the sale of intoxicants wholly out of private hands and entrusting it to public agents with fixed salaries not dependent on amount of sales. Each sale [is] to be at cost of goods and management, with a view to eliminating the motive of profit in stimulating sales.

In all cases when the substitution of public for private management of business is professed, the idea is involved not only that the business should be conducted at cost and not for profit, but also that the employees should have a fixed tenure of positions, with admissions to the service and promotions in it dependent upon fixed tests of merit and not upon favoritism, dismissals not to take place without cause and pensions to be provided in case of accident and old age. The idea is, that is to say, that, as each business shall pass under public control, it shall to some extent illustrate both by the greater cheapness of that method and the humane and secure conditions it promises the employee, what and how great are the advantages the full application of Nationalism would bring to all.

While the city of Boston was the cradle of the Nationalist agitation and is still perhaps its most important local center, the portion of the United States in which the population has been most generally favorable to Nationalism has been the great agricultural states west of the Mississippi and those upon the Pacific coast. In these newly settled regions the force of conservative prejudice is less than in the older communities on the Atlantic coast. These Western populations, having with their own hands made a new world out of wilderness within a generation's time, find nothing to daunt them in the idea of establishing a new industrial system.

Economical causes have also had much to do with the favorable attitudes of this agricultural population toward radical social reform. The farming lands of the West have within a decade largely become mortgaged to the capitalists of the Eastern States at rates of interest making it impossible for the farmer to live and fore-closures on an unprecedented scale have already transformed a large percentage of the formerly independent farming class into tenants.

In minds prepared by such bitter experiences the seed of *Looking Backward* found congenial soil and it is accordingly in the Far West that the Nationalist propaganda has shown the most amazing results. Scores of the farmers' newspapers in that region already show their adherence to the full program of Nationalism, and [they] declare that the only possible relief for the people will ultimately be found in its adoption of a new national political party, called the People's Party, [which] arose last year and the year before among the farmers of the Western States, with a view to seeking by political means a radical improvement in their condition. This year it is receiving the support also of the farmers of the Southern States, and has moreover effected a coalition with powerful artisans' organizations.

The platform of the party demands several of the most important measures professed by the Nationalists; namely, national conduct of the banking system, telegraph, telephone and railroads, together with others. Prominent Nationalists are in the highest councils of the new party and the Nationalists generally, while maintaining with unabated zeal their radical propaganda, are, as a piece of opportunist policy, doing all they can to help a movement which has adopted so much of their immediate policy.

While the Nationalist agitation is of too recent an origin to be much understood outside of the United States, it has a foothold in Canada, and is represented in England by a number of organizations under the name of a "Nationalization of Labour Societies," which are affiliated with the Nationalist clubs of America.

In concluding this very hasty and desultory statement, I think it not too much to say that the awakening of the American people to the necessity and possibility of radical, social

and industrial reform which has taken place in the last four
years, has been astonishing. Four years ago radical solutions
were debated only by a few small and unheard of groups. Today
they are discussed on every hand, and the land is full of the
expectation of great changes.

EDWARD BELLAMY

*Chicopee Falls*
*Massachusetts, U.S.A.*
March, 1892*

---

* The original manuscript of this letter is preserved in the Literary
Archives in Moscow; this copy was prepared by A. Nikoljukin. A
photograph of the first page of Bellamy's letter was also supplied
with the cooperation of the Maxim Gorky Institute of World Literature.

*Appendix II*

# "The Programme of the Nationalists"*

By

## EDWARD BELLAMY

Chicopee-Falls (Massachusetts)

## I.

The publication of the following article† in *Nord und Süd*
gives me the welcome opportunity to tell my German readers
of *Looking Backward* something about the movement for introducing a basically new system of economy, to the establishment
of which that book has contributed in the United States. Socialism is something old for Europe; for America, however, something new. Since the beginning of the modern democratic and
humanist movement, the drama of the economic misery of the
masses has caused the mind of well-meaning and thinking persons to think about possible social reorganisations, which would
effectively improve general welfare. The situation was entirely
different in the United States. Thanks to the vastness of our
not yet occupied continent, our immense material resources,
and our relatively small population there was no economic
misery among our people until lately. Everyone, who was able
and ready to work, hitherto was generally able to earn his living.
Therefore socialist ideas had absolutely no soil in this country.
Scholars of national economy and some groups of European

---

* Authorized translation into German was by Georg von Gizycki,
Berlin, the translator of *Looking Backward;* this translation into English is by Franz Riederer.

†The article published in *Nord und Süd* was Bellamy's "First Steps
toward Nationalism" which had been published in *The Forum* (October, 1890).

immigrants knew something about socialism; but people generally neither knew anything about this subject, nor did they want to know anything about it.

The following article describes briefly the accumulation of wealth by which in recent times the economic situation of this country became worse. Of course this change gradually must effect all branches of economy; but its suddenness and rapidity certainly raises it to a wonder in history. The extraordinary, general impression which *Looking Backward* made in this country by its description of a better social system founded on economic equality can be explained to the greatest part by the fact that its publication occurred in a time when the American people seriously became conscious about the change of their situation. Immediately dozens and hundreds of clubs and associations were formed all over the country with the aim of spreading the idea of economic equality, founded on a nationalized system of industry. A great many magazines developed this doctrine, in particular among the population of the countryside; the bigger and richer part of the press attacked them and tried to make them ridiculous; and the monthlies and quarterlies opened their columns for the discussion. This idea became one of the main topics of argument in society and in the newspapers; and also those clergymen, who wanted to keep up with the times, had to preach about it. In one word, socialism, about which nothing was heard before, suddenly became a subject which stood in the foreground of public interest. This position, gained so suddenly, socialism was able to maintain completely. Indeed, nothing else could have been possible among thinking people, who saw that the threatening power of the plutocracy—which had made people listen to *Looking Backward*—year by year, even month by month, increasingly acquired an undeniable character, until even yonder man, who most optimistically had believed in the plain fortune of the republic, no longer could deny its terrible danger. Today it seems that the argument between the idea of democracy and the economic absolutism of private capital will reach a decision in America sooner than anywhere else. In this moment of world history, in particular in America, where the basic attitude of the people is intensively democratic, there can be no doubt as to what decision will be taken; it will be a system of nationalized industries with the guarantee of inalienable economic equality. In America there exist no monarchical nor aristocratic institutions or traditions, which could resist the people, once they would stand up; and when the

Americans rise, then they are very fast and radical in their actions. In America there exists nothing above the people, as the Constitution is their creation and is subjected to unlimited legal modifications by the votes of the citizens. In view of this situation I do not hesitate to foretell that if by the end of this century the socialist order is not introduced in Europe, America will be the pioneer of the world towards economic equality, just as before America had brought the so-called political equality.

In regard to the difference between Nationalism and other forms of socialism, it may be said that the Nationalists differ from the many other brands of socialists by the fact that they not only demand the corporative organisation of industry instead of private capitalism, but that they also demand that this corporative organisation will be a national one, embracing the whole nation, with the prerequisite, however, that the nation already possesses a democratic form of government. Furthermore, while many other socialists are satisfied with the demand of a "just" distribution of products, whatever this may mean, the Nationalists demand an equal distribution. The maxim of some other schools of socialists, "To everybody according to his work," we deny because this norm would be both immoral in its idea and unrealizable in practice. In regard to production and distribution of products we want to use the national principle, as it is demonstrated by the relation of the modern state to its citizens; that is, the demand of contributions from the citizens under one equal law with the consideration individual inability, and the continuing equal participation of all in the resulting wealth, without any consideration to the inequality of the contributions, which is the result of relative inability. The equal distribution of equally raised but necessarily unequal contributions is the principle of all public administrations in civilized countries, and this principle we intend to apply in the expansion of the public administration to industrial affairs.

In our propaganda we try to avoid a hateful, bitter tone, as we are of the opinion that such a strong matter as ours does not need the violence of speech. We appeal to all classes in the same way and reject—at least in America, which may also be valid for other countries—the idea that the equalization of human life must be the work of one single class of socitey. We always try to emphasize the moral side of our arguments.

I may add that the Nationalists, though they eagerly endeavor to carry out their measures by political and legislative means, are not associated with one particular political party. Their propaganda, so to speak, has been a pedagogical one and addressed to the spirit of the people generally. Nationalists may be found in all parties; but, in particular, they are active in the recently founded People's Party, which has adopted their practical programme of action to such an extent, that it sometimes is, wrongly, called the Nationalists' Party.

# Notes

## Notes to Chapter One

### EDWARD BELLAMY, THE AMERICAN PROPHET

1. Letter of E. B. to Benjamin Ticknor, June 15, 1888.
2. *Ibid.*, August 11, 1887, quoted in Mason Green, *Edward Bellamy* MS.
3. Alan Seagar, *They Worked for a Better World* (New York, 1939), p. 78.
4. E. Bellamy, "Progress of Nationalism in the United States," *North American Review*, CLIV, 426 (June, 1892), p. 746.
5. *Looking Backward*, pp. 41-42, 44-45, 92-93, 163, 169. (All references are to the Modern Library edition.)
6. Letter of EB, June 17, 1888, to William D. Howells.
7. W. F. Phillips, "Edward Bellamy, Prophet of Nationalism," *Westminster Review*, CL, 5 (November, 1898), pp. 502-3.
8. Anonymous, "A Look Ahead," *The Literary World* (March 17, 1888), p. 86.
9. Charles Madison, "Edward Bellamy, Social Dreamer," *New England Quarterly*, XV (September, 1942), 451-52.
10. "A Look Ahead," p. 85.
11. Laurence Gronlund, "A Reply to Dr. Heber Newton," *Nationalist*, I, 4 (September, 1889), pp. 158-61.
12. EB, "The Secret of Power," *New Nation*, II, 14 (April 2, 1892), p. 212; John Dewey, "The Great American Prophet," *Common Sense* (April, 1934).
13. Joseph Dorfman, *The Economic Mind in American Civilization* (New York, 1949), pp. 141-42; A. W. Levi, "Edward Bellamy, Utopian," *Ethics*, LV (January, 1945), 131-44.
14. EB, "How I Came to Write *Looking Backward*," *Ladies' Home Journal* (April, 1894), p. 2.
15. T. W. Higginson, "Step by Step," *Nationalist*, I, 4 (September, 1889), p. 145.
16. "The Lesson from Bellamy," Chicago *Journal*, May 24, 1898.
17. Dorfman, *The Economic Mind . . .* , pp. 141-42.
18. "The Lesson from Bellamy."
19. EB, "In the Interest of a Clear Use of Terms," *New Nation*, I, 46 (Dec. 12, 1891), pp. 725-26.
20. *Ibid.*
21. *Ibid.*
22. *Ibid.*
23. *Ibid.*

24. Green, *Edward Bellamy* MS, pp. 2-3.

25. EB, "Four Distinctive Principles of Nationalism," *New Nation*, II, 2 (January 9, 1892), pp. 17-18. Also: EB, "Talks on Nationalism," *New Nation*, I, 27 (August 8, 1891), pp. 425-27; S. Baxter, "What is Nationalism," *The Nationalist*, I, 1 (May, 1889), pp. 2-12.

26. S. E. Bowman, *The Year 2000, A Critical Biography of EB* (New York, 1958), p. 256.

27. *Ibid.*, p. 189.

28. *Ibid.*, p. 266.

29. *Ibid.*, pp. 153-91.

30. EB, "Looking Forward," *Nationalist*, II, 1 (December, 1889), pp. 2-4.

31. Bowman, *The Year 2000*, pp. 220-25.

32. Letter of EB, June 17, 1888, to W. D. Howells.

33. EB, "Looking Forward," pp. 2-4.

34. Letter of EB, December 23, 1888, to T. W. Higginson.

35. EB, MS "To Whom This May Come," "But it is. . . ."

36. Dewey, "The Great American Prophet," p. 2.

37. Laurence Gronlund, "Nationalism," *The Arena*, I, 2 (January, 1890), p. 158.

38. Charles Madison, "EB, Social Dreamer," *New England Quarterly* (September, 1942), p. 465.

39. Levi, "EB, Utopian," p. 131.

40. EB, "Letter to the People's Party Ratification Meeting," *New Nation*, II, 43 (October 22, 1892), pp. 644-45.

41. EB, "Principles and Purposes of Nationalism," Nationalist Reprint, p. 2.

42. Robert Cushman, *The Sin and Danger of Self Love Described in a Sermon Preached at Plymouth in New England in 1621* (Plymouth, Mass.), p. 24.

43. Clive Day, "Capitalistic and Socialistic Tendencies in the Puritan Colonies," *Annual Report of the American Historical Association for the Year 1920* (Washington, D. C., 1925), pp. 228, 232-35.

44. Walter Taylor, *The Economic Novel in America* (Chapel Hill, 1942), p. 19.

45. F. C. Clark, "A Neglected Socialist, Wilhelm Weitling," *Publications of the American Academy of Political and Social Science*, No. 144 (April 9, 1893), p. 79.

46. EB, "Literary Notices," *Springfield Union* (Dec. 31, 1874), p. 6.

47. *Ibid.* (Dec. 11, 1875), p. 6.

48. EB, "Concerning the Founding of Nationalist Colonies," *The New Nation*, III, 38 (Sept. 23, 1893), p. 434.

49. John Orvis, "Social Transition," *Nationalist*, III, 1 (Aug., 1890), pp. 1-16.

50. James F. Hudson, "The Anthracite Coal Pool," *North American Review*, CXLIV, 362 (Jan., 1887), p. 54.

51. EB, "Collapse of the International," *Springfield Union* (Sept.

26, 1874), p. 4.

52. Richard Ely, *Socialism and Social Reform* (New York, 1894), p. 87.

53. Etienne Cabét, "Préface de la Deuxième Edition," *Voyage en Icarie* (Paris, 1842), p. ii.

54. Louis Hartz, *The Liberal Tradition in America* (New York, 1955), p. 233.

55. EB, "The Reign of Terror Ended," *Springfield Union* (March 17, 1877), p. 6.

56. Unsigned Letter, Washington, D. C. to EB, March 23, 1889, pp. 1-5.

57. Letter to EB from C. F. Willard, Boston, March 22, 1889, pp. 5-6.

58. EB, *Equality* (New York, 1933), p. 153. (All quotations are from this edition.)

59. W. T. Harris, "EB's Vision," *Forum*, VIII (Oct., 1889), 199-200.

60. EB, "Two Good Christians," *Springfield Union* (April 25, 1877), p. 6.

61. EB, "Death of a Chartist," *New Nation*, II, 33 (Aug. 13, 1892), p. 518.

62. EB, "Literary Notices," *Springfield Union* (Sept. 23, 1875), p. 6.

63. *Ibid.* (Nov. 13, 1873), p. 6.

64. EB, Notebook 4 [187?], p. 60.

65. EB, "Literary Notices," *Springfield Union* (April 15, 1876), p. 6.

66. *Ibid.*, (May 27, 1876), p. 6.

67. *Ibid.*, (Sept. 30, 1876), p. 6.

68. *Ibid.*, (June 1, 1876), p. 6.

69. EB, "Religion and Science," *Springfield Union* (March 30, 1875), p. 4.

70. EB, "Literary Notices," *Springfield Union* (May 8, 1875), p. 6.

71. EB Notebook, possessed by Marion Bellamy Earnshaw, Springfield, Mass.

72. EB, "Literary Notices," *Springfield Union* (April 21, 1877), p. 6.

73. *Looking Backward*, p. 107.

74. Hartz, *The Liberal Tradition* . . . , p. 50; quotes Gunnar Myrdal, p. 50.

75. Robert Spiller, *et al.*, *Literary History of the United States* (New York, 1953), p. 991.

76. Elizabeth Sadler, "One Book's Influence: Edward Bellamy's 'Looking Backward,'" *New England Quarterly*, XVII, 4 (Dec., 1944), pp. 530-55.

77. Louis Boudin, "A Marxian Looks at America, This Un-American Movement," *Our America* (January, 1933), pp. 1-2.

*Notes to Chapter Two*

A Little-Known Story:  Bellamy in Russia

1.  A detailed description of Isabel Hapgood's Russian literary contacts may be found in *Memoirs of I. I. Yanshul, 1864-1909,* (2nd ed.; St. Petersburg, 1911), II, 12-17. All titles of Russian books and articles are given in the English translation.

2.  L. N. Tolstoy, *Complete Works* (Moscow, 1952), L, 101. The translator friend was E. Mengden (1822-1902) but it is not certain that this translation was published.

3.  *Ibid.* (Moscow, 1953), LXIV, 335-36.

4.  Tolstoy marked pp. 459-61, 463, and 465 which describe West's dream in the copy of *Looking Backward* (Boston: Ticknor and Co., 1888), VI–470.

5.  Tolstoy, *op. cit.,* XXVIII, 27; L, 101-2; "The Slavery of Our Times," trans. from the Russian MS by A. Maude (London: Free Age Press, c1900), p. 50.

6.  From the archives of the Moscow Censorship Committee.

7.  From the archives of the Central Censorship Committee of Foreign Books and the Chief Press Department. In 1898 the circulation of a German translation by M. Jacobi of this novel by Bellamy was banned in Russia (Archives of the Moscow Censorship Committee).

8.  "New Utopian Dreams," *Novey Zhurnal Inostrannoi Literaturi,* 1897, No. 5, p. 235.

9.  *Novey Zhurnal Literaturi, Iskusstva i Nauki,* 1907, No. 10, p. 13.

10.  Before 1917 F. Zinin's translation of *Looking Backward* was published six times in from 3,000 to 5,100 copies; L. Gay's translation came out in two editions in from 2,000 to 3,000 copies; Klyukin's translation, two editions of 2,400 copies each; Efimov's edition, 3,000 copies; popular rendition by B. S. Mayevsky, twice in 3,000 copies each. In 1918, 10,000 copies were printed; the figures for the reprint of 1917 have been lost.

11.  V. Syvatlovsky, *The Russian Utopian Novel* (St. Petersburg, 1922), pp. 9, 50.

12.  Collection of documents and material entitled *Working Class Movement in Russia in the XIXth Century,* ed. A. M. Pankratova (Moscow, 1952), Vol. III, Part 2, p. 62.

13.  *Rizhsky Vestnik,* XLI, 1 (February 19, 1891).

14.  M. Tugan-Baranovsky, "The Socialist Order," *Ehemesyachny Zhurnal dlya Vsekh* (1906), No. 6, p. 362.

15.  *Ibid.,* p. 363.

16.  S. I. Mitskevich, *Revolutionary Moscow, 1888-1905* (Moscow: Khudozhestvennaya Literatura, 1940), p. 76.

17. N. A. Rubakin, *Studies of the Russian Reading Public. Facts, Figures and Observations* (St. Petersburg, 1895), pp. 244-45.

18. M. A. Bagayev, *Ten Years. The Social-Democratic Organization in Ivanovo-Voznesensk District, 1892-1902*, ed. by O. A. Varentsova, N. N. Kudryashev, and S. P. Shesternin (Ivanovo-Voznesensk: State Publishing House, Ivanovo Regional Branch, 1930). N. I. Makhov, *Past Life* (Ivanovo, 1939). S. P. Shesternin, *Reminiscences From the History of the Workers' and Revolutionary Movement of 1880-1900*, ed. and preface by O.A. Varentsova and M. A. Bagayev (Ivanovo: Gosizdat, 1940).

19. Bagayev, *op. cit.*, pp. 26, 36, 37.

20. Memoirs of N. Kudryashov, quoted from Bagayev, *op. cit.*, p. 35.

21. Makhov, *op. cit.*, p. 85.

22. Quoted from Shesternin, *op. cit.*, p. 118.

23. Makhov, *op. cit.*, p. 113.

24. "Nadejda Konstantinova Krupskaya," *Women of the Whole World* (March, 1960), pp. 42-43.

25. *Narodny utschitel*, No. 3, 1931, p. 79; republished in: *N. K. Krupskaya. Pedagogical Works*, IV (Moscow, 1959), 410.

26. For an example, see long article entitled "Utopia of the Modern Age," *Nablyudatel* (1898), Nos. 7, 8.

27. *Vestnik Yevropi* (1890), No. 5, pp. 202-3.

28. K. Golovin, *Socialism as a Positive Teaching* (St. Petersburg, 1892), p. 82.

29. Rtsi, *Sketches, An Evening of Black and White Magic (A Phantasy on the Theme of 'Looking Backward' by Bellamy)*, (Kiev, 1891), p. 14.

30. *Ibid.*, p. 7.

31. *Ibid.*, p. 14.

32. S. Sharapov, *Works* (Moscow, 1902), VIII, 3-4.

33. *Ibid.*

34. N. N. Shelonsky, *In the World of the Future, A Fantastic Novel* (Moscow, 1892), pp. 261, 226, 223.

35. *Ibid.*, p. 228.

36. *Ibid.*, pp. 203-4.

37. *Ibid.*, p. 211.

38. *Ibid.*, p. 244.

39. *Ibid.*, p. 293.

40. A. P. Chekhov, *Complete Works and Letters* (Moscow, 1949), XV, 136.

41. V. G. Korolenko, *Collected Works in Ten Volumes* (Moscow, 1956), X, 219. Books published in U. S. A.: *The Vagrant and Other Tales* (1887); *The Blind Musician* (1890); *Makar's Dream and Other Stories* (1916); *Birds of Heaven and Other Stories* (1919); *In A Strange Land* (1925).

42. A. M. Gorky, *Collected Works in Thirty Volumes* (Moscow, 1954), XXVIII, 258.

43. *The Press*, Philadelphia, May 29, 1906.

44. R. Ganelin, "M. Gorky and the American Public in 1906," *Appleton's Magazine* (1906), No. 8, p. 182; *Russkaya Literatura* (1958), No. 1, p. 221.


## Notes to Chapter Three

### A British Sensation

1. S. E. Bowman, *The Year 2000* . . . . (New York, 1958), p. 120.

2. A. H. Nethercot, *The First Five Lives of Annie Besant* (Chicago, 1960) contains many interesting sidelights on the people mentioned in this paragraph. For information about Joyce and "A. E." Russell, see Ellmann, *James Joyce* (Oxford University Press, 1959).

3. E. Sylvia Pankhurst, *The Suffragette Movement* (London, 1931).

4. Mrs. Edward Bellamy, "Interview," *Springfield Union*, Bellamy family clipping file.

5. Bowman, *op. cit.*, pp. 43-44.

6. Henry Holiday, *Reminiscences of my Life* (London, 1914), p. 347.

7. Dugald MacFayden, *Sir Ebenezer Howard and the Town Planning Movement*, (Manchester, 1933), p. 20.

8. Holiday, *op. cit.*, p. 351.

9. Helen Merrell Lynd, *England in the Eighteen-Eighties*, (New York, 1945), p. 369. No authority for this figure is given.

10. *The Review of Reviews*, I (1890), 230.

11. Holiday, *op. cit.*, pp. 350-51.

12. Bowman, *op. cit.*, p. 121.

13. Letter of Thomas Reynolds, London, August 5, 1897, to Edward Bellamy. The book Reynolds presented to Prince Khan is in the New York Public Library.

14. Holiday, *op. cit.*, p. 449.

15. A. L. Morton, *The English Utopia* (London, 1952), pp. 174-75.

16. M. L. Berneri, *Journey Through Utopia* (London, 1950), p. 238.

17. *Ibid.*, pp. 281-82.

18. Andreas Scheu to Alfred Russel Wallace, February 3, 1909, British Museum Add. MSS 46440.

19. J. Bruce Glasier, *William Morris and the Early Days of the Socialist Movement* . . . (London, 1921), pp. 149-51.

20. Morton, *op. cit.*, p. 155.

21. May Morris, *William Morris* . . . (Oxford, 1936), II, 501-7.

22. Morton, *op. cit.*, p. 161.

23. Berneri, *op. cit.*, p. 259.

24. "Mr. Bellamy's Critics," *Lend a Hand*, V, 1 (January, 1891), p. 4.

25. [E. Bellamy] "News from Nowhere," *New Nation*, I, 3 (February 14, 1891), p. 47.

26. Nethercot, *op. cit.*, pp. 299-300.

27. H. Pearson, *Oscar Wilde: His Life and Wit* (London, 1946), p. 141.

28. Oscar Wilde, *The Soul of Man Under Socialism* (Boston, n.d.), pp. 34-35.

29. *Ibid.*, pp. 33-34.

30. *Seed-Time*, 10 (October 1891).

31. Morton, *op. cit.*, p. 169.

32. John Orme, Letter to E. Bellamy.

33. *Nationalization News* (October 4, 1890). The account and quotations of the proceedings of the Society which follow are drawn from this source.

34. Ruth R. Lewis, "Kaweah: An Experiment in Cooperative Colonization," *Pacific Historical Review*, XVII (1948), pp. 429-41.

35. Edward R. Pease, *The History of the Fabian Society* (2nd ed.; London, 1925), p. 26.

36. Wm. Clarke quoted by Harry W. Laidler, *A History of Socialist Thought* (New York, 1927), p. 234.

37. Pease, *op. cit.*, pp. 28-35.

38. Laidler, *op. cit.*, p. 237.

39. Sidney Webb, *Socialism in England* (2nd ed.; London, 1893), p. 37.

40. *Ibid.*, pp. 88-89.

41. Nethercot, *op. cit.*, p. 270.

42. "Concerning Nationalism—Nationalist Meeting at Chicago," *New Nation*, III, 37 (September 16, 1893), p. 428.

43. E. Bellamy, "Introduction," *Socialism: The Fabian Essays* (Boston, 1894), pp. xv-xviii.

44. Laidler, *op. cit.*, p. 236.

45. Archibald Henderson, *Bernard Shaw, Playboy and Prophet* (New York, 1932), p. 182.

46. Sidney Webb, *Socialism True and False*, Fabian Tract 51 (London, 1894), pp. 10-12.

47. Sidney Webb, *The Difficulties of Individualism*, Fabian Tract 69 (London, 1896), p. 1.

48. *Report on Fabian Policy*, Fabian Tract 70 (London, 1896), p. 8; C. E. M. Joad (ed.), *Shaw and Society* (London, 1951), pp. 125-26.

49. Bowman, *op. cit.*, p. 140.

50. Holiday, *op. cit.*, p. 453.

51. *Review of Reviews*, 33 (1906), pp. 568-82.
52. G. D. H. Cole, *Socialist Thought Marxism and Anarchism 1850-1890* (London, 1954), p. 361.
53. Alexander Gray, *The Socialist Tradition* (London, 1946), p. 75.
54. R. C. K. Ensor, *England 1870-1914* (Oxford, 1936), p. 334.
55. Josiah C. Wedgwood, *Memoirs of a Fighting Life* (London, 1940), p. 33; C. V. Wedgwood, *The Last of the Radicals* (London, 1951), pp. 42-43.
56. Fenner Brockway, *Bermondsey Story* (London, 1949), p. 6.
57. Fenner Brockway, *Socialism over Sixty Years* . . . (London, 1946), p. 204.
58. H. M. Pelling, *The Origins of the Labour Party 1880-1900* (London, 1954), p. 141.
59. *Labour Annual, 1898* (London & Manchester, 1898), p. 211.
60. *Labour Annual* (Manchester, 1895), p. 187.
61. A. L. Morton, letter of February, 1957, to S. E. Bowman.
62. G. K. Chesterton, *Autobiography* (London, 1937), p. 25.
63. Holiday, *op. cit.*, p. 349.
64. *Ibid.*, pp. 350-51.
65. *Ibid.*, pp. 356-57.
66. H. Stanley Jevons, *Economic Equality in the Co-operative Commonwealth* (London, 1933), p. xx.
67. *Ibid.*, p. xvii.
68. Morton, *op. cit.*, p. 149.
69. Berneri, *op. cit.*, p. 243.
70. *Ibid.*, p. 244.
71. *Ibid.*, p. 230.
72. *Ibid.*, p. 252.
73. *Ibid.*, p. 253.
74. *Ibid.*, p. 255.
75. Alfred Russel Wallace, *My Life* . . . (London, 1908), pp. 326-27.
76. *Ibid.*, pp. 327-28.
77. Andreas Scheu to Wallace, February 3, 1909, February 11, 1909. British Museum Add. MSS 46440.
78. Macfayden, *op. cit.*, p. 21. Ebenezer Howard, *Garden Cities of Tomorrow*, F. J. Osborn (ed.) (London, 1946), pp. 20-21.
79. Lewis Mumford, *The Culture of Cities*, (3rd edition; London, 1944), pp. 397-98.
80. Harold Orlans, *Utopia Ltd.*, (New Haven, 1953), p. 7.
81. Julian Kaye, *Bernard Shaw and the Nineteenth Century* (Norman, Okla., 1958), pp. 145-52.
82. J. W. Cunliffe (ed.), *Writing of Today* . . . (New York, 1920), pp. 232-40.
83. Antonia Vallentin, *H. G. Wells* (New York, 1950), pp. 78-79, 106-7.
84. *Ibid.*, p. 126.

85. H. G. Wells, *A Modern Utopia* (London, 1905), p. 100.
86. Morton, *op. cit.*, p. 184.
87. Ensor, *op. cit.*, p. 334.
88. All the information about the literary influence of Bellamy was added by S. E. Bowman; any errors in this material about Wells, Shaw, Russell, Jevons, and Wilde are hers.—S. E. Bowman.

## Notes to Chapter Four

### THE AUSTRALIAN IMPACT

1. N. G. Butlin, "The Shape of the Australian Economy, 1860-1900," *Economic Record*, XXXIV, 67 (April, 1958).
2. *Ibid.*
3. T. A. Coghlen, *Wealth and Progress of New South Wales* (Sydney: N. S. W., Govt. Printer, 1891), pp. 770-71.
4. B. C. Fitzpatrick, *The British Empire in Australia* (Melbourne: M. U. P., 1949), p. 193.
5. Francis Adams, *The Australians* (London: Fisher Unwin, 1893), p. 165.
6. Russel Ward, *The Australian Legend* (Melbourne: O. U. P., 1958), pp. 193-94.
7. *Ibid.*, p. 167.
8. W. G. Spence, *Australia's Awakening: Thirty Years in the Life of an Australian Agitator* (Sydney: Worker Trustees, 1909), p. 78.
9. Ward, *The Australian Legend*, p. 208.
10. Adams, *The Australians*, p. 54.
11. Max O'Rell (pseud.), *John Bull & Co., the Great Colonial Branches of the Firm* (London, 1899), p. 189.
12. Adams, *The Australians*, p. 55.
13. *Ibid.*, p. 56.
14. *Bulletin*, Sept. 14, 1889.
15. *Ibid.*, Feb. 1, 1890.
16. *Ibid.*
17. *Worker*, Sept. 1, 1890.
18. *Worker*, May 1, 1890.
19. *Worker*, July 1, 1890.
20. *Ibid.*
21. *Worker*, Sept. 1, 1890.
22. *Ibid.*
23. *Worker*, Aug. 7, 1890.
24. *Worker*, Nov. 1, 1890.
25. *Worker*, Mar. 1, 1890.

26. *Worker,* July 1, 1890.
27. *Worker,* Aug. 7, 1890.
28. *Worker,* Sept. 1, 1890.
29. *Worker,* Oct. 1, 1890.
30. *Worker,* Oct. 18, 1890.
31. *Worker,* Aug. 7, 1890.
32. *Ibid.*
33. Ward, *The Australian Legend,* pp. 173ff.
34. N. S. W. *Royal Commission on Strikes* (Sydney: Government Printer, 1891). Evidence of Thomas Allwright Dibbs, question 4619.
35. *Worker,* May 1, 1890.
36. *Worker,* Oct. 22, 1892.
37. *Worker,* June 12, 1890.
38. *Worker,* Aug. 7, 1890.
39. *Worker,* April 16, 1891.
40. Lloyd Ross, *William Lane and the Australian Labor Movement* (Sydney Forward Press, n.d.).
41. See B. C. Fitzpatrick, *A Short History of the Australian Labor Movement* (Melbourne: Rawson, 1944); G. Greenwood (ed.), *Australia: A Social and Political History* (Sydney: Angus & Robertson, 1955); and R. Gollan, "The Trade Unions and Labour Parties, 1890-94," *Historical Studies,* VII, 25 (November, 1955).
42. N. S. W. *Royal Commission on Strikes,* q. 1810.
43. V. S. Clark, *The Labour Movement in Australia: A Study in Social-Democracy* (New York: Holt, 1906); S. & B. Webb, *Industrial Democracy* (Edinburgh: The Authors, 1913); A. Metin, *Le Socialisme sans Doctrines: Australie et Nouvelle Zelande* (Paris: Alcan, 1901).
44. Ross, *William Lane and the Australian Labor Movement.*
45. P. J. O'Farrell, "The Australian Socialist League and the Labour Movement, 1887-91," *Historical Studies,* VIII, 30.

## Notes to Chapter Five

### CANADIAN REACTION

1. This article is published in the appendix of this volume.
2. Paul Bellamy, quoted by Gordon Rigby in a letter to Alexander Scott, published in the *New Zealand Worker,* September 27, 1933, p. 1, col. 7.
3. Mrs. Edward Bellamy, Morgan Papers, No. XXXVIII, Houghton Library, Harvard University.
4. EB, *Looking Backward* (Toronto, n.d.).
5. EB, *Equality* (Toronto, 1897).
6. Herbert Clark, letter of September 25, 1958, to W. R. Fraser.

7. Harold Winch, letter of April 7, 1958, to W. R. Fraser.

8. Douglas Carr, letter of October 18, 1958, from Toronto, Canada, to S. E. Bowman.

9. J. A. M., "Looking Backward," *Knox College Monthly*, X, 4 (1896).

10. John A. Cooper, "Bellamy and Howells," *Canadian Magazine*, IX (1897).

11. W. A. Douglas, "Bellamy's Blunders," *Canadian Magazine*, X (January, 1898), 268, 269, 270.

12. James Edward Le Rossignol, "The March of Socialism," *The University Magazine*, XI, 3 (October, 1912), p. 432.

13. Sylvia Thrupp, "Review of Arthur Morgan's Edward Bellamy," *Canadian Forum* (January, 1945), p. 237.

14. Maurice Colbourne, *The Real George Bernard Shaw* (New York, 1949), p. 294.

15. Everett W. MacNair, *Edward Bellamy and the Nationalist Movement, 1889-1894* (Milwaukee, 1957), pp. 256, 259.

16. *Ibid.*, p. 256.

17. *Ibid.*, p. 259, quoted from *Wilshire's Magazine* (January, 1902), p. 3.

18. *Ibid.*, p. 258.

19. *Ibid.*, p. 256, quoted from Wilshire's address from *The Trust*, pp. 4 and 16.

20. Letter of October 20, 1958, of M. J. Coldwell to W. R. Fraser.

21. Letters of October 4, 1958, September 26, 1958, and April 7, 1959, from W. E. Peirce to W. R. Fraser.

22. Le Rossignol, *op. cit.*, p. 412.

23. Harold Winch, letter of October 20, 1958, to W. R. Fraser.

24. A. Andras, letter of October 1, 1958, to W. R. Fraser.

25. W. R. Fraser, *A White Stone* (New York, 1955), p. 4.

26. S. M. Lipset, *Agrarian Socialism*, p. 3.

27. J. S. Woodworth, Foreword, *Social Planning for Canada*.

28. F. R. Scott, "The C. C. F. Convention," *Canadian Forum* (September, 1933), pp. 447-48, quoted by Lipset, *Agrarian Socialism*.

29. Scott, *op. cit.*

30. Lipset, *Agrarian Socialism*, p. 3.

31. W. R. Fraser, *Journal*.

32. Stephen Leacock, letter of January 17, 1934, to Mrs. E. Bellamy, Bellamy Family Files, Springfield, Mass.

33. A. E. Morgan, *Edward Bellamy* (New York, 1944), pp. xi-xii; also letter of March 27, 1939, from Leacock to Morgan, Harvard Library, pp. 1-2.

34. Dr. R. H. Ross's address as reported in the Sherbrooke *Daily Record* of September 20, 1950.

35. Warren E. Brokaw, *Equitable Society and How to Create It* (New York, 1927), pp. 225-26.

# 460   EDWARD BELLAMY ABROAD

36. A. B. Davies, "Christocracy" (1948).
37. Mrs. Marion B. Earnshaw in an interview with Sylvia E. Bowman, September, 1958, as reported to W. R. Fraser.
38. Fraser, *A White Stone*, p. 167.
39. Fraser, "Distributive Justice and the 'Single Price,'" paper read to the Canadian Congress of Philosophy, June, 1958, at Edmonton, p. 5.


## Notes to Chapter Six

### THE GERMAN ACCEPTANCE AND REACTION

1. Arthur von Kirchenheim, "Schlaraffia Politica," *Geschichte der Dichtungen von besten Staate*, (1892), p. 259.
2. Bruno Schoenlank, "Socialism in Germany," *New Nation*, I, 8 (March 21, 1891), p. 130.
3. Today's Social-Democrat weekly *Vorwaerts*, central organ of the West German party, is the successor of the *Vorwaerts* published in Leipzig from 1876 to 1878 and of the publication of the same name of 1891, which originated from the *Berliner Volksblatt* founded in 1884.
4. George von Gizycki's translation was reprinted in Reclam's *Universal Bibliothek* in 1916 and 1937; it was also published by the house of Wolf and Ruthe of Magdeburg in 1919.
5. Until 1942 Reclam's Universal Library listed 7,500 books.
6. Luise Dornemann, *Clara Zetkin* (Dietz, 1958), p. 440.
7. "Nadejda Konstantinova Krupskaya," *Women of the Whole World*, (March 8, 1960), pp. 42-43.
8. Among the other books published by Clara Zetkin are: *Die Arbeiterinnen und die Frauenfrage der Gegenwart* (Berlin, 1889); *Geistiges Proletariat, Frauenfrage und Sozialismus* (Berlin, 1902); *Der Weg nach Moskau* (Moscow, 1920); *Das weltweite Taetigkeitsfeld der Kommunistischen Internationale* (Hamburg, 1924); *Die Bedeutung der aufbauenden Sowjetunion fuer die deutsche Arbeiterklasse* (Berlin, 1926); *Hungermai–Blutmai–Roter Mai* (Hamburg-Berlin, 1932); *Erinnerungen an Lenin* (Dietz Verlag, Berlin, 1957).
9. The title of the serial was *2000-1889. Ein Ruckblick aus dem zwanzigsten Jahrhundert;* and the magazine in which it was published was a family newspaper–*Familienblatt*–published by Gustav G. Steiner and Company of Vienna, Berlin, Leipzig, and New York. This serialization was mentioned by Dr. F. Kleinwaechter in *Die Staatsromane* (1891), which is also discussed in this study.
10. "Der juengste Zukunftsroman," *Die Neue Zeit* (June, 1889), p. 268.
11. *Looking Backward,* ed. Max Schippel (Berlin, 1889, 1893).

12. "Der Juengste Zukunftsroman," *op. cit.*, p. 270.
13. *Ibid.*, p. 271.
14. *Ibid.*, p. 273.
15. *Ibid.*
16. "Eine soziale Utopie," *Monatsschrift fuer christliche Social-reform*, XII (Vienna, 1890), 598.
17. Hans Gustav Erdmannsdoerffer, *Ein Phantasiestaat. Kritik von Bellamy's Rueckblick* (Leipzig, 1891), pp. 29-30.
18. Heinrich Fraenkel, *Gegen Bellamy* (Wuerzburg, 1891), p. 9.
19. Theodor Hertzka, *Freiland*, (Leipzig, 1890), pp. xxxiv, 677.
20. J. Jastrow, *Jahrbuch fuer Gesetzgebung, Verwaltung und Volkswirtschaft im Deutschen Reich*, XV (1891), 520.
21. Frederich Kleinwaechter, *Die Staatsromane—Ein Beitrag zur Lehre vom Communismus und Socialismus* (Wien, 1891), p. 4.
22. *Ibid.*, pp. 114, 118, 119.
23. Richard Loewenthal, *Der Staat Bellamy's und seine Nachfolge* (Berlin, 1892), p. 11.
24. Carl Tiburtius, *Bellamy als Lehrer* (Berlin, 1892), p. 6.
25. *Ibid.*, p. 26.
26. Moritz Brasch, "Bellamy's Vorgaenger," *Deutsche Revue*, I (1893), 256.
27. Franz Sintenis, *Literararische Ansichten in Vortraegen: H. Sudermann, H. Seidel, Bret Harte, Mark Twain, E. Bellamy* (Jurjew, 1894), p. 76.
28. *Ibid.*, p. 77.
29. *Ibid.*, p. 78.
30. *Ibid.*, p. 79.
31. Julie Romm, "Bellamy's Gleichheit," *Die Neue Zeit*, I (1898), 590.
32. *Ibid.*, p. 594.
33. *Ibid.*
34. Ernesto Gagliardi, "*Equality*. Eine neue Utopie von Bellamy," *Magazin fuer Litteratur* (Berlin, 1897), p. 1458.
35. Ottmar Weichmann, *Edward Bellamy's 'Ein Rueckblick aus dem Jahr 2000 auf 1887' im Zusammenhang mit den Staatsromanen der Vergangenheit* (Claw, 1908), p. 13.
36. Fritz Koch, *Bellamy's Zukunftsstaat* (Bonn, 1924), p. 130.
37. *Ibid.*, p. 133.
38. Edwin M. J. Kretzman, *The Pre-War German Utopian Novel, 1890-1914*. (Unpublished doctoral thesis, Brown University, 1936.) p. 76.
39. *Ibid.*, p. 72; also p. 161.
40. *Ibid.*, p. 72.
41. Dr. Herman Duncker, Introduction, *Looking Backward*, tr. by Clara Zetkin (1949), p. 5.
42. *Ibid.*, p. 7.
43. *Ibid.*
44. Rudolf Blueher, *Modern Utopien* (Bonn, 1920), p. 87.

45. *Ibid.*, p. 88.
46. *Ibid.*, p. 87.
47. Ernst Bloch, *Freiheit und Ordnung* (Berlin, 1947), p. 197.
48. "Mr. Bellamy's Critics," *Lend A Hand*, VI, 1 (Jan., 1891), pp. 2-3.
49. Richard Michaelis, *Ein Blick in die Zukunft. Eine Antwort auf: 'Ein Rueckblick' von Edward Bellamy* (Leipzig, 1891), pp. 80, 81.
50. Philipp Laicus [P. Wasserburg], *Etwas spaeter! Fortsetzung von Bellamy's Rueckblick aus dem Jahr 2000* (Mainz, 1891), p. 54.
51. *Ibid.*, p. 189.
52. Conrad Wilbrandt, *Der Herrn Friedrich Ost Erlebnisse in der Welt Bellamy's* (Wismar, 1891), p. 80.
53. *Ibid.*, p. 144.
54. Ernst Mueller, *Ein Rueckblick aus dem Jahre 2037 auf das Jahr 2000* (3rd. ed.; Berlin, 1891), p. 39.
55. *Ibid.*, p. 92.
56. Ferdinand Kemsies, *Sozialistische und ethische Erziehung im Jahre 2000* (Berlin, 1893), p. 27.
57. A. Reichardt, *Des Bellamy Zeitalter 2001-2010 Efindungen, Entdeckungen und Begebnisse* (Berlin, 1893), p. 60.
58. *Ibid.*, p. 161.
59. Theodor Herzl, *Altneuland* (Berlin, Wien, 1900), p. 165.
60. *Ibid.*, p. 329.
61. *Ibid.*, p. 300.
62. *Ibid.*, p. 334.
63. [Edward Bellamy] "Some Account of Eugen Richter's Anti-Socialist Romance," *New Nation*, III, 22 (June 3, 1893), pp. 273-75.
64. Mason Green, *Edward Bellamy* MS, Harvard Library, p. 123.
65. Eugen Richter, *Sozialdemokratische Zukunftsbilder* (Berlin, 1892), p. 8.
66. [Edward Bellamy] "Freeland: An Austrian *Looking Backward*," *New Nation*, I, 39 (October 24, 1891), pp. 614-15.
67. See back cover of *Das neunzehnte und zwanzigste Jahrhundert*, essays by L. B. Hellenbach, ed. Dr. Karl du Prel (Leipzig, 1893).
68. This volume was not available for study.
69. L. B. Hellenbach, *Die Insel Mellonta* (Leipzig, 1887), pp. 23, 226.
70. Wilhelm Schaefer, *Aus einem anarchischen Idealstaat* (Hanover, 1906), p. 16.
71. *Ibid.*, p. 35.
72. Kretzman, *op. cit.*, p. 76.
73. *Ibid.*, p. 75.
74. *Ibid.*, p. 121.
75. *Ibid.*, p. 122.
76. *Ibid.*, p. 123.
77. *Ibid.*, pp. 116-17.

78. Heinrich Stroebel, *Die erste Millarde der zweiten Billion* (Berlin, 1919), pp. 14, 227.

79. *Ibid.*, p. 270.

80. *Ibid.*, pp. 15, 18.

81. Fraenkel, *op. cit.*, p. 3.

82. Friedrich Engels, *Der Sozialismus von der Utopie zur Wissenschaft* (Muenchen, 1946), but the first edition was published in 1883.

83. Protocol of the negotiations at the Party Congress of the German Socialist Party in Berlin in 1890, quoted from *Das Erfurter Programm* (Muenchen, 1947), p. 40.

84. F. Engels, "Der Entwurf eines neuen Parteiprogrammes," *Die Neue Zeit* IX (1890-91), 724.

85. Fraenkel, *op. cit.*, p. 4.

86. August Bebel, *Die Frau und der Sozialismus* (9th ed.; Stuttgart, 1891), pp. vi-viii.

87. *Ibid.*, pp. vii, ix.

88. *Bebel und sein Zukunftsstaat vor dem Reichstag* (Koeln, 1893), p. 18.

89. *Ibid.*, p. 36.

90. *Ibid.*, p. 151.

91. Dr. Karl Renner, *Karl Kautsky* (Berlin, 1929), p. 95.

92. Karl Kautsky, *Die Soziale Revolution—II. Am Tage nach der sozialen Revolution* (2nd ed.; Berlin, 1907), p. 3.

93. Franz Laufkoetter, "Utopistische Ideen im Modernen Sozialismus," *Sozialistische Monatsheft*, III (September-December, 1908), 1342-44.

94. Dr. Kurt Schumacher, *Aufgaben und Ziele der Deutschen Sozialdemokratie* (Karlsruhe, 1946), p. 7.

95. *Das Heidelberger Programm,* (Muenchen, 1947), p. 3.

96. Vorstand der Sozialdemokratischen Partei Deutschlands (ed.), *Grundsatzprogramme der Sozialdemokratischen Partei Deutschlands* (Bonn, 1959), p. 26.

97. *Ibid.*, p. 7.

98. *Ibid.*, p. 8.

99. *Ibid.*, p. 14.

100. *Ibid.*, p. 15.

101. *Stimme der Arbeit,* organ of the free trade press of Hessen, No. 15, August, 1948.

102. Arthur Morgan, *Edward Bellamy* (New York, 1944), p. x.

103. *Ibid.*, p. x.

104. Dr. Rudolf Broda, *Die Kulturaufgaben des Jahrhunderts* (Berlin, 1914), p. 17.

105. "Die Einzelnen in der modernen Gesellschaft," *Muenchner Merkur* (Nov. 7, 1958), p. 7.

*Notes to Chapter Seven*

THE BELLAMY ASSOCIATION OF HOLLAND

All references for this chapter are included within the text.

*Notes to Chapter Eight*

BELLAMY SOCIETIES OF INDONESIA, SOUTH AFRICA, AND NEW ZEALAND

*Indonesia and South Africa*

1. *De Uitweg, V*, 8 (October, 1938), p. 66.
2. Letter of K. Zylstra, Ede, Holland, July 12, 1958, to Sylvia E. Bowman.
3. *Ibid.*
4. Telegram to Mrs. Edward Bellamy from Chairman Valdhuysen, Bandoeng, July 29, 1935.
5. Letters of Mrs. R. W. Hughes to Mrs. E. Bellamy, Wheaton, Illinois, June 13, 1939.
6. Letter of R. Neil Williams to Mrs. E. Bellamy, Bandoeng, Java, September 26, 1939.
7. Letter from R. F. Kennedy, City Librarian, Johannesburg, South Africa, to S. E. Bowman, December 10, 1957.
8. *The International Bellamy League* (South Africa), p. 4.
9. Telegram to Mrs. E. Bellamy from F. Bell, Johannesburg, October 14, 1933.
10. Typed MS of *Constitution of South African Section of the International Bellamy League,* October 11, 1932, pp. 1-4.
11. Letter from D. H. Varley, Secretary and Chief Librarian, South African Library, Capetown, May 28, 1956, to S. E. Bowman.
12. "What Do You Know About Edward Bellamy?" *The Cape Argus* (Capetown), November 17, 1934.
13. *The International Bellamy League* (South Africa), pp. 1-4.

*New Zealand*

1. William Pember Reeves, *State Experiments in Australia and New Zealand* (London, 1902), I, 74.
2. William Pember Reeves, *Some Historical Articles on Communism and Socialism* (Christchurch, 1890), p. 8.
3. *Ibid.,* p. 2.
4. Advertisement, *Auckland Star,* April 19, 1890.
5. *Auckland Star,* April 26, 1890.
6. *New Zealand Tablet* (Dunedin), May 30, 1890.

7. Advertisement, *Evening Star* (Dunedin), April 17, 1890.

8. Maurice William Richmond, "Looking Backward," *The Monthly Review* (Wellington), I, 448, (Sept., 1889).

9. William Freeman Kitchen, "Looking Backward, 2000-1887," *Zealandia* (Dunedin), I, 296-97 (Nov. 1889).

10. *New Zealand Tablet* (Dunedin), May 30, 1890.

11. *Ibid.*, June 6, 1890.

12. Editorial, "Will-o'-the-Wisp," *Typo* (Napier), IV, 106-7 (Sept. 27, 1890).

13. William Pember Reeves, *State Experiments in Australia and New Zealand* (London, 1902), I, 75.

14. Quoted in Sidney Wilfred Scott, *Outline History of the New Zealand Labour Movement* (3rd. ed.; Auckland, 1951), p. 14.

15. John Ballance, "The Altruistic State," *The Monthly Review* (Wellington), II, 218 (April, 1890).

16. *Ibid.*, p. 219.

17. David Low, *Autobiography* (London, 1956), p. 40.

18. Letter of A. Scott, May 14, 1933, to Upton Sinclair, reprinted in *The New Zealand Worker* (Wellington), Sept. 27, 1933.

19. *Ibid.*, September 27, 1933: A. Scott, "Bellamy's *Looking Backward.*"

20. *Ibid.*, n.d.: "*Looking Backward*/Bellamy's Famous . . . ."

21. Letter of A. Scott, March 27, 1934, to Mrs. E. Bellamy.

22. Letter of Wm. H. Auckland, April 3, 1935, to Upton Sinclair.

23. Alexander Scott, "Labour Wants the People's Mandate to End Poverty in N.Z.," *The New Zealand Worker* (Wellington), Aug. 28, 1935.

24. Alexander Scott, "Idealist, Philosopher, Psychologist and Seer," *The Standard* (Wellington), Dec. 24, 1935.

25. Letter of Mrs. E. Bellamy, April 24, 1936, to A. Scott, reprinted in *The Standard* (Wellington), June 17, 1936.

26. "Bellamy Society Notes," *The Standard* (Wellington), July 22, 1936.

27. William John Lyon, Reply (undated) to Edward Bellamy Society's Questionnaire of Aug. 15, 1936.

28. Letter of D. G. McMillan, Aug. 18, 1936, to Edward Bellamy Society.

29. "Bellamy Society Notes," *The Standard* (Wellington), Aug. 26, 1936.

30. Evidence of Edward Bellamy Society before the National Health and Superannuation Committee, 1938, *passim.*

31. *Ibid.*, p. 2 G 35.

32. New Zealand. Parliament. National Health and Superannuation Committee, *Report* (Wellington, 1938), p. 17. Universal superannuation at age sixty-five, regardless of income, was introduced in 1940. The amount payable has steadily increased until today (1960) it is of the same value as the Age Benefit. The latter, which is paid from the age of sixty, is, however, still subject to a means test. The

Family Benefit, a weekly payment for every child up to the age of sixteen (or eighteen, if full-time education is continued) was introduced in 1946. It is paid regardless of the parents' income.

33. Letter of A. Scott, April 17, 1938, to Mrs. E. Bellamy.
34. "Talk on Social Justice," by Alexander Scott, radioscript MS (1938), pp. 1-6.
35. "The Prophet Is Not Dead," radioscript MS by Alexander Scott (May 22, 1938), pp. 1-7.
36. "Two 'Books of the Age' As Well As 'Books of the Moment,'" by A. Scott, radioscript MS, pp. 1-7.
37. Letter of A. Scott, June 1, 1938, to Mrs. E. Bellamy.
38. Letter of A. Scott, April 9, 1937, p. 1.
39. Letter of A. Scott, Aug. 16, 1943, to Mrs. E. Bellamy.
40. Letter of R. S. Odell, July 12, 1946, to Miss J. Kliphuis. (This twenty-four-year old Dutch girl had written to the Prime Minister asking whether the Bellamy system was in force in New Zealand. A. Scott had been asked to draft the reply.)
41. Letter of A. E. Hollay, Sept. 6, 1960, to Miss S. E. Bowman.
42. The phrase was coined by an American, Professor Frank Parsons, in his *The Story of New Zealand* (Philadelphia, 1904).
43. Letter of A. Scott, September 15, 1960, to H. Roth.

## Notes to Chapter Nine

### A CONTRIBUTION TO SCANDINAVIAN SOCIALISM

1. Cf. Hj. Branting, "En svensk utopist," *Ur Dagens Krönika*, VII, 192-99 (1887); Ivar Vennerström, *Svenska utopister* (Stockholm: Tidens Förlag, 1913). In this study Bellamy's *Looking Backward* is mentioned among a number of other Utopian books (p. 111). For the emergence of socialism, see Carl Stegman & C. Hugo, *Handbuch des Socialismus* (Zurich, 1897).
2. *Illustrert Tidende* (1887-1888), pp. 503-5, 515-17, 527, 539-41, 551-53.
3. The Swedish translation, which followed the seventeenth American edition, was also published in 1889.
4. See S. Magelssen Groth, "Ko-operative Husholdninger," *Tilskueren*, pp. 920-32 (1892); Argus, "Socialisternas Fremtidsstat," *Ibid.*, pp. 241-48 (1892). See also *Tilskueren*, pp. 331-32, 332-34, 401-4, 567-70 (1892). Cf. Gerson Trier, "Anarkismen," *Ibid.*, pp. 307-27, 397-412, 493-504, 608-28 (1894); Frantz Pio, "Kommunesocialisme," *Ibid.*, pp. 223-41 (1898); and Gustaf Borg, *Den socialistiske Fremtidsstat* (Copenhagen, 1903).
5. U. Birkedal, "Utopier og Virkelighed," *Dansk Tidskrift*, pp. 513-41 (1899). The quotation is on page 537.

6. Bellamy's half-page excerpt began: "Let nobody falsely assume that I dream of happiness without struggle, abundance without work." Rousseau's motto read: "Jordens Frugter tilhøre alle, Jorden ingen."

7. Reidar Øksnevad's *Sambandsstatene i norsk litteratur* (Oslo, 1950) contains no reference to Bellamy. Nor was there any article about Bellamy in the leftist magazine *Klassekampen* (1912-1915).

8. See *Norsk Bogfortegnelse* (1888-1940) and *Årskatalog over Norsk litteratur* (1946-1956).

9. Report of Houghton Mifflin, Morgan Collection, Harvard University Library.

10. Professor Sigmund Skard, letter of April 23, 1959, Oslo, Norway, to S. E. Bowman.

11. *Kringsjaa*, III, 453-58 (March 17, 1894). The article was taken from *The Forum*.

12. "Det fabiske sambund," *Kringsjaa*, III, 566-73 (April 15, 1894); see particularly note on p. 569.

13. *Kringsjaa*, III, 711 (May 1, 1894).

14. There was a Danish society and a Norwegian branch which helped to support the Freiland experiment. See *Kringsjaa*, IV, 317-18 (1894). The California socialist colony of Altruria was discussed in *Kringsjaa*, V, 400, 921-23 (1895) and New Harmony in Indiana, *Ibid.*, pp. 407 ff.

15. "Socialisme i praksis," *Kringsjaa*, X, 759-63 (1897).

16. *Ibid.*, XII, 79 (1898).

17. See *Aschehougs Konversajons Leksikon* (Oslo, 1939) and *Norsk Allkunnebok* (Oslo, 1948).

18. *Arbeidernes Leksikon* (Oslo: Arbeidermagesinets Forlag, 1932).

19. Prof. Skard, *op. cit.*

20. This firm had earlier published *Furst Serebräny* by Tolstoy and *Klara Militsch* by Turgenev in addition to a number of historical romances.

21. Cf. Carl L. Anderson, *The Swedish Acceptance of American Literature* (Stockholm, 1957), p. 34.

22. The sale was pushed by advertisement. See, for instance, the cover of *Ur Dagens Krönika*, IX (December, 1889).

23. Karl Fernström, *Ungsocialismen. En krönika.* (Stockholm: Federative Förlag, 1950). *Karl Börjesson 1877-1941. En minnesbok.* (Stockholm: Svenska Antikvariatsföreningen, 1942).

24. Johan Leffler, "Hvad är socialism?" *Nordisk Tidskrift*, III, 89-108 (1890). Bellamy is discussed on pp. 102-3.

25. "Samhällsutopier," *Ute och Hemma*, II, 401 (1890).

26. Richard Hofstadter, *The Age of Reform* (New York, 1955), p. 68. Hofstadter adds on p. 70 that Donnelly "doubtless" intended his "fantasy . . . to say what would happen if the warnings of reformers" went unheeded.

27. L.H.Å., "Moderna utopier och framtidstankar," *Svensk Tid-*

*skrift.* In a review of Theodor Hertzka's Utopian *Freiland* (1890) a reference was made to *Looking Backward.* See Bredo Morgenstierne, "En tysk Henry George," *Nordisk Tidskrift,* IV, 249-65 (1891). See Algot Ruhe, "Konstens undergång," *Ord och Bild,* II, 563-68 (1893). An attack was also directed against Whitman's "monstrous" verse in this article.

28. Otto v. Zweigbergk, "Den sociala frågan i den moderna litteraturen," *Ord och Bild,* I, 370-73 (1892). The author discussed also Richter's *Socialdemokratiska framtidsbilder,* Donnelly's *Världens undergång,* Zola's *Germinal,* Per Sivle's *Strejk* and Paul Göhre's *Tre månader som fabriksarbetare.*

29. John Alexander, "Hur jag blef socialist," *Brand,* II, No. 9 (1899), p. 3.

30. *Katalog över Stockholms Arbetarbiblioteksförbunds Bibliotek.* No. 1. By Knut Tengdahl and Edm. Lindborg (Stockholm, 1892). Two books by Bellamy were listed under the title *Skönlitteratur,* namely *Doktor Heidenhoffs upptäckt,* No. 276, and *En återblick,* Nos. 275, 284, 420, 500. The Library also owned *Looking Backward* in English, No. 222. There were also four copies of Henry George's *Sociala spörsmål,* listed under the heading *Ekonomi, Statistik. Samhälleliga frågor. Socialism,* p. 31. The 1894 *Katalog* lists five copies of *En återblick,* p. 3. *En återblick* was listed as No. 2 of Stockholm's *Arbetarbiblioteksförbunds Vandringsbibliotek* (Stockholm, 1910).

31. The translator was probably Ann Gödecke. See unpublished letter of Anna Gödecke to Socialdemokratiska Partistyrelsen, March 29, 1901. Arbetarrörelsens Arkiv.

32. The four-page pamphlet entitled "Det nya samhället" by Bellamy was printed by Walfrid Wilhelmsson.

33. It was published in September, 1899.

34. *Brand,* I (December, 1898).

35. *Ibid.,* II, 3 (March, 1899).

36. *Ibid.,* II, 4 (March, 1899).

37. *Ibid.,* II, No. 9, p. 4 (1899).

38. See note 31.

39. "Utopier," *Stormklockan,* III, 3 (October 22, 1910).

40. Olof Lagercrantz, "Ett socialistiskt paradis," *Dagens Hyheter,* January 2, 1960.

41. Sigmund Skard, *American Studies in Europe,* II, 453 (Philadelphia, Pa., 1958). See also Leo Ehrnrooth, "Den nya riktningen inom den tyska social-demokratin" *Finsk Tidskrift,* LIV, 504-22 (1903) and the same author's "Synpunkter i var arbetarfraga," *Ibid.,* LV, 282-304 (1903).

42. *Finsk Tidskrift,* XXIX, 467-68 (1890).

43. *Ibid.,* XXXII, 172 (1892).

44. G. Enckell made his interesting comparison between Benjamin Kidd's *Den sociala utyecklingen* and *Looking Backward* in "Benjamin Kidds bok: Den sociala utvecklingen," *Humanitas,* III, 121-36, (1898).

45. Philip Durham and Tauno F. Mustanoja, *American Fiction in Finland: An Essay and Bibliography* (Helsinki, 1960), p. 55.

46. Danielsson referred to Bellamy's solution of the problem of distribution by means of credit cards in a speech delivered at a Stockholm labor club on May 25, 1891. See "Anarki eller socialism" (Anarchy or Socialism) in *Urval av Axel Danielssons skrifter*, ed. Bengt Lidforss (Malmo, 1908). Danielsson also lectured about More, Plato, and Bellamy.

47. This statement is from "Edvard Bellamy dod," which was unsigned, but which was probably written by Hj. Branting, the editor of the paper in which the notice appeared: *Social-Demokraten* (May 26, 1898).

## Notes to Chapter Ten

### CHANGING FRENCH ATTITUDES

1. Cyrille Arnavon, *Les Lettres américaines devant la Critique Française* (Paris, 1951), p. 11.

2. T. Bentzon (pseud. of Thérèse de Salms Blanc), "Les Nouveaux Romans Américains," *Revue des Deux-Mondes* (August 1, 1885), p. 15.

3. *Ibid.*; see also Introduction to R. Issant's translation of *Miss Ludington's Sister.*

4. Combes de Lestrade also wrote *Sicily under the Savoie Monarchy* (1894) and *The Monarchies of the German Empire* (1904).

5. Noted among Rey's works are: *Elliptics* (poems in prose with melodies by the author); *Ninarels* (1904); *Occitanian Poems; La Razurga.*

6. Arnavon, *op. cit.*, pp. 14-15.

7. "La Société de l'Avenir," *Revue des Deux-Mondes* (October 15, 1890), 30 pp.

8. *Ibid.*

9. T. Bentzon, "La Communisme en Amérique—Le Communisme dans la Fiction," *Revue des Deux-Mondes* (October 1, 1897), pp. 569-96.

10. Arnavon, *op. cit.*, p. 15.

11. Caro, "Etudes morales sur le temps présent" in *Les Meilleurs Ecrivains français, classiques et modernes, apologistes de la Foi chretienne*, ed. Mazuel (1898).

12. *Ibid.*, Etudes des Pères Jésuites (1895), Vol. II, No. 65.

13. Jaures, quoted in *Social Democrat Herald* (July 9, 1898).

14. "Le Socialisme en Amérique," *Revue des Revues* (1890), pp. 26-27.

15. *Ibid.*, January, 1891.

16. Marchioness San Carlos, "Les Américains chez Eux—Le Socialisme aux Etats-Unis," *La Nouvelle Revue* (May 15, 1890), pp. 280-307.

17. E. Grenard, "Choses et Gens d'Amérique" de T. Bentzon, *Polybiblion*, Vol. XLVIII (1899).

18. *Utopies de Justice* (Neufchatel, 1898).

19. An article was also published by Helene Burgues in *Population* (April-June, 1951) which contained about twenty-five lines about *Looking Backward*. Since the material is very general, it was not quoted.

20. Address of the M. F. A. is 30, rue Leningrad, Paris.

21. Cercle Civique Vosgien: 3, rue d'Alsace, Epinal.

22. There are two great Esperantist Associations: the first in date, the Universal Esperantist Association, is politically neutral; the second—Mondial A-National Association or S. A. T.—is the one which thinks that Esperanto should be used for political purposes.

23. The translation of *Looking Backward* was due to Mr. C. M. Hamaker; it was originally published by Cohen Brothers in Holland.

24. Mr. Cottereau, the editor of the French Esperanto bulletin and secretary of the group, also mentioned an article about an "appeal for the Abundance Section," which had been published in *The French Esperantist* (February, 1947). Other articles were— among the list presented—"About the Bellamy-Abundance Section," *Sennaciulo* (the A-National). June, 1955; "Distributive Economy," *Vegetarano* (The Vegetarian), Summer, 1958.

25. F. A. R. has the following address: 19, rue Milton, Paris IX; publishes *Agir*.

26. G.A.E.D. has the following address: 9 place Bonsergent, Paris X; publishes *Réagir*.

27. Secretary of the *Egalité* movement is Mr. A. Dufourd, 14, rue de Metz, Toulouse.

28. *Temps Nouveaux*, 40 rue de la Division Leclerc, Butry (S. et. O). The president of the association is Mr. J. M. Bugat; he is also the president of the "Friends of Law," director of the *Grandes Conferences de Paris* (Paris Great Lectures), and of the *Cahiers de la Quinzaine* (Bi-weekly Books). The Friendship Clubs were created to gather together the sympathizers of the Bi-weekly Books.

29. With such a vast subject, one may easily overlook information which should have been included. We hope that the reader will show understanding and that this chapter will open the way for further research.

## Notes to Chapter Eleven

### THE CATHOLIC, LIBERAL ATTACKS IN BELGIUM

1. For fuller information, see: Van Kalken, *Histoire de la Belgique* (Brussels, 1954); Terlinden *et autres, Histoire de la Belgique Contemporaine, 1830-1914*, Vol. I (Brussels, 1928); Van Kalken, *Commotions Populaires en Belgique (1834-1902)* (Brussels, 1936); Bertrand, *Le Parti Ouvrier Belge et son Programme* (Brussels, 1886); Bertrand, *Souvenirs d'un Meneur socialiste*, Vol. I (Brussels, 1927); Destrée et Vandervelde, *Le Socialisme en Belgique* (1st ed.; Paris, 1898); Daumont, *L'Evolution du Socialisme Belge* (Brussels, 1914).

2. Van Kalken, *Histoire de la Belgique*, p. 616.

3. L. Delsinne, *Le Parti Ouvrier Belge des Origines à 1894* (Brussels, 1955), pp. 69ff.

4. See: C. Huysmans, *La Plus-Value Immobilière* (Abonnement Germinal, 1909) which mentions the foreign collectivists, except Bellamy. *Manifeste des étudiants socialistes de l'Université de Gand* (Abonnement Germinal, March 1910): This apology of collectivism mentions such writers as Marx, Engels, Vandervelde, Solvay, Anseele, H. G. Wells, but not Bellamy. See also *L'Action Socialiste, Lettres d'E. Vandervelde à la Gazette de Bruxelles* (Abonnement Germinal, 1911); L. Bertrand, *Souvenirs d'un Meneur Socialiste* (Brussels, 1927); L. Bertrand, *Le Parti Ouvrier Belge et son Programme* (Brussels, 1886); E. Vandervelde, *Cours sur les Doctrines Sociales au 19ᵉ Siècle* (Extension Universitaire de Bruxelles, 1894); J. P. Koch, *Quelques Expériences collectivistes* (Brussels, 1947); "Let us skip over the first socialist authors, Proudhon, etc., and let us at once go over to the two genuine representatives—they might almost be called 'inventors'—of modern collectivism: Karl Marx and Lassalle" (Comte de Bousies, *Le Collectivisme et ses conséquences*, p. 21, in a chapter entitled: "La théorie collectiviste et ses promoteurs"). ("Passons les premiers auteurs socialistes: Proudhon, etc., pour arriver de suite aux deux veritables représentants—on pourrait presque dire inventeurs—du collectivisme actuel: Karl Marx et Lassalle.)

5. C. Huysmans, letter to author, December 25, 1958.

6. P. Geiregat, *Maatschappelijke Vraagstukken, Gedachten ontleend aan Edw. Bellamy, Em. de Laveleye en Ch. Richet* (Ghent, 1893), pp. 64-77: Bellamy door Em. de Laveleye beoordeeld.

7. *Ibid.*, p. 5.

8. *Ibid.*, p. 75.

9. *Ibid.*, p. 76.

10. *Ibid.*, pp. 76-77.

11. *Ibid.*, p. 77.

12. *Ibid.*

13. *Ibid.*, p. 21.

14. *Ibid.*, p. 67.
15. *Ibid.*, p. 69.
16. *Ibid.*
17. *Ibid.*, p. 66.
18. *Ibid.*, p. 67.
19. Van Kalken, *Histoire de Belgique,* p. 614.
20. Richter, *Socialisme au Pouvoir,* ed. A. Baisir, Foreword.
21. Jean Halleux, "Le Société de l'Avenir d'après Bellamy," *Revue Générale,* LV (June, 1892), 915.
22. *Ibid.*, p. 903.
23. *Ibid.*, pp. 906, 910.
24. *Ibid.*, p. 915.
25. "Un Journal du 21e Siècle," *Revue Générale,* LV (June 1892), 916.
26. *Ibid.*, p. 916.
27. *Ibid.*, p. 920.
28. Comte Eméric du Chastel, "Deux Romans à propos du Socialisme," *Revue Générale,* LIX (March, 1894), 114-15.
29. *Ibid.*, p. 114.
30. *Ibid.*, p. 104.
31. In 1895 the Comité de Propagande de la Presse Catholique published a pamphlet: *"Le Socialisme au Pouvoir"* by Richter (in the series *Bibliothèque de Propagande Antisocialiste,* n. 8) with the subtitle "Application a notre Pays," by A. Baisir, p. 366.
32. *Het Jaar 2000 of de Socialisten in Werking, door Ed. Bellamy; Uittreksels en Bemerkingen door Arthur Verhaegen* (Antisocialistische Propagandabibliotheek, *circum* 1895).
33. This group published material for only social and labor groups.
34. Van Kalken, *Histoire de Belgique,* p. 726.

> ("Ses chefs n'avaient plus tous confiance dans l'infaillibilité des theories marxistes. Les jeunes envisageaient des Plans, 'durs et neufs.' Ils abandonnaient l'internationalisme, le slogan du prolétariat exploité et la tactique révolutionnaire pour concentrer leurs efforts sur la nationalisation de quelques industries de base et sur la direction de l'économie du pays par l'Etat.")

35. *De Uitweg* (October, 1938), p. 66. This listing is as follows: "Belgie: Gent: Mej. Maria de Keyser, Sluizekens-Straat 4. Gent. Antwerpen: Frans de Craene, Haantjeslei 157, Antwerpen."
36. The following information about the "Bellamy Vereniging" is derived from an interview the author had with two founders of the association, Mrs. de Sweemer and Mr. Arpad Lödör, and from the minutes of the different meetings of the association, as well as from other material provided by the founders.
37. Minutes of the Ghent Bellamy Association, p. 1:

("1) het *propageeren van de ideeën,* voorgesteld in beide boeken van Bellamy, en dit aan *alle leden* der bevolking.

2) aantoonen der oorzaken van de tegenwoordige toestanden, voortvloeiende uit de actuele ekonomie.

3) aanwerven van interesseerende.")

38. Minutes of the Ghent Bellamy Association, p. 3.

39. Even the statutes of the Association were to be copied literally from the Dutch statutes.

40. "Argus," *De Dag,* October 27, 1939, p. 2, col. 2.

41. *Ibid.*

42. "Argus," *De Dag,* October 28, 1939, p. 10, col. 2.

43. A. Blavier, letter to author, January, 1959: "Mon expérience de bibliothécaire m'a permis de m'assurer d'une chose: c'est qu'il existe, aujourd'hui encore, une sorte de transmission orale et quasi franc-maconnique des vertus du livre de Bellamy. Ainsi, régulièrement, des individus qui ne lisent autrement rien, me demandent en grand mystère si j'ai *L'an 2000* et l'emportent radieux. C'est en gros la même catégorie de lecteurs que celle des spirites et autres adeptes de toutes les théosophies."

## Notes to Chapter Twelve

### THE ITALIAN CONTROVERSY

1. Much of this material about historical background is from Carlo Morandi's *I partiti Politici nella Storia d'Italia* (Florence, 1957).

2. Letter of P. Mazzoni, London, July 21, 1890, to Edward Bellamy, Houghton Library, Harvard University.

3. Paolo Mantegazza, *L'anno 3000* (Milan, 1897), p. 119.

4. *Ibid.,* p. 250.

5. *Ibid.,* pp. 39-42.

6. *Ibid.,* pp. 28-45.

7. *Ibid.,* pp. 48-49.

8. These quotations are from the translations of the German editions and are from John Kretzmann, *The Pre-War German Utopian Novel 1890-1914,* p. 139.

9. Mantegazza, *op. cit.,* p. 253.

10. F. S. Merlino, *Pro e Contro il Socialismo* (Milan, 1897), p. 173.

11. Merlino, *L'Utopia Collettivista* (Milan, 1898), p. 39.

12. *Ibid.,* pp. 51-52.

13. Dante, *Purgatorio,* XXI, 136.

14. *L'Avanti,* May 27, 1898.
15. *Corriere della Sera,* May 27-28, 1898.
16. Carlo Curcio, *Miti della Politica* (Rome, 1940), p. 296.
17. *Ibid.,* p. 301.
18. Benedetto Croce, *Storia d'Italia, 1871-1915* (Bari, 1928), p. 164.
19. *Gazzetta Padana,* October 26, 1957.
20. *Leggere,* No. 5, May, 1958.


## Notes to Chapter Thirteen

### In Other European Countries

1. *Encykopedja Powszecha,* p. 1.
2. *Ibid.*
3. *Glos,* No. 43 (November 3, 1890), p. 561.
4. H. Pac, Foreword, Henry George and Edward Bellamy . . . (MS, University of Warsaw, 1955).
5. *Ibid.,* pp. 66, 74.
6. *Ibid.,* pp. 63, 62, 60.
7. *Ibid.,* pp. 74, 53, 54-55.
8. *Ibid.,* p. 74.
9. *Ibid.,* pp. 74-75.
10. *Ibid.,* p. 75.
11. *Ibid.,* p. 76.
12. *Ibid.,* pp. 76-77.
13. *Ibid.,* p. 77.
14. *Ibid.,* pp. 77-78.
15. *Ibid.,* p. 81.
16. Dr. F. Backovsky, *Vzpominkovy Sbonik* (Prague, 1928), pp. 134, 203.
17. *Ibid.,* p. 134.
18. *Ibid.,* p. 211.
19. *Ibid.,* p. 213.
20. *Ibid.,* pp. 212, 217.
21. *Ibid.,* p. 199.
22. *Ibid.,* p. 201.
23. *Ibid.,* p. 203.
24. *Ibid.,* pp. 201, 134.
25. *Ibid.,* p. 34.
26. *Ibid.*

## Notes to Chapter Fourteen

### THE THEOSOPHICAL SOCIETY; THE ORIENT

*Letters cited in this chapter are listed in the bibliography only.*

1. Arthur Nethercot, *The First Five Lives of Annie Besant* (Chicago, 1960), p. 270.

2. Arthur Morgan, *Edward Bellamy* (New York, 1944), pp. 260-75, 269ff., 275.

3. Everett W. MacNair, *Edward Bellamy and the Nationalist Movement, 1889-1894* (Milwaukee, 1957), pp. 329-30.

4. Morgan, *op. cit.*, pp. 262-63.

5. See also the *Path*, October, 1889. In this article it is stated that Bellamy had *a* plan but not necessarily *the* plan; the writer thought the people would win a new state through revolution. Also quoted by MacNair, *op. cit.*, p. 329.

6. Nethercot, *op. cit.*, p. 349.

7. *Ibid.*

8. *Ibid*

9. *Ibid.*, p. 350.

10. *Ibid.*

11. *Ibid.*, p. 195.

12. J. Nehru, *Toward Freedom* (New York, 1941), pp. 28-29.

13. *Ibid.*, p. 38.

14. J. Nehru, *The Discovery of India* (New York, 1946), p. 534.

15. Donald Smith, *Nehru and Democracy* (Calcutta, 1958), pp. 112-13.

16. J. Nehru, *The Discovery of India*, p. 534.

17. Norman Cousins, *Talks with Nehru* (New York, 1951), p. 11.

18. Smith, *op. cit.*, p. 108.

19. *Ibid.*, p. 112.

## Notes to Chapter Fifteen

### PATTERNS OF CRITICISM, INFLUENCE, FUTURE RESEARCH

1. A. D. Vinton, *Looking Further Backward* (Albany, 1890), p. 50.

2. L. Gronlund, Preface, *The Co-operative Commonwealth* (2nd. ed.; Boston, 1890), p. viii.

3. General F. A. Walker, "Edward Bellamy and the New Nationalist Movement," *Atlantic Monthly* (February, 1890) quoted in E. Bellamy, "'Looking Backward' Again," *North American Review* (March, 1890), pp. 353, 357.

4. W. L. Garrison, "Mask of Tyranny," *Arena* (April, 1890), p. 555-56.

5. Joel Benton, article in *Social Economist* quoted by Bellamy in "What Mr. Joel Benton Thinks Nationalism is Like," *New Nation*, III, 3 (January 21, 1893), 34.

6. Edward Bellamy, "Talks on Nationalism," *New Nation*, I, 17 (May 23, 1891), 264-65. According to Mason Green, *Edward Bellamy* MS, Harvard University, Spencer's attack was in the preface to a volume of anti-socialistic essays.

7. Emile de Laveleye and others quoted by Bellamy, "What 'Nationalism' Means," *Contemporary Review* (July, 1890), pp. 8-9, 11.

8. Henry George, *Progress and Poverty*, (4th ed.), pp. xvi, xvii, 320.

9. William Morris, "Looking Backward," *The Commonweal* V, 180 (June 22, 1889), 194-95.

10. Garrison, *op. cit.*, p. 555.

11. W. T. Harris, "Edward Bellamy's Vision," *Forum* (October, 1889), p. 202.

12. Michael Maher, "Socialist's Dream," *The Month* (January, 1891), p. 14.

13. G. Smith, "Prophet of Unrest," *Forum* (August, 1890), pp. 604, 609. See also: John Rae, *Contemporary Socialism* (New York, 1910), pp. 403-4.

14. Richard Ely, *The Labor Movement in America* (New York, 1886), pp. 31, 186-87.

15. Max Georgii, "Co-operative Society of Ghent," *The Nationalist* (January, 1890), pp. 53-57.

16. Annie Besant, "Industry Under Socialism," *Fabian Essays* (Boston, 1894), pp. 150-51.

17. G. B. Shaw, *Fabian Essays* (Boston, 1894), p. 6.

18. C. R. Henderson, "Fact and Fiction in Social Study," *The Dial* (July 16, 1897), p. 49.

19. Mrs. Marie A. Brown, *The True Author of Looking Backward* (New York, 1890), p. 40.

20. Henry Austin, *Address of . . . Before the Second Nationalist Club of Boston at Twilight Hall*, August 25, 1890 (Boston, n.d.), p. 9.

21. Caroline Fairfield Corbin, *The Position of Women in Utopia* (Chicago, 1901), pp. 15-16.

22. Anna L. Dawes, "Mr. Bellamy and Christianity," *Andover Review* (April, 1891), pp. 413-18.

23. See the following articles:

William Higgs, "Bellamy: Objections to His Utopia," *New Englander and Yale Review* (March, 1890), pp. 231-39; Michael Maher, *op. cit.*, pp. 1-9, 320; (February, 1891), pp. 173-88; A. G. Sedgwick, "Bellamy's Utopia," *The Nation* (August 26, 1897), pp. 170-71.

24. Frances Willard, "An Interview with Edward Bellamy," *Our Day* (December, 1889), p. 542.

25. Henry George, cited in Bellamy MSS, Houghton Library, Harvard University, XXIV, 4, 5.

26. *Ibid.*, p. 7.

27. Brown, *op. cit.*, pp. 20-23.

28. Mason Green, Unpublished Biography of E. Bellamy, Houghton Library, Harvard, p. 4.

29. John Dewey, "American Prophet," *Common Sense*, III, 4 (April, 1934), p. 7.

30. H. A. Meyers, *Are Men Equal?* (Binghamton, N. Y.: 1955), p. 126.

31. Mason Green, "Unconscious Nationalism in Our American System of Government," *New Englander and Yale Review* (February, 1890), pp. 97-106.

32. [E. B.] "Points to be Remembered," *New Nation* (November 4, 1893), p. 483; " 'Looking Backward' Again," *North American Review* (March, 1890), p. 354.

33. *Ibid.*

34. [E. B.] "Talks on Nationalism," *New Nation* (May 23, 1891), pp. 264-65.

35. E. Bellamy, *Equality*, p. 407ff.

36. *Ibid.*, pp. 51, 145, 147-52, 282-85, 412.

37. William James, "The Moral Equivalent of War," quoted by Arthur Morgan, *Edward Bellamy* (New York, 1944), p. 326.

38. Dewey, *op. cit.*, p. 7.

39. Bowman, *The Year 2000*, pp. 102-4, 201-5.

40. *Ibid.*

41. *Ibid.*

42. Rensis Likert, "Motivation: The Core of Management" (New York, 1953), pp. 3-20.

43. F. C. Minaker, *Short Course in Supervision* (Chicago, 1956, 1958), pp. 38-39.

44. U. S. Chamber of Commerce, "The Washington Report," February 25, 1957.

45. C. Wright Mills, "On Reason and Freedom," *Identity and Anxiety*, ed. Maurice R. Stein, *et al.* (Glencoe, Illinois: The Free Press, 1960), pp. 114-19.

46. Bruno Bettelheim, *The Informed Heart* (Glencoe, Illinois), p. 289 fn.

47. *Ibid.*, pp. 14-15, 37, 38, 47.

48. *Ibid.*, pp. 87, 92, 105, 195, 198, 293, 293-94, 300.

49. *Ibid.*, p. 288.

50. *Ibid.*, p. 11.

51. *Ibid.*, p. viii.

52. Reinhold Niebuhr, *Moral Man and Immoral Society* (1931), pp. xvii-xxiii.

53. Ortega y Gasset, *The Revolt of the Masses* (1932), p. 47.

54. Alfred Cobban, *In Search of Humanity* (New York, 1960), p. 12.

55. Bettelheim, *op. cit.*, p. 62.

56. *Ibid.*, p. 57fn.

57. *Ibid.*, pp. 122-23.

58. A. A. Berle, Jr., "Dynamics of the Dollar," *Saturday Review* (July 9, 1960), p. 19.

59. Reports given at American Psychological Convention in Cincinnati, in 1959.

60. Letters of J. H. Hamilton, Indiana University, March 2, 1894, to Edward Bellamy. Bellamy MSS, Harvard University, 1181 (206).

61. Howard Quint, *The Forging of American Socialism* (Columbia, S. C., 1953), p. 126. See also Dombrowski and MacNair.

62. Mason Green, *Edward Bellamy*, pp. 108-9, unpublished MS in Harvard Bellamy Collection.

63. Alex Bein, *Theodor Herzl* (Philadelphia, 1943), pp. 121-227.

64. Quoted from *Nationalist* (1890) by Quint, *op. cit.*, p. 83.

65. Richard Hofstader, *The Age of Reform from Bryan to F. D. R.* (New York, 1956), p. 67.

66. Theodore Draper, *The Roots of American Communism* (New York, 1957), p. 14.

67. Max Lerner, *America As a Civilization* (New York, 1957), p. 33. Bellamy is also cited on page 718 as a contrast to those who "say that American thought has a feet-on-the-ground realism."

68. Stewart H. Holbrook, *Dreamers of the American Dream* (New York, 1957), p. 313.

69. Martin Buber, *Paths in Utopia* (London, 1949), p. 5.

70. *Ibid.*, p. 6.

71. Walter F. Taylor, *Literary History of the United States.* Eds., R. E. Spiller, W. Thorp, *et al.* (New York, 1953), p. 989.

# Bibliography

The international bibliography is arranged in alphabetical order by the names of countries in order to make reference to it easier for the reader or the researcher. Although this international listing of translations of Bellamy's novels, articles about him, Utopias written in reaction to his, and books influenced by him or mentioning him does not pretend to be complete, it is as complete as the current world situation and the fallibility of humanity could make it. The material listed under the section entitled "United States" contains only a listing of books and articles directly concerning Bellamy which were mentioned in chapters I and XV. Since *The Year 2000: A Critical Biography of Edward Bellamy* (1958) contains an almost complete bibliography—or at least the most extensive one ever compiled or published—it was thought futile to repeat the listings.

It is also hoped that readers in other countries who know of articles, translations, or books about, or written in reaction to Bellamy will generously contribute their information to the major author of the volume so that the international bibliography may someday be more complete.

S. E. B.

## AUSTRALIA

ADAMS, FRANCIS. *The Australians.* London: Fisher Unwin, 1893.
*The Bulletin* (Sydney) 1889——.
BUTLIN, N. G. "The Shape of the Australian Economy," *Economic Record,* Vol. XXXIV, No. 67, April 1958.
CHURCHWARD, LLOYD. "American Influence on the Australian Labour Movement," *Historical Studies, Australia and New Zealand* (November, 1952).
CLARK, V. S. *The Labour Movement in Australasia: A Study in Social Democracy.* New York: Holt, 1906.
COGHLEN, T. A. *Wealth and Progress of New South Wales.* Sydney: N.S.W. Govt. Printer, 1891.
FITZPATRICK, B. C. *The British Empire in Australia.* Melbourne: M.U.P., 1949.

————. *A Short History of the Australian Labour Movement.* Melbourne: Rawson, 1944.

GOLLAN, ROBIN. "The Trade Unions and Labour Parties, 1890-4," *Historical Studies,* Vol. 7, No. 25, Nov. 1955.

GRAHAME, STEWART. *Where Socialism Failed.* New York: McBride, Nast & Co., 1912.

GREENWOOD, G. (ed.) *Australia: A Social and Political History.* Sydney: Angus & Robertson, 1955.

MÉTIN, A. *Le Socialisme sans Doctrines: Australie et Nouvelle Zélande.* Paris: Alcan, 1901.

NEW SOUTH WALES, *Royal Commission on Strikes.* Sydney: Government Printer, 1891.

O'FARRELL, P. J. 'The Australian Socialist League and the Labour Movement, 1887-91,' *Historical Studies,* Vol. 8. No. 30.

O'RELL, MAX (pseud.) *John Bull & Co., the great Colonial Branches of the Firm.* London, 1899.

ROSS, LLOYD. *William Lane and the Australian Labour Movement.* Sydney: Forward Press, n.d.

SPENCE, W. G. *Australia's Awakening: Thirty years in the life of an Australian Agitator.* Sydney: Worker Trustees, 1909.

WARD, RUSSEL. *The Australian Legend.* Melbourne: O.U.P., 1958.

*The Worker* (Brisbane) 1890—.

## BELGIUM

### Bellamy Translations

BELLAMY, EDWARD. *Seul de son Siècle en l'an 2000,* Traduction et discussion du Roman Communiste "Looking Backward," par le Vicomte Combes de Lestrade. 2nd ed.; Paris: Guillaumin, 1891.

————. *Honderd Jaar Later.* Ghent: Volksdrukkerij, 1909 (no name of translator).

————. *Parabole du Réservoir d'Eau.* Ed. Pensée et Action. Brussels: 1946 (no name of translator).

### General Reference Works

BAIWIR, ALBERT. *Abrégé de l'histoire du Roman Américain.* Brussels: Editions Lumière, 1946.

DHONDT, J. *De Sociale Kwestie in Belgie (1840-1885). Algemene*

*Geschiedenis der Nederlanden.* 314-349. Utrecht-Antwerp, 1955.

PIRENNE, H. *Histoire de Belgique,* Vol. VII, Brussels, 1932.

ROBERT, V. *De Arbeidersbeweging in Belgie (1885-1914). Algemene Geschiedenis der Nederlanden.* XI, 24-59. Utrecht-Antwerp, 1956.

TERLINDEN and others. *Histoire de la Belgique Contemporaine, 1830-1914.* Vol. I. Brussels: A. Dewit, 1928.

VAN KALKEN, FRANS. *Commotions Populaires en Belgique (1834-1902).* Brussels: Office de Publicité, 1936.

————. *Histoire de la Belgique.* Brussels: Office de Publicité, 1954.

### Social Problems

BOURDEAU, J. *Evolution du Socialisme.* Paris: F. Alcan, 1901.

COMTE DE BOUSIES. *Le Collectivisme et ses Conséquences.* Brussels: Société Belge de Librairie, 1894.

BRANCART, L. *Socialisme Moral et Réformes Possibles.* Brussels: Editions de Belgique, 1934.

CHAUDOIR ROBERTI, M. *L'Autorité, Essai de Sociologie et d'Economie Politique.* Brussels: Office de Publicité, n.d.

DE LARIVIÈRE. *Collectivisme, Communism, Propriété Privée.* Brussels: n.p., 1908.

DE LAVELEYE, E. *Le Socialisme Contemporain.* Paris: Alcan, 1891.

DESTRÉE, J. *Les Socialistes et la Guerre Européenne 1914-1918.* Brussels: Van Oest., 1926.

DEVILLE, GABRIEL. *Aperçu sur le Socialisme Scientifique.* Brussels: Bibliothèque Populaire, 1896.

KERBY, W. J. *Le Socialisme aux Etats-Unis.* Brussels: Ecole des Sciences Politiques et Sociales de Louvain, 1897.

KOCH, J. P. *Quelques Expériences Collectivistes.* Brussels: Et. Généraux d'Imprimerie, 1947.

LAIDLER, H. W. *Social-Economic Movements.* London: Routledge and Kegan Paul, 1953.

LANGEROCK, H. *Essai sur le Collectivisme.* Brussels: Lebegue et Cie, 1895.

ONCLAIR, A. *Le Communisme dans l'Histoire et des Systèmes Socialistes d'à Présent.* Namur, n.p., 1895.

VANDERVELDE, E. *Cours sur les Doctrines Sociales au 19e Siècle.* Brussels: Extension Universitaire de Bruxelles, 1894.

VAN OVERBERGH, C. *Marx, sa vie, son oeuvre. Bilan du Marxisme.* Brussels: Office de Publicité, 1948.

## Belgian Socialism

BERTRAND, L. *Histoire de la démocratie et du socialisme en Belgique depuis 1830.* 2 vols. Brussels: 1906-1907.

————. *Le Parti Ouvrier Belge et son Programme.* Brussels: Bibliothèque Populaire [1886], 2nd ed.

————. *Souvenirs d'un Meneur Socialiste.* Vol. I. Brussels: L'Eglantine, 1927.

DAUMONT, F. *L'Evolution du Socialisme Belge.* Brussels: Librairie de l'Action Catholique, 1914.

DELSINNE, L. *Le Parti Ouvrier Belge des Origines à 1894.* Brussels: n.p., 1955 (coll. Notre Passe).

DESTRÉE, J. and VANDERVELDE, E. *Le Socialisme en Belgique.* Paris: Giard et Briere, 1898.

DES ESSARTS, S. MASY & M. *Histoire du Parti Ouvrier Belge.* Huy, 1938.

GEIREGAT, P. *Maatschappelijke Vraagstukken. Gedachten, ontleend aan Edw. Bellamy, Em. de Laveleye en Ch. Richet.* Ghent: Vuylsteke, 1893.

PIERSON, M. A. *Histoire du Socialisme en Belgique.* Brussels: n.p., 1953.

VANDERVELDE, E. *Dans la Mêlée.* Paris: Berger-Levrault, 1919.

## Periodicals

"Annales Parlementaires," *Abonnement Germinal.* Ghent: Volksdrukkerij, 1906.

DE LAVELEYE, EMILE. "Deux Utopies Nouvelles," *Revue de Belgique,* LXV (May 15, 1890), pp. 5-30.

DE MAREZ, HENDRIK. "In Het Jaar 2000, door Edw. Bellamy, Vertaling van F. Van der Goes," *Nederlandsch Museum* (Ghent), XVII, 2 (1891), pp. 244-46.

DU CHASTEL, COMTE EMERIC. "Deux Romans à propos du Socialisme," *Revue Générale,* LIX. (January, 1894), pp. 102-116; (March, 1894), pp. 349-367.

HALLEUX, J. "La Société de l'Avenir d'après Bellamy," *Revue Générale,* LV (June, 1892), 903-915.

HUYSMANS, C. "La Plus-Value Immobilière," *Abonnement Germinal.* Ghent: Volksdrukkerij, 1909.

"Manifeste des Etudiants Socialistes de l'Université de Gand." *Abonnement Germinal.* Ghent: Volksdrukkerij (March, 1910).

MERLINO, S. "Looking Backward, 2000-1887." La Société Nouvelle, II (1891), 222-225, 452-459.

PLEKHANOFF, G. "Anarchisme et Socialisme," *Abonnement Germinal.* Ghent: Volksdrukkerij, 1907.

RICHTER, E. "Le Socialisme au Pouvoir." *Bibliothèque de Propagande Antisocialiste,* No. 8. Brussels: Comité de Propagande de la Presse Catholique.

VAN DE VENNE, JEF. "Eene voorlezing over Amerikaansche Letterkunde, vooral met het Oog op Edward Bellamy's Werken: Dr. Heidenhoff's Process, Miss Ludington's Sister, Looking Backward," *Nederlandsch Museum* (Ghent), XVIII, 2 (1892), pp. 5-20, 65-83.

VANDERVELDE, E. "L'Action Socialiste," Lettres d'E. Vandervelde a la Gazette de Bruxelles. *Abonnement Germinal,* March, 1911. Ghent: Volksdrukkerij.

———. "Le Collectivisme," *Bibliothèque de Propagande Socialiste.* No. 5. Brussels, 1893.

———. "Lettre Collectiviste au Courrier de Bruxelles," *Bibliothèque de Propagande Socialiste.* Brussels, 1895.

VERHAEGEN, A. "Het Jaar 2000, of de Socialisten in Werking, door Ed. Bellamy; Uittreksels en Bemerkingen," *Antisocialistische Propaganda Bibliotheek,* Propagandacomiteit der Katholiek Pers, Brussels: no. 12, n.d.

WATTEZ, OMER. "Een Amerikaansch Schrijver: Edward Bellamy," *Nederlandsche Dichten Kunsthalle* (Antwerp and Amsterdam), XIV (1891-92), pp. 543-552.

### Newspapers

ARGUS, "De Verdeeling van den Overvloed," *De Dag* (October 31, 1939), p. 2, cols. 2, 3, 4.

———. "Een Keure voor een Nieuwe Samenleving," *De Dag,* (October 28, 1939), p. 10, cols. 2, 3, 4.

———. "Pan Europa en nog wat anders," *De Dag* (October 27, 1939), p. 2, cols. 2, 3, 4.

### Interview

FEBRUARY 22, 1959. Interview of the author with Mrs. De Sweemer and Mr. A. Lödör (founders of the Bellamy Association) in Ghent.

*Unpublished Materials*

BLAVIER, A., letter to Miss P. Michot, n.d. [January, 1959].
HUYSMANS, C., letter to Pierre Michel, dated December 25, 1958.
INSTITUT E. VANDERVELDE, letter to Miss P. Michot, December 22, 1958.
Minutes of the Ghent meetings of the Bellamy Vereniging; handwritten; 31 pages. Meetings of: Sept. 17, 19, Oct. 3, 16, 29, Nov. 13, Dec. 3, 18, 1939; of January 2, 15, 28, Feb. 12, 26, March 11, 28, and April 8, 1940.

### BULGARIA

### Translations

*Looking Backward:*

*Sled sto godini. Fantasticěski roman. Ot.* . . Prevel ot runski K. T. Bozveliev. Russe: pečatnitza Spiro Goulabčev, 1892.

*Nastojašteto razgledano ot potomstvoto ni i nadničano v napredǎka na bǎdašteto. S prevod i podražanie ot 415-to izdanie na pǎrvoobraznoto Looking Backward ot Edward Bellamy.* Pobǎlgaril Ilija S. Jovcev. Sofia: pecatnitza K. G. Cinkov, 1900.

*V kraja na XX vek. Fantastičen roman ot.* . . Prevel ot ruski K. T. Bozveliev. 2. izd. Sofia: Koop. d-vo Prosveta, 1921.

"Anarhističeski idei v literaturata. Iz romana 'Sled sto godini' ot E. Bellamy." — *S v o b o d n o  u c i l i s t e*, I, 1934, br. 3, p. 2. [A fragment of the original work].

*Utroto na truda.* /Hristijanski socializam/. Prevel A. G. (?), Sliven, Pečatnica Balgarsko zname, izd. N.D. Dimčevski, 1898. 24p. [On the title page, on the cover and in the Preface the author of this work is shown as F. Bellamy (sic!).]

### Stories

"Prikazka za vodata." — *V a r n e n s k i  r a b o t n i k*, I, 1919, br. 5, p. 2; br. 8, p. 2. [There is no indication of the original.]

### Books and Journals

Mihaelis, R. *Edin pogled vǎrhu bǎdesteto. Otgovor na "Edin pogled vǎrhu minaloto" ot Edward Bellamy.* Prevel ot nemski Bartolomej Robertovič. Razgrad, pec. S. Iv. Kilifarski, etc., 1893.

"Edward Bellamy." (A sketch with a portrait). *Bălgarska iljustracija*, I, 1925, br. 2, p. 2.

"Na 23/11 maj t.g. e počinal Edward Bellamy."— *Narod*, I, 1898, br. 31, p. 6.

## Unpublished

Letter to S. E. Bowman, from Acting Director of *Vassil Kolarov*, the National Library, November 15, 1957.

## CANADA

### Books by Bellamy or Mentioning Bellamy

BELLAMY, EDWARD. *Looking Backward: 2000-1887*. Toronto: Bryce, n.d.

——. *Equality*. Toronto: Morang, 1897.

FRASER, W. R. *A White Stone*. New York: Philosophical Library, 1955.

——. *Journal* (largely unpublished).

GALBRAITH, J. K *The Affluent Society*. Boston: Houghton Mifflin Co., 1958.

LEAGUE FOR SOCIAL RECONSTRUCTION. *Social Planning for Canada*. Toronto: Thomas Nelson and Sons, 2nd printing, Dec., 1935.

LIPSET, S. M. *Agrarian Socialism*. Berkeley and Los Angeles, California: University of California Press, 1950.

MACNAIR, EVERETT W. *Edward Bellamy and the Nationalist Movement, 1889 to 1894*. Milwaukee: The Fitzgerald Company, 1957.

THE CAMBRIDGE SOCIETY, LTD. *The Cambridge Encyclopaedia*. Montreal, 1932.

### Articles or Lectures Concerning Bellamy

COOPER, JOHN A. "Bellamy and Howells," *Canadian Magazine*, IX, 1897.

DOUGLAS, W. A. "Bellamy's Blunders," *Canadian Magazine*, X, Jan., 1898.

FRASER, W. R. "Distributive Justice and 'the Single Price,'" a paper read before the Canadian Philosophical Association at Edmonton, Alberta, June, 1958.

————. "Bellamy as a Social Philosopher," a lecture given each spring at Sir George Williams University.

GORDON, J. KING. "Socialism and Christianity," *Saskatchewan C.C.F. Research Review.* May, 1934, pp. 4-9.

IRVING, JOHN A. "Psychological Aspects of the Social Credit Movement in Alberta," *Canadian Journal of Psychology*, 1 (1947), Nos. 1, 2 and 3.

————. "The Evolution of the Social Credit Movement," *Canadian Journal of Economics and Political Science*, August, 1948, pp. 321-341.

J. A. M. "Looking Backward," *Knox College Monthly*, X, 4 (1889).

LE ROSSIGNOL, JAMES EDWARD. "The March of Socialism," *The University Magazine*, XI, October 3, 1912.

PEIRCE, W. E. "Hour for Hour Exchange," *Show Window* (Detroit, Michigan, December, 1947).

QUINN, H. F. "Nationalism and the Industrial Development of Quebec," Sir George Williams University, November 8, 1958.

THRUPP, SYLVIA L. "Edward Bellamy" (a review of Arthur E. Morgan's biography). *Canadian Forum* (January, 1945).

### Newspaper Clippings about Canadians

Editorial and Article (the latter on p. 14, col. 1 and col. 2), the Montreal *Star*, Feb. 10, 1955, on the life of Dr. H. S. Ross.

FRASER, W. R. Letter to the Editor, published Feb. 15, 1955, in the Montreal *Star*, on Dr. H. S. Ross and "the Single Price."

### Pamphlets by Canadians

DAVIES, A. B. "Christocracy," (Hamilton, Ontario: 1948).

GROULX, CANON LIONEL. "Why We Are Divided," tr. by Gordon Rothney (Montreal: L'Action Nationale, Nov., 1943).

### Interviews

Conversation by telephone with Mr. G. S. Mooney on October 24, 1958.

MARION BELLAMY EARNSHAW, September, 1958, by Sylvia E. Bowman.

## Unpublished Materials

(a) Letters, bearing on Edward Bellamy or on social affairs, were received by W. R. Fraser from: A. Andras, R. H. Blackburn, Mrs. R. Bobilya, R. W. Brockway, the late W. E. Brokaw, L. Brown, H. D. Clark, M. J. Coldwell, W. Courage, A. B. Davies, C. East, F. Flemington, E. Forsey, C. D. Goodwin, A. P. Hewett, B. C. Kierstead, A. Mac-Beth, H. MacLennan, W. K. Lamb, W. T. Nef, J. W. A. Nicholson, W. E. Peirce, A. Suddon, the late H. S. Ross, R. E. Watters, J. F. Williams, H. Winch, and F. M. Young.

(b) Manuscripts by Canadians stressing economic and social issues: Fraser, W. R., *Journal*. Goodwin, Craufurd David, *Canadian Economic Thought: 1814-1914* (a Ph.D. dissertation).

### CZECHOSLOVAKIA

#### Translations

*Looking Backward:*

> *Pohled do budouchiho ráje neboli Jaky usl bude svet, až zavládne vsude rovnost, volnost a bratství.* Prel. K. Sobička. 2 editions. Praha: Narodni tiskarna a nakladatelstvo, 1890. (Publisher was also publisher of the workingmen's newspaper in which the novel was serialized.)
> *Pohled do....* Praha: Frant. Backovsky, 1893.
> *Pohled do....* (Serialized) *Hlas Národa* (January 1, 1890-March, 1890).

*Equality:*

> *Rovnost. Roman.* Prelozil Jarolav Jirousek. Praha: Delnicka tiskarna a nakladatelstvi, 1898. (This publishing house was the official one of the Social Democrats which also published the *Pravo Lidu,* the official newspaper of the laborers and of the party.)

#### Articles

"Beseda—Edward Bellamy." *Pravo Lidu.* VII. 145 (1898), p. 1.
[Death Notice]. *Cas.* XII (1898), p. 390.
"Edward Bellamy Zemrál." *Hlas Národa,* May 25, 1898.
[*Equality*] *Pravo Lidu.* IV, 13 (April, 1898), 102.
[*Equality*] *Pravo Lidu.* V, 14 (May, 1898), 7.

"Moderni utopie sociálni." (*Looking Backward*: 2000-1887. 1889, 21. vyd.) *Cas*. Roc. IV. 1890. pp. 424-26, 520-25, 821-22.
"Pohled do boucí ho ráje od Edwarda Bellamyho, pré kla dem K. Sobičky." *Hlas Národa*. No. 18, January, 1890.

## Books

Dr. Frant. Backovsky: *Vzpominkovy Sbornik*. Prague: Jindr, Backovsky, 1948.
RICHTER, EUGENE. [*In the Future Social-Democrat State*.] Praha: Nărodní tiskárna a nakladatelstvi, 1892.

## DENMARK
(See Sweden for general works.)

### Translations of Bellamy

*Anno 2000-1889*. Et tilbageblik. Avtoris. overs. efter den ameri-kanske originals 16. oplag ved Fr. Winkel-Horn. København: J. H. Schubothe, 1889. 3:50.
*En Kjærlighedshistorie*. (*Illustreret Tidende*, 1887-88, 503-5, 515-17, 527, 539-41, 551-53.)
*Frøken Ludingtons Søster*. Overs. fra Engelsk af P.V. København: V.Pio, 1891. 2:50.
*Lighed*. Oversat fra engelsk af John Packness. København, 1905. 22 p. Pris 10 øre. (Udgivet af de københavnske socialistiske Ungdomsforeningers Forlag.)
*Om 100 Aar*. Aarhus, 1901. 164 p. (Føljeton til *Landarbejderen*).
*Tilbageblik Aar 2000*. Overs. af Eiler Jørgensen. København: Carit Andersen, 1946. 218 p. 8:75.

## ENGLAND
(A Selective Bibliography)

### Bellamy's Works

Dr. *Heidenhoff's Process* (Edinburgh, 1884). Reprinted Fred-erick Warne (London, 1891).
*Miss Ludington's Sister* (Edinburgh, 1884). Reprinted Fred-erick Warne (London, 1891)
*Looking Backward*. Editions and reprints by William Reeves (London, 1889); George Routledge (London, 1890); Fred-

erick Warne (London, 1891); W. Foulsham (London, 1925); Alvin Redman (London, 1948).

*Six to One. A Nantucket Idyl.* (London, 1890).

*Equality* (London, 1897).

*The Blindman's World* (London, 1898).

*The Duke of Stockbridge* (London, 1901).

## Publications Directly Related to Bellamy, Nationalism

Periodicals: *Nationalization News; Brotherhood; The Sower,* continued as *Seed-Time.*

Anon., *Atlantis A. D. 2050: Electrical Development at Atlantis* . . . London, 1890.

Anon., *Looking Ahead . . . Not by the Author of Looking Backward.* London, 1892.

CRUSOE, ROBINSON. *Looking Upwards . . . The Up Grade from Henry George past E. Bellamy.* London, 1892.

MICHAELIS, RICHARD. *A Sequel to Looking Backward or Looking Further Forward.* London, 1891.

O'BRIEN, M. D. *Socialism Tested by Facts . . . Containing a Criticism of 'Looking Backward'* . . . London, 1892.

REYNOLDS, THOMAS. *Preface and Notes . . . to Mr. E. Bellamy's Book, 'Looking Backward.'* London, 1890.

SANDERS, GEORGE A. *Reality . . . A Reply to E. Bellamy's 'Looking Backward' and 'Equality.'* London, 1898.

WEST, JULIAN. *My Afterdream . . .* London, 1900.

HOLIDAY, HENRY. "The Artistic Aspects of Edward Bellamy's *Looking Backward,*" *Transactions of the Guild and School of Handicraft.* I (London, 1890), 55-71.

ORME, JOHN. *Nationalisation of Labour.* London, 1890.

## Works Containing References to Bellamy

*Labour Annual*

*Review of Reviews*

BERNERI, MARIE L. *Journey Through Utopia.* London, 1950.

BROCKWAY, FENNER. *Bermondsey Story.* London, 1949.

————. *Socialism Over Sixty Years.* . . . London, 1946.

COLE, G. D. H. *A History of Socialist Thought.* London, 1953-58.

ENSOR, R. C. K. *England 1870-1914.* Oxford, 1936.

GERBER, RICHARD. *Utopian Fantasy: A Study of English Utopian Fiction Since the End of the Nineteenth Century.* London, 1955.

GLASIER, J. BRUCE. *William Morris and the Early Days of the Socialist Movement* . . . London, 1921.

GRAY, ALEXANDER. *The Socialist Tradition.* London, 1946.

HEINDEL, RICHARD HEATHCOTE. *The American Impact on Great Britain 1898-1914.* Philadelphia, 1940.

HENDERSON, ARCHIBALD. *Bernard Shaw, Playboy and Prophet.* New York, 1935.

HOLIDAY, HENRY. *Reminiscences of My Life.* London, 1914.

JEVONS, H. STANLEY. *Economic Equality in the Co-operative Commonwealth.* London, 1933.

KAYE, JULIAN. *Bernard Shaw and the Nineteenth Century.* Norman, Oklahoma: University of Oklahoma Press, 1958.

LAIDLER, HARRY W. *A History of Socialist Thought.* New York, 1927.

LYND, HELEN MERRELL. *England in the Eighteen-Eighties.* New York, 1945.

MACFAYDEN, DUGALD. *Sir Ebenezer Howard and the Town Planning Movement.* Manchester, 1933.

MANNIN, ETHEL. *Bread and Wine.* London, 1944.

MORRIS, MAY. *William Morris. Artist, Writer, Socialist.* Oxford, 1936.

MORTON, A. L. *The English Utopia.* London, 1952.

NETHERCOT, A. H. *The First Five Lives of Annie Besant.* Chicago, 1960.

ORLANS, HAROLD. *Utopia Ltd.* New Haven, 1953.

OSBORN, F. J. (ed.) EBENEZER HOWARD, *Garden Cities of Tomorrow.* London, 1946.

PEASE, EDWARD R. *The History of the Fabian Society.* 2nd ed., London, 1925.

PELLING, H. M. *The Origins of the Labour Party 1880-1900.* London, 1954.

VILLIERS, BROUGHAM. *The Socialist Movement in England.* London, 1908.

WALLACE, ALFRED RUSSEL. *My Life.* . . . London, 1908.

WEBB, SIDNEY. *Socialism in England.* Baltimore, 1889.

―――. *Socialism: True and False.* Fabian Tract 51. London, 1894.

―――. *The Difficulties of Individualism.* Fabian Tract 69. London, 1896.

WEDGWOOD, C. V. *The Last of the Radicals.* London, 1951.

WEDGWOOD, JOSIAH C. *Memoirs of a Fighting Life.* London, 1940.

FINLAND

(See Sweden for general works.)

*Translations of Bellamy*

*Vuonna 2000.* Katsaus vuoteen 1887. Saksasta suom. J. K. Kari.
Helsingissä, Työväen kp., 1902, 274 p. Työväen sanomalehti-
osakeyhtiö. 3.00. Ilmestyi 10 vihkossa a 0.30. [*Looking Backward.*]
*Vuonna 2000.* Katsaus vuoteen 1887. Kirjoittanut Edvard Bellamy. Saksasta Suom. J. K. Kari. Toinen painos. Helsinki,
Työväen sanomalehden O.Y., 1907. 274 p. 3:—.
*Yhdenvertaisuus.* Seitsemännestä painoksesta suomennettu. En-
simäinen-toinen nidos. Hancock, Mich., 1905-6. 159 p. —
160-399 p. Työmiehen kustannusyhtiö, doll. 1.00.
*Yhdenvertaisuus.* 1:nen nidos (Jatkoa teokseen Vuonna 2000.)
Seitsemännestä painoksesta suomennettu. Tampere, 1906.
216 p. M.V. Vuolukka. 1:25; Koruk. 2:—.

FRANCE

*Translations of Bellamy*

*Looking Backward:*
*En l'An 2000.* Trans. A. Berry. Paris: E. Flammarion, 1893.
————. Trans. Mrs. Poynter-Redfern. Paris: E. Flam-
marion, 1898.
*Cent Ans Après.* Trans. P. Rey; Introduction of T. Reinach.
Paris: E. Dentu, 1891.
————. 2nd ed. Introduction by E. Charpentier. Paris:
Editions Fustier, 1939.
*Seul de son Siècle, en l'an 2000.* Trans., preface G. Combes
de Lestrade. Paris: Guillaumin et Cie, 1891.
Serialized in *La Grande Relève*, March, 1955, Nos. 260-304;
in *Bellamy-Abundo Frakcio* (Esperanto), 1958.
*Miss Ludington's Sister.* Trans. Robert Issant. Preface, study
of American literature, by T. Bentzon. Paris: J. Hetzel,
1891.

*Books and Articles*

ARNAVON, CYRILLE. *Les Lettres américaines devant la Critique
française. Annales de l'Université de Lyon.* Paris: Société
d'Edition *Les Belles Lettres,* 1951.

BENTZON, THÉRÈSE. *Préface* (a study of American literature), *Miss Ludington's Sister*, Traduction de R. Issant. Paris: J. Hetzel, 1891.

————. "Les Nouveaux Romans Américains." *Revue des Deux-Mondes*, August 1, 1885.

————. "La Société de l'Avenir." *Revue des Deux-Mondes*, October 15, 1890.

————. "Le Communisme en Amérique." *Revue des Deux-Mondes*, October 1, 1897.

BERGUES, HELENE. "La Population vue par les Utopistes," *Population* (April-June, 1951).

BLOCH, MAURICE. *Les Suites d'une Grève*. Paris: Hachette, 1891.

BOWMAN, SYLVIA E. *Le Dévelopment des Idées d'Edouard Bellamy*. Thèse de doctorat (unpublished). Université de Paris: 1952.

BRUN, P. A. *Leur Utopie et la Mienne*. Paris: n.p., 1886.

CARO. "Etudes morales sur le temps presént." *Les Meilleurs Ecrivains français, classiques et modernes, apologistes de la Foi*. Ed. M. Mazuel, agrégé de l'Université. Paris: Société de Saint-Augustin, Desclée, de Broweret Cie, 1898.

CHARPENTIER, E. "Introduction." *Cent Ans Apres*. Paris: Editions Fustier, 1939.

COMBES DE LESTRADE, G. "Introduction." *Seul de son siècle, en l'an 2000*. Paris: Guillaumin et Cie, 1891.

LE DRIMEUR, ALAIN. *La Cité Future*. Paris: A. Savine, 1890.

DUBOIN, JACQUES. *Ce qu'on appelle la crise*. Paris, Libraire Ocia, 1934.

————. *En route vers l'abondance*. Paris, Librairie Ocia, 1935.

————. *Demain ou le Socialisme de l'abondance*. Paris, Librairie Ocia, 1940.

————. *Egalité économique*. Paris: Librairie Ocia, 1938.

————. *Économie distributive*. Paris: Librairie Ocia, 1946.

————. *Kou l'Ahuri*. Paris: Librairie Ocia, 1935.

————. *La Grande Relève des hommes par la machine*. Paris: Librairie Ocia, 1932.

————. *La Grande Révolution qui vient*. Paris: Librairie Ocia, 1934.

————. *Les Hommes sont-ils naturellement méchants?* Paris: Librairie Ocia, 1937.

————. *Lettre à tout le monde*. Paris: Librairie Ocia, 1937.

————. *Liberation*. Paris: Librairie Ocia, 1937.

————. *Nous faisons fausse route*. Préface de Joseph Caillaux. Paris: Librairie Ocia, 1932.

————. *Rareté et abondance*. Paris: Librairie Ocia, 1944.

————. *Réflexions d'un Français moyen*. Préface d'Henry de Jouvenal. Paris: Librairie Ocia, 1923.

————. Ed. *La Grande Relève*. Paris: 30 rue de Leningrad, 1932————.

————. Directeur, *Mouvement français pour l'Abondance*.

DUPONT, VICTOR. *L'Utopie et le Roman Utopique dans la Littérature anglaise*. Cahors: A. Couesland, 1941.

FORAY, ADRIEN. *La Société Idéale*. Paris: A. Savine, 1896.

FRANCE, ANATOLE. *Sur la Pierre blanche*. Paris: C. Levy, 1905.

FRISTOT, FATHER. "Le Rêve Collectiviste." *Etudes* des Peres Jesuites. II, 65 (1895).

GIDE, CHARLES. *Les Colonies Communistes et Cooperatives* (1928), translated into English by Ernest F. Row. London: George G. Harrap and Company, Ltd., 1930.

GRENARD, F. Revue de "Choses et Gens d'Amérique" de Th. Bentzon. *Polybiblion*, XLIX (1899). Paris: C. Levy, 1898.

GOURMAND, PAUL. "Lettres Anglaises." *La Plume*, October 1, 1897, p. 613.

HERTZKA, THEODOR. *Freiland* (1890): *Un Voyage à Terre-Libre, coup d'oeil sur la Société de l'Avenir*. Traduction de Teodor de Wyzewa. Paris: L. Chailly, 1894.

DE LAVELEYE, EMILE. "Deux Utopies Nouvelles." *Revue Socialiste*, July, 1890.

LEO XIII. Encyclical: "On the Condition of Labor," May 15, 1891.

LEROY-BEAULIEU, PAUL. Preface, Richter's *Where Does Socialism Lead?* (See Richter).

LOUIS, PAUL. *150 ans de Pensée socialiste. Bibliothèque des Sciences politiques et sociales*. 1953.

MAITRE, PIERRE-LOUIS. "Utopie d'hier, Réalité de demain." Lecture given on July 2, 1947, to the Cercle Civique Vosgien.

MARCHAND, VICTOR. *L'Utopiste*. Paris: n.p., 1882.

MERCIER, LOUIS-SEBASTIEN. *L'an 2440, rêve s'il en fut jamais*. Published in London, 1771; Paris, 1887; Netherlands; 1792.

*Mercure*, February 1, 1906, pp. 478-79.

NEULIF. *L'Utopie contemporaine, Notes de Voyage*. March, 1888.

PELLERIN, GEORGES. *Le Monde dans 2000 ans*. Paris: E. Dentu, 1878.

PERROT, JOSEPH. *Nos Utopies politiques et socialistes devant le sens commun ou Nos Cahiers en 1899*. Paris: n.p., 1899.

RADIOT, PAUL ENGINEER. *l'Elite. Cf. Revue Blanche*, December, 1891, "Chronique de la Litterature."

RICHET, CHARLES. *Dans Cent Ans.* Paris: P. Ollendorf, 1892.

RICHTER, EUGENE. *Ou mene le socialisme. Journal d'un ouvrier.* Traduction de P. Villard. Préface de Leroy Beaulieu. Paris: H. le Soudier, 1892.

ROBERT, FERNARD. *Pour un Monde Nouveau. L'Union des Hommes,* 1937.

RUYER, RAYMOND. *L'Utopie et les Utopies.* Paris: Presses Universitaires de France, 1950.

SAGOT, FRANÇOIS. *Le Communisme au Nouveau Monde.* Thèse de doctorat. Dijon, 1900.

SAN CARLOS, MARQUISE DE. "Les Américains chez eux. Le Socialisme aux Etats-Unis." *La Nouvelle Revue,* May 15, 1890, pp. 280-307.

SECRÉTAN, CHARLES. *Mon Utopie.* Paris: F. Alcan, 1892.

TARBOURIECH, ERNEST. *La Cité future, essai d'une Utopie scientifique.* Paris, 1902.

*Utopies de Justice.* Neufchatel: P. Attinger, 1898.

DE WYZEWA, TEODOR. Preface, Richter's *Freiland.* Paris: le Chailly, 1894.

GERMANY

*The Translations of Edward Bellamy's Works*

*Looking Backward:*

Tr. by Alexander Fleischmann. Leipzig: Otto Wigand, 1890.

Tr. by Richard George. Halle: Otto Hendel, 1890.

Tr. by Johannes Hoops. Leipzig: Joseph Meyer, 1891.

Tr. by Georg Malkowsky. Berlin: Ekstein Nachf, 1890.

Ed. by Max Schippel. Berlin: Verlag des "Vorwaerts," 1889, 1893.

Tr. by Georg von Gizycki. Leipzig: Philipp Reclam, Jr., 1890, 1916, 1937, Magburg: Wolf und Ruthe, 1919.

Tr. by Clara Zetkin. Stuttgart: J. H. W. Dietz, 1890, 1914, Berlin: Verlag volk und Welt, 1954.

Unsigned translation. Munich: Georg Mueller, 1919.

Unsigned translation. Zuerich: Verlag "Mensch und Arbeit," 1947.

Unsigned translation and serialized. *Die Illustration* (Vienna: Winter, 1889/90).

In English. Collection of British and American authors. Vol. 2690; Leipzig: B. Tauchnitz, 1890.

*Equality:*
> Tr. by M. Jacobi. Stuttgart: Deutsche Verlagsanstalt, 1898.
> [See note at the end of the bibliography.]

*Dr. Heidenhoff's Process:*
> Tr. by E. Wulkow. Berlin: Rosenbaum and Hart, 1890, 1895.
> Tr. by A. Zacher. Leipzig: Philipp Reclam, Jr., 1890.

*Miss Ludington's Sister:*
> Tr. by J. Noellenhoff. Leipzig: Philipp Reclam, Jr., 1891.
> Tr. by Clara Steinitz. Berlin: S. Fischer Verlag, 1890, 1891.

*An Echo of Antietam:*
> Tr. by Gustav Noël. Halle: Otto Hendel, 1891. This volume
> also contains "A Love Story Reversed."

"A Positive Romance":
> Unsigned translation, in *Bibliothek der fremden Zungen,*
> Nr. 10 (Stuttgart: Deutsche Verlagsanstalt, 1893).

"With the Eyes Shut":
> Tr. by Ottmar Dittrich, Leipzig: Joseph Meyer, 1894, p. 52.
> This volume also contains "Ein Schiffbruch," which is
> "To Whom This May Come."

"First Steps Towards Nationalism":
> With an introduction to German readers by Edward Bel-
> lamy, tr. by Georg V. Gizycki. *Nord und Sued,* Vol. 71,
> pp. 55-68 (Oct., Nov., Dec. 1894).

## Criticism

BITTMANN, K. "Bellamy's Idealstaat," *Ausgewaehlte kleinere Schriften,* XI (Jena: G. Fischer, 1920), 130-141.

BLOCH, ERNST. *Freiheit und Ordnung,* Berlin: Aufbau-Verlag, 1947.

BLUEHER, RUDOLF. *Moderne Utopien.* Bonn, Leipzig: Kurt Schroeder, 1920.

BRASCH, MORITZ. "Bellamy's Vorgaenger," *Deutsche Revue,* I (1893) 256-62.

"DER JUENGSTE ZUKUNFTSROMAN," Review of *Looking Backward, Die Neue Zeit,* 1889, p. 268.

"EINE SOZIALE UTOPIE," *Monatsschrift fuer christliche Social Reform,* XII (Vienna, 1890), 598.

ERDMANNSDOERFFER, H. G. *Ein Phantasiestaat. Kritik von Bellamy's Rueckblick.* Leipzig: Werther, 1891.

FRAENKEL, H. *Gegen Bellamy.* 12th ed.; Wuerzburg: A. Stuber, 1891.

GAGLIARDI, ERNESTO. *"Equality.* Eine neue Utopie von Bellamy." *Magazin fuer Litteratur.* (Berlin: S. Crombach; Weimar: Emil Felber, 1897), p. 1455 f.

HEISIG, KARL. *Edward Bellamy und William Morris als Utopisten.* (Zweite Staatsexamensarbeit, Breslau: 1926).

JASTROW, J. "Ein deutsches Utopien," *Jahrbuch fuer Gesetzgebung, Verwaltung und Volkswirtschaft im deutschen Reich,* XV (1891).

KOCH, FRITZ. "Bellamy's Zukunftsstaat." (Bonn: Ph. March 1, 1924).

LOEWENTHAL, RICHARD. *Der Staat Bellamy's und seine Nachfelge.* Berlin: Reform Verlag, 1895; 2nd and 3rd eds., Berlin: H. Muskalla, 1905.

MARWEIN, W. "Edward Bellamy, Der Weltverbesserer als Prophet," *Universum,* XXV (1925).

MUELLER, WOLF-DIETRICH. *Geschichte der Utopia-Romane der Weltliteratur* (Muenster: Ph. Feb. 23, 1938).

ROMM, JULIE. "Bellamy's Gleichheit," *Die Neue Zeit,* I (1898) 589-96.

SENGFELDER, KARL. *Utopische Erziehungsideale und praktische Schulreformversuche der neuesten Zeit.* (Erlangen: Ph. Dec. 31, 1929).

SINTENIS, FRANZ. *Literarische Ansichten in Vortraegen: H. Sudermann, H. Seidel, Bret Harte, Mark Twain, E. Bellamy.* Jurjew: E. J. Karow, 1894.

TIBURTIUS, CARL. *Bellamy als Lehrer.* Berlin: Verlag des Bibliographischen Bureaus, 1892, p. 38.

WEICHMANN, OTTMAR. *Ein Rueckblick sus dem Jahre 2000 auf 1887 im Zusammenhange mit den Staatsromanen der Vergangenheit* (Calw, 1908).

## Utopian Literature

[ANON.] *Auch ein Rueckblick aus dem Jahr 2000.* Dresden: Saechsische Druckerei und Verlagsanstalt F. W. Quidde u. Co., 1898.

GERMANUS. (pseudonym). *Die soziale Entwicklung Deutschlands im 20w. Jahrhundert. Ein Vortrag aus dem Jahre 2000.* Berlin: Hermann Walther Verlagsbuchhandlung (G.m.b.H.), 1906.

GREGOROVIUS, EMIL. *Der Himmel auf Erden.* Leipzig: Fr. Wilh. Grunow, 1892.

HELLENBACH, L. B. *Die Insel Mellonta.* 2nd ed.; Leipzig: Oswald Mutze, 1887.

HERTZKA, THEODOR. *Freiland.* Leipzig: Duncker u. Humblot, 1890.

————. *Entrueckt in die Zukunft.* Berlin: F. Duemmlers, 1895.

HERZL, THEODOR. *Altneuland.* Berlin, Wien: B. Harz, 1900.

————. *Der Judenstaat* (1896).

KEMSIES, FERDINAND. *Socialistische und ethische Erziehung im Jahre 2000.* Berlin: Verlag des Bibliographischen Bureaus, 1893.

KLEINWACHTER, FRIEDRICH. *Die Staatsromane-Ein Beitrag zur Lehre vom Communismus und Socialismus.* Wien: M. Breitensteins Verlagsbuchhandlung, 1891.

KRETZMANN, JOHN. *The Pre-War German Utopian Novel 1890-1914.* Ph.D. Dissertation. (Brown University, 1936).

LAICUS, PHILIPP [PHILIPP WASSERBURG]. *Etwas Spaeter! Fortsetzung von Bellamy Rueckblick aus dem Jahr 2000.* Mainz: Franz Kirchheim, 1891.

LENZ, OTTOMAR. *Der Himmel auf Erden.* Leipzig, 1892.

MICHAELIS, RICHARD. *Ein Blick in die Zukunft. Eine Antwort auf: Ein Rueckblick von Edward Bellamy.* Leipzig: Philipp Reclam, Jr., 1891.

MUELLER, ERNST. *Ein Rueckblick aus dem Jahre 2037 auf das Jahr 2000.* 3rd ed., Berlin: Ulrich und Co., 1891.

NECKEBEN, J. *Ein Vorblick auf das Jahr 2000, oder Ein Tag in einer Strafanstalt des 21. Jahrhunderts.* Breslau: n.p., 1891.

PULVERMANN, M. "Die Gleichheit des Zukunftstaates," Berlin: Reichsverbands-Verlag, 1906, p. 20.

REICHARDT, A. *Des Bellamy Zeitalter 2001-2010 Erfindungen, Entdeckungen und Begebnisse.* Berlin: R. v. Decker, 1893.

RICHTER, EUGEN. *Sozialdemokratische Zukunftsbilder.* Berlin: Verlag "Fortschritt," 1892.

SCHAEFER, WILHELM. *Aus einem anarchistischen Idealstaat.* Hannover: Goehmann, 1906, p. 40.

STROEBEL, HEINRICH. *Die erste Milliarde der zweiten Billion.* Berlin: Paul Cassirer, 1919, p. 350.

VOIGT, ROSA. *Anno Domini 2000.* Stuttgart: Mimir-Verlag, 1909, p. 168.

VON SUTTNER, BERTA. *Das Maschinenalter.* Zuerich: Verlags-Magazin, 1889.

WILBRANDT, CONRAD. *Des Herrn Friedrich Ost Erlebnisse in der Welt Bellamy's.* Wismar: Hinstorff, 1891.

## Social Democrats

BEBEL, AUGUST. *Aus meinem Leben*. 3 vols. Berlin: J.H.W. Dietz Nachf, 1946.

———. *Die Frau und der Sozialismus*. 9th ed., Stuttgart: J.H.W. Dietz, 1891.

*Bebel und sein Zukunftsstaat vor dem Reichstag*. Koeln: Commissionsverlag von J.P. Bachem, 1893.

BERNSTEIN, EDUARD. *Geschichte der Berliner Arbeiterbewegung*. 3 vols. Berlin: Verlag Buchhandlung Vorwaerts, 1907, 1910.

*Das Erfurter Programm*. Muenchen: Verlag Das Volk, 1947.

*Das Goerlitzer Programm*. Offenbach A.M.: Bollwerk-Verlag Karl Drott, 1947.

*Das Heidelberger Programm*. Muenchen: Verlag Das Volk, 1947.

*Das Heidelberger Programm*. Offenbach A.M.: Bollwerk-Verlag Karl Drott, 1947.

DORNEMANN, LUISE. *Clara Zetkin*. Berlin: Dietz Verlag, 1957.

ENGELS, FRIEDRICH. "Der Entwurf eines neuen Parteiprogrammes." *Die Neue Zeit*, IX, 2nd vol. (Stuttgart: 1890/91), p. 724.

———. *Der Sozialismus von der Utopie zur Wissenschaft*. Muenchen: Verlag der SPD, 1946.

———. "Ein Stueck Zukunftsstaat," *Monatsschrift fur christliche Social-Reform*. (Letter to Dr. Rud. Meyer of July 19, 1893), XIX (Wien, Leipzig, 1897), 133-36.

ERLER, FRITZ. *Sozialismus als Gegenwartsaufgabe*. Schwenningen /N. : Neckar-Verlag, 1947.

GROTEWOHL, OTTO. *Wo stehen wir? Wohin gehen wir? Weg und Ziel der deutschen Sozialdemokratie*. Berlin: Verlag Das Volk, 1945.

KAMPFMEYER, PAUL. *Die Sozialdemokratie im Lichte der Kulturentwicklung*. Berlin: Buchhandlung Vorwaerts, 1913.

KAUTSKY, KARL. *Die Soziale Revolution. II. Am Tage nach der Sozialen Revolution*. 2nd ed., Berlin: Buchhandlung Vorwaerts, 1907.

KLUEHS, F. *August Bebel, Der Mann und sein Werk*. Sozialistische Klassiker. Berlin: J.H.W. Dietz, 1923.

LAUFKOETTER, FRANZ. "Utopistische Ideen im modernen Sozialismus," *Sozialistische Monatshefte*, III, 1340-1345 (September-December, 1908).

LIEFMANN, ROBERT. *Geschichte und Kritik des Sozialismus*. Leipzig: Quelle und Meyer, 1922.

Lux, Heinrich. *Sozialpolitisches Handbuch.* Berlin: Verlag der Expedition des *Vorwaerts* Berliner Volksblatt, 1892.

Martini, Walter. *Die Wandlungen im Parteiprogramm der Sozialdemokratie seit 1875.* Erlangen: Junge und Sohn, 1908.

Mehring, Franz. *Geschichte der Deutschen Sozialdemokratie.* Stuttgart: J.H.W. Dietz, 1897.

Mitscherlich, Alexander, and Weber, Alfred. *Freier Sozialismus.* Heidelberg: Lambert, Schneider, 1946.

Renner, Dr. Karl. *Karl Kautsky.* Berlin: J.H.W. Dietz, 1929.

Schumacher, Dr. Kurt. *Aufgaben und Ziele der deutschen Sozialdemokratie.* Karlsruhe: Verlag Volk und Zeit, 1946.

Sombart, Werner. *Sozialismus und soziale Bewegung.* 7th ed. Jena: Gustav Fischer, 1919.

Surenhoefner, Karl. "Utopie und Sozialismus." (Muenchen). *Der Ruf, Blaetter der jungen Generation* (April 15, 1947), pp. 5/6.

Vorstand der Sozialdemokratischen Partei Deutschlands, ed. *Grundsatzprogramm der Sozialdemokratischen Partei Deutschlands.* Bonn, 1959.

Weidmann, Paul. *Die Programm der sozialdemokratischen Partei Deutschlands von Gotha bis Goerlitz.* (Dissertation, Hamburg, 1926).

## Other Social Reform Movements

Anderson, Evelyn. *Hammer oder Amboss.* Nuernberg: Nest Verlag, 1948.

Becker, Otto. *Entwicklung, Ideologie und Politik der wirtschaftsfriedlichen Arbeiterverbaende in Deutschland.* Halle/Saale: Dissertation, 1931.

Broda, Dr. Rudolf. *Die Kulturaufgaben des Jahrhunderts.* Berlin: Georg Reimer, 1914.

Faber, Ernst. *Die evangelischen Arbeitervereine und ihre Stellungnahme zu sozialpolitischen Problemen.* Dissertation. Leipzig: Erlangen, 1928.

Faulhaber, Alfons. *Die christliche Gewerkschaftsbewegung.* Dissertation. Erlangen, 1913.

Frings, Joseph. *Grundsaetze katholischer Sozialarbeit und zeitnahe Folgerungen.* Koeln: n.p., 1947.

Guilleband, Claude Williams. *The Social Policy of Nazi Germany.* Cambridge: Cambridge University Press, 1942.

Herz, Johannes, ed. *Friedrich Naumann nationales und soziales Christentum.* Berlin: Bott, 1935.

KALKUM, B. *Utopia 2048.* Muenchen: B. Rausch, 1948.

MILLER, DR. WILLY. *Das soziale Leben im neuen Deutschland unter besonderer Beruecksichtigung der Deutschen Arbeitsfront.* Berlin: Mittler, 1938.

OTTO, BERTHOLD. *Der Zukunftsstaat als sozialistische Monarchie.* Berlin: Verlag von Puttkammer und Muehlbrecht, 1910.

PEPPLER, CARL, ed. *N.S.-Sozialpolitik,* Stuttgart: n.p., 1933.

POPPER-LYNKEUS, JOSEF. *Die allgemeine Naehrpflicht als Loesung der sozialen Frage.* 2nd ed.; Wien, Leipzig, Muenchen: Rikola Verlag, 1923.

RIEKER, KARLHEINRICH. *Das Wirtschaftsprogramm des Nationalsozialismus.* Berlin: Carl Heymanns Verlag, 1933.

SCHANZ, JOHANN. *Sozialisierung und katholische Gesellschaftslehre.* Kleve-Niederrhein: Boss, 1951.

SCHIEFER, JACK. *Geschichte der deutschen Gewerkschaften,* Aachen, 1947.

SCHNEIDER, JOHANN. *Friedrich Naumanns Gedankenwelt.* Berlin, n.p., 1929.

SEIDEL, RICHARD. *Die deutschen Gewerkschaften.* Stuttgart: n.p., 1948.

VON NEUPAUER, DR. JOSEPH R. *Der Kollektivismus und die soziale Monarchie.* Dresden: Richard Lincke, 1909.

ZWING, KARL. *Geschichte der deutschen freien Gewerkschaften.* Jena, 1926.

### Background

BERGSTRAESSER, LUDWIG. *Geschichte der politischen Parteien in Deutschland.* Editions 8 and 9. Muenchen: Isar Verlag Dr. Guenter Olzog, 1955.

*Bibliographie der Sozialwissenschaften,* Vols. I-XXXII. Dresden-Berlin, 1904-1936.

*Bibliographie der Staats-und Wirtschaftswissenschaften,* Vols. XXXIII-XXXVIII. Berlin, 1937-1942.

BORKENAU, FRANZ, ed. *Karl Marx.* Frankfurt/Main: Fischer Buecherei K. G., 1956.

BOUHLER, PHILIPP, ed., *Nationalsozialistische Bibliographie,* Vols. I-VI. Muenchen-Berlin: Zentralverlag der NSDAP, Franz Eher Nachf. GmbH., 1936-1941.

BOWMAN, SYLVIA E. *The Year 2000.* New York: Bookman Associates, 1958.

BUEHLER, THEODOR. *Von der Utopie zum Sozialstaat.* Berlin: W. Kohlhammer Verlag, 1942.

DEMETZ, PETER. *Marx, Engels und die Dichter.* Stuttgart: Deutsche Verlagsanstalt, 1959.

DRAHN, ERNST, ed. *Fuehrer durch das Schrifttum der deutschen Sozialdemokratie.* Berlin: Verlag fuer Sozialwissenschaft, 1919.

FALKE, RITA. "Versuch einer Bibliographie der Utopien." *Romanistisches Jahrbuch,* VI (1956), 92-109.

FREYER, HANS. *Die politische Insel.* Leipzig: Bibliographisches Institut, 1936.

HELLENBACH, L. B. *Das neunzehnte und zwanzigste Jahrhundert.* Ed. Dr. Karl du Prel. Leipzig: Oswald Mutze, 1893.

MANNHEIM, KARL. *Ideologie und Utopie.* Bonn: Friedrich Cohen, 1929.

MORGAN, ARTHUR. *Edward Bellamy.* New York: Columbia University, 1944.

RITTER, GERHARD. *Machtstaat und Utopie.* Berlin: R. Oldenbourg, 1940.

STAMHAMMER, JOSEF, ed. *Bibliographie der Social-Politik.* Vols. I, II. Jena: Verlag von Gustav Fischer, 1896, 1912.

—————. *Bibliographie des Socialismus und Communismus.* Vols. I-III. Jena: Verlag von Gustav Fischer, 1893, 1900, 1909.

THEIMER, WALTER. *Von Bebel zu Ollenhauer.* Muenchen: Leo Lehnen Verlag, 1957.

VON KIRCHENHEIM, ARTHUR. *Schlaraffia politica.* Leipzig: Verlag von Fr. Wilh. Grunow, 1892.

VON NELL-BREUNING, OSWALD, S. J. and SACHER, DR. HERMANN, eds. *Woerterbuch der Politik.* Freiburg/Breisgau: Herder, 1954.

WELTY, EBERHARD, OP, ed. *Herders Sozialkatechismus.* Vols. I-III. Freiburg/Breisgau: Herder, 1951, 1953, 1958.

ZENTRALINSTITUT FUER BIBLIOTHEKSWESEN, ed. *Bibliographie zur Geschichte der deutschen Arbeiterbewegung.* Leipzig: Verlag fuer Buch und Bibliothekswesen, 1955.

*Note*: More editions of *Equality* might have appeared in Germany had it not been for a bilateral copyright contract of January 15, 1892, between Germany and the United States which became effective May 6, 1892, and which is still effective. For the text of this copyright, consult Dr. Ernst Roethlisberger, *Urheberrechtegesetze und Vertraege in al len Laendern* (3rd ed.; Leipzig: G. Hechler, 1914, pp. 454, 455) and *Gewerblicher Rechtsschutz und Urheberrecht,* a periodical of the German association for industrial, judicial protection of copyrights edited by Professor Dr. Eduard Reimer (1950, p. 414).

## HUNGARY

### Translations of Bellamy's Works

Looking Backward:

Visszapillantás 2000-1887. Trans. by Gyula Csernyei. Buda-
pest: O. Nagel, 1891.
Visszapillantás 2000-bol 1887-dik évre. Trans. by Dániel
Radványi. Budapest: Franklin-Tarsulat, 1892.
Egy szoczialisztikus regény. Budapest: Karoly Rozsnyai,
Samu Markus Press [1895]. This is a digested edition
of 32 pages.
Egy szoczialisztikus regény. Budapest: Karoly Rozsnyai,
1895.
Visszapillantás 2000-bol 1887-dik évre. Trans. by Dániel
Radványi. Budapest: Franklin-Tarsulat, 1898. There
were two imprints of this edition.
Visszapillantás 2000-bol 1887-dik évre. Trans. by Dániel
Radványi. Budapest: 2nd edition, Franklin-Tarsulat,
1911.
Visszapillantás 2000-bol 1887-dik évre. Trans. by Dániel
Radványi. Budapest: 3rd edition, Franklin-Tarsulat,
1920.

Equality:

"The Parable"—Mese a vizrol. Budapest: A Szocialista-Kom-
munista Munkasok Magyarorszagi Partja (The Social-
ist-Communist Party of Hungary), 1919.
Skazka o vode [Russian]. Budapest: n.p., 1919.
Miss Ludington's Sister:
Ida, Regény a halhatatlanságról. Trans. by A. S. Budapest:
Athenaeum, 1898.
Dr. Heidenhoff's Process:
A csodadoktor [The Miraculous Healer]. Trans. by Dezso
Naray. Mako: M. Vitez, 1898.

### Books

CSERNYEI, GYULA. A középpont. Budapest: Franklin Press, 1885.
KUBOWICH, GASPAR. A munkáskérdes memoranduma. Ungvár:
Kelet Press, 1890.
MADZSAR, JOZSEF. Mintajegyźek városi nyilvános konyvtarok
számára. Budapest: editions of 1892, 1911, 1913 mention
Bellamy.

Rózsa, Ignác. *Utmutató a szocialista irodalomba.* Vols. 1-3. Budapest: Karoly Rozsnyai, 1919.


## India

### Translations

Sophia Wadia reported that translations had been made in Hindu and Shindi of *Looking Backward;* no record of publication could, however, be found by librarians.


### Articles

Because the Theosophical world headquarters have for so long been in India, we are listing all articles from the journals of different countries here.

"Bellamy's 'Looking Backward,'" *Canadian Theosophist,* XIX (1938-39), 102, 226.

Earnshaw, Marion Bellamy. "Edward Bellamy," *Aryan Path* (India), XXI, 5 (May, 1950), pp. 195-99.

Fawcett, E. Douglas. "'Looking Backward' and the Socialist Movement," *Theosophist* (India), XI, 129 (June, 1890), pp. 476-85.

*The Link* (South Africa), (April-May, 1942), p. 15; (December, 1923), p. 514.

"Looking Backward Indeed!", Letter to the Editor, *Herald of the Star* (India).

"The Nationalist," *Lucifer* (London), IV, 23 (July, 1889), p. 440.

"Reflections and Refractions," *The Path* (London), III (March, 1912-13), 358.

Taylor, James. "'Looking Backward,'" *The Messenger* (U.S.A.), VII (June, 1919).

[Wadia, Sophia] "Editor's Note," "Edward Bellamy," by Marion B. Earnshaw, *Aryan Path* (India), XXXI, 5 (May, 1950), p. 195.

"The Wise Way," *Theosophical Review* (London, ed. by Annie Besant), XXXVII (September, 1905-February, 1906), p. 248.


### Books

Blavatsky, Helena. *The Key to Theosophy.* Point Loma, California: Theosophical University Press, 1939.

Cousins, Norman. *Talks with Nehru.* New York: John Day Co., 1951.

Gandhi, Mahatmas. *Home Rule.*

MacNair, Everett W. *Edward Bellamy and the Nationalist Movement.* Milwaukee: Fitzgerald Co., 1957.

Morais, Frank. *Jawaharlal Nehru.* New York: Macmillan Co., 1956.

Morgan, Arthur. *Edward Bellamy.* New York: Columbia University Press, 1944.

Nehru, Jawaharlal. *The Discovery of India.* New York: John Day Co., 1946.

————. *Independence and After.* New York: John Day Co., 1950.

————. *Toward Freedom.* New York: John Day Co., 1941

————. *Unity of India.* Intro. by V. K. Krishna Menon. New York: John Day Co., 1942.

————. *Visit to America.* New York: John Day Co., 1950.

Nethercot, Arthur H. *The First Five Years of Annie Besant.* Chicago: University of Chicago Press, 1960.

Radhakrishnan, S. "Culture of India." *The Annals of the American Academy of Political and Social Science* (May, 1944).

Smith, Donald E. *Nehru and Democracy.* Calcutta: Orient Longmans Private Ltd., 1958.

### Unpublished Material

Letters to Sylvia E. Bowman from:

Bose, B., Calcutta, June 8, 1959.

Chaturvedi, Dr. S. K., secretary of Shriman Narajan, New Delhi, April 13, 1960.

Pratap, Raja Mahendra, M. P., New Delhi, December 6, 1958.

Pyarelal, Shri, New Delhi, December 29, 1959; April 9, 1960.

Raghavachari, Professor D. V. K., Waltair University, September 5, 1956; September 20, 1956; September 28, 1956; June 24, 1957; July 13, 1957; April 21, 1959; September 29, 1959; January 23, 1960.

Stock, Professor A. G., University of Calcutta, May 26, 1956.

Trivedi, B. R., Librarian, Allabad, U. P., India, May 26, 1960.

Wadia, Sophia, Madras, September 15, 1959; October 3, 1959; November 10, 1959.

INDONESIA

*Published and Unpublished Material*

De Uitweg, Officeel Orgaan der Internationale Vereniging "Bellamy" (Dutch East Indies), V, 8 (October, 1938), pp. 59-66.

HUGHES, MRS. R. W. Wheaton, Illinois, June 13, 1939, letter to Mrs. E. Bellamy.

VALDHUYSEN, Chairman, Bellamy Society, telegram from Bandoeng, Java, July 29, 1935, to Mrs. E. Bellamy.

WILLIAMS, NEIL. Letter of September 26, 1939, from Bandoeng, Java, to Mrs. E. Bellamy.

ZYLSTRA, K. Letter from Ede, Holland, July 12, 1958, to S. E. Bowman.


ITALY

*Translations of Bellamy's Works*

*Equality:*

Eguaglianza. Anonymous translation. 2 vols. Palermo: Remo Sandron, 1898.

*Looking Backward:*

Guardando indietro (2000-1887). Translated by Evi Malagoli. Turin: U.T.E.T., 1957.

La vita sociale nel 2000. Translated by Giuseppe Oberosler. Milan: Max Kantorowicz, 1890.

L'uomo di 143 anni. Anonymous translation, published by installments in L'Italia del Popolo, a federalist-republican paper, printed in Milan, 16 via S. Pietro all'Orto, No. 2 (Sunday-Monday, June 8-9, 1890) to No. 35 (July 11-12, 1890).

Nell'anno 2000, Racconto Americano. Translation by Pietro Mazzoni. Milan: Treves, 1890.


*Other Works about Bellamy*

(We do not include in this list the various forewords, notes and advice of publishers or translators to be found in the volumes previously listed.)

A. CAM. (ALDO CAMERINO). Nell' 'anno 2000. Dizionario degli Autori, Milan: Bompiani, 1948, Vol. V, p. 41.

ANONYMOUS, "Ecco il duemila!" Gazzetta Padana (Ferrara). Oct. 26, 1957 (a review).

————. "Edward Bellamy." *Avanti!* (Rome). No. 315, May 27, 1898 (obituary).

————. "Il filosofo Negri" (debate). *L'Italia del Popolo* (Milan). No. 210, January 4-5, 1891.

————. "Il socialismo" (debate). *La Giustizia, Bifesa degli Sfruttati* (Reggio Emilia). No. 252, Feb. 15, 1891.

————. "La concorrenza" (debate). *La Giustizia* (Reggio Emilia). No. 250, Feb. 1, 1891.

————. "Le confessioni socialiste di un nuovo senatore moderato" (debate). *La Giustizia* (Reggio Emilia). No. 247, Jan. 11, 1891.

————. "L'uomo di 133 anni" (presentation). *L'Italia del Popolo* (Milan). No. 1, June 7-8, 1890.

BOGLIETTI, GIOVANNI. "Nuove Utopie americane: il libro di E. Bellamy *Looking Backward.*" Nuova Antologia. Vol. CXII, pp. 609-27. (August, 1890) (review).

BONOMI, IVANOE. "Due libri sul socialismo di Saverio Merlino." *Critica sociale* (Milan). Nos. 6 and 7 (March 16, April 1, 1898) (review).

BORELLI, GIOVANNI. "Edward Bellamy" (obituary). *Corriere della Sera* (Milan). Vol. XXIII, No. 144, May 27-28, 1898.

CAPRARELLI, G. "Edward Bellamy: Guardando indietro" (review). *Vivi tra i vivi* (Rome) (Dec., 1957).

————. "E. Bellamy: Guardando indietro" (review). *Corriere di Sicilia* (Catania) (Aug. 30, 1957).

COSTO, ANDREA. *Un sogno.* Rome: Edizioni dell'Avanguardia, 1914.

CROCE, BENEDETTO. *Storia d'Italia 1871-1915.* Bari: Laterza, 1918.

CURCIO, CARLO. *Miti della politica.* Rome: Cremonese, 1940.

D. C. "Edward Bellamy: Guardando indietro" (review). *Leggere* (Rome). No. 5 (May, 1958).

FEDERICI, BORTOLO. "Bibliografia: Nell'anno 2000" (review). *Il pensiero italiano* (Milan). Monthly periodical (Feb., 1891).

GAGLIARDI, ERNESTO. "Lo Stato transformato in Società cooperativa: un libro fortunato." *Corriere della Sera* (Milan). Vol. XV, No. 287, (Oct. 17-18, 1890) (correspondence).

IZZO, CARLO. *Storia della letteratura nord-americana.* Milan: Nuova Accademia, 1957; 1959.

L.R.L. (ind.) "Edward Bellamy" (article). *Dizionario degli Autori,* Vol. I. Milan: Bompiani, 1956, pp. 215-16.

MERLINO, FR. SAVERIO. *Pro e contro il socialismo.* Milan: Treves, 1897.

————. *L'utopia collettivista e la crisi del socialismo scientifico.* Milan: Treves, 1898, pp. 37-52.

NEGRI, GAETANO. *Un romanzo socialista* (review). *La Perseveranza*, daily morning paper, special supplement (Milan), (Dec. 25, 1890).

## JAPAN

### *Translations*

*Looking Backward:*

*Kaerimireba.* Trans. by Masayoski Yamamoto. Tokyo: Iwanami Shoten, 1953.

*Hyakunengo no Shakai.* Trans. by Kogoro Hirai. Tokyo: Keiseisha Shoten, 1903.

————. Trans. and abridged by Kosen Sakai. Heiminsha Press, 1904.

### *Unpublished Material*

Letters and translation of postscript of his translation of *Looking Backward,* Professor Masayoski Yamamoto, January, 1958.

Letters of Iyoji Aono, University of Tokyo Library, January 6, 1958; Shiro Sugai, National Diet Library, Tokyo, December 16, 1957.

Notes of S. E. Bowman of interview, September, 1958, with Mrs. Marion Bellamy Earnshaw, Springfield, Mass.

## JUGOSLAVIA

### (Croatia and Serbia)

### *Translations*

*Looking Backward:*

*U godini 2000. Osvrt na godinu 1887. Englezki napisao Edward Bellamy.* Zagreb: Tisak i naklada Knjizare Lav. Hartmana (St. Kugli), 1903.

*Jedan pogled iz godine 2000. na 1887.* Od Edvarda Belamija. *Zanatliski savez* (3/ 1894), No. 47, p. 3; No. 48, p. 2; No. 49, p. 3; No. 51, p. 2 (Extracts.)

*U. 2000-oj godini. Roman Edvarda Belami-a.* Trans. H. S. D. [Hajim S. Davico] *Trgovinski glasnik* (11/1901), pp. 136-214. (Extracts.)

*Pogled iz 2000-te godine. Jedna slika sociajalisticke buduc-
nosti. Roman Edvarda Belamia. Radnicke novine* (8/
1908—9/1909). (This is the most complete serialization,
but it was obviously translated from the German translation of Georg Malkowsky because of the omissions.)

*Equality:*

"Štrajkači." E. Belami. *Radničke novine* (10/1910), No. 85,
p. 2; No. 86, p. 2; No. 87, pp. 2-3. (An extract.)
"Mali ratovi i veliki rat." E. Belami. *Radničke novine* (10/
1910), No. 50, pp. 2-3. (A small part of the novel
*Equality.*)

## Articles

B. M., "Edvard Belami, američki socijalista." *Zanatliski savez*
(3/1894), No. 45, p. 3 [Biography.]
BALUGDŽIĆ, ŽIVOJIN. "Jedan Pogled iz godine 2000 na 1887."
*Zanatliski savez,* (3/1894), No. 38, p. 2.
GRGEC, PETAR. "Po receptu Bellamy-a. Čovjek je mnogo zamršeniji
stvor, nego što misle neki romanopisci. Zivot ima svoju
logiku.—Mastanje utopističkog pisca Bellamy-a izriče srčiku
komunističkog programa. Neostvarivost komunističke uto-
pije." *Hrvatska straža* (6/1934), Vol. VI, No. 135, p. 4,
cols. 1-4.

## Unpublished Materials

Letters to S. E. BOWMAN from:

Hanz, Branko, University Library, Zagreb, April 3, 1959;
February 10, 1959; July 10, 1960.
Rojnic, Matko, Director, University Library, Zagreb, April
4, 1958. November 12, 1957.
Nednadovic, Ljubica, Narodna Biblioteka, Beograd, August
2, 1958.

## NEW ZEALAND

### Bellamy's Works

BELLAMY, EDWARD. *Looking Backward 2000-1887.* Dunedin:
James Horsburgh, 1890.
————. *Looking Backward 2000-1887.* Christchurch: Whit-
combe and Tombs, 1890.

509

——. *Looking Backward 2000-1887*. Serialized, *The Stand-*
*ard*, Jan. 29 to July 8, 1936.
——. *The Parable of the Water Tank*. Lower Hutt:
H. & P. C. Printers, 1932?
——. *The Parable of the Water Tank*. Wellington: N. Z.
Worker, 1932?

### Articles and Books

BALLANCE, JOHN. "*The Altruistic State.*" *The Monthly Review*
(Wellington) II, 217-19 (April, 1890).
BEERE, WYNFORD ORMSBY. *Prospectus of New Zealand Limited*.
Wellington: Edward Bellamy Society (N.Z.), 1937 (1) p.
DONNELLY, MARTIN. "*Looking Backward*, some Objections to
Mr. Bellamy's Gospel (An Essay Read before the Catholic
Literary Society, Christchurch)." *Weekly Press* (Christ-
church), June 6 and 13, 1890.
Edward Bellamy Society (N.Z.) (Incorporated) *Constitution
and Rules*. Wellington: Standard Print, 1938. (8) p.
*The Edward Bellamy Society of N.Z.* Wellington: 1936. (1) p.
FREEMAN, WILLIAM (i.e., Kitchen, William Freeman) "*Look-
ing Backward, 2000-1887.*" *Zealandia* (Dunedin) I, 296-97
(Nov., 1889).
"Idealist, Philosopher, Psychologist, and Seer. . . ." Wellington,
N. Z., *Standard*, December, 1935, cols. 1-6.
RICHMOND, MAURICE WILLIAM. "*Looking Backward.*" *The
Monthly Review* (Wellington) I, 444-48 (Sept., 1889).
SCOTT, ALEXANDER. *The Immortal Edward Bellamy: an Intro-
duction to the Man and his Books—"Looking Backward"
and "Equality.*" Wellington, The Labour Bookroom, 1937.
(5) p. portrait on cover.
——. "'Looking Backward'/Bellamy's Famous Book/No
Funds Obtainable for Film Version/Banker Controlled
Companies Decline Production," New Zealand *Worker*,
September 27, 1933, p. 1.
——. "Bellamy's 'Looking Backward,'" New Zealand
*Worker*, September 27, 1933, p. 1.
"Socialism Cure/A Roosevelt Expert." New Zealand *Worker*,
Sept. 27, 1933.
"U. S. A.'s Economic Revolution." New Zealand *Worker*, Sept.
27, 1933, p. 2, col. 5.
WALKER, FRANCIS AMASA. "*Mr. Bellamy and the New Nationalist
Party. A Criticism of the Views Contained in 'Looking
Backward.'*" Auckland, W. Wildman, 1890. 34 pp.

## Unpublished Materials

Edward Bellamy Society (N.Z.)* *Minute Books.* I (July 9, 1936 to Feb. 9, 1938).
————. *Minute Books.* II (March 24, 1938 to Sept. 30, 1941).
————. *Outward Letter Book* (Feb. 1, 1937 to May 27, 1938).
————. *Clippings Books*
————. *Miscellaneous Files* (containing Inward Letters, Circulars, Overseas Correspondence, etc., etc.).
SCOTT, ALEXANDER. Letters from Wellington, N.Z., to Mrs. Edward Bellamy, March 27, 1934; April 17, 1938; April 9, 1937; June 1, 1938: to Gordon Rigby, January 12, 1936.
————. Radio Scripts MSS: "Talk on Social Justice," 1938; "The Prophet Is Not Dead," May 22, 1938; "Two 'Books of the Age' as well as 'Books of the Moment,'" May 22, 1938.
WILLIAMSON, W. H. Letter from Auckland, New Zealand, April 3, 1935, to Upton Sinclair, in Bellamy Files.

### THE NETHERLANDS

The following bibliography of material about Edward Bellamy is necessarily limited because all Bellamy material—books, documents, records—was confiscated and destroyed by the Nazi secret police during the German occupation (1940-1945). The entire library and papers of Mr. P. Yssel de Schepper, President of the Bellamy Association, were destroyed by the Germans; Mr. Yssel de Schepper died from a nervous breakdown in 1943. Mr. Zylstra, the man in charge of the central administration of the association, was under arrest for some months and then released. Mr. Gertenbach, the printer of the Bellamy publications, was arrested and then executed by a firing squad because of his having printed political publications—and his chief assistant was also arrested and sentenced to life imprisonment. The Cohen Brothers, publishers of Bellamy, were Jews; they perished in a gas chamber.

### Translations of Bellamy's Books

BELLAMY, EDWARD. *Economische Gelijkheid.* Translator unknown. Bussum: "Phoenix," 1946.
————. *Gelijkheid voor Allen.* Translation of *Equality* by A.C.B. Den Haag: A. Abrams, 1897.

* (*All in Possession of Mr. A. Scott, Lower Hutt*)

————. *Gelijkheid voor Allen*. Revised by H. Nolles. Amsterdam: Cohen Brothers, 1934.

————. *Het jaar 2000*. Translated by Frank van der Goes. Amsterdam: S. L. van Looy, 1890.

————. *Het jaar 2000*. Translated by Frank van der Goes. Amsterdam: Cohen Brothers, 1919.

————. *Het jaar 2000*. Translated by Henri Polak. Amsterdam: Cohen Brothers, 1930.

————. *Het jaar 2000*. Translator unknown. Zandvoort: Bibliotheek voor Ontwikkeling en Ontspanning, 1935.

————. *Rigardante Malantauen*. Translation into Esperanto by C. M. Hamaker. Amsterdam: Cohen Brothers, 1937.

————. *Terugblik uit het jaar 2000*. Translated by T. Stillebroer, Ede: Stichting Centrale Administratie Bellamy, 1951.

### Articles, Books, Reviews

BANNING, W. and BARENTS, J. *Socialistische Documenten van een Eeuw*. Amsterdam: De Arbeiderspers, 1953.

*Bellamy: Economische Gelijkheid*. Den Haag: Internationale Vereniging Bellamy: 1933.

*Bellamy: Een wereld zonder geld, Gelijkheid voor Allen*. Den Haag: De Internationale Vereniging Bellamy, 1933.

*Bellamy-Nieuws. Officieel Sociaal Economisch Orgaan van de Internationale Vereniging Bellamy*. Published from 1933 to present. Velsen.

BOS, C. G. *Kan Bellamy ons redden?* 1939. Publisher unknown.

BURGERS, P. J. *De oplossing der Crisis*. Founder of the Internationale Vereniging Bellamy, 1932.

DE KADT, J. "Commentaar op: Socialistische Documenten van een Eeuw." *Parool* (Amsterdam), February 11, 1933.

*Economic Verities, in Twenty-eight Pictures*. Paris: Mouvement pour L'Abondance, 1952.

*Liberigo de Mizero: Bulteno de la Krakcio*. Bellamy-Abundo. (Paris, France). Nos. 23/24, September-November, 1958.

NIEKEL, J. H. and VERMAAS, E.A.V. *De Bellamy Beweging*. Hilversum: Paul Brand, Publishers, 1939.

POLAK, F. L. *De Toekomst is Verleden Tijd*. Utrecht: De Haan, 1955.

POLAK, SIEGFRIED. *Beknopte Geschiedenis der Staathuishoudkunde in theorie en praktijk*. (Vol. I.) Amsterdam: Mij. voor goedeen goedkope lectuur, 1919.

QUAK, H.P.G. *De Socialisten, Personen en Stelsels*. Amsterdam. P.N.v.Kampen & Zoon, 1901.

VAN DER GOES, FRANK. "Voorbericht," *Het jaar 2000*. Amsterdam: Cohen Brothers, 1890.
VAN EEDEN, FREDERIK. *Studies*. Amsterdam: S. L. van Looy, 1890.

Reviews of: *Het Jaar 2000* (1950)

*De Jonge Kerk* (Amsterdam), September 1, 1951.
*Delftsche Courant* (Delft), July 21, 1951.
*De Vlam*. (Amsterdam), February 24, 1951.
*Gelderlander/Noordooster*. (Nijmegen), January 25, 1951.
*Laarder Courant* (Laren), March 23, 1951.
*Nieuwe Noordhollandse Courant*, January 26, 1951.
*Nieuwsblad voor Zuidholland en Utrecht* (Schoonhoven), February 28, 1951.
*Zandvoortse Courant*. December 20, 1950.


NORWAY

(See Sweden for general works.)

*Translations of Bellamy*

*Det nationalistiske program*. *Kringsjaa*, III, 453-58 (March 17, 1894).


POLAND

*Translations of Bellamy*

*Looking Backward:*

Z *przeszlosci*, 2000-1887. Paryz: Aleksander Okecki, 1891.
Z *przeszlosci*, 2000-1887. Genewa: "Przedswit," 1891. [Biblioteka Robotnika Polskiego. Nowa seria. Tomik czwarty.]
W *wicku XXI*. Przedmowa i tlumaczenie przez K.O.R. Krakow: Wl. L. Anczyc, 1890.
W *roku 2000*. Tlomaczyl J. K. Potocki. Warszawa: *Glos*, 1890. [Tlum. Jozef Karol Potocki.]
*In hundert johr arum*. Iberzect durch Dawid Druk. Warszawa: "Progres," 1905? [Alfabet zydowdki.]
*In hundert johr arum*. Iberzect durch Dawid Druk. Warszawa: "Progres," 1906.
*Excerpts:* "Sklery W XXI Wiekv" (Shops). *Prawda Tygodnik Polityczny*.

*Spokeczny i Literracki* (Warsaw), 1890, pp. 254-56; "Restauracye W XXI Wiekv" (Restaurants), 1890, pp. 266-68.

Chapter I, *Antologia Tekstow Do Nauki Jezyka Angiel-Skiego*. Kl. XI. Edited by Professor S. Helsztynski. Warszawa, 1950.

*Miss Ludington's Sister:*
*Siostra panny Ludington*. Warszawa: "Przeglad tygodniowy," 1891.

*Dr. Heidenhoff's Process:*
*Sposob dra Heidenhoffa*. Odbitka z "Glosu." Warszawa: (druk. M. Ziemkiewiczowej), 1891.

"With the Eyes Shut":
"Ze Swiata Prvszkosci," *Czytanie z Zamknietymi Oczyma przez Edwarda Bellamy' Ego, Przeglad Tygodniowv* (Warsaw), Nos. 2, 3 (1891), pp. 25, 41.


### Articles and Books

"Bellamyego Wr. 2000," (Krakow) *Przeglad Polaki* (1890).

*Encykopedia Powszechna*, Vol. II. Warszawa: Wydawnict Wo Ultima Thule, 1928.

G. "W roku 2000," *Biblioteka warszawska*. LXVI (1890), 133-37.

Korbut, Gabrjel. *Literatura Polska od Poczatkow Do Wojny Swiatowes*, Vol. IV. Od Roku 1864 Do R. 1914. Warszawa: Sklad Glowny W Kasie Im. Mianowskiego, Palac Staszica, 1931.

————. "O Energii Spolecznej." Warsaw: 1900.

————. "Wspolzawodnictwo i Wspoldzialanie." Lwow (Krakow): 1900.

["Literary Chronicle"] *Przeglad Rolski* (Krakow), XCVIII (1890), 306-9.

"Utopia Amerykanska," *Przeglad Tygodniowy*, No. 6 (January 27, 1890), pp. 81-82.

Zyg, Piet. "Az Dwa." (Warsaw) *Prawda*. (1890), pp. 450-51.

Zywicki, K. R. "Nationalist League Agitation." *Prawda*. No. 22 (1890), pp. 254-56.


### Unpublished Material

Pać, Henryk. *Henry George and Edward Bellamy, Two Anti-Capitalistic American Writers*. Unpublished dissertation for the M. A., University of Warsaw, 1955.

## PORTUGAL

*Looking Backward: D'Aqui a Cem Anos.* Translated by M. Pinhero Chagas. Lisbon: Comp. Esitora, 1891.

## RUMANIA

BELLAMY, ED. *In anul 2000. Ua privire retrospectivă din anul 2000 asupra secolului nostru.* (Looking Backward). Bucuresci: Tip. Romanulu V.C.A. Rosetti, 1891. (Biblioteca Romanului) [Translator unknown.]
————. *In anul 2000.* Roman Traducere de Sarina Cassvan. Bucuresci: Cercul de editura socialistă, 1920. [On the cover: Fantezie instorica. Note: Abbreviated translation.]

## RUSSIA

### Translations of Edward Bellamy's Works Into the Languages of the Peoples of the USSR

*Dr. Heidenhoff's Process:*
RUSSIAN: Trans. by R. O. and B. F. Kazan, 1893, 147 pp.
GEORGIAN: Trans. by D. Ghiorgobiani. *Moambre,* 1894, NN 8-9.

*Miss Ludington's Sister:*
RUSSIAN: Abridged trans. by Ú. K. *Illustrirovanny mir,* 1885, NN 46-47; Complete trans. St. Petersburg, 1891. 103 pp.

*Looking Backward 2000-1887:*
RUSSIAN: Abridged trans. St. Petersburg, 1889, 176 pp.; *Knishky "Nedely,"* 1890, May-July. Trans. by L. Gay. St. Petersburg, 1891. IV, 334 pp.; 2nd ed., 1891. Trans. by F. Zinin. St. Petersburg, 1891. IV, 312 pp.; 2nd ed. rev., 1891. 314 pp.; 3rd ed., 1893. 320 pp.; 4th ed., 1901. 328 pp.; 5th ed., 1905; 6th ed., 1908; Moscow: Klyukin [1899]. 333 pp.; 2nd ed. [1906]. 232 pp. Moscow: Efomov [1900]. VIII, 357 pp.; Abridged by B. S. Mayevsky. Moscow, 1905. 64 pp.; 2nd ed., 1913; Abridged by A. A. Nikolayev. [St. Petersburg, 1906]. 140 pp.; Petrograd, 1917. 112 pp.; 1918. 106 pp.
GEORGIAN: Trans. by D. Calandariashvili. Tiflis, 1896.
LITHUANIAN: Chapter I of the novel. *Varpas,* 1896, N 4. *Vienybe lietuoninky* (USA), 1897, NN 30-50; 1898, NN 1, 3-45. (Separate ed. in 1910, in the USA).
JEWISH: Abridged trans. Berdichef, 1898. 76 pp.

ESTONIAN: Chapters I and II. Trans. by V. Lüdig. *Voitleja*, 1905. NN 1-2. Chapters I-II. Trans. by A. Kitzberg. *Album 1906-1907*. NN 1-5.
UKRAINIAN: Lwow, 1932. 124 pp.

*With the Eyes Shut* (*Harper's Monthly*, October, 1889):
RUSSIAN: Trans. by B——sky. *Russky vedomosty*, 1890, N 336.

*What Nationalism Means* (*The Contemporary Review*, July, 1890):
RUSSIAN: *Nedela*, 1891, NN 3-34.

*Some Account of the Propaganda. Work in America Which Has Followed Looking Backward* (Not published in English except in Appendix of this book):
RUSSIAN: Trans. from the MS by L. K. Davidova. *Pomoch.* St. Petersburg, 1892, pp. 222-29.

*Equality:*
RUSSIAN: Trans. by B. Vinnizkaya. Moscow, 1907. VIII, 671, 1V pp.; *Idem*, n.d.

*The Parable of the Water Tank* (Chapter XXIII of *Equality*):
LITHUANIAN: *Vienybe lietuoninky* (USA), 1904, NN 41-42.
LETTISH: Riga, 1905. 15 pp. *Arodnieks*, 1925, NN 2-3.
RUSSIAN: Trans. from the French by N. B. St. Petersburg, 1906. 15 pp. Trans. from the German by E. I. Reidemeister. Ed. by I. V. Vladislavlev. Moscow. 1917. 13 pp. Trans. from the English [Petrograd, 1917]. 14 pp.; Moscow, 1918. 16 pp.; Kiev, 1919. 16 pp.; n.p., 1919; Ekaterinoslav, 1922, 16 pp.
GEORGIAN: Trans. by Dadvadze. Tiflis, 1906. 16 pp.
TARTAR: Trans. by S. Tagirov. Kazan, 1906. 19 pp.
JEWISH: Vilna, 1906. 11 pp.; Trans. by M. Moscow, 1918. 14 pp.
BYELORUSSIAN: Trans. by A. B. Vilna, 1907. 15 pp.
UKRAINIAN: Trans. by I. Savkin. Winnipeg, 1911. 30 pp.
SLOVENIAN: Moscow, 1919. 15 pp.

*Books and Chapters in Books* (*in Russian*)

RTSI [ROMANOV I. F.] Chernovye nabrosky. Vecher chernoy i beloy magii. (Fantasia na temu "Cherez sto let" Bellamy). Kiev, I. N. Kushnerev, 1891. 14 str.
GOLOVIN K. Sotsialism kak polozhitelnoe uchenie. St. Petersburg, 1892. VI, 246 str. *Idem*, 2nd edition, 1894. VI, 246 str.

SHELONSKY N. N. V mire budushego. Fantastichesky roman. Moskva, I. D. Sitin, 1892. 315, III str.

SHARAPOV S. Cherez polveka. Fantastichesky politikosotsialni roman. Chast pervaya. Moskva, A. V. Vasilyev, 1902. 80 str.

ANICHKOV E. William Morris i ego utopichesky roman.–In: Anichkov E. Predtechy i sovremenniky. I. Na Zapade. St. Petersburg, "Osvobozhdenie" [1910], str. 168-69.

SVYATLOVSKY V. Russki utopichesky roman. Petrograd, Gosizdat, 1922, 53 str.

SVYATLOVSKY V. V. Katalog utopy. Moskva-Petrograd, Gosizdat, 1923. 100 str.

KRUPSKAYA N. Iz dalekih vremen. Politprosvetrabota sredi peterburgskih rabochih v 90-e godi. Moskva-Leningrad, Gosizdat, 1930. 15 str.

BAGAEV M. A. Za desyat let. Sotsial-democraticheskaya organizatsiya v Ivanovo-Voznesenskom rayone v 1892-1902 gg. Pod red. O. A. Varentsovoy, N. N. Kudryasheva, S. P. Shesternina. Ivanovo-Voznesensk, Gosizdat, 1930. 160 str.

MAKHOV N. I. Zhisn minuvshaya. Ivanovo, 1939. 144 str.

SHESTERNIN S. P. Perezhitoe. Iz istorii rabochego i revolutsionnogo dvizheniya 1880-1900 g.g. Pod. red. i spred. O. A. Varentsovoy i M. A. Bagaeva. Ivanovo, Gosizdat, 1940. 224 str.

MITSKEWICH S. I. Revolutsionnaya Moskva. 1888-1905. Moskva, Goslitizdat, 1940. 493 str.

Istoria angliyskoy literaturi, tom. III, Moskva, Akademia Nauk SSSR, 1958, str. 318-19 (Institut mirovoy literaturi imeni A. M. Gorkogo).

## Periodicals (in Russian)

YANSHUL I. Novaya fantaziya na staruyu temu. Vestnik Yevropi, 1890, N 4, str. 553-89; N 5, str. 173-203. Idem in: Yanshul I. V poiskah luchego budushego. Sotsialnie etudi. St. Petersburg, "Prosveshenie," 1908, str. 103-80.

Cherez sto let. Fantastichesky roman E. Bellamy. St. Petersburg, 1891. Niva, 1890 [sic!], N 47 (24.XI), str. 1192.

SHARAPOV S. V 2000-m godu. Blagovest, 1890, vip. 9(15.XII), str. 254-58.

Cherez sto let. Sotsiologichesky roman E. Bellamy. St. Petersburg, F. Pavlenkov, 1891. Severny Vestnik, 1890 [sic!], N 12, otd. II, str. 115-18.

EDWARD BELLAMY. "Cherez sto let." Fantastichesky roman.

St. Petersburg [F. Pavlenkov, 1891], *Russkoe bogatstvo,*
1890 [*sic!*], N 12, str. 175-76.

M. EDWARD BELLAMY. Budushy vek. Roman. Per. L. Gay. St.
Petersburg, 1891. *Sotrudnik,* 1891, kn. 1, str. 134-35.

Budushy vek, rom. Edwarda Bellamy. Per. L. Gay. 1891.
*Zhivopisnoe obozrenie,* 1891, N 7(17.II), str. 126.

Roman Bellamy "Looking Backward" i koe chto o sotsialnom
dvizhenii v Soedinennih Shtatah Sev. Ameriky. *Rizhsky
Vestnik,* 1891, N 41 (19.II), str. 1-2.

Budushy vek. Roman Edwarda Bellamy. Per. L. Gay. St.
Petersburg, 1891. *Nablyudatel,* 1891, N 4, str. 18-21 (Sov-
remennoe obozrenie).

[SLONIMSKAYA L. S.] Ein Rückblick aus dem Jahre 2037 auf das
Jahr 2000. Aus dem Erinnerungen des Herrn Julian West.
Herausgegeben von Dr. Ernst Müller, Berlin, 1891 [Rec.].
*Vestnik Yevropi,* 1891, N 8, str. 858-62. Signed: L. S.

[SLONIMSKAYA L. S.] Des Herrn Friedrich Ost Erlebnisse in
der Welt Bellamy's. Mittheilungen aus den Jahren 2001
und 2002. Herausg, von Conrad Wilbrandt. Wismar, 1891.
212 str. *Vestnik Yevropi,* 1891, N 10, str. 857-58.

SEMENTKOVSKY R. K. GOLOVIN. Sotsialism kak polozhitelnoe
uchenie. St. Petersburg, 1892. *Istorichesky vestnik,* 1892,
t. 49, N 9, str. 727-31.

N. [*sic.*] GOLOVIN. Sotsialism kak polozhitelnoe uchenie. St.
Petersburg, 1894. *Severny vestnik,* 1894, N 9, otd. II, str.
65-68.

Novye utopicheskie grezi. *Novy zhurnal inostrannoi literaturi,*
1897, N 5 (XI), str. 235-39. [After Th. Bentzon's "Le
communisme en Amerique. Le communisme dans la fiction" in *Revue des deux monds,* October 15, 1897].

E. BELLAMY. [Obituary.] *Vsemirnaya illustratsiya,* 1898, N 1533,
(13.VI), str. 564-65.

EDWARD BELLAMY. [Obituary.] *Zhivopisnoe obozrenie,* 1898,
N 25, (21.VI), str. 508.

[Obituary.] *Knizhki "Nedeli,"* 1898, VI, str. 215-16.

EDWARD BELLAMY. [Obituary.] *Literaturnie semeinye vechera,*
1898, N 7, str. 450-51.

[KOGAN P. S.] Utopii novogo vremeni. *Nablyudatel,* 1898, N 7,
str. 79-83; N 8, str. 236-50. Signed : K.

ILISH R. Iz putevih vpechatleny. Madyarskie silueti. *Voshod,*
1898, N 8, str. 129-33.

TUGAN-BARANOVSKY M. Sotsialistichesky obshestvenny stroi.
*Ezhemesyachny Zhurnal dlya vseh,* 1906, N 6, str. 355-63.

NIKITIN A. N. Noveishie utopii (Po romanam Bellamy). *Novy Zhurnal Literaturi, Iskusstva i Nauki*, 1907, N 10, str. 4-26; N 11, str. 100-26.

DINAMOV S. Literatura sovremennoi Ameriki *Narodny uchitel*, 1929, N 12, str. 132-41.

KRUPSKAYA N. K. Po Bellamy. *Narodny uchitel*, 1931. N 3, str. 79.

SHENGELI G. Gorod utopistov. *Kommunalnoe hozyaistvo*, 1932, N 7, str. 4-16.

LEITES A. Rozhdenie gumanizma. I. Sudba odnogo zhanra. *Znamya*, 1935, N 5, str. 224-46.

LEITES A. Puteshestvenniki v budushee (Sudba utopii v zapad-no-evropeiskoi literature). *Internatsionalnaya literatura*, 1938, N 7, str. 146-59.

## SOUTH AFRICA

### Published and Unpublished

BELL, FRED. Johannesburg, S. Africa, October 14, 1933, telegram to Mrs. E. Bellamy.

Constitution of South Africa Section of International Bellamy League, typed MS, October 11, 1932.

KENNEDY, R. F., City Librarian, Johannesburg, S. Africa, December 10, 1957, letter to S. E. Bowman.

VARLEY, D. H. Chief Librarian, South Africa Library, Capetown, letter of May 28, 1956, to S. E. Bowman.

"What Do You Know about Edward Bellamy?" *The Cape Argus* (Capetown), November 17, 1934.

## SPAIN

### Translations

*Looking Backward:*

*El Año 2000*. Traducción de Ricardo Francia. Ilustraciones de J. Pedraza. Madrid: Ricardo Fé, n.d.

————. Traducción por José Esteben Aranguren. Barcelona: Imprenta "La Luz," 1905.

*Cien ãños despues*. Barcelona: Carbonell y Esteve, n.d. Tomos VI de "Los grandes novelistas."

————. Valencia: Cosmos, 1939. [In the Institute for Social History, Amsterdam.]

————. Genoa, Italy: Carlos Maucci, n.d. Contains the
preface of the French edition by T. Reinach.

*Unpublished Material*

Letters to Mrs. Edward Bellamy: M. Elena Gamoy, Asociacion
Cristiana de Jovenes, Montevideo, Uruguay, November 15,
1937; Alvaro A. Araujo, Montevideo, Uruguay, April 7,
1934.
Letters to S. E. Bowman: I. Flamm, Beverly Hills, California,
September 18, 1959; contains a listing of the holding of
Bellamy books in the Institute for Social History, Amsterdam; Justo Garcia Morales, National Library, Madrid, Nov.
19, 1957; Dec. 21, 1957; and Juan R. Parellada, Cultural
Counselor, Spanish Embassy, Washington, D.C., February
27, 1957.

SWEDEN

*Translations of Bellamy*

*År 2000.* Sociala iakttagelser efter ett uppvaknande år 2000. Ny
öfv. l:a hft. Stockholm: Socialistiska ungdomsförbundet,
1899. 16 p. 10 öre.
*En återblick.* Sociala iakttagelser efter ett uppvaknande år 2000
af Edward Bellamy. Öfversättning från det amerikanska
originalets sjuttonde upplaga af Gustaf F. Steffen. Stockholm: Looström & Komp:s Förlag, 1889. 405 p. 3 kr.
*En återblick.* Sociala iakttagelser efter ett uppvaknande år 2000
af Edward Bellamy. Öfversättning från engelskan. Folkupplaga. Stockholm: Bohlin & Co., 1901. 256 p. 75 öre.
*En återblick.* Sociala iakttagelser efter ett uppvaknande år 2000
af Edward Bellamy. Öfversättning från engelskan. Svensk
billighetsupplaga. Stockholm: Björk [sic] & Börjesson, 1906,
256 p. 75 öre. (*Berömda Böcker 2.*)
*En återblick.* Sociala iakttagelser efter ett uppvaknande år 2000
av Edward Bellamy. Översättning från engelskan. Stockholm: Björck & Börjesson, 1919. 212 p. 2:75. (*Berömda
Böcker* No. 82).
*Doktor Heidenhoffs upptäckt.* En psykologisk novell af Edward
Bellamy. Öfversättning från det amerikanska originalet af
Gustaf F. Steffen. Stockholm: Looström & Komp:s Förlag,
1890. 188 p. 1:75 kr.
"Det nationalistiske program," *Kringsjaa,* III, 711 (May 1, 1894).

*Det mya samhället.* Af Edv. Bellamy. (Utilistiska propagandans skrifter). Stockholm: G. Walfrid Wilhelmsson, 1891. 4 p. 2 öre.

*Vattentornet. Övers. från engelskan.* Karlstad: Klasskampens Förlag, 1918, 13 p.

### Selective Bibliography of Scandinavian Material

Anon. "Bellamys dröm förverkligad." *Arbetet* (February 25, 1890).

————. "Framtidens samhälle." *Ibid.* (April 8, 1890).

————. "Georg Brandes om socialismen." *Ibid.* (October 25, 1890).

————. "Den socialistiska framtidsstaten." *Ibid.* (November 6, 1890).

————. "Nationalisterna." *Ibid.* (December 19, 1890).

————. Review of Tor Hedberg's *Ett eldprov.* (Comparison with Bellamy's *Doktor Heidenhoffs upptäckt.*) *Ibid.* (December 19, 1890).

————. "Nationalekonomiens Jules Verne." *Ibid.* (May 28, 1898).

————. "En socialistdebatt i Uppsala." *Social-Demokraten* (April 8, 1892).

————. "En svensk-amerikansk nationalist." *Ibid.* (May 30, 1890).

————. "Nationalister och socialister." *Ibid.* (August 5, 1890).

————. "Socialister och nationalister." *Ibid.* (August 15, 1890).

————. "Socialismens 'tvångsstat.'" *Ibid.* (October 2, 1890).

————. "Socialdemokratin och dess framtidsstat." *Ibid.* (November 8, 1890).

————. "Edvard Bellamy död." *Ibid.* (May 26, 1898).

————. "Två berömda socialistböcker." *Ibid.* (October 22, 1919).

————. "Forskjellige meddelelser." [Death of Bellamy.] *Kringsjaa,* XII, 79 (1898).

————. "Utopier." *Stormklockan,* III, 3 (October 22, 1910).

ALEXANDER, JOHN. "Hur jag blef socialist." *Brand,* II, 3 (1899).

ANDERSON, CARL L. *The Swedish Acceptance of American Literature.* Stockholm: Almqvist & Wiksell, 1957.

ARGUS. "Socialisternas Fremtidsstat." *Tilskueren,* pp. 241-48 (1892).

[BERG, C. O.] *Efteråt.* En blick på den socialistiska framtidsstaten. (Efter en tysk ide.) Stockholm: Arbetarens väns expedition, 1902.

BIRKEDAL, U. "Utopier og Virkelighed." *Dansk Tidskrift*, pp. 513-41 (1899).

BLOMBERG, ERNST. *Vid öfvergången till ett nytt samhälle*. Stockholm: Socialdemokratisk Arbetarepartiets Förlag, 1905.

BORG, GUSTAF. *Den socialistiske Fremtidsstat*. Copenhagen, 1903.

BÖRJESSON, KARL. "Edward Bellamy." *Brand*, VII, 3 (1899).

BRANDES, GEORG. Review of Ibsen's *Hedda Gabler*. *Verdens Gang* (February 24, 1891).

BRANTING, HJALMAR. "En svensk utopist." *Ur Dagens Krönika*, VII, 192-99 (1887).

————. *Socialismen*. En historisk framställning. Stockholm: Albert Bonniers Förlag, 1892.

DANIELSSON, AXEL. "Brandsyn." *Arbetet* (January 25, 1890).

————. *Främlingen*. Ett besök i det nya samhället. Malmö: Malmö socialdemokratiska förenings förlag, 1892.

————. "Hvad en bok kan åstadkomma." *Arbetet* (January 16, 1890).

————. "Platons 'Stat,' Th. Mores' 'Utopia' och Bellamys 'Återblick.'" *Arbetet* (September 30, 1890).

DONNELLY, IGNATIUS. Review of *Caesar's Column*. *Finsk Tidskrift*, XXXII, 172 (1892).

DONNER, H. W. *Introduction to Utopia*. London: 1945.

DURHAM, PHILIP, and MUSTANOJA, TAUNO F. *American Fiction in Finland: An Essay and Bibliography*. Helsinki: Société Néophilologique, 1960.

EHRNROOTH, LEO. "Den nya riktningen inom den tyska socialdemokratin." *Finsk Tidskrift*, LIV, 504-22 (1903).

————. "Synpunkter i vår arbetarfråga." *Ibid.*, LV, 282-304 (1903).

ENCKELL, G. "Benjamin Kidds bok: Den sociala utvecklingen." *Humanitas*, III, 121-36 (1898).

FERNSTROM, KARL. *Ungsocialismen*. En krönika. Stockholm: Federativs Förlag, 1950.

GROTH, S. Magelssen. "Ko-operative Husholdninger," *Tilskueren*, 920-32 (1892).

HEIKINHEIMO, ILMARI. *Suomen Elämä-Kerrasto*. Helsinki: Werner Söderström Osakeyhtiö, 1955.

HERMANSON, V. Review of *Doktor Heidenhoffs upptäckt*. *Finsk Tidskrift*, XXIX, 467-68 (1890).

HERTZKA, THEODOR. *En resa till Friland*. Stockholm, 1895.

JUNGEN, ERNST. *Studiet av socialismen*. Göteborg: Framåt, 1928.

*Karl Börjesson 1877-1941*. En minnesbok. Stockholm: Svenska Antikvariats-föreningen, 1942.

KIRK, HANS. "Om den sociala ønskedrøm i litteraturen." *Kritisk Revy*, pp. 26-27 (1927).

LAGERCRANTZ, OLOF. "Ett socialistiskt paradis." *Dagens Nyheter* (January 2, 1960).

————. "Framtiden som mardröm." *Ibid.* (January 5, 1960).

————. "Den nya fanatismen och förnuftet." *Ibid.* (January 10, 1960).

LEFFLER, JOHN. "Hvad är socialism?" *Nordisk Tidskrift*, III, 89-108 (1890).

LIDFORSS, BENGT (ed.). *Urval av Axel Danielssons skrifter. Med levnadsteckning och karaktäristik.* Malmö: Förlagsaktiebolaget 'Fram,' 1908.

LILLIESTAM, ÅKE. *Gustaf Steffen: samhällsteoretiker och idépolitiker.* Göteborg: Akademiförlaget-Gumperts, 1960.

MORGENSTIERNE, BREDO. "En tysk Henry George." *Nordisk Tidskrift*, IV, 249-65 (1891).

ØKSNEVAD, REIDAR. *Sambandsstatene i norsk litteratur.* Oslo, 1950.

PETTER. "Utopier." *Social-Demokraten* (August 31, 1889).

PIO, FRANTZ. "Kommunesocialisme." *Tilskueren*, pp. 223-41 (1898).

QUERCUS. "Om hundra år." *Social-Demokraten* (January 5, 1889).

[Review of *Dr. Heidenhoff's Process*] *Finsk Tidskrift*, XXIX, 467-68 (1890).

RUHE, ALGOT. "Konstens undergång." *Ord och Bild*, II, 563-68 (1893).

"Samhällsutopier," *Ute och Hemma*, II, 401 (1890).

SKARD, SIGMUND. *American Studies in Europe*, II, 453. Philadelphia, Pa., 1958.

"Socialisme i praksis," *Kringsjaa*, X, 759-63 (1897): see also in the same publication, XII, 79 (1898).

STEGMAN, CARL, and HUGO, Co. *Handbuch des Socialismus.* Zurich, 1897.

TENGDAHL, KNUT, and LINDBORG, EDM. *Katalog over Stockholms Arbetarbiblioteksförbunds Bibliotek.* No. I. Stockholm, 1892.

TRIER, GERSON. "Anarkismen." *Tilskueren*, pp. 307-27, 397-412, 493-504, 608-28 (1894).

VENNERSTRÖM, IVAR. *Svenska utopister.* Stockholm: Tidens Förlag, 1913.

ZWEIGBERGK, OTTO v. "Den sociala frågan i den moderna litteraturen." *Ord och Bild*, I, 370-73 (1892).

SWITZERLAND*

*Looking Backward:*

    *Erlebnisse im Jahr 2000.* Zurich: Verlag Mensch und Arbeit, 1947.

    ————. Serialized in *Anzeiger aus de Bezirk Affoltern* (1947).

    ————. Serialized in *Merkur* (Zurich).

BELLAMY, EDOUARD. *Parabole du Réservoir d'Eau.* (Tirage á part du Réveil socialiste-anarchiste, 6e Annee, Nr. 122 et 123, 11 et 25 Mars 1905, distribue le Premier Mai 1905) 16 p. Genève, Ed. du Réveil, (Imp. Commerciale).

C. BELLAMIABEL, ed., *Zukunftszeitung,* Organ des Germanischen Völkerbundes (Organ of the Germanic League of Nations) Wien, Stockholm, London, Zürich, den 1. Mai 3000. (May 1st, 3000), Zurich: Caesar Schmidt, (July, August), 1891; 4 p.

## Unpublished Material

Report of Dr. W. Bleuler, Zurich, Switzerland; and letters of April 11, 1957; December 26, 1956; January 30, 1957; August 21, 1957; August 7, 1957; September 2, 1958; July 23, 1959.

Letters of Werner Reist, Zurich, to S. E. Bowman, May 28th, 1959; June 30, 1959; August 16, 1959; September 14, 1960.

Letter of Franz Riederer, Munich, Germany, to S. E. Bowman, November 10, 1960, containing additional bibliographical information about Switzerland. In fact, the bibliography of Switzerland must be attributed to Mr. Riederer.

## UNITED STATES

(This bibliography contains only books and articles mentioned in chapters I and XV; for a nearly complete listing, see the extensive bibliography in *The Year 2000: A Critical Biography of Edward Bellamy* [1958].)

BAXTER, SYLVESTER. "What is Nationalism?" I, 1 (May, 1889), pp. 2-12.

---

\* Although reviews were published of Bellamy's books in Switzerland, they were not listed in the bibliographies consulted by Mr. Riederer; and Mr. Reist and Dr. Bleuler could not supply them or list them.

BELLAMY, EDWARD. *Equality.* New York: D. Appleton & Co., 1933.

————. *Looking Backward.* Modern Library Edition. New York: Random House, n.d.

————. "Concerning the Founding of Nationalist Colonies." *New Nation,* III, 38 (Sept. 23, 1893), p. 434.

————. "Collapse of the International," *Springfield Union* (September 26, 1874), p. 4.

————. "Death of a Chartist," *New Nation,* II, 33 (August 13, 1892), p. 518.

————. "Four Distinctive Principles of Nationalism," *New Nation* (January 9, 1892), pp. 17-18.

————. "How I Came to Write *Looking Backward,*" *Ladies' Home Journal,* (April 1, 1894), p. 2.

————. "In the Interest of a Clear Use of Terms," *New Nation,* I, 46 (December 12, 1891), pp. 725-26.

————. "Letter to the People's Ratification Meeting," *New Nation,* II, 43 (October 22, 1892), pp. 644-45.

————. "Literary Notices," *Springfield Union* (December 31, 1874), p. 6; (December 11, 1875), p. 6; (September 23, 1875), p. 6; (November 13, 1873), p. 6; (April 15, 1876), p. 6; (May 27, 1876), p. 6; (September 30, 1876), p. 6; (June 1, 1876), p. 6; (May 8, 1875), p. 6; (April 21, 1877), p. 6.

————. "Looking Backward Again," *The North American Review,* CL, 400 (March, 1890), pp. 351-63.

————. "Looking Forward," *Nationalist,* II, 1 (December, 1889), pp. 2-4.

————. "Progress of Nationalism in the United States," *North American Review,* CLIV, 426 (June, 1892), pp. 742-52.

————. "The Reign of Terror Ended," *Springfield Union* (March 17, 1877), p. 6.

————. "Religion and Science," *Springfield Union* (March 30, 1875), p. 4.

————. "Talks on Nationalism," *New Nation* (May 23, 1891), pp. 264-65; (August 8, 1891), pp. 425-27.

————. "Two Good Christians," *Springfield Union* (April 25, 1877), p. 6.

————. "What Mr. Joel Benton Thinks Nationalism is Like," *New Nation,* III, 3 (January 21, 1893), p. 34.

————. "What 'Nationalism' Means" *Contemporary Review* (July, 1890), pp. 1-18.

BESANT, ANNIE. "Industry Under Socialism," *Socialism: Fabian Essays.* Boston: Charles E. Brown & Co., 1894.

BOUDIN, LOUIS. "A Marxian Looks at America, This Un-American Movement," *Our America* (January, 1933), pp. 1-2.

BOWMAN, SYLVIA E. *The Year 2000: A Critical Biography of Edward Bellamy.* New York: Bookman Associates, 1958.

BROWN, MARIE A. [Mrs. John B. Shipley]. *The True Author of Looking Backward.* New York: John B. Alden, Publisher, 1890.

CABET, ETIENNE. "Préface de la Deuxième Edition," *Voyage en Icarie.* Paris: J. Mollet et Cie, 1842.

CLARK, F. C. "A Neglected Socialist, Wilhelm Weitling," *Publications of the American Academy of Political and Social Science,* No. 144 (April 9, 1893), p. 79.

CORBIN, CAROLINE FAIRFIELD. *The Position of Women in Utopia.* Chicago: n.p., 1901.

CUSHMAN, ROBERT. *The Sin and Danger of Self Love Described in a Sermon Preached at Plimouth in New England in 1621.* Plymouth, Massachusetts: Reprinted by Nathaniel Coverly, MDCCLXXXVIII.

DAWES, ANNA L. "Mr. Bellamy and Christianity," *Andover Review,* CL, 88 (April, 1891), pp. 413-18.

DAY, CLIVE. "Capitalistic and Socialistic Tendencies in the Puritan Colonies" *Annual Report of the American Historical Association for the Year 1920.* Washington, D. C., 1925.

DE LAVELEYE, EMILE. "Two New Utopias," *Littell's Living Age,* CLXXXIV, 2381 (February 15, 1890), pp. 381-99. See also: *Contemporary Review* (January, 1890).

DEWEY, JOHN. "A Great American Prophet," *Common Sense,* III, 4 (April, 1934).

DORFMAN, JOSEPH. *The Economic Mind in American Civilization.* New York: Viking Press, 1949.

DRAPER, THEODORE. *The Roots of American Communism.* New York: Viking Press, 1957.

EGBERT, DONALD D., and PERSONS, STOW. *Socialism and American Life.* Vol. I. Princeton: Princeton University Press, 1952.

ELY, RICHARD. *The Labor Movement in America.* New York: Thomas Y. Crowell & Co., 1886.

————. *Socialism and Social Reform.* New York: Thomas Y. Crowell & Co., 1894.

FORBES, ALYN. "The Literary Quest for Utopias," *Social Forces,* VI, 2 (December, 1927), pp. 179-189.

GARRISON, WM. L. "The Mask of Tyranny," *Arena,* I, 5 (April, 1890), pp. 553-59.

GRONLUND, L. "Preface," *The Co-operative Commonwealth.* 2nd. ed.; Boston: Lee and Shepard, 1890.

————. "Nationalism," *The Arena,* I, 2 (January, 1890), pp. 153-65.

————. "A Reply to Dr. Heber Newton," *Nationalist,* I, 4 (September, 1889), pp. 158-61.

GEORGII, MAX. "Co-operative Society of Ghent," *Nationalist,* II, 2 (January, 1890), pp. 53-57.

GREEN, MASON. *Edward Bellamy.* Unpublished manuscript, Houghton Library, Harvard University.

————. "Unconscious Nationalism in Our American System of Government." *New Englander and Yale Review,* n.s. XVI, 229 (February, 1890), pp. 97-196.

HARTZ, LOUIS. *The Liberal Tradition in America.* New York: Harcourt, Brace and Company, 1955.

HARRIS, W. T. "Edward Bellamy's Vision." *Forum,* VIII (October, 1889), pp. 199-200.

HENDERSON, C. R. "Fact and Fiction in Social Study," *The Dial,* XXIII, 266 (July 16, 1897), pp. 48-50.

HIGGINSON, T. W. "Step by Step," *Nationalist,* I, 4 (September, 1889), pp. 145-48.

HIGGS, WILLARD. "Bellamy: Objections to His Utopia," *New Englander and Yale Review,* LII, 240 (March, 1890), pp. 231-39.

HOFSTADER, RICHARD. *The Age of Reform from Bryan to F. D. R.* New York: Alfred A. Knopf, 1956.

HOLBROOK, STEWARD H. *Dreamers of the American Dream.* New York: Doubleday & Company, 1957.

HUDSON, JAMES F. "The Anthracite Coal Pool," *North American Review.* CXLIV, 362 (January, 1887), p. 54.

LERNER, MAX. *America as a Civilization.* New York: Simon and Schuster, 1957.

"Lesson from Bellamy," Chicago *Journal,* May 24, 1898.

LEVI, A. W. "Edward Bellamy, Utopian," *Ethics,* LV (January, 1945), pp. 131-44.

"A Look Ahead," *The Literary World,* XIX, 6 (March 7, 1888), pp. 85-86.

MACNAIR, EVERETT W. *Edward Bellamy and the Nationalist Movement, 1889 to 1894.* Milwaukee, Wisconsin: The Fitzgerald Company, 1957.

MADISON, CHARLES. "Edward Bellamy, Social Dreamer," *New England Quarterly,* XV (September, 1942), pp. 444-46.

MAHER, MICHAEL. "Socialist's Dream," *The Month,* LXXII, 319 (January, 1891), pp. 1-9, 320; (February, 1891), pp. 173-88.

MEYERS, H. A. *Are Men Equal?* Great Seal Books, Cornell University Press. Binghamton, N. Y.: Vail-Ballou, 1955.

MORGAN, ARTHUR. *Edward Bellamy.* New York: Columbia University Press, 1944.

ORVIS, JOHN. "Social Transition," *Nationalist,* III, 1 (August, 1890), pp. 1-16.

PHILLIPS, W. F. "Edward Bellamy, Prophet of Nationalism," *Westminster Review,* CL, 5 (November, 1898), pp. 502-3.

QUINT, HOWARD. *The Forging of American Socialism.* Columbia, S.C.: University of South Carolina Press, 1953.

ROE, JOHN. *Contemporary Socialism.* New York: Charles Scribners' Sons, 1910.

RIDEOUT, WALTER B. *The Radical Novel in the United States.* Cambridge: Harvard University Press, 1956.

RUSSELL, FRANCES T. *Touring Utopia: the Realm of Constructive Humanism.* New York: Dial Press, 1932.

SADLER, ELIZABETH. "One Book's Influence: Edward Bellamy's Looking Backward," *New England Quarterly,* XVII, 4 (December, 1944), pp. 530-55.

SEAGAR, ALAN. *They Worked for a Better World.* New York: Macmillan Co., 1939.

SEDGWICK, A. G. "Bellamy's Utopia," *The Nation,* LXV, 1678 (August 26, 1897), pp. 170-71.

SMITH, GOLDWIN. "Prophet of Unrest," *Forum,* IX, 6 (August 1890), pp. 599-614

SPILLER, ROBERT, *et al. Literary History of the United States.* New York: Macmillan Co., 1953.

TAYLOR, WALTER. *The Economic Novel in America.* Chapel Hill: University of North Carolina Press, 1942.

VINTON, A. D. *Looking Further Backward.* Albany, N. Y.: Albany Book Company, 1890.

WALKER, F. A. "Edward Bellamy and the New Nationalist Movement." *Atlantic Monthly,* LXV, 388 (February, 1890), pp. 248-62.

### Unpublished Material

EDWARD BELLAMY, June 15, 1888, to Benjamin Ticknor, Bellamy Collection, Harvard University.

E. BELLAMY, June 17, 1888, to Wm. D. Howells, Howells Collection, Harvard University.

E. BELLAMY, December 23, 1888, to Thomas W. Higginson, Higginson Collection, Harvard University.

E. BELLAMY, "To Whom This May Come" MS, Harvard Library.

E. BELLAMY, Notebook 4 [187-?], p. 60, Harvard University.

E. BELLAMY, Notebook, possessed by M. B. Earnshaw, Springfield, Mass.

Letter, signature page missing, March 23, 1889, to E. B., from
Washington, D. C., Harvard Collection.

C. F. WILLARD, to E. B., Boston, March 22, 1889, Harvard
Collection.

H. HAMILTON, to E. B., Indiana University, March 2, 1894,
Bellamy MS, Harvard University.

# Who's Who of *Edward Bellamy Abroad*

*Sylvia E. Bowman*

Associate professor of English of Indiana University, is the author of *The Year 2000: A Critical Biography of Edward Bellamy,* which, published in 1958, was the first volume of her proposed three-volume study of the life, ideas, and influence abroad and at home of Edward Bellamy. The world authority on Bellamy and a specialist in the novel, Professor Bowman is also the author of many articles and book reviews published in both scholarly and popular publications. She has written introductions for such books as A. Mordell's *Discovery of a Genius: Howells and James;* and the following 1961 Twayne United States Classic was edited and contains an introduction written by her: Edgar Watson Howe's *Story of a Country Town.* Professor Bowman is editor of Twayne's U. S. Authors Series for which more than a hundred professors of the United States are writing books; she is also the general editor of Twayne's United States Classics Series and editor of Twayne's English Authors Series.

*Lars Ahnebrink*

*Docent* of American literature at the University of Uppsala, Uppsala, Sweden, is already well known in the United States for his study *The Beginnings of Naturalism in American Fiction: A study of the works of . . . Garland . . . Crane and . . . Norris with special reference to some European influences, 1891-1903.*

*Guido Fink*

Teacher in a secondary school at Argenta (Ferrara) and the assistant of Professor Carlo Izzo at the University of Bologna, received his doctorate in 1958 from the University of Bologna. He is the translator into Italian of Ford Madox Ford's *The Good Soldier,* and he is now preparing an Italian version of Samuel Taylor Coleridge's *Biographia Literaria* and a book of critical essays about Erich von Stroheim, the late movie director and actor.

### William R. Fraser

Professor of philosophy at Sir George Williams University of Canada, has published many articles and a novel, *The White Stone*. He is now writing another philosophical novel concerned with the ideas of Marx, Bellamy, and others.

### Robin Allenby Gollan

Research fellow in history at the Australian National University, is working on a history of the Australian Labour Movements (1887-1914). Dr. Gollan received his master's degree from Sydney and his doctorate from the University of London where he studied from 1948-1950 under Harold Laski and others. His thesis was about the radical and working class movements of Australia from 1850 to 1910.

### Maurice le Breton

Director of the Institute of English and American Studies of the University of Paris and the editor of *Etudes Anglaises*. Professor le Breton is widely known for his work in English and American studies, and has frequently lectured in the United States.

### Georges Levin

A specialist in English language and literature, professor of English at Lycée Ampère (Lyon), and an assistant professor at the University of Lyon and at the National Institute of Applied Science. Professor Levin, the author of many articles about the United States and its literature, has also taught and studied in America. From 1948 to 1950, he was an exchange teacher who taught at the State University of Michigan in Lansing. He returned to the United States in 1959 as a result of receiving a Smith-Mundt grant to do research on the social evolution of the United States in the last sixty years. He is presently working for his state doctoral and his thesis topic is *Utopia in the American Novel from 1869 to 1907*. Professor Levin passed the *agrégation* in 1948, after having served in the armed forces for four years.

### Peter Marshall

Received his education at Oxford University and at Yale University, is a lecturer in history at the University of Bristol and the author of many essays and reviews published in scholarly journals of the United States and of

Great Britain: *English Historical Review, Past and Present, Antioch Review, Confluence,* and *William and Mary Quarterly.*

### Pierre Michel

Now associated with the University of Liège of Belgium, is well known for many reviews and articles. He is now preparing a study of the novels of James G. Cozzens. A specialist in American literature and civilization, Professor Michel studied also at the Mercersburg Academy in Pennsylvania in 1952.

### Alexander Nikoljukin

A graduate of the University of Moscow where he presented his doctoral thesis on English poetry about the masses in the eighteenth century and the beginning of the nineteenth, is now associated with the Maxim Gorky Institute of World Literature in Moscow. He has published articles in *Izvestia otdeljenia literaturi i jazika, Voprosi literaturi,* and the *Berliner Zeitschrift fur Anglistik und Amerikanistik.*

### Franz Riederer

A graduate student and journalist, was selected by the *Amerika Institut* of the University of Munich to prepare a study for *Bellamy Abroad;* the institute awarded him a scholarship for his research. His study of Bellamy in Germany was presented as a thesis for his doctoral degree.

### Herbert Otto Roth

The chief of the reference section of the National Library, Wellington, is a specialist in socialist and labor movements who has published widely in periodicals in Holland, Austria, and New Zealand. Mr. Roth received his education at the University of Paris, the University of Grenoble, and the University of Wellington, New Zealand.

### K. Zylstra and J. Bogaard

Both of Holland, were, and are officials of the Bellamy Association of their country. Both are businessmen and both have traveled widely. Zylstra published many pamphlets and articles for the Bellamy Association; Bogaard has given many, many lectures about the American Utopian's ideas.

# Index